International Politics

International Politics

Enduring Concepts and Contemporary Issues

FOURTH EDITION

Robert J. Art
Brandeis University

Robert Jervis
Columbia University

HarperCollins*CollegePublishers*

Acquisitions Editor/Executive Editor: Leo A.W. Wiegman
Project and Art Coordination, Cover Design: York Production Services
Cover Designer: Scott Russo
Manufacturing Manager: Hilda Koparanian
Electronic Page Makeup: R.R. Donnelley and Sons Company, Inc.
Printer and Binder: R.R. Donnelley and Sons Company, Inc.
Cover Printer: Color-Imetry Corp

International Politics: Enduring Concepts and Contemporary Issues, 4/E.

Library of Congress Cataloging-in-Publication Data

International politics: enduring concepts and contemporary issues/[edited by]
Robert J. Art, Robert Jervis.—4th ed.
p. cm.
Includes bibliographical references.
ISBN 0–673–52441–8
1. International relations. I. Art, Robert J. II. Jervis, Robert, 1940–.
JX1395.I576 1995
327.1—dc20   95–19392
                                                                                      CIP

95 96 97 98 9 8 7 6 5 4 3 2 1

Brief Contents

Detailed Contents

PART TWO

THE USES OF FORCE   149

THE POLITICAL USES OF FORCE   149

THE POLITICAL UTILITY OF NUCLEAR WEAPONS   204

THE POLITICAL UTILITY OF FORCE IN THE CURRENT ERA   236

PART THREE

THE INTERNATIONAL POLITICAL ECONOMY

PART FOUR

Preface

The first edition of *International Politics* appeared in 1973. Since then, the field of international relations has experienced a dramatic enrichment in the subjects studied and the quality of works published. Political economy came into its own as an important subfield in the 1970s. New and important works in the field of security studies appeared. The literature on cooperation among states flourished in the early 1980s, and important studies about the environment began to appear in the mid–1980s. Feminist, post-modernist, and constructivist critiques of the mainstream made their appearance also. With the end of the Cold War, issues of morality, human rights, and the tension between state sovereignty and the obligations of the international community came to the fore. The growing diversity of the field has closely mirrored the actual developments in international relations.

In fashioning the fourth edition, we have kept in mind both the new developments in world politics and the literature that has accompanied them. Central to this edition, though, as for the other three, is our belief that the realm of international politics differs fundamentally from that of domestic politics. Therefore, we have continued to put both the developments and the literature in the context of the patterns that still remain valid for understanding the differences between politics within anarchy and politics under a government. The theme for this edition continues to revolve around enduring concepts and contemporary issues in world politics.

The fourth edition makes moderate changes in the first three parts of the reader. We have retained the sections on anarchy, the use of force, and international political economy, but have changed some of the selections. In order to make room for the rapid changes in the contemporary world, we have had to omit the section on decision making that was in the third edition. We were reluctant to do so, but we felt the subjects of Part Four were sufficiently important and grew so naturally out of the first three parts that the decision was a wise one.

The fourth edition of *International Politics* is roughly one-third different from the third. But it continues to follow the four principles that have guided us throughout all previous editions:

1. A selection of subjects that, even though they do not exhaustively cover the field of international politics, nevertheless encompasses most of the essential topics that we teach in our introductory courses.
2. Individual readings that are mainly analytical in content, that take issue with one another, and that thereby introduce the student to the fundamental debates and points of view in the field.
3. Editors' introductions to each part that summarize the central concepts the student must master, that organize the central themes of each part, and that relate the readings to one another.
4. A reader that can be used either as the core around which to design an introductory course or as the primary supplement to enrich an assigned text.

Finally, in putting together the fourth edition, we received excellent advice from the following colleagues, whom we would like to thank for the time and care they took: Andrew Bennett, Timothy McKeown, Roslin Simowitz, and Robert J. Griffiths.

Robert J. Art

Robert Jervis

International Politics

PART
One

ANARCHY AND ITS CONSEQUENCES

Unlike domestic politics, international politics takes place in an arena that has no central governing body. From this central fact flow important consequences for the behavior of states. In Part One, we explore three of them: the role that morality can and should play in statecraft; the effects that anarchy has on how states view and relate to one another; and the ways that the harsher edges of anarchy can be mitigated, even if not wholly removed.

THE ROLE OF MORALITY IN STATECRAFT

Citizens, students, and scholars alike often take up the study of international politics because they want their country to behave as morally as possible. But they soon discover that morality and statecraft do not easily mix. Why should this be? Is it inevitable? Can and should states seek to do good in the world? Will they endanger themselves and harm others if they try?

The end of the Cold War has brought these questions once again to the fore of international politics. But they are timeless questions, having been asked by observers of international politics in nearly every previous era. They therefore make a good starting point for thinking about the nature of international politics and the choices states face in our era. Hans J. Morgenthau, one of the leading proponents of the approach known as Realism (also known as power politics), takes the classic Realist position: morality cannot be an invariable guide to statecraft. Although morality must be present if foreign policies are to be effective, both the nature of human beings and the nature of international politics mean that political behavior can never truly be moral. J. Ann Tickner, commenting on the primacy of power in Morgenthau's writings, explains that what he considers to be a realistic description of international politics is only a picture of the past and therefore not a prediction about the future. A world in which women play a greater role, she

1

argues, might be more cooperative and pose fewer conflicts between the dictates of morality and the power of self-interest.

Especially today, much of the argument about the role that morality should play in international politics turns on whether states should press others to respect their conception of human rights. Some argue that such altruism is not only out of place, but also that it will backfire because others will resist intervention in their internal affairs. Others argue that it is a moral error to apply the values and standards of one society to others that have different values, cultures, and political systems. Rhoda E. Howard and Jack Donnelly dispute both positions. They argue that, although cultures and systems differ, each individual human being still has a set of rights by virtue of being human. The difficulty, they note, is not with the definition of human rights but with their implementation. In the absence of effective international government, there is no choice but to rely on states for the enforcement of human rights. This reliance raises two difficult problems for the fostering of human rights internationally. First, what specific set of rights will a state try to enforce on another? Second, will a state pursue its human rights agenda at the cost of all the other goals that it legitimately holds?

PERSPECTIVES ON THE NATURE OF ANARCHY

Even those who argue that morality should play a large role in statecraft acknowledge that international politics is not like domestic politics. In the latter, there is government; in the former, there is none. As a consequence, no agency exists above the individual states with authority and power to make laws and settle disputes. States can make commitments and treaties, but no sovereign power ensures compliance and punishes deviations. This—the absence of a supreme power—is what is meant by the anarchic environment of international politics. Anarchy is therefore said to constitute a *state of war:* When all else fails, force is the *ultima ratio*—the final and legitimate arbiter of disputes among states.

The state of war does not mean that every nation is constantly at the brink of war or actually at war with other nations. Most countries, though, do feel threatened by some states at some time, and every state has experienced periods of intense insecurity. No two contiguous states, moreover, have had a history of close, friendly relations uninterrupted by severe tension if not outright war. Because a nation cannot look to a supreme body to enforce laws, nor count on other nations for constant aid and support, it must rely on its own efforts, particularly for defense against attack. Coexistence in an anarchic environment thus requires *self-help*. The psychological outlook that self-help breeds is best described by a saying common among British statesmen since Palmerston: "Great Britain has no permanent enemies or permanent friends, she has only permanent interests."

Although states must provide the wherewithal to achieve their own ends, they do not always reach their foreign policy goals. The goals may be grandiose; the means available, meager. The goals may be attainable; the means selected, inappropriate. But even if the goals are realistic and the means both available and appropriate, a state can be frustrated in pursuit of its ends. The reason is simple, but fundamental to an understanding of international politics: What one state does will inevitably impinge on some other states—on some beneficially, but on others adversely. What one state desires another may covet. What one thinks its just due another may find threatening. Steps that a state takes to achieve its goals may be rendered useless by the countersteps others take. No state, therefore, can afford to disregard the effects its actions will have on other nations' behavior. In this sense state behavior is contingent: What one state does is dependent in part upon what others do. Mutual dependence means that each must take the others into account. Kenneth Waltz explores this point more fully and shows why "in anarchy there is no automatic harmony."

Mutual dependence affects nothing more powerfully than it does security—the measures states take to protect their territory. Like other foreign-policy goals, the security of one state is contingent upon the behavior of other states. Herein lies the *security dilemma* to which each state is subject: In its efforts to preserve or enhance its own security, one state can take measures that decrease the security of other states and cause them to take countermeasures that neutralize the actions of the first state and that may even menace it. The first state may feel impelled to take additional actions that will provoke additional countermeasures . . . and so forth. The security dilemma means that an action-reaction spiral can occur between two states or among several of them so that each is forced to spend even larger sums on arms and be no more secure than before. All will run faster merely to stay where they were.

At the heart of the security dilemma are these two constraints: the inherent difficulty in distinguishing between offensive and defensive postures and the inability of one state to bank on the fact that another state's present pacific intentions will remain so. The capability to defend can also provide the capability to attack. In adding to its arms, state A may know that its aim is defensive, that its intentions are peaceful, and therefore that it has no aggressive designs on state B. In a world where states must look to themselves for protection, however, B will examine A's actions carefully and suspiciously. B may think that A will attack him when A's arms become powerful enough and that A's protestations of friendship are designed to lull him into lowering his guard. But even if B believes A's actions are not directed against him, B cannot assume that A's intentions will remain peaceful. B must allow for the possibility that what A can do to him, A sometime might do. The need to assess capabilities along with intentions, or, the equivalent, to allow for a change in intentions, makes statesmen profoundly conservative. They prefer to err on the side of safety, to have too much rather than too little. Because security is the basis of existence and the prerequisite for the achievement of all other goals, statesmen must be acutely sensitive to the security actions of others. The security dilemma thus means that statesmen cannot risk *not* reacting to the security actions of other states, but that in so reacting they can produce circumstances that leave them worse off than before.

The anarchic environment of international politics, then, allows every state to be the final judge of its own interests, but requires that each provide the means to attain them. Because the absence of a central authority permits wars to occur, security considerations become paramount. Because of the effects of the security dilemma, efforts of statesmen to protect their peoples can lead to severe tension and war even when all parties sincerely desire peace. Two states, or two groups of states, each satisfied with the status quo and seeking only security, may not be able to achieve it. Conflicts and wars with no economic or ideological basis can occur. The outbreak of war, therefore, does not necessarily mean that some or all states seek expansion, or that men have an innate drive for power. That states go to war when none of them wants to, however, does not imply that they never seek war. The security dilemma may explain some wars; it does not explain all wars. States often do experience conflicts of interest over trade, real estate, ideology, and prestige. For example, when someone asked Francis I what differences led to his constant wars with Charles V, he replied: "None whatever. We agree perfectly. We both want control of Italy!" (Cited in Frederick L. Schuman, *International Politics,* 7th ed., New York, 1953, p. 283.) If states cannot obtain what they want by blackmail, bribery, or threats, they may resort to war. Wars can occur when no one wants them; wars do occur when someone wants them.

Even under propitious circumstances, international cooperation is difficult to achieve, Realists argue. Joseph Grieco points out that in anarchy, states are often more concerned with relative advantages than with absolute gains. That is, because international politics is a self-help system in which each state must be prepared to rely on its own resources and strength to further its interests, statesmen often seek to become more powerful than their potential adversaries. Cooperation is then made difficult not only by the fear that others will cheat and fail to live up to their agreements, but also by the felt need to gain a superior position. The reason is not that statesmen are concerned with status, but that they fear that arrangements which benefit all, but provide greater benefits to others than to them, will render their country vulnerable to pressure and coercion in the future.

In an anarchic condition the better question to ask is not "Why does war occur?" but "Why does war not occur more frequently than it does?" Instead of asking "Why do states not cooperate more to achieve common interests?" we should ask "Given anarchy and the security dilemma, how is it that states are able to cooperate at all?" This Realist perspective is not without its critics. As Milner notes, the absence of a formal international authority and world government may mean that international politics is technically anarchic, but it does not mean that the contrast to domestic politics is as extreme as Realists claim. States are tied together by a complex web of interests and values. Attacking or even menacing others often is not a prudent policy, even for a state that is more powerful than its neighbors. We should not exaggerate either the insecurities or the opportunities created by the international system.

THE MITIGATION OF ANARCHY

Even Realists note that conflict and warfare is not a constant characteristic of international politics. Most states remain at peace with most others most of the time. Statesmen have developed a number of ways of coping with anarchy, of gaining more than a modicum of security, of regulating their competition with other states, and of developing patterns that contain, although not eliminate, the dangers of aggression. Summarizing a great deal of recent research, Kenneth Oye shows that even if anarchy and the security dilemma inhibit cooperation, they do not prevent it. A number of conditions and national strategies can make it easier for states to achieve common ends. Cooperation is usually easier if there are a small number of actors. Not only can each more carefully observe the others, but all actors know that their impact on the system is great enough so that if they fail to cooperate with others, joint enterprises are likely to fail. Furthermore, when the number of actors is large, there may be mechanisms and institutions that group them together, thereby reproducing some of the advantages of small numbers. The conditions actors face also influence their fates. The barriers of anarchy are more likely to be overcome when actors have long time horizons, when even successfully exploiting others produces an outcome that is only a little better than mutual cooperation, when being exploited by others is only slightly worse than mutual noncooperation, and when mutual cooperation is much better than unrestricted competition. Under such circumstances, states are particularly likely to undertake contingent strategies such as tit-for-tat. That is, they will cooperate with others if others do likewise and refuse to cooperate if others have refused to cooperate with them.

Most strikingly, it appears that democracies have never gone to war against each other. This is not to say, as Woodrow Wilson did, that democracies are inherently peaceful. They seem to fight as many wars as do dictatorships. But, as Michael Doyle shows, they do not fight each other. If this is correct—and, of course, both the evidence and the reasons are open to dispute—it implies that anarchy and the security dilemma do not prevent peaceful and even harmonious relations among states that share certain common values and beliefs.

Democracies are relatively recent developments. For a longer period of time, two specific devices—international law and diplomacy—have proven useful in resolving conflicts among states. Although not enforced by a world government, international law can provide norms for behavior and mechanisms for settling disputes. The effectiveness of international law derives from the willingness of states to observe it. Its power extends no further than the disposition of states "to agree to agree." Where less than vital interests are at stake, statesmen may accept settlements that are not entirely satisfactory because they think the precedents or principles justify the compromises made. Much of international law reflects a consensus among states on what is of equal benefit to all, as, for example, the rules regulating international communications. Diplomacy, too, can facilitate cooperation and resolve disputes. Particularly if diplomacy is skillful, that is, if the legitimate interests of the parties in dispute are taken into account, understandings can often be reached on issues that might otherwise lead to war. These points and others are explored more fully by Stanley Hoffmann and Hans Morgenthau.

Statesmen use these two traditional tools within a balance-of-power system. Much maligned by President Wilson and his followers and often misunderstood by many others, balance of power refers to the manner in which stability can be the outcome of the efforts of individual states, whether or not any or all of them deliberately pursue that goal. Just as Adam Smith argued that if every individual pursued his or her own self-interest, the interaction of individual egoisms would enhance national wealth, so international relations theorists have argued that even if every state seeks power at the expense of the others, no one state will likely dominate. In both cases a general good can be the unintended product of selfish individual actions. Moreover, even if most states desire only to keep what they have, their own interests dictate that they band together in order to resist any state or coalition of states that threatens to dominate them.

The balance-of-power system is likely to prevent any one state's acquiring hegemony. It will not, however, benefit all states equally nor maintain the peace permanently. Rewards will be unequal because of inequalities in power and expertise. Wars will occur because they are one of the means by which states can preserve what they have or acquire what they covet. Small states may even be eliminated by their more powerful neighbors. The international system will be unstable, however, only if states flock to what they think is the strongest side. What is called *bandwagoning* or the *domino theory* argues that the international system is precarious because successful aggression will attract many followers, either out of fear or out of a desire to share the spoils of victory. Stephen Walt disagrees, drawing on balance-of-power theory and historical evidence to argue that rather than bandwagoning, under most conditions states balance against emerging threats. They do not throw in their lot with the stronger side. Instead, they join with others to prevent any state from becoming so strong that it could dominate the system.

Power balancing is a strategy followed by individual states acting on their own. Other ways of coping with anarchy which may supplement or exist alongside this impulse, are more explicitly collective. Regimes and institutions can help overcome anarchy and facilitate cooperation. When states agree on the principles, rules, and norms that should govern behavior, they can often ameliorate the security dilemma and increase the scope for cooperation. Institutions may not only embody common understandings but, as Robert Keohane argues, they can also help states work toward mutually desired outcomes by providing a framework for long-run agreements, making it easier for each state to see whether others are living up to their promises, and increasing the costs the state will pay if it cheats. In the security area, the United Nations has the potential to be an especially important institution.

As Bruce Russett and James Sutterlin note, the end of the Cold War opens up new possibilities for the internationalization of deterrence and force in the service of common security.

The Role of Morality in Statecraft

The Moral Blindness of Scientific Man

Hans J. Morgenthau

The age of science misunderstands the nature of man in that it attributes to man's reason, in its relation to the social world, a power of knowledge and control which reason does not have. It misunderstands the nature of man in yet another respect; for it does not see that understanding, and action according to understanding, is not the only dimension in which man faces the social world. Not only does man try to know what the social world is about and to act according to his knowledge, he also reflects and renders judgments on its nature and value and on the nature and value of his social actions and of his existence in society. In brief, man is also a moral being. It is this side of man which the age of science has obscured and distorted, if not obliterated, by trying to reduce moral problems to scientific propositions.

Man is a political animal by nature; he is a scientist by chance or choice; he is a moralist because he is a man. Man is born to seek power, yet his actual condition makes him a slave to the power of others. Man is born a slave, but everywhere he wants to be a master. Out of this discord between man's desire and his actual condition arises the moral issue of power, that is, the problem of justifying and limiting the power which man has over man. Hence, the history of political thought is the history of the moral evaluation of political power. . . .

The argument starts with the observation that man as an actor on the political scene does certain things in violation of ethical principles, which he does not do, or at least not so frequently and habitually, when he acts in a private capacity. There, he lies, deceives, and betrays; and he does so quite often. Here he does so, if at all, only as an exception and under extraordinary circumstances. From this starting-point the argument leads to the conclusion that man acts differently in the political and in the private spheres because ethics allows him to act differently. In other words, there is one ethics for the political sphere and there is another ethics for the

Portions of the text and some footnotes have been omitted.

7

private sphere, and the former allows him to do certain things there which the latter does not allow him to do here. Political acts are subject to one ethical standard;
private acts are subject to another. What the latter condemns, the former may
approve. "If we had done for ourselves," exclaimed Cavour, "what we did for Italy,
what scoundrels we would have been!"

No civilization can be satisfied with such a dual morality; for through it the
domain of politics is not only made morally inferior to the private sphere but this
inferiority is recognized as legitimate and made respectable by a particular system
of political ethics. Hence, the very age that conceived the problem of political
ethics in terms of a dual morality has endeavored either to overcome the duality of
standards or to justify it in the light of a higher principle.

The attempt at overcoming the cleavage between private and political morality starts with the assumption that the morality of the political sphere, viewed from
the standards of individual ethics, is a residue from an immoral age which has been
overcome in the individual sphere but still leads a ghost-like existence in the realm
of politics. Political ethics, in other words, is in a retarded stage of development.
The particular ethics of political action is the manifestation of what the sociologists
call a "cultural lag." If this is so, then the conclusion is inevitable that the forward
march of civilization will sooner or later subject political action to the same moral
standards by which private action is already judged. A deliberate effort at reform
will bridge over the gulf which still separates political and private morality.
Woodrow Wilson, in his address to Congress on the declaration of war in 1917,
thought that he could detect "the beginning of an age in which it will be insisted
that the same standards of conduct and of responsibility for wrong shall be
observed among nations and their governments that are observed among the individual citizens of civilized states." Thus, this conception culminates in a perfectionist ethics which tries to solve the problem of political ethics by minimizing the
conflict between ethical standards and political reality and by obscuring its intrinsic relation to the existence of man in society.

THE END JUSTIFIES THE MEANS

It is on a higher level of insight that this cleavage is being recognized as inevitable
yet justified in the light of a higher principle. Here harmony is sought not in the
reality of actual behavior but in ethical judgment. The harmony derives from the
subordination of certain otherwise immoral acts as means to certain ends in whose
moral value the former partake. Since we are under a moral obligation to realize
these ends and since we cannot do so without using those in themselves immoral
means, we are confronted with the dilemma either of renouncing the attainment
of moral ends in order to avoid the evil of the means or of doing what would otherwise be evil in order to attain the good of the end. It is the latter alternative, we
are told, that we have to choose. For as the means are subordinated functionally to
the end, so they are ethically. A good end must be sought for and an evil end must
be avoided—in both cases regardless of the means employed. The end taints the

means employed for its attainment with its own ethical color and thus justifies or condemns that which, considered by itself, would merit the opposite valuation.

The end which, above all others, is considered to justify whatever means are employed in its behalf is the state as the repository of the common good. What a man would not be allowed to do for himself, that is, in behalf of his own limited interests as the end of his action, he is allowed and even obligated to do when his act would further the welfare of the state and thus promote the common good. The action which would make him a scoundrel and a criminal there, will make him a hero and a statesman here. Cavour's statement, quoted above as an expression of dual morality, may be quoted here again; and the justification of means by ends, if limited to the political sphere, is indeed identical with, and only a particular manifestation of, the conception of a dual morality discussed above.

Actually, however, the tendency to justify otherwise immoral actions by the ends they serve is universal. It is merely most conspicuous in politics. It has been said that there are just wars but no just armies. One might as well say that there are just foreign policies but no just diplomats. The particular discrepancy between ethics and political action and its quantitative dimension cannot escape our attention, and we are all vaguely aware of the problem when we read a dispatch such as the following: "Snapped Lady Astor: 'When are you going to stop killing people?' Said Stalin: 'When it is no longer necessary.' To an English newspaperman who asked him about the millions of peasants who had died during the collectivization drive, Stalin answered with the question: 'How many died in the Great War?' Over 7,500,000. Said Stalin: 'Over 7,500,000 deaths for no purpose at all. Then you must acknowledge that our losses are small, because your war ended in chaos, while we are engaged in a work which will benefit the whole of humanity.' "

What is called the "ethics of capitalism" offers less striking, yet no less typical, examples of the same attempt at reconciling action with ethics. They appear to us to be less striking only because they do not operate in a world seemingly different from our own and in dimensions which qualitatively and quantitatively transcend our own individual experience, but are a familiar part of this very experience. The Puritan identification of worldly success with virtue and divine blessings is interpreted in such a way as to signify that the means employed on the road to success, whatever they may be, partake of the ethical dignity of the latter. The belief of laisser faire liberalism that the natural harmony of interests, that is, the common good in economic terms, results from the free interplay of the enlightened self-interest of individuals bestows upon individual egotism an ethical value which it would not possess apart from its subservience to the ethical goal of social harmony. The ethical life of the individual himself is a continued series of attempts to justify manifestations of individual egotism in terms of an ethically valuable goal and thus to prove that what has the appearance of egotism transcends actually the individual interest. The promotion of the latter is only incidental, an inevitable step toward the realization of a good of higher ethical value than the interests of any single individual.

The harmony thus achieved between ethical standard and human action is, however, apparent rather than real, ambiguous rather than definite. In order to achieve it, one must weigh the immorality of the means against the ethical value of the end and establish a fixed relationship between them. This is impossible. One may argue from the point of view of a particular political philosophy, but one cannot prove from the point of view of universal and objective ethical standards that the good of the end ought to prevail over the evil of the means; for there is no objective standard by which to compare two kinds of happiness or of misery or the happiness of one man with the misery of another. That the welfare of one group is or is not too dearly paid for by the misery of another has always been asserted but has never been demonstrated. The analysis of the artificial and partial character of the end-means relation will make this clear. . . . The means-end relation itself therefore has no objectivity and is relative to the social vantage point of the observer. Kant and Marx have decried the use of man by man as a means to an end, proclaiming the ethical maxim that every man be treated as an end in himself, and the disinherited have taken up the cry. Yet from Plato and Aristotle to Spencer and Hitler, philosophers and practitioners of government alike have maintained the claim that certain men are born to serve as means for the ends of others, and this claim the disinherited themselves support once they have risen to the top and then determine for themselves what is end and what is means.

On the other hand, the end-means relation is ambiguous and relative also in that whatever we call "means" in view of the end of a chain of actions is itself an end if we consider it as the final point of a chain of actions. Conversely, what we call "end" is a point at which a chain of actions is supposed to come to a stop, while it proceeds actually beyond it; in view of this "beyond," the end transforms itself into a means. All action is, therefore, at the same time means and end; and it is only by an arbitrary separation of a certain chain of actions from what precedes and follows it that we can attribute to certain actions the exclusive quality of means and end. Actually, however, the totality of human actions presents itself as a hierarchy of actions each of which is the end of the preceding and a means for the following. This hierarchy culminates in the ultimate goal of all human activity which is identical with the absolute good—be it God, humanity, the state, or the individual himself. This is the only end that is nothing but end and hence does not serve as a means to a further end. Viewed from this end, all human activity appears as means to the ultimate goal.

In the last analysis, then, the doctrine that the ethical end justifies unethical means leads to the negation of absolute ethical judgments altogether. For if the ethical end justifies unethical means, the ultimate and absolute good which all human activity serves as means to an end justifies all human actions. Among them there may be differences in degree, there can be none in kind. Whatever is done *ad majorem dei gloriam* partakes of the sanctity of its ultimate goal. The harmony thus established between ethical norm and reality is indeed complete. However, the solution of the problem is again apparent rather than real. For the dilemma which disturbs the consciences of men and raises this problem in their minds concerns primarily not the relation between human action and the absolute good but the relation between human actions and limited objectives, the former presumably evil, the latter presumably good. The question which man is anxious to answer is therefore not, at least not within the context of an end-means discussion, how we can explain the apparently inevitable evilness of all human action in the light of the absolute good but how we can explain the apparently inevitable evilness of some, especially political, actions in the light of the relative good they are intended to serve. . . .

THE CORRUPTION OF MAN

It is the common mark of all these attempts at solving the problem of political ethics that they try to create a harmony which the facts do not warrant, either because there is no discord in the first place or because the existing discord is final. All these attempts start with the assumption that the individual sphere is ethically superior to politics. They idealize the individual sphere and erect it into a model, if not of ethical perfection, at least of approximation to it. In contrast with it, political action appears sinister and evil and in need of being elevated to the ethical level of individual action. At the basis of this juxtaposition there is the optimistic belief in the intrinsic goodness of the rational individual and the pessimistic conviction that politics is the seat of all irrationality and evil.

One might note from the outset that the opposition between man and society, individual and political action, is a mere figure of speech in so far as the individual actor is confronted with a collectivity which is supposed likewise to act. It is always the individual who acts, either with reference to his own ends alone or with reference to the ends of others. The action of society, of the nation, or of any other collectivity, political or otherwise, as such has no empirical existence at all. What empirically exist are always the actions of individuals who perform identical or different actions with reference to a common end. The most that can be said concerning the moral character of a private, as over against a political, action is that an individual acting in one capacity may be more or less moral than when acting in the other. Once the opposition between man and society, between private and political action, is reduced to the opposition between different kinds of individual actions, it becomes obvious that the difference in moral character between the two kinds of actions is at best a relative one and is devoid of the absoluteness which contemporary doctrine attributes to it.

The examination of the moral character of individual action, furthermore, shows that all action is, at least potentially, immoral and that this immorality inherent in all human action is to a higher degree and more obviously present in political than in private action, owing to the particular conditions under which political action proceeds. The at least potential immorality of human action, regardless of the level on which it proceeds, becomes evident when we measure, not one action by another one (e.g., the political by the private) but all actions by the intention in which they originate. Such a comparison shows that our intentions are generally good, whereas the consequences of our actions generally are not. As soon as we leave the realm of our thoughts and aspirations, we are inevitably involved in sin and guilt. While our hand carries the good intent to what seems to be its consummation, the fruit of evil grows from the seed of noble thought. We want peace among nations and harmony among individuals, yet our actions end in conflict and war. We want to see all men free, but our actions put others in chains as others do to us. We believe in the equality of all men, and our very demands on society make others unequal. Oedipus tries to obviate the oracle's prophecy of future crimes and by doing so makes the fulfilment of the prophecy inevitable. Brutus' actions intend to preserve Roman liberty but bring about its destruction. Lincoln's purpose is to make all Americans free, yet his actions destroy the lives of many and make the freedom of others a legal fiction and an actual mockery. Hamlet, aware of this tragic tension between the ethics of our minds and the ethics of our actions, resolves to act only when he can act as ethically as his intention demands and thus despairs of acting at all, and, when he finally acts, his actions and fate are devoid of ethical meaning.

"He who acts," Goethe remarks to Eckermann, "is always unjust; nobody is just but the one who reflects." The very act of acting destroys our moral integrity. Whoever wants to retain his moral innocence must forsake action altogether and, following Hamlet's advice to Ophelia, "go. . . . to a nunnery." Why is this so with respect to all actions and particularly so with respect to political actions?

First of all, because of its natural limitations, the human intellect is unable to calculate and to control completely the results of human action. Once the action is performed, it becomes an independent force creating changes, provoking actions, and colliding with other forces, which the actor may or may not have foreseen and which he can control but to a small degree. . . .

While, however, good intention is corrupted before it reaches its intended goal in the world of action, it may not even leave the world of thought without corruption. The demands which life in society makes on our good intentions surpass our faculty to satisfy them all. While satisfying one, we must neglect others, and the satisfaction of one may even imply the positive violation of another. Thus the incompatibility, in the light of our own limitations, of the demands which morality makes upon us compels us to choose between different equally legitimate demands. Whatever choice we make, we must do evil while we try to do good; for we must abandon one moral end in favor of another. While trying to render to Caesar what is Caesar's and to God what is God's, we will at best strike a precarious balance which will ever waver between both, never completely satisfying either. In the extreme, we will abandon one completely in order fully to satisfy the other. The typical solution, however, will be a compromise which puts the struggle at rest without putting conscience at ease.

The same incompatibility of two contradictory ethical demands, ending in one of these three alternative solutions, corrupts good intentions on all levels of human actions. Loyalty to the nation comes into conflict with our duties to humanity. Even though most men will in our age resolve the conflict easily in favor of the nation, the conflict is nevertheless a real one; and there are more individuals than the war literature would let us suspect who bore as a heavy burden the dual duty to kill in the name of their country and to respect in their fellow-men the image of God. Punishment of children as well as of criminals gives rise to a similar moral conflict between the duty owed to all men to understand their weaknesses and to forgive rather than to judge them and the duty owed to a certain individual or to a group of individuals to protect them against infringement of their rights. By killing the killer, we fulfil the latter duty, while our conscience keeps asking whether it was the killer alone who was guilty or whether his guilt was shared by the one whom he killed and perhaps by all other men as well. There is no end to examples of such insoluble conflicts and of the consequent corruption of good intentions. The daughter perceives, like Desdemona, "a divided duty" between parents and husband. The father must choose between two children, the friend between two friends; and, finally and above all, a man must choose between himself and others. It is here that the inevitability of evil becomes paramount. . . .

There are two reasons why the egotism of one must come into conflict with the egotism of the other. What the one wants for himself, the other already possesses or wants, too. Struggle and competition ensue. Finding that all his relations with his fellow-men contain at least the germs of such conflicts of interest, man can no longer seek the goodness of his intentions in the almost complete absence of selfishness and of the concomitant harm to others but only in the limitations which conscience puts upon the drive toward evil. Man cannot hope to be good but must be content with being not too evil.

The other root of conflict and concomitant evil stems from the *animus dominandi*, the desire for power. This lust for power manifests itself as the desire to maintain range of one's own person with regard to others, to increase it, or to demonstrate it. In whatever disguises it may appear, its ultimate essence and aim is in one of these particular references of one person to others. Centered as it is upon the person of the actor in relation to others, the desire for power is closely related to the selfishness of which we have spoken but is not identical with it. For the typical goals of selfishness, such as food, shelter, security, and the means by which they are obtained, such as money, jobs, marriage, and the like, have an objective relation to the vital needs of the individual; their attainment offers the best chances for survival under the particular natural and social conditions under which the individual lives.

The desire for power, on the other hand, concerns itself not with the individual's survival but with his position among his fellows once his survival has been secured. Consequently, the selfishness of man has limits; his will to power has none. For while man's vital needs are capable of satisfaction, his lust for power would be satisfied only if the last man became an object of his domination, there being nobody above or beside him, that is, if he became like God. "The fact is," as Aristotle put it, "that the greatest crimes are caused by excess and not by necessity. Men do not become tyrants in order that they may not suffer cold.". . .

To the degree in which the essence and aim of politics is power over man, politics is evil; for it is to this degree that it degrades man to a means for other men. It follows that the prototype of this corruption through power is to be found on the political scene. For here the *animus dominandi* is not merely blended with dominant aims of a different kind but is the very essence of the intention, the very lifeblood of the action, the constitutive principle of politics as a distinct sphere of human activity. Politics is a struggle for power over men, and whatever its ultimate aim may be, power is its immediate goal and the modes of acquiring, maintaining, and demonstrating it determine the technique of political action.

The evil that corrupts political action is the same evil that corrupts all action, but the corruption of political action is indeed the paradigm and the prototype of all possible corruption. The distinction between private and political action is not one between innocence and guilt, morality and immorality, goodness and evil, but lies in the degree alone in which the two types of action deviate from the ethical norm. Nor is the distinction of a normative character at all. To hold differently, as the school of the dual standard does, is to confound the moral obligations of man and his actual behavior with respect to these obligations. From the fact that the political acts of a person differ from his private ones, it does not follow that he recognizes different moral precepts in the different spheres of action. There is not one kind of ethical precept applying to political action and another one to the private sphere, but one and the same ethical standard applies to both—observed and observable, however, by either with unequal compliance.

That political action and doing evil are inevitably linked becomes fully clear only when we recognize not only that ethical standards are empirically violated on the political scene, and this to a particular degree, but that it is unattainable for an action at the same time to conform to the rules of the political art (i.e., to achieve political success) and to conform to the rules of ethics (i.e., to be good in itself). The test of political success is the degree to which one is able to maintain, to increase, or to demonstrate one's power over others. The test of a morally good action is the degree to which it is capable of treating others not as means to the actor's ends but as ends in themselves. It is for this reason alone inevitable that, whereas nonpolitical action is ever exposed to corruption by selfishness and lust for power, this corruption is inherent in the very nature of the political act.

Only the greatest dissenters of the age have been clearly aware of this necessary evilness of the political act. The great nonliberal thinkers writing in the liberal age will find, with Lord Acton, that "power corrupts. . . . absolute power corrupts absolutely"; or they will see, with Jacob Burckhardt, in politics the "absolute evil"; or they will agree with Emerson that force is "a practical lie" and that "every actual state is corrupt."

THE PARTICULAR CORRUPTION OF POLITICAL MAN

The scope of this corruption, which, as such, is a permanent element of human existence and therefore operates regardless of historic circumstances everywhere and at all times, is broadened and its intensity strengthened by the particular conditions under which political action proceeds in the modern nation state. The state has become in the secular sphere the most exalted object of loyalty on the part of the individual and at the same time the most effective organization for the exercise of power over the individual. These two qualities enable the modern state to accentuate the corruption of the political sphere both qualitatively and quantitatively. This is accomplished by two complementary processes.

The state as the receptacle of the highest secular loyalty and power devaluates and actually delimits the manifestations of the individual desire for power. The individual, power-hungry for his own sake, is held in low public esteem; and the mores and laws of society endeavor to strengthen through positive sanctions the moral condemnation of individual aspirations for power, to limit their modes and sphere of action, and to suppress them altogether. While, however, the state is ideologically and physically incomparably more powerful than its citizens, it is free from all effective restraint from above. The state's collective desire for power is limited, aside from self-chosen limitations, only by the ruins of an old, and the rudiments of a new, normative order, both too feeble to offer more than a mere intimation of actual restraint. Above it, there is no centralized authority beyond the mechanics of the balance of power, which could impose actual limits upon the manifestations of its collective desire for domination. The state has become indeed a "mortal God," and for an age that believes no longer in an immortal God, the state becomes the only God there is.

Moreover, what the individual is not allowed to want for himself, he is encouraged to seek for the legal fiction called "the state." The impulses which both ethics and the state do not allow the individual to satisfy for his own sake are directed by the state itself toward its own ends. By transferring his egotism and power impulses to the nation, the individual gives his inhibited aspirations not only a vicarious satisfaction. The process of transference transforms also the ethical significance of the satisfaction. What was egotism—and hence ignoble and immoral—there becomes patriotism and therefore noble and altruistic here. While society puts liabilities upon aspirations for individual power, it places contributions to the collective power of the state at the top of the hierarchy of values. . . .

THE LESSER EVIL

The lust for power as ubiquitous empirical fact and its denial as universal ethical norm are the two poles between which, as between the poles of an electric field, this antinomy is suspended. The antinomy is insoluble because the poles creating it are perennial. There can be no renunciation of the ethical denial without renouncing the human nature of man. "We," Benedetto Croce quotes an Italian as saying to a German, "with our bad faith, at least keep the intellect lucid, and we remain bad men, but men: whereas you lose it altogether and become beasts." There can be no actual denial of the lust for power without denying the very conditions of human existence in this world. . . .

There is no escape from the evil of power, regardless of what one does. Whenever we act with reference to our fellow men, we must sin, and we must still sin when we refuse to act; for the refusal to be involved in the evil of action carries with it the breach of the obligation to do one's duty. No ivory tower is remote enough to offer protection against the guilt in which the actor and the bystander, the oppressor and the oppressed, the murderer and his victim are inextricably enmeshed. Political ethics is indeed the ethics of doing evil. While it condemns politics as the domain of evil par excellence, it must reconcile itself to the enduring presence of evil in all political action. Its last resort, then, is the endeavor to choose, since evil there must be, among several possible actions the one that is least evil.

It is indeed trivial, in the face of so tragic a choice, to invoke justice against expediency and to condemn whatever political action is chosen because of its lack of justice. Such an attitude is but another example of the superficiality of a civilization which, blind to the tragic complexities of human existence, contents itself with an unreal and hypocritical solution of the problem of political ethics. In fact, the invocation of justice pure and simple against a political action makes of justice a mockery; for, since all political actions needs must fall short of justice, the argument against one political action holds true for all. By avoiding a political action because it is unjust, the perfectionist does nothing but exchange blindly one injustice for another which might even be worse than the former. He shrinks from the lesser evil because he does not want to do evil at all. Yet his personal abstention from evil, which is actually a subtle form of egotism with a good conscience, does not at all affect the existence of evil in the world but only destroys the faculty of discriminating between different evils. The perfectionist thus becomes finally a source of greater evil. "Man," in the words of Pascal, "is neither angel nor beast and his misery is that he who would act the angel acts the brute." Here again it is only the awareness of the tragic presence of evil in all political action which at least enables man to choose the lesser evil and to be as good as he can be in an evil world.

Neither science nor ethics nor politics can resolve the conflict between politics and ethics into harmony. We have no choice between power and the common good. To act successfully, that is, according to the rules of the political art, is political wisdom. To know with despair that the political act is inevitably evil, and to act nevertheless, is moral courage. To choose among several expedient actions the least evil one is moral judgment. In the combination of political wisdom, moral courage, and moral judgment, man reconciles his political nature with his moral destiny. That this conciliation is nothing more than a *modus vivendi*, uneasy, precarious, and even paradoxical, can disappoint only those who prefer to gloss over and to distort the tragic contradictions of human existence with the soothing logic of a specious concord.

A Critique of Morgenthau's Principles of Political Realism

J. Ann Tickner

It is not in giving life but in risking life that man is raised above the animal: that is why superiority has been accorded in humanity not to the sex that brings forth but to that which kills

Simone de Beauvoir[1]

International politics is a man's world, a world of power and conflict in which warfare is a privileged activity. Traditionally, diplomacy, military service and the science of international politics have been largely male domains. In the past women have rarely been included in the ranks of professional diplomats or the military; of the relatively few women who specialize in the academic discipline of international relations, few are security specialists. Women political scientists who do study international relations tend to focus on areas such as international political economy, North–South relations and matters of distributive justice.

Today, in the United States, where women are entering the military and the foreign service in greater numbers than ever before, they are rarely to be found in positions of military leadership or at the top of the foreign policy establishment.[2] One notable exception, Jeane Kirkpatrick, who was U.S. ambassador to the United Nations in the early 1980s, has described herself as 'a mouse in a man's world'; for, in spite of her authoritative and forceful public style and strong conservative credentials, Kirkpatrick maintains that she failed to win the respect or attention of her male colleagues on matters of foreign policy.[3]

Kirkpatrick's story could serve to illustrate the discrimination that women often encounter when they rise to high political office. However, the doubts as to

---

Portions of the text and some footnotes have been omitted.

whether a woman would be strong enough to press the nuclear button, (an issue raised when a tearful Patricia Schroeder was pictured sobbing on her husband's shoulder as she bowed out of the 1988 U.S. presidential race) suggest that there may be an even more fundamental barrier to women's entry into the highest ranks of the military or of foreign policy making. Nuclear strategy, with its vocabulary of power, threat, force and deterrence, has a distinctly masculine ring;[4] moreover, women are stereotypically judged to be lacking in qualities which these terms evoke. It has also been suggested that, although more women are entering the world of public policy, they are more comfortable dealing with domestic issues such as social welfare that are more compatible with their nurturing skills. Yet the large number of women in the ranks of the peace movement suggests that women are not uninterested in issues of war and peace, although their frequent dissent from national security policy has often branded them as naive, uninformed or even unpatriotic.

In this chapter I propose to explore the question of why international politics is perceived as a man's world and why women remain so underrepresented in the higher echelons of the foreign policy establishment, the military and the academic discipline of international relations. Since I believe that there is something about this field that renders it particularly inhospitable and unattractive to women, I intend to focus on the nature of the discipline itself rather than on possible strategies to remove barriers to women's access to high policy positions. As I have already suggested, the issues that are given priority in foreign policy are issues with which men have had a special affinity. Moreover, if it is primarily men who are describing these issues and constructing theories to explain the workings of the international system, might we not expect to find a masculine perspective in the academic discipline also? If this were so then it could be argued that the exclusion of women has operated not only at the level of discrimination but also through a process of self-selection which begins with the way in which we are taught about international relations.

In order to investigate this claim that the discipline of international relations, as it has traditionally been defined by realism, is based on a masculine world view, I propose to examine the six principles of political realism formulated by Hans Morgenthau in his classic work *Politics Among Nations*. I shall use some ideas from feminist theory to show that the way in which Morgenthau describes and explains international politics, and the prescriptions that ensue are embedded in a masculine perspective. Then I shall suggest some ways in which feminist theory might help us begin to conceptualize a world view from a feminine perspective and to formulate a feminist epistemology of international relations. Drawing on these observations I shall conclude with a reformulation of Morgenthau's six principles. Male critics of contemporary realism have already raised many of the same questions about realism that I shall address. However, in undertaking this exercise, I hope to make a link between a growing critical perspective on international relations theory and feminist writers interested in global issues. Adding a feminist perspective to its discourse could also help to make the field of international relations more accessible to women scholars and practitioners.

HANS MORGENTHAU'S PRINCIPLES OF POLITICAL REALISM: A MASCULINE PERSPECTIVE?

I have chosen to focus on Hans Morgenthau's six principles of political realism because they represent one of the most important statements of contemporary realism from which several generations of scholars and practitioners of international relations in the United States have been nourished. Although Morgenthau has frequently been criticized for his lack of scientific rigour and ambiguous use of language, these six principles have significantly framed the way in which the majority of international relations scholars and practitioners in the West have thought about international politics since 1945.[5]

Morgenthau's principles of political realism can be summarized as follows:

1. Politics, like society in general, is governed by objective laws that have their roots in human nature, which is unchanging: therefore it is possible to develop a rational theory that reflects these objective laws.
2. The main signpost of political realism is the concept of interest defined in terms of power which infuses rational order into the subject matter of politics, and thus makes the theoretical understanding of politics possible. Political realism stresses the rational, objective and unemotional.
3. Realism assumes that interest defined as power is an objective category which is universally valid but not with a meaning that is fixed once and for all. Power is the control of man over man.
4. Political realism is aware of the moral significance of political action. It is also aware of the tension between the moral command and the requirements of successful political action.
5. Political realism refuses to identify the moral aspirations of a particular nation with the moral laws that govern the universe. It is the concept of interest defined in terms of power that saves us from moral excess and political folly.
6. The political realist maintains the autonomy of the political sphere; he asks 'How does this policy affect the power of the nation?' Political realism is based on a pluralistic conception of human nature. A man who was nothing but 'political man' would be a beast, for he would be completely lacking in moral restraints. But, in order to develop an autonomous theory of political behaviour, 'political man' must be abstracted from other aspects of human nature.[6]

I am not going to argue that Morgenthau is incorrect in his portrayal of the international system. I do believe, however, that it is a partial description of international politics because it is based on assumptions about human nature that are partial and that privilege masculinity. First, it is necessary to define masculinity and femininity. According to almost all feminist theorists, masculinity and femininity refer to a set of socially constructed categories, which vary in time and place, rather than to biological determinants. In the West, conceptual dichotomies such as objectivity vs subjectivity, reason vs emotion, mind vs body, culture vs nature, self vs other or autonomy vs relatedness, knowing vs being and public vs private have typically been used to describe male/female differences by feminists and non-feminists alike.[7] In the United States, psychological tests conducted across different socioeconomic groups confirm that individuals perceive these dichotomies as masculine and feminine and also that the characteristics associated with masculinity are more highly valued by men and women alike.[8] It is important to stress, however, that these characteristics are stereotypical; they do not necessarily describe individual men or women, who can exhibit characteristics and modes of thought associated with the opposite sex.

Using a vocabulary that contains many of the words associated with masculinity as I have identified it, Morgenthau asserts that it is possible to develop a rational (and unemotional) theory of international politics based on objective laws that have their roots in human nature. Since Morgenthau wrote the first edition of *Politics Among Nations* in 1948, this search for an objective science of international politics based on the model of the natural sciences has been an important part of the realist and neorealist agenda. In her feminist critique of the natural sciences, Evelyn Fox Keller points out that most scientific communities share the 'assumption that the universe they study is directly accessible, represented by concepts and shaped not by language but only by the demands of logic and experiment'.[9] The laws of nature, according to this view of science, are 'beyond the relativity of language'. Like most feminists, Keller rejects this view of science which, she asserts, imposes a coercive, hierarchical and conformist pattern on scientific inquiry. Feminists in general are sceptical about the possibility of finding a universal and objective foundation for knowledge, which Morgenthau claims is possible. Most share the belief that knowledge is socially constructed: since it is language that transmits knowledge, the use of language and its claims to objectivity must continually be questioned.

Keller argues that objectivity, as it is usually defined in our culture, is associated with masculinity. She identifies it as 'a network of interactions between gender development, a belief system that equates objectivity with masculinity, and a set of cultural values that simultaneously (and cojointly) elevates what is defined as scientific and what is defined as masculine'.[10] Keller links the separation of self from other, an important stage of masculine gender development, with this notion of objectivity. Translated into scientific inquiry this becomes the striving for the separation of subject and object, an important goal of modern science and one which, Keller asserts, is based on the need for control; hence objectivity becomes associated with power and domination.

The need for control has been an important motivating force for modern realism. To begin his search for an objective, rational theory of international politics, which could impose order on a chaotic and conflictual world, Morgenthau constructs an abstraction which he calls political man, a beast completely lacking in moral restraints. Morgenthau is deeply aware that real men, like real states, are both moral and bestial but, because states do not live up to the universal moral laws that govern the universe, those who behave morally in international politics are doomed to failure because of the immoral actions of others. To solve this tension Morgenthau postulates a realm of international politics in which the amoral behaviour of political man is not only permissible but prudent. It is a Hobbesian world, separate and distinct from the world of domestic order. In it, states may act like beasts, for survival depends on a maximization of power and a willingness to fight.

Having long argued that the personal is political, most feminist theory would reject the validity of constructing an autonomous political sphere around which boundaries of permissible modes of conduct have been drawn. As Keller maintains, 'the demarcation between public and private not only defines and defends the boundaries of the political but also helps form its content and style'.[11] Morgenthau's political man is a social construct based on a partial representation of human nature. One might well ask where the women were in Hobbes's state of nature; presumably they must have been involved in reproduction and childrearing, rather than warfare, if life was to go on for more than one generation.[12] Morgenthau's emphasis on the conflictual aspects of the international system contributes to a tendency, shared by other realists, to de-emphasize elements of cooperation and regeneration which are also aspects of international relations.[13]

Morgenthau's construction of an amoral realm of international power politics is an attempt to resolve what he sees as a fundamental tension between the moral laws that govern the universe and the requirements of successful political action in a world where states use morality as a cloak to justify the pursuit of their own national interests. Morgenthau's universalistic morality postulates the highest form of morality as an abstract ideal, similar to the Golden Rule, to which states seldom adhere: the morality of states, by contrast, is an instrumental morality guided by self-interest.

Morgenthau's hierarchical ordering of morality contains parallels with the work of psychologist Lawrence Kohlberg. Based on a study of the moral development of 84 American boys, Kohlberg concludes that the highest stage of human moral development (which he calls stage 6) is the ability to recognize abstract universal principles of justice; lower on the scale (stage 2) is an instrumental morality concerned with serving one's own interests while recognizing that others have interests too. Between these two is an interpersonal morality which is contextual and characterized by sensitivity to the needs of others (stage 3).[14]

In her critique of Kohlberg's stages of moral development, Carol Gilligan argues that they are based on a masculine conception of morality. On Kohlberg's scale women rarely rise above the third or contextual stage. Gilligan claims that this is not a sign of inferiority but of difference. Since women are socialized into a mode of thinking which is contextual and narrative, rather than formal and abstract, they tend to see issues in contextual rather than in abstract terms.[15] In international relations the tendency to think about morality either in terms of abstract, universal and unattainable standards or as purely instrumental, as Morgenthau does, detracts from our ability to tolerate cultural differences and to seek potential for building community in spite of these differences.

Using examples from feminist literature I have suggested that Morgenthau's attempt to construct an objective, universal theory of international politics is rooted in assumptions about human nature and morality that, in modern Western culture, are associated with masculinity. Further evidence that Morgenthau's principles are not the basis for a universalistic and objective theory is contained in his frequent references to the failure of what he calls the 'legalistic–moralistic' or idealist approach to world politics which he claims was largely responsible for both the world wars. Having laid the blame for the Second World War on the misguided morality of appeasement, Morgenthau's *realpolitik* prescriptions for successful political action appear as prescriptions for avoiding the mistakes of the 1930s rather than as prescriptions with timeless applicability.

If Morgenthau's world view is embedded in the traumas of the Second World War, are his prescriptions still valid as we move further away from this event? I share with other critics of realism the view that, in a rapidly changing world, we must begin to search for modes of behaviour different from those prescribed by Morgenthau. Given that any war between the major powers is likely to be nuclear, increasing security by increasing power could be suicidal.[16] Moreover, the nation state, the primary constitutive element of the international system for Morgenthau and other realists, is no longer able to deal with an increasingly pluralistic array of problems ranging from economic interdependence to environmental degradation. Could feminist theory make a contribution to international relations theory by constructing an alternative, feminist perspective on international politics that might help us to search for more appropriate solutions?

A FEMINIST PERSPECTIVE ON INTERNATIONAL RELATIONS?

If the way in which we describe reality has an effect on the ways we perceive and act upon our environment, new perspectives might lead us to consider alternative courses of action. With this in mind I shall first examine two important concepts in international relations, power and security, from a feminist perspective and then discuss some feminist approaches to conflict resolution.

Morgenthau's definition of power, the control of man over man, is typical of the way power is usually defined in international relations. Nancy Hartsock argues that this type of power-as-domination has always been associated with masculinity, since the exercise of power has generally been a masculine activity: rarely have women exercised legitimized power in the public domain. When women write about power they stress energy, capacity and potential, says Hartsock. She notes that women theorists, even when they have little else in common, offer similar definitions of power which differ substantially from the understanding of power as domination.[17]

Hannah Arendt, frequently cited by feminists writing about power, defines power as the human ability to act in concert, or to take action in connection with others who share similar concerns.[18] This definition of power is similar to that of psychologist David McClelland's portrayal of female power, which he describes as shared rather than assertive.[19] Jane Jaquette argues that, since women have had less access to the instruments of coercion, they have been more apt to rely on power as persuasion; she compares women's domestic activities to coalition building.[20]

All of these writers are portraying power as a relationship of mutual enablement. Tying her definition of female power to international relations, Jaquette sees similarities between female strategies of persuasion and strategies of small states operating from a position of weakness in the international system. There are also examples of states' behaviour that contain elements of the female strategy of coalition building. One such example is the Southern African Development Coordination Conference (SADCC), which is designed to build regional infrastructure based on mutual cooperation and collective self-reliance in order to decrease dependence on the South African economy. Another is the European Community, which has had considerable success in building mutual cooperation in an area of the world whose history would not predict such a course of events.[21] It is rare, however, that cooperative outcomes in international relations are described in these terms, although Karl Deutsch's notion of pluralistic security communities might be one such example where power is associated with building community.[22] I am not denying that power as domination is a pervasive reality in international relations. However, there are also instances of cooperation in inter-state relations, which tend to be obscured when power is seen solely as domination. Thinking about power in this multidimensional sense may help us to think constructively about the potential for cooperation as well as conflict, an aspect of international relations generally played down by realism.

Redefining national security is another way in which feminist theory could contribute to new thinking about international relations.[23] Traditionally in the West, the concept of national security has been tied to military strength and its role in the physical protection of the nation state from external threats. Morgenthau's notion of defending the national interest in terms of power is consistent with this definition. But this traditional definition of national security is partial at best in today's world.[24] The technologically advanced states are highly interdependent, and rely on weapons whose effects would be equally devastating to winners and losers alike. For them to defend national security by relying on war as the last resort no longer appears very useful. Moreover, if one thinks of security in North–South rather than East–West terms, for a large portion of the world's population security has as much to do with the satisfaction of basic material needs as with military threats. According to Johan Galtung's notion of structural violence, to suffer a lower life expectancy by virtue of one's place of birth is a form of violence whose effects can be as devastating as war.[25]

Basic needs satisfaction has a great deal to do with women, but only recently have women's roles as providers of basic needs, and in development more generally, become visible as important components in development strategies.[26] Traditionally the development literature has focused on aspects of the development process that are in the public sphere, are technologically complex and are usually undertaken by men. Thinking about the role of women in development and the way in which we can define development and basic needs satisfaction to be inclusive of women's roles and needs are topics that deserve higher priority on the international agenda. Typically, however, this is an area about which traditional international relations theory, with the priority it gives to order over justice, has had very little to say.

A further threat to national security, more broadly defined, which has also been missing from the agenda of traditional international relations, concerns the environment. Carolyn Merchant argues that a mechanistic view of nature, contained in modern science, has helped to guide an industrial and technological development which has resulted in environmental damage that has now become a matter of global concern. In the introduction to her book *The Death of Nature*, Merchant suggests that, 'Women and nature have an age-old association—an affiliation that has persisted throughout culture, language, and history.'[27] Hence she maintains that the ecology movement, which is growing up in response to environmental threats, and the women's movement are deeply interconnected. Both stress living in equilibrium with nature rather than dominating it, both see nature as a living non-hierarchical entity in which each part is mutually dependent on the whole. Ecologists, as well as many feminists, are now suggesting that only such a fundamental change of world view will allow the human species to survive the damage it is inflicting on the environment.

Thinking about military, economic and environmental security in interdependent terms suggests the need for new methods of conflict resolution that seek to achieve mutually beneficial, rather than zero sum, outcomes. One such method comes from Sara Ruddick's work on 'maternal thinking'.[28] Ruddick describes maternal thinking as focused on the preservation of life and the growth of children. To foster a domestic environment conducive to these goals, tranquility must be preserved by avoiding conflict where possible, engaging in it non-violently and restoring community when it is over. In such an environment the ends for which disputes are fought are subordinate to the means by which they are resolved. This method of conflict resolution involves making contextual judgements rather than appealing to absolute standards and thus has much in common with Gilligan's definition of female morality.

While non-violent resolution of conflict in the domestic sphere is a widely accepted norm, passive resistance in the public realm is regarded as deviant. But, as Ruddick argues, the peaceful resolution of conflict by mothers does not usually extend to the children of one's enemies, an important reason why women have been ready to support men's wars.[29] The question for Ruddick then becomes how to get maternal thinking, a mode of thinking which she believes can be found in men as well as women, out into the public realm. Ruddick believes that finding a common humanity among one's opponents has become a condition of survival in the nuclear age when the notion of winners and losers has become questionable.[30] Portraying the adversary as less than human has all too often been a technique of the nation state to command loyalty and to increase its legitimacy in the eyes of its citizens. Such behaviour in an age of weapons of mass destruction may be self-defeating.

We might also look to Gilligan's work for a feminist perspective on conflict resolution. Reporting on a study of playground behaviour of American boys and girls, Gilligan argues that girls are less able to tolerate high levels of conflict, and more likely than boys to play games that involve taking turns and in which the success of one does not depend on the failure of another.[31] While Gilligan's study does not take into account attitudes toward other groups (racial, ethnic, economic or national), it does suggest the validity of investigating whether girls are socialized to use different modes of problem solving when dealing with conflict, and whether such behaviour might be useful in thinking about international conflict resolution.

[handwritten note in margin: - In short, girls are "socialized differently, meaning that the world has been socialized to be what it is.]

TOWARD A FEMINIST EPISTEMOLOGY OF INTERNATIONAL RELATIONS

I am deeply aware that there is no *one* feminist approach but many, which come out of various disciplines and intellectual traditions. Yet there are common themes in the different feminist literatures that I have reviewed which could help us to begin to formulate a feminist epistemology of international relations. Morgenthau encourages us to try to stand back from the world and to think about theory building in terms of constructing a rational outline or map that has universal applications. In contrast, the feminist literature reviewed here emphasizes connection and contingency. Keller argues for a form of knowledge, which she calls 'dynamic objectivity', 'that grants to the world around us its independent integrity, but does so in a way that remains cognizant of, indeed relies on, our connectivity with that world'.[32] Keller illustrates this mode of thinking in her study of Barbara McClintock, whose work on genetic transposition won her a Nobel prize after many years of marginalization by the scientific community.[33] McClintock, Keller argues, was a scientist with a respect for complexity, diversity and individual difference whose methodology allowed her data to speak rather than imposing explanations on it.

Keller's portrayal of McClintock's science contains parallels with what Sandra Harding calls an African world view.[34] Harding tells us that the Western liberal notion of rational economic man, an individualist and a welfare maximizer, similar to the image of rational political man on which realism has based its theoretical investigations, does not make any sense in the African world view where the individual is seen as part of the social order acting within that order rather than upon it. Harding believes that this view of human behaviour has much in common with a feminist perspective. If we combine this view of human behaviour with Merchant's holistic perspective which stresses the interconnectedness of all things, including nature, it may help us to begin to think from a more global perspective. Such a perspective appreciates cultural diversity but at the same time recognizes a growing interdependence, which makes anachronistic the exclusionary thinking fostered by the nation state system.

Keller's dynamic objectivity, Harding's African world view and Merchant's ecological thinking all point us in the direction of an appreciation of the 'other' as a subject whose views are as legitimate as our own, a way of thinking that has been sadly lacking in the history of international relations. Just as Keller cautions us against the construction of a feminist science which could perpetuate similar exclusionary attitudes, Harding warns us against schema that contrast people by race, gender or class and that originate within projects of social domination. Feminist thinkers generally dislike dichotomization and the distancing of subject from object that goes with abstract thinking, both of which, they believe, encourage a we/they attitude characteristic of international relations. Instead, feminist literature urges us to construct epistemologies that value ambiguity and difference. These qualities could stand us in good stead as we begin to build a human or ungendered theory of international relations which contains elements of both masculine and feminine modes of thought.

MORGENTHAU'S PRINCIPLES OF POLITICAL REALISM: A FEMINIST REFORMULATION

The first part of this paper used feminist theory to develop a critique of Morgenthau's principles of political realism in order to demonstrate how the theory and practice of international relations may exhibit a masculine bias. The second part suggested some contributions that feminist theory might make to reconceptualizing some important elements in international relations and to thinking about a feminist epistemology. Drawing on these observations, this conclusion will present a feminist reformulation of Morgenthau's six principles of political realism, outlined earlier in this paper, which might help us to begin to think differently about international relations. I shall not use the term realism since feminists believe that there are multiple realities: a truly realistic picture of international politics must recognize elements of cooperation as well as conflict, morality as well as *realpolitik*, and the strivings for justice as well as order.[35] This reformulation may help us to think in these multidimensional terms.

1. A feminist perspective believes that objectivity, as it is culturally defined, is associated with masculinity. Therefore, supposedly 'objective' laws of human nature are based on a partial, masculine view of human nature. Human nature is both masculine and feminine; it contains elements of social reproduction and development as well as political domination. Dynamic objectivity offers us a more connected view of objectivity with less potential for domination.

2. A feminist perspective believes that the national interest is multidimensional and contextually contingent. Therefore, it cannot be defined solely in terms of power. In the contemporary world the national interest demands cooperative rather than zero sum solutions to a set of interdependent global problems which include nuclear war, economic well-being and environmental degradation.

3. Power cannot be infused with meaning that is universally valid. Power as domination and control privileges masculinity and ignores the possibility of collective empowerment, another aspect of power often associated with femininity.

4. A feminist perspective rejects the possibility of separating moral command from political action. All political action has moral significance. The realist agenda for maximizing order through power and control gives priority to the moral command of order over those of justice and the satisfaction of basic needs necessary to ensure social reproduction.

5. While recognizing that the moral aspirations of particular nations cannot be equated with universal moral principles, a feminist perspective seeks to find common moral elements in human aspirations which could become the basis for de-escalating international conflict and building international community.

6. A feminist perspective denies the autonomy of the political. Since autonomy is associated with masculinity in Western culture, disciplinary efforts to construct a world view which does not rest on a pluralistic conception of human nature are partial and masculine. Building boundaries around a narrowly defined political realm defines political in a way that excludes the concerns and contributions of women.

To construct this feminist alternative is not to deny the validity of Morgenthau's work. But adding a feminist perspective to the epistemology of international relations is a stage through which we must pass if we are to think about constructing an ungendered or human science of international politics which is sensitive to, but goes beyond, both masculine and feminine perspectives. Such inclusionary thinking, as Simone de Beauvoir tells us, values the bringing forth of life as much as the risking of life; it is becoming imperative in a world in which the technology of war and a fragile natural environment threaten human existence. An ungendered, or human, discourse becomes possible only when women are adequately represented in the discipline and when there is equal respect for the contributions of women and men alike.

NOTES

An earlier version of this paper was presented at a symposium on Gender and International Relations at the London School of Economics in June 1988. I would like to thank the editors of *Millennium*, who organized this symposium, for encouraging me to undertake this rewriting. I am also grateful to Hayward Alker Jr and Susan Okin for their careful reading of the manuscript and helpful suggestions.

1. Quoted in Sandra Harding, *The Science Question in Feminism* (Ithaca, N.Y.: Cornell University Press, 1986), p. 148.
2. In 1987 only 4.8 per cent of the top career Foreign Service employees were women. Statement of Patricia Schroeder before the Committee on Foreign Affairs, U.S. House of Representatives, p. 4; *Women's Perspectives on U.S. Foreign Policy: A Compilation of Views* (Washington, D.C.: U.S. Government Printing Office, 1988). For an analysis of women's roles in the American military, see Cynthia Enloe, *Does Khaki Become You? The Militarisation of Women's Lives* (London: Pluto Press, 1983).
3. Edward P. Crapol (ed.), *Women and American Foreign Policy* (Westport, Conn.: Greenwood Press, 1987), p. 167.
4. For an analysis of the role of masculine language in shaping strategic thinking see Carol Cohn, 'Sex and death in the rational world of defense intellectuals', *Signs: Journal of Women in Culture and Society* (Vol. 12, No. 4, Summer 1987).
5. The claim for the dominance of the realist paradigm is supported by John A. Vasquez, 'Colouring it Morgenthau: new evidence for an old thesis on quantitative international

studies', *British Journal of International Studies* (Vol. 3, No. 5, October 1979), pp. 210–28. For a critique of Morgenthau's ambiguous use of language see Inis L. Claude Jr, *Power and International Relations* (New York: Random House, 1962), especially pp. 25–37.

6. These are drawn from Hans Morgenthau, *Politics Among Nations: The Struggle for Power and Peace,* 5th revised edition (New York: Alfred Knopf, 1973), pp. 4–15. I am aware that these principles embody only a partial statement of Morgenthau's very rich study of international politics, a study which deserves a much more detailed analysis than I can give here.

7. This list is a composite of the male/female dichotomies which appear in Evelyn Fox Keller's *Reflections on Gender and Science* (New Haven, Conn.: Yale University Press, 1985) and Harding, *op. cit.*

8. Inge K. Broverman, Susan R. Vogel, Donald M. Broverman, Frank E. Clarkson and Paul S. Rosenkranz, 'Sex-role stereotypes: a current appraisal', *Journal of Social Issues* (Vol. 28, No. 2, 1972), pp. 59–78. Replication of this research in the 1980s confirms that these perceptions still hold.

9. Keller, *op. cit.*, p. 130.

10. *Ibid.*, p. 89.

11. *Ibid.*, p. 9.

12. Sara Ann Ketchum, 'Female culture, woman culture and conceptual change: toward a philosophy of women's studies', *Social Theory and Practice* (Vol. 6, No. 2, Summer 1980).

13. Others have questioned whether Hobbes's state of nature provides an accurate description of the international system. See for example Charles Beitz, *Political Theory and International Relations* (Princeton, N.J.: Princeton University Press, 1979), pp. 35–50 and Stanley Hoffmann, *Duties Beyond Borders* (Syracuse, N.Y.: Syracuse University Press, 1981), chap. 1.

14. Kohlberg's stages of moral development are described and discussed in Robert Kegan, *The Evolving Self: Problem and Process in Human Development* (Cambridge, Mass.: Harvard University Press, 1982), chap. 2.

15. Carol Gilligan, *In a Different Voice: Psychological Theory and Women's Development* (Cambridge, Mass.: Harvard University Press, 1982). See chap. 1 for Gilligan's critique of Kohlberg.

16. There is evidence that, toward the end of his life, Morgenthau himself was aware that his own prescriptions were becoming anachronistic. In a seminar presentation in 1978 he suggested that power politics as the guiding principle for the conduct of international relations had become fatally defective. For a description of this seminar presentation see Francis Anthony Boyle, *World Politics and International Law* (Durham, N.C.: Duke University Press, 1985), pp. 70–4.

17. Nancy C. M. Hartsock, *Money, Sex and Power: Toward a Feminist Historical Materialism* (Boston: Northeastern University Press, 1983), p. 210.

18. Hannah Arendt, *On Violence* (New York: Harcourt, Brace and World, 1969), p. 44. Arendt's definition of power, as it relates to international relations, is discussed more extensively in Jean Bethke Elshtain's 'Reflections on war and political discourse: realism, just war, and feminism in a nuclear age', *Political Theory* (Vol. 13, No. 1, February 1985), pp. 39–57.

19. David McClelland, 'Power and the feminine role', in David McClelland, *Power, The Inner Experience* (New York: Wiley, 1975).

20. Jane S. Jaquette, 'Power as ideology: a feminist analysis', in Judith H. Stiehm (ed.), *Women's Views of the Political World of Men* (Dobbs Ferry, N.Y.: Transnational Publishers, 1984).

21. These examples are cited by Christine Sylvester, 'The emperor's theories and transformations: looking at the field through feminist lenses', in Dennis Pirages and Christine

Sylvester (eds), *Transformations in the Global Political Economy* (Basingstoke: Macmillan, 1989).

22. Karl W. Deutsch *et al., Political Community and the North Atlantic Area* (Princeton, N.J.: Princeton University Press, 1957).

23. New thinking is a term that is also being used in the Soviet Union to describe foreign policy reformulations under Gorbachev. There are indications that the Soviets are beginning to conceptualize security in the multidimensional terms described here. See Margot Light, *The Soviet Theory of International Relations* (New York: St Martin's Press, 1988), chap. 10.

24. This is the argument made by Edward Azar and Chung-in Moon, 'Third World national security: toward a new conceptual framework', *International Interactions* (Vol. 11, No. 2, 1984), pp. 103–35.

25. Johan Galtung, 'Violence, peace, and peace research', in Galtung, *Essays in Peace Research,* Vol. I (Copenhagen: Christian Ejlers, 1975).

26. See, for example, Gita Sen and Caren Grown, *Development, Crises and Alternative Visions: Third World Women's Perspectives* (New York: Monthly Review Press, 1987). This is an example of a growing literature on women and development which deserves more attention from the international relations community.

27. Carolyn Merchant, *The Death of Nature: Women, Ecology and the Scientific Revolution* (New York: Harper and Row, 1982), p. xv.

28. Sara Ruddick, 'Maternal thinking' and 'Preservative love and military destruction: some reflections on mothering and peace', in Joyce Treblicot, *Mothering: Essays in Feminist Theory* (Totowa, N.J.: Rowman and Allenhead, 1984).

29. For a more extensive analysis of this issue see Jean Bethke Elshtain, *Women and War* (New York: Basic Books, 1987).

30. This type of conflict resolution contains similarities with the problem solving approach of Edward Azar, John Burton and Herbert Kelman. See, for example, Edward E. Azar and John W. Burton, *International Conflict Resolution: Theory and Practice* (Brighton: Wheatsheaf, 1986) and Herbert C. Kelman, 'Interactive problem solving: a social-psychological approach to conflict resolution', in W. Klassen (ed.), *Dialogue Toward Inter-Faith Understanding* (Tantur/Jerusalem: Ecumenical Institute for Theoretical Research, 1986), pp. 293–314.

31. Gilligan, *op. cit.*, pp. 9–10.

32. Keller, *op. cit.*, p. 117.

33. Evelyn Fox Keller, *A Feeling for the Organism: The Life and Work of Barbara McClintock* (New York: Freeman, 1983).

34. Harding, *op. cit.*, chap. 7.

35. 'Utopia and reality are . . . the two facets of political science. Sound political thought and sound political life will be found only where both have their place': E. H. Carr, *The Twenty Years Crisis: 1919–1939* (New York: Harper and Row, 1964), p. 10.

Human Rights in World Politics

Rhoda E. Howard and Jack Donnelly

WHAT ARE HUMAN RIGHTS?

The International Human Rights Covenants[1] note that human rights "derive from the inherent dignity of the human person." But while the struggle to assure a life of dignity is probably as old as human society itself, reliance on human rights as a mechanism to realize that dignity is a relatively recent development.

Human rights are, by definition, the rights one has simply because one is a human being. This simple and relatively uncontroversial definition, though, is more complicated than it may appear on the surface. It identifies human rights as *rights,* in the strict and strong sense of that term, and it establishes that they are held simply by virtue of being human.

The term "right" in English has a variety of meanings, but two are of special moral importance. On the one hand, "right" may refer to something that is (morally) correct or demanded, the fact of something being right. In this sense, "right" refers to conformity with moral standards; righteousness; moral rectitude. On the other hand, "right" may refer to the entitlement of a person, the special title one has to a good or opportunity. Such titles ground special and particularly strong claims against those who would deny the right; as Ronald Dworkin[2] puts it, rights in ordinary circumstances "trump" other moral and political considerations. It is in this sense that one *has* a right. And it is in this sense that one has human rights.

The sense of moral standards, must be as old as the notion of moral standards themselves. In the Western tradition of moral and political discourse there have been a variety of theories resting on this sense of right, but perhaps the most popular has been the theory of natural law. Natural law theories hold that there is an objective moral law (given by God and/or grasped by human reason). This natural law binds all men and women and provides a standard for evaluating human practices, including political practices. A regime that transgresses the natural law is guilty of serious crimes and, in severe instances, loses its moral and political legitimacy.

Perhaps the most highly developed theory of natural law was that of St. Thomas Aquinas (1225–1274), who sought to combine Christian doctrine with the philosophical ideas of classical antiquity, especially those of Aristotle. For Aquinas, all law is the expression of divine reason, which is made available to mankind in two principal forms: "divine law," or the revelation of the Bible, and "natural law," the imprint of divine reason, directly available to all through the exercise of reason. What Aquinas calls "human law," the ordinary sorts of law made by legislators, is legitimate to the extent that it conforms to the natural law, of which it ought to be merely a practical political expression.[3]

Such theories in the Western world go back explicitly at least as far as Cicero (106–43 B.C.), and they may be seen as implicit in the writings of Plato and Aristotle. They also extend well into the modern era; even John Locke, one of the most important early modern natural rights theorists, has an explicit theory of natural law.[4] Today, natural law ideas still receive the support of a number of respected philosophers and have considerable popular appeal, particularly, but not entirely, in certain religious circles.

Furthermore, such ideas have been the norm in most premodern or preindustrial societies throughout the world. For example, the Chinese emperor was held to rule through a mandate from heaven, and thus was held to be accountable to heaven for his actions. Similarly, Islam provides a very detailed set of substantive norms, expressed in the Koran and in Sharia law, to which rulers are required to conform. In very few societies have rulers been conceived of as truly absolute and unconstrained; even the Ancien Régime monarchs of France who claimed to rule by divine right acknowledged an obligation to conform their rule to the dictates of divine justice. Whatever the deviations in practice, almost all rulers in preindustrial societies ruled under what in the West was usually referred to as natural law. Most traditional societies, Western and non-Western alike, have conceived of justice primarily in terms of conformity with substantive principles of right (although usually known through tradition, not apprehended directly by reason).

The political leverage that natural law provides citizens against the state—that is, the ability to indict a violator of natural law as one who transgresses objective principles of justice, not merely the preferences or interests of a particular person or group—should not be denigrated. For example, a tyrannical ruler in medieval Europe or imperial China would stand condemned in the eyes of God and the objective principles of law and justice; a ruler could be held accountable to objective standards. But the difference between natural *law* and natural or human *right* indictments is quite important, both theoretically and practically.

A state that violates the natural law is guilty of moral crimes, but it has not necessarily violated the rights of its citizens. Natural law does not necessarily give rise to natural rights, one has "by nature," simply as a human being. In fact, while some recent natural law theorists (most prominently, Jacques Maritain[5]) link natural law with natural or human rights, historically such a linkage is quite rare; it certainly is not made by figures such as Cicero, Aquinas, and Richard Hooker. Typically, regimes that stand condemned by the natural law do not face citizens whose natural *rights* have been violated, and thus the kinds of actions that are justified to remedy the injustice are quite different.

In particular, without natural (or legal) rights against the government, citizens are not *entitled* to seek redress; natural law by itself gives no one any right to enforce its injunctions. For that they must have natural or human (or legal) *rights* in the strong sense of entitlements that ground claims that have a special force. If the state violates their rights, citizens may claim not only that injustice is perpetrated against them but that their rights have been violated. This gives considerable additional force to these claims. In addition, and no less important, it puts the process of redress under their control, as rights-holders who are entitled to press claims of rights. When those rights are natural or human rights, rights one has simply because one is a human being, the moral offense is of the greatest magnitude.

This understanding of states being constrained by the *rights* of citizens, which are morally prior to and above the state, is historically of relatively recent date, distinctively "modern." Thomas Hobbes, in *Leviathan* (1655), speaks of the "right of nature," a precursor of our conception of natural rights, but he explicitly denies that such rights limit the sovereign's power.[6] By the time of Locke's *Second Treatise of Government* (1688),[7] a clear and explicit theory of natural rights exists side by side with a fairly traditional theory of natural law. By the time of the American and French revolutions, ideas of natural rights—or, in the language of the era, the rights of man—are not only politically central but have replaced natural law both in popular revolutionary discourse and in the writings of figures such as Thomas Jefferson and Thomas Paine.[8]

As is clear from the authors already cited, the human rights tradition is, in its inception at least, closely tied to contractarian political thought. In the social contract tradition, individuals are seen as possessors of natural rights entirely independent of the state; their basic rights derive "from (human) nature," not from the state, politics, God, or tradition. In fact, the state (and society) are seen as products of a contract among individuals to protect natural rights and provide the social and political conditions that will allow individuals to realize them. As such, the state is letigimate only if it respects, enforces, and permits the fuller realization of natural rights. And if it fails to discharge its part of the contract—if it grossly and systematically violates human rights—citizens, either individually or collectively, are entitled to revolt. For example, Locke recognizes and defends a right to revolution held by society against governments that systematically violate natural rights; Jefferson in the American Declaration of Independence justifies the revolution by the British denial of natural rights; and the French Declaration of the Rights and the Citizen explicitly includes a right to revolution.

Natural law and other (nonhuman rights) theories of justice certainly are capable of denying the legitimacy of corrupt or vicious governments. The grounds of the denial, however, and the position in the fact of such a government, are quite different in the absence of natural rights.

For example, Aquinas holds that tyrants are illegitimate because they have grossly and systematically violated the natural law. But citizens, lacking natural *rights* that this law be respected, are not entitled to revolt or even press rights-claims against the tyrant.[9] When, however, it is considered legitimate for citizens to react not only against the injustice of violations of the natural law but also in defense of their natural rights, the state is guilty of additional and particularly severe affronts to human dignity. Not only are its practices unjust, but they also violate human rights. And citizens are entitled to act to restore their rights. A natural or human rights conception of politics places individual citizens and their rights at the heart of politics, which is viewed as ultimately a device for the vindication of natural rights.

As we have already indicated, there is nothing necessary about such a conception of persons or politics. Elsewhere we have argued in some detail that most societies at most times (including Western society in previous eras) have had quite different views.[10] But this is what is entailed by a human rights conception. And the nearly universal acceptance of the idea (if not the practice) of human rights by virtually all states in all areas of the contemporary world gives this conception a validity that cannot be ignored. . . .

WHAT RIGHTS DO WE HAVE?

The definition of human or natural rights as the rights of each person simply as a human being specifies their character; they are rights. The definition also specifies their source: (human) nature. We have already talked briefly about human rights as rights. A few words are necessary about the claim that human *nature* gives rise to human rights, as well as the particular list that results.

What is it in human nature that gives rise to human rights? There are two basic answers to this question. On the one hand, many people argue that human rights arise from human needs, from the naturally given requisites for physical and mental health and well-being. On the other hand, many argue that human rights reflect the minimum requirements for human dignity or *moral* personality.[11] These latter arguments derive from essentially philosophical theories of human "nature," dignity, or moral personality.

Needs theories of human rights run into the problem of empirical confirmations; the simple fact is that there is sound scientific evidence only for a very narrow list of human needs. But if we use "needs" in a broader, in part nonscientific, sense, then the two theories overlap. We can thus say that people have human rights to those things "needed" for a life of dignity, for the full development of their moral personality. The "nature" that gives rise to human rights is thus *moral* nature.

This moral nature is, in part, a social creation. Human nature, in the relevant sense, is an amalgam consisting both of psycho-biological facts (constraints and possibilities) and of the social structures and experiences that are no less a part of the essential nature of men and women. Human beings are not isolated individuals, but rather individuals who are essentially social creatures, in part even social creations. Therefore, a theory of human rights must recognize both the essential

see
Rawls
v.
Walzer

universality of human nature and the no less essential particularity arising from cultural and socioeconomic traditions and institutions.

Human rights are, by their nature, universal; it is not coincidental that we have a *Universal* Declaration of Human Rights, for human rights are the rights of all men and women. Therefore, in its basic outlines a list of human rights must apply at least more or less "across the board." But the nature of human beings is also shaped by the particular societies in which they live. Thus the universality of human rights must be qualified in at least two important ways.

First, the forms in which universal rights are institutionalized are subject to some legitimate cultural and political variation. For example, what counts as popular participation in government may vary, within a certain range, from society to society. Both multiparty and single-party regimes may reflect legitimate notions of political participation. Although the ruling party cannot be removed from power, in some one-party states individual representatives can be changed and electoral pressure may result in significant policy changes.

Second, and no less important, the universality (in principle) of human rights is qualified by the obvious fact that any particular list, no matter how broad its cross-cultural and international acceptance, reflects the necessarily contingent understandings of a particular era. For example, in the seventeenth and eighteenth centuries, the rights of man were indeed the rights of men, not women, and social and economic rights (other than the right to private property) were unheard of. Thus we must expect a gradual evolution of even a consensual list of human rights, as collective understandings of the essential elements of human dignity, the conditions of moral personality, evolve in response to changing ideas and material circumstances.

In other words, human rights are by their essential nature universal in form. They are, by definition, the rights held by each (and every) person simply as a human being. But any universal list of human rights is subject to a variety of justifiable implementations.

In our time, the Universal Declaration of Human Rights (1948) is a minimum list that is nearly universally accepted, although additional rights have been added (e.g., self-determination) and further new rights (e.g., the right to nondiscrimination on the grounds of sexual orientation or the right to peace) may be added in the future. We are in no position to offer a philosophical defense of the list of rights in the Universal Declaration. To do so would require an account of the source of human rights—human nature—that would certainly exceed the space available to us. Nonetheless, the Universal Declaration is nearly universally accepted by states. For practical political purposes we can treat it as authoritative. All the contributors to this volume have agreed to do precisely that. Therefore a brief review of the list of rights contained in the Universal Declaration . . . is appropriate here.

It is conventional to divide human rights into two major classes, civil and political rights, and economic, social, and cultural rights. Such a division is rather crude and unenlightening. It also has too often been the basis for partisan arguments, by left and right alike, for granting priority to one category or the other, arguments that often simply attempt to cloak the abuse of rights. Nevertheless, it is a common and convenient categorization.

The civil and political rights enumerated in the Universal Declaration include rights to life; nationality; recognition before the law; protection against cruel, degrading, or inhuman treatment or punishment; and protection against racial, ethnic, sexual, or religious discrimination. They also include such legal rights as access to remedies for violations of basic rights; the presumption of innocence; the guarantee of fair and impartial public trials; prohibition of ex post facto laws; and protections against arbitrary arrest, detention or exile, and arbitrary interference with one's family, home, or reputation. Civil liberties enumerated include rights to freedom of thought, conscience and religion, opinion and expression, movement and residence, and peaceful assembly and association. Finally, political rights include the rights to take part in government and to periodic and genuine elections with universal and equal suffrage. Economic, social, and cultural rights recognized in the Declaration include the rights to food and a standard of living adequate for the health and well-being of oneself and one's family; the rights to work, rest and leisure, and social security; and rights to education and to participation in the cultural life of the community.

There are occasional claims still made, especially by political conservatives in the West, that only civil and political rights are really rights.[12] Likewise, one still runs across no less one-sided arguments, made principally by Soviet bloc and Third World politicians and scholars, that economic and social rights have priority over civil and political rights.[13] But virtually all states are explicitly committed to the view that all the rights recognized in the Universal Declaration are interdependent and indivisible. . . .

INTERNATIONAL HUMAN RIGHTS INSTITUTIONS

The international context of national practices deserves some attention.[14] There are, as we have already noted, international human rights standards that are widely accepted—in principle at least—by states. Thus the discussion and evaluation of national practices take place within an overarching set of international standards to which virtually all states have explicitly committed themselves. Whatever the force of claims of national sovereignty, with its attendant legal immunity from international action, the evaluation of national human rights practices from the perspective of the international standards of the Universal Declaration thus is certainly appropriate, even if one is uncomfortable with the moral claim sketched above that such universalistic scrutiny is demanded by the very idea of human rights.

In the literature on international relations it has recently become fashionable to talk of "international regimes," that is, norms and decision-making procedures accepted by states in a given issue area. National human rights practices do take place within the broader context of an international human rights regime centered on the United Nations.

We have already sketched the principal norms of this regime—the list of rights in the Universal Declaration. These norms/rights are further elaborated in two major treaties, the International Covenant on Economic, Social and Cultural

Rights and the International Covenant on Civil and Political Rights, which were opened for signature and ratification in 1966 and came into force in 1976. Almost all of the countries studied in this volume have ratified (become a party to) both the Covenant on Civil and Political Rights and the Covenant on Economic, Social and Cultural Rights. . . . Even the countries that are not parties to the Covenants often accept the principles of the Universal Declaration. In addition, there are a variety of single-issue treaties that have been formulated under UN auspices on topics such as racial discrimination, the rights of women, and torture. These later Covenants and Conventions go into much greater detail than the Universal Declaration and include a few important changes. For example, the Covenants prominently include a right to national self-determination, which is absent in the Universal Declaration, but do not include a right to private property. Nevertheless, for the most part they can be seen simply as elaborations on the Universal Declaration, which remains the central normative document in the international human rights regime.

What is the legal and political force of these norms? The Universal Declaration of Human Rights was proclaimed in 1948 by the United Nations General Assembly. As such, it has no force of law. Resolutions of the General Assembly, even solemn declarations, are merely recommendations to states; the General Assembly has no international legislative powers. Over the years, however, the Universal Declaration has come to be something more than a mere recommendation.

There are two principal sources of international law, namely, treaty and custom. Although today we tend to think first of treaty, historically custom is at least as important. A rule or principle attains the force of customary international law when it can meet two tests. First, the principle or rule must reflect the general practice of the overwhelming majority of states. Second, what lawyers call *opinio juris*, the sense of obligation, must be taken into account. Is the customary practice seen by states as an obligation, rather than a mere convenience or courtesy? Today it is a common view of international lawyers that the Universal Declaration has attained something of the status of customary international law, so that the rights it contains are in some important sense binding on states.

Furthermore, the International Human Rights Covenants are treaties and as such do have the force of international law, but only for the parties to the treaties, that is, those states that have (voluntarily) ratified or acceded to the treaties. The same is true of the single-issue treaties that round out the regime's norms. It is perhaps possible that the norms of the Covenants are coming to acquire the force of customary international law even for states that are not parties. But in either case, the fundamental weakness of international law is underscored: Virtually all international legal obligations are voluntarily accepted.

This is obviously the case for treaties: states are free to become parties or not entirely as they choose. It is no less true, though, of custom, where the tests of state practice and *opinio juris* likewise assure that international legal obligation is only voluntarily acquired. In fact, a state that explicitly rejects a practice during the process of custom formation is exempt even from customary international legal obligations. For example, Saudi Arabia's objection to the provisions on the equal rights of women during the drafting of the Universal Declaration might be held to

exempt it from such a norm, even if the norm is accepted internationally as customarily binding. Such considerations are particularly important when we ask what
force there is to international law and what mechanisms exist to implement and
enforce the rights specified in the Universal Declaration and the Covenants.

Acceptance of an obligation by states does not carry with it acceptance of any
method of international enforcement. Quite the contrary. Unless there is an explicit enforcement mechanism attached to the obligation, its enforcement rests simply
on the good faith of the parties. The Universal Declaration contains no enforcement mechanisms of any sort. Even if we accept it as having the force of international law, its implementation is left entirely in the hands of individual states. The
Covenants do have some implementation machinery, but the machinery's practical
weakness is perhaps its most striking feature.

Under the provisions of the International Covenant on Civil and Political
Rights, a Human Rights Committee of independent experts was created in the
United Nations to supervise the Covenant's implementation.[15] The Committee's
principal function, however, is simply to review periodic reports submitted by the
different states who are party to the Covenant concerning their practices with
respect to the enumerated rights. While the reports of states are examined in public, the most the Committee can do is raise questions and request further information. It is powerless to compel more than pro forma compliance with the requirement of periodic reporting, and even that sometimes cannot be achieved.
Furthermore, even this minimal international scrutiny applies only to the parties to
the Covenant, which numbered only eighty—about half the countries of the
world—in 1985.

An Optional Protocol to the Civil/Political Covenant permits the Human
Rights Committee to receive and examine complaints from individuals. The Committee receives about two dozen complaints a year, about half of which are admissible and receive substantive scrutiny. But even here the most that the Committee
can do is state its views on whether a violation has occurred. In other words, even
in this, probably the strongest procedure in the international human rights regime,
there is only international monitoring of state practice. Enforcement remains
entirely national. And by 1985 only thirty-five countries had accepted the provisions of the Optional Protocol. Not surprisingly, almost none of those covered are
major human rights violators. Thus relatively strong procedures apply primarily
where they are least needed—which is not at all surprising given that participation
in these procedures is entirely voluntary.

The procedures under the International Covenant on Economic, Social and
Cultural Rights are even weaker. Periodic reports are reviewed not by an independent committee of experts but by a working group of the UN Economic and Social
Council (ECOSOC), a body of political delegates representing the views of their
governments. (A new committee of experts was established in 1986, but it has yet
to meet.) In addition, there is no individual complaint procedure.

The single-issue treaties on racial discrimination, torture and women's rights
also contain periodic reporting procedures, as well as various complaint procedures, but the coverage of the first two is narrow and their provisions not significantly stronger than those of the Civil and Political Covenant. The International

Labour Organization, which provided the model for the reporting procedures adopted in the field of human rights, also has similar powers for the workers' rights issues within its purview, but once more the furthest the system goes is voluntarily accepted monitoring of voluntarily accepted obligations. There is no real international enforcement of any sort.[16]

The one other major locus of activity in the international human rights regime is the UN Commission on Human Rights. In addition to being the body that played the principal role in the formulation of the Universal Declaration, the Covenants, and most of the major single-issue human rights treaties, it has some weak implementation powers. Its public discussion of human rights situations in various countries can help to mobilize international public opinion, which is not always utterly useless in helping to reform national practice. For example, in the 1970s the Commission played a major role in publicizing the human rights conditions in Chile, Israel, and South Africa. Furthermore, it is empowered by ECOSOC resolution 1503 (1970) to investigate communications (complaints) from individuals and groups that "appear to reveal a consistent pattern of gross and reliably attested violations of human rights."

The 1503 procedure, however, is at least as thoroughly hemmed in by constraints as are the other enforcement mechanisms that we have considered.[17] Although individuals may communicate grievances, the 1503 procedure deals only with "*situations*" of gross and systematic violations, not the particular cases of individuals. Individuals cannot even obtain an international judgment in their particular case, let alone international enforcement of the human rights obligations of their government. Furthermore, the entire procedure remains confidential until a case is concluded, although the Commission does publicly announce a "blacklist" of countries being studied. In only four cases (Equatorial Guinea, Haiti, Malawi, and Uruguay) has the Commission gone public with a 1503 case. Its most forceful conclusion was a 1980 resolution provoked by the plight of Jehovah's Witnesses in Malawi, which merely expressed the hope that all human rights were being respected in Malawi.

In addition to this global human rights regime, there are regional regimes.[18] The 1981 African Charter of Human and Peoples' Rights, drawn up by the Organization of African Unity, provides for a Human Rights Commission, but it is not yet functioning. In Europe and the Americas there are highly developed systems involving both commissions with very strong investigatory powers and regional human rights courts with the authority to make legally binding decisions on complaints by individuals (although only eight states have accepted the jurisdiction of the Inter-American Court of Human Rights).

Even in Europe and the Americas, however, implementation and enforcement remain primarily national. In nearly thirty years the European Commission of Human Rights has considered only about 350 cases, while the European Court of Human Rights has handled only one-fifth that number. Such regional powers certainly should not be ignored or denigrated. They provide authoritative interpretations in cases of genuine disagreements and a powerful check on backsliding and occasional deviations by states. But the real force of even the European regime lies in the voluntary acceptance of human rights by the states in question, which has infinitely more to do with domestic politics than with international procedures.

In sum, at the international level there are comprehensive, authoritative human rights norms that are widely accepted as binding on all states. Implementation and enforcement of these norms, however, both in theory and in practice, are left to states. The international context of national human rights practices certainly cannot be ignored. Furthermore, international norms may have an important socializing effect on national leaders and be useful to national advocates of improved domestic human rights practices. But the real work of implementing and enforcing human rights takes place at the national level. . . . Before the level of the nation-state is discussed, however, one final element of the international context needs to be considered, namely, human rights as an issue in national foreign policies.

HUMAN RIGHTS AND FOREIGN POLICY

Beyond the human rights related activities of states in international institutions such as those discussed in the preceding section, many states have chosen to make human rights a concern in their bilateral foreign relations.[19] In fact, much of the surge of interest in human rights in the last decade can be traced to the catalyzing effect of President Jimmy Carter's (1977–1981) efforts to make international human rights an objective of U.S. foreign policy.

In a discussion of human rights as an issue in national foreign policy, at least three problems need to be considered. First, a nation must select a particular set of rights to pursue. Second, the legal and moral issues raised by intervention on behalf of human rights abroad need to be explored. Third, human rights concerns must be integrated into the nation's broader foreign policy, since human rights are at best only one of several foreign policy objectives.

The international normative consensus on human rights noted above largely solves the problem of the choice of a set of rights to pursue, for unless a state chooses a list very similar to that of the Universal Declaration, its efforts are almost certain to be dismissed as fatally flawed by partisan or ideological bias. Thus, for example, claims by officials of the Reagan administration that economic and social rights are not really true human rights are almost universally denounced. By the same token, the Carter administration's serious attention to economic and social rights, even if it was ultimately subordinate to a concern for civil and political rights, greatly contributed to the international perception of its policy as genuinely concerned with human rights, not just a new rhetoric for the Cold War or neo-colonialism. Such an international perception is almost a necessary condition—although by no means a sufficient condition—for an effective international human rights policy.

A state is, of course, free to pursue any objectives it wishes in its foreign policy. If it wishes its human rights policy to be taken seriously, however, the policy must at least be enunciated in terms consistent with the international consensus that has been forged around the Universal Declaration. In practice, some rights must be given particular prominence in a nation's foreign policy, given the limited material resources and international political capital of even the most powerful state, but the basic contours of policy must be set by the Universal Declaration.

After the rights to be pursued have been selected, the second problem, that of intervention on behalf of human rights, arises. When state A pursues human rights in its relations with state B, A usually will be seeking to alter the way that B treats its own citizens. This is, by definition, a matter essentially within the domestic jurisdiction of B and thus outside the legitimate jurisdiction of A. A's action, therefore, is vulnerable to the charge of intervention, a charge that carries considerable legal, moral, and political force in a world, such as ours, that is structured at the international level around sovereign nation-states.

The legal problems raised by foreign policy action on behalf of human rights abroad are probably the most troubling. Sovereignty entails the principle of nonintervention; to say that A has sovereign jurisdiction over X is essentially equivalent to saying that no one else may intervene in A with respect to X. Because sovereignty is the foundation of international law, any foreign policy action that amounts to intervention is prohibited by international law. On the face of it at least, this prohibition applies to action on behalf of human rights as much as any other activity.

It might be suggested that we can circumvent the legal proscription of intervention in the case of human rights by reference to particular treaties or even the general international normative consensus discussed above. International norms per se, however, do not authorize even international organizations, let alone individual states acting independently, to enforce those norms. Even if all states are legally bound to implement the rights enumerated in the Universal Declaration, it simply does not follow, in logic or in law, that any particular state or group of states is entitled to enforce that obligation. States are perfectly free to accept international legal obligations that have no enforcement mechanisms attached.

This does not imply, though, that for a state to comply with international law it must stand by idly in the face of human rights violations abroad. International law prohibits intervention. It does, however, leave considerable room for *action*—perhaps even interference—on behalf of human rights.

Intervention is most often defined as coercive interference (especially by the threat or use of force) in the internal affairs of another country. But there are many kinds of noncoercive "interference," which is the stuff of foreign policy. For example, barring explicit treaty commitments to the contrary, no state is under an international legal obligation to deal with any other state. Should state A choose to deny B the benefits of its friendly relations, A is perfectly free, as a matter of international law, to reduce or eliminate its relations with B. And should A decide to do so on the basis of B's human rights performance, A is legally within its rights.

Scrupulously avoiding intervention (coercive interference) thus still leaves considerable room for international action at improving the human rights performance of a foreign country. Quiet diplomacy, public protests or condemnations, downgrading or breaking diplomatic relations, reducing or halting foreign aid, and selective or comprehensive restrictions of trade and other forms of interation are all actions that fall short of intervention. Thus in most circumstances they will be legally permissible actions on behalf of human rights abroad.

An international legal perspective on humanitarian intervention, however, does not exhaust the subject. Recently, several authors have argued, strongly and we believe convincingly, that moral considerations in at least some circumstances justify humanitarian intervention on behalf of human rights.[20] Michael Walzer, whose book *Just and Unjust Wars* has provoked much of the recent moral discussion of humanitarian intervention, can be taken as illustrative of such arguments.

Walzer presents a strong defense of the morality of the general international principle of nonintervention, arguing that it gives force to the basic right of peoples to self-determination, which in turn rests on the rights of individuals, acting in concert as a community, to choose their own government. Walzer has been criticized for interpreting this principle in a way that is excessively favorable to states by arguing that the presumption of legitimacy (and thus against intervention) should hold in all but the most extreme circumstances. Nonetheless, even Walzer allows that intervention must be permitted "when the violation of human rights is so terrible that it makes talk of community or self-determination . . . seem cynical and irrelevant,"[21] when gross, persistent, and systematic violations of human rights shock the moral conscience of mankind.

The idea underlying such arguments is that human rights are of such paramount moral importance that gross and systematic violations present a moral justification for remedial international action. If the international community as a whole cannot or will not act—and above we have shown that an effective collective international response will usually be impossible—then one or more states may be morally justified in acting ad hoc on behalf of the international community.

International law and morality thus lead to different and conflicting conclusions in at least some cases. One of the functions of international politics is to help to resolve such a conflict; political considerations will play a substantial role in determining how a state will respond in its foreign policy to the competing moral and legal demands placed on it. But the political dimensions of such decisions point to the practical dangers by moral arguments in favor of humanitarian intervention.

If we search the historical record it is very hard to find a clear example of humanitarian intervention in practice. In the last twenty-five years, the two leading candidates are the 1971 Indian intervention in East Pakistan (which soon became Bangladesh) in response to the massacre of Bengalis by the government, and the 1979 Tanzanian intervention in Uganda to topple Amin. But even here it must be noted that India intervened so as to partition its archenemy, Pakistan, and Tanzania intervened only after almost a decade of extremely poor Ugandan-Tanzanian relations, and close on the heels of a failed Ugandan invasion of Tanzanian territory. By contrast, the use of the language of humanitarian intervention to cloak partisan political adventurism—for example, in the U.S. interventions in the Dominican Republic in 1965, Grenada in 1983, and Nicaragua in the mid–1980s—is distressingly common.

Reasonable people may disagree on whether the danger of abuse outweighs the benefits of openly acknowledging and advocating a right to coercive humanitarian intervention. At the very least it should be noted that such a right is at best a very dangerous double-edged sword. Our preference would be to keep that particular sword sheathed and focus the pursuit of human rights in national foreign policy instead on actions short of military intervention. Such nonmilitary actions are legally and morally relatively unproblematic, and far less subject to catastrophic political abuse.

Having selected the rights to be pursued and satisfied itself that the means to be employed in that pursuit are, all things considered, acceptable, a state still faces the fact that human rights are only one part of its foreign policy, and a part that is not always consistent with other parts of the national interest. The relationship between human rights and the rest of the national interest, however, is neither as clear nor as simple as critics often make it out to be. In fact, a concern for human rights may enhance the national security, as a few examples from recent U.S. foreign policy clearly indicate.

In the late seventies, the United States "lost" Nicaragua and Iran in large measure as a result of its support of repressive rulers who managed to alienate virtually their entire populations and provoke genuine popular revolutions. A few years earlier, Angola was "lost" because of the colonial policy and human rights abuses of the U.S.-backed Portuguese regime. More recently, the cost of supporting dictators has been underscored by the fall of Marcos in the Philippines: Any problems faced by the United States in this strategically important country are not only almost entirely of its own making but also largely the result of a misguided subordination of human rights concerns.

Human rights may be moral concerns, but often they are not *merely* moral concerns. Morality and realism are not necessarily incompatible, and to treat them as if they always were can harm not only a state's human rights policy but its broader foreign policy as well.

Sometimes a country can afford to act on its human rights concerns; other times it cannot. Politics involves compromise, as a result of multiple and not always compatible goals that are pursued and the resistance of a world that more often than not is unsupportive of the particular objectives being sought. Human rights, like other goals of foreign policy, must at times be compromised. In some instances there is little that a country can afford to do even in the face of major human rights violations. . . .

If such variations in the treatment of human rights violators are to be part of a consistent policy, human rights concerns need to be explicitly and coherently integrated into the broader framework of foreign policy. A human rights policy must be an integral part of, not just something tacked on to, a country's overall foreign policy.

Difficult decisions have to be made about the relative weights to be given to human rights, as well as other foreign policy goals, and at least rough rules for making trade-offs need to be formulated. Furthermore, such decisions need to be made early in the process of working out a policy, and as a matter of principle. Ad hoc responses to immediate problems and crises, which have been the rule in the human rights policies of countries such as Canada and the United States, are almost sure to lead to inconsistencies and incoherence, both in appearance and in fact. Without such efforts to integrate human rights into the structure of national foreign policy, any trade-offs that are made will remain, literally, unprincipled.

Standards will be undeniably difficult to formulate, and their application will raise no less severe problems. Hard cases and exceptions are unavoidable. So are gray areas and fuzzy boundaries. Unless such efforts are seriously undertaken, however, the resulting policy is likely to appear baseless or inconsistent, and probably will be so in fact as well.

There are many opportunities for foreign policy action on behalf of human rights in foreign countries, but effective action requires the same sort of care and attention required for success in any area of foreign policy. . . .

Culture and Human Rights

This view of the creation of the individual, with individual needs for human rights, is criticized by many advocates of the "cultural relativist" school of human rights. They present the argument that human rights are a "Western construct with limited [universal] applicability."[22] But cultural relativism, as applied to human rights, fails to grasp the nature of culture. A number of erroneous assumptions underlie this viewpoint.

Criticism of the universality of human rights often stems from erroneous perceptions of the persistence of traditional societies, societies in which principles of social justice are based not on rights but on status and on the intermixture of privilege and responsibility. Often anthropologically anachronistic pictures are presented of premodern societies, taking no account whatsoever of the social changes we have described above. It is assumed that culture is a static entity. But culture—like the individual—is adaptive. One can accept the principle that customs, values, and norms do indeed glue society together, and that they will endure, without assuming cultural stasis. Even though elements of culture have a strong hold on people's individual psyches, cultures can and do change. Individuals are actors who can influence their own fate, even if their range of choice is circumscribed by the prevalent social structure, culture, or ideology.

Cultural relativist arguments also often assume that culture is a unitary and unique whole; that is, that one is born into, and will always be, a part of a distinctive, comprehensive, and integrated set of cultural values and institutions that cannot be changed incrementally or only in part. Since in each culture the social norms and roles vary, so, it is argued, human rights must vary. The norms of each society are held to be both valuable in and of their own right, and so firmly rooted as to be impervious to challenge. Therefore, such arguments are applicable only to certain Western societies; to impose them on other societies from which they did not originally arise would do serious and irreparable damage to those cultures. In fact, though, people are quite adept cultural accommodationists; they are able to choose which aspects of a "new" culture they wish to adopt and which aspects of the "old" they wish to retain. For example, the marabouts (priests), who lead Senegal's traditional Muslim brotherhoods, have become leading political figures and have acquired considerable wealth and power through the peanut trade.

3

Still another assumption of the cultural relativism school is that culture is unaffected by social structure. But structure does affect culture. To a significant extent cultures and values reflect the basic economic and political organization of a society. For example, a society such as Tokugawa Japan, that moves from a feudal structure to an organized bureaucratic state is bound to experience changes in values. Or the amalgamation of many different ethnic groups into one nation-state inevitably changes the way that individuals view themselves: For example, state-sponsored retention of ethnic customs, as under Canada's multicultural policy of preserving ethnic communities, cannot mask the fact that most of those communities are merging into the larger Canadian society.

4

A final assumption of the cultural relativist view of human rights is that cultural practices are neutral in their impact on different individuals and groups. Yet very few social practices, whether cultural or otherwise, distribute the same benefits to each member of a group. In considering any cultural practice it is useful to ask, who benefits from its retention? Those who speak for the group are usually those most capable of articulating the group's values to the outside world. But such spokesmen are likely to stress, in their articulation of "group" values, those particular values that are most to their own advantage. Both those who choose to adopt "new" ideals, such as political democracy or atheism, and those who choose to retain "old" ideals, such as a God-fearing political consensus, may be doing so in their own interests. Culture is both influenced by, and an instrument of, conflict among individuals or social groups. Just as those who attempt to modify or change customs may have personal interests in so doing, so also do those who attempt to preserve them. Quite often, relativist arguments are adopted principally to protect the interests of those in power.

This is a weak criticism of cultural relativism

Thus the notion that human rights cannot be applied across cultures violates both the principle of human rights and its practice. Human rights mean precisely that: rights held by virtue of being human. Human rights do not mean human dignity, nor do they represent the sum of personal resources (material, moral, or spiritual) that an individual might hold. Cultural variances that do not violate basic human rights undoubtedly enrich the world. But to permit the interests of the powerful to masquerade behind spurious defenses of cultural relativity is merely to lessen the chance that the victims of their policies will be able to complain. In the modern world, concepts such as cultural relativity, which deny to individuals the moral right to make comparisons and to insist on universal standards of right and wrong, are happily adopted by those who control the state.

THIRD WORLD CRITICISMS

In recent years a number of commentators from the Third World have criticized the concept of universal human rights. Frequently, the intention of the criticisms appears to be to exempt some Third World governments from the standard of judgment generated by the concept of universal human rights. Much of the criticism in fact serves to cover abuses of human rights by state corporatist, developmental dictatorship, or allegedly "socialist" regimes.

A common criticism of the concept of universal human rights is that since it is Western in origin, it must be limited in its applicability to the Western world. Both logically and empirically, this criticism is invalid. Knowledge is not limited in its applicability to its place or people of origin—one does not assume, for example, that medicines discovered in the developed Western world will cure only people of European origin. Nor is it reasonable to state that knowledge or thought of a certain kind—about social arrangements instead of about human biology or natural science—is limited to its place of origin. Those same Third World critics who reject universal concepts of human rights often happily accept Marxist socialism, which also originated in the Western world, in the mind of a German Jew.

The fact that human rights is originally a liberal notion, rooted in the rise of a class of bourgeois citizens in Europe who demanded individual rights against the power of kings and nobility, does not make human rights inapplicable to the rest of the world. As we argue above, all over the world there are now formal states, whose citizens are increasingly individualized. All over the world, therefore, there are people who need protections against the depradations of class-ruled governments.

Moreover, whatever the liberal origins of human rights, the list now accepted as universal includes a wide range of economic and social rights that were first advocated by socialist and social-democratic critics of liberalism. Although eighteenth-century liberals stressed the right to private property, the 1966 International Human Rights Covenants do not mention it, substituting instead the right to sovereignty over national resources. . . . To attribute the idea of universal human rights to an outdated liberalism, unaffected by later notions of welfare democracy and uninfluenced by socialist concerns with economic rights, is simply incorrect.

The absence of a right to private property in the Covenants indicates a sensitivity to the legitimate preoccupations of socialist and postcolonial Third World governments. Conservative critics of recent trends in international human rights in fact deplore the right to national sovereignty over resources, as some of them also deplore any attention to the economic rights of the individual. We certainly do not share this view of rights; we believe that the economic rights of the individual are as important as civil and political rights. But it is the individual we are concerned with. We would like to see a world in which *every individual* has enough to eat, not merely a world in which every *state* has the right to economic sovereignty.

We are skeptical, therefore, of the radical Third Worldist assertion that "group" rights ought to be more important than individual rights. Too often, the "group" in question proves to be the state. Why allocate rights to a social institution that is already the chief violator of individuals' rights? Similarly, we fear the expression "peoples' rights." The communal rights of individuals to practice their own religion, speak their own language, and indulge in their own ancestral customs are protected in the Covenant on Civil and Political Rights. Individuals are free to come together in groups to engage in those cultural practices which are meaningful to them. On the other hand, often a "group" right can simply mean that the individual is subordinate to the group—for example, that the individual Christian fundamentalist in the Soviet Union risks arrest because of the desire of the larger "group" to enforce official atheism.

The one compelling use that we can envisage for the term "group rights" is in protection of native peoples, usually hunter-gatherers, pastoralists, or subsistence agriculturalists, whose property rights as collectivities are being violated by the larger state societies that encroach upon them. Such groups are fighting a battle against the forces of modernization and the state's accumulative tendencies. For example, native peoples in Canada began in the 1970s to object to state development projects, such as the James Bay Hydroelectric project in Quebec, which deprived them of their traditional lands. At the moment, there is no international human rights protection for such groups or their "way of life."

One way to protect such group rights would be to incorporate the group as a legal entity in order to preserve their land claims. However, even if the law protects such group rights, individual members of the group may prefer to move into the larger society in response to the processes of modernization discussed above. Both opinions must be protected.

If the purpose of group rights is to protect large, established groups of people who share the same territory, customs, language, religion, and ancestry, then such protection could only occur at the expense of states' rights. These groups, under international human rights law, do not have the right to withdraw from the states that enfold them. Moreover, it is clearly not the intention of Third World defenders of group rights to allow such a right to secession. A first principle of the Organization of African Unity, for example, is to preserve the sovereignty of all its member states not only against outside attack but also against internal attempts at secession. Group rights appear to mean, in practice, states' rights. But the rights of states are the rights of the individuals and classes who control the state.

Many Third World and socialist regimes also argue that rights ought to be tied to duties. A citizen's rights, it is argued, ought to be contingent upon his duties toward the society at large—privilege is contingent on responsibility. Such a view of rights made sense in nonstate societies in which each "person" fulfilled his roles along with others, all of the roles together creating a close-knit, tradition-bound group. But in modern state societies, to tie rights to duties is to risk the former's complete disappearance. All duties will be aimed toward the preservation of the state and of the interests of those who control it.

It is true that no human rights are absolute; even in societies that adhere in principle to the liberal ethos, individuals are frequently deprived of rights, especially in wartime or if they are convicted of criminal acts. However, such deprivations can legitimately be made only after the most scrupulous protection of civil and political rights under the rule of law. The difficulty with tying rights to duties without the intermediate step of scrutiny by a genuinely independent judiciary is the likelihood of wholesale cancellation of rights by the ruling class. But if one has rights merely because one is human, and for no other reason, then it is much more difficult, in principle, for the state to cancel them. It cannot legitimate the denial of rights by saying that only certain types of human beings, exhibiting certain kinds of behavior, are entitled to them.

One final criticism of the view of universal human rights embedded in the International Covenants is that an undue stress is laid on civil and political rights, whereas the overriding rights priority in the Third World is economic rights. In this view, the state as the agent of economic development—and hence, presumably, of eventual distribution of economic goods or "rights" to the masses—should not be bothered with problems of guaranteeing political participation in decision making, or of protecting people's basic civil rights. These rights, it is argued, come "after" development is completed. The empirical basis for this argument is weak. . . . Economic development per se will not guarantee future human rights, whether of an economic or any other kind. Often, development means economic growth, but without equitable distributive measures. Moreover, development strategies often fail because of insufficient attention to citizens' needs and views. Finally, development plans are often a cover for the continued violations of citizens' rights by the ruling class.

Thus we return to where we started: the rights of all men and women against all governments to treatment as free, equal, materially and physically secure persons. This is what human dignity means and requires in our era. And the individual human rights of the Universal Declaration and the Covenants are the means by which individuals today carry out the struggle to achieve their dignity. . . .

NOTES

1. The International Bill of Human Rights includes the Universal Declaration of Human Rights (1948: reprinted below as appendix 1), the International Covenant on Economic, Social and Cultural Rights (1966), the International Covenant on Civil and Political Rights (1966), and the Optional Protocol to the latter Covenant.
2. Ronald Dworkin, *Taking Rights Seriously* (Cambridge: Harvard University Press, 1977), pp. xi, 90.
3. Thomas Aquinas, *The Political Ideas of St. Thomas Aquinas,* ed. Dino Bigongiari (New York: Hafner Press, 1953).
4. John Locke, *Essays on the Law of Nature* (Oxford: Clarendon Press, 1954); *Two Treatises of Government* (Cambridge: Cambridge University Press, 1967), *Second Treatise,* para. 6, 12, 16, 57, 59, 60, 118, 124, 135, 172.
5. Jacques Maritain, *The Rights of Man and Natural Law* (New York: Charles Scribner's Sons, 1947); *Man and the State* (Chicago: University of Chicago Press, 1951).
6. Thomas Hobbes, *Leviathan* (Baltimore: Penguin Books, 1971).
7. Locke, *Second Treatise.*
8. Thomas Jefferson, *The Life and Selected Writings of Thomas Jefferson,* ed. Adrienne Koch and William Peden (New York: Modern Library, 1944); Thomas Paine, *Rights of Man* (New York: Penguin Books, 1984).
9. See Jack Donnelly, "Natural Law and Right in Aquinas' Political Thought," *Western Political Quarterly* 33 (December 1980); 520–35.
10. Rhoda E. Howard and Jack Donnelly, "Human Dignity, Human Rights and Political Regimes," *American Political Science Review* 80 (September 1986); 51–63; Jack Donnelly, "Human Rights and Human Dignity: An Analytic Critique of Non-Western Human Rights Conceptions," *American Political Science Review* 76 (June 1982); 303–16; Rhoda E. Howard, *Human Rights in Commonwealth Africa* (Totowa, N.J.: Rowman and Littlefield, 1986), chap. 2.
11. See Jack Donnelly, *The Concept of Human Rights* (London: Croom Helm; New York: St. Martin's, 1985), chap. 3 and the sources cited therein.

12. See, for example, Marc F. Plattner, ed., *Human Rights in Our Time: Essays in Memory of Victor Baras* (Boulder, Col.: Westview Press, 1984); Maurice Cranston, "Are There Any Human Rights?" *Daedalus* 112 (Fall 1983); 1–17; Jeane J. Kirkpatrick, "Establishing a Viable Human Rights Policy," in *Human Rights and U.S. Human Rights Policy,* Howard J. Wiarda, ed. (Washington, D.C.: American Enterprise Institute, 1982).

13. See, for example, H. Klenner, "Freedom and Human Rights," *GDR Committee for Human Rights Bulletin* 10, no. 1 (1984); 13–21; A. G. Egorov, "Socialism and the Individual: Rights and Freedoms," *Soviet Studies in Philosophy* 18 (Fall 1979); 3–51; and UN document number A/C.3/32/SR.51.

14. This section is a very much abbreviated version of Jack Donnelly, "International Human Rights: A Regime Analysis," *International Organization* 40 (Summer 1986); 599–642.

15. See Farrokh Jhabvala, "The Practice of the Covenant's Human Rights Committee, 1976–82; Review of State Party Reports," *Human Rights Quarterly* 6 (February 1984); 81–106; Dana D. Fischer, "Reporting under the Covenant on Civil and Political Rights: The First Five Years of the Human Rights Committee," *American Journal of International Law* 76 (January 1982); 142–53; and Donnelly "International Human Rights," pp. 609–11.

16. See Donnelly, "International Human Rights," pp. 628–33 and the works cited there.

17. Howard Tolley, "The Concealed Crack in the Citadel: The United Nations Commission on Human Rights' Response to Confidential Communications," *Human Rights Quarterly* 6 (November 1984); 420–62.

18. See Donnelly, "International Human Rights," pp. 620–28 and the works cited there.

19. This section draws heavily on Jack Donnelly, "Human Rights and Foreign Policy," *World Politics* 34 (July 1982); 574–95, and "Human Rights, Humanitarian Intervention and American Foreign Policy: Law, Morality and Politics," *Journal of International Affairs* 37 (Winter 1984); 311–28.

20. See, for example, Jerome Slater and Terry Nardin, "Nonintervention and Human Rights," *Journal of Politics* 48 (February 1986); 86–96; Charles R. Beitz, "Nonintervention and Communal Integrity," *Philosophy and Public Affairs* 9 (Summer 1980); 385–91; and Robert Matthews and Cranford Pratt, "Human Rights and Foreign Policy: Principles and Canadian Practice," *Human Rights Quarterly* 7 (May 1985); 159–88.

21. Michael Walzer, *Just and Unjust Wars* (New York: Basic Books, 1977), p. 90. For criticisms of Walzer see Slater and Nardin, "Nonintervention;" Beitz, "Nonintervention"; and David Luban, "The Romance of the Nation State," *Philosophy and Public Affairs* 9 (Summer 1980); 392–97.

22. Adamantia Pollis and Peter Schwab, "Human Rights: A Western Concept with Limited Applicability," in *Human Rights: Cultural and Ideological Perspectives,* Pollis and Schwab, ed. (New York: Praeger, 1979), pp. 1–18.

Perspectives on the Nature of Anarchy

The Anarchic Structure of World Politics

Kenneth N. Waltz

POLITICAL STRUCTURES

Only through some sort of systems theory can international politics be understood. To be a success, such a theory has to show how international politics can be conceived of as a domain distinct from the economic, social, and other international domains that one may conceive of. To mark international-political systems off from other international systems, and to distinguish systems-level from unit-level forces, requires showing how political structures are generated and how they affect, and are affected by, the units of the system. How can we conceive of international politics as a distinct system? What is it that intervenes between interacting units and the results that their acts and interactions produce? To answer these questions, this chapter first examines the concept of social structure and then defines structure as a concept appropriate for national and for international politics.

A system is composed of a structure and of interacting units. The structure is the system-wide component that makes it possible to think of the system as a whole. The problem is . . . to contrive a definition of structure free of the attributes and the interactions of units. Definitions of structure must leave aside, or abstract from, the characteristics of units, their behavior, and their interactions. Why must those obviously important matters be omitted? They must be omitted so that we can distinguish between variables at the level of the units and variables at the level of the system. The problem is to develop theoretically useful concepts to

From Kenneth N. Waltz, *Theory of International Politics,* © 1979, Addison-Wesley, Reading, Massachusetts, pp. 79–106. Reprinted with permission. Portions of the text and some footnotes have been omitted.

replace the vague and varying systemic notions that are customarily employed—notions such as environment, situation, context, and milieu. Structure is a useful concept if it gives clear and fixed meaning to such vague and varying terms.

We know what we have to omit from any definition of structure if the definition is to be useful theoretically. Abstracting from the attributes of units means leaving aside questions about the kinds of political leaders, social and economic institutions, and ideological commitments states may have. Abstracting from relations means leaving aside questions about the cultural, economic, political, and military interactions of states. To say what is to be left out does not indicate what is to be put in. The negative point is important nevertheless because the instruction to omit attributes is often violated and the instruction to omit interactions almost always goes unobserved. But if attributes and interactions are omitted, what is left? The question is answered by considering the double meaning of the term "relation." As S. F. Nadel points out, ordinary language obscures a distinction that is important in theory. "Relation" is used to mean both the interaction of units and the positions they occupy vis-à-vis each other.[1] To define a structure requires ignoring how units relate with one another (how they interact) and concentrating on how they stand in relation to one another (how they are arranged or positioned). Interactions, as I have insisted, take place at the level of the units. How units stand in relation to one another, the way they are arranged or positioned, is not a property of the units. The arrangement of units is a property of the system.

By leaving aside the personality of actors, their behavior, and their interactions, one arrives at a purely positional picture of society. Three propositions follow from this. First, structures may endure while personality, behavior, and interactions vary widely. Structure is sharply distinguished from actions and interactions. Second, a structural definition applies to realms of widely different substance so long as the arrangement of parts is similar.[2] Third, because this is so, theories developed for one realm may with some modification be applicable to other realms as well. . . .

The concept of structure is based on the fact that units differently juxtaposed and combined behave differently and in interacting produce different outcomes. I first want to show how internal political structure can be defined. In a book on international-political theory, domestic political structure has to be examined in order to draw a distinction between expectations about behavior and outcomes in the internal and external realms. Moreover, considering domestic political structure now will make the elusive international-political structure easier to catch later on.

Structure defines the arrangement, or the ordering, of the parts of a system. Structure is not a collection of political institutions but rather the arrangement of them. How is the arrangement defined? The constitution of a state describes some parts of the arrangement, but political structures as they develop are not identical with formal constitutions. In defining structures, the first question to answer is this: What is the principle by which the parts are arranged?

Domestic politics is hierarchically ordered. The units—institutions and agencies—stand vis à vis each other in relations of super- and subordination. The ordering principle of a system gives the first, and basic, bit of information about how the parts of a realm are related to each other. In a polity the hierarchy of offices is by no means completely articulated, nor are all ambiguities about relations of super- and subordination removed. Nevertheless, political actors are formally differentiated according to the degrees of their authority, and their distinct functions are specified. By "specified" I do not mean that the law of the land fully describes the duties that different agencies perform, but only that broad agreement prevails on the tasks that various parts of a government are to undertake and on the extent of the power they legitimately wield. Thus Congress supplies the military forces; the President commands them. Congress makes the laws; the executive branch enforces them; agencies administer laws; judges interpret them. Such specification of roles and differentiation of functions is found in any state, the more fully so as the state is more highly developed. The specification of functions of formally differentiated parts gives the second bit of structural information. This second part of the definition adds some content to the structure, but only enough to say more fully how the units stand in relation to one another. The roles and the functions of the British Prime Minister and Parliament, for example, differ from those of the American President and Congress. When offices are juxtaposed and functions are combined in different ways, different behaviors and outcomes result, as I shall shortly show.

The placement of units in relation to one another is not fully defined by a system's ordering principle and by the formal differentiation of its parts. The standing of the units also changes with changes in their relative capabilities. In the performance of their functions, agencies may gain capabilities or lose them. The relation of Prime Minister to Parliament and of President to Congress depends on, and varies with, their relative capabilities. The third part of the definition of structure acknowledges that even while specified functions remain unchanged, units come to stand in different relation to each other through changes in relative capability.

A domestic political structure is thus defined: first, according to the principle by which it is ordered; second, by specification of the functions of formally differentiated units; and third, by the distribution of capabilities across those units. Structure is a highly abstract notion, but the definition of structure does not abstract from everything. To do so would be to leave everything aside and to include nothing at all. The three-part definition of structure includes only what is required to show how the units of the system are positioned or arranged. Everything else is omitted. Concern for tradition and culture, analysis of the character and personality of political actors, consideration of the conflictive and accommodative processes of politics, description of the making and execution of policy— all such matters are left aside. Their omission does not imply their unimportance. They are omitted because we want to figure out the expected effects of structure on process and of process on structure. That can be done only if structure and process are distinctly defined.

I defined domestic political structures first by the principle according to which they are organized or ordered, second by the differentiation of units and the specification of their functions, and third by the distribution of capabilities across units. Let us see how the three terms of the definition apply to international politics.

1. Ordering Principles

Structural questions are questions about the arrangement of the parts of a system. The parts of domestic political systems stand in relations of super- and subordination. Some are entitled to command; others are required to obey. Domestic systems are centralized and hierarchic. The parts of international-political systems stand in relations of coordination. Formally, each is the equal of all the others. None is entitled to command; none is required to obey. International systems are decentralized and anarchic. The ordering principles of the two structures are distinctly different, indeed, contrary to each other. Domestic political structures have governmental institutions and offices as their concrete counterparts. International politics, in contrast, has been called "politics in the absence of government."[3] International organizations do exist, and in ever-growing numbers. Supranational agents able to act effectively, however, either themselves acquire some of the attributes and capabilities of states, as did the medieval papacy in the era of Innocent III, or they soon reveal their inability to act in important ways except with the support, or at least the acquiescence, of the principal states concerned with the matters at hand. Whatever elements of authority emerge internationally are barely once removed from the capability that provides the foundation for the appearance of those elements. Authority quickly reduces to a particular expression of capability. In the absence of agents with system-wide authority, formal relations of super- and subordination fail to develop.

The first term of a structural definition states the principle by which the system is ordered. Structure is an organizational concept. The prominent characteristic of international politics, however, seems to be the lack of order and of organization. How can one think of international politics as being any kind of an order at all? The anarchy of politics internationally is often referred to. If structure is an organizational concept, the terms "structure" and "anarchy" seem to be in contradiction. If international politics is "politics in the absence of government," what are we in the presence of? In looking for international structure, one is brought face to face with the invisible, an uncomfortable position to be in.

The problem is this: how to conceive of an order without an orderer and of organizational effects where formal organization is lacking. Because these are difficult questions, I shall answer them through analogy with microeconomic theory. Reasoning by analogy is helpful where one can move from a domain for which theory is well developed to one where it is not. Reasoning by analogy is permissible where different domains are structurally similar.

Classical economic theory, developed by Adam Smith and his followers, is microtheory. Political scientists tend to think that microtheory is theory about small-scale matters, a usage that ill accords with its established meaning. The term "micro" in economic theory indicates the way in which the theory is constructed rather than the scope of the matters it pertains to. Microeconomic theory describes how an order is spontaneously formed from the self-interested acts and interactions of individual units—in this case, persons and firms. The theory then turns upon the two central concepts of the economic units and of the market. Economic units and economic markets are concepts, not descriptive realities or concrete entities. This must be emphasized since from the early eighteenth century to the present, from the sociologist Auguste Comte to the psychologist George Katona, economic theory has been faulted because its assumptions fail to correspond with realities.[4] Unrealistically, economic theorists conceive of an economy operating in isolation from its society and polity. Unrealistically, economists assume that the economic world is the world of the world. Unrealistically, economists think of the acting unit, the famous "economic man," as a single-minded profit maximizer. They single out one aspect of man and leave aside the wondrous variety of human life. As any moderately sensible economist knows, "economic man" does not exist. Anyone who asks businessmen how they make their decisions will find that the assumption that men are economic maximizers grossly distorts their characters. The assumption that men behave as economic men, which is known to be false as a descriptive statement, turns out to be useful in the construction of theory.

Markets are the second major concept invented by microeconomic theorists. Two general questions must be asked about markets: How are they formed? How do they work? The answer to the first question is this: The market of a decentralized economy is individualist in origin, spontaneously generated, and unintended. The market arises out of the activities of separate units—persons and firms—whose aims and efforts are directed not toward creating an order but rather toward fulfilling their own internally defined interests by whatever means they can muster. The individual unit acts for itself. From the coaction of like units emerges a structure that affects and constrains all of them. Once formed, a market becomes a force in itself, and a force that the constitutive units acting singly or in small numbers cannot control. Instead, in lesser or greater degree as market conditions vary, the creators become the creatures of the market that their activity gave rise to. Adam Smith's great achievement was to show how self-interested, greed-driven actions may produce good social outcomes if only political and social conditions permit free competition. If a laissez-faire economy is harmonious, it is so because the intentions of actors do not correspond with the outcomes their actions produce. What intervenes between the actors and the objects of their action in order to thwart their purposes? To account for the unexpectedly favorable outcomes of selfish acts, the concept of a market is brought into play. Each unit seeks its own good; the result of a number of units simultaneously doing so transcends the motives and the aims of the separate units. Each would like to work less hard and price his product higher. Taken together, all have to work harder and price their products lower. Each firm seeks to increase its profit; the result of many firms doing so drives the profit rate downward. Each man seeks his own end, and, in doing so, produces a result that was no part of his intention. Out of the mean ambition of its members, the greater good of society is produced.

The market is a cause interposed between the economic actors and the results they produce. It conditions their calculations, their behaviors, and their interactions. It is not an agent in the sense of A being the agent that produces outcome X. Rather it is a structural cause. A market constrains the units that comprise it from taking certain actions and disposes them toward taking others. The market, created by self-directed interacting economic units, selects behaviors according to their consequences. The market rewards some with high profits and assigns others to bankruptcy. Since a market is not an institution or an agent in any concrete or palpable sense, such statements become impressive only if they can be reliably inferred from a theory as part of a set of more elaborate expectations. They can be. Microeconomic theory explains how an economy operates and why certain effects are to be expected. . . .

International-political systems, like economic markets, are formed by the coaction of self-regarding units. International structures are defined in terms of the primary political units of an era, be they city states, empires, or nations. Structures emerge from the coexistence of states. No state intends to participate in the formation of a structure by which it and others will be constrained. International-political systems, like economic markets, are individualist in origin, spontaneously generated, and unintended. In both systems, structures are formed by the coaction of their units. Whether those units live, prosper, or die depends on their own efforts. Both systems are formed and maintained on a principle of self-help that applies to the units. . . .

In a microtheory, whether of international politics or of economics, the motivation of the actors is assumed rather than realistically described. I assume that states seek to ensure their survival. The assumption is a radical simplification made for the sake of constructing theory. The question to ask of the assumption, as ever, is not whether it is true but whether it is the most sensible and useful one that can be made. Whether it is a useful assumption depends on whether a theory based on the assumption can be contrived, a theory from which important consequences not otherwise obvious can be inferred. Whether it is a sensible assumption can be directly discussed.

Beyond the survival motive, the aims of states may be endlessly varied; they may range from the ambition to conquer the world to the desire merely to be left alone. Survival is a prerequisite to achieving any goals that states may have, other than the goal of promoting their own disappearance as political entities. The survival motive is taken as the ground of action in a world where the security of states is not assured, rather than as a realistic description of the impulse that lies behind every act of state. The assumption allows for the fact that no state always acts exclusively to ensure its survival. It allows for the fact that some states may persistently seek goals that they value more highly than survival; they may, for example, prefer amalgamation with other states to their own survival in form. It allows for the fact that in pursuit of its security no state will act with perfect knowledge and wisdom—if indeed we could know what those terms might mean. . . .

Actors may perceive the structure that constrains them and understand how it serves to reward some kinds of behavior and to penalize others. But then again they either may not see it or, seeing it, may for any of many reasons fail to conform their actions to the patterns that are most often rewarded and least often punished. To say that "the structure selects" means simply that those who conform to accepted and successful practices more often rise to the top and are likelier to stay there. The game one has to win is defined by the structure that determines the kind of player who is likely to prosper. . . .

2. The Character of the Units

The second term in the definition of domestic political structure specifies the functions performed by differentiated units. Hierarchy entails relations of super- and subordination among a system's parts, and that implies their differentiation. In defining domestic political structure the second term, like the first and third, is needed because each term points to a possible source of structural variation. The states that are the units of international-political systems are not formally differentiated by the functions they perform. Anarchy entails relations of coordination among a system's units, and that implies their sameness. The second term is not needed in defining international-political structure, because, so long as anarchy endures, states remain like units. International structures vary only through a change of organizing principle or, failing that, through variations in the capabilities of units. Nevertheless I shall discuss these like units here, because it is by their interactions that international-politics structures are generated.

Two questions arise: Why should states be taken as the units of the system? Given a wide variety of states, how can one call them "like units"? Questioning the choice of states as the primary units of international-political systems became popular in the 1960s and 1970s as it was at the turn of the century. Once one understands what is logically involved, the issue is easily resolved. Those who question the state-centric view do so for two main reasons. First, states are not the only actors of importance on the international scene. Second, states are declining in importance, and other actors are gaining, or so it is said. Neither reason is cogent, as the following discussion shows.

States are not and never have been the only international actors. But then structures are defined not by all of the actors that flourish within them but by the major ones. In defining a system's structure one chooses one or some of the infinitely many objects comprising the system and defines its structure in terms of them. For international-political systems, as for any system, one must first decide which units to take as being the parts of the system. Here the economic analogy will help again. The structure of a market is defined by the number of firms competing. If many roughly equal firms contend, a condition of perfect competition is approximated. If a few firms dominate the market, competition is said to be oligopolistic even though many smaller firms may also be in the field. But we are told that definitions of this sort cannot be applied to international politics because of the interpenetration of states, because of their inability to control the environment of their action, and because rising multinational corporations and other nonstate actors are difficult to regulate and may rival some states in influence. The importance of nonstate actors and the extent of transnational activities are obvious. The conclusion that the state-centric conception of international politics is made obsolete by them does not follow. That economists and economically minded politics scientists have thought that it does is ironic. The irony lies in the fact that all of the reasons given for scrapping the state-centric concept can be related more strongly and applied to firms. Firms competing with numerous others have no hope of controlling their market, and oligopolistic firms constantly struggle with imperfect success to do so. Firms interpenetrate, merge, and buy each up at a merry pace. Moreover, firms are constantly threatened and regulated by, shall we say, "non-firm" actors. Some governments encourage concentration; others work to prevent it. The market structure of parts of an economy may move from a wider to a narrower competition or may move in the opposite direction, but whatever the extent and the frequency of change, market structures, generated by the interaction of firms, are defined in terms of them.

Just as economists define markets in terms of firms, so I define international-political structures in terms of states. If Charles P. Kindleberger were right in saying that "the nation-state is just about through as an economic unit,"[5] then the structure of international politics would have to be redefined. That would be necessary because economic capabilities cannot be separated from the other capabilities of states. The distinction frequently drawn between matters of high and low politics is misplaced. States use economic means for military and political ends; and military and political means for the achievement of economic interests.

An amended version of Kindleberger's statement may hold: Some states may be nearly washed up as economic entities, and others not. That poses no problem for international-political theory since international politics is mostly about inequalities anyway. So long as the major states are the major actors, the structure of international politics is defined in terms of them. That theoretical statement is of course borne out in practice. States set the scene in which they, along with nonstate actors, state their dramas or carry on their humdrum affairs, Though they may choose to interfere little in the affairs of nonstate actors for long periods of time, states nevertheless set the terms of intercourse, whether by passively permitting informal rules to develop or by actively intervening to change rules that no longer suit them. When the crunch comes, states remake the rules by which other actors operate. Indeed, one may be struck by the ability of weak states to impede the operation of strong international corporations and by the attention the latter pay to the wishes of the former. . . .

States are the units whose interactions form the structure of international-political systems. They will long remain so. The death rate among states is remarkably low. Few states die; many firms do. . . . To call states "like units" is to say that each state is like all other states in being an autonomous political unit. It is another way of saying that states are sovereign. But sovereignty is also a bothersome concept. Many believe, as the anthropologist M. G. Smith has said, that "in a system of sovereign states no state is sovereign."[6] The error lies in identifying the sovereignty of states with their ability to do as they wish. To say that states are sovereign is not to say that they can do as they please, that they are free of others' influence, that they are able to get what they want. Sovereign states may be hardpressed all around, constrained to act in ways they would like to avoid, and able to do hardly anything just as they would like to. The sovereignty of states has never entailed their insulation from the effects of other states' actions. To be sovereign and to be dependent are not contradictory conditions. Sovereign states have seldom led free and easy lives. What then is sovereignty? To say that a state is sovereign means that it decides for itself how it will cope with its internal and external problems, including whether or not to seek assistance from others and in doing so to limit its freedom by making commitments to them. States develop their own strategies, chart their own courses, make their own decisions about how to meet whatever needs they experience and whatever desires they develop. It is no more contradictory to say that sovereign states are always constrained and often tightly so than it is to say that free individuals often make decisions under the heavy pressure of events.

Each state, like every other state, is a sovereign political entity. And yet the differences across states, from Costa Rica to the Soviet Union, from Gambia to the United States, are immense. States are alike, and they are also different. So are corporations, apples, universities, and people. Whenever we put two or more objects in the same category, we are saying that they are alike not in all respects but in some. No two objects in this world are identical, yet they can often be usefully compared and combined. "You can't add apples and oranges" is an old saying that seems to be especially popular among salesmen who do not want you to compare their wares with others. But we all know that the trick of adding dissimilar objects is to express the result in terms of a category that comprises them. Three apples plus four oranges equals seven pieces of fruit. The only interesting question is whether the category that classifies objects according to their common qualities is useful. One can add up a large number of widely varied objects and say that one has eight million things, but seldom need one do that.

States vary widely in size, wealth, power, and form. And yet variations in these and in other respects are variations among like units. In what way are they like units? How can they be placed in a single category? States are alike in the tasks that they face, though not in their abilities to perform them. The differences are of capability, not of function. States perform or try to perform tasks, most of which are common to all of them; the ends they aspire to are similar. Each state duplicates the activities of other states at least to a considerable extent. Each state has its agencies for making, executing, and interpreting laws and regulations, for raising revenues, and for defending itself. Each state supplies out of its own resources and by its own means most of the food, clothing, housing, transportation, and amenities consumed and used by its citizens. All states, except the smallest ones, do much more of their business at home than abroad. One has to be impressed with the functional similarity of states and, now more than ever before, with the similar lines their development follows. From the rich to the poor states, from the old to the new ones, nearly all of them take a larger hand in matters of economic regulation, of education, health, and housing, of culture and the arts, and so on almost endlessly. The increase of the activities of states is a strong and strikingly uniform international trend. The functions of states are similar, and distinctions among them arise principally from their varied capabilities. International politics consists of like units duplicating one another's activities.

3. The Distribution of Capabilities

The parts of a hierarchic system are related to one another in ways that are determined both by their functional differentiation and by the extent of their capabilities. The units of an anarchic system are functionally undifferentiated. The units of such an order are then distinguished primarily by their greater or lesser capabilities for performing similar tasks. This states formally what students of international politics have long noticed. The great powers of an era have always been marked off from others by practitioners and theorists alike. Students of national government make such distinctions as that between parliamentary and presidential systems; governmental systems differ in form. Students of international politics make distinctions between international-political systems only according to the number of their great powers. The structure of a system changes with changes in the distribution of capabilities across the system's units. And changes in structure change expectations about how the units of the system will behave and about the outcomes their interactions will produce. Domestically, the differentiated parts of a system may perform similar tasks. We know from observing the American government that executives sometimes legislate and legislatures sometimes execute. Internationally, like units sometimes perform different tasks . . . but two problems should be considered.

The first problem is this: Capability tells us something about units. Defining structure partly in terms of the distribution of capabilities seems to violate my instruction to keep unit attributes out of structural definitions. As I remarked earlier, structure is a highly but not entirely abstract concept. The maximum of abstraction allows a minimum of content, and that minimum is what is needed to enable one to say how the units stand in relation to one another. States are differently placed by their power. And yet one may wonder why only *capability* is included in the third part of the definition, and not such characteristics as ideology, form of government, peacefulness, bellicosity, or whatever. The answer is this: Power is estimated by comparing the capabilities of a number of units. Although capabilities are attributes of units, the distribution of capabilities across units is not. The distribution of capabilities is not a unit attribute, but rather a system-wide concept. . . .

The second problem is this: Though relations defined in terms of interactions must be excluded from structural definitions, relations defined in terms of grouping of states do seem to tell us something about how states are placed in the system. Why not specify how states stand in relation to one another by considering the alliances they form? Would doing so not be comparable to defining national political structures partly in terms of how presidents and prime ministers are related to other political agents? It would not be. Nationally as internationally, structural definitions deal with the relation of agents and agencies in terms of the organization of realms and not in terms of the accommodations and conflicts that may occur within them or the groupings that may now and then form. Parts of a government may draw together or pull apart, may oppose each other or cooperate in greater or lesser degree. These are the relations that form and dissolve within a system rather than structural alterations that mark a change from one system to another. This is made clear by the example that runs nicely parallel to the case alliances. Distinguishing systems of political parties according to their number is common. A multiparty system changes if, say, eight parties become two, but not if two groupings of the eight form merely for the occasion of fighting an election. By the same logic, an international-political system in which three or more great powers have split into two alliances remains a multipolar system—structurally distinct from a bipolar system, a system in which no third power is able to challenge the top two. . . .

In defining international-political structures we take states with whatever traditions, habits, objectives, desires, and forms of government they may have. We do not ask whether states are revolutionary or legitimate, authoritarian or democratic, ideological or pragmatic. We abstract from every attribute of states except their capabilities. Nor in thinking about structure do we ask about the relations of states—their feelings of friendship and hostility, their diplomatic exchanges, the alliances they form, and the extent of the contacts and exchanges among them. We ask what range of expectations arises merely from looking at the type of order that prevails among them and at the distribution of capabilities within that order. We abstract from any particular qualities of states and from all of their concrete connections. What emerges is a positional picture, a general description of the ordered overall arrangement of a society written in terms of the placement of units rather than in terms of their qualities. . . .

ANARCHIC STRUCTURES AND BALANCES OF POWER

[We must now] examine the characteristics of anarchy and the expectations about outcomes associated with anarchic realms. . . . [This] is best accomplished by drawing some comparisons between behavior and outcomes in anarchic and hierarchic realms.

4. Violence at Home and Abroad

The state among states, it is often said, conducts its affairs in the brooding shadow of violence. Because some states may at any time use force, all states must be prepared to do so—or live at the mercy of their militarily more vigorous neighbors. Among states, the state of nature is a state of war. This is meant not in the sense that war constantly occurs but in the sense that, with each state deciding for itself whether or not to use force, war may at any time break out. Whether in the family, the community, or the world at large, contact without at least occasional conflict is inconceivable; and the hope that in the absence of an agent to manage or to manipulate conflicting parties the use of force will always be avoided cannot be realistically entertained. Among men as among states, anarchy, or the absence of government, is associated with the occurrence of violence.

The threat of violence and the recurrent use of force are said to distinguish international from national affairs. But in the history of the world surely most rulers have had to bear in mind that their subjects might use force to resist or overthrow them. If the absence of government is associated with the threat of violence, so also is its presence. A haphazard list of national tragedies illustrates the point all too well. The most destructive wars of the hundred years following the defeat of Napoleon took place not among states but *within* them. Estimates of deaths in China's Taiping Rebellion, which began in 1851 and lasted 13 years, range as high as 20 million. In the American Civil War some 600 thousand people lost their lives. In more recent history, forced collectivation and Stalin's purges eliminated 5 million Russians, and Hitler exterminated 6 million Jews. In some Latin American countries, coups d'états and rebellions have been normal features of national life.

Between 1948 and 1957, for example, 200 thousand Colombians were killed in civil strife. In the middle 1970s most inhabitants of Idi Amin's Uganda must have felt their lives becoming nasty, brutish, and short, quite as in Thomas Hobbes's state of nature. If such cases constitute aberrations, they are uncomfortably common ones. We easily lose sight of the fact that struggles to achieve and maintain power, to establish order, and to contrive a kind of justice within states may be bloodier than wars among them.

If anarchy is identified with chaos, destruction, and death, then the distinction between anarchy and government does not tell us much. Which is more precarious: the life of a state among states, or of a government in relation to its subjects? The answer varies with time and place. Among some states at some times, the actual or expected occurrence of violence is low. Within some states at some times, the actual or expected occurrence of violence is high. The use of force, or the constant fear of its use, are not sufficient grounds for distinguishing international from domestic affairs. If the possible and the actual use of force mark both national and international orders, then no durable distinction between the two realms can be drawn in terms of the use or the nonuse of force. No human order is proof against violence.

To discover qualitative differences between internal and external affairs one must look for a criterion other than the occurrence of violence. The distinction between international and national realms of politics is not found in the use or the nonuse of force but in their different structures. But if the dangers of being violently attacked are greater, say, in taking an evening stroll through downtown Detroit than they are in picnicking along the French and German border, what practical difference does the difference of structure make? Nationally as internationally, contact generates conflict and at times issues in violence. The difference between national and international politics lies not in the use of force but in the different modes of organization for doing something about it. A government, ruling by some standard of legitimacy, arrogates to itself the right to use force—that is, to apply a variety of sanctions to control the use of force by its subjects. If some use private force, others may appeal to the government. A government has no monopoly on the use of force, as is all too evident. An effective government, however, has a monopoly on the *legitimate* use of force, and legitimate here means that public agents are organized to prevent and to counter the private use of force. Citizens need not prepare to defend themselves. Public agencies do that. A national system is not one of self-help. The international system is.

5. Interdependence and Integration

The political significance of interdependence varies depending on whether a realm is organized, with relations of authority specified and established, or remains formally unorganized. Insofar as a realm is formally organized, its units are free to specialize, to pursue their own interests without concern for developing the means of maintaining their identity and preserving their security in the presence of others. They are free to specialize because they have no reason to fear the increased interdependence that goes with specialization. If those who specialize most benefit most, then competition in specialization ensues. Goods are manufactured, grain is produced, law and order are maintained, commerce is conducted, and financial services are provided by people who ever more narrowly specialize. In simple economic terms, the cobbler depends on the tailor for his pants and the tailor on the cobbler for his shoes, and each would be ill-clad without the services of the other. In simple political terms, Kansas depends on Washington for protection and regulation and Washington depends on Kansas for beef and wheat. In saying that in such situations interdependence is close, one need not maintain that the one part could not learn to live without the other. One need only say that the cost of breaking the interdependent relation would be high. Persons and institutions depend heavily on one another because of the different tasks they perform and the different goods they produce and exchange. The parts of a polity bind themselves together by their differences.[7]

Differences between national and international structures are reflected in the ways the units of each system define their ends and develop the means for reaching them. In anarchic realms, like units coact. In hierarchic realms, unlike units interact. In an anarchic realm, the units are functionally similar and tend to remain so. Like units work to maintain a measure of independence and may even strive for autarchy. In a hierarchic realm, the units are differentiated, and they tend to increase the extent of their specialization. Differentiated units become closely interdependent, the more closely so as their specialization proceeds. Because of the difference of structure, interdependence within and interdependence among nations are two distinct concepts. So as to follow the logicians' admonition to keep a single meaning for a given term throughout one's discourse, I shall use "integration" to describe the condition within nations and "interdependence" to describe the condition among them.

Although states are like units functionally, they differ vastly in their capabilities. Out of such differences something of a division of labor develops. The division of labor across nations, however, is slight in comparison with the highly articulated division of labor within them. Integration draws the parts of a nation closely together. Interdependence among nations leaves them loosely connected. Although the integration of nations is often talked about, it seldom takes place. Nations could mutually enrich themselves by further dividing not just the labor that goes into the production of goods but also some of the other tasks they perform, such as political management and military defense. Why does their integration not take place? The structure of international politics limits the cooperation of states in two ways.

In a self-help system each of the units spends a portion of its effort, not in forwarding its own good, but in providing the means of protecting itself against others. Specialization in a system of divided labor works to everyone's advantage, though not equally so. Inequality in the expected distribution of the increased product works strongly against extension of the division of labor internationally. When faced with the possibility of cooperating for mutual gain, states that feel insecure must ask how the gain will be divided. They are compelled to ask not "Will both of us gain?" but "Who will gain more?" If an expected gain is to be divided, say, in the ratio of two to one, one state may use its disproportionate gain to implement a policy intended to damage or destroy the other. Even the prospect of large absolute gains for both parties does not elicit their cooperation so long as each fears how the other will use its increased capabilities. Notice that the impediments to collaboration may not lie in the character and the immediate intention of either party. Instead, the condition of insecurity—at the least, the uncertainty of each about the other's future intentions and actions—works against their cooperation. . . .

A state worries about a division of possible gains that may favor others more than itself. That is the first way in which the structure of international politics limits the cooperation of states. A state also worries lest it become dependent on others through cooperative endeavors and exchanges of goods and services. That is the second way in which the structure of international politics limits the cooperation of states. The more a state specializes, the more it relies on others to supply the materials and goods that it is not producing. The larger a state's imports and exports, the more it depends on others. The world's well-being would be increased if an ever more elaborate division of labor were developed, but states would thereby place themselves in situations of ever closer interdependence. Some states may not resist that. For small and ill-endowed states the costs of doing so are excessively high. But states that can resist becoming ever more enmeshed with others ordinarily do so in either or both of two ways. States that are heavily dependent, or closely interdependent, worry about securing that which they depend on. The high interdependence of states means that the states in question experience, or are subject to, the common vulnerability that high interdependence entails. Like other organizations, states seek to control what they depend on or to lessen the extent of their dependency. This simple thought explains quite a bit of the behavior of states: their imperial thrusts to widen the scope of their control and their autarchic strivings toward greater self-sufficiency.

Structures encourage certain behaviors and penalize those who do not respond to the encouragement. Nationally, many lament the extreme development of the division of labor, a development that results in the allocation of ever narrower tasks to individuals. And yet specialization proceeds, and its extent is a measure of the development of societies. In a formally organized realm a premium is put on each unit's being able to specialize in order to increase its value to others in a system of divided labor. The domestic imperative is "specialize"! Internationally, many lament the resources states spend unproductively for their own defense and the opportunities they miss to enhance the welfare of their people through cooperation with other states. And yet the ways of states change little. In an unorganized realm each unit's incentive is to put itself in a position to be able to take care of itself since no one else can be counted on to do so. The international imperative is "take care of yourself"! Some leaders of nations may understand that the well-being of all of them would increase through their participation in a fuller division of labor. But to act on the idea would be to act on a domestic imperative, an imperative that does not run internationally. What one might want to do in the absence of structural constraints is different from what one is encouraged to do in their presence. States do not willingly place themselves in situations of increased dependence. In a self-help system, considerations of security subordinate economic gain to political interest. . . .

6. Structures and Strategies

That motives and outcomes may well be disjoined should now be easily seen. Structures cause nations to have consequences they were not intended to have. Surely most of the actors will notice that, and at least some of them will be able to figure out why. They may develop a pretty good sense of just how structures work their effects. Will they not then be able to achieve their original ends by appropriately adjusting their strategies? Unfortunately, they often cannot. To show why this is so I shall give only a few examples; once the point is made, the reader will easily think of others.

If shortage of a commodity is expected, all are collectively better off if they buy less of it in order to moderate price increases and to distribute shortages equitably. But because some will be better off if they lay in extra supplies quickly, all have a strong incentive to do so. If one expects others to make a run on a bank, one's prudent course is to run faster then they do even while knowing that if few others run, the bank will remain solvent, and if many run, it will fail. In such cases, pursuit of individual interest produces collective results that nobody wants, yet individuals by behaving differently will hurt themselves without altering outcomes. These two much used examples establish the main point. Some courses of action I cannot sensibly follow unless we are pretty sure that many others will as well. . . .

We may well notice that our behavior produces unwanted outcomes, but we are also likely to see that such instances as these are examples of what Alfred E. Kahn describes as "large" changes that are brought about by the accumulation of "small" decisions. In such situations people are victims of the "tyranny of small decisions," a phrase suggesting that "if one hundred consumers choose option x, and this causes the market to make decision X (where X equals $100x$), it is not necessarily true that those same consumers would have voted for that outcome if that large decision had ever been presented for their explicit consideration."[8] If the market does not present the large question for decision, then individuals are doomed to making decisions that are sensible within their narrow contexts even though they know all the while that in making such decisions they are bringing about a result that most of them do not want. Either that or they organize to overcome some of the effects of the market by changing its structure—for example, by bringing consumer units roughly up to the size of the units that are making producers' decisions. This nicely makes the point: So long as one leaves the structure unaffected it is not possible for changes in the intentions and the actions of particular actors to produce desirable outcomes or to avoid undesirable ones. . . . The only remedies for strong structural effects are structural changes.

Structural constraints cannot be wished away, although many fail to understand this. In every age and place, the units of self-help systems—nations, corporations, or whatever—are told that the greater good, along with their own, requires them to act for the sake of the system and not for their own narrowly defined advantage. In the 1950s, as fear of the world's destruction in nuclear war grew, some concluded that the alternative to world destruction was world disarmament. In the 1970s, with the rapid growth of population, poverty, and pollution, some concluded, as one political scientist put it, that "states must meet the needs of the political ecosystem in its global dimensions or court annihilation."[9] The international interest must be served; and if that means anything at all, it means that national interests are subordinate to it. The problems are found at the global level. Solutions to the problems continue to depend on national policies. What are the conditions that would make nations more or less willing to obey the injunctions that are so often laid on them? How can they resolve the tension between pursuing their own interests and acting for the sake of the system? No one has shown how that can be done, although many wring their hands and plead for rational behavior. The very problem, however, is that rational behavior, given structural constraints, does not lead to the wanted results. With each country constrained to take care of itself, no one can take care of the system.[10]

A strong sense of peril and doom may lead to a clear definition of ends that must be achieved. Their achievement is not thereby made possible. The possibility of effective action depends on the ability to provide necessary means. It depends even more so on the existence of conditions that permit nations and other organizations to follow appropriate policies and strategies. World-shaking problems cry for global solutions, but there is no global agency to provide them. Necessities do not create possibilities. Wishing that final causes were efficient ones does not make them so.

Great tasks can be accomplished only by agents of great capability. That is why states, and especially the major ones, are called on to do what is necessary for the world's survival. But states have to do whatever they think necessary for their own preservation, since no one can be relied on to do it for them. Why the advice to place the international interest above national interests is meaningless can be explained precisely in terms of the distinction between micro- and macrotheories. . . .

Some have hoped that changes in the awareness and purpose, in the organization and ideology of states would change the quality of international life. Over the centuries states have changed in many ways, but the quality of international life has remained much the same. States may seek reasonable and worthy ends, but they cannot figure out how to reach them. The problem is not in their stupidity or ill will, although one does not want to claim that those qualities are lacking. The depth of the difficulty is not understood until one realizes that intelligence and goodwill cannot discover and act on adequate programs. Early in this century Winston Churchill observed that the British-German naval race promised disaster *and* that Britain had no realistic choice other than to run it. States facing global problems are like individual consumers trapped by the "tyranny of small decisions." States, like consumers, can get out of the trap only by changing the structure of their field of activity. The message bears repeating: The only remedy for a strong structural effect is a structural change.

7. The Virtues of Anarchy

To achieve their objectives and maintain their security, units in a condition of anarchy—be they people, corporations, states, or whatever—must rely on the means they can generate and the arrangements they can make for themselves. Self-help is necessarily the principle of action in an anarchic order. A self-help situation is one of high risk—of bankruptcy in the economic realm and of war in a world of free states. It is also one in which organizational costs are low. Within an economy or within an international order, risks may be avoided or lessened by moving from a situation of coordinate action to one of super- and subordination, that is, by erecting agencies with effective authority and extending a system of rules. Government emerges where the functions of regulation and management themselves become distinct and specialized tasks. The costs of maintaining a hierarchic order are frequently ignored by those who deplore its absence. Organizations have at least two aims: to get something done and to maintain themselves as organizations. Many of their activities are directed toward the second purpose. The leaders of organizations, and political leaders preeminently, are not masters of the matters their organizations deal with. They have become leaders not by being experts on one thing or another but by excelling in the organizational arts—in maintaining control of a group's members, in eliciting predictable and satisfactory efforts from them, in holding a group together. In making political decisions, the first and most important concern is not to achieve the aims the members of an organization may have but to secure the continuity and health of the organization itself.[11]

Along with the advantages of hierarchic orders go the costs. In hierarchic orders, moreover, the means of control become an object of struggle. Substantive issues become entwined with efforts to influence or control the controllers. The hierarchic ordering of politics adds one to the already numerous objects of struggle, and the object added is at a new order of magnitude.

If the risks of war are unbearably high, can they be reduced by organizing to manage the affairs of nations? At a minimum, management requires controlling the military forces that are at the disposal of states. Within nations, organizations have to work to maintain themselves. As organizations, nations, in working to maintain themselves, sometimes have to use force against dissident elements and areas. As hierarchical systems, governments nationally or globally are disrupted by the defection of major parts. In a society of states with little coherence, attempts at world government would founder on the inability of an emerging central authority to mobilize the resources needed to create and maintain the unity of the system by regulating and managing its parts. The prospect of world government would be an invitation to prepare for world civil war. . . . States cannot entrust managerial powers to a central agency unless that agency is able to protect its client states. The more powerful the clients and the more the power of each of them appears as a threat to the others, the greater the power lodged in the center must be. The greater the power of the center, the stronger the incentive for states to engage in a struggle to control it.

States, like people, are insecure in proportion to the extent of their freedom. If freedom is wanted, insecurity must be accepted. Organizations that establish relations of authority and control may increase insecurity as they decrease freedom. If might does not make right, whether among people or states, then some institution or agency has intervened to lift them out of nature's realm. The more influential the agency, the stronger the desire to control it becomes. In contrast, units in an anarchic order act for their own sakes and not for the sake of preserving an organization and furthering their fortunes within it. Force is used for one's own interest. In the absence of organization, people or states are free to leave one another alone. Even when they do not do so, they are better able, in the absence of the politics of the organization, to concentrate on the politics of the problem and to aim for a minimum agreement that will permit their separate existence rather than a maximum agreement for the sake of maintaining unity. If might decides, then bloody struggles over right can more easily be avoided.

Nationally, the force of a government is exercised in the name of right and justice. Internationally, the force of a state is employed for the sake of its own protection and advantage. Rebels challenge a government's claim to authority; they question the rightfulness of its rule. Wars among states cannot settle questions of authority and right; they can only determine the allocation of gains and losses among contenders and settle for a time the question of who is the stronger. Nationally, relations of authority are established. Internationally, only relations of strength result. Nationally, private force used against a government threatens the political system. Force used by a state—a public body—is, from the international perspective, the private use of force; but there is no government to overthrow and no governmental apparatus to capture. Short of a drive toward world hegemony, the private use of force does not threaten the system of international politics, only some of its members. War pits some states against others in a struggle among similarly constituted entities. The power of the strong may deter the weak from asserting their claims, not because the weak recognize a kind of rightfulness of rule on the part of the strong, but simply because it is not sensible to tangle with them. Conversely, the weak may enjoy considerable freedom of action if they are so far removed in their capabilities from the strong that the latter are not much bothered by their actions or much concerned by marginal increases in their capabilities.

National politics is the realm of authority, of administration, and of law. International politics is the realm of power, of struggle, and of accommodation. The international realm is preeminently a political one. The national realm is variously described as being hierarchic, vertical, centralized, heterogeneous, directed, and contrived; the international realm, as being anarchic, horizontal, decentralized, homogeneous, undirected and mutually adaptive. The more centralized the order, the nearer to the top the locus of decisions ascends. Internationally, decisions are made at the bottom level, there being scarcely any other. In the vertical horizontal dichotomy, international structures assume the prone position. Adjustments are made internationally, but they are made without a formal or authoritative adjuster. Adjustment and accommodation proceed by mutual adaptation.[12] Action and reaction, and reaction to the reaction, proceed by a piecemeal process. The parties feel each other out, so to speak, and define a situation simultaneously with its development. Among coordinate units, adjustment is achieved and accommodations arrived at by the exchange of "considerations," in a condition, as Chester Barnard put it, "in which the duty of command and the desire to obey are essentially absent."[13] Where the contest is over considerations, the parties seek to maintain or improve their positions by maneuvering, by bargaining, or by fighting. The manner and intensity of the competition is determined by the desires and the abilities of parties that are at once separate and interacting.

Whether or not by force, each state plots the course it thinks will best serve its interests. If force is used by one state or its use is expected, the recourse of other states is to use force or be prepared to use it singly or in combination. No appeal can be made to a higher entity clothed with the authority and equipped with the ability to act on its own initiative. Under such conditions the possibility that force will be used by one or another of the parties looms always as a threat in the background. In politics force is said to be the *ultima ratio*. In international politics force serves, not only as the *ultima ratio*, but indeed as the first and constant one. To limit force to being the *ultima ratio* of politics implies, in the words of Ortega y Gasset, "the previous submission of force to methods of reason."[14] The constant possibility that force will be used limits manipulations, moderates demands, and serves as an incentive for the settlement of disputes. One who knows that pressing too hard may lead to war has strong reason to consider whether possible gains are worth the risks entailed. The threat of force internationally is comparable to the role of the strike in labor and management bargaining. "The few strikes that take place are in a sense," as Livernash has said, "the cost of the strike option which produces settlements in the large mass of negotiations."[15] Even if workers seldom strike, their doing so is always a possibility. The possibility of industrial disputes leading to long and costly strikes encourages labor and management to face difficult issues, to try to understand each other's problems, and to work hard to find accommodations. The possibility that conflicts among nations may lead to long and costly wars has similarly sobering effects.

8. Anarchy and Hierarchy

I have described anarchies and hierarchies as though every political order were of one type or the other. Many, and I suppose most, political scientists who write of structures allow for a greater, and sometimes for a bewildering, variety of types. Anarchy is seen as one end of a continuum whose other end is marked by the presence of a legitimate and competent government. International politics is then described as being flecked with particles of government and alloyed with elements of community—supranational organizations whether universal or regional, alliances, multinational corporations, networks of trade, and whatnot. International-political systems are thought of as being more or less anarchic.

Those who view the world as a modified anarchy do so, it seems, for two reasons. First, anarchy is taken to mean not just the absence of government but also the presence of disorder and chaos. Since world politics, although not reliably peaceful, falls short of unrelieved chaos, students are inclined to see a lessening of anarchy in each outbreak of peace. Since world politics, although not formally organized, is not entirely without institutions and orderly procedures, students are inclined to see a lessening of anarchy when alliances form, when transactions across national borders increase, and when international agencies multiply. Such views confuse structure with process, and I have drawn attention to that error often enough.

Second, the two simple categories of anarchy and hierarchy do not seem to accommodate the infinite social variety our senses record. Why insist on reducing the types of structure to two instead of allowing for a greater variety? Anarchies are ordered by the juxtaposition of similar units, but those similar units are not identical. Some specialization by function develops among them. Hierarchies are ordered by the social division of labor among units specializing in different tasks,

but the resemblance of units does not vanish. Much duplication of effort continues. All societies are organized segmentally or hierarchically in greater or lesser
degree. Why not, then, define additional social types according to the mixture of
organizing principles they embody? One might conceive of some societies
approaching the purely anarchic, of others approaching the purely hierarchic, and
of still others reflecting specified mixes of the two organizational types. In anarchies the exact likeness of units and the determination of relations by capability
alone would describe a realm wholly of politics and power with none of the interaction of units guided by administration and conditioned by authority. In hierarchies the complete differentiation of parts and the full specification of their functions would produce a realm wholly of authority and administration with none of
the interaction of parts affected by politics and power. Although such pure orders
do not exist, to distinguish realms by their organizing principles is nevertheless
proper and important.

Increasing the number of categories would bring the classification of societies
closer to reality. But that would be to move away from a theory claiming explanatory power to a less theoretical system promising greater descriptive accuracy. One
who wishes to explain rather than to describe should resist moving in that direction
if resistance is reasonable. Is it? What does one gain by insisting on two types when
admitting three or four would still be to simplify boldly? One gains clarity and
economy of concepts. A new concept should be introduced only to cover matters
that existing concepts do not reach. If some societies are neither anarchic or hierarchic, if their structures are defined by some third ordering principle, then we
would have to define a third system.[16] All societies are mixed. Elements in them
represent both of the ordering principles. That does not mean that some societies
are ordered according to a third principle. Usually one can easily identify the principle by which a society is ordered. The appearance of anarchic sectors within hierarchies does not alter and should not obscure the ordering principle of the larger
system, for those sectors are anarchic only within limits. The attributes and behavior of the units populating those sectors within the larger system differ, moreover,
from what they should be and how they would behave outside of it. Firms in oligopolistic markets again are perfect examples of this. They struggle against one
another, but because they need not prepare to defend themselves physically, they
can afford to specialize and to participate more fully in the division of economic
labor than states can. Nor do the states that populate an anarchic world find it
impossible to work with one another, to make agreements limiting their arms, and
to cooperate in establishing organizations. Hierarchic elements within international structures limit and restrain the exercise of sovereignty but only in ways strongly conditioned by the anarchy of the larger system. The anarchy of that order
strongly affects the likelihood of cooperation, the extent of arms agreements, and
the jurisdiction of international organizations. . . .

NOTES

1. S. F. Nadel, *The Theory of Social Structure* (Glencoe, Ill.: Free Press, 1957), pp. 8–11.
2. *Ibid.*, pp. 104–9.

3. William T. R. Fox, "The Uses of International Relations Theory," in William T. R. Fox, ed., *Theoretical Aspects of International Relations* (Notre Dame, Ind.: University of Notre Dame Press, 1959), p. 35.

4. Marriet Martineau, *The Positive Philosophy of Auguste Comte: Freely Translated and Condensed,* 3rd ed. (London: Kegan Paul, Trench, Trubner, 1983), vol. 2, pp. 51–53; George Katona, "Rational Behavior and Economic Behavior," *Psychological Review* 60 (September 1953).

5. Charles P. Kindleberger, *American Business Abroad* (New Haven, Ct.: Yale University Press, 1969), p. 207.

6. Smith should know better. Translated into terms that he has himself so effectively used, to say that states are sovereign is to say that they are segments of a plural society. See his "A Structural Approach to Comparative Politics" in David Easton, ed., *Varieties of Politics Theories* (Englewood Cliffs, N.J.: Prentice-Hall, 1966), p. 122; cf. his "On Segmentary Lineage Systems," *Journal of the Royal Anthropological Society of Great Britain and Ireland* 86 (July–December 1956).

7. Emile Durkheim, *The Division of Labor in Society,* trans. George Simpson (New York: Free Press, 1964), p. 212.

8. Alfred E. Kahn, "The Tyranny of Small Decision: Market Failure, Imperfections and Limits of Econometrics," in Bruce M. Russett, ed., *Economic Theories of International Relations* (Chicago, Ill.: Markham, 1966), p. 23.

9. Richard W. Sterling, *Macropolitics: International Relations in a Global Society* (New York: Knopf, 1974), p. 336.

10. Put differently, states face a "prisoners' dilemma." If each of two parties follows his own interest, both end up worse off than if each acted to achieve joint interests. For thorough examination of the logic of such situations, see Glenn H. Snyder and Paul Diesing, *Conflict among Nations* (Princeton, N.J.: Princeton University Press, 1977); for brief and suggestive international applications, see Robert Jervis, "Cooperation under the Security Dilemma," *World Politics* 30 (January 1978).

11. Cf. Paul Diesing, *Reason in Society* (Urbana, Ill.: University of Illinois Press, 1962), pp. 198–204; Anthony Downs, *Inside Bureaucracy* (Boston: Little, Brown, 1967), pp. 262–70.

12. Cf. Chester I. Barnard, "On Planning for World Government," in Chester I. Barnard, ed., *Organization and Management* (Cambridge, Mass.: Harvard University Press, 1948), pp. 148–152; Michael Polanyi, "The Growth of Thought in Society," *Economica* 8 (November 1941), pp. 428–456.

13. Barnard, "On Planning," pp. 150–51.

14. Quoted in Chalmers A. Johnson, *Revolutionary Change* (Boston: Little, Brown, 1966), p. 13.

15. E. R. Livernash, "The Relation of Power to the Structure and Process of Collective Bargaining," in Bruce M. Russett, ed., *Economic Theories of International Politics* (Chicago, Ill.: Markham, 1963), p. 430.

16. Emile Durkheim's depiction of solidary and mechanical societies still provides the best explication of the two ordering principles, and his logic in limiting the types of society to two continues to be compelling despite the efforts of his many critics to overthrow it (see esp. *The Division of Labor in Society*).

A Critique of Anarchy

Helen V. Milner

Anarchy *is one of the most vague and ambiguous words in language.*
George Cornewall Lewis, 1832.

In much current theorizing, anarchy has once again been declared to be the fundamental assumption about international politics. Over the last decade, numerous scholars, especially those in the Neorealist tradition, have posited anarchy as the single most important characteristic underlying international relations. This article explores implications of such an assumption. In doing so, it reopens older debates about the nature of international politics. . . .

The . . . focus on anarchy in international politics has led to the creation of a sharp distinction between domestic and international politics. Politics internationally is seen as characterized primarily by anarchy, while domestically centralized authority prevails. One of the most explicit statements of this position is in Waltz's *Theory of International Politics.* His powerful articulation of this dichotomy is interesting to examine closely since it is the clearest logical statement of the consequences of the anarchy assumption.

Waltz makes three separate claims about the distinction between the two areas. First, anarchy as a lack of central authority implies that international politics is a decentralized competition among sovereign equals. . . . A second distinction flows from the assumption of anarchy. As a lack of centralized control over force, anarchy implies that world politics is a self-help system reliant primarily on force. This also distinguishes international from national politics. . . . Finally, international politics is seen as the only true "politics". . . .

A very sharp distinction is drawn between the two political arenas on a number of different grounds, all of which flow from the assumption of anarchy. While some

From "The Assumption of Anarchy in International Relations Theory" by Helen Milner from *The Review of International Studies* (1991). Reprinted by permission of Helen Milner and Cambridge University Press. Portions of the text and some footnotes have been omitted.

societies may possess elements of both ordering principles—anarchy and hierar-chy—the conclusion of many is that such a rigid dichotomy is empirically feasible and theoretically useful. This section examines the utility of such a distinction. Is it empirically and heuristically helpful? To answer this question, it is important to examine Waltz's three distinctions because they represent the logical outcome of adopting the assumption of anarchy as the basis of international politics. While his views are the most explicit and perhaps extreme statement of this dichotomy, they do reflect the implicit understanding of Neorealist theory in general.

The first line of demarcation between domestic and international politics is the claim that centralization prevails in the former and decentralization in the lat-ter. What is meant by centralization or its opposite? Centralization seems related to hierarchy. As Waltz notes, "The units—institutions and agencies—stand vis à vis each other in relations of super- and subordination."[1] Apparently, it refers to the number of, and relationship among, recognized centers of authority in a system. Domestic politics has fewer, more well-defined centers that are hierarchically ordered, while in international politics many centers exist and they are not so ordered. What counts as a center of authority, however? Waltz resorts to the legal-istic notion of sovereignty to make his count internationally. He also assumes that domestically a well-defined hierarchy of authority exists. . . .

Such a view of domestic politics is hard to maintain. Who is the highest author-ity in the United States? The people, the states, the Constitution, the President, the Supreme Court, or even Congress? De jure, the Constitution is; but, de facto, it depends upon the issue. There is no single hierarchy of authority, as in some ideal military organization. Authority for deciding different issues rests with differ-ent groups in society. Authority is not highly concentrated; it is diffused. This was the intention of the writers of the Constitution, who wanted a system where power was not concentrated but rather dispersed. It was dispersed not only functionally through a structure of countervailing "checks and balances," but also geographi-cally through federalism.[2]

Moreover, this decentralization is not unique to the United States. One of the main concerns in comparative politics has been to locate the centers of authority in various nations and plot their differing degrees of political centralization and decentralization along some continuum. Authority in some states may be fairly centralized, while in others it is highly decentralized, as demonstrated in the debate over "strong" and "weak" states.[3] But the central point is that states exhibit a very broad range of values along this continuum, and not all of them—or perhaps even the majority—may be more centralized than the international system.

A second issue is to what extent the international system is decentralized. The point made above that the concentration of authority in any system is best gauged along a continuum, and not a dichotomy, is relevant. Where along the continuum does the international system fit? The answer to this depends on two factors: What issue we are discussing (e.g., fishing rights, the use of nuclear weapons, or control of the seas) and what time period we have in mind. The first factor raises the issue of the fungibility of power. Curiously, Waltz assumes it is highly fungible: Force dom-inates and a hierarchy of power exists internationally, that is, "great powers" are identifiable. This view centralizes power much more than does the assumption that it is infungible. The issue of change over time is also important. The international system may evince different levels of centralization and decentralization, e.g., the nineteenth century Concert of Europe versus the post–World War II system.

To deal with these issues, Waltz has to relinquish his more legalistic notion of the international system as one of sovereign equals. At times, he indeed does this. In discussing anarchy, he posits that all states are equal and thus that authority internationally is highly decentralized. But, when talking of the distribution of capabilities, he recognizes that states are not equal and that only a few great powers count. In this latter discussion, he implies that capabilities are highly centralized in the international system. Waltz himself then does *not* find the assumption that all states are equal and thus that power is highly decentralized to be either empirically true or heuristically useful. As a "good" realist, he focuses upon the few strong powers in the system. . . .

The issue of the centralization of power internationally touches on another distinction between domestic and international politics. . . . The argument is that states are sovereign, implying that they are functionally equal and hence not interdependent. They are duplicates who do not need one another. Domestically, the units within states are differentiated, each filling some niche in the chain of command. For many domestic systems this is not accurate. For instance, in federal systems each state is functionally equal and no generally agreed-upon chain of command between the states and the national government exists. On some issues at some times, states have the final say; on others, the central government.

On the other hand, there is the question of whether all nation-states are functionally equivalent. If states are all "like units," why only examine the great powers? Waltz realizes this is a problem. He admits that "internationally, like units sometimes perform different tasks." Moreover, "the likelihood of their doing so, varies with their capabilities."[4] Thus he acknowledges that states with different capabilities perform different functions; hence, they are not all "like" units. Later he takes the point further:

> Although states are like units functionally, they differ vastly in their capabilities. Out of such differences something of a division of labor develops. . . . The division of labor across nations, however, is slight in comparison with the highly articulated division of labor within them.[5]

His position is that states do not perform the same tasks, that some international division of labor exists, but that this differentiation is *empirically* unimportant relative to that domestically. The dilemma is that two of Waltz's three central assumptions/ordering principles conflict. It is difficult to assume both that all states are equal (principles 1 and 2) *and* that all states are not equal as a result of the distribution of their capabilities (principle 3). Waltz might claim that they are equal in function but not in capabilities; however, as he himself states, one's capabilities shape one's functions. The point is, as others have noted before, the distribution of resources internationally creates a division of labor among states; differentiation and hierarchy exist and provide governing mechanisms for states, just as they do for individuals within states. Most importantly, the distinction among different international systems and within nation-states over the degree of centralization of authority as well as over the degree of differentiation among their units is variable and should be viewed along a continuum, rather than as a dichotomy.

A second means of separating domestic and international politics is to differentiate the role and importance of force in the two arenas. For Waltz, domestically, force is less important as a means of control and is used to serve justice; internationally, force is widespread and serves no higher goal than to help the state using it. But is the importance of force so different in the two realms?. . . . For theorists like Waltz, Carr, and Weber, the threat of the use of force—in effect, deterrence— is ultimately the means of social control domestically. Threats of sanctions are the state's means of enforcement, as they are internationally. When norms and institutions fail to maintain social control, states internally and externally resort to threats of force. It may be that norms and institutions are more prevalent forms of control domestically than internationally. But this depends on the state in question. In some countries, belief in the legitimacy of government and institutions, being widespread and well-developed, might suffice to maintain control. However, the fact that more civil wars have been fought in this century than international ones and that since 1945 more have died in the former should make one pause when declaiming about the relative use of force in the two realms.[6]

Since at times the frequency of violence domestically is acknowledged, perhaps the point is that force is legitimate and serves justice domestically and not internationally.[7] Again, this depends upon the perceived legitimacy of the government and the particular instance of use. Have the majority of people in the Soviet Union, Poland, Ethiopia, South Africa, Iran, or the Philippines—to name just a few—felt that the state's use of force serves justice (all of the time? some of the time?)? Whether force serves justice domestically is an issue to be studied, not a given to be assumed. On the other hand, does force never serve justice internationally? Is it always, or most of the time, "for the sake of [the state's] own protection and advantage"? States have been known to intervene forcefully for larger purposes. The fight against Germany in World War II by the United States, for example, helped serve justice regardless of whether the United States' own protection was a factor. The distinction between international and domestic politics on this issue does not appear as clear as is claimed.

A third dichotomy between the two arenas asserts that power and politics operate internationally. Domestically, authority, administration, and law prevail; internationally, it is power, struggle, and accommodation. For some, the latter alone is politics. This distinction is the hardest to maintain. Disputes among political parties, local and national officials, the executive and the legislature, different geographic regions, different races, capital and labor, industry and finance, organized and unorganized groups, etc., over who gets how much and when occur constantly within the nation. Morgenthau recognizes this:

> The essence of international politics is identical with its domestic counterpart. Both domestic and international politics are a struggle for power, modified only by the different conditions under which this struggle takes place in the domestic and in the international spheres.
>
> The tendency to dominate, in particular, is an element of all human associations, from the family through fraternal and professional associations and local political

organizations, to the state. . . . Finally, the whole political life of a nation, particularly of a democratic nation, from the local to the national level, is a continuous struggle for power.[8]

E. H. Carr, another realist, also disagrees with Waltz. Like Morgenthau, he sees the national and world arenas as being based on the same principles and processes: power politics. In talking of domestic politics, he echoes Thucydides' Melian dialogue: "The majority rules because it is stronger, the minority submits because it is weaker."[9] He maintains that the factors which supposedly distinguish domestic politics—for example, legitimacy, morality, ideology, and law—are just as political nationally as internationally.

Theories of social morality are always the product of a

> dominant group which identifies itself with the community as a whole, and which possesses facilities denied to subordinate groups or individuals for imposing its view of life on the community. Theories of international morality are, for the same reason and in virtue of the same process, the product of dominant nations or groups of nations.[10]

As an example of this, Carr notes that "laissez-faire, in international relations as in those between capital and labor, is the paradise of the economically strong."[11] He points out that even law, another factor that is supposed to make politics within the nation different, is merely a manifestation of power:

> Behind all law there is this necessary political background. The ultimate authority of law derives from politics.[12]

Others would reject Carr's insistence that law and morality spring from power, but would nonetheless agree that politics within nations and among them are similar. These authors see authority, law, and morality being as important to international relations as to domestic ones. For instance, Inis Claude holds that international order is maintained by a balance of power among opposing forces, just as it is domestically. In attacking the notion that governments maintain peace through some monopoly of force, Claude returns to Morgenthau to make his point:

> Morgenthau's espousal of the concept of the state's "monopoly of organized violence" is contradicted by his general conception of politics: "Domestic and international politics are but two different manifestations of the same phenomenon: the struggle for power." In his terms, "The balance of power . . . is indeed a perennial element of all pluralistic societies."[13]

For him, as for Morgenthau, societies are pluralistic, and thus the role of government is "the delicate task of promoting and presiding over a constantly shifting equilibrium."[14] Politics domestically and internationally is about balancing power. To assume that a state has a monopoly of power and that this is "the key to the effectiveness of [it] as an order-keeping institution may lead to an exaggerated notion of the degree to which actual states can and do rely upon coercion."[15] Unlike Morgenthau and other realists, Claude sees factors other than coercion—such as, norms and institutions—as being more important both domestically and internationally to the maintenance of order, but like them he views the balance of power as fundamental to the two realms. Unlike Waltz, all of these authors find relations within nations and among them to be political and to be based on similar political processes. . . .

A second and related heuristic problem is the tendency implicit in this separation of the two fields to view all states as being the same. Waltz, for one, wants us to conceive of states as like units and to avoid looking within them at their internal arrangements. His is a systemic level theory. But the issue is whether it is possible and/or fruitful to abstract from all of domestic politics. All states are not the same, and their internal characteristics, including their goals and capabilities, affect international politics importantly, as Waltz is forced to admit. This is reflected in the tension between his ordering principles, the first two of which give primacy to structural pressures while the third makes certain agents key. Using systemic theory, he wants to "tell us about the forces the units are subject to," but he also notes that "in international politics, as in any self-help system, the units of greatest capability set the scene of action for others as well as for themselves.[16] The units do matter.

NOTES

1. Kenneth Waltz, *Theory of International Politics* (Reading, Mass.: Addison-Wesley, 1979), p. 81.
2. Waltz recognizes this: see *Theory of International Politics*, p. 81. But it never influences his very sharp distinction between the ordering of domestic and international politics.
3. See, for example, Peter Katzenstein, ed., *Between Power and Plenty* (Ithaca, N.Y.: Cornell University Press, 1978).
4. Waltz, *Theory of International Politics*, p. 47.
5. *Ibid.*, p. 105.
6. Melvin Small and J. David Singer, *Explaining War* (Beverly Hills: Sage, 1979), pp. 63, 65, 68–69.
7. Waltz, *Theory of International Politics*, p. 103.
8. Hans Morgenthau, *Politics Among Nations*. 6th ed. (New York: Knopf, 1985), pp. 39–40.
9. E. H. Carr, *The Twenty Years' Crisis* (New York: Harper and Row, 1964), p. 41.
10. *Ibid.*, p. 79.
11. *Ibid.*, p. 60.
12. *Ibid.*, p. 180.
13. Inis Claude, *Power and International Relations* (New York: Random House, 1962), p. 231.
14. *Ibid.*
15. *Ibid.*, p. 234.
16. Waltz, *Theory of International Politics*, p. 72.

Anarchy and the Limits of Cooperation

Joseph M. Grieco

Realism has dominated international relations theory at least since World War II. For realists, international anarchy fosters competition and conflict among states and inhibits their willingness to cooperate even when they share common interests. Realist theory also argues that international institutions are unable to mitigate anarchy's constraining effects on interstate cooperation. Realism, then, presents a pessimistic analysis of the prospects for international cooperation and of the capabilities of international institutions.

The major challenger to realism has been what I shall call *liberal institutionalism....* The new liberal institutionalists basically argue that even if the realists are correct in believing that anarchy constrains the willingness of states to cooperate, states nevertheless can work together and can do so especially with the assistance of international institutions.[1]

This point is crucial for students of international relations. If neoliberal institutionalists are correct, then they have dealt realism a major blow while providing the intellectual justification for treating their own approach, and the tradition from which it emerges, as the most effective for understanding world politics.

This essay's principal argument is that, in fact, neoliberal institutionalism misconstrues the realist analysis of international anarchy and therefore it misunderstands the realist analysis of the impact of anarchy on the preferences and actions of states. Indeed, the new liberal institutionalism fails to address a major constraint on the willingness of states to cooperate, which is generated by international anarchy and which is identified by realism. As a result, the new theory's optimism about international cooperation is likely to be proven wrong.

Neoliberalism's claims about cooperation are based on its belief that states are atomistic actors. It argues that states seek to maximize their individual *absolute* gains and are indifferent to the gains achieved by others. Cheating, the new theory suggests, is the greatest impediment to cooperation among rationally egoistic states, but international institutions, the new theory also suggests, can help states overcome this barrier to joint action. Realists understand that states seek absolute gains and worry about compliance. However, realists find that states are *positional*, not atomistic, in character, and therefore realists argue that, in addition to concerns about cheating, states in cooperative arrangements also worry that their partners might gain more from cooperation than they do. For realists, a state will focus both on its absolute and relative gains from cooperation, and a state that is satisfied with a partner's compliance in a joint arrangement might nevertheless exit from it because the partner is achieving relatively greater gains. Realism, then, finds that there are at least two major barriers to international cooperation: state concerns about cheating and state concerns about relative achievements of gains. Neoliberal institutionalism pays attention exclusively to the former, and is unable to identify, analyze, or account for the latter.

Realism's identification of the relative gains problem for cooperation is based on its insight that states in anarchy fear for their survival as independent actors. According to realists, states worry that today's friend may be tomorrow's enemy in war, and fear that achievements of joint gains that advantage a friend in the present might produce a more dangerous *potential* foe in the future. As a result, states must give serious attention to the gains of partners. Neoliberals fail to consider the threat of war arising from international anarchy, and this allows them to ignore the matter of relative gains and to assume that states only desire absolute gains. Yet, in doing so, they fail to identify a major source of state inhibitions about international cooperation. . . .

Neoliberals begin with assertions of acceptance of several key realist propositions; however, they end with a rejection of realism and with claims of affirmation of the central tenets of the liberal institutionalist tradition. To develop this argument, neoliberals first observe that states in anarchy often faced mixed interests and, in particular, situations that can be depicted by Prisoners' Dilemma. In the game, each state prefers mutual cooperation to mutual noncooperation (CC > DD), but also successful cheating to mutual cooperation (DC > CC) and mutual defection to victimization by another's cheating (DD > CD); overall, then, DC > CC > DD > CD. In these circumstances, and in the absence of a centralized authority or some other countervailing force to bind states to their promises, each defects regardless of what it expects the other to do.

However, neoliberals stress that countervailing forces often do exist—forces that cause states to keep their promises and thus to resolve the Prisoners' Dilemma. They argue that states may pursue a strategy of tit-for-tat and cooperate on a conditional basis—that is, each adheres to its promises so long as partners do so. They also suggest that conditional cooperation is more likely to occur in Prisoners' Dilemma if the game is highly iterated, since states that interact repeatedly in either a mutually beneficial or harmful manner are likely to find that mutual cooperation is their best long-term strategy. Finally, conditional cooperation is more attractive to states if the costs of verifying one another's compliance, and of sanctioning cheaters, are low compared to the benefits of joint action. Thus, conditional cooperation among states may evolve in the face of international anarchy and mixed interests through strategies of reciprocity, extended time horizons, and reduced verification and sanctioning costs.

Neoliberals find that one way states manage verification and sanctioning problems is to restrict the number of partners in a cooperative arrangement.[2] However, neoliberals place much greater emphasis on a second factor—international institutions. In particular, neoliberals argue that institutions reduce verification costs, create iterativeness, and make it easier to punish cheaters. As Keohane suggests, "in general, regimes make it more sensible to cooperate by lowering the likelihood of being double-crossed."[3] Similarly, Axelrod and Keohane assert that "international regimes do not substitute for reciprocity; rather, they reinforce and institutionalize it. Regimes incorporating the norm of reciprocity delegitimize defection and thereby make it more costly."[4] In addition, finding that "coordination conventions" are often an element of conditional cooperation in Prisoners' Dilemma, Charles Lipson suggests that "in international relations, such conventions, which are typically grounded in ongoing reciprocal exchange, range from international law to regime rules."[5] Finally, Arthur Stein argues that, just as societies "create" states to resolve collective action problems among individuals, so too "regimes in the international arena are also created to deal with the collective suboptimality that can emerge from individual [state] behavior."[6] Hegemonic power may be necessary to establish cooperation among states, neoliberals argue, but it may endure after hegemony with the aid of institutions. As Keohane concludes, "When we think about cooperation after hegemony, we need to think about institutions."[7]

The new liberals assert that they can accept key realist views about states and anarchy and still sustain classic liberal arguments about institutions and international cooperation. Yet, in fact, realist and neoliberal perspectives on states and anarchy differ profoundly, and the former provides a more complete understanding of the problem of cooperation than the latter.

Neoliberals assume that states have only one goal in mixed-interest interactions: to achieve the greatest possible individual gain. For example, Axelrod suggests that the key issue in selecting a "best strategy" in Prisoners' Dilemma— offered by neoliberals as a powerful model of the problem of state cooperation in the face of anarchy and mixed interests—is to determine "what strategy will yield a player the highest possible score."[8] Similarly, Lipson observes that cheating is attractive in a single play of Prisoners' Dilemma because each player believes that defecting "can maximize his own reward," and, in turning to iterated plays, Lipson retains the assumption that players seek to maximize individual payoffs over the long run.[9] Indeed, reliance upon conventional Prisoners' Dilemma to depict international relationships and upon iteration to solve the dilemma unambiguously requires neoliberalism to adhere to an individualistic payoff maximization assumption, for a player responds to an iterated conventional Prisoners' Dilemma with conditional cooperation *solely out of a desire to maximize its individual long-term total payoffs.* . . .

Given its understanding of anarchy, realism argues that individual well-being is not the key interest of states; instead, it finds that *survival* is their core interest. Raymond Aron, for example, suggested that "politics, insofar as it concerns relations among states, seems to signify—in both ideal and objective terms—simply the survival of states confronting the potential threat created by the existence of other states."[10] Similarly, Robert Gilpin observes that individuals and groups may seek truth, beauty, and justice, but he emphasizes that "all these more noble goals will be lost unless one makes provision for one's security in the power struggle among groups."[11]

Driven by an interest in survival, states are acutely sensitive to any erosion of their relative capabilities, which are the ultimate basis for their security and independence in an anarchical, self-help international context. Thus, realists find that the major goal of states in any relationship is not to attain the highest possible individual gain or payoff. Instead, *the fundamental goal of states in any relationship is to prevent others from achieving advances in their relative capabilities.* For example, E. H. Carr suggested that "the most serious wars are fought in order to make one's own country militarily stronger or, *more often,* to prevent another from becoming militarily stronger."[12] Along the same lines, Gilpin finds that the international system "stimulates, and may compel, a state to increase its power; at the least, it necessitates that the prudent state prevent relative increases in the power of competitor states."[13] Indeed, states may even forego increases in their absolute capabilities if doing so prevents others from achieving even greater gains. This is because, as Waltz suggests, "the first concern of states is not to maximize power but to maintain their position in the system."[14]

States seek to prevent increases in others' relative capabilities. As a result, states always assess their performance in any relationship in terms of the performance of others.[15] Thus, I suggest that states are positional, not atomistic, in character. Most significantly, *state positionality may constrain the willingness of states to cooperate.* States fear that their partners will achieve relatively greater gains; that, as a result, the partners will surge ahead of them in relative capabilities; and, finally, that their increasingly powerful partners in the present could become all the more formidable foes at some point in the future.

State positionality, then, engenders a "relative gains problem" for cooperation. That is, a state will decline to join, will leave, or will sharply limit its commitment to a cooperative arrangement if it believes that partners are achieving, or are likely to achieve, relatively greater gains. It will eschew cooperation even though participation in the arrangement was providing it, or would have provided it, with large absolute gains. Moreover, a state concerned about relative gains may decline to cooperate even if it is confident that partners will keep their commitments to a joint arrangement. Indeed, if a state believed that a proposed arrangement would provide all parties absolute gains, but would also generate gains favoring partners, then greater certainty that partners would adhere to the terms of the arrangement would only accentuate its relative-gains concerns. Thus, a state worried about relative gains might respond to greater certainty that partners would keep their promises with a lower, rather than a higher, willingness to cooperate.

NOTES

1. See Robert Axelrod, *The Evolution of Cooperation* (New York: Basic Books, 1984); Axelrod and Robert O. Keohane, "Achieving Cooperation under Anarchy: Strategies and Institutions," *World Politics* 38 (October 1985), pp. 226–54; Keohane, *After Hegemony: Cooperation and Discord in the World Political Economy* (Princeton, N.J.: Princeton University Press, 1984); Charles Lipson, "International Cooperation in Economic and Security Affairs," *World Politics* 37 (October 1984), pp. 1–23; and Arthur Stein, "Coordination and Collaboration: Regimes in an Anarchic World," in Stephen D. Krasner, ed., *International Regimes* (Ithaca, N.Y.: Cornell University Press, 1983), pp. 115–40.
2. See Keohane, *After Hegemony*, p. 77; Axelrod and Keohane, "Achieving Cooperation," pp. 234–38. For a demonstration, see Lipson, "Bankers' Dilemmas."
3. Keohane, *After Hegemony*, p. 97.
4. Axelrod and Keohane, "Achieving Cooperation," p. 250.
5. Lipson, "International Cooperation," p. 6.
6. Stein, "Coordination and Collaboration," p. 123.
7. Keohane, *After Hegemony*, p. 246.
8. Axelrod, *Evolution of Cooperation*, pp. 6, 14. Stein acknowledges that he employs an absolute-gains assumption and that the latter "is very much a liberal, not mercantilist, view of self-interest; it suggests that actors focus on their own returns and compare different outcomes with an eye to maximizing their own gains." See Stein, "Coordination and Collaboration," p. 134. It is difficult to see how Stein can employ a "liberal" assumption of state interest and assert that his theory of regimes, as noted earlier in note 34, is based on the "classic [realist?] characterization" of international politics.
9. Lipson, "International Cooperation," pp. 2, 5.
10. Raymond Aron, *International Relations: A Theory of Peace and War*, trans. Richard Howard and Annette Baker Fox (Garden City, N.J.: Doubleday, 1973), p. 7; also see pp. 64–65.
11. Robert Gilpin, "The Richness of the Tradition of Political Realism," in Robert O. Keohane, ed., *Neorealism and Its Critics* (New York: Columbia University Press, 1986), p. 305. Similarly, Waltz indicates that "in anarchy, security is the highest end. Only if survival is assured can states safely seek such other goals as tranquility, profit, and power." See Kenneth Waltz, *Theory of International Politics* (Reading, Mass.: Addison-Wesley, 1979), p. 126. Also see pp. 91–92, and Waltz, "Reflections on Theory of International Politics: A Response to My Critics," in Keohane, ed., *Neorealism and Its Critics*, p. 334.
12. E. H. Carr, *Twenty Years Crisis, 1919–1939: An Introduction to the Study of International Relations* (London and New York: Harper Torchbooks, 1964), p. 111, emphasis added.
13. Robert Gilpin, *War and Change in World Politics* (Cambridge: Cambridge University Press, 1981), pp. 87–88.
14. Waltz, *Theory of International Politics*, p. 126; see also Waltz, "Reflections," p. 334.
15. On the tendency of states to compare performance levels, see Oran Young, "International Regimes: Toward a New Theory of Institutions," *World Politics* 39 (October 1986), p. 118.

The Mitigation of Anarchy

The Conditions for Cooperation in World Politics

Kenneth A. Oye

I. INTRODUCTION

Nations dwell in perpetual anarchy, for no central authority imposes limits on the pursuit of sovereign interests. This common condition gives rise to diverse outcomes. Relations among states are marked by war and concert, arms races and arms control, trade wars and tariff truces, financial panics and rescues, competitive devaluation and monetary stabilization. At times, the absence of centralized international authority precludes attainment of common goals. Because, as states, they cannot cede ultimate control over their conduct to an supranational sovereign, they cannot guarantee that they will adhere to their promises. The possibility of a breach of promise can impede cooperation even when cooperation would leave all better off. Yet, at other times, states do realize common goals through cooperation under anarchy. Despite the absence of any ultimate international authority, governments often bind themselves to mutually advantageous courses of action. And, though no international sovereign stands ready to enforce the terms of agreement, states can realize common interests through tacit cooperation, formal bilateral and multilateral negotiation, and the creation of international regimes. The question is: if international relations can approximate both a Hobbesian state of nature and a Lockean evil society, why does cooperation emerge in some cases and not in others?

"Explaining Cooperation under Anarchy: Hypothesis and Strategies" by Kenneth A. Oye from *World Politics*. Reprinted by permission of Johns Hopkins University Press. Portions of the text and some footnotes have been omitted.

[Scholars] address both explanatory and prescriptive aspects of this perennial question. *First, what circumstances favor the emergence of cooperation under anarchy?* Given the lack of a central authority to guarantee adherence to agreements, what features of situations encourage or permit states to bind themselves to mutually beneficial courses of action? What features of situations preclude cooperation? *Second, what strategies can states adopt to foster the emergence of cooperation by altering the circumstances they confront?* Governments need not necessarily accept circumstances as given. To what extent are situational impediments to cooperation subject to willful modification? Through what higher order strategies can states create the preconditions for cooperation?. . .

I submit that three circumstantial dimensions serve both as proximate explanations of cooperation and as targets of longer-term strategies to promote cooperation. Each of the three major sections of this piece defines a dimension, explains how that dimension accounts for the incidence of cooperation and conflict in the absence of centralized authority, and examines associated strategies for enhancing the prospects for cooperation.

In the section entitled "Payoff Structure: Mutual and Conflicting Preferences," I discuss how payoffs affect the prospects for cooperation and present strategies to improve the prospects for cooperation by altering payoffs. Orthodox game theorists identify optimal strategies *given* ordinally defined classes of games, and their familiar insights provide the starting point for the discussion. Recent works in security studies, institutional microeconomics, and international political economy suggest strategies to *alter* payoff structures and thereby improve the prospects for cooperation.[1]

In the next section, entitled "Shadow of the Future: Single-play and Iterated Games," I discuss how the prospect of continuing interaction affects the likelihood of cooperation; examine how strategies of reciprocity can provide direct paths to cooperative outcomes under iterated conditions; and suggest strategies to lengthen the shadow of the future.[2] In addition, this section shows that recognition and control capabilities—the ability to distinguish between cooperation and defection by others and to respond in kind—can affect the power of reciprocity, and suggests strategies to improve recognition capabilities.

In the third section, "Number of Players: Two-Person and N-Person Games," I explain why cooperation becomes more difficult as the number of actors increases; present strategies for promoting cooperation in N-actor situations; and offer strategies for promoting cooperation by reducing the number of actors necessary to the realization of common interests. Game theorists and oligopoly theorists have long noted that cooperation becomes more difficult as numbers increase, and their insights provide a starting point for discussion. Recent work in political economy focuses on two strategies for promoting cooperation in thorny N-person situations: functionalist analysts of regimes suggest strategies for increasing the likelihood and robustness of cooperation *given* large numbers of actors,[3] analysts of *ad hoc* bargaining in international political economy suggest strategies of bilateral and regional decomposition to *reduce* the number of actors necessary to the realization of some mutual interests, at the expense of the magnitude of gains from cooperation. . . .[4]

II. PLAYOFF STRUCTURE: MUTUAL AND CONFLICTING PREFERENCES

The structure of payoffs in a given round of play—the benefits of mutual cooperation (CC) relative to mutual defection (DD) and the benefits of unilateral defection (DC) relative to unrequited cooperation (CD)—is fundamental to the analysis of cooperation. The argument proceeds in three stages. First, how does payoff structure affect the significance of cooperation? More narrowly, when is cooperation, defined in terms of conscious policy coordination, necessary to the realization of mutual interests? Second, how does payoff structure affect the likelihood and robustness of cooperation? Third, through what strategies can states increase the long-term prospects for cooperation by altering payoff structures?

Before turning to these questions, consider briefly some tangible and intangible determinants of payoff structures. The security and political economy literatures examine the effects of military force structure and doctrine, economic ideology, the size of currency reserves, macroeconomic circumstance, and a host of other factors on national assessments of national interests. In "Cooperation under the Security Dilemma," Robert Jervis has explained how the diffusion of offensive military technology and strategies can increase rewards from defection and thereby reduce the prospects for cooperation. In "International Regimes, Transactions, and Chance: Embedded Liberalism in the Postwar Economic Order," John Ruggie has demonstrated how the diffusion of liberal economic ideas increased the perceived benefits of mutual economic openness over mutual closure (CC-DD), and diminished the perceived rewards from asymmetric defection relative to asymmetric cooperation (DC-CD). In "Firms and Tariff Regime Change," Timothy McKeown has shown how downturns in the business cycle alter national tastes for protection and thereby decrease the perceived benefits of mutual openness relative to mutual closure and increase the perceived rewards of asymmetric defection. . . .[5]

A. Payoff Structure and Cooperation

How does payoff structure determine the significance of cooperation? More narrowly, when is *cooperation,* defined in terms of conscious policy coordination, *necessary* to the realization of *mutual benefits?* For a *mutual benefit* to exist, actors must prefer mutual cooperation (CC) to mutual defection (DD). For coordination to be *necessary* to the realization of the mutual benefit, actors must prefer unilateral defection (DC) to unrequited cooperation (CD). These preference orderings are consistent with the familiar games of Prisoners' Dilemma, Stag Hunt, and Chicken. Indeed, these games have attracted a disproportionate share of scholarly attention precisely because cooperation is desirable but not automatic. In these cases, the capacity of states to cooperate under anarchy, to bind themselves to mutually beneficial courses of action without resort to any ultimate central authority, is vital to the realization of a common good. . . .

In the class of games—including Prisoners' Dilemma, Stag Hunt, and Chicken—where cooperation is necessary to the realization of mutual benefits, how does payoff structure affect the likelihood and robustness of cooperation in these situations? Cooperation will be less likely in Prisoners' Dilemma than in Stag Hunt or Chicken. To understand why, consider each of these games in conjunction with the illustrative stories from which they derive their names.

Prisoners' Dilemma: Two prisoners are suspected of a major crime. The authorities possess evidence to secure conviction on only a minor charge. If neither prisoner squeals, both will draw a light sentence on the minor charge (CC). If one prisoner squeals and the other stonewalls, the rat will go free (DC) and the sucker will draw a very heavy sentence (CD). If both squeal, both will draw a moderate sentence (DD). Each prisoner's preference ordering is: DC > CC > DD > CD. If the prisoners expect to "play" only one time, each prisoner will be better off squealing than stonewalling, no matter what his partner chooses to do (DC > CC and DD > CD). The temptation of the rat payoff and fear of the sucker payoff will drive single-play Prisoners' Dilemmas toward mutual defection. Unfortunately, if both prisoners act on this reasoning, they will draw a moderate sentence on the major charge, while cooperation could have led to a light sentence on the minor charge (CC > DD). In single-play Prisoners' Dilemmas, individually rational actions produce a collectively suboptimal outcome.

Stag Hunt: A group of hunters surround a stag. If all cooperate to trap the stag, all will eat well (CC). If one person defects to chase a passing rabbit, the stag will escape. The defector will eat lightly (DC) and none of the others will eat at all (CD). If all chase rabbits, all will have some chance of catching a rabbit and eating lightly (DD). Each hunter's preference ordering is: CC > DC > DD > CD. The mutual interest in plentiful venison (CC) relative to all other outcomes militates strongly against defection. However, because a rabbit in the hand (DC) is better than a stag in the bush (CD), cooperation will be assured only if each hunter believes that all hunters will cooperate. In single-play Stag Hunt, the temptation to defect to protect against the defection of others is balanced by the strong universal preference for stag over rabbit.

Chicken: Two drivers race down the center of a road from opposite directions. If one swerves and the other does not, then the first will suffer the stigma of being known as a chicken (CD) while the second will enjoy being known as a hero (DC). If neither swerves, both will suffer grievously in the ensuing collision (DD). If both swerve, damage to the reputation of each will be limited (CC). Each driver's preference ordering is: DC > CC > CD > DD. If each believes that the other will swerve, then each will be tempted to defect by continuing down the center of the road. Better to be a live hero than a live chicken. If both succumb to this temptation, however, defection will result in collision. The fear that the other driver may not swerve decreases the appeal of continuing down the center of the road. In single-play Chicken, the temptations of unilateral defection are balanced by fear of mutual defection.

In games that are not repeated, only ordinally defined preferences matter. Under single-play conditions, interval-level payoffs in ordinally defined categories of games cannot (in theory) affect the likelihood of cooperation. In the illustrations above, discussions of dominant strategies do not hinge on the magnitude of differences among the payoffs. Yet the magnitude of differences between CC and DD and between DC and CD can be large or small, if not precisely measurable, and can increase or decrease. Changes in the magnitude of differences in the value placed on outcomes can influence the prospects for cooperation through two paths.

First, changes in the value attached to outcomes can transform situations from one ordinally defined class of game into another. For example, in "Cooperation under the Security Dilemma," Robert Jervis described how difficult Prisoners' Dilemmas may evolve into less challenging Stag Hunts if the gains from mutual cooperation (CC) increase relative to the gains from exploitation (DC). He related the structure of payoffs to traditional concepts of offensive and defensive dominance, and offensive and defensive dominance to technological and doctrinal shifts. Ernst Haas, Mary Pat Williams, and Don Babai have emphasized the importance of cognitive congruence as a determinant of technological cooperation. The diffusion of common conceptions of the nature and effects of technology enhanced perceived gains from cooperation and diminished perceived gains from defection, and may have transformed some Prisoners' Dilemmas into Harmony.[6]

Second, under iterated conditions, the magnitude of differences among payoffs *within* a given class of games can be an important determinant of cooperation. The more substantial the gains from mutual cooperation (CC-DD) and the less substantial the gains from unilateral defection (DC-CD), the greater the likelihood of cooperation. In iterated situations, the magnitude of the difference between CC and DD and between DC and CD in present and future rounds of play affects the likelihood of cooperation in the present. This point is developed at length in the section on the shadow of the future.

B. Strategies to Alter Payoff Structure

If payoff structure affects the likelihood of cooperation, to what extent can states alter situations by modifying payoff structures, and thereby increase the long-term likelihood of cooperation? Many of the tangible and intangible determinants of payoff structure, discussed at the outset of this section, are subject to willful modification through unilateral, bilateral, and multilateral strategies. In "Cooperation under the Security Dilemma," Robert Jervis has offered specific suggestions for altering payoff structures through unilateral strategies. Procurement policy can affect the prospects for cooperation. If one superpower favors procurement of defensive over offensive weapons, it can reduce its own gains from exploitation through surprise attack (DC) and reduce its adversary's fear of exploitation (CD). Members of alliances have often resorted to the device of deploying troops on troubled frontiers to increase the likelihood of cooperation. A state's use of troops as hostages is designed to diminish the payoff from its own defection—to reduce its gains from exploitation (DC)—and thereby render defensive defection by its partner less likely. Publicizing an agreement diminishes payoffs associated with defection from the agreement, and thereby lessens gains from exploitation. These observations in international relations are paralleled by recent developments in microeconomics. Oliver Williamson has identified unilateral and bilateral techniques used by firms to facilitate interfirm cooperation by diminishing gains from exploitation. He distinguishes between specific and nonspecific costs associated with adherence to agreements. Specific costs, such as specialized training, machine tools, and construction, cannot be recovered in the event of the break-down of an agreement. When parties to an agreement incur high specific costs, repudiation of commitments will entail substantial losses. Firms can thus reduce their gains from exploitation through the technique of acquiring dedicated assets that serve as hostages to continuing cooperation. Nonspecific assets, such as general-purpose trucks and airplanes, are salvageable if agreements break down; firms can reduce their fear of being exploited by maximizing the use of nonspecific assets, but such assets cannot diminish gains from exploitation by serving as hostages.[7] Unilateral strategies can improve the prospects of cooperation by reducing both the costs of being exploited (CD) and the gains from exploitation (DC). The new literature on interfirm cooperation indirectly raises an old question on the costs of unilateral strategies to promote cooperation in international relations.

In many instances, unilateral actions that limit one's gains from exploitation may have the effect of increasing one's vulnerability to exploitation by others. For example, a state could limit gains from defection from liberal international economic norms by permitting the expansion of sectors of comparative advantage and by permitting liquidation of inefficient sectors. Because a specialized economy is a hostage to international economic cooperation, this strategy would unquestionably increase the credibility of the nation's commitment to liberalism. It also has the effect, however, of increasing the nation's vulnerability to protection by others. In the troops-as-hostage example, the government that stations troops may promote cooperation by diminishing an ally's fear of abandonment, but in so doing it raises its own fears of exploitation by the ally. . . .

Unilateral strategies do not exhaust the range of options that states may use to alter payoff structures. Bilateral strategies—most significantly strategies of issue linkage—can be used to alter payoff structures by combining dissimilar games. Because resort to issue linkage generally assumes iteration, analysis of how issue linkage can be used to alter payoffs is presented in the section on the shadow of the future. Furthermore, bilateral "instructional" strategies can aim at altering another country's understanding of cause-and-effect relationships, and result in altered perceptions of interest. For example, American negotiators in SALT I sought to instruct their Soviet counterparts on the logic of mutual assured destruction.[8]

Multilateral strategies, centering on the formation of international regimes, can be used to alter payoff structures in two ways. First, norms generated by regimes may be internalized by states, and thereby alter payoff structure. Second, information generated by regimes may alter states' understanding of their interests. As Ernst Haas argues, new regimes may gather and distribute information that can highlight cause-and-effect relationships not previously understood. Changing perceptions of means-ends hierarchies can, in turn, result in changing perceptions of interest.[9]

III. THE SHADOW OF THE FUTURE: SINGLE-PLAY AND ITERATED GAMES

The distinction between cases in which similar transactions among parties are unlikely to be repeated and cases in which the expectation of future interaction can influence decisions in the present is fundamental to the emergence of cooperation among egotists. As the previous section suggests, states confronting strategic situations that resemble single-play Prisoners' Dilemma and, to a lesser extent, single-play Stag Hunt and Chicken, are constantly tempted by immediate gains from unilateral defection, and fearful of immediate losses from unrequited cooperation. How does continuing interaction affect prospects for cooperation? The argument proceeds in four stages. First, why do iterated conditions improve the prospects for cooperation in Prisoners' Dilemma and Stag Hunt while diminishing the prospects for cooperation in Chicken? Second, how do strategies of reciprocity improve the prospects for cooperation under iterated conditions? Third, why does the effectiveness of reciprocity hinge on conditions of play—the ability of actors to distinguish reliably between cooperation and defection by others and to respond in kind? Fourth, through what strategies can states improve conditions of play and lengthen the shadow of the future?[10]

Before turning to these questions, consider the attributes of iterated situations. First, states must expect to continue dealing with each other. This condition is, in practice, not particularly restrictive. With the possible exception of global thermonuclear war, international politics is characterized by the expectation of future interaction. Second, payoff structures must not change substantially over time. In other words, each round of play should not alter the structure of the game in the future. This condition is, in practice, quite restrictive. For example, states considering surprise attack when offense is dominant are in a situation that has many of the characteristics of a single-play game: Attack alters options and payoffs in future rounds of interaction. Conversely, nations considering increases or decreases in their military budgets are in a situation that has many of the characteristics of an iterated game: Spending options and associated marginal increases or decreases in military strength are likely to remain fairly stable over future rounds of interaction. In international monetary affairs, governments considering or fearing devaluation under a gold-exchange standard are in a situation that has many of the characteristics of a single-play game: Devaluation may diminish the value of another state's foreign currency reserves on a one-time basis, while reductions in holdings of reserves would diminish possible losses on a one-time basis. Conversely, governments considering intervention under a floating system with minimal reserves are in a situation that has many of the characteristics of an iterated game: Depreciation or appreciation of a currency would not produce substantial one-time losses or gains. Third, the size of the discount rate applied to the future affects the iterativeness of games. If a government places little value on future payoffs, its situation has many of the characteristics of a single-play game. If it places a high value on future payoffs, its situation may have many of the characteristics of an interated game. For example, political leaders in their final term are likely to discount the future more substantially than political leaders running for, or certain of, reelection.

A. The Shadow of the Future and Cooperation

How does the shadow of the future affect the likelihood of cooperation? Under single-play conditions without a sovereign, adherence to agreements is often irrational. Consider the single-play Prisoners' Dilemma. Each prisoner is better off squealing, whether or not his partner decides to squeal. In the absence of continuing interaction, defection would emerge as the dominant strategy. Because the prisoners can neither turn to a central authority for enforcement of an agreement to cooperate nor rely on the anticipation of retaliation to deter present defection, cooperation will be unlikely under single-play conditions. If the prisoners expect to be placed in similar situations in the future, the prospects for cooperation improve. Experimental evidence suggests that under iterated Prisoners' Dilemma the incidence of cooperation rises substantially.[11] Even in the absence of centralized authority, tacit agreements to cooperate through mutual stonewalling are frequently reached and maintained. Under iterated Prisoners' Dilemma, a potential defector compares the immediate gain from squealing with the possible sacrifice of future gains that may result from squealing. In single-play Stag Hunt, each hunter is tempted to defect in order to defend himself against the possibility of defection by others. A reputation for reliability, for resisting temptation, reduces the likelihood of defection. If the hunters are a permanent group, and expect to hunt together again, the immediate gains from unilateral defection relative to unrequited cooperation must be balanced against the cost of diminished cooperation in the future. In both Prisoners' Dilemma and Stag Hunt, defection in the present *decreases* the likelihood of cooperation in the future. In both, therefore, iteration improves the prospects for cooperation. In Chicken, iteration may decrease the prospects for cooperation. Under single-play conditions, the temptation of unilateral defection is balanced by the fear of the collision that follows from mutual defection. How does iteration affect this balance? If the game is repeated indefinitely, then each driver may refrain from swerving in the present to coerce the other driver into swerving in the future. Each driver may seek to acquire a reputation for not swerving to cause the other driver to swerve. In iterated Chicken, one driver's defection in the present may decrease the likelihood of the other driver's defection in the future.

B. Strategies of Reciprocity and Conditions of Play

It is at this juncture that strategy enters the explanation. Although the expectation of continuing interaction has varying effects on the likelihood of cooperation in the illustrations above, an iterated environment permits resort to strategies of reciprocity that may improve the prospects of cooperation in Chicken as well as in Prisoners' Dilemma and Stag Hunt. Robert Axelrod argues that strategies of reciprocity have the effect of promoting cooperation by establishing a direct connection between an actor's present behavior and anticipated future benefits. Tit-for-tat, or conditional cooperation, can increase the likelihood of joint cooperation by shaping the future consequences of present cooperation or defection.

In iterated Prisoners' Dilemma and Stag Hunt, reciprocity underscores the future consequences of present cooperation and defection. The argument presented above—that iteration enhances the prospects for cooperation in these games—rests on the assumption that defection in the present will decrease the likelihood of cooperation in the future. Adoption of an implicit or explicit strategy of matching stonewalling with stonewalling, squealing with squealing, rabbit chasing with rabbit chasing, and cooperative hunting with cooperative hunting validates the assumption. In iterated Chicken, a strategy of reciprocity can offset the perverse effects of reputational considerations on the prospects for cooperation. Recall that in iterated Chicken, each driver may refrain from swerving in the present to coerce the other driver into swerving in the future. Adoption of an implicit or explicit strategy of tit-for-tat in iterated games of Chicken alters the failure stream of benefits associated with present defection. If a strategy of reciprocity is credible, then the mutual losses associated with future collisions can encourage present swerving. In all three games, a premise to respond to present cooperation with future cooperation and a threat to respond to present defection with future defection can improve the prospects for cooperation.

The effectiveness of strategies of reciprocity hinges on conditions of play—the ability of actors to distinguish reliably between cooperation and defection by others and to respond in kind. In the illustrations provided above, the meaning of "defect" and "cooperate" is unambiguous. Dichotomous choices—between squeal and stonewall, chase the rabbit or capture the stag, continue down the road or swerve—limit the likelihood of misperception. Further, the actions of all are transparent. Given the definitions of the situations, prisoners, hunters, and drivers can reliably detect defection and cooperation by other actors. Finally, the definition of the actors eliminates the possibility of control problems. Unitary prisoners, hunters, and drivers do not suffer from factional, organizational, or bureaucratic dysfunctions that might hinder implementation of strategies of reciprocity.

In international relations, conditions of play can limit the effectiveness of reciprocity. The definition of cooperation and defection may be ambiguous. For example, the Soviet Union and the United States hold to markedly different definitions of "defection" from the terms of détente as presented in the Basic Principles Agreement;[12] the European Community and the United States differ over whether domestic sectoral policies comprise indirect export subsidies. Further, actions may not be transparent. For example, governments may not be able to detect one another's violations of arms control agreements or indirect export subsidies. If defection cannot be reliably detected, the effect of present cooperation on possible future reprisals will erode. Together, ambiguous definitions and a lack of transparency can limit the ability of states to recognize cooperation and defection by others.

Because reciprocity requires flexibility, control is as important as recognition. Internal factional, organizational, and bureaucratic dysfunctions may limit the ability of nations to implement tit-for-tat strategies. It may be easier to sell one unvarying line of policy than to sell a strategy of shifting between lines of policy in response to the actions of others. For example, arms suppliers and defense planners tend to resist the cancellation of weapons systems even if the cancellation is a response to the actions of a rival. Import-competing industries tend to resist the removal of barriers to imports, even if trade liberalization is in response to liberalization by another state. At times, national decision makers may be unable to implement strategies of reciprocity. On other occasions, they must invest heavily in selling reciprocity. For these reasons, national decision makers may display a bias against conditional strategies: The domestic costs of pursuing such strategies may partially offset the value of the discounted stream of future benefits that conditional policies are expected to yield. . . .

C. Strategies to Improve Recognition and Lengthen the Shadow of the Future

To what extent can governments promote cooperation by creating favorable conditions of play and by lengthening the shadow of the future? The literature on international regimes offers several techniques for creating favorable conditions of play. Explicit codification of norms can limit definitional ambiguity. The very act of clarifying standards of conduct, of defining cooperative and uncooperative behavior, can permit more effective resort to strategies of reciprocity. Further, provisions for surveillance—for example, mechanisms for verification in arms control agreements or for sharing information on the nature and effects of domestic sectoral policies—can increase transparency. In practice, the goal of enhancing recognition capabilities is often central to negotiations under anarchy.

The game-theoretic and institutional microeconomic literatures offer several approaches to increasing the iterative character of situations. Thomas Schelling and Robert Axelrod suggest tactics of decomposition over time to lengthen the shadow of the future.[13] For example, the temptation to defect in a deal promising thirty billion dollars for a billion barrels of oil may be reduced if the deal is sliced up into a series of payments and deliveries. Cooperation in arms reduction or in territorial disengagement may be difficult if the reduction or disengagement must be achieved in one jump. If a reduction or disengagement can be sliced up into increments, the problem of cooperation may be rendered more tractable. Finally, strategies of issue linkage can be used to alter payoff structures and to interject elements of iterativeness into single-play situations. Relations among states are rarely limited to one single-play issue of overriding importance. When nations confront a single-play game on one issue, present defection may be deterred by threats of retaliation on other iterated issues. In international monetary affairs, for instance, a government fearing one-time reserve losses if another state devalues its currency may link devaluation to an iterated trade game. By establishing a direct connection between present behavior in a single-play game and future benefits in an iterated game, tacit or explicit cross-issue linkage can lengthen the shadow of the future. . . .

IV. NUMBER OF PLAYERS: TWO-PERSON AND N-PERSON GAMES

Up to now, I have discussed the effects of payoff structure and the shadow of the future on the prospects of cooperation in terms of two-person situations. What happens to the prospects for cooperation as the number of significant actors rises? In this section, I explain why the prospects for cooperation diminish as the number of players increases; examine the function of international regimes as a response to the problems created by large numbers; and offer strategies to improve the prospects for cooperation by altering situations to diminish the number of significant players.

The numbers problem is central to many areas of the social sciences. Mancur Olson's theory of collective action focuses on N-person versions of Prisoners' Dilemma. The optimism of our earlier discussions of cooperation under iterated Prisoners' Dilemma gives way to the pessimism of analyses of cooperation in the provision of public goods. Applications of Olsonian theory to problems ranging from cartelization to the provision of public goods in alliances underscore the significance of "free-riding" as an impediment to cooperation.[14] In international relations, the numbers problem has been central to two debates. The longstanding controversy over the stability of bipolar versus multipolar systems reduces to a debate over the impact of the number of significant actors on international conflict.[15] A more recent controversy, between proponents of the theory of hegemonic stability and advocates of international regimes, reduces to a debate over the effects of large numbers on the robustness of cooperation.[16]

A. Number of Players and Cooperation

How do numbers affect the likelihood of cooperation? There are at least three important channels of influence.[17] First, cooperation requires recognition of opportunities for the advancement of mutual interests, as well as policy coordination once these opportunities have been identified. As the number of players increases, transactions and information costs rise. In simple terms, the complexity of N-person situations militates against identification and realization of common interests. Avoiding nuclear war during the Cuban missile crisis called for cooperation by the Soviet Union and the United States. The transaction and information costs in this particularly harrowing crisis, though substantial, did not preclude cooperation. By contrast, the problem of identifying significant actors, defining interests, and negotiating agreements that embodied mutual interests in the N-actor case of 1914 was far more difficult. These secondary costs associated with attaining cooperative outcomes in N-actor cases erode the difference between CC and DD. More significantly, the intrinsic difficulty of anticipating the behavior of other players and of weighing the value of the future goes up with the number of players. The complexity of solving N-person games, even in the purely deductive sense, has stunted the development of formal work on the problem. This complexity is even greater in real situations, and operates against multilateral cooperation.

Second, as the number of players increases, the likelihood of autonomous defection and of recognition and control problems increases. Cooperative behavior rests on calculations of expected utility—merging discount rates, payoff structures, and anticipated behavior of other players. Discount rates and approaches to calculation are likely to vary across actors, and the prospects for mutual cooperation may decline as the number of players and probable heterogeneity of actors increases. The chances of including a state that discounts the future heavily, that is too weak (domestically) to detect, react, or implement a strategy of reciprocity, that cannot distinguish reliably between cooperation and defection by other states, or that departs from even minimal standards of rationality increase with the number of states in a game. For example, many pessimistic analyses of the consequences of nuclear proliferation focus on how breakdowns of deterrence may become more likely as the number of countries with nuclear weapons increases.

Third, as the number of players increases, the feasibility of sanctioning defectors diminishes. Strategies of reciprocity become more difficult to implement without triggering a collapse of cooperation. In two-person games, tit-for-tat works well because the costs of defection are focused on only one other party. If defection imposes costs on all parties in an N-person game, however, the power of strategies of reciprocity is underminded. The infeasibility of sanctioning defectors creates the possibility of free-riding. What happens if we increase the number of actors in the iterated Prisoners' Dilemma from 2 to 20? Confession by any one of them could lead to the conviction of all on the major charge; therefore, the threat to retaliate against defection in the present with defection in the future will impose costs on all prisoners, and could lead to wholesale defection in subsequent rounds. For example, under the 1914 system of alliances, retaliation against one member of the alliance was the equivalent of retaliation against all. In N-person games, a strategy of conditional defection can have the effect of spreading, rather than containing, defection.

B. Strategies of Institutionalization and Decomposition

Given a large number of players, what strategies can states use to increase the likelihood of cooperation? Regime creation can increase the likelihood of cooperation in N-person games. First, conventions provide rules of thumb that can diminish transaction and information costs. Second, collective enforcement mechanisms both decrease the likelihood of autonomous defection and permit selective punishment of violators of norms. These two functions of international regimes directly address problems created by large numbers of players. For example, Japan and the members of NATO profess a mutual interest in limiting flows of militarily useful goods and technology to the Soviet Union. Obviously, all suppliers of militarily useful goods and technology must cooperate to deny the Soviet Union access to such items. Although governments differ in their assessment of the military value of some goods and technologies, there is consensus on a rather lengthy list of prohibited items. By facilitating agreement of the prohibited list, the Coordinating Committee on the Consultative Group of NATO (CoCom) provides a relatively clear definition of what exports would constitute defection. By defining the scope of defection, the CoCom list forestalls the necessity of retaliation against nations that ship technology or goods that do not fall within the consensual definition of defection. Generally, cooperation is a prerequisite of regime creation. The creation of rules of thumb and mechanisms of collective enforcement and the maintenance and administration of regimes can demand an extraordinary degree of cooperation. This problem may limit the range of situations susceptible to modification through regimist strategies.

What strategies can reduce the number of significant players in a game and thereby render cooperation more likely? When governments are unable to cooperate on a global scale, they often turn to discriminatory strategies to encourage bilateral or regional cooperation. Tactics of decomposition across actors can, at times, improve the prospects for cooperation. Both the possibilities and the limits of strategies to reduce the number of players are evident in the discussions that follow. First, reductions in the number of actors can usually be purchased at the expense of the magnitude of gains from cooperation. The benefits of regional openness are smaller than the gains from global openness. A bilateral clearing arrangement is less economically efficient than a multilateral clearing arrangement. Strategies to reduce the number of players in a game generally diminish the gains from cooperation while they increase the likelihood and robustness of cooperation. Second, strategies to reduce the number of players generally impose substantial costs on third parties. These externalities may motivate third parties to undermine the limited area of cooperation or may serve as an impetus for a third party to enlarge the zone of cooperation. In the 1930s, for example, wholesale resort to discriminatory trading policies facilitated creation of exclusive zones of commercial openness. When confronted by a shrinking market share, Great Britain adopted a less liberal and more discriminatory commercial policy in order to secure preferential access to its empire and to undermine preferential agreements between other countries. As the American market share diminished, the United States adopted a more liberal and more discriminatory commercial policy to increase its access to export markets. It is not possible, however, to reduce the number of players in all situations. For example, compare the example of limited commercial openness with the example of a limited strategic embargo. To reduce the number of actors in a trade war, market access can simply be offered to only one country and withheld from others. By contrast, defection by only one supplier can permit the target of a strategic embargo to obtain a critical technology. These problems may limit the range of situations susceptible to modification through strategies that reduce the number of players in games.

NOTES

1. For examples, see Robert Jervis, "Cooperation under the Security Dilemma," *World Politics* 30 (January 1978), pp. 167–214; Oliver E. Williamson, "Credible Commitments: Using Hostages to Support Exchange," *American Economic Review* (September 1983), pp. 519–40; John Gerard Ruggie, "International Regimes, Transactions, and Change: Embedded Liberalism in the Postwar Economic Order," in Stephen D. Krasner, ed., *International Regimes* (Ithaca, N.Y.: Cornell University Press, 1983).
2. For orthodox game-theoretic analyses of the importance of iteration, see R. Duncan Luce and Howard Raiffa, *Games and Decisions* (New York: Wiley, 1957), Appendix 8, and David M. Kreps, Paul Milgram, John Roberts, and Robert Wilson, "Rational Cooperation in Finitely-Repeated Prisoner's Dilemma," *Journal of Economic Theory* 27 (August 1982), pp. 245–52. For the results of laboratory experiments, see Robert Radlow, "An Experimental Study of Cooperation in the Prisoner's Dilemma Game," *Journal of Conflict Resolution* 9 (June 1965), pp. 221–27. On the importance of indefinite iteration to the emergence of cooperation in business transactions, see Robert Telsor "A Theory of Self-Enforcing Agreements," *Journal of Business* 53 (January 1980), pp. 27–44.
3. See Robert O. Keohane, *After Hegemony: Cooperation and Discord in the World Political Economy* (Princeton, N.J.: Princeton University Press, 1984), and Krasner (fn. 5).

4. See John A. C. Conybeare, "International Organization and the Theory of Property Rights," *International Organization* 34 (Summer 1980), pp. 307–34, and Kenneth A. Oye, "Belief Systems, Bargaining, and Breakdown: International Political Economy 1929–1936," Ph.D. diss. (Harvard University, 1983), chap. 3.
5. See Jervis (fn. 1); Ruggie (fn. 1); Timothy J. McKeown, "Firms and Tariff Regime Change: Explaining the Demand for Protection," *World Politics* 36 (January 1984), pp. 215–33. On the effects of *ambiguity* of preferences on the prospects of cooperation, see the concluding sections of Jervis (fn. 1).
6. Haas, Williams, and Babai, *Scientists and World Order: The Uses of Technical Knowledge in International Organizations* (Berkeley: University of California Press, 1977).
7. Williamson (fn. 1).
8. See John Newhouse, *Cold Dawn: The Story of SALT I* (New York: Holt, Rinehart & Winston, 1973).
9. See Haas, "Words Can Hurt You; Or Who Said What to Whom About Regimes," in Krasner (fn. 5).
10. This section is derived largely from Axelrod (fn. 2) and Telsor (fn. 2).
11. See Anatol Rapoport and Albert Chammah, *Prisoner's Dilemma* (Ann Arbor: University of Michigan Press, 1965), and subsequent essays in *Journal of Conflict Resolution*.
12. See Alexander L. George, *Managing U.S.-Soviet Rivalry: Problems of Crisis Prevention* (Boulder, Colo.: Westview, 1983).
13. Schelling, *Strategy of Conflict* (Cambridge, Mass.: Harvard University Press, 1960), pp. 43–46, and Axelrod (fn. 2), pp. 126–132.
14. See Mancur Olson, Jr., *The Logic of Collective Action: Public Goods and the Theory of Groups* (Cambridge, Mass.: Harvard University Press, 1965), and Mancur Olson and Richard Zeckhauser, "An Economic Theory of Alliances," *Review of Economics and Statistics* 48 (August 1966), pp. 266–79. For a recent elegant summary and extension of the large literature on dilemmas of collective action, see Russell Hardin, *Collective Action* (Baltimore: Johns Hopkins University Press, 1982).
15. See Kenneth N. Waltz, "The Stability of a Bipolar World," *Daedalus* 93 (Summer 1964), and Richard N. Rosecrance, "Bipolarity, Multipolarity, and the Future," *Journal of Conflict Resolution* (September 1966), pp. 314–27.
16. On hegemony, see Robert Gilpin, *U.S. Power and the Multinational Corporation* (New York: Basic Books, 1975), pp. 258–59. On duopoly, see Timothy McKeown, "Hegemonic Stability Theory and 19th-Century Tariff Levels in Europe," *International Organization* 37 (Winter 1983), pp. 73–91.
17. See Keohane (fn. 3), chap. 6, for extensions of these points.

Kant, Liberal Legacies, and Foreign Affairs

Michael W. Doyle

I

What difference do liberal principles and institutions make to the conduct of the foreign affairs of liberal states? A thicket of conflicting judgments suggests that the legacies of liberalism have not been clearly appreciated. For many citizens of liberal states, liberal principles and institutions have so fully absorbed domestic politics that their influence on foreign affairs tends to be either overlooked altogether or, when perceived, exaggerated. Liberalism becomes either unselfconsciously patriotic or inherently "peace-loving." For many scholars and diplomats, the relations among independent states appear to differ so significantly from domestic politics that influences of liberal principles and domestic liberal institutions are denied or denigrated. They judge that international relations are governed by perceptions of national security and the balance of power; liberal principles and institutions, when they do intrude, confuse and disrupt the pursuit of balance-of-power politics.

Although liberalism is misinterpreted from both these points of view, a crucial aspect of the liberal legacy is captured by each. Liberalism is a distinct ideology and set of institutions that has shaped the perceptions of and capacities for foreign relations of political societies that range from social welfare or social democratic to laissez faire. It defines much of the content of the liberal patriot's nationalism. Liberalism does appear to disrupt the pursuit of balance-of-power politics. Thus its foreign relations cannot be adequately explained (or prescribed) by a sole reliance on the balance of power. But liberalism is not inherently "peace-loving"; nor is it consistently restrained or peaceful in intent. Furthermore, liberal practice may reduce the probability that states will successfully exercise the consistent restraint and peaceful intentions that a world peace may well require in the nuclear age. Yet the peaceful intent and restraint that liberalism does manifest in limited aspects of its foreign affairs announces the possibility of a world peace this side of the grave or of world conquest. It has strengthened the prospects for a world peace established by the steady expansion of a separate peace among liberal societies. . . .

II

Liberalism has been identified with an essential principle—the importance of the freedom of the individual. Above all, this is a belief in the importance of moral freedom, of the right to be treated and a duty to treat others as ethical subjects, and not as objects or means only. This principle has generated rights and institutions.

A commitment to a threefold set of rights forms the foundation of liberalism. Liberalism calls for freedom from arbitrary authority, often called "negative freedom," which includes freedom of conscience, a free press and free speech, equality under the law, and the right to hold, and therefore to exchange, property without fear of arbitrary seizure. Liberalism also calls for those rights necessary to protect and promote the capacity and opportunity for freedom, the "positive freedoms." Such social and economic rights as equality of opportunity in education and rights to health care and employment, necessary for effective self-expression and participation, are thus among liberal rights. A third liberal right, democratic participation or representation, is necessary to guarantee the other two. To ensure that morally autonomous individuals remain free in those areas of social action where public authority is needed, public legislation has to express the will of the citizens making laws for their own community.

These three sets of rights, taken together, seem to meet the challenge that Kant identified:

> To organize a group of rational beings who demand general laws for their survival, but of whom each inclines toward exempting himself, and to establish their constitution in such a way that, in spite of the fact their private attitudes are opposed, these private attitudes mutually impede each other in such a manner that [their] public behavior is the same as if they did not have such evil attitudes.[1]

But the dilemma within liberalism is how to reconcile the three sets of liberal rights. The right to private property, for example, can conflict with equality of opportunity and both rights can be violated by democratic legislation. During the 180 years since Kant wrote, the liberal tradition has evolved two high roads to individual freedom and social order; one is laissez-faire, or "conservative," liberalism and the other is social welfare, or social democratic, or "liberal," liberalism. Both reconcile these conflicting rights (though in differing ways) by successfully organizing free individuals into a political order.

The political order of laissez-faire and social welfare liberals is marked by a shared commitment to four essential institutions. First, citizens possess juridical equality and other fundamental civil rights such as freedom of religion and the press. Second, the effective sovereigns of the state are representative legislatures deriving their authority from the consent of the electorate and exercising their authority free from all restraint apart from the requirement that basic civic rights be preserved. Most pertinently for the impact of liberalism on foreign affairs, the state is subject to neither the external authority of other states nor to the internal authority of special prerogatives held, for example, by monarchs or military castes over foreign policy. Third, the economy rests on a recognition of the rights of private property including the ownership of means of production. Property is justified by individual acquisition (for example, by labor) or by social agreement or social utility. This excludes state socialism or state capitalism, but it need not exclude market socialism or various forms of the mixed economy. Fourth, economic decisions are predominantly shaped by the forces of supply and demand, domestically and internationally, and are free from strict control by bureaucracies. . . .

III

In foreign affairs liberalism has shown, as it has in the domestic realm, serious weaknesses. But unlike liberalism's domestic realm, its foreign affairs have experienced startling but less than fully appreciated successes. Together they shape an unrecognized dilemma, for both these successes and weaknesses in large part spring from the same cause: the international implications of liberal principles and institutions.

The basic postulate of liberal international theory holds that states have the right to be free from foreign intervention. Since morally autonomous citizens hold rights to liberty, the states that democratically represent them have the right to exercise political independence. Mutual respect for these rights then becomes the touchstone of international liberal theory. When states respect each other's rights, individuals are free to establish private international ties without state interference. Profitable exchange between merchants and educational exchanges among scholars then create a web of mutual advantages and commitments that bolsters sentiments of public respect.

These conventions of mutual respect have formed a cooperative foundation for relations among liberal democracies of a remarkably effective kind. *Even though liberal states have become involved in numerous wars with nonliberal states, constitutionally secure liberal states have yet to engage in war with one another.*[2] No one should argue that such wars are impossible; but preliminary evidence does appear to indicate that there exists a significant predisposition against warfare between liberal states. Indeed, threats of war also have been regarded as illegitimate. A liberal zone of peace, a pacific union, has been maintained and has expanded despite numerous particular conflicts of economic and strategic interest. . . .

Statistically, war between any two states (in any single year or other short period of time) is a low probability event. War between any two adjacent states, considered over a long period of time, may be somewhat more probable. The apparent absence of war among the more clearly liberal states, whether adjacent or not, for almost two hundred years thus has some significance. Politically more significant, perhaps, is that, when states are forced to decide, by the pressure of an impinging world war, on which side of a world contest they will fight, liberal states wind up all on the same side, despite the real complexity of the historical, economic, and political factors that affect their foreign policies. And historically, we should recall that medieval and early modern Europe were the warring cockpits of states, wherein France and England and the Low Countries engaged in near constant strife. Then in the late eighteenth century there began to emerge liberal regimes. At first hesitant and confused, and later clear and confident as liberal regimes gained deeper domestic foundations and longer international experience, a pacific union of these liberal states became established.

The realist model of international relations, which provides a plausible explanation of the general insecurity of states, offers little guidance in explaining the pacification of the liberal world. Realism, in its classical formation, holds that the state is and should be formally sovereign, effectively unbounded by individual rights nationally and thus capable of determining its own scope of authority. (This determination can be made democratically, oligarchically, or autocratically.) Internationally, the sovereign state exists in an anarchical society in which it is radically independent, neither bounded nor protected by international "law" or treaties or duties, and hence, insecure. Hobbes, one of the seventeenth-century founders of the realist approach drew the international implications of realism when he argued that the existence of international anarchy, the very independence of states, best

TABLE 1   WARS INVOLVING LIBERAL REGIMES

Period	Liberal regimes and the pacific union (by date "liberal")[a]	Total number
18th century	Swiss Cantons[b] French Republic 1790–1795 the United States[b] 1776–	3
1800–1850	Swiss Confederation, the United States France 1830–1849 Belgium 1830– Great Britain 1832– Netherlands 1848– Piedmont 1848– Denmark 1849–	8
1850–1900	Switzerland, the United States, Belgium, Great Britain, Netherlands Piedmont 1861, Italy 1861– Denmark 1866 Sweden 1864– Greece 1864– Canada 1867– France 1871– Argentina 1880– Chile 1891–	13

Table 1 (Continued)

Period	Liberal regimes and the pacific union (by date "liberal")[a]	Total number
1900–1945	Switzerland, the United States, Great Britain, Sweden, Canada,	29
	Greece 1911, 1928–1936	
	Italy 1922	
	Belgium 1940	
	Netherlands 1940	
	Argentina 1943	
	France 1940	
	Chile 1924, 1932	
	Australia 1901–	
	Norway 1905–1940	
	New Zealand 1907–	
	Colombia 1910–1949	
	Denmark 1914–1940	
	Poland 1917–1935	
	Latvia 1922–1934	
	Germany 1918–1932	
	Austria 1918–1934	
	Estonia 1919–1934	
	Finland 1919–	
	Uruguay 1919–	
	Costa Rica 1919–	
	Czechoslovakia 1920–1939	
	Ireland 1920–	
	Mexico 1928–	
	Lebanon 1944–	
1945[c]–	Switzerland, the United States, Great Britain, Sweden, Canada, Australia, New Zealand, Finland, Ireland, Mexico	49
	Uruguay 1973	
	Chile 1973	
	Lebanon 1975	
	Costa Rica 1948, 1953–	
	Iceland 1944–	
	France 1945–	
	Denmark 1945–	
	Norway 1945–	
	Austria 1945–	
	Brazil 1945–1954, 1955–1964	
	Belgium 1946–	
	Luxemburg 1946–	
	Netherlands 1946–	
	Italy 1946–	
	Philippines 1946–1972	

99

Table 1 (Continued)

Period	Liberal regimes and the pacific union (by date "liberal")[a]	Total number
	India 1947–1975, 1977–	
	Sri Lanka 1948–1961, 1963–1977, 1978–	
	Ecuador 1948–1963, 1979–	
	Israel 1949–	
	West Germany 1949–	
	Peru 1950–1962, 1963–1968, 1980–	
	El Salvador 1950–1961	
	Turkey 1950–1960, 1966–1971	
	Japan 1951–	
	Bolivia 1956–1969	
	Colombia 1958–	
	Venezuela 1959–	
	Nigeria 1961–1964, 1979–	
	Jamaica 1962–	
	Trinidad 1962–	
	Senegal 1963–	
	Malaysia 1963–	
	South Korea 1963–1972	
	Botswana 1966–	
	Singapore 1965–	
	Greece 1975–	
	Portugal 1976–	
	Spain 1978–	
	Dominican Republic 1978–	

[a]I have drawn up this approximate list of "Liberal Regimes" according to the four institutions described as essential: market and private property economies; politics that are extremely sovereign; citizens who possess juridical rights; and "republican" (whether republican or monarchical), representative, government. This latter includes the requirement that the legislative branch have an effective role in public policy and be formally and competitively, either potentially or actually, elected. Furthermore, I have taken into account whether male suffrage is wide (that is, 30 percent) or open to "achievement" by inhabitants (for example, to poll-tax payers or householders) of the national or metropolitan territory. Female suffrage is granted within a generation of its being demanded; and representative government is internally sovereign (for example, including and especially over military and foreign affairs) as well as stable (in existence for at least three years).

[b]There are domestic variations within these liberal regimes. For example, Switzerland was liberal only in certain cantons; the United States was liberal only north of the Mason-Dixon line until 1865, when it became liberal throughout. These lists also exclude ancient "republics," since none appear to fit Kant's criteria. See Stephen Holmes, "Aristippus in and out of Athens," *American Political Science Review* 73, no. 1 (March 1979).

[c]Selected list, excludes liberal regimes with populations less than one million.

Sources: Arthur Banks and W. Overstreet, eds., *The Political Handbook of the World,* 1980 (New York: McGraw-Hill, 1980; Foreign and Commonwealth Office. *A Year Book of the Commonwealth* 1980 (London: HMSO, 1980); *Europa Yearbook* 1981 (London: Europe, 1981); W. L. Langer, *An Encyclopedia of World History* (Boston: Houghton-Mifflin, 1968); Department of State, *Country Reports on Human Rights Practices* (Washington, D.C.: U.S. Government Printing Office, 1981); and *Freedom at Issue,* no. 54 (January–February 1980).

TABLE 2   INTERNATIONAL WARS LISTED CHRONOLOGICALLY*

British-Maharattan (1817–1818)
Greek (1821–1828)
Franco-Spanish (1823)
First Anglo-Burmese (1823–1826)
Javanese (1825–1830)
Russo-Persian (1826–1828)
Russo-Turkish (1828–1829)
First Polish (1831)
First Syrian (1831–1832)
Texan (1835–1836)
First British-Afghan (1838–1842)
Second Syrian (1839–1840)
Franco-Algerian (1839–1847)
Peruvian-Bolivian (1841)
First British-Sikh (1845–1846)
Mexican-American (1846–1848)
Austro-Sardinian (1848–1849)
First Schleswig-Holstein (1848–1849)
Hungarian (1848–1849)
Second British-Sikh (1848–1849)
Roman Republic (1849)
La Plata (1851–1852)
First Turco-Montenegran (1852–1853)
Crimean (1853–1856)
Anglo-Persian (1856–1857)
Sepoy (1857–1859)
Second Turco-Montenegran (1858–1859)
Italian Unification (1859)
Spanish-Moroccan (1859–1860)
Italo-Roman (1860)
Italo-Sicilian (1860–1861)
Franco-Mexican (1862–1867)
Ecuadorian-Colombian (1863)
Second Polish (1863–1864)
Spanish-Santo Dominican (1863–1865)
Second Schleswig-Holstein (1864)
Lopez (1864–1870)
Spanish-Chilean (1865–1866)
Seven Weeks (1866)
Ten Years (1868–1878)
Franco-Prussian (1870–1871)
Dutch-Achinese (1873–1878)
Balkan (1875–1877)
Russo-Turkish (1877–1878)
Bosnian (1878)
Madagascan (1947–1948)
First Kashmir (1947–1949)

Second British-Afghan (1878–1880)
Pacific (1879–1880)
British-Zulu (1879)
Franco-Indochinese (1882–1884)
Mahdist (1882–1885)
Sino-French (1884–1885)
Central American (1885)
Serbo-Bulgarian (1885)
Sino-Japanese (1894–1895)
Franco-Madagascan (1894–1895)
Cuban (1895–1896)
Italo-Ethiopian (1895–1896)
First Philippine (1896–1898)
Greco-Turkish (1897)
Spanish-American (1898)
Second Philippine (1899–1902)
Boer (1899–1902)
Boxer Rebellion (1900)
Ilinden (1903)
Russo-Japanese (1904–1905)
Central American (1906)
Central American (1907)
Spanish-Moroccan (1909–1910)
Italo-Turkish (1911–1912)
First Balkan (1912–1913)
Second Balkan (1913)
World War I (1914–1918)
Russian Nationalities (1917–1921)
Russo-Polish (1919–1920)
Hungarian-Allies (1919)
Greco-Turkish (1919–1922)
Riffian (1921–1926)
Druze (1925–1927)
Sino-Soviet (1929)
Manchurian (1931–1933)
Chaco (1932–1935)
Italo-Ethiopian (1935–1936)
Sino-Japanese (1937–1941)
Changkufeng (1938)
Nomohan (1939)
World War II (1939–1945)
Russo-Finnish (1939–1940)
Franco-Thai (1940–1941)
Indonesian (1945–1946)
Indochinese (1945–1954)
Palestine (1948–1949)
Hyderabad (1948)

TABLE 2 (Continued)

Korean (1950–1953)	Philippine-MNLF (1972-)
Algerian (1954–1962	Yom Kippur (1973)
Russo-Hungarian (1956)	Turco-Cypriot (1974)
Sinai (1956)	Ethiopian-Eritrean (1974-)
Tibetan (1956–1959)	Vietnamese-Cambodian (1975-)
Sino-Indian (1962)	Timor (1975-)
Vietnamese (1965–1975)	Saharan (1975-)
Second Kashmir (1965)	Ogaden (1976-)
Six Day (1967)	Ugandan-Tanzanian (1978–1979)
Israeli-Egyptian (1969–1970)	Sino-Vietnamese (1979)
Football (1969)	Russo-Afghan (1979–1989)
Bangladesh (1971)	Irani-Iraqi (1980–1988)

*The table is reprinted by permission from Melvin Small and J. David Singer from *Resort to Arms* (Beverly Hills, Calif.: Sage Publications, 1962), pp. 79–80. This is a partial list of international wars fought between 1816 and 1980. In Appendices A and B of *Resort to Arms,* Small and Singer identify a total of 575 wars in this period, but approximately 159 of them appear to be largely domestic or civil wars.

   This definition of war excludes covert interventions, some of which have been directed by liberal regimes against other liberal regimes. One example is the United States' effort to destabilize the Chilean election and Allende's government. Nonetheless, it is significant (as will be apparent below) that such interventions are not pursued publicly as acknowledged policy. The covert destabilization campaign against Chile is recounted in U.S. Congress, Senate, Select Committee to Study Governmental Operations with Respect to Intelligence Activities, *Covert Action in Chile,* 1963–73, 94th Congress, 1st Session (Washington, D.C.: U.S. Government Printing Office, 1975).

accounts for the competition, the fear, and the temptation toward preventive war that characterize international relations. Politics among nations is not a continuous combat, but it is in this view a "state of war . . . a tract of time, wherein the will to contend by battle is sufficiently known"[3]. . . .

   Finding that all states, including liberal states, do engage in war, the realist concludes that the effects of differing domestic regimes (whether liberal or not) are overridden by the international anarchy under which all states live[4]. . . . But the ends that shape the international state of war are decreed for the realist by the anarchy of the international order and the fundamental quest for power that directs the policy of all states, irrespective of differences in their domestic regimes. As Rousseau argued, international peace therefore depends on the abolition of international relations either by the achievement of a world state or by a radical isolationism (Corsica). Realists judge neither to be possible.

   Recent additions to game theory specify some of the circumstances under which prudence could lead to peace. Experience; geography; expectations of cooperation and belief patterns; and the differing payoffs to cooperation (peace) or conflict associated with various types of military technology all appear to influence the calculus.[5] But when it comes to acquiring the techniques of peaceable interaction, nations appear to be slow, or at least erratic, learners. The balance of power (more below) is regarded as a primary lesson in the realist primer, but centuries of experience did not prevent either France (Louis XIV, Napoleon I) or Germany (Wilhelm II, Hitler) from attempting to conquer Europe, twice each. Yet some, very new, black African states appear to have achieved a twenty-year-old system of impressively effective standards of mutual toleration. These standards are not completely effective (as in Tanzania's invasion of Uganda); but they have confounded expectations of a scramble to redivide Africa.[6] Geography—"insular security" and "continental insecurity"—may affect foreign policy attitudes; but it does not appear to determine behavior, as the bellicose records of England and Japan suggest. Beliefs, expectations, and attitudes of leaders and masses should influence strategic behavior. . . . Nevertheless, it would be difficult to determine if liberal leaders have had more peaceable attitudes than leaders who lead nonliberal states. But even if one did make that discovery, he also would have to account for why these peaceable attitudes only appear to be effective in relations with other liberals (since wars with nonliberals have not been uniformly defensive). . . .

Second, at the level of social determinants, some might argue that relations among any group of states with similar social structures or with compatible values would be peaceful. But again, the evidence for feudal societies, communist societies, fascist societies, or socialist societies does not support this conclusion. Feudal warfare was frequent and very much a sport of the monarchs and nobility. There have not been enough truly totalitarian, fascist powers (nor have they lasted long enough) to test fairly their pacific compatibility; but fascist powers in the wider sense of nationalist, capitalist, military dictatorships fought each other in the 1930s. Communist powers have engaged in wars more recently in East Asia. And we have not had enough socialist societies to consider the relevance of socialist pacification. The more abstract category of pluralism does not suffice. Certainly Germany was pluralist when it engaged in war with liberal states in 1914; Japan as well in 1941. But they were not liberal.

And third, at the level of interstate relations, neither specific regional attributes nor historic alliances or friendships can account for the wide reach of the liberal peace. The peace extends as far as, and no further than, the relations among liberal states, not including nonliberal states in an otherwise liberal region (such as the north Atlantic in the 1930s) nor excluding liberal states in a nonliberal region (such as Central America or Africa).

At this level, Raymond Aron has identified three types of interstate peace: empire, hegemony, and equilibrium.[7] An empire generally succeeds in creating an internal peace, but this is not an explanation of peace among independent liberal states. Hegemony can create peace by over-awing potential rivals. Although far from perfect and certainly precarious, United States hegemony, as Aron notes, might account for the interstate peace in South America in the postwar period during the height of the Cold War conflict. However, the liberal peace cannot be attributed merely to effective international policing by a predominant hegemon— Britain in the nineteenth century, the United States in the postwar period. Even though a hegemon might well have an interest in enforcing a peace for the sake of commerce or investments or as a means of enhancing its prestige or security; hegemons such as seventeenth-century France were not peace-enforcing police, and the liberal peace persisted in the interwar period when international society lacked a predominant hegemonic power. Moreover, this explanation overestimates hegemonic control in both periods. Neither England nor the United States was able to prevent direct challenges to its interests (colonial competition in the nineteenth century, Middle East diplomacy and conflicts over trading with the enemy in the postwar period). Where then was the capacity to prevent all armed conflicts between liberal regimes, many of which were remote and others strategically or economically insignificant? Liberal hegemony and leadership are important, but they are not sufficient to explain a liberal peace. . . .

Finally, some realists might suggest that the liberal peace simply reflects the absence of deep conflicts of interest among liberal states. Wars occur outside the liberal zone because conflicts of interest are deeper there. But this argument does nothing more than raise the question of why liberal states have fewer or less fundamental conflicts of interest with other liberal states than liberal states have with nonliberal, or nonliberal states have with other nonliberals. We must therefore examine the workings of liberalism among its own kind—a special pacification of the "state of war" resting on liberalism and nothing either more specific or more general.

IV

Most liberal theorists have offered inadequate guidance in understanding the exceptional nature of liberal pacification. Some have argued that democratic states would be inherently peaceful simply and solely because in these states citizens rule the polity and bear the costs of wars. Unlike monarchs, citizens are not able to indulge their aggressive passions and have the consequences suffered by someone else. Other liberals have argued that laissez-faire capitalism contains an inherent tendency toward rationalism, and that, since war is irrational, liberal capitalisms will be pacifistic. Others still, such as Montesquieu, claim that "commerce is the cure for the most destructive prejudices," and "Peace is the natural effect of trade."[8] While these developments can help account for the liberal peace, they do not explain the fact that liberal states are peaceful only in relations with other liberal states. France and England fought expansionist, colonial wars throughout the nineteenth century (in the 1830s and 1840s against Algeria and China); the United States fought a similar war with Mexico in 1848 and intervened again in 1914 under President Wilson. Liberal states are as aggressive and war prone as any other form of government or society in their relations with nonliberal states.

Immanuel Kant offers the best guidance. "Perpetual Peace," written in 1795, predicts the ever-widening pacification of the liberal pacific union, explains that pacification, and at the same time suggests why liberal states are not pacific in their relations with nonliberal states. . . .

Kant shows how republics, once established, lead to peaceful relations. He argues that once the aggressive interests of absolutist monarchies are tamed and once the habit of respect for individual rights is engrained by republican government, wars would appear as the disaster to the people's welfare that he and the other liberals thought them to be. The fundamental reason is this:

> If the consent of the citizens is required in order to decide that war should be declared (and in this constitution it cannot but be the case), nothing is more natural than that they would be very cautious in commencing such a poor game, decreeing for themselves all the calamities of war. Among the latter would be: having to fight, having to pay the costs of war from their own resources, having painfully to repair the devastation war leaves behind, and, to fill up the measure of evils, load themselves with a heavy national debt that would embitter peace itself and that can never be liquidated on account of constant wars in the future. But, on the other hand, in a constitution which is not republican, and under which the subjects are not citizens, a declaration of war is the easiest thing in the world to decide upon, because war does not require of the ruler, who is the proprietor and not a member of the state, the least sacrifice of the pleasure of his table, the chase, his country houses, his court functions, and the like. He may, therefore, resolve on war as on a pleasure party for the most trivial reasons, and with perfect indifference leave the justification which decency requires to the diplomatic corps who are ever ready to provide it.[9]

One could add to Kant's list another source of pacification specific to liberal constitutions. The regular rotation of office in liberal democratic polities is a nontrivial device that helps ensure that personal animosities among heads of government provide no lasting, escalating source of tension.

These domestic republican restraints do not end war. If they did, liberal states would not be warlike, which is far from the case. They do introduce Kant's "caution" in place of monarchical caprice. Liberal wars are only fought for popular, liberal purposes. To see how this removes the occasion of wars among liberal states and not wars between liberal and nonliberal states, we need to shift our attention from constitutional law to international law, Kant's second source.

Complementing the constitutional guarantee of caution, *international law* adds a second source—a guarantee of respect. The separation of nations that asocial sociability encourages is reinforced by the development of separate languages and religions. These further guarantee a world of separate states—an essential condition needed to avoid a "global, soul-less despotism." Yet, at the same time, they also morally integrate liberal states "as culture progresses and men gradually come closer together toward a greater agreement on principles for peace and understanding."[10] As republics emerge (the first source) and as culture progresses, an understanding of the legitimate rights of all citizens and of all republics comes into play; and this, now that caution characterizes policy, sets up the moral foundations for the liberal peace. Correspondingly, international law highlights the importance of Kantian publicity. Domestically, publicity helps ensure that the officials of republics act according to the principles they profess to hold just and according to the interests of the electors they claim to represent. Internationally, free speech and the effective communication of accurate conceptions of the political life of foreign peoples is essential to establish and preserve the understanding on which the guarantee of respect depends. In short, domestically just republics, which rest on consent, presume foreign republics to be also consensual, just, and therefore deserving of accommodation. The experience of cooperation helps engender further cooperative behavior when the consequences of state policy are unclear but (potentially) mutually beneficial.[11]

Lastly, *cosmopolitan law* adds material incentives to moral commitments. The cosmopolitan right to hospitality permits the "spirit of commerce" sooner or later to take hold of very nation, thus impelling states to promote peace and to try to avert war.

Liberal economic theory holds that these cosmopolitan ties derive from a cooperative international division of labor and free trade according to comparative advantage. Each economy is said to be better off than it would have been under autarky; each thus acquires an incentive to avoid policies that would lead the other to break these economic ties. Since keeping open markets rests upon the assumption that the next set of transactions will also be determined by prices rather than coercion, a sense of mutual security is vital to avoid security-motivated searches for economic autarky. Thus, avoiding a challenge to another liberal state's security or even enhancing each other's security by means of alliance naturally follows economic interdependence.

A further cosmopolitan source of liberal peace is that the international market removes difficult decisions of production and distribution from the direct sphere of state policy. A foreign state thus does not appear directly responsible for these outcomes; states can stand aside from, and to some degree above, these contentious market rivalries and be ready to step in to resolve crises. Furthermore, the interdependence of commerce and the connections of state officials help create crosscutting transnational ties that serve as lobbies for mutual accommodation. According to modern liberal scholars, international financiers and transnational, bureaucratic, and domestic organizations create interests in favor of accommodation and have ensured by their variety that no single conflict sours an entire relationship.[12]

No one of these constitutional, international or cosmopolitan sources is alone sufficient, but together (and only where together) they plausibly connect the characteristics of liberal politics and economies with sustained liberal peace. Liberal states have not escaped from the realists' "security dilemma," the insecurity caused by anarchy in the world political system considered as a whole. But the effects of international anarchy have been tamed in the relations among states of a similarly liberal character. Alliances of purely mutual strategic interest among liberal and nonliberal states have been broken, economic ties between liberal and nonliberal states have proven fragile, but the political bond of liberal rights and interests has proven a remarkably firm foundation for mutual nonaggression. A separate peace exists among liberal states.

NOTES

1. Immanuel Kant, "Perpetual Peace" (1795), in *The Philosophy of Kant,* ed. Carl J. Friedrich (New York: Modern Library, 1949), p. 453.
2. There appear to be some exceptions to the tendency for liberal states not to engage in a war with each other. Peru and Ecuador, for example, entered into conflict. But for each, the war came within one to three years after the establishment of a liberal regime, that is, before the pacifying effects of liberalism could become deeply ingrained. The Palestinians and the Israelis clashed frequently along the Lebanese border, which Lebanon could not hold secure from either belligerent. But at the beginning of the 1967 War, Lebanon seems to have sent a flight of its own jets into Israel. The jets were repulsed. Alone among Israel's Arab neighbors, Lebanon engaged in no further hostilities with

Israel. Israel's recent attack on the territory of Lebanon was an attack on a country that had already been occupied by Syria (and the P.L.O.). Whether Israel actually will withdraw (if Syria withdraws) and restore an independent Lebanon is yet to be determined.

3. Thomas Hobbes, *Leviathan* (New York: Penguin, 1980), I, chap. 13, 62, p. 186.

4. Kenneth N. Waltz, *Man, the State, and War* (New York: Columbia University Press, 1954, 1959), pp. 120–23; and see his *Theory of International Politics* (Reading, Mass.: Addison-Wesley, 1979). The classic sources of this form of Realism are Hobbes and, more particularly, Rousseau's "Essay on St. Pierre's Peace Project" and his "State of War" in *A Lasting Peace* (London: Constable, 1917), E. H. Carr's *The Twenty Year's Crisis: 1919–1939* (London: Macmillan & Co., 1951), and the works of Hans Morgenthau.

5. Jervis, "Cooperation under the Security Dilemma," *World Politics* 30, no. 1 (January 1978), pp. 172–86.

6. Robert H. Jackson and Carl G. Rosberg, "Why West Africa's Weak States Persist," *World Politics* 35, no. 1 (October 1962).

7. Raymond Aron, *Peace and War* (New York: Praeger, 1968) pp. 151–54.

8. The incompatibility of democracy and war is forcefully asserted by Paine in *The Rights of Man.* The connection between liberal capitalism, democracy, and peace is argued by, among others, Joseph Schumpeter in *Imperialism and Social Classes* (New York: Meridian, 1955); and Montesquieu, *Spirit of the Laws* I, bk. 20, chap. 1. This literature is surveyed and analyzed by Albert Hirschman, "Rival Interpretations of Market Society: Civilizing, Destructive, or Feeble?" *Journal of Economic Literature* 20 (December 1982).

9. Immanuel Kant, "Perpetual Peace," in *The Enlightenment,* ed. Peter Gay (New York: Simon & Schuster, 1974), pp. 790–92.

10. Kant, *The Philosophy of Kant,* p. 454. These factors also have a bearing on Karl Deutsch's "compatibility of values" and "predictability of behavior" (see n. 20).

11. A highly stylized version of this effect can be found in the realist's "Prisoners' Dilemma" game. There, a failure of mutual trust and the incentives to enhance one's own position produce a noncooperative solution that makes both parties worse off. Contrarily, cooperation, a commitment to avoid exploiting the other party, produces joint gains. The significance of the game in this context is the character of its participants. The "prisoners" are presumed to be felonious, unrelated apart from their partnership in crime, and lacking in mutual trust—competitive nation-states in an anarchic world. A similar game between fraternal or sororal twins—Kant's republics—would be likely to lead to different results. See Robert Jervis, "Hypotheses on Misperception," *World Politics* 20, no. 3 (April 1968), for an exposition of the role of presumptions; and "Cooperation under the Security Dilemma," *World Politics* 30, no. 2 (January 1978), for the factors realists see as mitigating the security dilemma caused by anarchy.

    Also, expectations (including theory and history) can influence behavior, making liberal states expect (and fulfill) pacific policies toward each other. These effects are explored at a theoretical level in R. Dacey, "Some Implications of 'Theory Absorption' for Economic Theory and the Economics Information," in *Philosophical Dimensions of Economics,* ed. J Pitt (Dordrecht, Holland: D. Reidel, 1980).

12. Karl Polanyi, *The Great Transformation* (Boston: Beacon Press, 1944), chaps. 1–2 and Samuel Huntington and Z. Brzezinski, *Political Power: USA/USSR* (New York: Viking Press, 1963, 1964), chap. 9. And see Richard Neustadt, *Alliance Politics* (New York: Columbia University Press, 1970) for a detailed case study of interliberal politics.

Alliances: Balancing and Bandwagoning

Stephen M. Walt

When confronted by a significant external threat, states may either balance or bandwagon. *Balancing* is defined as allying with others against the prevailing threat; *bandwagoning* refers to alignment with the source of danger. Thus two distinct hypotheses about how states will select their alliance partners can be identified on the basis of whether the states ally against or with the principal external threat.[1]

These two hypotheses depict very different worlds. If balancing is more common than bandwagoning, then states are more secure, because aggressors will face combined opposition. But if bandwagoning is the dominant tendency, then security is scarce, because successful aggressors will attract additional allies, enhancing their power while reducing that of their opponents. . . .

BALANCING BEHAVIOR

The belief that states form alliances in order to prevent stronger powers from dominating them lies at the heart of traditional balance-of-power theory. According to this view, states join alliances to protect themselves from states or coalitions whose superior resources could pose a threat. States choose to balance for two main reasons.

First, they place their survival at risk if they fail to curb a potential hegemon before it becomes too strong. To ally with the dominant power means placing one's trust in its continued benevolence. The safer strategy is to join with those who cannot readily dominate their allies, in order to avoid being dominated by those who can. As Winston Churchill explained Britain's traditional alliance policy: "For four hundred years the foreign policy of England has been to oppose the strongest, most aggressive, most dominating power on the Continent. . . . [I]t would have been easy . . . and tempting to join with the stronger and share the fruits of his conquest. However, we always took the harder course, joined with the less strong powers, . . . and thus defeated the Continental military tyrant whoever he was."[2] More recently, Henry Kissinger advocated a rapprochement with China, because he believed that in a triangular relationship, it was better to align with the weaker side.

Second, joining the weaker side increases the new member's influence within the alliance, because the weaker side has greater need for assistance. Allying with the strong side, by contrast, gives the new member little influence (because it adds relatively less to the coalition) and leaves it vulnerable to the whims of its partners. Joining the weaker side should be the preferred choice.

BANDWAGONING BEHAVIOR

The belief that states will balance is unsurprising, given the many familiar examples of states joining together to resist a threatening state or coalition. Yet, despite the powerful evidence that history provides in support of the balancing hypothesis, the belief that the opposite response is more likely is widespread. According to one scholar: "In international politics, nothing succeeds like success. Momentum accrues to the gainer and accelerates his movement. The appearance of irreversibility in his gains enfeebles one side and stimulates the other all the more. The bandwagon collects those on the sidelines."[3]

The bandwagoning hypothesis is especially popular with statesmen seeking to justify overseas involvements or increased military budgets. For example, German admiral Alfred von Tirpitz's famous risk theory rested on this type of logic. By building a great battle fleet, Tirpitz argued, Germany could force England into neutrality or alliance with her by posing a threat to England's vital maritime supremacy.

Bandwagoning beliefs have also been a recurring theme throughout the Cold War. Soviet efforts to intimidate both Norway and Turkey into not joining NATO reveal the Soviet conviction that states will accommodate readily to threats, although these moves merely encouraged Norway and Turkey to align more closely with the West.[4] Soviet officials made a similar error in believing that the growth of Soviet military power in the 1960s and 1970s would lead to a permanent shift in the correlation of forces against the West. Instead, it contributed to a Sino-American rapprochement in the 1970s and the largest peacetime increase in U.S. military power in the 1980s.

American officials have been equally fond of bandwagoning notions. According to NSC–68, the classified study that helped justify a major U.S. military buildup in the 1950s: "In the absence of an affirmative decision [to increase U.S. military capabilities] . . . our friends will become more than a liability to us, they will become a positive increment to Soviet power."[5] President John F. Kennedy once claimed that "if the United States were to falter, the whole world . . . would inevitably begin to move toward the Communist bloc."[6] And though Henry Kissinger often argued that the United States should form balancing alliances to contain the Soviet Union, he apparently believed that U.S. allies were likely to bandwagon. As he put it, "If leaders around the world . . . assume that the U.S. lacked either the forces or the will . . . they will accommodate themselves to what they will regard as the dominant trend."[7] Ronald Reagan's claim, "If we cannot defend ourselves [in Central America] . . . then we cannot expect to prevail else-where. . . . [O]ur credibility will collapse and our alliances will crumble," reveals the same logic in a familiar role—that of justifying overseas intervention.[8]

Balancing and bandwagoning are usually framed solely in terms of capabilities. Balancing is alignment with the weaker side, bandwagoning with the stronger. This conception should be revised, however, to account for the other factors that statemen consider when deciding with whom to ally. Although power is an important part of the equation, it is not the only one. It is more accurate to say that states tend to ally with or against the foreign power that poses the greatest threat. For example, states may balance by allying with other strong states if a weaker power is more dangerous for other reasons. Thus the coalitions that defeated Germany in World War I and World War II were vastly superior in total resources, but they came together when it became clear that the aggressive aims of the Wilhelmines and Nazis posed the greater danger. Because balancing and bandwagoning are more accurately viewed as a response to threats, it is important to consider other factors that will affect the level of threat that states may pose: aggregate power, geographic proximity, offensive power, and aggressive intentions. . . .

By defining the basic hypotheses in terms of threats rather than power alone, we gain a more complete picture of the factors that statesmen will consider when making alliance choices. One cannot determine a priori, however, which sources of threat will be most important in any given case; one can say only that all of them are likely to play a role. And the greater the threat, the greater the probability that the vulnerable state will seek an alliance.

THE IMPLICATIONS OF BALANCING AND BANDWAGONING

The two general hypotheses of balancing and bandwagoning paint starkly contrasting pictures of international politics. Resolving the question of which hypothesis is more accurate is especially important, because each implies very different policy prescriptions. What sort of world does each depict, and what policies are implied?

If balancing is the dominant tendency, then threatening states will provoke others to align against them. Because those who seek to dominate others will attract widespread opposition, status quo states can take a relatively sanguine view of threats. Credibility is less important in a balancing world, because one's allies will resist threatening states out of their own self-interest, not because they expect others to do it for them. Thus the fear of allies defecting will decline.

Moreover, if balancing is the norm and if statesmen understand this tendency, aggression will be discouraged because those who contemplate it will anticipate resistance.

In a balancing world, policies that convey restraint and benevolence are best. Strong states may be valued as allies because they have much to offer their partners, but they must take particular care to avoid appearing aggressive. Foreign and defense policies that minimize the threat one poses to others make the most sense in such a world.

A bandwagoning world, by contrast, is much more competitive. If states tend to ally with those who seem most dangerous, then great powers will be rewarded if they appear both strong and potentially aggressive. International rivalries will be more intense, because a single defeat may signal the decline of one side and the ascendancy of the other. This situation is especially alarming in a bandwagoning world, because additional defections and a further decline in position are to be expected. Moreover, if statesmen believe that bandwagoning is widespread, they will be more inclined to use force. This tendency is true for both aggressors and status quo powers. The former will use force because they will assume that others will be unlikely to balance against them and because they can attract more allies through belligerence or brinkmanship. The latter will follow suit because they will fear the gains their opponents will make by appearing powerful and resolute.[9]

Finally, misperceiving the relative propensity to balance or bandwagon is dangerous, because the policies that are appropriate for one situation will backfire in the other. If statesmen follow the balancing prescription in a bandwagoning world, their moderate responses and relaxed view of threats will encourage their allies to defect, leaving them isolated against an overwhelming coalition. Conversely, following the bandwagoning prescription in a world of balancers (employing power and threats frequently) will lead others to oppose you more and more vigorously.[10]

These concerns are not merely theoretical. In the 1930s, France failed to recognize that her allies in the Little Entente were prone to bandwagon, a tendency that French military and diplomatic policies reinforced. As noted earlier, Soviet attempts to intimidate Turkey and Norway after World War II reveal the opposite error; they merely provoked a greater U.S. commitment to these regions and cemented their entry into NATO. Likewise, the self-encircling bellicosity of Wilhelmine Germany and Imperial Japan reflected the assumption, prevalent in both states, that bandwagoning was the dominant tendency in international affairs.

WHEN DO STATES BALANCE? WHEN DO THEY BANDWAGON?

These examples highlight the importance of identifying whether states are more likely to balance or bandwagon and which sources of threat have the greatest impact on the decision. . . . In general, we should expect balancing behavior to be much more common than bandwagoning, and we should expect bandwagoning to occur only under certain identifiable conditions.

Although many statesmen fear that potential allies will align with the strongest side, this fear receives little support from most of international history. For example, every attempt to achieve hegemony in Europe since the Thirty Years War has been thwarted by a defensive coalition formed precisely for the purpose of defeating the potential hegemon. Other examples are equally telling. Although isolated cases of bandwagoning do occur, the great powers have shown a remarkable tendency to ignore other temptations and follow the balancing prescription when necessary.

This tendency should not surprise us. Balancing should be preferred for the simple reason that no statesman can be completely sure of what another will do. Bandwagoning is dangerous because it increases the resources available to a threatening power and requires placing trust in its continued forbearance. Because perceptions are unreliable and intentions can change, it is safer to balance against potential threats than to rely on the hope that a state will remain benevolently disposed.

But if balancing is to be expected, bandwagoning remains a possibility. Several factors may affect the relative propensity for states to select this course.

Strong Versus Weak States

In general, the weaker the state, the more likely it is to bandwagon rather than balance. This situation occurs because weak states add little to the strength of a defensive coalition but incur the wrath of the more threatening states nonetheless. Because weak states can do little to affect the outcome (and may suffer grievously in the process), they must choose the winning side. Only when their decision can affect the outcome is it rational for them to join the weaker alliance. By contrast, strong states can turn a losing coalition into a winning one. And because their decision may mean the difference between victory and defeat, they are likely to be amply rewarded for their contribution.

Weak states are also likely to be especially sensitive to proximate power. Where great powers have both global interests and global capabilities, weak states will be concerned primarily with events in their immediate vicinity. Moreover, weak states can be exceped to balance when threatened by states with roughly equal capabilities but they will be tempted to bandwagon when threatened by a great power. Obviously, when the great power is capable of rapid and effective action (i.e., when its offensive capabilities are especially strong), this temptation will be even greater.

The Availability of Allies

States will also be tempted to bandwagon when allies are simply unavailable. This statement is not simply tautological, because states may balance by mobilizing their own resources instead of relying on allied support. They are more likely to do so, however, when they are confident that allied assistance will be available. Thus a further prerequisite for balancing behavior is an effective system of diplomatic communication. The ability to communicate enables potential allies to recognize their shared interests and coordinate their responses. If weak states see no possibility of outside assistance, however, they may be forced to accommodate the most imminent threat. Thus the first Shah of Iran saw the British withdrawal from Kandahar in 1881 as a signal to bandwagon with Russia. As he told the British representative, all he had received from Great Britain was "good advice and honeyed words—nothing else."[11] Finland's policy of partial alignment with the Soviet Union suggests the same lesson. When Finland joined forces with Nazi Germany during World War II, it alienated the potential allies (the United States and Great Britain) that might otherwise have helped protect it from Soviet pressure after the war.

Of course, excessive confidence in allied support will encourage weak states to free-ride, relying on the efforts of others to provide security. Free-riding is the optimal policy for a weak state, because its efforts will contribute little in any case. Among the great powers, the belief that allies are readily available encourages buck-passing; states that are threatened strive to pass to others the burdens of standing up to the aggressor. Neither response is a form of bandwagoning, but both suggest that effective balancing behavior is more likely to occur when members of an alliance are not convinced that their partners are unconditionally loyal.

Taken together, these factors help explain the formation of spheres of influence surrounding the great powers. Although strong neighbors of strong states are likely to balance, small and weak neighbors of the great powers may be more inclined to bandwagon. Because they will be the first victims of expansion, because they lack the capabilities to stand alone, and because a defensive alliance may operate too slowly to do them much good, accommodating a threatening great power may be tempting.

Peace and War

Finally, the context in which alliance choices are made will affect decisions to balance or bandwagon. States are more likely to balance in peacetime or in the early stages of a war, as they seek to deter or defeat the powers posing the greatest threat. But once the outcome appears certain, some will be tempted to defect from the losing side at an opportune moment. Thus both Rumania and Bulgaria allied with Nazi Germany initially and then abandoned Germany for the Allies, as the tides of war ebbed and flowed across Europe in World War II.

The restoration of peace, however, restores the incentive to balance. As many observers have noted, victorious coalitions are likely to disintegrate with the conclusion of peace. Prominent examples include Austria and Prussia after their war with Denmark in 1864. Britain and France after World War I, the Soviet Union and the United States after World War II, and China and Vietnam after the U.S. withdrawal from Vietnam. This recurring pattern provides further support for the proposition that balancing is the dominant tendency in international politics and that bandwagoning is the opportunistic exception.

SUMMARY OF HYPOTHESES ON BALANCING AND BANDWAGONING

Hypotheses on Balancing

1. *General form:* States facing an external threat will align with others to oppose the states posing the threat.
2. The greater the threatening state's aggregate power, the greater the tendency for others to align against it.
3. The nearer a powerful state, the greater the tendency for those nearby to align against it. Therefore, neighboring states are less likely to be allies than are states separated by at least one other power.
4. The greater a state's offensive capabilities, the greater the tendency for others to align against it. Therefore, states with offensively oriented military capabilities are likely to provoke other states to form defensive coalitions.
5. The more aggressive a state's perceived intentions, the more likely others are to align against that state.
6. Alliances formed during wartime will disintegrate when the enemy is defeated.

Hypotheses on Bandwagoning

The hypotheses on bandwagoning are the opposite of those on balancing.

1. *General form:* States facing an external threat will ally with the most threatening power.
2. The greater a state's aggregate capabilities, the greater the tendency for others to align with it.
3. The nearer a powerful state, the greater the tendency for those nearby to align with it.
4. The greater a state's offensive capabilities, the greater the tendency for others to align with it.
5. The more aggressive a state's perceived intentions, the less likely other states are to align against it.
6. Alliances formed to oppose a threat will disintegrate when the threat becomes serious.

Hypotheses on the Conditions Favoring Balancing or Bandwagoning

1. Balancing is more common than bandwagoning.
2. The stronger the state, the greater its tendency to balance. Weak states will balance against other weak states but may bandwagon when threatened by great powers.
3. The greater the probability of allied support, the greater the tendency to balance. When adequate allied support is certain, however, the tendency for free-riding or buck-passing increases.

4. The more unalterably aggressive a state is perceived to be, the greater the tendency for others to balance against it.

5. In wartime, the closer one side is to victory, the greater the tendency for others to bandwagon with it.

NOTES

1. My use of the terms *balancing* and *bandwagoning* follows that of Kenneth Waltz (who credits it to Stephen Van Evera) in his *Theory of International Politics* (Reading, Mass., 1979). Arnold Wolfers uses a similar terminology in his essay "The Balance of Power in Theory and Practice," in *Discord and Collaboration: Essays on International Politics* (Baltimore, Md., 1962), pp. 122–24.

2. Winston S. Churchill, *The Second World War,* vol. 1: *The Gathering Storm* (Boston, 1948), pp. 207–8.

3. W. Scott Thompson, "The Communist International System," *Orbis* 20, no. 4 (1977).

4. For the effects of the Soviet pressure on Turkey, see George Lenczowski, *The Middle East in World Affairs,* 4th ed. (Ithaca, 1980), pp. 134–38; and Bruce R. Kuniholm, *The Origins of the Cold War in the Near East* (Princeton, N.J., 1980), pp. 355–78. For the Norwegian response to Soviet pressure, see Herbert Feis, *From Trust to Terror: The Onset of the Cold War, 1945–50* (New York, 1970), p. 381; and Geir Lundestad, *America, Scandinavia, and the Cold War: 1945–1949* (New York, 1980), pp. 308–9.

5. NSC–68 ("United States Objectives and Programs for National Security"), reprinted in Gaddis and Etzold, *Containment,* p. 404. Similar passages can be found on pp. 389, 414, and 434.

6. Quoted in Seyom Brown, *The Faces of Power: Constancy and Change in United States Foreign Policy from Truman to Johnson* (New York, 1968), p. 217.

7. Quoted in U.S. House Committee on Foreign Affairs, *The Soviet Union and the Third World: Watershed in Great Power Policy?* 97th Cong., 1st sess., 1977, pp. 157–58.

8. *New York Times,* April 28, 1983, p. A12. In the same speech, Reagan also said: "If Central America were to fall, what would the consequences be for our position in Asia and Europe and for alliances such as NATO? . . . Which ally, which friend would trust us then?"

9. It is worth noting that Napoleon and Hitler underestimated the costs of aggression by assuming that their potential enemies would bandwagon. After Munich, for example, Hitler dismissed the possibility of opposition by claiming that British and French statesmen were "little worms." Napoleon apparently believed that England could not "reasonably make war on us unaided" and assumed that the Peace of Amiens guaranteed that England had abandoned its opposition to France. On these points, see Fest, *Hitler,* pp. 594–95; Liska, *Nations in Alliance,* p. 45; and Geoffrey Bruun, *Europe and the French Imperium: 1799–1814* (New York, 1938), p. 118. Because Hitler and Napoleon believed in a bandwagoning world, they were excessively eager to go to war.

10. This situation is analogous to Robert Jervis's distinction between the deterrence model and the spiral model. The former calls for opposition to a suspected aggressor, the latter for appeasement. Balancing and bandwagoning are the alliance equivalents of deterring and appeasing. See Robert Jervis, *Perception and Misperception in International Politics* (Princeton, N.J., 1976), chap. 3.

11. Quoted in C. J. Lowe, *The Reluctant Imperialists* (New York, 1967), p. 85.

The Future of Diplomacy

Hans J. Morgenthau

FOUR TASKS OF DIPLOMACY

. . . Diplomacy [is] an element of national power. The importance of diplomacy for the preservation of international peace is but a particular aspect of that general function. For a diplomacy that ends in war has failed in its primary objective: the promotion of the national interest by peaceful means. This has always been so and is particularly so in view of the destructive potentialities of total war.

Taken in its widest meaning, comprising the whole range of foreign policy, the task of diplomacy is fourfold: (1) Diplomacy must determine its objectives in the light of the power actually and potentially available for the pursuit of these objectives. (2) Diplomacy must assess the objectives of other nations and the power actually and potentially available for the pursuit of these objectives. (3) Diplomacy must determine to what extent these different objectives are compatible with each other. (4) Diplomacy must employ the means suited to the pursuit of its objectives. Failure in any one of these tasks may jeopardize the success of foreign policy and with it the peace of the world.

A nation that sets itself goals which it has not the power to attain may have to face the risk of war on two counts. Such a nation is likely to dissipate its strength and not to be strong enough at all points of friction to deter a hostile nation from challenging it beyond endurance. The failure of its foreign policy may force the nation to retrace its steps and to redefine its objectives in view of its actual strength. Yet it is more likely that, under the pressure of an inflamed public opinion, such a nation will go forward on the road toward an unattainable goal, strain all its resources to achieve it, and finally, confounding the national interest with that goal, seek in war the solution to a problem that cannot be solved by peaceful means.

A nation will also invite war if its diplomacy wrongly assesses the objectives of other nations and the power at their disposal. . . . A nation that mistakes a policy of imperialism for a policy of the status quo will be unprepared to meet the threat to its own existence which the other nation's policy entails. Its weakness will invite attack and may make war inevitable. A nation that mistakes a policy of the status quo for a policy of imperialism will evoke through its disproportionate reaction the very danger of war which it is trying to avoid. For as A mistakes B's policy for imperialism, so B might mistake A's defensive reaction for imperialism. Thus both nations, each intent upon forestalling imaginary aggression from the other side, will rush to arms. Similarly, the confusion of one type of imperialism with another may call for disproportionate reaction and thus evoke the risk of war.

As for the assessment of the power of other nations, either to overrate or to underrate it may be equally fatal to the cause of peace. By overrating the power of B, A may prefer to yield to B's demands until, finally, A is forced to fight for its very existence under the most unfavorable conditions. By underrating the power of B, A may become overconfident in its assumed superiority. A may advance demands and impose conditions upon B which the latter is supposedly too weak to resist. Unsuspecting B's actual power of resistance, A may be faced with the alternative of either retreating and conceding defeat or of advancing and risking war.

A nation that seeks to pursue an intelligent and peaceful foreign policy cannot cease comparing its own objectives and the objectives of other nations in the light of their compatibility. If they are compatible, no problem arises. If they are not compatible, nation A must determine whether its objectives are so vital to itself that they must be pursued despite that incompatibility with the objectives of B. If it is found that A's vital interests can be safeguarded without the attainment of these objectives, they ought to be abandoned. On the other hand, if A finds that these objectives are essential for its vital interests, A must then ask itself whether B's objectives, incompatible with its own, are essential for B's vital interests. If the answer seems to be in the negative, A must try to induce B to abandon its objectives, offering B equivalents not vital to A. In other words, through diplomatic bargaining, the give and take of compromise, a way must be sought by which the interests of A and B can be reconciled.

Finally, if the incompatible objectives of A and B should prove to be vital to either side, a way might still be sought in which the vital interests of A and B might be redefined, reconciled, and their objectives thus made compatible with each other. Here, however—even provided that both sides pursue intelligent and peaceful policies—A and B are moving dangerously close to the brink of war.

It is the final task of an intelligent diplomacy, intent upon preserving peace, to choose the appropriate means for pursuing its objectives. The means at the disposal of diplomacy are three: persuasion, compromise, and threat of force. No diplomacy relying only upon the threat of force can claim to be both intelligent and peaceful. No diplomacy that would stake everything on persuasion and compromise deserves to be called intelligent. Rarely, if ever, in the conduct of the foreign policy of a great power is there justification for using only one method to the exclusion of the others. Generally, the diplomatic representative of a great power, in order to be able to serve both the interests of his country and the interests of peace, must at the same time use persuasion, hold out the advantages of a compromise, and impress the other side with the military strength of his country.

The art of diplomacy consists in putting the right emphasis at any particular moment on each of these three means at its disposal. A diplomacy that has been successfully discharged in its other functions may well fail in advancing the national interest and preserving peace if it stresses persuasion when the give and take of compromise is primarily required by the circumstances of the case. A diplomacy that puts most of its eggs in the basket of compromise when the military might of the nation should be predominantly displayed, or stresses military might when the political situation calls for persuasion and compromise, will likewise fail. . . .

The Promise of Diplomacy: Its Nine Rules[1]

Diplomacy could revive if it would part with [the] vices, which in recent years have well-nigh destroyed its usefulness, and if it would restore the techniques which have controlled the mutual relations of nations since time immemorial. By doing so, however, diplomacy would realize only one of the preconditions for the preservation of peace. The contribution of a revived diplomacy to the cause of peace would depend upon the methods and purposes of its use. . . .

We have already formulated the four main tasks with which a foreign policy must cope successfully in order to be able to promote the national interest and preserve peace. It remains for us now to reformulate those tasks in the light of the special problems with which contemporary world politics confront diplomacy. . . .

The main reason for [the] threatening aspect of contemporary world politics [lies] in the character of modern war, which has changed profoundly under the impact of nationalistic universalism* and modern technology. The effects of modern technology cannot be undone. The only variable that remains subject to deliberate manipulation is the new moral force of nationalistic universalism. The attempt to reverse the trend toward war through the techniques of a revived diplomacy must start with this phenomenon. That means, in negative terms, that a revived diplomacy will have a chance to preserve peace only when it is not used as the instrument of a political religion aiming at universal dominion.

Four Fundamental Rules

Diplomacy Must Be Divested of the Crusading Spirit   This is the first of the rules that diplomacy can neglect only at the risk of war. In the words of William Graham Sumner:

> If you want war, nourish a doctrine. Doctrines are the most frightful tyrants to which men ever are subject, because doctrines get inside of a man's own reason and betray him against himself. Civilised men have done their fiercest fighting for doctrines. The reconquest of the Holy Sepulcher, "the balance of power," "no universal dominion," "trade follows the flag," "he who holds the land will hold the sea," "the throne and the altar," the revolution, the faith—these are the things for which men have given their lives. . . . Now when any doctrine arrives at that degree of authority, the name of it is a

---

*[Editors' Note: By this term Professor Morgenthau refers to the injection of ideology into international politics and to each nation's claim that its own ethical code would serve as the basis of international conduct for all nations.]

club which any demagogue may swing over you at any time and apropos of anything. In order to describe a doctrine, we must have resource to theological language. A doctrine is an article of faith. It is something which you are bound to believe, not because you have some rational grounds for believing it is true, but because you belong to such and such a church or denomination. . . . A policy in a state we can understand; for instance, it was the policy of the United States at the end of the eighteenth century to get the free navigation of the Mississippi to its mouth, even at the expense of war with Spain. That policy had reason and justice in it; it was founded in our interests; it had positive form and definite scope. A doctrine is an abstract principle; it necessarily absolute in its scope and abstruse in its terms; it is metaphysical assertion. It is never true, because it is absolute, and the affairs of men are all conditioned and relative. . . . Now to turn back to politics, just think what an abomination in statecraft an abstract doctrine must be. Any politician or editor can, at any moment, put a new extension on it. The people acquiesce in the doctrine and applaud it because they hear the politicians and editors repeat it, and the politicians and editors repeat it because they think it is popular. So it grows. . . . It may mean anything or nothing, at any moment, and no one knows how it will be. You accede to it now, within the vague limits of what you suppose it to be; therefore, you will have to accede to it tomorrow when the same name is made to cover something which you never have heard or thought of. If you allow a political catchword to go on and grow, you will awaken some day to find it standing over you, the arbiter of your destiny, against which you are powerless, as men are powerless against delusions. . . . What can be more contrary to sound statesmanship and common sense than to put forth an abstract assertion which has no definite relation to any interest of ours now at stake, but which has in it any number of possibilities of producing complications which we cannot foresee, but which are sure to be embarrassing when they arise![2]

The Wars of Religion have shown that the attempt to impose one's own religion as the only true one upon the rest of the world is as futile as it is costly. A century of almost unprecedented bloodshed, devastation, and barbarization was needed to convince the contestants that the two religions could live together in mutual toleration. The two political religions of our time have taken the place of the two great Christian denominations of the sixteenth and seventeenth centuries. Will the political religions of our time need the lesson of the Thirty Years' War, or will they rid themselves in time of the universalistic aspirations that inevitably issue in inconclusive war?

Upon the answer to that question depends the cause of peace. For only if it is answered in the affirmative can a moral consensus, emerging from shared convictions and common values, develop—a moral consensus within which a peace-preserving diplomacy will have a chance to grow. Only then will diplomacy have a chance to face the concrete political problems that require peaceful solution. If the objectives of foreign policy are not to be defined in terms of a world-embracing political religion, how are they to be defined? This is a fundamental problem to be solved once the crusading aspirations of nationalistic universalism have been discarded.

The Objectives of Foreign Policy Must Be Defined in Terms of the National Interest and Must Be Supported with Adequate Power   This is the second rule of a peace-preserving diplomacy. The national interest of a peace-loving nation can only be defined in terms of national security, and national security must be defined as integrity of the national territory and of its institutions. National security, then, is the irreducible minimum that diplomacy must defend with adequate power without compromise. But diplomacy must ever be alive to the radical transformation that national security has undergone under the impact of the nuclear age. Until the advent of that age, a nation could use its diplomacy to purchase its security at the expense of another nation. Today, short of a radical change in the atomic balance of power in favor of a particular nation, diplomacy, in order to make one nation secure from nuclear destruction, must make them all secure. With the national interest defined in such restrictive and transcendent terms, diplomacy must observe the third of its rules.

Diplomacy Must Look at the Political Scene from the Point of View of Other Nations   "Nothing is so fatal to a nation as an extreme of self-partiality, and the total want of consideration of what others will naturally hope or fear."[3] What are the national interests of other nations in terms of national security and are they compatible with one's own? The definition of the national interest in terms of national security is easier, and the interests of the two opposing nations are more likely to be compatible in a bipolar system than in any other system of the balance of power. The bipolar system, as we have seen, is more unsafe from the point of view of peace than any other, when both blocs are in competitive contact throughout the world and the ambition of both is fired by the crusading zeal of a universal mission. ". . . Vicinity, or nearness of situation, constitutes nations natural enemies."[4]

Yet once they have defined their national interests in terms of national security, they can draw back from their outlying positions, located close to, or within, the sphere of national security of the other side, and retreat into their respective spheres, each self-contained within its orbit. Those outlying positions add nothing to national security; they are but liabilities, positions that cannot be held in case of war. Each bloc will be the more secure the wider it makes the distance that separates both spheres of national security. Each side can draw a line far distant from each other, making it understood that to touch or even to approach it means war. What then about the interjacent spaces, stretching between the two lines of demarcation? Here the fourth rule of diplomacy applies.

Nations Must Be Willing to Compromise on All Issues that Are Not Vital to Them

> All government, indeed every human benefit and enjoyment, every virtue and every prudent act, is founded on compromise and barter. We balance inconveniences; we give and take; we remit some rights, that we may enjoy others; and we choose rather to be happy citizens than subtle disputants. As we must give away some natural liberties, for the advantages to be derived from the communion and fellowship of a great empire. But, in all fair dealings, the thing bought must bear some proportion to the purchase paid. None will barter away the immediate jewel of his soul.[5]

Here diplomacy meets its most difficult task. For minds not beclouded by the crusading zeal of a political religion and capable of viewing the national interests of both sides with objectivity, the delimitation of these vital interests should not prove too difficult. Compromise on secondary issues is a different matter. Here the task is not to separate and define interests that by their very nature already tend toward separation and definition, but to keep in balance interests that touch each other at many points and may be intertwined beyond the possibility of separation. It is an immense task to allow the other side a certain influence in those interjacent spaces without allowing them to be absorbed into the orbit of the other side. It is hardly a less immense task to keep the other side's influence as small as possible in the regions close to one's own security zone without absorbing those regions into one's own orbit. For the performance of these tasks, no formula stands ready for automatic application. It is only through a continuous process of adaptation, supported both by firmness and self-restraint, that compromise on secondary issues can be made to work. It is, however, possible to indicate a priori what approaches will facilitate or hamper the success of policies of compromise.

First of all, it is worth noting to what extent the success of compromise—that is, compliance with the fourth rule—depends upon compliance with the other three rules, which in turn are similarly interdependent. As the compliance with the second rule depends upon the realization of the first, so the third rule must await its realization from compliance with the second. A nation can only take a rational view of its national interests after it has parted company with the crusading spirit of a political creed. A nation is able to consider the national interests of the other side with objectivity only after it has become secure in what it considers its own national interests. Compromise on any issue, however minor, is impossible so long as both sides are not secure in their national interests. Thus nations cannot hope to comply with the fourth rule if they are not willing to comply with the other three. Both morality and expediency require compliance with these four fundamental rules.

Compliance makes compromise possible, but it does not assure its success. To give compromise, made possible through compliance with the first three rules, a chance to succeed, five other rules must be observed.

Five Prerequisites of Compromise

Give up the Shadow of Worthless Rights for the Substance of Real Advantage   A diplomacy that thinks in legalistic and propagandistic terms is particularly tempted to insist upon the letter of the law, as it interprets the law, and to lose sight of the consequences such insistence may have for its own nation and for humanity. Since there are rights to be defended, this kind of diplomacy thinks that the issue cannot be compromised. Yet the choice that confronts the diplomat is not between legality and illegality, but between political wisdom and political folly. "The question with me," said Edmund Burke, "is not whether you have a right to render your people miserable, but whether it is not your interest to make them happy. It is not what a lawyer tells me I *may* do, but what humanity, reason and justice tell me I ought to do."[6]

Never Put Yourself in a Position from Which You Cannot Retreat Without Losing Face and from Which You Cannot Advance Without Grave Risks   The violation of this rule often results from disregard for the preceding one. A diplomacy that confounds the shadow of legal right with the actuality of political advantage is likely to find itself in a position where it may have a legal right, but no political business, to be. In other words, a nation may identify itself with a position, which it may or may not have a right to hold, regardless of the political consequences. And again compromise becomes a difficult matter. A nation cannot retreat from that position without incurring a serious loss of prestige. It cannot advance from that position without exposing itself to political risks, perhaps even the risk of war. That heedless rush into untenable positions and, more particularly, the stubborn refusal to extricate oneself from them in time is the earmark of incompetent diplomacy. Its classic examples are the policy of Napoleon III on the eve of the Franco-Prussian War of 1870 and the policies of Austria and Germany on the eve of the First World War. These examples also show how closely the risk of war is allied with the violation of this rule.

Never Allow a Weak Ally to Make Decisions for You   Strong nations that are oblivious to the preceding rules are particularly susceptible to violating this one. They lose their freedom of action by identifying their own national interests completely with those of the weak ally. Secure in the support of its powerful friend, the weak ally can choose the objectives and methods of its foreign policy to suit itself. The powerful nation then finds that it must support interests not its own and that it is unable to compromise on issues that are vital not to itself, but only to its ally.

The classic example of the violation of this rule is to be found in the way in which Turkey forced the hand of Great Britain and France on the eve of the Crimean War in 1853. The Concert of Europe had virtually agreed upon a compromise settling the conflict between Russia and Turkey, when Turkey, knowing that the Western powers would support it in a war with Russia, did its best to provoke that war and thus involved Great Britain and France in it against their will. Thus Turkey went far in deciding the issue of war and peace for Great Britain and France according to its own national interests. Great Britain and France had to accept that decision even though their national interests did not require war with Russia and they had almost succeeded in preventing its outbreak. They had surrendered their freedom of action to a weak ally, which used its control over their policies for its own purposes.

The Armed Forces Are the Instrument of Foreign Policy, Not Its Master
No successful and no peaceful foreign policy is possible without observance of this rule. No nation can pursue a policy of compromise with the military determining the ends and means of foreign policy. The armed forces are instruments of war; foreign policy is an instrument of peace. It is true that the ultimate objectives of the conduct of war and of the conduct of foreign policy are identical: Both serve the national interest. Both, however, differ fundamentally in their immediate objective, in the means they employ, and in the modes of thought they bring to bear upon their respective tasks.

The objective of war is simple and unconditional: to break the will of the enemy. Its methods are equally simple and unconditional: to bring the greatest amount of violence to bear upon the most vulnerable spot in the enemy's armor. Consequently, the military leader must think in absolute terms. He lives in the present and in the immediate future. The sole question before him is how to win victories as cheaply and quickly as possible and how to avoid defeat.

The objective of foreign policy is relative and conditional: to bend, not to break, the will of the other side as far as necessary in order to safeguard one's own vital interests without hurting those of the other side. The methods of foreign policy are relative and conditional: not to advance by destroying the obstacles in one's way, but to retreat before them, to circumvent them, to maneuver around them, to soften and dissolve them slowly by means of persuasion, negotiation, and pressure. In consequence, the mind of the diplomat is complicated and subtle. It sees the issue in hand as a moment in history, and beyond the victory of tomorrow it anticipates the incalculable possibilities of the future. In the words of Bolingbroke:

> Here let me only say, that the glory of taking towns, and winning battles, is to be measured by the utility that results from those victories. Victories that bring honour to the arms, may bring shame to the councils, of a nation. To win a battle, to take a town, is the glory of a general, and of an army. . . . But the glow of a nation is to proportion the ends she proposes, to her interest and her strength; the means she employs to the ends she proposes, and the vigour she exerts to both.[7]

To surrender the conduct of foreign affairs to the military, then, is to destroy the possibility of compromise and thus surrender the cause of peace. The military mind knows how to operate between the absolutes of victory and defeat. It knows nothing of that patient intricate and subtle maneuvering of diplomacy, whose main purpose is to avoid the absolutes of victory and defeat and meet the other side on the middle ground of negotiated compromise. A foreign policy conducted by military men according to the rules of the military art can only end in war, for "what we prepare for is what we shall get."[8]

For nations conscious of the potentialities of modern war, peace must be the goal of their foreign policies. Foreign policy must be conducted in such a way as to make the preservation of peace possible and not make the outbreak of war inevitable. In a society of sovereign nations, military force is a necessary instrument of foreign policy. Yet the instrument of foreign policy should not become the master of foreign policy. As war is fought in order to make peace possible, foreign policy should be conducted in order to make peace permanent. For the performance of both tasks, the subordination of the military under the civilian authorities which are constitutionally responsible for the conduct of foreign affairs is an indispensable prerequisite.

The Government Is the Leader of Public Opinion, Not Its Slave   Those responsible for the conduct of foreign policy will not be able to comply with the foregoing principles of diplomacy if they do not keep this principle constantly in mind. As has been pointed out above in greater detail, the rational requirements of good foreign policy cannot from the outset count upon the support of a public opinion whose preferences are emotional rather than rational. This is bound to be particularly true of a foreign policy whose goal is compromise, and which, therefore, must concede some of the objectives of the other side and give up some of its own. Especially when foreign policy is conducted under conditions of democratic control and is inspired by the crusading zeal of a political religion, statesmen are always tempted to sacrifice the requirements of good foreign policy to the applause of the masses. On the other hand, the statesmen who would defend the integrity of these requirements against even the slightest contamination with popular passion would seal his own doom as a political leader and, with it, the doom of his foreign policy, for he would lose the popular support which put and keeps him in power.

The statesman, then, is allowed neither to surrender to popular passions nor disregard them. He must strike a prudent balance between adapting himself to them and marshaling them to the support of his policies. In one word, he must lead. He must perform that highest feat of statesmanship: trimming his sails to the winds of popular passion while using them to carry the ship to the port of good foreign policy, on however roundabout and zigzag a course.

CONCLUSION

The road to international peace which we have outlined cannot compete in inspirational qualities with the simple and fascinating formulae that for a century and a half have fired the imagination of a war-weary world. There is something spectacular in the radial simplicity of a formula that with one sweep seems to dispose of the problem of war once and for all. This has been the promise of such solutions as free trade, arbitration, disarmament, collective security, universal socialism, international government, and the world state. There is nothing spectacular, fascinating, or inspiring, at least for the people at large, in the business of diplomacy.

We have made the point, however, that these solutions, insofar as they deal with the real problem and not merely with some of its symptoms, presuppose the existence of an integrated international society, which actually does not exist. To bring into existence such an international society and keep it in being, the accommodating techniques of diplomacy are required. As the integration of domestic society and its peace develop from the unspectacular and almost unnoticed day-by-day operations of the techniques of accommodation and change, so the ultimate ideal of international life—that is, to transcend itself in a supranational society—must await its realization from the techniques of persuasion, negotiation, and pressure, which are the traditional instruments of diplomacy.

The reader who has followed us to this point may well ask: But has not diplomacy failed in preventing war in the past? To that legitimate question two answers can be given.

Diplomacy has failed many times, and it has succeeded many times, in its peace-preserving task. It has failed sometimes because nobody wanted it to succeed. We have seen how different in their objectives and methods the limited wars of the past have been from the total war of our time. When war was the normal activity of kings, the task of diplomacy was not to prevent it, but to bring it about at the most propitious moment.

On the other hand, when nations have used diplomacy for the purpose of preventing war, they have often succeeded. The outstanding example of a successful war-preventing diplomacy in modern times is the Congress of Berlin of 1878. By the peaceful means of an accommodating diplomacy, that Congress settled, or at least made susceptible of settlement, the issues that had separated Great Britain and Russia since the end of the Napoleonic Wars. During the better part of the nineteenth century, the conflict between Great Britain and Russia over the Balkans, the Dardanelles, and the Eastern Mediterranean hung like a suspended sword over the peace of the world. Yet, during the fifty years following the Crimean War, though hostilities between Great Britain and Russia threatened to break out time and again, they never actually did break out. The main credit for the preservation of peace must go to the techniques of an accommodating diplomacy which culminated in the Congress of Berlin. When British Prime Minister Disraeli returned from that Congress to London, he declared with pride that he was bringing home "peace . . . with honor." In fact, he had brought peace for later generations, too; for a century there has been no war between Great Britain and Russia.

We have, however, recognized the precariousness of peace in a society of sovereign nations. The continuing success of diplomacy in preserving peace depends, as we have seen, upon extraordinary moral and intellectual qualities that all the leading participants must possess. A mistake in the evaluation of one of the elements of national power, made by one or the other of the leading statesmen, may spell the difference between peace and war. So may an accident spoiling a plan or a power calculation.

Diplomacy is the best means of preserving peace which a society of sovereign nations has to offer, but, especially under the conditions of contemporary world politics and of contemporary war, it is not good enough. It is only when nations have surrendered to a higher authority the means of destruction which modern technology has put in their hands—when they have given up their sovereignty—that international peace can be made as secure as domestic peace. Diplomacy, can make peace more secure than it is today, and the world state can make peace more secure than it would be if nations were to abide by the rules of diplomacy. Yet, as there can be no permanent peace without a world state, there can be no world state without the peace-preserving and community-building processes of diplomacy. For the world state to be more than a dim vision, the accommodating processes of diplomacy, mitigating and minimizing conflicts, must be revived. Whatever one's conception of the ultimate state of international affairs may be, in the recognition of that need and in the demand that it be met all men of good will can join.

NOTES

1. We by no means intend to give here an exhaustive account of rules of diplomacy. We propose to discuss only those which seem to have a special bearing upon the contemporary situation.
2. "War." *Essays of William Graham Sumner* (New Haven, Conn.: Yale University Press, 1934), vol. I, pp. 169 ff.

3. Edmund Burke, "Remarks on the Policy of the Allies with Respect to France" (1793), *Works,* vol. IV (Boston: Little, Brown and Company, 1889), p. 447.
4. *The Federalist,* no. 6.
5. Edmund Burke, "Speech on the Conciliation with America," *loc. cit.,* vol. II, p. 169.
6. "Speech on Conciliation with the Colonies" (1775), *The Works of Edmund Burke,* vol. II (Boston: Little, Brown and Company, 1865), p. 140.
7. *Bolingbroke's Defense of the Treaty of Utrecht* (Cambridge: Cambridge University Press, 1932), p. 95.
8. William Graham Sumner, *op. cit.,* p. 173.

The Uses and Limits of International Law

Stanley Hoffmann

The student of international law who examines its functions in the present international system and in the foreign policy of states will, unless he takes refuge in the comforting seclusion from reality that the pure theory of law once provided, be reduced to one of three attitudes. He will become a cynic, if he chooses to stress, like Giraudoux in *Tiger at the Gates,* the way in which legal claims are shaped to support any position a state deems useful or necessary on nonlegal grounds, or if he gets fascinated by the combination of cacophony and silence that characterizes international law as a system of world public order. He will become a hypocrite, if he chooses to rationalize either the conflicting interpretations and uses of law by states as a somehow converging effort destined to lead to some such system endowed with sufficient stability and solidity, or else if he endorses one particular construction (that of his own statesmen) as a privileged and enlightened contribution to the achievement of such a system, He will be overcome by consternation, if he reflects upon the gap between, on the one hand, the ideal of a world in which traditional self-help will be at least moderated by procedures and rules made even more indispensable by the proliferation both of states and of lethal weapons, and, on the other hand, the realities of inexpiable conflicts, sacred egoisms, and mutual recriminations. . . .

1. Some of the functions of international law constitute *assets both for the policy maker and from the viewpoint of world order,* i.e., of providing the international milieu with a framework of predictability and with procedures for the transaction of interstate business.

(a) International law is an instrument of *communication*. To present one's claims in legal terms means, 1, to signal to one's partner or opponent which "basic conduct norms" (to use Professor Scheinman's expression) one considers relevant or essential, and 2, to indicate which procedures one intends to follow and would like the other side to follow. At a time when both the size of a highly heterogeneous international milieu and the imperatives of prudence in the resort to force make communication essential and often turn international relations into a psychological contest, international law provides a kind of common language that does not amount to a common code of legitimacy yet can serve as a joint frame of reference. (One must however remember, one, that communication is no guarantee against misperception and, two, that what is being communicated may well determine the other side's response to the message: If "we" communicate to "them" an understanding of the situation that threatens their basic values or goals—like our interpretation of the war in South Vietnam as a case of aggression—there will be no joint frame of reference at all, and in fact the competition may become fiercer.)

(b) International law affords means of *channeling conflict*—of diverting inevitable tensions and clashes from the resort to force. Whenever there have been strong independent reasons for avoiding armed conflict—in an international system in which the superpowers in particular have excellent reasons for "managing" their confrontations, either by keeping them nonviolent, or by using proxies—international law has provided statesmen both with alibis for shunning force and with alternatives to violence. . . . In Berlin, both the Soviets and the West shaped their moves in such a way as to leave to the other side full responsibility for a first use of force, and to avoid the kind of frontal collision with the other side's legal claim that could have obliged the opponent to resort to force in order not to lose power or face. Thus, today as in earlier periods, law can indeed . . . serve as an alternative to confrontation whenever states are eager or forced to look for an alternative.

2. International law also plays various useful roles in the policy process, which however do not ipso facto contribute to world order. Here, we are concerned with *law as a tool of policy* in the competition of state visions, objectives, and tactics.

(a) The establishment of a network of rights and obligations, or the resort to legal arguments can be useful for the *protection or enhancement of a position:* if one wants to give oneself a full range of means with which to buttress a threatened status quo (cf. the present position of the West in Berlin; this is also what treaties of alliance frequently are for); if one wants to enhance one's power in a way that is demonstrably authorized by principles in international law (cf. Nasser's claim when he nationalized the Suez Canal, and Sukarno's invocation of the principle of self-determination against Malaysia); if one wants to restore a political position badly battered by an adversary's move, so that the resort to legal arguments becomes part of a strategy of restoring the status quo ante (Western position during the

Berlin blockade; Kennedy's strategy during the Cuban missile crisis; Western powers' attempts during the first phase of the Suez crisis; Soviet tactics in the U.N. General Assembly debates on the financing of peace-keeping operations).

(b) In all those instances, policy makers use law as a way of putting pressure on an opponent by *mobilizing international support* behind the legal rules invoked: law serves as a focal point, as the tool for "internationalizing" a national interest and as the cement of a political coalition. States that may have political misgivings about pledging direct support to a certain power whose interests only partly coincide with theirs, or because they do not want to antagonize another power thereby, may find it both easier and useful to rally to the defense of a legal principle in whose maintenance or promotion they may have a stake.

(c) . . . A policy maker who ignores international law leaves the field of political-competition-through-legal-manipulation open to his opponents or rivals. International law provides one of the numerous *chessboards* on which state contests occur.

3. Obviously, this indicates not only that to the statesmen international law provides an instrument rather than a guide for action, but also that this tool is often *not used,* when resort to it would hamper the state's interest as defined by the policy maker.

(a) One of the reasons why international law often serves as a technique of political mobilization is the appeal of reciprocity: "You must support my invocation of the ride against him, because if you let the rule be violated at my expense, someday it may be breached at yours; and we both have an interest in its preservation." But *reciprocity cuts both ways:* My using a certain legal argument to buttress my case against him may encourage him, now or later, to resort to the same argument against me; I may therefore be unwise to play on a chessboard in which, given the solemn and abstract nature of legal rights and obligations, I may not be able to make the kind of distinction between my (good) case and your (bad) one that can best be made by resort to ad hoc, political and circumstantial evidence that is irrelevant or ruled out in legal argumentation. Thus . . . during the Cuban crisis, when the United States tried to distinguish between Soviet missiles in Cuba and American ones in Turkey in order to build its case and get support, America's use of the OAS [Organization of American States] Charter as the legal basis for its "quarantine" established a dangerous precedent which the Soviets could use some day, against the U.S. or its allies, on behalf of the Warsaw Pact. And in the tragicomedy of the battle over Article 19 of the U.N. Charter, one reason why the U.S. finally climbed down from its high legal horse and gave up the attempt to deprive the Soviets of their right to vote, unless they paid their share, was the growing awareness of the peril which the principle of the exercise of the U.N. taxing power by the General Assembly could constitute some day for the United States if it lost control of the Assembly.

(b) One of the things that international law "communicates" is the solemnity of a commitment: a treaty, or a provision of the Charter, serves as a kind of tripwire or burglar alarm. When it fails to deter, the victim and third parties have a fateful choice between upholding the legal principle by all means, at the cost of a possible escalation in violence, and choosing to settle the dispute more peacefully, at the cost of *fuzzing the legal issue*. For excellent political reasons, the latter course is frequently adopted . . . in the form of dropping any reference to the legal principle at stake. . . .

(c) The very *ambiguity* of international law, which in many essential areas displays either gaping holes or conflicting principles, allows policy makers in an emergency to act as if international law were irrelevant—as if it were neither a restraint nor a guide. . . .

However, precisely because there is a legal chessboard for state competition, the fact that international law does not, in a crisis, really restrict one's freedom of action, does not mean that one will forgo legal rationalizations of the moves selected. Here we come to the last set of considerations about the role of law:

4. The resort to legal arguments by policy makers may be *detrimental to world order and thereby counterproductive for the state* that used such arguments.

(a) In the legal vacuum or confusion which prevails in areas as vital to states as internal war or the use of force, each state tries to justify its conduct with legal rationalizations. The result is a kind of *escalation of claims and counterclaims*, whose consequence, in turn, is both a further devaluation of international law and a "credibility gap" at the expense of those states who have debased the currency. America's rather indiscriminate resort to highly debatable legal arguments to support its Vietnam policy is a case in point. The unsubtle reduction of international law to a mere storehouse of convenient *ex post* justifications (as in the case of British intervention at Suez, or American interventions in Santo Domingo and Vietnam) undermines the very pretense of contributing to world order with which these states have tried to justify their unilateral acts.

(b) Much of contemporary international law authorizes states to *increase their power*. In this connection, Nasser's nationalization of the Suez Canal Company was probably quite legal, and those who accept the rather tortured argument put forth by the State Department legal advisers to justify the Cuban "quarantine" have concluded that this partial blockade was authorized by the OAS Charter and not in contradiction with the U.N. Charter. Yet it is obvious that a full exploitation by all states of all permissions granted by international law would be a perfect recipe for chaos.

(c) *Attempts to enforce or to strengthen international law,* far from consolidating a system of desirable restraints on state (mis)behavior, may actually *backfire* if the political conditions are not ripe. This is the central lesson of the long story of the financing of U.N. peace-keeping operations. American self-intoxication with the importance of the rule of law, fed by misleading analogies between the U.N. Charter and the U.S. Constitution, resulted ultimately in a weakening of the influence of the World Court (which largely followed America's line of reasoning), and in an overplaying of America's hand during the "non-session" of the General Assembly in the fall of 1964 and winter of 1965.

These are sobering considerations. But what they tell us is not, as so many political scientists seem to believe, that international law is, at best, a farce, and, at worst, even a potential danger; what they tell us is that *the nature of the international system condemns international law to all the weaknesses and perversions that it is so easy to deride.* International law is merely a magnifying mirror that reflects faithfully and cruelly the essence and the logic of international politics. In a fragmented world, there is no "global perspective" from which anyone can authoritatively assess, endorse, or reject the separate national efforts at making international law serve national interests above all. Like the somber universe of Albert Camus' Caligula, this is a judgeless world where no one is innocent. . . .

The permanent plight of international law is that, now as before, it shows on its body of rules all the scars inflicted by the international state of war. The tragedy of contemporary international law is that of a double divorce: first, between the old liberal dream of a world rule of law, and the realities of an international system of multiple minidramas that always threaten to become major catastrophes; second, between the old dream and the new requirements of moderation which in the circumstances of the present system suggest a *down-playing* of formal law in the realm of peace-and-war issues, and an *upgrading* of more flexible techniques, until the system has become less fierce. The interest of international law for the political scientist is that there is no better way of grasping the continuing differences between order within a national society and the fragile order of international affairs than to study how and when states use legal language, symbols, and documents, and with what results. . . .

A Functional Theory of Regimes

Robert O. Keohane

COOPERATION IN THEORY

. . . Since governments put a high value on the maintenance of their own autonomy, it is usually impossible to establish international institutions that exercise authority over states. This fact is widely recognized by officials of international organizations and their advocates in national governments as well as by scholars. It would therefore be mistaken to regard international regimes, or the organizations that constitute elements of them, as characteristically unsuccessful attempts to institutionalize centralized authority in world politics. They cannot establish patterns of legal liability that are as solid as those developed within well-ordered societies, and their architects are well aware of this limitation.

Of course, the lack of a hierarchical structure of world politics does not prevent regimes from developing bits and pieces of law. But the principal significance of international regimes does not lie in their formal legal status, since any patterns of legal liability and property rights established in world politics are subject to being overturned by the actions of sovereign states. . . . These arrangements . . . are designed not to implement centralized enforcement of agreements, but rather to establish stable mutual expectations about others, patterns of behavior and to develop working relationships that will allow the parties to adapt their practices to new situations. Contracts, conventions, and quasi-agreements provide information and generate patterns of transaction costs: Costs of reneging on commitments are increased, and the costs of operating within these frameworks are reduced.

Both these arrangements and international regimes are often weak and fragile. Like contracts and quasi-agreements, international regimes are frequently

From "A Functional Theory of Regimes," pp. 31–46, 88–103, from *After Hegemony: Cooperation and Discord in the World Political Economy* by Robert O. Keohane. Copyright © 1984 by Princeton University Press. Reprinted by permission of Princeton University Press. Portions of the text and some footnotes have been omitted.

altered: Their rules are changed, bent, or broken to meet the exigencies of the moment. They are rarely enforced automatically, and they are not self-executing. Indeed, they are often matters for negotiation and renegotiation. . . .

Transaction Costs

Like oligopolistic quasi-agreements, international regimes alter the relative costs of transactions. Certain agreements are forbidden. Under the provisions of the General Agreement on Tariffs and Trade (GATT), for instance, it is not permitted to make discriminatory trade arrangements except under specific conditions. Since there is no centralized government, states can nevertheless implement such actions, but their lack of legitimacy means that such measures are likely to be costly. Under GATT rules, for instance, retaliation against such behavior is justified. By elevating injunctions to the level of principles and rules, furthermore, regimes construct linkages between issues. No longer does a specific discriminatory agreement constitute merely a particular act without general significance; on the contrary, it becomes a "violation of GATT" with serious implications for a large number of other issues. In the terms of Prisoners' Dilemma, the situation has been transformed from a single-play to an iterated game. In market-failure terms, the transaction costs of certain possible bargains have been increased, while the costs of others have been reduced. In either case, the result is the same: Incentives to violate regime principles are reduced. International regimes reduce transaction costs of legitimate bargains and increase them for illegitimate ones.

International regimes also affect transaction costs in the more mundane sense of making it cheaper for governments to get together to negotiate agreements. It is more convenient to make agreements within a regime than outside of one. International economic regimes usually incorporate international organizations that provide forums for meetings and secretariats that can act as catalysts for agreement. Insofar as their principles and rules can be applied to a wide variety of particular issues, they are efficient: Establishing the rules and principles at the outset makes it unnecessary to renegotiate them each time a specific question arises.

International regimes thus allow governments to take advantage of potential economies of scale. Once a regime has been established, the marginal cost of dealing with each additional issue will be lower than it would be without a regime. If a policy area is sufficiently dense, establishing a regime will be worthwhile. Up to a point there may even be what economists call "increasing returns to scale." In such a situation, each additional issue could be included under the regime at lower cost than the previous one. . . . In world politics, we should expect increasing returns to scale to lead to more extensive international regimes.

In view of the benefits of economies of scale, it is not surprising that specific agreements tend to be "nested" within regimes. For instance, an agreement by the United States, Japan, and the European Community in the Multilateral Trade Negotiations to reduce a particular tariff will be affected by the rules and principles of GATT—that is, by the trade regime. The trade regime, in turn, is nested within a set of other arrangements, including those for monetary relations, energy, foreign investment, aid to developing countries, and other issues, which together constitute a complex and interlinked pattern of relations among the advance market-economy countries. These, in turn, are related to military-security relations among the major states.[1]

The nesting patterns of international regimes affect transaction costs by making it easier or more difficult to link particular issues and to arrange side-payments, giving someone something on one issue in return for her help on another. Clustering of issues under a regime facilitates side-payments among these issues: more potential *quids* are available for the *quo*. Without international regimes linking clusters of issues to one another, side-payments and linkages would be difficult to arrange in world politics; in the absence of a price system for the exchange of favors, institutional barriers would hinder the construction of mutually beneficial bargains.

Suppose, for instance, that each issue were handled separately from all others, by a different governmental bureau in each country. Since a side-payment or linkage always means that a government must give up something on one dimension to get something on another, there would always be a bureaucratic loser within each government. Bureaus that would lose from proposed side-payments, on issues that matter to them, would be unlikely to bear the costs of these linkages willingly on the basis of other agencies' claims that the national interest required it.

Of course, each issue is not considered separately by a different governmental department or bureau. On the contrary, issues are grouped together, in functionally organized departments such as Treasury, Commerce, and Energy (in the United States). Furthermore, how governments organize themselves to deal with foreign policy is affected by how issues are organized internationally; issues considered by different regimes are often dealt with by different bureaucracies at home. Linkages and side-payments among issues grouped in the same regime thus become easier, since the necessary internal tradeoffs will tend to take place within rather than across bureaus; but linkages among issues falling into different regimes will remain difficult, or even become more so (since the natural linkages on those issues will be with issues within the same regime).

Insofar as issues are dealt with separately from one another on the international level, it is often hard, in simply bureaucratic terms, to arrange for them to be considered together. There are bound to be difficulties in coordinating policies of different international organizations—GATT, the IMF, and the IEA all have different memberships and different operating styles—in addition to the resistance that will appear to such a move within member governments. Within regimes, by contrast, side-payments are facilitated by the fact that regimes bring together negotiators to consider sets of issues that may well lie within the negotiators' bureaucratic bailiwicks at home. GATT negotiations, as well as deliberations on the international monetary system, have been characterized by extensive bargaining over side-payments and the politics of issue-linkage. The well-known literature on "spillover" in bargaining, relating to the European Community and other integration schemes, can also be interpreted as concerned with side-payments. According to these writings, expectations that an integration arrangement can be expanded to new issue-areas permit the broadening of potential side-payments, thus facilitating agreement.

We conclude that international regimes affect the costs of transactions. The value of a potential agreement to its prospective participants will depend, in part, on how consistent it is with principles of legitimacy embodied in international regimes. Transactions that violate these principles will be costly. Regimes also affect bureaucratic costs of transactions: successful regimes organize issue-areas so that productive linkages (those that facilitate agreements consistent with the principles of the regime) are facilitated, while destructive linkages and bargains that are inconsistent with regime principles are discouraged.

Uncertainty and Information

From the perspective of market-failure theories, the informational functions of regimes are the most important of all. . . . Even in games of pure coordination with stable equilibria, this may be a problem. Conventions—commuters meeting under the clock at Grand Central Station, suburban families on a shopping trip "meeting at the car"—become important. But in simple games of coordination, severe information problems are not embedded in the structure of relationships, since actors have incentives to reveal information and their own preferences fully to one another. In these games the problem is to reach some point of agreement; but it may not matter much which of several possible points is chosen. Conventions are important and ingenuity may be required, but serious systemic impediments to the acquisition and exchange of information are lacking.

Yet as we have seen in our discussions of collective action and Prisoners' Dilemma, many situations—both in game theory and in world politics—are characterized by conflicts of interest as well as common interests. In such situations, actors have to worry about being deceived and double-crossed, just as the buyer of a used car has to guard against purchasing a "lemon." The literature on market failure elaborates on its most fundamental contention—that, in the absence of appropriate institutions, some mutually advantageous bargains will not be made because of uncertainty—by pointing to three particularly important sources of difficulty: *assymetrical information; moral hazard;* and *irresponsibility.*

Asymmetrical Information   Some actors may know more about a situation than others. Expecting that the resulting bargains would be unfair, "outsiders" will be reluctant to make agreements with "insiders." This is essentially the problem of "quality uncertainty" as discussed by Akerlof.[2] This is a problem not merely of insufficient information, but rather of *systematically biased* patterns of information, which are recognized in advance of any agreement both by the holder of more information (the seller of the used car) and by its less well-informed prospective partner (the potential buyer of the "lemon" or "creampuff," as the case may be). Awareness that others have greater knowledge than oneself, and are therefore capable of manipulating a relationship or even engaging successful deception and double-cross, is a barrier to making agreements. When this suspicion is unfounded—that is, the agreement would be mutually benefical—it is an obstacle to improving welfare through cooperation.

This problem of asymmetrical information only appears when dishonest behavior is possible. In a society of saints, communication would be open and no one would take advantage of superior information. In our imperfect world, however, asymmetries of information are not rectified simply by communication. Not all communication reduces uncertainty, since communication may lead to asymmetrical or unfair bargaining outcomes as a result of deception. Effective communication is not measured well by the amount of talking that used-car salespersons do to customers or that governmental officials do to one another in negotiating international regimes! The information that is required in entering into an international regime is not merely information about other governments' resources and formal negotiating positions, but also accurate knowledge of their future positions. In part, this is a matter of estimating whether they will keep their commitments. As the "market for lemons" example suggests, . . . a government's reputation therefore becomes an important asset in persuading others to enter into agreements with it. International regimes help governments to assess others' reputations by providing standards of behavior against which performance can be measured, by linking these standards to specific issues, and by providing forums, often through international organizations, in which these evaluations can be made. Regimes may also include international organizations whose secretariats act not only as mediators but as providers of unbiased information that is made available, more or less equally to all members. By reducing asymmetries of information through a process of upgrading the general level of available information, international regimes reduce uncertainty. Agreements based on misapprehension and deception may be avoided; mutually beneficial agreements are more likely to be made. . . .

The significance of asymmetrical information and quality uncertainty in theories of market failure therefore calls attention to the importance not only of international regimes but also of variations in the degree of closure of different states' decision-making processes. Some governments maintain secrecy much more zealously than others. American officials, for example, often lament that the U.S. government leaks information "like a sieve" and claim that this openness puts the United States at a disadvantage vis à vis its rivals.

Surely there are disadvantages in openness. The real or apparent incoherence in policy that often accompanies it may lead the open government's partners to view it as unreliable because its top leaders, whatever their intentions, are incapable of carrying out their agreements. A cacophony of messages may render all of them uninterpretable. But some reflection on the problem of making agreements in world politics suggests that there are advantages for the open government that cannot be duplicated by countries with more tightly closed bureaucracies. Governments that cannot provide detailed and reliable information about their intentions—for instance, because their decision-making processes are closed to the outside world and their officials are prevented from developing frank informal relationships with their foreign counterparts—may be unable convincingly to persuade their potential partners of their commitment to the contemplated arrangements. Observers from other countries will be uncertain about the genuineness of officials' enthusiasm or the depth of their support for the cooperative scheme under consideration. These potential partners will therefore insist on discounting the value of prospective agreements to take account of their uncertainty. As in the "market for lemons," some potential agreements, which would be beneficial to all parties, will not be made because of "quality uncertainty"—about the quality of the closed government's commitment to the accord.

Moral Hazard   Agreements may alter incentives in such a way as to encourage less cooperative behavior. Insurance companies face this problem of "moral hazard." Property insurance, for instance, may make people less careful with their property and therefore increase the risk of loss. The problem of moral hazard arises quite sharply in international banking. The solvency of a major country's largest banks may be essential to its financial system, or even to the stability of the entire international banking network. As a result, the country's central bank may have to intervene if one of these banks is threatened. The U.S. Federal Reserve, for instance, could hardly stand idly by while the Bank of America or Citibank became unable to meet its liabilities. Yet this responsibility creates a problem of moral hazard, since the largest banks, in effect, have automatic insurance against disastrous consequences of risky but (in the short run at least) profitable loans. They have incentives to follow risk-seeking rather than risk-averse behavior at the expense of the central bank.

Irresponsibility   Some actors may be irresponsible, making commitments that they may not be able to carry out. Governments or firms may enter into agreements that they intend to keep, assuming that the environment will continue to be benign; if adversity sets in, they may be unable to keep their commitments. Banks regularly face this problem, leading them to devise standards of creditworthiness. Large governments trying to gain adherents to international agreements may face similar difficulties: countries that are enthusiastic about cooperation are likely to be those that expect to gain more, proportionately, than they contribute. This is a problem of self-selection, as discussed in the market-failure literature. For instance, if rates are not properly adjusted, people with high risks of heart attack will seek life insurance more avidly that those with longer life expectancies; people who purchased "lemons" will tend to sell them earlier on the used-car market than people with "creampuffs." In international politics, self-selection means that for certain types of activities—such as sharing research and development information—weak states (with much to gain but little to give) may have more incentive to participate than strong ones, but less incentive actually to spend funds on research and development. Without the strong states, the enterprise as a whole will fail. . . .

Regimes and Market Failure

International regimes help states to deal with all of these problems. As the principles and rules of a regime reduce the range of expected behavior, uncertainty declines, and as information becomes more widely available, the asymmetry of its distribution is likely to lessen. Arrangements within regimes to monitor actors' behavior . . . mitigate problems of moral hazard. Linkages among particular issues within the context of regimes raise the costs of deception and irresponsibility, since the consequences of such behavior are likely to extend beyond the issue on which they are manifested. Close ties among officials involved in managing international regimes increase the ability of governments to make mutually beneficial agreements, because intergovernmental relationships characterized by ongoing communication among working-level officials, informal as well as formal, are inherently more conducive to exchange of information than are traditional relationships between closed bureaucracies. In general, regimes make it more sensible to cooperate by lowering the likelihood of being double-crossed. . . .

Thus international regimes are useful to governments. Far from being threats to governments (in which case it would be hard to understand why they exist at all), they permit governments to attain objectives that would otherwise be unattainable. They do so in part by facilitating intergovernmental agreements. Regimes facilitate agreements by raising the anticipated costs of violating others' property rights, by altering transaction costs through the clustering of issues, and by providing reliable information to members. Regimes are relatively efficient institutions, compared with the alternative of having a myriad of unrelated agreements, since their principles, rules, and institutions create linkages among issues that give actors incentives to reach mutually beneficial agreements. They thrive in situations where states have common as well as conflicting interests on multiple, overlapping issues and where externalities are difficult but not impossible to deal with through bargaining. Where these conditions exist, international regimes can be of value to states.

NOTES

1. For the idea of "nesting," I am indebted to Vinod Aggarwal, *Liberal Protectionism: The International Politics of Organized Textile Trade* (Berkeley: University of California Press, 1985).
2. Oliver Williamson, *Markets and Hierarchies: Analysis and Anti-Trust Implications* (New York: Free Press, 1975), pp. 31–33; George Akerlof "The Market for 'Lemons'" *Quarterly Journal of Economics,* vol. 84 (August 1970), pp. 488–500.

The U.N. in a New World Order

Bruce Russett and James S. Sutterlin

The new world order envisioned by Presidents Bush and Gorbachev would be founded on the rule of law and on the principle of collective security. That principle necessarily entails the possibility of military enforcement measures by the United Nations. Twice in its history the Security Council has authorized such action. The first instance was in the Korean War in 1950; the second was in the Persian Gulf in 1990. More occasions are likely to follow.

The U.N. Charter gives the Security Council the authority "to maintain or restore international peace and security," and to enforce the will of the council on a state that has broken the peace. Use of military force by the council for these purposes was foreseen by the founders of the United Nations. Indeed it was seen almost half a century ago as an essential element in the world order that the United Nations was intended to establish. Should the need arise, countries would be protected from aggression by forces provided to the Security Council by member states, serving as a U.N. army at the council's will. Military forces, however, have not been available to the council on this basis and improvisation has therefore been required. The action taken by the Security Council in response to the Iraqi invasion of Kuwait amounted to just that—an improvisation to permit enforcement of the council's will without the specific means provided in the charter for that purpose.

Military force has much more frequently been used by the United Nations for the purpose of peacekeeping, something not foreseen in the charter at all. This improvisation was first devised in haste to facilitate an end to the 1956 hostilities in the Middle East. Since that beginning, which amply demonstrated the value of the technique, U.N. use of military and civilian personnel provided by member states for peacekeeping has become a well-established practice now supported by all the major powers.

The use of military force by the United Nations for both of these purposes—enforcement and peacekeeping—is surely essential to a world order in which international security is heavily dependent on the Security Council. The experience of the Gulf War and of the more distant past offers important lessons and raises trenchant questions as to how this can most effectively be done in the gulf (as action moves from military victory to the maintenance of peace in the region) and wherever else peace may be endangered.

Since the Suez crisis of 1956, the United Nations has developed a notable elasticity in using peacekeeping forces, to the point that it is now difficult to formulate a precise definition—or the limits—of what peacekeeping functions may be. The original role of standing between hostile forces has been expanded to encompass, among other functions, the maintenance of security or stability within a given area (as in southern Lebanon), the monitoring of elections (Namibia, Haiti), the provision of humanitarian assistance (Cyprus), and the disarmament of insurgents (Nicaragua). This flexibility greatly increases the value of peacekeeping forces as an instrument available to the Security Council in dealing with potential or existing conflicts. For example, the permanent members of the Security Council have recently developed a plan to bring peace to Cambodia that would use peacekeeping forces—both military and civilian—for broad purposes of pacification, stabilization, and administration.

Three limitations on the use of peacekeeping have been consistently honored: (1) peacekeeping has been interpreted, as originally articulated by U.N. Secretary General Dag Hammarskjöld, as a provisional measure under the U.N. Charter, that is, as a measure undertaken without prejudice to the rights, claims, or positions of the parties concerned; (2) peacekeeping operations have been undertaken only with the consent of all the parties concerned; (3) peacekeeping forces may use arms only in self-defense. Again, in accordance with the original decision by Hammarskjöld, U.S. and Soviet troops have never been included in peacekeeping forces.

In domestic conflicts the consent of all the parties is likely to remain a compelling requirement. It was clearly shown in non–U.N. peacekeeping undertakings, in Lebanon in 1983–84 and more recently in Liberia, that without the consent of the parties grave risks are involved and the results can be disastrous. This may not, however, be the case in interstate conflicts. When peacekeeping forces are deployed between hostile forces after a truce or ceasefire has been achieved, an essential purpose is to deter a renewal of hostilities. In this sense deterrence is already an accepted function of peacekeeping. Yet in interstate conflicts a situation could well rise in which peacekeeping forces are needed for deterrence purposes but the consent of one of the parties is not obtainable. This should not, a priori, preclude a Security Council decision to deploy them if the other characteristic limitations are maintained. . . .

It is worth emphasizing that nothing in the charter prohibits the Security Council from deploying peacekeeping forces without the consent of all the parties, or from including troop contingents from the permanent members of the council in such forces where the need for deterrence arises. (U.S. and Soviet military personnel already serve in U.N. military observer missions.) Such action would still fall under the definition of a provisional measure to be taken by the council "to prevent an aggravation of the situation" before deciding on enforcement action as foreseen in Articles 41 and 42 of the U.N. Charter. The provision of troops by member states for such deterrence operations would remain voluntary, as in other peacekeeping missions, with financing determined on an ad hoc basis by the council, either through assessment of all members or through payment of the cost by the countries requesting the deployment, as could be the case in a situation like the gulf where wealthy states are involved as parties. . . .

A good number of countries might well oppose in principle the idea of deploying peacekeeping forces without the consent of all the parties concerned, fearing that it would open the way to action contrary to their own national interests. Unlike the United States and the other four permanent members of the Security Council, they would not enjoy the protection of the veto. When a similar idea was put forward some years ago, in the course of confidential consultations in the Security Council on how its effectiveness might be enhanced, there was little response. The Gulf War has served, however, to heighten interest in effective deterrence using multilateral means not under the domination of one or several U.N. members. There is certainly now a broad recognition that adequate means of deterrence will be essential to a peaceful world order.

The second broad purpose for the Security Council's use of military force falls largely under the heading of compellence, or coercion, rather than simply deterrence. In the context of the Security Council such action is best understood as enforcement action. Use of "air, sea or land forces" for enforcement is specifically foreseen in Chapter VII, Articles 39–46 of the U.N. Charter, in which all members undertake to make available to the Security Council "on its call and in accordance with a special agreement or agreements, armed forces, assistance and facilities, including rights of passage, necessary for the purpose of maintaining international peace and security."

Since no such special agreements have been concluded, no standing multilateral force has been available to the Security Council. Therefore the Security Council authorized the use of ad hoc forces to restore international peace in Korea and the Persian Gulf. When the North Korean attacks on South Korea were formally brought to the Security Council's attention, the council's resolution of July 7, 1950—adopted in the temporary absence of the Soviet Union—called on member states to assist South Korea in resisting the North Korean aggression. It recommended "that all members providing military forces and other assistance pursuant to the aforesaid Security Council resolutions make such forces and other assistance available to a unified command under the United States." It requested further that the United States designate the commander of such forces. The same resolution authorized use of the U.N. flag.

Thus in the case of Korea the Security Council requested one member state to lead a combined effort on behalf of the United Nations to resist aggression. Notwithstanding his designation as commander of U.N. forces in Korea, General

Douglas MacArthur, the commander named by the United States, never reported directly to the Security Council. (Routine, unclassified status reports were provided by the United States.) Neither the Military Staff Committee—a body composed of military representatives of the five permanent members intended to advise the council on military matters—nor the council itself had any role in directing military operations of the unified command. The General Assembly did, however, establish a three-nation ceasefire committee that sought a formula to end the war, and the secretary general suggested the procedure of direct talks between the military commanders that was ultimately followed and through which an armistice was achieved.

The advantages offered by this procedures were:

—Expeditious action to resist aggression. Only the United States had troops deployed in South Korea capable of taking quick military action.

—The unambiguous command structure needed for large-scale field operations.

—A practical way to meet the responsibilities of the United Nations under the charter in the absence of a multilateral force under the Security Council for which the necessary agreements with member states had not been reached.

—Validation of the concept of collective security, since states acted jointly in response to Security Council (and subsequently General Assembly) decisions.

The disadvantages of this procedure (which became more evident in the course of time) were:

—The United Nations lacked control or influence over the course of military action or the precise purposes for which it was exercised (e.g., to repel and punish aggression, to reunify the country).

—The military operation became identified with the policy of the nation leading the effort rather than with the United Nations.

—Divisive forces within the United Nations were encouraged by the dominant role of one member state pursuing goals not universally shared.

—Opportunities were afforded the aggressor to identify the struggle with one country, the United States, rather than with the international community as a whole.

All of these disadvantages were intensified in the Korean case by the bitter disagreements that prevailed at the time between the Soviet Union and the United States. Under conditions of harmony among the permanent members of the Security Council, these various disadvantages could have considered less force.

In the Persian Gulf crisis the Security Council authorized, albeit in oblique language, the use of force for enforcement in another interstate conflict. After imposing a comprehensive embargo in order to bring about Iraqi withdrawal from Kuwait and the restoration of its legitimate government, the council called upon "those member states cooperating with the government of Kuwait which are deploying maritime forces to the area to use such measures commensurate to the specific circumstances as may be necessary under the authority of the Security Council . . . to ensure strict implementation" of the provisions laid down in the resolution relating to economic sanctions. Then, in Resolution 678 of November 29, 1990, the Security Council authorized "member states cooperating with the government of Kuwait . . . to use all necessary means to uphold and implement Security Council Resolution 660 and all subsequent relevant resolutions and to restore international peace and security in the area." All states were requested to provide appropriate support for "the actions undertaken."

This action, with specific reference to Chapter VII of the charter, constituted a new approach to implementation of the collective security concept. As in the earlier enforcement action in Korea, when there was no reference to Chapter VII, a basis for the council to mobilize a U.N. force for military enforcement action did not exist. Therefore the council again turned to member states to act in its behalf through such measures as might be necessary. But this time no unified command was established, and the use of the U.N. flag was not authorized.

The gulf action became possible because the permanent members of the Security Council cooperated on a matter of peace and security in the way originally foreseen when the United Nations was founded. Representatives of the United States and the Soviet Union have repeatedly suggested that such action is an important element in a new world order; that is, a world in which nations will be secure because of the capacity of the United Nations to guarantee their security through collective measures. This fundamental goal of the United Nations is unquestionably brought closer through the sustained cooperation and a notably increased commonality of interests among the major powers, evident not only in the Gulf War but also in other conflicts such as Cambodia and Angola. Two questions nonetheless warrant careful examination: Is the approach that was taken to enforce the council's decisions with regard to the Iraq-Kuwait crisis necessarily a viable model for implementing collective security in the future? Is there a realistic alternative that would offer greater advantages?

With regard to the first question, it is clear that the Security Council, in deciding on action to counter the Iraqi aggression, prescribed action for all member states. While it authorized individual states to take "the necessary action," it requested "all states to provide appropriate support for the actions undertaken." Thus all states were called on to assist in defending one state, Kuwait, from aggression. Actions to be taken for this purpose would seem clearly to constitute "effective collective measures for the prevention and removal of threats to the peace, and for the suppression of acts of aggression" as foreseen in Article 1 of the charter.

But the procedure adopted is not without its difficulties. The Security Council has no means of controlling when, how, or in what degree the collective measures are applied. In the gulf case, the states concerned were only requested "to keep the council regularly informed"; some measures taken might not have had majority support in the Security Council or the General Assembly. The state that is in command may have from the outset an interpretation of U.N. goals different from that of other Security Council members, or its aims may become more expansive in the course of the operation. The latter happened in Korea with the U.S. decision to cross the 38th parallel and try to reunify the country by force. It would have been the case in the gulf had the United States pursued military action beyond the Kuwaiti theater of operations.

If the measures taken cease to have the endorsement of the majority of the Security Council, can they still be considered collective measures taken in the council's behalf? This problem is inherent in a procedure in which action is taken on behalf of the council but without any council control over the nature, timing, or extent of the action. The major danger is that the entire undertaking will be identified with the country or countries actually involved in military action rather than with the United Nations. In any case, many U.N. members will not view the military action as an appropriate application of collective security if the action appears to conflict with the Security Council's goals.

The gulf operation and the terms for ending military action against Iraq offer a case in point. None of the 12 Security Council resolutions called for eliminating Iraq's war-making capability or deposing Saddam Hussein. But the former clearly became a goal of some coalition members, and the latter was widely suspected. President Bush and the coalition partners felt free to give their own interpretation to the Security Council resolutions. Those members, including the Soviet Union, that interpreted the resolutions more narrowly may be reluctant next time to give such unconstrained authority to member states acting on the council's behalf. In any operation, if the Security Council has asserted no control over the military action authorized, will it be possible for it to assert control over the terms of peace?

Such questions indicate the problems that can arise when a procedure such as that developed for the Gulf War is followed. Moreover, the approach adopted in the gulf case is not likely to be viable unless vital interests of one or more major military powers are at risk. For example, the United States might not be interested in deploying substantial forces, even if authorized to do so by the Security Council, to deter or repel an Egyptian attack on Libya.

There are alternative procedures that might in the future be followed by the Security Council, ones that would offer the prospect of effective enforcement action without the disadvantages and problems associated with according responsibility to individual member states.

One would be a variant of the procedure followed in Korea. National forces could be brought together in ad hoc fashion under a unified U.N. command, with the commander designated by whichever happened to be the major troop-contributing country. The problems that arose in the Korean case could conceivably be alleviated if the unified commander were required to consult with the Security Council, or with some form of military authority appointed by the council, on the mission of the military operation and the basic strategy to be followed in achieving it. The country supplying the major troop contingent can be expected to resist such a procedure as inhibiting unacceptably the freedom of action of the commander and subjecting its forces to perilous uncertainties. But if favorable relations among the permanent members of the Security Council persist, such a consultative, though not command, procedure might be feasible. It would have the distinct advantage of maintaining a close U.N. identification with all action taken and of giving the Security Council some influence, if not control, over any military action.

The other alternative is the procedure defined in Articles 42 and 43 of the U.N. Charter, according to which all members of the United Nations undertake "to make available to the Security Council on its call in accordance with a special agreement or agreements, armed forces, facilities and assistance." In the Korean War, the "uniting for peace" resolution of 1950 recommended that each member maintain within its armed forces earmarked units so trained that they could promptly be made available for service "as a United Nations unit or units."

The hostile relations between the United States and the Soviet Union were long perceived as the major obstacle in implementing such provisions. If after the Gulf War the two countries remain in accord on using the United Nations, that obstacle may be lifted. The willingness of member states to commit themselves in advance to provide troops and facilities at the request of the Security Council for enforcement purposes has never been tested. It can be argued that such commitment is inherent in U.N. membership, a condition for which is acceptance of the obligations contained in the charter and ability and willingness to carry out those obligations. For such a commitment to be reliable, however, it must be embodied in agreements between the Security Council and those member states prepared to assume the obligations. Such commitments will not be undertaken lightly.

The subject was discussed in detail in 1945 in the U.S. Senate when the U.N. Charter was under consideration. John Foster Dulles, a member of the U.S. delegation to the San Francisco conference at which the charter was signed, told the Senate Foreign Relations Committee that an agreement with the United Nations on the provision of troops should be regarded as a treaty requiring approval of a two-thirds majority of the Senate. The recorded comments of the senators indicate wide agreement with that interpretation. It was also discussed whether the president would need to obtain the consent of Congress to provide troops, when called upon by the United Nations after completion of an agreement. No consensus emerged on the question, but one senator suggested at the time that the size of the force requested could be decisive. Two or three thousand troops for "police action" would not need congressional approval, whereas a battle force would.

Soviet representatives have recently expressed a positive view of a U.N. agreement on the provision of troops for enforcement purposes, but they have emphasized that in no case could the troops be provided without the specific approval of the Soviet parliament.

Once agreements on the provision of troops were completed with a fair portion of member states, the Security Council would have the capacity to call into being a multilateral force (land, sea, and air) under a U.N. commander "to maintain or restore international peace and security." In military operations the commander would presumably have full tactical authority but would operate under the guidance of the Security Council or a body established by the council to serve this purpose. Subsequent understandings would be required on command, intelligence, logistics, and other more or less centralized functions. The Military Staff Committee could, as foreseen 46 years ago, "advise and assist the Security Council on all questions relating to military requirements." It could do this without acquiring any command authority, which would be advisable since it functions on the basis of consensus.

In some ways a U.N. force of this type would be quite similar to a peacekeeping force, since it would be made up of troops provided by member states and would have a U.N. commander. It would differ markedly, however, in mission, armament, composition, and command.

A U.N. force of this nature would not entail the problems and disadvantages that the other identified approaches could present. Identification with the United Nations from initiation to end of any operation would be assured, and control could be clearly in the hands of the Security Council. The likelihood of sustained support among U.N. members for the action undertaken would be strong. Yet in this approach, too, likely problems can be identified.

First of all, it is not clear how many states will be willing to conclude the agreements foreseen in the U.N. Charter—or how long this will take. It can only be said that international circumstances, especially in the wake of the Gulf War, appear more favorable than at any time since 1945. It is also questionable whether a force as large and elaborately equipped as one needed to maintain peace in the gulf, for example, could have been organized quickly on this basis. Any very large operation is bound to depend heavily on a major contingent from one or more of the principal military powers; the larger and more sophisticated the contingent provided, the less likely the contributing country will be willing to place it under non-national command.

Organization and deployment of multilateral force by the Security Council would likely require more time than if action were delegated to one or more member states, especialy if a large-scale operation were foreseen. To shorten the lead time, the secretary general might be given authority, not subject to the veto, to send an unarmed observer corps to any international border at any time. According to Article 99 of the U.N. Charter, the secretary general "may bring to the attention of the Security Council any matter which in his opinion may threaten the maintenance of international peace and security." To do so he needs to be informed. An authorization to send observers without specific consent of the parties raises difficulties, but it would allow the Security Council to be forewarned and to make quick preparations if an enforcement action were required. The very presence of observers can have a deterrent effect, possibly avoiding the need for subsequent enforcement.

Then, too, there is a very basic question as to whether a military action can be successfully carried out under multilateral strategic command, or as successfully as under national command. Administrative aspects of managing the use of force by the Security Council have received little attention. . . .

One question inherent in any big multilateral action concerns the level at which integration of command of multinational forces would occur. The distinction in U.S. military terminology between command and operational control (OPCON) is useful in this respect. Command applies to such matters as discipline, pay, morale, and logistics; most of these (perhaps not logistics) would be carried out at the level of the national military contingents. OPCON is likely to be different.

If U.S. troops were involved there would probably have to be, under an overall U.N. commander from some country, a U.S. "component commander" operating with substantial independence. OPCON can be decentralized by confining each member's forces to a specific sector, physically dividing up the ground, as has been done in most U.N. peacekeeping operations.

Some other functions may be even harder to divide than OPCON. Intelligence gathering for example, will be dominated by states with vast technological capacities for overhead electronic surveillance. In the gulf operation other coalition members presumably accepted U.S. control of intelligence, but if there were substantial Soviet participation the Soviets would likely not accept it. Secure communications would be required among participating forces in the field, either through sharing encryption (politically very sensitive) or cumbersome procedures for transmission and delivery. It is likely that some states will be unable or unwilling to provide adequate logistical support for their troops, and that those with the motivation and ability to do so will have to provide for others. Some U.N. "headquarters" personnel and facilities will be required for these functions, probably drawing on the experience and capabilities of the secretary general's staff.

The problem of financing such military actions demands careful attention. The history of financing past peacekeeping efforts by voluntary contribution is, to say the least, not encouraging. The gulf operation was heavily dependent on the willingness and ability of the most deeply involved states—the United States, Saudi Arabia, and Kuwait—to pay most of the immediate costs, and in turn their willingness depended upon their ability to control the means and ends of military operations. A future operation that less directly engaged the interests of such states would have to rely on broader support, probably through an assessment of all member governments. Reasonably complete and prompt payment of those assessments would have to be assured.

Such problems may be equally severe for the peacetime maintenance of standing earmarked forces. Unless any additional costs incurred can be covered by the United Nations, Third World states may be unable to participate. Certain central (non-state-specific) services, such as administration, intelligence, command, and control, perhaps logistics and transport, must be prepared and institutionalized in advance. Provision in the regular budget of the United Nations might cover such ongoing costs of multilateral readiness, with special assessments made to cover the cost of any enforcement actions undertaken.

The credibility of U.N. action to repel aggression and restore international peace and security, as foreseen in the U.N. Charter, has been profoundly affected by the response to the Iraqi invasion of Kuwait. The Security Council showed itself capable of taking decisive action. Its ability to impose comprehensive sanctions and see them enforced was clearly demonstrated, even though the ultimate effectiveness of the sanctions was not adequately tested. By authorizing the use of military force the council gained compliance with all of its relevant resolutions. The Security Council has shown that it has the capacity to initiate collective measures essential for the maintenance of peace in a new world order.

This development can enhance the United Nations' ability not just to restore the status quo as it existed prior to a breach of the peace, but also to change the parameters of the global order to something more favorable than existed under the prior status quo. In this it may even go beyond the vision of the U.N. founders. Furthermore, knowledge that the United Nations has such a capability will also enhance its ability to deter breaches of the peace, and so make actual enforcement or later peacekeeping less necessary. Collective security may suppress incipient acts of aggression as well as defeat or punish those that do emerge.

Nevertheless, it should not be assumed that any U.N. role in enforcement during the 1990s will be automatic. It will require a deliberate political judgment that can only be made by members of the Security Council acting collectively, and will depend on some continuing commonality of interests among the five permanent members of the council—the United States and the Soviet Union in particular. The effectiveness of the United Nations in dealing with international security problems, whether by enforcement measures, peacekeeping or mediation, will always be sensitive to the nature of relations between these two superpowers. A United Nations whose credibility in dealing with aggression and threats to peace has been restored, however, can serve to moderate any revival of tension between them by lessening the need for, or likelihood of, unilateral intervention in regional crises.

The manner in which the gulf military action was executed by the United States and its coalition partners will likely limit the willingness of council members to follow a similar procedure in the future—a procedure that leaves council members little control over the course of military operations and over the conclusion of hostilities. Neither the United States nor any other country will be ready to act under all circumstances to preserve or restore peace. Nor will other states always be ready to endorse unilateral actions. Some states may not wish to contribute to an operation, and the council may not always wish to depend disproportionately on a particular state's contribution.

Some U.N. capacity to carry out these functions on a permanent basis will therefore be desirable. For this reason, as well as others previously mentioned, the Security Council should be able to mobilize a force to serve under U.N. command for enforcement purposes. That capacity may be virtually indispensable in an emergent world order. The chance to achieve it should not be missed.

PART
Two

THE USES OF FORCE

With the end of both the Cold War and the Soviet Union, the nightmare of an all-out nuclear war between the superpowers that so dominated world politics since 1945 has ended. It is not likely that a new danger of the same magnitude will arise, at least for the economically developed democracies of North America, Japan, and Western Europe. Indeed, for the first time since the formation of these nation states, the citizens of these countries may live out their lives without worrying that they or their children will have to die or kill in a major war.

This fact, however, does not mean that we should no longer be concerned with how states use force. Even if the optimistic prediction is correct, we still need to understand previous eras in which warfare played such a large role. To take the recent past, we cannot understand the course of the Cold War without studying the role nuclear weapons played in it. Moreover, an understanding of the role that nuclear weapons played in that era is central for determining the role they will play in this era. This is so for no other reason than that national leaders' views of the present are heavily influenced by their reading of the past. Furthermore, even within the developed rich world, where a great power war is unlikely, military power still remains useful to the conduct of statecraft. If it were not, these states would have already disarmed. They have not because the use of force must always be available, even if it is not always necessary. For much of the rest of the world, unfortunately, circumstances are different. Threats to security of states remain real, and war among them has not been abolished. For all states, then—those likely to enjoy peace and those that will have to endure war—what has changed is not the utility of military power so much as how it can be usefully employed.

THE POLITICAL USES OF FORCE

The use of force almost always represents the partial failure of a policy. The exception, of course, is the case in which fighting is valued for its own sake—when it is believed that war brings out manly values and purifies individuals and cultures, or when fighting is seen as entertainment. Changes in states' values and the increased destructiveness of war, however, have led statesmen to view armed conflicts as the last resort. Threats are a second choice to diplomatic maneuvers; actual use of force follows only if the threats fail.

Because of the high costs of violence, its use is tempered by restraints and bargaining. As bloody as most wars are, they could always be bloodier. Brutalities are limited in part by the combatants shared interests, if not by their scruples. Because two states differ enough to go to war, it does not follow that they have no common interests. Only when everything that is good for one side is bad for the other (a "zero-sum" situation), do the opponents gain nothing by bargaining. In most cases, however, some outcomes are clearly bad for both sides; and therefore, even though they are at war, each side shares an interest in avoiding them.

The shared nature of the interest, as Thomas Schelling points out, stems from the fact that it is easier to destroy than to create. Force can be used to take—or to bargain. If you can take what you want, you do not need your adversary's cooperation and do not have to bargain with him. A country may use force to seize disputed territory just as a robber may kill you to get your wallet. Most of the things people and nations want, however, cannot be taken in this way. A nation not only wants to take territory, it wants to govern and exploit it. A nation may want others to stop menacing it; it may even want others to adopt its values. Brute force alone cannot achieve these goals. A nation that wants to stop others from menacing it may not want to fight them in order to remove the threat. A nation that wants others to adopt its values cannot impose them solely through conquest. Where the cooperation of an adversary is needed, bargaining will ensue. The robber does not need the cooperation of his victim if he kills him to get his wallet. The thief, however, who must obtain the combination of a safe from the hostage, who carries it only in his head, does need such cooperation. The thief may use force to demonstrate that the hostage can lose his life if he does not surrender the combination. But the thief no more wishes to kill the hostage and lose the combination than the hostage wishes to die. The hostage may trade the combination for his life. The bargain may be unequal or unfair, but it is still a bargain.

The mutual avoidance of certain outcomes explains why past wars have not been as bloody as they could have been; but an analysis of why wars were not more destructive should not blind us to the factors that made them as destructive as they were. By 1914, for example, all the statesmen of Europe believed a war inevitable, and all were ready to exploit it. None, however, imagined the staggering losses that their respective nations would inflict and bear in the field, or the extent to which noncombatants would be attacked. Yet by the second year of the war, the same men were accepting the deaths of hundreds or thousands for a few yards, gain in the front lines; and by the end of the war, they were planning large-scale aerial gas attacks on each other's major cities. The German bombing of Guernica in 1937 and Rotterdam in 1940 shocked statesmen and citizens alike, but by the middle of the war both were accepting as routine the total destruction of German and Japanese cities.

Three factors largely account for the increasing destructiveness of the wars of the last two centuries. First was the steady technological improvement in weaponry. Weapons such as machine guns, submarines, poison gas, and aircraft made it feasible to maim or kill large numbers of people quickly. The rapidity of destruction that is possible with nuclear weapons is only the most recent, albeit biggest, advance. Second was the growth in the capacity, and thus the need, of states to field ever larger numbers of forces. As states became more industrialized and centralized, they acquired the wealth and developed the administrative apparatus to move men on a grand scale. Concomitant with the increase in military potential was the necessity to realize the potential. As soon as one state expanded the forces at its disposal, all other states had to follow suit. Thus when Prussia instituted universal conscription and the general-staff system and then demonstrated their advantages by her swift victories over Austria and France, the rest of the continent quickly adopted her methods. Because of the security dilemma, an increase in the potential power of states led to an increase in their standing power.

Third was the gradual "democratization" of war: the expansion of the battlefield and hence the indiscriminate mass killing of noncombatants. Everyone, citizens and soldiers alike, began fighting and dying. World War II, with its extensive use of airpower, marked not the debut but the zenith of this mass killing. Once war became the burden of the masses, not the province of the princes, the distinction between combatants and noncombatants increasingly blurred. Most of the wars of the eighteenth century did impinge upon the citizenry, but mainly financially; few civilians died in them. With the widespread use of conscription in the nineteenth and twentieth centuries, however, more citizens became soldiers. With the advent of industrialization and with the increasing division of labor, the citizens who did not fight remained behind to produce weapons. Now a nation not only had to conquer its enemy's armies, but also to destroy the industrial plant that supplied their weapons. Gradually the total energy of a country was diverted into waging wars. And, of course, as the costs of wars increased, so did the justifications given for them and the benefits claimed to derive from them. The greater the sacrifices asked, the larger the victory spoils demanded. Because wars became literally wars of, by, and for the people, governments depended increasingly upon the support of their citizens. As wars became democratized, so too did they become popularized and propagandized.

The readings in the first section explore how force has been and can be used in a changing world. Robert Art notes that the threat and use of force has four distinct functions and shows how their relative importance varies from one situation to another. Thomas Schelling examines the differences between the uses of conventional and nuclear weapons and the links between force and foreign policy goals. Robert Jervis argues that the extent to which states can make themselves more secure without menacing others depends in large part on whether offensive postures can be distinguished from defensive ones and whether the offense is believed to be more efficacious than the defense.

THE POLITICAL UTILITY OF NUCLEAR WEAPONS

The fundamental change in the use of military force among the great powers since 1945 is the premium put on deterrence. Before 1945, military planners concentrated, not on preventing the next general war, but on winning it. In the contingency planning prior to World War I, for example, the military staffs of Europe became obsessed with the swift strike that would knock the opponent out of the war. These men concentrated on victory partly because they believed that the first strike, if properly executed, could be militarily decisive and that the side that conquered the other's military forces could in the process protect its own population. The possibility of nuclear retaliation makes this no longer feasible; in a nuclear war neither side could save itself. Nuclear weapons have brought, not overkill, but *mutual* kill. Because each side can destroy the other no matter which attacks first, each has an interest in avoiding all-out war. But this raises the question of what exactly is the utility of force in the contemporary world.

The standard argument about nuclear weapons is that, by vastly increasing the costs of war, they played a major role in seeing that the Cold War never turned into a general war. John Mueller, however, argues that nuclear weapons were not all that important for the sustained peace between the superpowers. Conventional war would have been so enormously destructive that this prospect would have been sufficient to have produced peace. Furthermore, because both the United States and the USSR were satisfied with the status quo, they had little reason to fight. Robert Jervis finds this argument not sufficient to explain superpower peace and points to those special characteristics of nuclear weapons that enhance deterrence. But even if nuclear weapons have played a significant role in ensuring that neither the United States nor the USSR attacked the other, did they help these states reach other goals? Were they useful bargaining instruments and tools of statecraft? McGeorge Bundy's analysis of the historical record indicates that they have not. With the passing of the Cold War, we will gain increasing evidence about these questions, but continuing debates rather than definitive answers are likely.

THE POLITICAL UTILITY OF FORCE IN THE CURRENT ERA

It is a mistake to examine the possible use of force in a vacuum. As Clausewitz stressed, force is an instrument for reaching political goals. Its utility, as well as the likelihood of its use, depends not only on the costs and perceived benefits of fighting, but on the general political context, the values statesmen and citizens hold, the alternative policy instruments available, and the objectives sought. Robert Keohane and Joseph Nye contrast the models or "ideal types" of Realism and complex interdependence in dealing with the role of force and military threats. Realism, represented in many of the readings in Part One, stresses the importance of military power. Complex interdependence, by contrast, is designed to capture relations, not among military adversaries, but among those states with close economic and political ties. In the latter case, so argue Keohane and Nye, military force is likely to play a smaller role; and international organizations, economic issues and resources, and relations among nongovernmental groups, a larger one. They argue that what was true for the relations between America and her major allies during the Cold War is likely to characterize relations among developed democracies in the future.

As Caroline Thomas shows, states that are not advanced democracies—the Third World—are likely to face greater security threats. In a few cases, nuclear weapons may endanger them. But rather than being menaced by foreign bombs and armies, the threat is more often likely to arise from the nature of these states themselves: Most of them contain potentially adversarial ethnic groups and lack the legitimacy and administrative strength that permits effective government. The line between domestic and international politics, between civil wars and international wars, is likely to be blurred, as it is in the conflict in the former Yugoslavia. Furthermore, force cannot protect Third World states against the pressing threats of economic underdevelopment and environmental degradation.

The Political Uses of Force

The Four Functions
of Force

Robert J. Art

In view of what is likely to be before us, it is vital to think carefully and precisely about the uses and limits of military power. That is the purpose of this essay. It is intended as a backdrop for policy debates, not a prescription of specific policies. It consciously eschews elaborate detail on the requisite military forces for scenarios *a* . . . *n* and focuses instead on what military power has and has not done, can and cannot do. Every model of how the world works has policy implications. But not every policy is based on a clear view of how the world works. What, then, are the uses to which military power can be put? How have nuclear weapons affected these uses? And what is the future of force in a world of nuclear parity and increasing economic interdependence?

WHAT ARE THE USES OF FORCE?

The goals that states pursue range widely and vary considerably from case to case. Military power is more useful for realizing some goals than others, though it is generally considered of some use by most states for all of the goals that they hold. If we attempt, however, to be descriptively accurate, to enumerate all of the purposes for which states use force, we shall simply end up with a bewildering list. Descriptive accuracy is not a virtue *per se* for analysis. In fact, descriptive accuracy is generally bought at the cost of analytical utility. (A concept that is descriptively accurate is usually analytically useless.) Therefore, rather than compile an exhaustive list of such purposes, I have selected four categories that themselves analytically exhaust the functions that force can serve: defense, deterrence, compellence, and "swaggering."[1]

From "To What Ends Military Power" by Robert J. Art, in *International Security,* vol. 4 (Spring 1980), pp. 4–35. Portions of the text and some footnotes have been omitted.

Not all four functions are necessarily well or equally served by a given military posture. In fact, usually only the great powers have the wherewithal to develop military forces that can serve more than two functions at once. Even then, this is achieved only vis à vis smaller powers, not vis à vis the other great ones. The measure of the capabilities of a state's military forces must be made relative to those of another state, not with reference to some absolute scale. A state that can compel another state can also defend against it and usually deter it. A state that can defend against another state cannot thereby automatically deter or compel it. A state can deter another state without having the ability to either defend against or compel it. A state that can swagger vis à vis another may or may not be able to perform any of the other three functions relative to it. Where feasible, defense is the goal that all states aim for first. If defense is not possible, deterrence is generally the next priority. Swaggering is the function most difficult to pin down analytically; deterrence, the one whose achievement is the most difficult to demonstrate; compellence, the easiest to demonstrate but among the hardest to achieve. The following discussion develops these points more fully.

The *defensive* use of force is the deployment of military power so as to be able to do two things—to ward off an attack and to minimize damage to oneself if attacked. For defensive purposes, a state will direct its forces against those of a potential or actual attacker, but not against his unarmed population. For defensive purposes, a state can deploy its forces in place prior to an attack, use them after an attack has occurred to repel it, or strike first if it believes that an attack upon it is imminent or inevitable. The defensive use of force can thus involve both peaceful and physical employment and both repellent (second) strikes and offensive (first) strikes.[2] If a state strikes first when it believes an attack upon it is imminent, it is launching a preemptive blow. If it strikes first when it believes an attack is inevitable but not momentary, it is launching a preventive blow. Preemptive and preventive blows are undertaken when a state calculates, first, that others plan to attack it and, second, that to delay in striking offensively is against its interests. A state preempts in order to wrest the advantage of the first strike from an opponent. A state launches a preventive attack because it believes that others will attack it when the balance of forces turns in their favor and therefore attacks while the balance of forces is in its favor. In both cases it is better to strike first than to be struck first. The major distinction between preemption and prevention is the calculation about when an opponent's attack will occur. For preemption, it is a matter of hours, days, or even a few weeks at the most; for prevention, months or even a few years. In the case of preemption, the state has almost no control over the timing of its attack; in the case of prevention, the state can in a more leisurely way contemplate the timing of its attack. For both cases, it is the belief in the certainty of war that governs the offensive, defensive attack. For both cases, the maxim, "the best defense is a good offense," makes good sense.

The *deterrent* use of force is the deployment of military power so as to be able to prevent an adversary from doing something that one does not want him to do and that he might otherwise be tempted to do by threatening him with unacceptable punishment if he does it. Deterrence is thus the threat of retaliation. Its purpose is to prevent something undesirable from happening. The threat of punishment is directed at the adversary's population and/or industrial infrastructure. The effectiveness of the threat depends upon a state's ability to convince a potential adversary that it has both the will and power to punish him severely if he undertakes the undesirable action in question. Deterrence therefore employs force peacefully. It is the threat to resort to force in order to punish that is the essence of deterrence. If the threat has to be carried out, deterrence by definition has failed. A deterrent threat is made precisely with the intent that it will not have to be carried out. Threats are made to prevent actions from being undertaken. If the threat has to be implemented, the action has already been undertaken. Hence deterrence can be judged successful only if the retaliatory threats have not been implemented.

Deterrence and defense are alike in that both are intended to protect the state or its closest allies from physical attacks. The purpose of both is dissuasion—persuading others *not* to undertake actions harmful to oneself. The defensive use of force dissuades by convincing an adversary that he cannot conquer one's military forces. The deterrent use of force dissuades by convincing the adversary that his population and territory will suffer terrible damage if he initiates the undesirable action. Defense dissuades by presenting an unvanquishable military force. Deterrence dissuades by presenting the certainty of retaliatory devastation.

Defense is possible without deterrence, and deterrence is possible without defense. A state can have the military wherewithall to repel an invasion without also being able to threaten devastation to the invader's population or territory. Similarly, a state can have the wherewithall credibly to threaten an adversary with such devastation and yet be unable to repel his invading force. Defense, therefore, does not necessarily buy deterrence, nor deterrence defense. A state that can defend itself from attack, moreover, will have little need to develop the wherewithall to deter. If physical attacks can be repelled or if the damage from them drastically minimized, the incentive to develop a retaliatory capability is low. A state that cannot defend itself, however, will try to develop an effective deterrent if that be possible. No state will leave its population and territory open to attack if it has the means to redress the situation. Whether a given state can defend or deter or do both vis à vis another depends upon two factors: (1) the quantitative balance of forces between it and its adversary; and (2) the qualitative balance of forces, that is, whether the extant military technology favors the offense or the defense. These two factors are situation-specific and therefore require careful analysis of the case at hand.

The *compellent* use of force is the deployment of military power so as to be able either to stop an adversary from doing something that he has already undertaken or to get him to do something that he has not yet undertaken. Compellence, in Schelling's words, "involves initiating an action . . . that can cease, or become harmless, only if the opponent responds."[3] Compellence can employ force either physically or peacefully. A state can start actually harming another with physical destruction until the latter abides by the former's wishes. Or, a state can take actions against another that do not cause physical harm but that require the latter to pay some type of significant price until it changes its behavior. America's bombing of North Vietnam in early 1965 was an example of physical compellence; Tirpitz's building of a German fleet aimed against England's in the two decades before

World War I, an example of peaceful compellence. In the first case, the United
States started bombing North Vietnam in order to compel it to stop assisting the
Vietcong forces in South Vietnam. In the latter case, Germany built a battlefleet
that in an engagement threatened to cripple England's in order to compel her to
make a general political settlement advantageous to Germany. In both cases, one
state initiated some type of action against another precisely so as to be able to stop
it, to bargain it away for the appropriate response from the "put upon" state.

The distinction between compellence and deterrence is one between the
active and passive use of force. The success of a deterrent threat is measured by its
not having to be used. The success of a compellent action is measured by how
closely and quickly the adversary conforms to one's stipulated wishes. In the case
of successful deterrence, one is trying to demonstrate a negative, to show why
something did not happen. It can never be clear whether one's actions were crucial
to, or irrelevant to, why another state chose *not* to do something. In the case of successful compellence, the clear sequence of actions and reactions lends a compelling plausibility to the centrality of one's actions. Figure 1 illustrates the distinction. In successful compellence, state B can claim that its pressure deflected state
A from its course of action. In successful deterrence, state B has no change in state
A's behavior to point to, but instead must resort to claiming that its threats were
responsible for the continuity in A's behavior. State A may have changed its behavior for reasons other than state B's compellent action. State A may have continued
with its same behavior for reasons other than state B's deterrent threat. "Proving"
the importance of B's influence on A for either case is not easy, but it is more plausible to claim that B influenced A when there is a change in A's behavior than when
there is not. Explaining why something did not happen is more difficult than
explaining why something did.

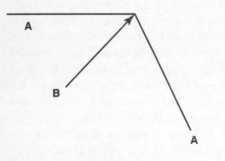

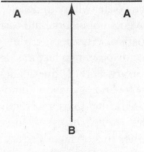

Compellence

(1) A is doing something that B cannot
tolerate

(2) B initiates action against A in order to
get him to stop his intolerable actions

(3) A stops his intolerable actions and B
stops his (or both cease simultaneously)

Deterrence

(1) A is presently not doing anything that
B finds intolerable

(2) B tells A that if A changes his behavior
and does something intolerable, B will
punish him

(3) A continues not to do anything B finds
intolerable

Figure 1

Compellence may be easier to demonstrate than deterrence, but it is harder to achieve. Schelling argues that compellent actions tend to be vaguer in their objectives than deterrent threats and for that reason more difficult to attain.[4] If an adversary has a hard time understanding what it is that one wished him to do, his compliance with one's wishes is made more difficult. There is, however, no inherent reason why a compellent action must be vaguer than a deterrent threat with regard to how clearly the adversary understands what is wanted from him. "Do not attack me" is not any clearer in its ultimate meaning than "stop attacking my friend." A state can be as confused or as clear about what it wishes to prevent as it can be about what it wishes to stop. The clarity, or lack of it, of the objectives of compellent actions and deterrent threats does not vary according to whether the given action is compellent or deterrent in nature, but rather according to a welter of particularities associated with the given action. Some objectives, for example, are inherently clearer and hence easier to perceive than others. Some statesmen communicate more clearly than others. Some states have more power to bring to bear for a given objective than others. It is the specifics of a given situation, not any intrinsic difference between compellence and deterrence, that determines the clarity with which an objective is perceived.

We must, therefore, look elsewhere for the reason as to why compellence is comparatively harder to achieve than deterrence. It lies, not in what one asks another to do, but in *how* one asks. With deterrence, state B asks something of state A in this fashion: "Do not take action X; for if you do, I will bash you over the head with this club." With compellence, state B asks something of state A in this fashion: "I am now going to bash you over the head with this club and will continue to do so until you do what I want." In the former case, state A can easily deny with great plausibility any intention of having planned to take action X. In the latter case, state A cannot deny either that it is engaged in a given course of action or that it is being subjected to pressure by state B. If they are to be successful, compellent actions require a state to alter its behavior in a manner quite visible to all in response to an equally visible forceful initiative taken by another state. In contrast to compellent actions, deterrent threats are both easier to appear to have ignored or easier to acquiesce to without great loss of face. In contrast to deterrent threats, compellent actions more directly engage the prestige and the passions of the put-upon state. Less prestige is lost in not doing something than in clearly altering behavior due to pressure from another. In the case of compellence, a state has publicly committed its prestige and resources to a given line of conduct that it is now asked to give up. This is not so for deterrence. Thus, compellence is intrinsically harder to attain than deterrence, not because its objectives are vaguer, but because it demands mere humiliation from the compelled state.

The fourth purpose to which military power can be put is the most difficult to be precise about. *Swaggering* is in part a residual category, the deployment of military power for purposes other than defense, deterrence, or compellence. Force is not aimed directly at dissuading another state from attacking, at repelling attacks, nor at compelling it to do something specific. The objectives for swaggering are more diffuse, ill-defined, and problematic than that. Swaggering almost always involves only the peaceful use of force and is expressed usually in one of two ways: displaying one's military might at military exercises and national demonstrations and buying or building the era's most prestigious weapons. The swagger use of force is the most egoistic: It aims to enhance the national pride of a people or to satisfy the personal ambitions of its ruler. A state or statesman swaggers in order to look and feel more powerful and important, to be taken seriously by others in the councils of international decision making, to enhance the nation's image in the eyes of others. If its image is enhanced, the nation's defense, deterrent, and compellent capabilities may also be enhanced; but swaggering is not undertaken solely or even primarily for these specific purposes. Swaggering is pursued because it offers to bring prestige "on the cheap." Swaggering is pursued because of the fundamental yearning of states and statesmen for respect and prestige. Swaggering is more something to be enjoyed for itself than to be employed for a specific, consciously thought-out end.

And yet, the instrumental role of swaggering cannot be totally discounted because of the fundamental relation between force and foreign policy that obtains in an anarchic environment. Because there is a connection between the military might that a nation is thought to possess and the success that it achieves in attaining its objectives, the enhancement of a state's stature in the eyes of others can always be justified on *realpolitik* lines. If swaggering causes other states to take one's interests more seriously into account, then the general interests of the state will benefit. Even in its instrumental role, however, swaggering is undertaken less for any given end than for all ends. The swaggering function of military power is thus at one and the same time the most comprehensive and the most diffuse, the most versatile in its efects and the least focused in its immediate aims, the most instrumental in the long run and the least instrumental in the short run, easy to justify on hardheaded grounds and often undertaken on emotional grounds. Swaggering mixes the rational and irrational more than the other three functions of military power and, for that reason, remains both pervasive in international relations and elusive to describe.

Defense, deterrence, compellence, and swaggering—these are the four general purposes for which force can be employed. Discriminating among them analytically, however, is easier than applying them in practice. This is due to two factors. First, we need to know the motives behind an act in order to judge its purpose; but the problem is that motives cannot be readily inferred from actions because several motives can be served by the same action. But neither can one readily infer the motives of a state from what it publicly or officially proclaims them to be. Such statements should not necessarily be taken at face value because of the role that bluff and dissimulation play in statecraft. Such statements are also often concocted with domestic political, not foreign audiences in mind, or else are deliberate exercises in studied ambiguity. Motives are important in order to interpret actions, but neither actions nor words always clearly delineate motives.

It is, moreover, especially difficult to distinguish defensive from compellent actions and deterrent from swaggering ones unless we know the reasons for which they were undertaken. Peaceful defensive preparations often look largely the same as peaceful compellent ones. Defensive attacks are nearly indistinguishable from compellent ones. Is he who attacks first the defender or the compeller? Deterrence and swaggering both involve the acquisition and display of an era's prestigious weapons. Are such weapons acquired to enhance prestige or to dissuade an attack?

Second, to make matters worse, consider the following example. Germany launched an attack upon France and Russia at the end of July 1914 and thereby began World War I. There are two schools of thought as to why Germany did this. One holds that its motives were aggressive—territorial aggrandizement, economic gain, and elevation to the status of a world empire. Another holds that her motives were preventive and hence defensive. She struck first because she feared encirclement, slow strangulation, and then inevitable attack by her two powerful neighbors, foes whom she felt were daily increasing their military might faster than she was. She struck while she had the chance to win.

It is not simple to decide which school is the more nearly correct because both can marshall evidence to build a powerful case. Assume for the moment, though, that the second is closer to the truth. There are then two possibilities to consider: (1) Germany launched an attack because it *was* the case that her foes were planning to attack her ultimately, and Germany had the evidence to prove it; or (2) Germany felt she had reasonable evidence of her foes' *intent* to attack her eventually, but in fact her evidence was wrong because she misperceived their intent from their actions. If the first was the case, then we must ask this question: How responsible was Germany's diplomacy in the fifteen years before 1914, aggressive and blundering as it was, in breeding hostility in her neighbors? Germany attacked in the knowledge that they would eventually have struck her, but if her fifteen-year diplomatic record was a significant factor in causing them to lay these plans, must we conclude that Germany in 1914 was merely acting defensively? Must we confine our judgment about the defensive or aggressive nature of the act to the month or even the year in which it occurred? If not, how many years back in history do we go in order to make a judgment? If the second was the case, then we must ask this question: If Germany attacked in the belief, mistakenly as it turns out, that she would be attacked, must we conclude that Germany was acting defensively? Must we confine our judgment about the defensive or aggressive nature of the act simply to Germany's beliefs about others' intent, without reference to their actual intent?

It is not easy to answer these questions. Fortunately, we do not have to. Asking them is enough because it illustrates that an assessment of the *legitimacy* of a state's motives in using force is integral to the task of determining what its motives are. One cannot, that is, specify motives without at the same time making judgments about their legitimacy. The root cause of this need lies in the nature of state action. In anarchy every state is a valid judge of the legitimacy of its goals because there is no supranational authority to enforce agreed upon rules. Because of the lack of universal standards, we are forced to examine each case within its given context and to make individual judgments about the meaning of the particulars. When individual judgment is exercised, individuals may well differ. Definitive answers are more likely to be the exception rather than the rule.

Where does all of this leave us? Our four categories tell us what are the four possible purposes for which states can employ military power. The attributes of each alert us to the types of evidence for which to search. But because the context of an action is crucial in order to judge its ultimate purpose, these four categories cannot be applied mindlessly and ahistorically. Each state's purpose in using force in a given instance must fall into one of these four categories. We know *a priori* what the possibilities are. Which one it is, is an exercise in judgment, an exercise that depends as much upon the particulars of the given case as it does upon the general features of the given category. . . . (See Table 1).

WHAT IS THE FUTURE OF FORCE?

If the past be any guide to the future, then military power will remain central to the course of international relations. Those states that do not have the wherewithall to field large forces (for example, Denmark) or those that choose to field forces far smaller than their economies can bear (for example, Japan) will pay the price. Both will find themselves with less control over their own fate than would otherwise be the case. Those states that field powerful military forces will find themselves in greater control, but also that their great military power can produce unintended effects and that such power is not a solution to all their problems. For both the strong and the weak, however, as long as anarchy obtains, force will remain the final arbiter to resolve the disputes that arise among them. As has always been the case, most disputes will be settled short of the physical use of force. But as long as the physical use of force remains a viable option, military power will vitally affect the manner in which all states in peacetime deal with one another.

This is a conclusion not universally nor even widely held today. Three schools of thought challenge it. First are those who argue that nuclear weapons make war, nuclear or conventional, between American and Russia or between the NATO Alliance and the Warsaw Pact unthinkable. Hopefully, that is the case. But, as we have argued, one does not measure the utility of force simply by the frequency with which it is used physically. To argue that force is on the wane because war in Europe has not occurred is to confuse effect with cause. The probability of war between America and Russia or between NATO and the Warsaw Pact is practically nil precisely because the military planning and deployments of each, together with the fears of escalation to general nuclear war, keep it that way. The absence of war in the European theater does not thereby signify the irrelevance of military power to East-West relations but rather the opposite. The estimates of relative strength between these two sets of forces, moreover, intimately affect the political and economic relations between Eastern and Western Europe. A stable balance of forces creates a political climate conducive to trade. An unstable balance of forces heightens political tensions that are disruptive to trade. The chances for general war are quite small, but the fact that it nevertheless remains possible vitally shapes the peacetime relations of the European powers to one another and to their superpower protectors.

Second are those who argue that the common problems of mankind, such as pollution, energy and other raw material scarcities, have made war and military power passé. In fact, their argument is stronger: The common problems that all nations now confront make it *imperative* that they cooperate in order to solve

TABLE 1 THE PURPOSES OF FORCE

Type	Purpose	Mode	Targets	Characteristics
Defensive	Fend off attacks and/or reduce damage of an attack	Peaceful and physical	Primarily military Secondarily industrial	Defensive preparations can have dissuasion value; Defensive preparations can look aggressive; First strikes can be taken for defense.
Deterrent	Prevent adversary from initiating an action	Peaceful	Primarily civilian Secondarily industrial Tertiarily military	Threats of retaliation made so as not to have to be carried out; Second strike preparations can be viewed as first strike preparations.
Compellent	Get adversary to stop doing something or start doing something	Peaceful and physical	All three with no clear ranking	Easy to recognize but hard to achieve; Competent actions can be justified on defensive grounds.
Swaggering	Enhance prestige	Peaceful	None	Difficult to describe because of instrumental and irrational nature; Swaggering can be threatening.

them. This argument, however, is less a statement of fact about the present than a fervent hope for the future. Unfortunately, proof of how the future will look is not available in the present. Cooperation among nations today, such as it is, should not make us sanguine about their ability to surmount their conflicts for the good of all. It takes a strong imagination, moreover, to assume that what some nations term common problems are viewed as such by all. One man's overpopulation, for example, is another man's source of strength. China and India are rightly concerned about the deleterious effects of their population growth on their standard of living. But Nigeria, whose source of power and influence within Africa rests partly on a population that is huge by African standards, is not. The elemental rule of international relations is that the circumstances of states differ. Hence so too do their interests and perspectives. Not only do they have different solutions to the same problem, they do not always or often agree on what are the problems. As long as anarchy obtains, therefore, there will be no agency above states powerful enough to create and enforce a consensus. As long as anarchy obtains, therefore, military power deployed by individual states will play a vital role both in defining what are the problems and in hastening or delaying their solutions. Only when world government arrives will the ability of every nation to resort to force cease to be an option. But even then, the importance of force will endure. For every government has need of an army.

Finally, there are those who proclaim that the nations of the world have become so economically intertwined that military power is no longer of use because its use is no longer credible. A nation whose economic interests are deeply entangled with another's cannot use force against it because to do so would be to harm itself in the process. Interests intertwined render force unusable—so believe the "interdependencia theorists.". . . This view of the world is odd. . . . American military power has created and sustained the political preconditions necessary for the evolutionary intertwining of the American, Canadian, Japanese, and Western European economies. . . . Military preeminence has never ensured political and economic preeminence. But it does put one nation in a stronger bargaining position that, if skillfully exploited, can be fashioned for non-military goals. Force cannot be irrelevant as a tool of policy for America's economic relations with her great power allies: America's military preeminence politically pervades these relations. It is the cement of economic interdependence.

A simple example will clarify the point. In 1945, convinced that competitive devaluations of currencies made the depression of the 1930s deeper and longer than need be, America pushed for fixed exchange rates. Her view prevailed, and the Bretton Woods structure of fixed exchange rates, with small permissible variations monitored by the International Monetary Fund, was set up and lasted until 1971. In that year, because of the huge outflow of dollars over a twenty-five year period, the United States found it to its best interests to close the gold window—that is, to suspend the commitment to pay out gold for dollars that any nation turned in. Under Bretton Woods the relations of the free world's currencies to one another were fixed in the relation of each to the dollar, which in turn was fixed in value by its relation to the standard "one ounce of gold equals thirty-five dollars." By closing the gold window, the United States shattered that standard, caused the price of an ounce of gold in dollars to soar, destroyed the fixed benchmark according to which all currencies were measured, and ushered in the era of floating exchange rates. In sum, America both made and unmade the Bretton Woods system. In 1945 she persuaded her allies. In 1971 she acted unilaterally and against their wishes.

Under both fixed and floating exchange rates, moreover, the United States has confronted her great power allies with an unpleasant choice. Either they could accept and hold onto the dollars flowing out of the United States and thereby add to their inflation at home by increasing their money supplies; or they could refuse the dollars, watch the value of their currencies in relation to the dollar rise, make their exports more expensive (exports upon which all these nations heavily rely), and threaten a decline in exports with the concomitant risk of a recession. America's economic and military strength has enabled her for over twenty years to confront her great power allies with the choice of inflation or recession for their economies. America did not have to use her military power directly to structure the choice this way, nor to make and break the system. Her economic strength, still greater than that of most of her great power allies combined, gave her considerable bargaining power. But without her military preeminence and their military dependence, she could never have acted as she did. America used her military power politically to cope with her dollar valuation problem.

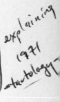

explaining 1971 tautology

In a similar vein, others argue that the United States can no longer use its military power against key Third World nations to achieve its aims because of its dependence on their raw materials or because of its needs to sell them manufactured goods. In order to assess the validity of this argument, four factors must be kept in mind. First, the efficacy of military power should not be confused with the will to use it. In the mid- and late 1970s, as a consequence of the experience with Vietnam, America's foreign policy elite was reluctant to commit American conventional forces to combat. Its calculation has been that the American public would not tolerate such actions, except for the most compelling and extreme of circumstances. The non-use of American military power in Asia, Africa, and Latin American in the late 1970s stems as much from American domestic political restraints as from anything else.

Second, it is important to recall a point made earlier about the inherent limits of military power to achieve economic objectives. A superior military. position can give one state a bargaining edge over another in the conduct of their bilateral economic relations, but bargains must still be struck. And that requires compromise by both parties. Only by conquest, occupation, and rule, or by a credible threat to that effect, can one state guarantee that another will conduct its economic relations on terms most favorable to the (would-be) conqueror. Short of that, the economic relations between two states are settled on the basis of each state's perception of its own economic interests, on differences in the strength, size, and diversity, of their economies, on differences in the degree to which each state coordinates the activities of its interest groups and hence centrally manages its economy, and on the differential in their military capabilities. Because military power is only one of the ingredients that determine the economic relations between two states, its rule is not always, nor usually, overriding. By itself superiority in arms does not guarantee,

superior arms alone does not guarantee econ. leverage

nor has it ever guaranteed, superiority, in economic leverage. In this sense, although there may be clear limits on what the United States through its military power can achieve in its economic relations with the Third World, much of the constraint stems from the limits that inhere in translating military power into economic ends.

Third, America's economic power relative to others has waned in the 1970s. The 1950s were characterized by a United States whose economic and military power far surpassed that of any other nation. With the emergence of the Soviet Union as a global military power in the 1970s, America's freedom to intervene militarily around the world, unimpeded by concerns about the counteractions of another global power, has drastically declined. But America's economic freedom worldwide has also waned. Whether measured by the diminished role of the dollar as the world's reserve currency, by the persistent lack of a favorable trade balance, by a smaller percentage of the world's trade accounted for by American imports and exports, by a decline in the productivity of its labor force, or by a greater dependence on imported raw materials, the United States economy is not as self-sufficient and immune from economic events beyond its borders as it once was. Analysts disagree over the extent to which, and the reasons why, the health of the American economy has become more dependent on the actions of other nations; but they do not disagree on the fact of greater dependence. If the hallmark of the fifties and sixties was America's military and economic preeminence, the hallmark of the seventies has been America's passing the zenith of her power and the consequent waning of this dual preeminence.

A diminishment in the economic power of a state is not easily compensated for by an edge in military capability. When that military edge also wanes, such compensation becomes even more difficult. Although the United States remains the world's strongest economic *and* military power, the gap between her strength in each dimension and that of other nations has narrowed in the seventies from that which was the case in the fifties and sixties. It is therefore wrongheaded to assert that America's diminished ability to get what it wants economically from allies and neutrals is due solely to the devaluation of military power. It is wrongheaded to assert that military power is devalued because it cannot solve economic problems when economic problems have never been readily or totally solved by military measures. It is wrongheaded to blame on military power that which has military and economic causes. The utility of force to a state for compellent purposes does diminish as the relative military power of a state declines. But the utility of force for compellent economic purposes declines even more when a state's economic bargaining power concomitantly wanes.

Fourth, force cannot be efficiently used to achieve goals when ambivalence exists over the goal to be attained. . . . It would be absurd to deny the fact that the potency of the Third World's virulent nationalism has restrained the great powers in their military adventures against those nations. It would be absurd to deny that the 1970s are not different from the 1870s and 1880s, when the European great powers, restrained only by their fears of each other's counteractions, intervened militarily at will in Asia and Africa against poorly armed and politically fragmented "nations." Clearly the political and military conditions for great power military intervention in such areas have drastically changed since then. . . .

The efficacy of force endures. It must. For in anarchy, force and politics are connected. By itself, military power guarantees neither survival nor prosperity. But it is almost always the essential ingredient for both. Because resort to force is the ultimate card of all states, the seriousness of a state's intentions is conveyed fundamentally by its having a credible military posture. Without it, a state's diplomacy generally lacks effectiveness. For the need not be physically used to be politically useful. Threats need not be overtly made to be communicated. The mere presence of a credible military option is often sufficient to make the point. It is the capability to resort to military force if all else fails that serves as the most effective brake against having to do so. Lurking behind the scenes, unstated but explicit, lies the military muscle that gives meaning to the posturings of the diplomats. Diplomacy is the striking of compromises by parties with differing perspectives and clashing interests. The ultimate ability of each to resort to force disciplines the diplomats. Precisely because each knows that all can come to blows if they do not strike compromises do the diplomats engage in the hard work necessary to construct them. There is truth to the old adage: "The best way to keep the peace is first to prepare for war."

Realism

NOTES

1. The term "compellence" was coined by Thomas C. Schelling in his *Arms and Influence* (New Haven: Yale University Press, 1966). Part of my discussion of compellence and deterrence draws upon his as it appears in Chapter 2 (pp. 69–86), but, as will be made clear below, I disagree with some of his conclusions.
2. Military power can be used in one of two modes—"physically" and "peacefully." The physical use of force refers to its actual employment against an adversary, usually but not always in a mutual exchange of blows. The peaceful use of force refers either to an explicit threat to resort to force, or to the implicit threat to use it that is communicated simply by a state's having it available for use. The physical use of force means that one nation is literally engaged in harming, destroying, or crippling those possessions which another nation holds dear, including its military forces. The peaceful use of force is referred to as such because, while force is "used" in the sense that it is employed explicitly or implicitly for the assistance it is thought to render in achieving a given goal, it does not result in any physical destruction to another nation's valued possessions. There is obviously a gray area between these two modes of use—the one in which a nation prepares (that is, gears up or mobilizes or moves about) its military forces for use against another nation but has not yet committed them such that they are inflicting damage.
3. Schelling, *Arms and Influence*, p. 72.
4. *Ibid.*, pp. 72–73.

The Diplomacy of Violence

Thomas C. Schelling

The usual distinction between diplomacy and force is not merely in the instruments, words or bullets, but in the relation between adversaries—in the interplay of motives and the role of communication, understandings, compromise, and restraint. Diplomacy is bargaining; it seeks outcomes that, though not ideal for either party, are better for both than some of the alternatives. In diplomacy each party somewhat controls what the other wants, and can get more by compromise, exchange, or collaboration than by taking things in his own hands and ignoring the other's wishes. The bargaining can be polite or rude, entail threats as well as offers, assume a status quo or ignore all rights and privileges, and assume mistrust rather than trust. But whether polite or impolite, constructive or aggressive, respectful or vicious, whether it occurs among friends or antagonists and whether or not there is a basis for trust and goodwill, there must be some common interest, if only in the avoidance of mutual damage, and an awareness of the need to make the other party prefer an outcome acceptable to oneself.

With enough military force a country may not need to bargain. Some things a country wants it can take, and some things it has it can keep, by sheer strength, skill, and ingenuity. It can do this *forcibly*, accommodating only to opposing strength, skill, and ingenuity and without trying to appeal to an enemy's wishes. Forcibly a country can repel and expel, penetrate and occupy, seize, exterminate, disarm and disable, confine, deny access, and directly frustrate intrusion or attack. It can, that is, if it has enough strength. "Enough" depends on how much an opponent has.

There is something else, though, the force can do. It is less military, less heroic, less impersonal, and less unilateral; it is uglier, and has received less attention in Western military strategy. In addition to seizing and holding, disarming and confining, penetrating and obstructing, and all that, military force can be used to *hurt*. In addition to taking and protecting things of value it can destroy value. In addition to weakening an enemy militarily it can cause an enemy plain suffering. . . .

THE CONTRAST OF BRUTE FORCE WITH COERCION

There is a difference between taking what you want and making someone give it to you, between fending off assault and making someone afraid to assault you, between holding what people are trying to take and making them afraid to take it, between losing what someone can forcibly take and giving it up to avoid risk or damage. It is the difference between defense and deterrence, between brute force and intimidation, between conquest and blackmail, between action and threats. It is the difference between the unilateral, "undiplomatic" recourse to strength, and coercive diplomacy based on the power to hurt.

The contrasts are several. The purely "military" or "undiplomatic" recourse to forcible action is concerned with enemy strength, not enemy interests; the coercive use of the power to hurt, though, is the very exploitation of enemy wants and fears. And brute strength is usually measured relative to enemy strength, the one directly opposing the other, while the power to hurt is typically not reduced by the enemy's power to hurt in return. Opposing strengths may cancel each other, pain and grief do not. The willingness to hurt, the credibility of a threat, and the ability to exploit the power to hurt will indeed depend on how much the adversary can hurt in return but there is little or nothing about an adversary's pain or grief that directly reduces one's own. Two sides cannot both overcome each other with superior strength; they may both be able to hurt each other. With strength they can dispute objects of value; with sheer violence they can destroy them.

And brute force succeeds when it is used, whereas the power to hurt is most successful when held in reserve. It is the *threat* of damage, or of more damage to come, that can make someone yield or comply. It is *latent* violence that can influence someone's choice—violence that can still be withheld or inflicted or that a victim believes can be withheld or inflicted. The threat of pain tries to structure someone's motives, while brute forces tries to overcome his strength. Unhappily, the power to hurt is often communicated by some performance of it. Whether it is sheer terroristic violence to induce an irrational response, or cool premeditated violence to persuade somebody that you mean it and may do it again, it is not the pain and damage itself but its influence on somebody's behavior that matters. It is the expectation of *more* violence that gets the wanted behavior, if the power to hurt can get it at all.

To exploit a capacity for hurting and inflicting damage one needs to know what an adversary treasures and what scares him and one needs the adversary to understand what behavior of his will cause the violence to be inflicted and what will cause it to be withheld. The victim has to know what is wanted, and he may have to be assured of what is not wanted. The pain and suffering have to appear *contingent* on his behavior; it is not alone the threat that is effective—the threat of pain or loss if he fails to comply—but the corresponding assurance, possibly an implicit one, that he can avoid the pain or loss if he does comply. The prospect of certain death may stun him, but it gives him no choice.

Coercion by threat of damage also requires that our interests and our opponent's not be absolutely opposed. If his pain were our greatest delight and our satisfaction his great woe, we would just proceed to hurt and to frustrate each other. It is when his pain gives us little or no satisfaction compared with what he can do for us, and the action or inaction that satisfies us costs him less than the pain we can cause, that there is room for coercion. Coercion requires finding a bargain, arranging for him to be better off doing what we want—worse off not . . . doing what we want—when he takes the threatened penalty into account. . . .

This difference between coercion and brute force is as often in the intent as in the instrument. To hunt down Comanches and to exterminate them was brute force; to raid their villages to make them behave was coercive diplomacy, based on the power to hurt. The pain and loss to the Indians might have looked much the same one way as the other; the difference was one of purpose and effect. If Indians were killed because they were in the way, or somebody wanted their land, or the authorities despaired of making them behave and could not confine them and decided to exterminate them, that was pure unilateral force. If *some* Indians were killed to make *other* Indians behave, that was coercive violence—or intended to be, whether or not it was effective. The Germans at Verdun perceived themselves to be chewing up hundreds of thousands of French soldiers in a gruesome "meat-grinder." If the purpose was to eliminate a military obstacle—the French infantry-man, viewed as a military "asset" rather than as a warm human being—the offensive at Verdun was a unilateral exercise of military force. If instead the object was to make the loss of young men—not of impersonal "effectives," but of sons, husbands, fathers and the pride of French manhood—so anguishing as to be unendurable, to make surrender a welcome relief and to spoil the foretaste of an Allied victory, then it was an exercise in coercion, in applied violence, intended to offer relief upon accommodation. And of course, since any use of force tends to be brutal, thoughtless, vengeful, or plain obstinate, the motives themselves can be mixed and confused. The fact that heroism and brutality can be either coercive diplomacy or a contest in pure strength does not promise that the distinction will be made, and the strategies enlightened by the distinction, every time some vicious enterprise gets launched. . . .

. . . . War appears to be, or threatens to be, not so much a contest of strength as one of endurance, nerve, obstinacy, and pain. It appears to be, and threatens to be, not so much a contest of military strength as a bargaining process—dirty, extortionate, and often quite reluctant bargaining on one side or both—nevertheless a bargaining process.

The difference cannot quite be expressed as one between the *use* of force and the *threat* of force. The actions involved in forcible accomplishment, on the one hand, and in fulfilling a threat, on the other, can be quite different. Sometimes the most effective direct action inflicts enough cost or pain on the enemy to serve as a threat, sometimes not. The United States threatens the Soviet Union with virtual destruction of its society in the event of a surprise attack on the United States; a hundred million deaths are awesome as pure damage, but they are useless in stopping the Soviet attack–especially if the threat is to do it all afterward anyway. So it is worthwhile to keep the concepts distinct—to distinguish forcible action from the threat of pain—recognizing that some actions serve as both a means of forcible accomplishment and a means of inflicting pure damage; some do not. Hostages tend to entail almost pure pain and damage, as do all forms of reprisal after the fact. Some modes of self-defense may exact so little in blood or treasure as to entail negligible violence; and some forcible actions entail so much violence that their threat can be effective by itself.

The power to hurt, though it can usually accomplish nothing directly, is potentially more versatile than a straightforward capacity for forcible accomplishment. By force alone we cannot even lead a horse to water—we have to drag him—much less make him drink. Any affirmative action, any collaboration, almost anything but physical exclusion, expulsion, or extermination, requires that an opponent or a victim do something, even if only to stop or get out. The threat of pain and damage may make him want to do it, and anything he can do is potentially susceptible to inducement. Brute force can only accomplish what requires no collaboration. The principle is illustrated by a technique of unarmed combat: One can disable a man by various stunning, fracturing, or killing blows, but to take him to jail one has to exploit the man's own efforts. "Come-along" holds are those that threaten pain or disablement, giving relief as long as the victim complies, giving him the option of using his own legs to get to jail. . . .

The fact that violence—pure pain and damage—can be used or threatened to coerce and to deter, to intimidate and to blackmail, to demoralize and to paralyze, in a conscious process of dirty bargaining, does not by any means imply that violence is not often wanton and meaningless or, even when purposive, in danger of getting out of hand. Ancient wars were often quite "total" for the loser, the men being put to death, the women sold as slaves, the boys castrated, the cattle slaughtered, and the buildings leveled, for the sake of revenge, justice, personal gain, or merely custom. If an enemy bombs a city, by design or by carelessness, we usually bomb his if we can. In the excitement and fatigue of warfare, revenge is one of the few satisfactions that can be savored. . . . Pure violence, like fire, can be harnessed to a purpose; that does not mean that behind every holocaust is a shrewd intention successfully fulfilled.

But if the occurrence of violence does not always bespeak a shrewd purpose, the absence of pain and destruction is no sign that violence was idle. Violence is most purposive and most successful when it is threatened and not used. Successful threats are those that do not have to be carried out. . . .

THE STRATEGIC ROLE OF PAIN AND DAMAGE

Pure violence, nonmilitary violence, appears most conspicuously in relations between unequal countries, where there is no substantial military challenge and the outcome of military engagement is not in question: Hitler could make his threats contemptuously and brutally against Austria; he could make them, if he wished, in a more refined way against Denmark. It is noteworthy that it was Hitler, not his generals, who used this kind of language; proud military establishments do not like to think of themselves as extortionists. Their favorite job is to deliver victory, to dispose of opposing military force and to leave most of the civilian violence to politics and diplomacy. But if there is no room for doubt how a contest in strength will come out, it may be possible to bypass the military stage altogether and to proceed at once to the coercive bargaining.

A typical confrontation of unequal forces occurs at the *end* of a war, between victor and vanquished. Where Austria was vulnerable before a shot was fired, France was vulnerable after its military shield had collapsed in 1940. Surrender negotiations are the place where the threat of civil violence can come to the fore. Surrender negotiations are often so one-sided, or the potential violence so unmistakable, that bargaining succeeds and the violence remains in reserve. But the fact that most of the actual damage was done during the military stage of the war, prior to victory and defeat, does not mean that violence was idle in the aftermath, only that it was latent and the threat of it successful. . . .

. . . The Russians crushed Budapest in 1956 and cowed Poland and other neighboring countries. There was a lag of ten years between military victory and this show of violence, but the principle was the one [just] explained. . . . Military victory is often the prelude to violence, not the end of it, and the fact that successful violence is usually held in reserve should not deceive us about the role it plays.

What about pure violence during war itself, the infliction of pain and suffering as a military technique? Is the threat of pain involved only in the political use of victory, or is it a decisive technique of war itself?

Evidently between unequal powers it has been part of warfare. Colonial conquest has often been a matter of "punitive expeditions" rather than genuine military engagements. If the tribesmen escape into the brush you can burn their villages without them until they assent to receive what, in strikingly modern language, used to be known as the Queen's "protection.". . .

Pure hurting, as a military tactic, appeared in some of the military actions against the plains Indians. In 1868, during the war with the Cheyennes, General Sheridan decided that his best hope was to attack the Indians in their winter camps. His reasoning was that the Indians could maraud as they pleased during the seasons when their ponies could subsist on grass, and in the winter hide away in remote places. "To disabuse their minds from the idea that they were secure from punishment, and to strike at a period when they were helpless to move their stock and villages, a winter campaign was projected against the large bands hiding away in the Indian territory."[1]

These were not military engagements; they were punitive attacks on people. They were an effort to subdue by the use of violence, without a futile attempt to draw the enemy's military forces into decisive battle. They were "massive retaliation" on a diminutive scale, with local effects not unlike those of Hiroshima. The Indians themselves totally lacked organization and discipline, and typically could not afford enough ammunitions for target practice and were no military match for the calvary; their own rudimentary strategy was at best one of harassment and reprisal. Half a century of Indian fighting in the West left us a legacy of cavalry tactics; but it is hard to find a serious treatise on American strategy against the Indians or Indian strategy against the whites. The twentieth is not the first century in which "retaliation" has been part of our strategy, but it is the first in which we have systematically recognized it. . . .

Making it "terrible beyond endurance" is what we associate with Algeria and Palestine, the crushing of Budapest, and the tribal warfare in Central Africa. But in the great wars of the last hundred years it was usually military victory, not the hurting of the people, that was decisive; General Sherman's attempt to make war hell for the Southern people did not come to epitomize military strategy for the century to follow. To seek out and destroy the enemy's military force, to achieve a crushing victory over enemy armies, was still the avowed purpose and the central aim of American strategy in both world wars. Military action was seen as an *alternative* to bargaining, not a *process* of bargaining.

The reason is not that civilized countries are so averse to huting people that they prefer "purely military" wars. (Nor were all of the participants in these wars entirely civilized.) The reason is apparently that the technology and geography of warfare, at least for a war between anything like equal powers during the century ending in World War II, kept coercive violence from being decisive before military victory was achieved. Blockade indeed was aimed at the whole enemy nation, not concentrated on its military forces; the German civilians who died of influenza in the First World War were victims directed at the whole country. It has never been quite clear whether blockade—of the South in the Civil War or of the Central Powers in both world wars, or submarine warfare against Britain—was expected to make war unendurable for the people or just to weaken the enemy forces by denying economic support. Both arguments were made, but there was no need to be clear about the purpose as long as either purpose was regarded as legitimate and either might be served. "Strategic bombing" of enemy homelands was also occasionally rationalized in terms of the pain and privation it could inflict on people and the civil damage it could do to the nation, as an effort to display either to the population or to the enemy leadership that surrender was better than persistence in view of the damage that could be done. It was also rationalized in more "military" terms, as a way of selectively denying war material to the troops or as a way of generally weakening the economy on which the military effort rested.

But terrorism—as violence intended to coerce the enemy rather than to weaken him militarily—blockade and strategic bombing by themselves were not quite up to the job in either world war in Europe. (They might have been sufficient in the war with Japan after straightforward military action had brought American aircraft into range.) Airplanes could not quite make punitive, coercive violence decisive in Europe, at least on a tolerable time schedule, and preclude the need to defeat or to destroy enemy forces as long as they had nothing but conventional explosives and incendiaries to carry. Hitler's V–1 buzz bomb and his V–2 rocket are fairly pure cases of weapons whose purpose was to intimidate, to hurt Britain itself rather than Allied military forces. What the V–2 needed was a punitive payload worth carrying, and the Germans did not have it. Some of the expectations in the 1920s and the 1930s that another major war would be one of pure civilian violence, of shock and terror from the skies, were not borne out by the available technology. The threat of punitive violence kept occupied countries quiescent; but the wars were won in Europe on the basis of brute strength and skill and not by intimidation, not by the threat of civilian violence but by the application of military force. Military victory was still the price of admission. Latent violence against people was reserved for the politics of surrender and occupation.

The great exception was the two atomic bombs on Japanese cities. These were weapons of terror and shock. They hurt, and promised more hurt, and that was their purpose. The few "small" weapons we had were undoubtedly of some direct military value but their enormous advantage was in pure violence. In a military sense the United States could gain a little by destruction of two Japanese industrial cities; in a civilian sense, the Japanese could lose much. The bomb that hit Hiroshima was a threat aimed at all of Japan. The political target of the bomb was not the dead of Hiroshima or the factories they worked in, but the survivors of Tokyo. The two bombs were in the tradition of Sheridan against the Comanches and Sherman in Georgia. Whether in the end those two bombs saved lives or wasted them, Japanese lives or American lives; whether punitive coercive violence is uglier than straightforward military force or more civilized; whether terror is more or less humane than military destruction; we can at least perceive that the bombs on Hiroshima and Nagasaki represented violence against the country itself and not mainly an attack on Japan's material strength. The effect of the bombs, and their purpose, was not mainly the military destruction they accomplished but the pain and the shock and the promise of more.

THE NUCLEAR CONTRIBUTION TO TERROR AND VIOLENCE

Man has, it is said, for the first time in history enough military power to eliminate his species from the earth, weapons against which there is no conceivable defense. War has become, it is said, so destructive and terrible that it ceases to be an instrument of national power. "For the first time in human history," says Max Lerner in a book whose title, *The Age of Overkill,* conveys the point, "men have bottled up a power . . . which they have thus far not dared to use." And Soviet military authorities, whose party dislikes having to accommodate an entire theory of history to a single technological event, have had to re-examine a set of principles that had been given the embarrassing name of "permanently operating factors" in warfare. Indeed, our era is epitomized by words like "the first time in human history," and by the abdication of what was "permanent."

For dramatic impact these statements are splendid. Some of them display a tendency, not at all necessary, to belittle the catastrophe of earlier wars. They may exaggerate the historical novelty of deterrence and the balance of terror.[2] More important, they do not help to identify just what is new about war when so much destructive energy can be packed in warheads at a price that permits advanced countries to have them in large numbers. Nuclear warheads are incomparably more devastating than anything packaged before. What does that imply about war?

It is not true that for the first time in history man has the capability to destroy a large fraction, even the major part, of the human race. Japan was defenseless by

August 1945. With a combination of bombing and blockade, eventually invasion, and if necessary the deliberate spread of disease, the United States could probably have exterminated the population of the Japanese islands without nuclear weapons. . . .

It is a grisly thing to talk about. We did not do it and it is not imaginable that we would have done it. We had no reason; if we had had a reason, we would not have the persistence of purpose once the fury of war had been dissipated in victory and we had taken on the task of the executioner. If we and our enemies might do such a thing to each other now, and to others as well, it is not because nuclear weapons have for the first time made it feasible.

Nuclear weapons can do it quickly. . . . To compress a catastrophic war within the span of time that a man can stay awake drastically changes the politics of war, the process of decision, the possibility of central control and restraint, the motivations of people in charge, and the capacity to think and reflect while war is in progress. It *is* imaginable that we might destroy 200,000,000 Russians in a war of the present, though not 80,000,000 Japanese in a war of the past. It is not only imaginable, it is imagined. It is imaginable because it could be done "in a moment, in the twinkling of an eye, at the last trumpet."

This may be why there is so little discussion of how an all-out war might be brought to a close. People do not expect it to be "brought" to a close, but just to come to an end when everything has been spent. It is also why the idea of "limited war" has become so explicit in recent years. Earlier wars, like the World Wars I and II or the Franco-Prussian War, were limited by *termination*, by an ending that occurred before the period of greatest potential violence, by negotiation that brought the *threat* of pain and privation to bear but often precluded the massive *exercise* of civilian violence. With nuclear weapons available, the restraint of violence cannot await the outcome of a contest of military strength; restraint, to occur at all, must occur during war itself.

This is a difference between nuclear weapons and bayonets. It is not in the number of people they can eventually kill but in the speed with which it can be done, in the centralization of decision, in the divorce of the war from political process, and in computerized programs that threaten to take the war out of human hands once it begins.

That nuclear weapons make it *possible* to compress the fury of global war into a few hours does not mean that they make it *inevitable*. We have still to ask whether that is the way a major nuclear war would be fought, or ought to be fought. Nevertheless, that the whole war might go off like one big string of firecrackers makes a critical difference between our conception of nuclear war and the world wars we have experienced. . . .

There is another difference. In the past it has usually been the victors who could do what they pleased to the enemy. War has often been "total war" for the loser. With deadly monotony the Persians, Greeks and Romans "put to death all men of military age, and sold the women and children into slavery," leaving the defeated territory nothing but its name until new settlers arrived sometime later. But the defeated could not do the same to their victors. The boys could be castrated and sold only after the war had been won, and only on the side that lost it. The power to hurt could be brought to bear only after military strength had achieved victory. The same sequence characterized the great wars of this century; for reasons of technology and geography, military force has usually had to penetrate, to exhaust, or to collapse opposing military force—to achieve military victory— before it could be brought to bear on the enemy nation itself. The Allies in World War I could not inflict coercive pain and suffering directly on the Germans in a decisive way until they could defeat the German army; and the Germans could not coerce the French people with bayonets unless they first beat the Allied troops that stood in their way. With two-dimensional warfare, there is a tendency for troops to confront each other, shielding their own lands while attempting to press into each other's. Small penetrations could not do major damage to the people; large penetrations were so destructive of military organization that they usually ended the military phase of the war.

Nuclear weapons make it possible to do monstrous violence to the enemy without first achieving victory. With nuclear weapons and today's means of delivery, one expects to penetrate an enemy homeland without first collapsing his military force. What nuclear weapons have done, or appear to do, is to promote this kind of warfare to first place. Nuclear weapons threaten to make war less military, and are responsible for the lowered status of "military victory" at the present time. *Victory is no longer a prerequisite for hurting the enemy.* And it is no assurance against being terribly hurt. One need not wait until he has won the war before inflicting "unendurable" damages on his enemy. One need not wait until he has lost the war. There was a time when the assurance of victory—false or genuine assurance—could make national leaders not just willing but sometimes enthusiastic about war. Not now.

Not only *can* nuclear weapons hurt the enemy before the war has been won, and perhaps hurt decisively enough to make the military engagement academic, but it is widely assumed that in a major war that is *all* they can do. Major war is often discussed as though it would be only a contest in national destruction. If this is indeed the case—if the destruction of cities and their populations has become, with nuclear weapons, the primary object in an all-out war—the sequence of war has been reversed. Instead of destroying enemy forces as a prelude to imposing one's will on the enemy nation, one would have to destroy the nation as a means or a prelude to destroying the enemy forces. If one cannot disable enemy forces without virtually destroying the country, the victor does not even have the option of sparing the conquered nation. He has already destroyed it. Even with blockade and strategic bombing it could be supposed that a country would be defeated before it was destroyed, or would elect surrender before annihilation had gone far. In the Civil War it could be hoped that the South would become too weak to fight before it became too weak to survive. For "all-out" war, nuclear weapons threaten to reverse this sequence.

So nuclear weapons do make a differnce, marking an epoch in warfare. The difference is not just in the amount of destruction that can be accomplished but in the role of destruction and in the decision process. Nuclear weapons can change the speed of events, the control of events, the sequence of events, the relation of victor to vanquished, and the relation of homeland to fighting front. Deterrence

rests today on the threat of pain and extinction, not just on the threat of military
defeat. We may argue about the wisdom of announcing "unconditional surrender"
as an aim in the last major war, but seem to expect "unconditional destruction" as
a matter of course in another one.

Something like the same destruction always *could* be done. With nuclear
weapons there is an expectation that it would be done. . . . What is new is . . . the
idea that major war might be just a contest in the killing of countries, or not even a
contest but just two parallel exercises in devastation.

That is the difference nuclear weapons make. At least they *may* make the difference. They also may not. If the weapons themselves are vulnerable to attack, or
the machines that carry them, a successful surprise might eliminate the opponent's
means of retribution. That an enormous explosion can be packaged in a single
bomb does not by itself guarantee that the victor will receive deadly punishment.
Two gunfighters facing each other in a Western town had an unquestioned capacity to kill one another; that did not guarantee that both would die in a gunfight—
only the slower of the two. Less deadly weapons, permitting an injured one to
shoot back before he died, might have been more conducive to a restraining balance of terror, or of caution. The very efficiency of nuclear weapons could make
them ideal for starting war, if they can suddenly eliminate the enemy's capability to
shoot back.

And there is a contrary possibility: that nuclear weapons are not vulnerable to
attack and prove not to be terribly effective against each other, posing no need to
shoot them quickly for fear they will be destroyed before they are launched, and
with no task available but the systematic destruction of the enemy country and no
necessary reason to do it fast rather than slowly. Imagine that nuclear destruction
had to go slowly—that the bombs could be dropped only one per day. The prospect
would look very different, something like the most terroristic guerilla warfare on a
massive scale. It happens that nuclear war does not have to go slowly; but it may
also not have to go speedily. The mere existence of nuclear weapons does not itself
determine that everything must go off in a blinding flash, any more than that it
must go slowly. Nuclear weapons do not simplify things quite that much. . . .

In World Wars I and II one went to work on enemy military forces, not his
people, because until the enemy's military forces had been taken care of there was
typically not anything decisive that one could do to the enemy nation itself. The
Germans did not, in World War I, refrain from bayoneting French citizens by the
millions in the hopes that the Allies would abstain from shooting up the German
population. They could not get at the French citizens until they had breached the
Allied lines. Hitler tried to terrorize London and did not make it. The Allied air
forces took the war straight to Hitler's territory, with at least some thought of doing
in Germany what Sherman recognized he was doing in Georgia; but with the
bombing technology of World War II one could not afford to bypass the troops and
go exclusively for enemy populations—not, anyway, in Germany. With nuclear
weapons one has that alternative.

To concentrate on the enemy's military installations while deliberately holding
in reserve a massive capacity for destroying his cities, for exterminating his people
and eliminating his society, on condition that the enemy observe similar restraint

with respect to one's own society is not the "conventional approach." In World Wars I and II the first order of business was to destroy enemy armed forces because that was the only promising way to make him surrender. To fight a purely military engagement "all-out" while holding in reserve a decisive capacity for violence, on condition the enemy do likewise, is not the way military operations have traditionally been approached.

. . . In the present era noncombatants appear to be not only deliberate targets but primary targets. . . . In fact, noncombatants appeared to be primary targets at both ends of the scale of warfare; thermonuclear war threatened to be a contest in the destruction of cities and populations; and, at the other end of the scale, insurgency is almost entirely terroristic. We live in an era of dirty war.

Why is this so? Is war properly a military affair among combatants, and is it a depravity peculiar to the twentieth century that we cannot keep it within decent bounds? Or is war inherently dirty?

To answer this question it is useful to distinguish three stages in the involvement of noncombatants—of plain people and their possessions—in the fury of war. These stages are worth distinguishing; but their sequence is merely descriptive of Western Europe during the past three hundred years, not a historical generalization. The first stage is that in which the people may get hurt by inconsiderate combatants. This is the status that people had during the period of "civilized warfare" that the International Committee had in mind.

From about 1648 to the Napoleonic era, war in much of Western Europe was something superimposed on society. It was a contest engaged in by monarchies for stakes that were measured in territories, and, occasionally, money or dynastic claims. The troops were mostly mercenaries and the motivation for war was confined to the aristocratic elite. Monarchs fought for bits of territory, but the residents of disputed terrain were more concerned with protecting their crops and their daughters from marauding troops than with whom they owed allegiance to. They were, as Quincy Wright remarked in his classic *Study of War,* little concerned that the territory in which they lived had a new sovereign.[3] Furthermore, as far as the King of Prussia and the Emperor of Austria were concerned, the loyalty and enthusiasm of the Bohemian farmer were not decisive considerations. It is an exaggeration to refer to European war during this period as a sport of kings, but not a gross exaggeration. And the military logistics of those days confined military operations to a scale that did not require the enthusiasm of a multitude.

Hurting people was not a decisive instrument in warfare. Hurting people or destroying property only reduced the value of things that were being fought over, to the disadvantage of both sides. Furthermore, the monarchs who conducted wars often did not want to discredit the social institutions they shared with their enemies. Bypassing an enemy monarch and taking the war straight to his people would have had revolutionary implications. Destroying the opposing monarchy was often not in the interest of either side; opposing sovereigns had much more in common with each other than with their own subjects, and to discredit the claims of a monarchy might have produced a disastrous backlash. It is not surprising—or, if it is surprising, not altogether astonishing—that on the European continent in that particular era war was fairly well confined to military activity.

One could still, in those days and in that part of the world, be concerned for the rights of noncombatants and hope to devise rules that both sides in the war might observe. The rules might well be observed because both sides had something to gain from preserving social order and not destroying the enemy. Rules might be a nuisance, but if they restricted both sides the disadvantages might cancel out.

This was changed during the Napoleonic wars. In Napoleon's France, people cared about the outcome. The nation was mobilized. The war was a national effort, not just an activity of the elite. It was both political and military genius on the part of Napoleon and his ministers that an entire nation could be mobilized for war. Propaganda became a tool of warfare, and war became vulgarized.

Many writers deplored this popularization of war, this involvement of the democratic masses. In fact, the horrors we attribute to thermonuclear war were already foreseen by many commentators, some before the First World War and more after it, but the new "weapon" to which these terrors were ascribed was people, millions of people, passionately engaged in national wars, spending themselves in a quest for total victory and desperate to avoid total defeat. Today we are impressed that a small number of highly trained pilots can carry enough energy to blast and burn tens of millions of people and the buildings they live in; two or three generations ago there was concern that tens of millions of people using bayonets and barbed wire, machine guns and shrapnel, could create the same kind of destruction and disorder.

That was the second stage in the relation of people to war, the second in Europe since the middle of the seventeenth century. In the first stage people had been neutral but their welfare might be disregarded; in the second stage people were involved because it was *their* war. Some fought, some produced materials of war, some produced food, and some took care of children; but they were all part of a war-making nation. When Hitler attacked Poland in 1939, the Poles had reason to care about the outcome. When Churchill said the British would fight on the beaches, he spoke for the British and not for a mercenary army. The war was about something that mattered. If people would rather fight a dirty war than lose a clean one, the war will be between nations and not just between governments. If people have an influence on whether the war is continued or on the terms of a truce, making the war hurt people serves a purpose. It is a dirty purpose, but war itself is often about something dirty. The Poles and the Norwegians, the Russians and the British, had reason to believe that if they lost the war the consequences would be dirty. This is so evident in modern civil wars—civil wars that involve popular feelings—that we expect them to be bloody and violent. To hope that they would be fought cleanly with no violence to people would be a little like hoping for clean race riot.

There is another way to put it that helps to bring out the sequence of events. If a modern war were a clean one, the violence would not be ruled out but merely saved for the postwar period. Once the army has been defeated in the clean war, the victorious enemy can be as brutally coercive as he wishes. A clean war would determine which side gets to use its power to hurt coercively after victory, and it is likely to be worth some violence to avoid being the loser.

"Surrender" is the process following military hostilities in which the power to hurt is brought to bear. If surrender negotiations are successful and not followed by overt violence, it is because the capacity to inflict pain and damage was successfully used in the bargaining process. On the losing side, prospective pain and damage were averted by concessions; on the winning side, the capacity for inflicting further harm was traded for concessions. The same is true in a successful kidnapping. It only reminds us that the purpose of pure pain and damage is extortion; it is *latent* violence that can be used to advantage. A well-behaved occupied country is not one in which violence plays no part; it may be one in which latent violence is used so skillfully that it need not be spent in punishment.

This brings us to the third stage in the relation of civilian violence to warfare. If the pain and damage can be inflicted during war itself, they need not wait for the surrender negotiation that succeeds a military decision. If one can coerce people and their governments while war is going on, one does not need to wait until he has achieved victory or risk losing that coercive power by spending it all in a losing war. General Sherman's march through Georgia might have made as much sense, possibly more, had the North been losing the war, just as the German buzz bombs and V–2 rockets can be thought of as coercive instruments to get the war stopped before suffering military defeat.

In the present era, since at least the major East-West powers are capable of massive civilian violence during war itself beyond anything available during the Second World War, the occasion for restraint does not await the achievement of military victory or truce. The principal restraint during the Second World War was a temporal boundary, the date of surrender. In the present era we find the violence dramatically restrained during war itself. The Korean War was furiously "all-out" in the fighting, not only on the peninsular battlefield but in the resources used by both sides. It was "all-out," though, only within some dramatic restraints; no nuclear weapons, no Russians, no Chinese territory, no Japanese territory, no bombing of ships at sea or even airfields on the United Nations side of the line. It was a contest in military strength circumscribed by the threat of unprecedented civilian violence. Korea may or may not be a good model for speculation on limited war in the age of nuclear violence, but it was dramatic evidence that the capacity for violence can be consciously restrained even under the provocation of war that measures its military dead in tens of thousands and that fully preoccupies two of the largest countries in the world.

A consequence of this third stage is that "victory" inadequately expresses what a nation wants from its military forces. Mostly it wants, in these times, the influence that resides in latent force. It wants the bargaining power that comes from its capacity to hurt, not just the direct consequence of successful military action. Even total victory over an enemy provides at best an opportunity for unopposed violence against the enemy population. How to use that opportunity in the national interest, or in some wider interest, can be just as important as the achievement of victory itself; but traditional military science does not tell us how to use that capacity for inflicting pain. And if a nation, victor or potential loser, is going to use its capacity for pure violence to influence the enemy, there may be no need to await the achievement of total victory.

Actually, this third stage can be analyzed into two quite different variants. In one, sheer pain and damage are primary instruments of coercive warfare and may actually be applied, to intimidate or to deter. In the other, pain and destruction *in* war are expected to serve little or no purpose but *prior threats* of sheer violence, even of automatic and uncontrolled violence, are coupled to military force. The difference is in the all-or-none character of deterrence and intimidation. Two acute dilemmas arise. One is the choice of making prospective violence as frightening as possible or hedging with some capacity for reciprocated restraint. The other is the choice of making retaliation as automatic as possible or keeping deliberate control over the fateful decisions. The choices are determined partly by governments, partly by technology. Both variants are characterized by the coercive role of pain and destruction—of threatened (not inflicted) pain and destruction. But in one the threat either succeeds or fails altogether, and any ensuing violence is gratuitous; in the other, progressive pain and damage may actually be used to threaten more. The present era, for countries possessing nuclear weapons, is a complex and uncertain blend of the two. . . .

The power to hurt is nothing new in warfare, but for the United States modern technology has drastically enhanced the strategic importance of pure, unconstructive, unacquisitive pain and damage, whether used against us or in our own defense. This in turn enhances the importance of war and threats of war as techniques of influence, not of destruction; of coercion and deterrence, not of conquest and defense; of bargaining and intimidation. . . .

War no longer looks like just a contest of strength. War and the brink of war are more a contest of nerve and risk-taking, of pain and endurance. Small wars embody the threat of a larger war; they are not just military engagements but "crisis diplomacy." The threat of war has always been somewhere underneath international diplomacy, but for Americans it is now much nearer the surface. Like the threat of a strike in industrial relations, the threat of divorce in a family dispute, or the threat of bolting the party at a political convention, the threat of violence continuously circumscribes international politics. Neither strength nor goodwill procures immunity.

Military strategy can no longer be thought of, as it could for some countries in some eras, as the science of military victory. It is now equally, if not more, the art of coercion, of intimidation and deterrence. The instruments of war are more punitive than acquisitive. Military strategy, whether we like it or not, has become the diplomacy of violence.

NOTES

1. Paul I. Wellman, *Death on the Prairie* (New York: Macmillan, 1934), p. 82.
2. Winston Churchill is often credited with the term, "balance of terror," and the following quotation succinctly expresses the familiar notion of nuclear mutual deterrence. This, though, is from a speech in Commons in November 1934. "The fact remains that when all is said and done as regards defensive methods, pending some new discovery the only direct measure of defense upon a great scale is the certainty of being able to inflict

simultaneously upon the enemy as great damage as he can inflict upon ourselves. Do not let us undervalue the efficiency of this procedure. It may well prove in practice—I admit I cannot prove it in theory—capable of giving complete immunity. If two Powers show themselves equally capable of inflicting damage upon each other by some particular process of war, so that neither gains an advantage from its adoption and both suffer the most hideous reciprocal injuries, it is not only possible but it seems probable that neither will employ that means. . . ."

3. (Chicago: University of Chicago Press), 1942, p. 296.

Offense, Defense, and the Security Dilemma

Robert Jervis

Another approach starts with the central point of the security dilemma—that an increase in one state's security decreases the security of others—and examines the conditions under which this proposition holds. Two crucial variables are involved: whether defensive weapons and policies can be distinguished from offensive one's, and whether the defense or the offense has the advantage. The definitions are not always clear, and many cases are difficult to judge, but these two variables shed a great deal of light on the question of whether status-quo powers will adopt compatible security policies. All the variables discussed so far leave the heart of the problem untouched. But when defensive weapons differ from offensive ones, it is possible for a state to make itself more secure without making others less secure. And when the defense has the advantage over the offense, a large increase in one state's security only slightly decreases the security of the others, and status-quo powers can all enjoy a high level of security and largely escape from the state of nature.

OFFENSE-DEFENSE BALANCE

When we say that the offense has the advantage, we simply mean that it is easier to destroy the other's army and take its territory than it is to defend one's own. When the defense has the advantage, it is easier to protect and to hold than it is to move forward, destroy, and take. If effective defenses can be erected quickly, an attacker may be able to keep territory he has taken in an initial victory. Thus, the dominance of the defense made it very hard for Britain and France to push Germany

From "Cooperation Under the Security Dilemma" from *World Politics,* vol. 30, no. 2 (Jan. 1978), pp. 186–214 by Robert Jervis. Reprinted with permission of Johns Hopkins University Press. Portions of the text and some footnotes have been omitted.

out of France in World War I. But when superior defenses are difficult for an aggressor to improvise on the battlefield and must be constructed during peacetime, they provide no direct assistance to him.

The security dilemma is at its most vicious when commitments, strategy, or technology dictate that the only route to security lies through expansion. Status-quo powers must then act like aggressors: the fact that they would gladly agree to forego the opportunity for expansion in return for guarantees for their security has no implications for their behavior. Even if expansion is not sought as a goal in itself, there will be quick and drastic changes in the distribution of territory and influence. Conversely, when the defense has the advantage, status-quo states can make themselves more secure without gravely endangering others.[1] Indeed, if the defense has enough of an advantage and if the states are of roughly equal size, not only will the security dilemma cease to inhibit status-quo states from cooperating, but aggression will be next to impossible, thus rendering international anarchy relatively unimportant. If states cannot conquer each other, then the lack of sovereignty, although it presents problems of collective goods in a number of areas, no longer forces states to devote their primary attention to self-preservation. Although, if force were not usable, there would be fewer restraints on the use of nonmilitary instruments, these are rarely powerful enough to threaten the vital interests of a major state.

Two questions of the offense-defense balance can be separated. First, does the state have to spend more or less than one dollar on defensive forces to offset each dollar spent by the other side on forces that could be used to attack? If the state has one dollar to spend on increasing its security, should it put it into offensive or defensive forces? Second, with a given inventory of forces, is it better to attack or to defend? Is there an incentive to strike first or to absorb the other's blow? These two aspects are often linked: If each dollar spent on offense can overcome each dollar spent on defense, and if both sides have the same defense budgets, then both are likely to build offensive forces and find it attractive to attack rather than to wait for the adversary to strike.

These aspects affect the security dilemma in different ways. The first has its greatest impact on arms races. If the defense has the advantage, and if the status-quo powers have reasonable subjective security requirements, they can probably avoid an arms race. Although an increase in one side's arms and security will still decrease the other's security, the former's increase will be larger than the latter's decrease. So if one side increases its arms, the other can bring its security back up to its previous level by adding a smaller amount to its forces. And if the first side reacts to this change, its increase will also be smaller than the stimulus that produced it. Thus a stable equilibrium will be reached. Shifting from dynamics to statics, each side can be quite secure with forces roughly equal to those of the other. Indeed, if the defense is much more potent than the offense, each side can be willing to have forces much smaller than the other's, and can be indifferent to a wide range of the other's defense policies.

The second aspect—whether it is better to attack or to defend—influences short-run stability. When the offense has the advantage, a state's reaction to international tension will increase the chances of war. The incentives for preemption and the "reciprocal fear of surprise attack" in this situation have been made clear by analyses of the dangers that exist when two countries have first-strike capabilities.[2] There is no way for the state to increase its security without menacing, or even attacking, the other. Even Bismarck, who once called preventive war "committing suicide from fear of death," said that "no government, if it regards war as inevitable even if it does not want it, would be so foolish as to leave to the enemy the choice of time and occasion and to wait for the moment which is most convenient for the enemy."[3] In another arena, the same dilemma applies to the policeman in a dark alley confronting a suspected criminal who appears to be holding a weapon. Though racism may indeed be present, the security dilemma can account for many of the tragic shootings of innocent people in the ghettos.

Beliefs about the course of a war in which the offense has the advantage further deepen the security dilemma. When there are incentives to strike first, a successful attack will usually so weaken the other side that victory will be relatively quick, bloodless, and decisive. It is in these periods when conquest is possible and attractive that states consolidate power internally—for instance, by destroying the feudal barons—and expand externally. There are several consequences that decrease the chance of cooperation among status-quo states. First, war will be profitable for the winner. The costs will be low and the benefits high. Of course, losers will suffer; the fear of losing could induce states to try to form stable cooperative arrangements, but the temptation of victory will make this particularly difficult. Second, because wars are expected to be both frequent and short, there will be incentives for high levels of arms, and quick and strong reaction to the other's increases in arms. The state cannot afford to wait until there is unambiguous evidence that the other is building new weapons. Even large states that have faith in their economic strength cannot wait, because the war will be over before their products can reach the army. Third, when wars are quick, states will have to recruit allies in advance.[4] Without the opportunity for bargaining and realignments during the opening stages of hostilities, peacetime diplomacy loses a degree of the fluidity that facilitates balance-of-power policies. Because alliances must be secured during peacetime, the international system is more likely to become bipolar. It is hard to say whether war therefore becomes more or less likely, but this bipolarity increases tension between the two camps and makes it harder for status-quo states to gain the benefits of cooperation. Fourth, if wars are frequent, statesmen's perceptual thresholds will be adjusted accordingly and they will be quick to perceive ambiguous evidence as indicating that others are aggressive. Thus, there will be more cases of status-quo powers arming against each other in the incorrect belief that the other is hostile.

When the defense has the advantage, all the foregoing is reversed. The state that fears attack does not preempt—since that would be a wasteful use of its military resources—but rather prepares to receive an attack. Doing so does not decrease the security of others, and several states can do it simultaneously; the situation will therefore be stable, and status-quo powers will be able to cooperate. When Herman Kahn argues that ultimatums "are vastly too dangerous to give because . . . they are quite likely to touch off a pre-emptive strike,"[5] he incorrectly assumes that it is always advantageous to strike first.

More is involved than short-run dynamics. When the defense is dominant, wars are likely to become stalemates and can be won only at enormous cost. Relatively small and weak states can hold off larger and stronger ones, or can deter attack by raising the costs of conquest to an unacceptable level. States then approach equality in what they can do to each other. Like the .45-caliber pistol in the American West, fortifications were the "great equalizer" in some periods. Changes in the status quo are less frequent and cooperation is more common wherever the security dilemma is thereby reduced.

Many of these arguments can be illustrated by the major powers' policies in the periods preceding the two world wars. Bismarck's wars surprised statesmen by showing that the offense had the advantage, and by being quick, relatively cheap, and quite decisive. Falling into a common error, observers projected this pattern into the future.[6] The resulting expectations had several effects. First, states sought semi-permanent allies. In the early stages of the Franco-Prussian War, Napoleon III had thought that there would be plenty of time to recruit Austria to his side. Now, others were not going to repeat this mistake. Second, defense budgets were high and reacted quite sharply to increases on the other side. It is not surprising that Richardson's theory of arms races fits this period well. Third, most decision makers thought that the next European war would not cost much blood and treasure.[7] That is one reason why war was generally seen as inevitable and why mass opinion was so bellicose. Fourth, once war seemed likely, there were strong pressures to preempt. Both sides believed that whoever moved first could penetrate the other deep enough to disrupt mobilization and thus gain an insurmountable advantage. (There was no such belief about the use of naval forces. Although Churchill made an ill-advised speech saying that if German ships "do not come out and fight in time of war they will be dug out like rats in a hole,"[8] everyone knew that submarines, mines and coastal fortifications made this impossible. So at the start of the war each navy prepared to defend itself rather than attack, and the short-run destabilizing forces that launched the armies toward each other did not operate.)[9] Furthermore, each side knew that the other saw the situation the same way, thus increasing the perceived danger that the other would attack, and giving each added reasons to precipitate a war if conditions seemed favorable. In the long and the short run, there were thus both offensive and defensive incentives to strike. This situation casts light on the common question about German motives in 1914: "Did Germany unleash the war deliberately to become a world power or did she support Austria merely to defend a weakening ally," thereby protecting her own position?[10] To some extent, this question is misleading. Because of the perceived advantage of the offense, war was seen as the best route both to gaining expansion and to avoiding drastic loss of influence. There seemed to be no way for Germany merely to retain and safeguard her existing position.

Of course the war showed these beliefs to have been wrong on all points. Trenches and machine guns gave the defense an overwhelming advantage. The fighting became deadlocked and produced horrendous casualties. It made no sense for the combatants to bleed themselves to death. If they had known the power of the defense beforehand, they would have rushed for their own trenches rather than for the enemy's territory. Each side could have done this without increasing the other's incentives to strike. War might have broken out anyway; but at least the pressures of time and the fear of allowing the other to get the first blow would not have contributed to this end. And, had both sides known the costs of the war, they would have negotiated much more seriously. The obvious question is why the states did not seek a negotiated settlement as soon as the shape of the war became clear. Schlieffen had said that if his plan failed, peace should be sought.[11] The answer is complex, uncertain, and largely outside of the scope of our concerns. But part of the reason was the hope and sometimes the expectation that break-throughs could be made and the dominance of the offensive restored. Without that hope, the political and psychological pressures to fight to a decisive victory might have been overcome.

The politics of the interwar period were shaped by the memories of the previous conflict and the belief that any future war would resemble it. Political and military lessons reinforced each other in ameliorating the security dilemma. Because it was believed that the First World War had been a mistake that could have been avoided by skillful conciliation, both Britain and, to a lesser extent, France were highly sensitive to the possibility that interwar Germany was not a real threat to peace, and alert to the danger that reacting quickly and strongly to her arms could create unnecessary conflict. And because Britain and France expected the defense to continue to dominate, they concluded that it was safe to adopt a more relaxed and nonthreatening military posture.[12] Britain also felt less need to maintain tight alliance bonds. The Allies' military posture then constituted only a slight danger to Germany; had the latter been content with the status quo, it would have been easy for both sides to have felt secure behind their lines of fortifications. Of course the Germans were not content, so it is not surprising that they devoted their money and attention to finding ways out of a defense-dominated stalemate. *Blitzkrieg* tactics were necessary if they were to use force to change the status quo.

The initial stages of the war on the Western Front also contrasted with the First World War. Only with the new air arm were there any incentives to strike first, and these forces were too weak to carry out the grandiose plans that had been both dreamed and feared. The armies, still the main instrument, rushed to defensive positions. Perhaps the allies could have successfully attacked while the Germans were occupied in Poland.[13] But belief in the defense was so great that this was never seriously contemplated. Three months after the start of the war, the French Prime Minister summed up the view held by almost everyone but Hitler: on the Western Front there is "deadlock. Two Forces of equal strength and the one that attacks seeing such enormous casualties that it cannot move without endangering the continuation of the war or of the aftermath."[14] The Allies were caught in a dilemma they never fully recognized, let alone solved. On the one hand, they had very high war aims; although unconditional surrender had not yet been adopted, the British had decided from the start that the removal of Hitler was a necessary condition for peace.[15] On the other hand, there were no realistic plans or instruments for allowing the Allies to impose their will on the other side. The British Chief of the Imperial General Staff noted, "The French have no intention of carrying out an offensive for years, if at all"; the British were only slightly bolder.[16] So the Allies looked to a long war that would wear the Germans down, cause civilian suffering through shortages, and eventually undermine Hitler. There was little analysis to support this view—and indeed it probably was not supportable—but as long as the defense was dominant and the numbers on each side relatively equal, what else could the Allies do?

To summarize, the security dilemma was much less powerful after World War I than it had been before. In the later period, the expected power of the defense allowed status-quo states to pursue compatible security policies and avoid arms races. Furthermore, high tension and fear of war did not set off short-run dynamics by which each state, trying to increase its security, inadvertently acted to make war more likely. The expected high costs of war, however, led the Allies to believe that no sane German leader would run the risks entailed in an attempt to dominate the Continent, and discouraged them from risking war themselves.

Technology and Geography

Technology and geography are the two main factors that determine whether the offense or the defense has the advantage. As Brodie notes, "On the tactical level, as a rule, few physical factors favor the attacker but many favor the defender. The defender usually has the advantage of cover. He characteristically fires from behind some form of shelter while his opponent crosses open ground."[17] Anything that increases the amount of ground the attacked has to cross, or impedes his progress across it, or makes him more vulnerable while crossing, increases the advantage accruing to the defense. When states are separated by barriers that produce these effects, the security dilemma is eased, since both can have forces adequate for defense without being able to attack. Impenetrable barriers would actually prevent war; in reality, decision makers have to settle for a good deal less. Buffer zones slow the attacker's progress; they thereby give the defender time to prepare, increase problems of logistics, and reduce the number of soldiers available for the final assault. At the end of the nineteenth century, Arthur Balfour noted Afghanistan's "non-conducting" qualities. "So long as it possesses few roads, and no railroads, it will be impossible for Russia to make effective use of her great numerical superiority at any point immediately vital to the Empire." The Russians valued buffers for the same reasons; it is not surprising that when Persia was being divided into Russian and British spheres of influence some years later, the Russians sought assurances that the British would refrain from building potentially menacing railroads in their sphere. Indeed, since railroad construction radically altered the abilities of countries to defend themselves and to attack others, many diplomatic notes and much intelligence activity in the late nineteenth century centered on this subject.[18]

Oceans, large rivers, and mountain ranges serve the same function as buffer zones. Being hard to cross, they allow defense against superior numbers. The defender has merely to stay on his side of the barrier and so can utilize all the men he can bring up to it. The attacker's men, however, can cross only a few at a time, and they are very vulnerable when doing so. If all states were self-sufficient islands, anarchy would be much less of a problem. A small investment in shore defenses and a small army would be sufficient to repel invasion. Only very weak states would be vulnerable, and only very large ones could menace others. As noted above, the United States, and to a lesser extent Great Britain, have partly been able to escape from the state of nature because their geographical positions approximated this ideal.

Although geography cannot be changed to conform to borders, borders can and do change to conform to geography. Borders across which an attack is easy tend to be unstable. States living within them are likely to expand or be absorbed. Frequent wars are almost inevitable since attacking will often seem the best way to protect what one has. This process will stop, or at least slow down, when the state's borders reach—by expansion or contraction—a line of natural obstacles. Security without attack will then be possible. Furthermore, these lines constitute salient solutions to bargaining problems and, to the extent that they are barriers to migration, are likely to divide ethnic groups, thereby raising the costs and lowering the incentives for conquest.

Attachment to one's state and its land reinforce one quasi-geographical aid to the defense. Conquest usually becomes more difficult the deeper the attacker pushes into the other's territory. Nationalism spurs the defenders to fight harder; advancing not only lengthens the attacker's supply lines, but takes him through unfamiliar and often devastated lands that require troops for garrison duty. These stabilizing dynamics will not operate, however, if the defender's war matériel is situated near its borders, or if the people do not care about their state, but only about being on the winning side. In such cases, positive feedback will be at work and initial defeats will be insurmountable.[19]

Imitating geography, men have tried to create barriers. Treaties may provide for demilitarized zones on both sides of the border, although such zones will rarely be deep enough to provide more than warning. Even this was not possible in Europe, but the Russians adopted a gauge for their railroads that was broader than that of the neighboring states, thereby complicating the logistics problems of any attacker—including Russia.

Perhaps the most ambitious and at least temporarily successful attempts to construct a system that would aid the defenses of both sides were the interwar naval treaties, as they affected Japanese-American relations. As mentioned earlier, the problem was that the United States could not defend the Philippines without denying Japan the ability to protect her home islands.[20] (In 1941 this dilemma became insoluble when Japan sought to extend her control to Malaya and the Dutch East Indies. If the Philippines had been invulnerable, they could have provided a secure base from which the United States could interdict Japanese shipping between the homeland and the areas she was trying to conquer.) In the 1920s and early 1930s each side would have been willing to grant the other security for its possessions in return for a reciprocal grant, and the Washington Naval Conference agreements were designed to approach this goal. As a Japanese diplomat later put it, their country's "fundamental principle" was to have "a strength insufficient for attack and adequate for defense,"[21] Thus Japan agreed in 1922 to accept a navy only three-fifths as large as that of the United States, and the United States agreed not to fortify its Pacific islands.[22] (Japan had earlier been forced to agree not to fortify the islands she had taken from Germany in World War I.) Japan's navy would not be large enough to defeat America's anywhere other than close to the home islands. Although the Japanese could still take the Philippines, not only would they be unable to move farther, but they might be weakened enough by their efforts to be vulnerable to counterattack. Japan, however, gained security. An American attack was rendered more difficult because the American bases were unprotected and because, until 1930, Japan was allowed unlimited numbers of cruisers, destroyers, and submarines that could weaken the American fleet as it made its way across the ocean.[23]

The other major determinant of the offense-defense balance is technology. When weapons are highly vulnerable, they must be employed before they are attacked. Others can remain quite invulnerable in their bases. The former characteristics are embodied in unprotected missiles and many kinds of bombers. (It should be noted that it is not vulnerability *per se* that is crucial, but the location of the vulnerability. Bombers and missiles that are easy to destroy only after having been launched toward their targets do not create destabilizing dynamics.) Incentives to strike first are usually absent for naval forces that are threatened by a naval attack. Like missiles in hardened silos, they are usually well protected when in their bases. Both sides can then simultaneously be prepared to defend themselves successfully.

In ground warfare under some conditions, forts, trenches, and small groups of men in prepared positions can hold off large numbers of attackers. Less frequently, a few attackers can storm the defenses. By and large, it is a contest between fortifications and supporting light weapons on the one hand, and mobility and heavier weapons that clear the way for the attack on the other. As the erroneous views held before the two world wars show, there is no simple way to determine which is dominant. "[T]hese oscillations are not smooth and predictable like those of a swinging pendulum. They are uneven in both extent and time. Some occur in the course of a single battle or campaign, others in the course of a war, still others during a series of wars." Longer-term oscillations can also be detected:

> The early Gothic age, from the twelfth to the late thirteenth century, with its wonderful cathedrals and fortified places, was a period during which the attackers in Europe generally met serious and increasing difficulties, because the improvement in the strength of fortresses outran the advance in the power of destruction. Later, with the spread of firearms at the end of the fifteenth century, old fortresses lost their power to resist. An age ensued during which the offense possessed, apart from short-term setbacks, new advantages. Then, during the seventeenth century, especially after about 1660, and until at least the outbreak of the War of the Austrian Succession in 1740, the defense regained much of the ground it had lost since the great medieval fortresses had proved unable to meet the bombardment of the new and more numerous artillery.[24]

Another scholar has continued the argument: "The offensive gained an advantage with new forms of heavy mobile artillery in the nineteenth century, but the stalemate of World War I created the impression that the defense again had an advantage; the German invasion in World War II, however, indicated the offensive superiority of highly mechanized armies in the field."[25]

The situation today with respect to conventional weapons is unclear. Until recently it was believed that tanks and tactical air power gave the attacker an advantage. The initial analyses of the 1973 Arab-Israeli war indicated that new anti-tank and anti-aircraft weapons have restored the primacy of the defense. These weapons are cheap, easy to use, and can destroy a high proportion of the attacking vehicles and planes that are sighted. It then would make sense for a status-quo power to buy lots of $20,000 missiles rather than buy a few half-million dollar fighter-bombers. Defense would be possible even against a large and well-equipped force; states that care primarily about self-protection would not need to engage in arms races. But further examinations of the new technologies and the history of the October War cast doubt on these optimistic conclusions and leave us unable to render any firm judgment.[26]

Concerning nuclear weapons, it is generally agreed that defense is impossible—a triumph not of the offense, but of deterrence. Attack makes no sense, not because it can be beaten off, but because the attacker will be destroyed in turn. In terms of the questions under consideration here, the result is the equivalent of the primacy of the defense. First, security is relatively cheap. Less than one percent of the G.N.P. is devoted to deterring a direct attack on the United States; most of it is spent on acquiring redundant systems to provide a lot of insurance against the worst conceivable contingencies. Second, both sides can simultaneously gain security in the form of second-strike capability. Third, and related to the foregoing, second-strike capability can be maintained in the face of wide variations in the other side's military posture. There is no purely military reason why each side has to react quickly and strongly to the other's increases in arms. Any spending that the other devotes to trying to achieve first-strike capability can be neutralized by the state's spending much smaller sums on protecting its second-strike capability. Fourth, there are no incentives to strike first in a crisis.

Important problems remain, of course. Both sides have interests that go well beyond defense of the homeland. The protection of these interests creates conflicts even if neither side desires expansion. Furthermore, the shift from defense to deterrence has greatly increased the importance and perceptions of resolve. Security now rests on each side's belief that the other would prefer to run high risks of total destruction rather than sacrifice its vital interests. Aspects of the security dilemma thus appear in a new form. Are weapons procurements used as an index of resolve? Must they be so used? If one side fails to respond to the other's buildup, will it appear weak and thereby invite predation? Can both sides simultaneously have images of high resolve or is there a zero-sum element involved? Although these problems are real, they are not as severe as those in the prenuclear era: There are many indices of resolve, and states do not so much judge images of resolve in the abstract as ask how likely it is that the other will stand firm in a particular dispute. Since states are most likely to stand firm on matters which concern them most, it is quite possible for both to demonstrate their resolve to protect their own security simultaneously.

OFFENSE-DEFENSE DIFFERENTIATION

The other major variable that affects how strongly the security dilemma operates is whether weapons and policies that protect the state also provide the capability for attack. If they do not, the basic postulate of the security dilemma no longer applies.

A state can increase its own security without decreasing that of others. The advantage of the defense can only ameliorate the security dilemma. A differentiation between offensive and defensive stances comes close to abolishing it. Such differentiation does not mean, however, that all security problems will be abolished. If the offense has the advantage, conquest and aggression will still be possible. And if the offense's advantage is great enough, status-quo powers may find it too expensive to protect themselves by defensive forces and decide to procure offensive weapons even though this will menace others. Furthermore, states will still have to worry that even if the other's military posture shows that it is peaceful now, it may develop aggressive intentions in the future.

Assuming that the defense is at least as potent as the offense, the differentiation between them allows status-quo states to behave in ways that are clearly different from those of aggressors. Three beneficial consequences follow. First, status-quo powers can identify each other, thus laying the foundations for cooperation. Conflicts growing out of the mistaken belief that the other side is expansionist will be less frequent. Second, status-quo states will obtain advance warning when others plan aggression. Before a state can attack, it has to develop and deploy offensive weapons. If procurement of these weapons cannot be disguised and takes a fair amount of time, as it almost always does, a status-quo state will have the time to take countermeasures. It need not maintain a high level of defensive arms as long as its potential adversaries are adopting a peaceful posture. (Although being so armed should not, with the one important exception noted below, alarm other status-quo powers.) States do, in fact, pay special attention to actions that they believe would not be taken by a status-quo state because they feel that states exhibiting such behavior are aggressive. Thus the seizure or development of transportation facilities will alarm others more if these facilities have no commercial value, and therefore can only be wanted for military reasons. In 1906, the British rejected a Russian protest about their activities in a district of Persia by claiming that this area was "only of [strategic] importance [to the Russians] if they wished to attack the Indian frontier, or to put pressure upon us by making us think that they intend to attack it."[27]

The same inferences are drawn when a state acquires more weapons than observers feel are needed for defense. Thus, the Japanese spokesman at the 1930 London naval conference said that his country was alarmed by the American refusal to give Japan a 70 percent ratio (in place of a 60 percent ratio) in heavy cruisers: "As long as America held that ten percent advantage, it was possible for her to attack. So when America insisted on sixty percent instead of seventy percent, the idea would exist that they were trying to keep that possibility, and the Japanese people could not accept that."[28] Similarly, when Mussolini told Chamberlain in January 1939 that Hitler's arms program was motivated by defensive considerations, the Prime Minister replied that "German military forces were now so strong as to make it impossible for any Power or combination of Powers to attack her successfully. She could not want any further armaments for defensive purposes; what then did she want them for?"[29]

Of course these inferences can be wrong—as they are especially likely to be because states underestimate the degree to which they menace others.[30] And when they are wrong, the security dilemma is deepened. Because the state thinks it has received notice that the other is aggressive, its own arms building will be less restrained and the chances of cooperation will be decreased. But the dangers of incorrect inferences should not obscure the main point: When offensive and defensive postures are different, much of the uncertainty about the other's intentions that contributes to the security dilemma is removed.

The third beneficial consequence of a difference between offensive and defensive weapons is that if all states support the status quo, an obvious arms control agreement is a ban on weapons that are useful for attacking. As President Roosevelt put it in his message to the Geneva Disarmament Conference in 1933: "If all nations will agree wholly to eliminate from possession and use the weapons which make possible a successful attack, defenses automatically will become impregnable, and the frontiers and independence of every nation will become secure."[31] The fact that such treaties have been rare—the Washington naval agreements discussed above and the anti-ABM treaty can be cited as examples—shows either that states are not always willing to guarantee the security of others, or that it is hard to distinguish offensive from defensive weapons.

Is such a distinction possible? Salvador de Madariaga, the Spanish statesman active in the disarmament negotiations of the interwar years, thought not: "A weapon is either offensive or defensive according to which end of it you are looking at." The French Foreign Minister agreed (although French policy did not always follow this view): "Every arm can be employed offensively or defensively in turn. . . . The only way to discover whether arms are intended for purely defensive purposes or are held in a spirit of aggression is in all cases to enquire into the intentions of the country concerned." Some evidence for the validity of this argument is provided by the fact that much time in these unsuccessful negotiations was devoted to separating offensive from defensive weapons. Indeed, no simple and unambiguous definition is possible and in many cases no judgment can be reached. Before the American entry into World War I, Woodrow Wilson wanted to arm merchantmen only with guns in the back of the ship so they could not initiate a fight, but this expedient cannot be applied to more common forms of armaments.[32]

There are several problems. Even when a differentiation is possible, a status-quo power will want offensive arms under any of three conditions: (1) If the offense has a great advantage over the defense, protection through defensive forces will be too expensive. (2) Status-quo states may need offensive weapons to regain territory lost in the opening stages of war. It might be possible, however, for a state to wait to procure these weapons until war seems likely, and they might be needed only in relatively small numbers, unless the aggressor was able to construct strong defenses quickly in the occupied areas. (3) The state may feel that it must be prepared to take the offensive either because the other side will make peace only if it loses territory or because the state has commitments to attack if the other makes war on a third party. As noted above, status-quo states with extensive commitments are often forced to behave like aggressors. Even when they lack such commitments, status-quo states must worry about the possibility that if they are able to hold off an attack, they will still not be able to end the war unless they move into the other's territory to damage its military forces and inflict pain. Many American naval officers after the Civil War, for example, believed that "only by destroying the commerce of the opponent could the United States bring him to terms."[33]

A further complication is introduced by the fact that aggressors as well as status-quo powers require defensive forces as a prelude to acquiring offensive ones, to protect one frontier while attacking another, or for insurance in case the war goes badly. Criminals as well as policemen can use bulletproof vests. Hitler as well as Maginot built a line of forts. Indeed, Churchill reports that in 1936 the German Foreign Minister said: "As soon as our fortifications are constructed [on our western borders] and the countries in Central Europe realize that France cannot enter German territory, all these countries will begin to feel very differently about their foreign policies, and a new constellation will develop."[34] So a state may not necessarily be reassured if its neighbor constructs strong defenses.

More central difficulties are created by the fact that whether a weapon is offensive or defensive often depends on the particular situation—for instance, the geographical setting and the way in which the weapon is used. "Tanks . . . spearheaded the fateful German thrust through the Ardennes in 1940, but if the French had disposed of a properly concentrated armored reserve, it would have provided the best means for their cutting off the penetration and turning into a disaster for the Germans what became instead an overwhelming victory."[35] Anti-aircraft weapons seem obviously defensive—to be used, they must wait for the other side to come to them. But the Egyptian attack on Israel in 1973 would have been impossible without effective air defenses that covered the battlefield. Nevertheless, some distinctions are possible. Sir John Simon, then the British Foreign Secretary, in response to the views cited earlier, stated that just because a fine line could not be drawn, "that was no reason for saying that there were not stretches of territory on either side which all practical men and women knew to be well on this or that side of the line." Although there are almost no weapons and strategies that are useful only for attacking, there are some that are almost exclusively defensive. Aggressors could want them for protection, but a state that relied mostly on them could not menace others. More frequently, we cannot "determine the absolute character of a weapon, but [we can] make a comparison . . . [and] discover whether or not the offensive potentialities predominate, whether a weapon is more useful in attack or in defense."[36]

The essence of defense is keeping the other side out of your territory. A purely defensive weapon is one that can do this without being able to penetrate the enemy's land. Thus a committee of military experts in an interwar disarmament conference declared that armaments "incapable of mobility by means of self-contained power," or movable only after long delay, were "only capable of being used for the defense of a State's territory."[37] The most obvious examples are fortifications. They can shelter attacking forces, especially when they are built right along the frontier,[38] but they cannot occupy enemy territory. A state with only a strong line of forts, fixed guns, and a small army to man them would not be much of a menace. Anything else that can serve only as a barrier against attacking troops is similarly defensive. In this category are systems that provide warning of an attack, the Russian's adoption of a different railroad gauge, and nuclear land mines that can seal off invasion routes.

If total immobility clearly defines a system that is defensive only, limited
mobility is unfortunately ambiguous. As noted above, short-range fighter aircraft
and anti-aircraft missiles can be used to cover an attack. And, unlike forts, they can
advance with the troops. Still, their inability to reach deep into enemy territory
does make them more useful for the defense than for the offense. Thus, the United States and Israel would have been more alarmed in the early 1970s had the Russians provided the Egyptians with long-range instead of short-range aircraft. Naval
forces are particularly difficult to classify in these terms, but those that are very
short-legged can be used only for coastal defense.

Any forces that for various reasons fight well only when on their own soil in
effect lack mobility and therefore are defensive. The most extreme example would
be passive resistance. Noncooperation can thwart an aggressor, but it is very hard
for large numbers of people to cross the border and stage a sit-in on another's territory. Morocco's recent march on the Spanish Sahara approached this tactic, but
its success depended on special circumstances. Similarly, guerrilla warfare is
defensive to the extent to which it requires civilian support that is likely to be forthcoming only in opposition to a foreign invasion. Indeed, if guerrilla warfare were
easily exportable and if it took ten defenders to destroy each guerrilla, then this
weapon would not only be one which could be used as easily to attack the other's
territory as to defend one's own, but one in which the offense had the advantage:
so the security dilemma would operate especially strongly.

If guerrillas are unable to fight on foreign soil, other kinds of armies may be
unwilling to do so. An army imbued with the idea that only defensive wars were
just would fight less effectively, if at all, if the goal were conquest. Citizen militias
may lack both the ability and the will for aggression. The weapons employed, the
short term of service, the time required for mobilization, and the spirit of repelling
attacks on the homeland, all lend themselves much more to defense than to attacks
on foreign territory.[39]

Less idealistic motives can produce the same result. A leading student of
medieval warfare has described the armies of that period as follows: "Assembled
with difficulty, insubordinate, unable to maneuver, ready to melt away from its
standard the moment that its short period of service was over, a feudal force presented an assemblage of unsoldierlike qualities such as have seldom been known to
coexist. Primarily intended to defend its own borders from the Magyar, the North-
man, or the Saracen . . . , the institution was utterly unadapted to take the offensive."[40] Some political groupings can be similarly described. International coalitions are more readily held together by fear than by hope of gain. Thus Castlereagh
was not being entirely self-serving when in 1816 he argued that the Quadruple
Alliance "could only have owed its origin to a sense of common danger; in its very
nature it must be conservative; it cannot threaten either the security or the liberties of other States."[41] It is no accident that most of the major campaigns of expansion have been waged by one dominant nation (for example, Napoleon's France
and Hitler's Germany), and that coalitions among relative equals are usually found
defending the status quo. Most gains from conquest are too uncertain and raise too
many questions of future squabbles among the victors to hold an alliance together
for long. Although defensive coalitions are by no means easy to maintain—conflicting national objectives and the free-rider problem partly explain why three of

them dissolved before Napoleon was defeated—the common interest of seeing that no state dominates provides a strong incentive for solidarity.

Weapons that are particularly effective in reducing fortifications and barriers are of great value to the offense. This is not to deny that a defensive power will want some of those weapons if the other side has them: Brodie is certainly correct to argue that while their tanks allowed the Germans to conquer France, properly used French tanks could have halted the attack. But France would not have needed these weapons if Germany had not acquired them, whereas even if France had no tanks, Germany could not have foregone them since they provided the only chance of breaking through the French lines. Mobile heavy artillery is, similarly, especially useful in destroying fortifications. The defender, while needing artillery to fight off attacking troops or to counterattack, can usually use lighter guns since they do not need to penetrate such massive obstacles. So it is not surprising that one of the few things that most nations at the interwar disarmament conferences were able to agree on was that heavy tanks and mobile heavy guns were particularly valuable to a state planning an attack.[42]

Weapons and strategies that depend for their effectiveness on surprise are almost always offensive. That fact was recognized by some of the delegates to the interwar disarmament conferences and is the principle behind the common national ban on concealed weapons. An earlier representative of this widespread view was the mid-nineteenth-century Philadelphia newspaper that argued: "As a measure of defense, knives, dirks, and sword canes are entirely useless. They are fit only for attack, and all such attacks are of murderous character. Whoever carries such a weapon has prepared himself for homicide."[43]

It is, of course, not always possible to distinguish between forces that are most effective for holding territory and forces optimally designed for taking it. Such a distinction could not have been made for the strategies and weapons in Europe during most of the period between the Franco-Prussian War and World War I. Neither naval forces nor tactical air forces can be readily classified in these terms. But the point here is that when such a distinction is possible, the central characteristic of the security dilemma no longer holds, and one of the most troublesome consequences of anarchy is removed.

Offense-Defense Differentiation and Strategic Nuclear Weapons

In the interwar period, most statesmen held the reasonable position that weapons that threatened civilians were offensive.[44] But when neither side can protect its civilians, a counter-city posture is defensive because the state can credibly threaten to retaliate only in response to an attack on itself or its closest allies. The costs of this strike are so high that the state could not threaten to use it for the less-than-vital interest of compelling the other to abandon an established position.

In the context of deterrence, offensive weapons are those that provide defense. In the now familiar reversal of common sense, the state that could take its population out of hostage, either by active or passive defense or by destroying the other's strategic weapons on the ground, would be able to alter the status quo. The desire to prevent such a situation was one of the rationales for the anti-ABM agreements; it explains why some arms controllers opposed building ABMs to protect cities, but favored sites that covered ICBM fields. Similarly, many analysts wanted to limit warhead accuracy and favored multiple re-entry vehicles (MRVs), but opposed multiple independently targetable re-entry vehicles (MIRVs). The former are more useful than single warheads for penetrating city defenses, and ensure that the state has a second-strike capability. MIRVs enhance counterforce capabilities. . . .

What is most important for the argument here is that land-based ICBMs are both offensive and defensive, but when both sides rely on Polaris-type systems (SLBMs), offense and defense use different weapons. ICBMs can be used either to destroy the other's cities in retaliation or to initiate hostilities by attacking the other's strategic missiles. Some measures—for instance, hardening of missile sites and warning systems—are purely defensive, since they do not make a first strike easier. Others are predominantly offensive—for instance, passive or active city defenses, and highly accurate warheads. But ICBMs themselves are useful for both purposes. And because states seek a high level of insurance, the desire for protection as well as the contemplation of a counterforce strike can explain the acquisition of extremely large numbers of missiles. So it is very difficult to infer the other's intentions from its military posture. Each side's efforts to increase its own security by procuring more missiles decreases, to an extent determined by the relative efficacy of the offense and the defense, the other side's security. That is not the case when both sides use SLBMs. The point is not that sea-based systems are less vulnerable than land-based ones (this bears on the offense-defense ratio) but that SLBMs are defensive, retaliatory weapons. . . . SLBMs are not the main instrument of attack against other SLBMs. The hardest problem confronting a state that wants to take its cities out of hostage is to locate the other's SLBMs, a job that requires not SLBMs but anti-submarine weapons. A state might use SLBMs to attack the other's submarines (although other weapons would probably be more efficient), but without anti-submarine warfare (ASW) capability the task cannot be performed. A status-quo state that wanted to forego offensive capability could simply forego ASW research and procurement. . . .

When both sides rely on ICBMs, one side's missiles can attack the other's, and so the state cannot be indifferent to the other's building program. But because one side's SLBMs do not menace the other's, each side can build as many as it wants and the other need not respond. Each side's decision on the size of its force depends on technical questions, its judgment about how much destruction is enough to deter, and the amount of insurance it is willing to pay for—and these considerations are independent of the size of the other's strategic force. Thus the crucial nexus in the arms race is severed. . . .

FOUR WORLDS

The two variables we have been discussing—whether the offense or the defense has the advantage, and whether offensive postures can be distinguished from defensive ones—can be combined to yield four possible worlds.

The first world is the worst for status-quo states. These is no way to get security without menacing others, and security through defense is terribly difficult to obtain. Because offensive and defensive postures are the same, status-quo states acquire the same kind of arms that are sought by aggressors. And because the offense has the advantage over the defense, attacking is the best route to protecting what you have; status-quo states will therefore behave like aggressors. The situation will be unstable. Arms races are likely. Incentives to strike first will turn crises into wars. Decisive victories and conquests will be common. States will grow and shrink rapidly, and it will be hard for any state to maintain its size and influence without trying to increase them. Cooperation among status-quo powers will be extremely hard to achieve.

There are no cases that totally fit this picture, but it bears more than a passing resemblance to Europe before World War I. Britain and Germany, although in many respects natural allies, ended up as enemies. Of course much of the explanation lies in Germany's ill-chosen policy. And from the perspective of our theory, the powers' ability to avoid war in a series of earlier crises cannot be easily explained. Nevertheless, much of the behavior in this period was the product of technology and beliefs that magnified the security dilemma. Decision makers thought that the offense had a big advantage and saw little difference between offensive and defensive military postures. The era was characterized by arms races. And once war seemed likely, mobilization races created powerful incentives to strike first.

In the nuclear era, the first world would be one in which each side relied on vulnerable weapons that were aimed at similar forces and each side understood the situation. In this case, the incentives to strike first would be very high—so high that status-quo powers as well as aggressors would be sorely tempted to preempt. And since the forces could be used to change the status quo as well as to preserve it, there would be no way for both sides to increase their security simultaneously.

TABLE 1

	Offense has the advantage	Defense has the advantage
Offensive posture not distinguishable from defensive one	1 Doubly dangerous	2 Security dilemma, but security requirements may be compatible
Offensive posture distinguishable from defensive one	3 No security dilemma, but aggression possible Status-quo states can follow different policy than aggressors Warning given	4 Doubly stable

Now the familiar logic of deterrence leads both sides to see the dangers in this world. Indeed, the new understanding of this situation was one reason why vulnerable bombers and missiles were replaced. Ironically, the 1950s would have been more hazardous if the decision makers had been aware of the dangers of their posture and had therefore felt greater pressure to strike first.

In the second world, the security dilemma operates because offensive and defensive postures cannot be distinguished; but it does not operate as strongly as in the first world because the defense has the advantage, and so an increment in one side's strength increases its security more than it decreases the other's. So, if both sides have reasonable subjective security requirements, are of roughly equal power, and the variables discussed earlier are favorable, it is quite likely that status-quo states can adopt compatible security policies. Although a state will not be able to judge the other's intentions from the kinds of weapons it procures, the level of arms spending will give important evidence. Of course a state that seeks a high level of arms might be not an aggressor but merely an insecure state, which if conciliated will reduce its arms, and if confronted will reply in kind. To assume that the apparently excessive level of arms indicates aggressiveness could therefore lead to a response that would deepen the dilemma and create needless conflict. But empathy and skillful statesmanship can reduce this danger. Furthermore, the advantageous position of the defense means that a status-quo state can often maintain a high degree of security with a level of arms lower than that of its expected adversary. Such a state demonstrates that it lacks the ability or desire to alter the status quo, at least at the present time. The strength of the defense also allows states to react slowly and with restraint when they fear that others are menacing them. So, although status-quo powers will to some extent be threatening to others, that extent will be limited.

This world is the one that comes closest to matching most periods in history. Attacking is usually harder than defending because of the strength of fortifications and obstacles. But purely defensive postures are rarely possible because fortifications are usually supplemented by armies and mobile guns which can support an attack. In the nuclear era, this world would be one in which both sides relied on relatively invulnerable ICBMs and believed that limited nuclear war was impossible. Assuming no MIRVs, it would take more than one attacking missile to destroy one of the adversary's. Preemption is therefore unattractive. If both sides have large inventories, they can ignore all but drastic increases on the other side. A world of either ICBMs or SLBMs in which both sides adopted the policy of limited nuclear war would probably fit in this category too. The means of preserving the status quo would also be the means of changing it, as we discussed earlier. And the defense usually would have the advantage, because compellence is more difficult than deterrence. Although a state might succeed in changing the status quo on issues that matter much more to it than to others, status-quo powers could deter major provocations under most circumstances.

In the third world there may be no security dilemma, but there are security problems. Because states can procure defensive systems that do not threaten others, the dilemma need not operate. But because the offense has the advantage, aggression is possible, and perhaps easy. If the offense has less of an advantage, stability and cooperation are likely because the status-quo states will procure defensive forces. They need not react to others who are similarly armed, but can wait for the warning they would receive if others started to deploy offensive weapons. But each state will have to watch the others carefully, and there is room for false suspicions. The costliness of the defense and the allure of the offense can lead to unnecessary mistrust, hostility, and war, unless some of the variables discussed earlier are operating to restrain defection.

A hypothetical nuclear world that would fit this description would be one in which both sides relied on SLBMs, but in which ASW techniques were very effective. Offense and defense would be different, but the former would have the advantage. This situation is not likely to occur; but if it did, a status-quo state could show its lack of desire to exploit the other by refraining from threatening its submarines. The desire to have more protecting you than merely the other side's fear of retaliation is a strong one, however, and a state that knows that it would not expand even if its cities were safe is likely to believe that the other would not feel threatened by its ASW program. It is easy to see how such a world could become unstable, and how spirals of tensions and conflict could develop.

The fourth world is doubly safe. The differentiation between offensive and defensive systems permits a way out of the security dilemma; the advantage of the defense disposes of the problems discussed in the previous paragraphs. There is no reason for a status-quo power to be tempted to procure offensive forces, and aggressors give notice of their intentions by the posture they adopt. Indeed, if the advantage of the defense is great enough, there are no security problems. The loss of the ultimate form of the power to alter the status quo would allow greater scope for the exercise of nonmilitary means and probably would tend to freeze the distribution of values.

This world would have existed in the first decade of the twentieth century if the decision makers had understood the available technology. In that case, the European powers would have followed different policies both in the long run and in the summer of 1914. Even Germany, facing powerful enemies on both sides, could have made herself secure by developing strong defenses. France could also have made her frontier almost impregnable. Furthermore, when crises arose, no one would have had incentives to strike first. There would have been no competitive mobilization races reducing the time available for negotiations.

In the nuclear era, this world would be one in which the superpowers relied on SLBMs, ASW technology was not up to its task, and limited nuclear options were not taken seriously. . . . Because the problem of violence below the nuclear threshold would remain, on issues other than defense of the homeland, there would still be security dilemmas and security problems. But the world would nevertheless be safer than it has usually been.

NOTES

1. Thus, when Wolfers argues that a status-quo state that settles for rough equality of power with its adversary, rather than seeking preponderance, may be able to convince the other to reciprocate by showing that it wants only to protect itself, not menace the

other, he assumes that the defense has an advantage. See Arnold Wolfers, *Discord and Collaboration* (Baltimore: Johns Hopkins Press, 1962), p. 126.

2. Thomas Schelling, *The Strategy of Conflict* (New York: Oxford University Press, 1963), chap. 9.

3. Quoted in Fritz Fischer, *War of Illusions* (New York: Norton, 1975), pp. 377, 461.

4. George Quester, *Offense and Defense in the International System* (New York: John Wiley, 1977), p. 105.

5. Herman Kahn, *On Thermonuclear War* (Princeton, N.J.: Princeton University Press, 1960), p. 211 (also see p. 144).

6. For a general discussion of such mistaken learning from the past, see Jervis, *Perception and Misperception in International Relations* (Princeton, N.J.: Princeton University Press, 1976), chap. 6. The important and still not completely understood question of why this belief formed and was maintained throughout the war is examined in Bernard Brodie, *War and Politics* (New York: Macmillan, 1973), pp. 262–70; Brodie: "Technological Change, Strategic Doctrine, and Political Outcomes," in Klaus Knorr, ed., *Historical Dimensions of National Security Problems* (Lawrence: University Press of Kansas, 1976), pp. 290–92; and Douglas Porch. "The French Army and the Spirit of the Offensive, 1900–14," in Brian Bond and Ian Roy, eds., *War and Society* (New York: Holmes & Meier, 1975), pp. 117–43.

7. Some were not so optimistic. Grey's remark is well-known: "The lamps are going out all over Europe; we shall not see them lit again in our life-time." The German Prime Minister, Bethmann Hollweg, also feared the consequences of the war. But the controlling view was that it would certainly pay for the winner.

8. Quoted in Martin Gilbert, *Winston S. Churchill*, III, *The Challenge of War, 1914–1916* (Boston: Houghton Mifflin, 1971), p. 84.

9. Quester (fn. 4), pp. 98–99. Robert Art, *The Influence of Foreign Policy on Seapower*, II (Beverly Hills: Sage Professional Papers in International Studies Series, 1973), pp. 14–18, pp. 26–28.

10. Konrad Jarausch, "The Illusion of Limited War: Chancellor Bethmann Hollweg's Calculated Risk, July 1914," *Central European History*, II (March 1969): p. 50.

11. Brodie, *War and Politics* (New York: Macmillan, 1973), p. 58.

12. President Roosevelt and the American delegates to the League of Nations Disarmament Conference maintained that the tank and the mobile heavy artillery had reestablished the dominance of the offensive, thus making disarmament more urgent (Marion Boggs, *Attempts to Define and Limit "Aggressive" Armament in Diplomacy and Strategy* [Columbia: University of Missouri Studies, XVI, no. 1, 1941]: pp. 31, 108), but this was a minority position and may not even have been believed by the Americans. The reduced prestige and influence of the military, and the high pressures to cut government spending throughout this period also contributed to the lowering of defense budgets.

13. Jon Kimche, *The Unfought Battle* (New York: Stein, 1968); Nicholas William Bethell, *The War Hitler Won: The Fall of Poland, September 1939* (New York: Holt, 1972); Alan Alexandroff and Richard Rosecrance, "Deterrence in 1939," *World Politics*, XXIX (April 1977): pp. 404–24.

14. Roderick Macleod and Denis Kelly, eds., *Time Unguarded: The Ironside Diaries, 1937–1940* (New York; McKay, 1962), p. 173.

15. For a short time, as France was falling, the British Cabinet did discuss reaching a negotiated peace with Hitler. The official history downplays this, but it is covered in P.M.H. Bell, *A Certain Eventuality* (Farnborough, England: Saxon House, 1974), pp. 40–48.

16. MacLeod and Kelly (fn. 14), 174. In flat contradiction to common sense and almost everything they believed about modern warfare, the Allies planned an expedition to

Scandinavia to cut the supply of iron ore to Germany and to aid Finland against the Russians. But the dominant mood was the one described above.

17. Brodie (fn. 11), p. 179.
18. Arthur Balfour, "Memorandum," Committee on Imperial Defence, April 30, 1903, pp. 2–3; see the telegrams by Sir Arthur Nicolson, in G.P. Gooch and Harold Temperley, eds., *British Documents on the Origins of the War,* vol. 4 (London: H.M.S.O., 1929): pp. 429, 524. These barriers do not prevent the passage of long-range aircraft; but even in the air, distance usually aids the defender.
19. See, for example, the discussion of warfare among Chinese warlords in Hsi-Sheng Chi, "The Chinese Warlord System as an International System," in Morton Kaplan, ed., *New Approaches to International Relations* (New York: St. Martin's 1968), pp. 405–25.
20. Some American decision makers, including military officers, thought that the best way out of the dilemma was to abandon the Philippines.
21. Quoted in Elting Morrison, *Turmoil and Tradition: A Study of the Life and Times of Henry L. Stimson* (Boston: Houghton Mifflin, 1960), p. 326.
22. The U.S. "refused to consider limitations on Hawaiian defenses, since these works posed no threat to Japan." William Braisted, *The United States Navy in the Pacific, 1909–1922* (Austin: University of Texas Press, 1971), p. 612.
23. That is part of the reason why the Japanese admirals strongly objected when the civilian leaders decided to accept a seven-to-ten ratio in lighter craft in 1930. Stephen Pelz, *Race to Pearl Harbor* (Cambridge, Mass.: Harvard University Press, 1974), p. 3.
24. John Nef, *War and Human Progress* (New York: Norton, 1963), p. 185. Also see *ibid.*, pp. 237, 242–43, and 323; C. W. Oman, *The Art of War in the Middle Ages* (Ithaca, N.Y.: Cornell University Press, 1953), pp. 70–72; John Beeler, *Warfare in Feudal Europe,* pp. 730–1200 (Ithaca, N.Y.: Cornell University Press, 1971), 212–14; Michael Howard, *War in European History* (London: Oxford University Press 1976), pp. 33–37.
25. Quincy Wright, *A Study of War* (abridged ed.; Chicago: University of Chicago Press, 1964), p. 142. Also see pp. 63–70, 74–75. There are important exceptions to these generalizations—the American Civil War, for instance, falls in the middle of the period Wright says is dominated by the offense.
26. Geoffrey Kemp, Robert Pfaltzgraff, and Uri Ra'anan, eds., *The Other Arms Race* (Lexington, Mass.: D.C. Heath, 1975); James Foster, "The Future of Conventional Arms Control," *Policy Sciences,* no. 8 (Spring 1977): pp. 1–19.
27. Richard Challener, *Admirals, Generals, and American Foreign Policy, 1898–1914* (Princeton, N.J.: Princeton University Press, 1973); Grey to Nicolson, in Gooch and Temperley (fn. 18), p. 414.
28. Quoted in James Crowley, *Japan's Quest for Autonomy* (Princeton, N.J.: Princeton University Press, 1966), p. 49. American naval officers agreed with the Japanese that a ten-to-six ratio would endanger Japan's supremacy in her home waters.
29. E. L. Woodward and R. Butler, ed., *Documents on British Foreign Policy, 1919–1939.* 3d ser. III (London: H.M.S.O., 1950); p. 526.
30. Jervis (fn. 6), pp. 69–72, 352–55.
31. Quoted in Merze Tate, *The United States and Armaments* (Cambridge, Mass.: Harvard University Press, 1948), p. 108.
32. Boggs (fn. 12), pp. 15, 40.
33. Kenneth Hagan, *American Gunboat Diplomacy and the Old Navy, 1877–1899* (Westport, Conn.: Greenwood Press, 1973), p. 20.
34. Winston Churchill, *The Gathering Storm* (Boston: Houghton, 1948), p. 206.
35. Brodie, *War and Politics* (fn. 6), p. 325.

36. Boggs (fn. 12), pp. 42, 83. For a good argument about the possible differentiation between offensive and defensive weapons in the 1930s, see Basil Liddell Hart, "Aggression and the Problem of Weapons," *English Review*, 55 (July 1932): pp. 71–78.
37. Quoted in Boggs (fn. 12), p. 39.
38. On these grounds, the Germans claimed in 1932 that the French forts were offensive (*ibid.*, p. 49). Similarly, fortified forward naval bases can be necessary for launching an attack; see Braisted (fn. 22), p. 643.
39. The French made this argument in the interwar period; see Richard Challener, *The French Theory of the Nation in Arms* (New York: Columbia University Press, 1955), pp. 181–82. The Germans disagreed; see Boggs (fn. 12), pp. 44–45.
40. Oman (fn. 24), pp. 57–58.
41. Quoted in Charles Webster, *The Foreign Policy of Castlereagh*, II, *1815–1822* (London: G. Bell and Sons, 1963), p. 510.
42. Boggs (fn. 12), pp. 14–15, 47–48, 60.
43. Quoted in Philip Jordan, *Frontier Law and Order* (Lincoln: University of Nebraska Press, 1970), p. 7; also see pp. 16–17.
44. Boggs (fn. 12), pp. 20, 28.

The Political Utility of Nuclear Weapons

The Obsolescence of War in the Modern Industrialized World

John Mueller

It is widely assumed that, for better or worse, the existence of nuclear weapons has profoundly shaped our lives and destinies. Some find the weapons supremely beneficial. Defense analyst Edward Luttwak says, "we have lived since 1945 without another world war precisely because rational minds . . . extracted a durable peace from the very terror of nuclear weapons."[1] And Robert Art and Kenneth Waltz conclude, "the probability of war between America and Russia or between NATO and the Warsaw Pact is practically nil precisely because the military planning and deployments of each, together with the fear of escalation to general nuclear war, keep it that way."[2] Others argue that, while we may have been lucky so far, the continued existence of the weapons promises eventual calamity: The doomsday clock on the cover of the *Bulletin of the Atomic Scientists* has been pointedly hovering near midnight for over 40 years now, and in his influential bestseller, *The Fate of the Earth,* Jonathan Schell dramatically concludes that if we do not "rise up and cleanse the earth of nuclear weapons," we will "sink into the final coma and end it all."[3]

This article takes issue with both of these points of view and concludes that nuclear weapons neither crucially define a fundamental stability nor threaten severely to disturb it.

The paper is in two parts. In the first it is argued that, while nuclear weapons may have substantially influenced political rhetoric, public discourse, and defense

International Security, Fall 1988 (Vol. 13, No. 2). © 1988 by the President and Fellows of Harvard College and of the Massachusetts Institute of Technology. Portions of the text and some footnotes have been omitted.

budgets and planning, it is not at all clear that they have had a significant impact on the history of world affairs since World War II. They do not seem to have been necessary to deter World War III, to determine alliance patterns, or to cause the United States and the Soviet Union to behave cautiously.

In the second part, these notions are broadened to a discussion of stability in the postwar world. It is concluded that there may be a long-term trend away from war among developed countries and that the long peace since World War II is less a peculiarity of the nuclear age than the logical conclusion of a substantial historical process. Seen broadly, deterrence seems to be remarkably firm; major war—a war among developed countries, like World War II or worse—is so improbable as to be obsolescent; imbalances in weapons systems are unlikely to have much impact on anything except budgets; and the nuclear arms competition may eventually come under control not so much out of conscious design as out of atrophy born of boredom.

THE IMPACT OF NUCLEAR WEAPONS

The postwar world might well have turned out much the same even in the absence of nuclear weapons. Without them, world war would have been discouraged by the memory of World War II, by superpower contentment with the postwar status quo, by the nature of Soviet ideology, and by the fear of escalation. Nor do the weapons seem to have been the crucial determinants of Cold War developments, of alliance patterns, or of the way the major powers have behaved in crises.

Deterrence of World War

It is true that there has been no world war since 1945 and it is also true that nuclear weapons have been developed and deployed in part to deter such a conflict. It does not follow, however, that it is the weapons that have prevented the war—that peace has been, in Winston Churchill's memorable construction, "the sturdy child of [nuclear] terror." To assert that the ominous presence of nuclear weapons has prevented a war between the two power blocs, one must assume that there would have been a war had these weapons not existed. This assumption ignores several other important war-discouraging factors in the postwar world.

The Memory of World War II   A nuclear war would certainly be vastly destructive, but for the most part nuclear weapons simply compound and dramatize a military reality that by 1945 had already become appalling. Few with the experience of World War II behind them would contemplate its repetition with anything other than horror. Even before the bomb had been perfected, world war had become spectacularly costly and destructive, killing some 50 million worldwide. . . .

Postwar Contentment   For many of the combatants, World War I was as destructive as World War II, but its memory did not prevent another world war. Of course, as will be discussed more fully in the second half of this article, most nations *did* conclude from the horrors of World War I that such an event must never be repeated. If the only nations capable of starting World War II had been Britain, France, the Soviet Union, and the United States, the war would probably never have occurred. Unfortunately other major nations sought direct territorial expansion, and conflicts over these desires finally led to war.

Unlike the situation after World War I, however, the only powers capable of creating another world war since 1945 have been the big victors, the United States and the Soviet Union, each of which has emerged confortably dominant in its respective sphere. As Waltz has observed, "the United States, and the Soviet Union as well, have more reason to be satisfied with the status quo than most earlier great powers had."[4] (Indeed, except for the dismemberment of Germany, even Hitler might have been content with the empire his archenemy Stalin controlled at the end of the war.) While there have been many disputes since the war, neither power has had a grievance so essential as to make a world war—whether nuclear or not—an attractive means for removing the grievance.

Soviet Ideology   Although the Soviet Union and international communism have visions of changing the world in a direction they prefer, their ideology stresses revolutionary procedures over major war. The Soviet Union may have hegemonic desires as many have argued but, with a few exceptions (especially the Korean War) to be discussed below, its tactics, inspired by the cautiously pragmatic Lenin, have stressed subversion, revolution, diplomatic and economic pressure, seduction, guerrilla warfare, local uprising, and civil war—levels at which nuclear weapons have little relevance. The communist powers have never—before or after the invention of nuclear weapons—subscribed to a Hitler-style theory of direct, Armageddon-risking conquest, and they have been extremely wary of provoking Western powers into large-scale war. Moreover, if the memory of World War II deters anyone, it probably does so to an extreme degree for the Soviets. Officially and unofficially they seem obsessed by the memory of the destruction they suffered. . . .

The Belief in Escalation   Those who started World Wars I and II did so not because they felt that costly wars of attrition were desirable, but because they felt that escalation to wars of attrition could be avoided. In World War I the offensive was believed to be dominant, and it was widely assumed that conflict would be short and decisive.[5] In World War II, both Germany and Japan experienced repeated success with bluster, short wars in peripheral areas, and blitzkrieg, aided by the counterproductive effects of their opponents' appeasement and inaction.

World war in the post–1945 era has been prevented not so much by visions of nuclear horror as by the generally accepted belief that conflict can easily escalate to a level, nuclear or not, that the essentially satisfied major powers would find intolerably costly.

To deal with the crucial issue of escalation, it is useful to assess two important phenomena of the early postwar years: the Soviet preponderance in conventional arms and the Korean War.

First, it has been argued that the Soviets would have been tempted to take advantage of their conventional strength after World War II to snap up a prize like

Western Europe if its chief defender, the United States, had not possessed nuclear weapons. As Winston Churchill put it in 1950, "nothing preserves Europe from an overwhelming military attack except the devastating resources of the United States in this awful weapon."[6]

This argument requires at least three questionable assumptions: (1) that the Soviets really think of Western Europe as a prize worth taking risks for; (2) that, even without the atomic bomb to rely on, the United States would have disarmed after 1945 as substantially as it did; and (3) that the Soviets have actually ever had the strength to be quickly and overwhelmingly successful in a conventional attack in Western Europe.[7]

However, even if one accepts these assumptions, the Soviet Union would in all probability still have been deterred from attacking Western Europe by the enormous potential of the American war machine. Even if the USSR had the ability to blitz Western Europe, it could not have stopped the United States from repeating what it did after 1941: mobilizing with deliberate speed, putting its economy onto a wartime footing, and wearing the enemy down in a protracted conventional major war of attrition massively supplied from its unapproachable rear base.

The economic achievement of the United States during the war was astounding. While holding off one major enemy, it concentrated with its allies on defeating another, then turned back to the first. Meanwhile, it supplied everybody. With 8 million of its ablest men out of the labor market, it increased industrial production 15 percent per year and agricultural production 30 percent overall. Before the end of 1943 it was producing so much that some munitions plants were closed down, and even so it ended the war with a substantial surplus of wheat and over $90 billion in surplus war goods. (National governmental expenditures in the first peacetime year, 1946, were only about $60 billion.) As Denis Brogan observed at the time, "to the Americans war is a business, not an art."[8]

If anyone was in a position to appreciate this, it was the Soviets. By various circuitous routes the United States supplied the Soviet Union with, among other things, 409,526 trucks; 12,161 combat vehicles (more than the Germans had in 1939); 32,200 motorcycles; 1,966 locomotives; 16,000,000 pairs of boots (in two sizes); and over one-half pound of food for every Soviet soldier for every day of the war (much of it Spam).[9] It is the kind of feat that concentrates the mind, and it is extremely difficult to imagine the Soviets willingly taking on this somewhat lethargic, but ultimately hugely effective juggernaut. That Stalin was fully aware of the American achievement—and deeply impressed by it—is clear. Adam Ulam has observed that Stalin had "great respect for the United States' vast economic and hence military potential, quite apart from the bomb," and that his "whole career as dictator had been a testimony to his belief that production figures were a direct indicator of a given country's power."[10] As a member of the Joint Chiefs of Staff put it in 1949, "if there is any single factor today which would deter a nation seeking world domination, it would be the great industrial capacity of this country rather than its armed strength."[11] Or, as Hugh Thomas has concluded, "if the atomic bomb had not existed, Stalin would still have feared the success of the U.S. wartime economy."[12]

After a successful attack on Western Europe the Soviets would have been in a position similar to that of Japan after Pearl Harbor: They might have gains aplenty, but they would have no way to stop the United States (and its major unapproachable allies, Canada and Japan) from eventually gearing up for, and then launching, a war of attrition. All they could hope for, like the Japanese in 1941, would be that their victories would cause the Americans to lose their fighting spirit. But if Japan's Asian and Pacific gains in 1941 propelled the United States into war, it is to be expected that the United States would find a Soviet military takeover of an area of far greater importance to it—Western Europe—to be alarming in the extreme. Not only would the United States be outraged at the American casualties in such an attack and at the loss of an important geographic area, but it would very likely conclude (as many Americans did conclude in the late 1940s even without a Soviet attack) that an eventual attack on the United States itself was inevitable. . . .

Second, there is the important issue of the Korean War. Despite the vast American superiority in atomic weapons in 1950, Stalin was willing to order, approve, or at least acquiesce in an outright attack by a communist state on a noncommunist one, and it must be assumed that he would have done so at least as readily had nuclear weapons not existed. The American response was essentially the result of the lessons learned from the experiences of the 1930s: Comparing this to similar incursions in Manchuria, Ethiopia, and Czechoslovakia (and partly also to previous Soviet incursions into neighboring states in East Europe and the Baltic area), Western leaders resolved that such provocations must be nipped in the bud. If they were allowed to succeed, they would only encourage more aggression in more important locales later. Consequently it seems likely that the Korean War would have occurred in much the same way had nuclear weapons not existed.

For the Soviets the lessons of the Korean War must have enhanced those of World War II: Once again the United States was caught surprised and underarmed, once again it rushed hastily into action, once again it soon applied itself in a forceful way to combat—in this case for an area that it had previously declared to be of only peripheral concern. If the Korean War was a limited probe of Western resolve, it seems the Soviets drew the lessons the Truman administration intended. . . .

The Korean experience may have posed a somewhat similar lesson for the United States. In 1950, amid talk of "rolling back" communism and sometimes even of liberating China, American-led forces invaded North Korea. This venture led to a costly and demoralizing, if limited, war with China, and resulted in a considerable reduction in American enthusiasm for such maneuvers. Had the United States been successful in taking over North Korea, there might well have been noisy calls for similar ventures elsewhere—though, of course, these calls might well have gone unheeded by the leadership.

It is not at all clear that the United States and the Soviet Union needed the Korean War to become viscerally convinced that escalation was dangerously easy. But the war probably reinforced that belief for both of them and, to the degree that it did, Korea was an important stabilizing event.

Cold War and Crisis

If nuclear weapons have been unnecessary to prevent world war, they also do not seem to have crucially affected other important developments, including develop-

ment of the Cold War and patterns of alliance, as well as behavior of the superpowers in crisis.

The Cold War and Alliance Patterns   The Cold War was an outgrowth of various disagreements between the United States and the USSR over ideology and
over the destinies of Eastern, Central, and Southern Europe. The American reaction to the perceived Soviet threat in this period mainly reflects prenuclear thinking, especially the lessons of Munich.

For example, the formation of the North Atlantic Treaty Organization and the
division of the world into alliances centered on Washington and Moscow suggests
that the participants were chiefly influenced by the experience of World War II. If
the major determinant of these alliance patterns had been nuclear strategy, one
might expect the United States and, to a lesser extent, the Soviet Union, to be only
lukewarm members, for in general the alliances include nations that contribute little to nuclear defense but possess the capability unilaterally of getting the core
powers into trouble. And one would expect the small countries in each alliance to
tie themselves as tightly as possible to the core nuclear power in order to have maximum protection from its nuclear weapons. However, the weakening of the
alliance which has taken place over the last three decades has not come from the
major partners.

The structure of the alliances therefore better reflects political and ideological
bipolarity than sound nuclear strategy. As military economist (and later Defense
Secretary) James Schlesinger has noted, the Western alliance "was based on some
rather obsolescent notions regarding the strength and importance of the European
nations and the direct contribution that they could make to the security of the
United States. There was a striking failure to recognize the revolutionary impact
that nuclear forces would make with respect to the earlier beliefs regarding European defense."[13] Or, as Warner Schilling has observed, American policies in
Europe were "essentially pre-nuclear in their rationale. The advent of nuclear
weapons had not influenced the American determination to restore the European
balance of power. It was, in fact, an objective which the United States would have
had an even greater incentive to undertake if the fission bomb had not been developed."[14]

Crisis Behavior   Because of the harrowing image of nuclear war, it is sometimes
argued, the United States and the Soviet Union have been notably more restrained
than they might otherwise have been, and thus crises that might have escalated to
dangerous levels have been resolved safely at low levels.[15]

There is, of course, no definitive way to refute this notion since we are unable
to run the events of the last forty years over, this time without nuclear weapons.
And it is certainly the case that decision makers are well aware of the horrors of
nuclear war and cannot be expected to ignore the possibility that a crisis could lead
to such devastation.

However, this idea—that it is the fear of nuclear war that has kept behavior
restrained—looks far less convincing when its underlying assumption is directly

confronted: that the major powers would have allowed their various crises to escalate if all they had to fear at the end of the escalatory ladder was something like a
repetition of World War II. Whatever the rhetoric in these crises, it is difficult to
see why the unaugmented horror of repeating World War II, combined with considerable comfort with the status quo, wouldn't have been enough to inspire
restraint.

Once again, escalation is the key: What deters is the belief that escalation to
something intolerable will occur, not so much what the details of the ultimate
unbearable punishment are believed to be. Where the belief that the conflict will
escalate is absent, nuclear countries *have* been militarily challenged with war—as
in Korea, Vietnam, Afghanistan, Algeria, and the Falklands.

To be clear: None of this is meant to deny that the sheer horror of nuclear war
is impressive and mind-concentratingly dramatic, particularly in the speed with
which it could bring about massive destruction. Nor is it meant to deny that decision makers, both in times of crisis and otherwise, are fully conscious of how hor-
ribly destructive a nuclear war could be. It is simply to stress that the sheer horror
of repeating World War II is not all that much *less* impressive or dramatic, and that
powers essentially satisfied with the status quo will strive to avoid anything that
they feel could lead to *either* calamity. World War II did not cause total destruction
in the world, but it did utterly annihilate the three national regimes that brought it
about. It is probably quite a bit more terrifying to think about a jump from the 50th
floor than about a jump from the 5th floor, but anyone who finds life even minimally satisfying is extremely unlikely to do either.

Did the existence of nuclear weapons keep the Korean conflict restrained? As
noted, the communist venture there seems to have been a limited probe—though
somewhat more adventurous than usual and one that got out of hand with the massive American and Chinese involvement. As such, there was no particular reason—
or meaningful military opportunity—for the Soviets to escalate the war further. In
justifying *their* restraint, the Americans continually stressed the danger of escalating to a war with the Soviet Union—something of major concern whether or not
the Soviets possessed nuclear weapons. . . .

Much the same could be said about other instances in which there was a real or
implied threat that nuclear weapons might be brought into play: the Taiwan Straits
crises of 1954–55 and 1958, the Berlin blockade of 1948–49, the Soviet-Chinese confrontation of 1969, the Six-Day War in 1967, the Yom Kippur War of 1973, Cold War
disagreements over Lebanaon in 1958, Berlin in 1958 and 1961, offensive weapons in
Cuba in 1962. All were resolved, or allowed to dissipate, at rather low rungs on the
escalatory ladder. While the horror of a possible nuclear war was doubtless clear to the
participants, it is certainly not apparent that they would have been much more casual
about escalation if the worst they had to visualize was a repetition of World War II.

Of course nuclear weapons add new elements to international politics: new
pieces for the players to move around the board (missiles in and out of Cuba, for
example), new terrors to contemplate. But in counter to the remark attributed to
Albert Einstein that nuclear weapons have changed everything except our way of
thinking, it might be suggested that nuclear weapons have changed little except
our way of talking, gesturing, and spending money.

STABILITY

The argument thus far leads to the conclusion that stability is overdetermined—that the postwar situation contains redundant sources of stability. The United States and the Soviet Union have been essentially satisfied with their lot and, fearing escalation to another costly war, have been quite willing to keep their conflicts limited. Nuclear weapons may well have enhanced this stability—they are certainly dramatic reminders of how horrible a big war could be. But it seems highly unlikely that, in their absence, the leaders of the major powers would be so unimaginative as to need such reminding. Wars are not begun out of casual caprice or idle fancy, but because one country or another decides that it can profit from (not simply win) the war—the combination of risk, gain, and cost appears preferable to peace. Even allowing considerably for stupidity, ineptness, miscalculation, and self-deception in these considerations, it does not appear that a large war, nuclear or otherwise, has been remotely in the interest of the essentially contented, risk-averse, escalation-anticipating powers that have dominated world affairs since 1945.

It is *conceivable* of course that the leadership of a major power could be seized by a lucky, clever, risk-acceptant, aggressive fanatic like Hitler; or that an unprecedentedly monumental crisis could break out in an area, like Central Europe, that is of vital importance to both sides; or that a major power could be compelled toward war because it is consumed by desperate fears that it is on the verge of catastrophically losing the arms race. It is not obvious that any of these circumstances would necessarily escalate to a major war, but the existence of nuclear weapons probably does make such an escalation less likely; thus there are imaginable circumstances under which it might be useful to have nuclear weapons around. In the world we've actually lived in, however, those extreme conditions haven't come about, and they haven't every really even been in the cards. This enhancement of stability is, therefore, purely theoretical—extra insurance against unlikely calamity.

Crisis Stability, General Stability, and Deterrence

In further assessing these issues, it seems useful to distinguish crisis stability from a more general form of stability. Much of the literature on defense policy has concentrated on crisis stability, the notion that it is desirable for both sides in a crisis to be so secure that each is able to wait out a surprise attack fully confident that it would be able to respond with a punishing counterattack. In an ideal world, because of its fear of punishing retaliation, neither side would have an incentive to start a war no matter how large or desperate the disagreement, no matter how intense the crisis. Many have argued that crisis stability is "delicate": easily upset by technological or economic shifts.[16]

There is a more general form of stability, on the other hand, that is concerned with balance derived from broader needs, desires, and concerns. It prevails when two powers, taking all potential benefits, costs, and risks into account, greatly prefer peace to war—in the extreme, even to victorious war—whether crisis stability exists or not. For example, it can be said that general stability prevails in the relationship between the United States and Canada. The United States enjoys a massive military advantage over its northern neighbor since it could attack at any time with little concern about punishing military retaliation or about the possibility of losing the war (that is, it has a full "first strike capability"), yet the danger that the United States will attack Canada is nil. General stability prevails.

Although the deterrence literature is preoccupied with military considerations, the deterrence concept may be more useful if it is broadened to include nonmilitary incentives and disincentives. For example, it seems meaningful to suggest that the United States is "deterred" from attacking Canada, but not, obviously, by the Canadians' military might. If anyone in Washington currently were even to contemplate a war against Canada (a country, it might be noted, with which the United States has been at war in the past and where, not too long ago, many Americans felt their "manifest destiny" lay), the planner would doubtless be dissuaded by nonmilitary factors. For example, the war would disrupt a beneficial economic relationship; the United States would have the task of occupying a vast new area with sullen and uncooperative inhabitants; the venture would produce political turmoil in the United States. Similar cases can be found in the Soviet sphere. Despite an overwhelming military superiority, the USSR has been far from anxious to attack such troublesome neighboring states as Poland and Romania. It seems likely that the vast majority of wars that never take place are caused by factors that have little to do with military considerations. . . .

If a kind of overwhelming general stability really prevails, it may well be that the concerns about arms and the arms race are substantially overdone. That is, the often-exquisite numerology of the nuclear arms race has probably had little to do with the important dynamics of the Cold War era, most of which have taken place at militarily subtle levels such as subversion, guerrilla war, local uprising, civil war, and diplomatic posturing. As Benjamin Lambeth has observed, "it is perhaps one of the notable ironies of the nuclear age that while both Washington and Moscow have often lauded superiority as a military force-posture goal, neither has ever behaved as though it really believed superiority significantly mattered in the resolution of international conflicts.[17] In their extensive study of the use of the threat and force since World War II, Blechman and Kaplan conclude that, "especially noteworthy is the fact that our data do not support a hypothesis that the strategic weapons balance between the United States and the USSR influences outcomes."[18]

A special danger of weapons imbalance is often cited: A dominant country might be emboldened to use its superiority for purposes of pressure and intimidation. But unless its satisfaction with the status quo falls enormously and unless its opponent's ability to respond becomes very low as well, the superior power is unlikely to push its advantage very far, and certainly not anywhere near the point of major war. Even if the war could be kept nonnuclear and even if that power had a high probability of winning, the gains are likely to be far too low, the costs far too high.

Stability: Trends

Curiously, in the last twenty-five years crisis stability between the United States and the USSR has probably gotten worse while general stability has probably improved.

With the development of highly accurate multiple warhead missiles, there is a danger that one side might be able to obtain a first-strike counterforce capability, at least against the other side's land-based missiles and bombers, or that it might become able to cripple the other's command and control operations. At the same time, however, it almost seems—to put it very boldly—that the two major powers have forgotten how to get into a war. Although on occasion they still remember how to say nasty things about each other, there hasn't been a true, bone-crunching confrontational crisis for over a quarter-century. Furthermore, as Bernard Brodie notes, even the last crisis, over missiles in Cuba, was "remarkably different . . . from any previous one in history" in its "unprecedented candor, direct personal contact, and at the same time mutual respect between the chief actors."[19] Events since then that seem to have had some warlike potential, such as the military alert that attended the Yom Kippur War of 1973, fizzled while still at extremely low levels. . . .

It seems reasonable, though perhaps risky, to extrapolate from this trend and to suggest that, whatever happens with crisis stability in the future, general stability is here to stay for quite some time. That is, major war—war among developed countries—seems so unlikely that it may well be appropriate to consider it obsolescent. Perhaps World War II was indeed the war to end war—at least war of that scale and type.

The Hollandization Phenomenon   There are, of course, other possibilities. Contentment with the status-quo could diminish in time and, whatever the traumas of World War II, its lessons could eventually wear off, especially as postwar generations come to power. Somehow the fear of escalation could diminish, and small, cheap wars among major countries could again seem viable and attractive. We could get so used to living with the bomb that its use becomes almost casual. Some sort of conventional war could reemerge as a viable possibility under nuclear stalemate. But, as noted, the trends seem to be substantially in the opposite direction: Discontent does not seem to be on the rise, and visceral hostility seems to be on the decline.

Moreover, it might be instructive to look at some broad historical patterns. For centuries now, various countries, once warlike and militaristic, have been quietly dropping out of the war system to pursue neutrality and, insofar as they are allowed to do so, perpetual peace. Their existence tends to go unremarked because chroniclers have preferred to concentrate on the antics of the "Great Powers." "The story of international politics," observes Waltz, "is written in terms of the great powers of an era."[20] But it may be instructive for the story to include Holland, a country which chose in 1713, centuries before the invention of nuclear weapons, to abandon the fabled "struggle for power," or Sweden, which followed Holland's lead in 1721. Spain and Denmark dropped out too, as did Switzerland, a country which fought its last battle in 1798 and has shown a "curious indifference" to "political or territorial aggrandizement," as one historian has put it.[21]

While Holland's bandwagon was quietly gathering riders, an organized movement in opposition to war was arising. The first significant peace organizations in Western history emerged in the wake of the Napoleonic Wars in 1815, and during the next century they sought to promote the idea that war was immoral, repugnant, inefficient, uncivilized, and futile. They also proposed remedies like disarmament, arbitration, and international law and organization, and began to give out prizes for prominent peaceable behavior. They had become a noticeable force by 1914 but, as one of their number, Norman Angell, has recalled, they tended to be dismissed as "cranks and faddists . . . who go about in sandals and long beards, live on nuts."[22] Their problem was that most people living within the great power system were inclined to disagree with their central premise: that war was bad. As Michael Howard has observed, "before 1914 war was almost universally considered an acceptable, perhaps an inevitable and for many people a desirable way of settling international differences."[23] One could easily find many prominent thinkers declaring that war was progressive, beneficial, and necessary; or that war was a thrilling test of manhood and a means of moral purification and spiritual enlargement, a promoter of such virtues as orderliness, cleanliness, and personal valor.

It should be remembered that a most powerful effect of World War I on the countries that fought it was to replace that sort of thinking with a revulsion against wars and with an overwhelming, and so far permanent, if not wholly successful, desire to prevent similar wars from taking place. Suddenly, after World War I, peace advocates were a decided majority. As A.A. Milne put it in 1935, "in 1913, with a few exceptions we all thought war was a natural and fine thing to happen, so long as we were well prepared for it and had no doubt about coming out the victor. Now, with a few exceptions, we have lost our illusions; we are agreed that war is neither natural nor fine, and that the victor suffers from it equally with the vanquished."[24]

For the few who didn't get the point, the lesson was substantially reinforced by World War II. In fact, it almost seems that after World War I the only person left in Europe who was willing to risk another total war was Adolf Hitler. He had a vision of expansion and carried it out with ruthless and single-minded determination. Many Germans found his vision appealing, but unlike the situation in 1914 where enthusiasm for war was common, Hitler found enormous reluctance at all levels within Germany to use war to quest after the vision. As Gerhard Weinberg has concluded, "whether any other German leader would indeed have taken the plunge is surely doubtful, and the very warnings Hitler received from some of his generals can only have reinforced his belief in his personal role as the one man able, willing, and even eager to lead Germany and drag the world into war."[25] Hitler himself told his generals in 1939 "in all modesty" that he alone possessed the nerve required to lead Germany to fulfill what he took to be its mission. In Italy, Benito Mussolini also sought war, but only a small one, and he had to deceive his own generals to get that.[26] Only in Japan, barely touched by World War I, was the willingness to risk major war fairly widespread.

Since 1945 the major nuclear powers have stayed out of war with each other, but equally interesting is the fact that warfare of *all* sorts seems to have lost its appeal within the developed world. With only minor and fleeting exceptions (the Falklands War of 1982, the Soviet invasions of Hungary and Czechoslovakia), there have been no wars among the 48 wealthiest countries in all that time. Never before have so many well-armed countries spent so much time not using their arms against each other. This phenomenon surely goes well beyond the issue of nuclear weapons; they have probably been no more crucial to the non-war between, say, Spain and Italy than they have been to the near-war between Greece and Turkey or to the small war between Britain and Argentina.

Consider the remarkable cases of France and Germany, important countries which spent decades and centuries either fighting each other or planning to do so. For this age-old antagonism, World War II was indeed the war to end war. Like Greece and Turkey, they certainly retained the creativity to discover a motivation for war if they had really wanted to, even under an over-arching superpower balance; yet they have now lived side-by-side for nearly half a century, perhaps with some bitterness and recrimination, but without even a glimmer of war fever. They have become Hollandized with respect to one another. The case of Japan is also instructive: Another formerly aggressive major power seems now to have embraced fully the virtues and profits of peace.

The existence of nuclear weapons also does not help very much to explain the complete absence since 1945 of civil war in the developed world (with the possible exception of the 1944–49 Greek civil war, which could be viewed instead as an unsettled carryover of World War II). The sporadic violence in Northern Ireland or the Basque region of Spain has not really been sustained enough to be considered civil war, nor have the spurts of terrorism carried out by tiny bands of self-styled revolutionaries elsewhere in Western Europe. Except for the case of Hungary in 1956, Europeans under Soviet domination have not (so far) resorted to major violence, no matter how desperate their disaffection. . . .

As a form of activity, war in the developed world may be following once-fashionable dueling into obsolescence: The perceived wisdom, value, and efficacy of war may have moved gradually toward terminal disrepute. Where war was often casually seen as beneficial, virtuous, progressive, and glorious, or at least as necessary or inevitable, the conviction has now become widespread that war in the developed world would be intolerably costly, unwise, futile, and debased.

World war would be catastrophic, of course, and so it is sensible to be concerned about it even if its probability is microscopic. Yet general stability seems so firm and the trends so comforting that the concerns of Schell and others about our eventual "final coma" seem substantially overwrought. By themselves, weapons do not start wars, and if nuclear weapons haven't had much difference, reducing their numbers probably won't either. They may be menacing, but a major war seems so spectacularly unlikely that for those who seek to save lives it may make sense to spend less time worrying about something so improbable as major war and more time dealing with limited conventional wars outside the developed world, where war still can seem cheap and tempting, where romantic notions about holy war and purifying revolution still persist and sometimes prevail, and where developed countries sometimes still fight carefully delimited surrogate wars. Wars of that sort are still far from obsolete and have killed millions since 1945.

Over a quarter century ago, strategist Herman Kahn declared that "it is most unlikely that the world can live with an uncontrolled arms race lasting for several decades." He expressed his "firm belief" that "we are not going to reach the year 2000—and maybe not even the year 1965—without a cataclysm" unless we have "much better mechanisms than we have had for forward thinking."[27] Reflecting again on the cases of the United States and Canada, of Sweden and Denmark, of Holland, of Spain and Switzerland, of France and Germany, and of Japan, it might be suggested that there is a long-term solution to the arms competition between the United States and the Soviet Union, and that it doesn't have much to do with "mechanisms." Should political tensions decline, as to a considerable degree they have since the classic Cold War era of 1945–63, it may be that the arms race will gradually dissipate. And it seems possible that this condition might be brought about not principally by ingenious agreements over arms control, but by atrophy stemming from a dawning realization that, since preparations for major war are essentially irrelevant, they are profoundly foolish.

NOTES

1. Edward N. Luttwak, "Of Bombs and Men," *Commentary*, August 1983, p. 82.
2. Robert J. Art and Kenneth N. Waltz, "Technology, Strategy, and the Uses of Force." in Robert J. Art and Kenneth N. Waltz, eds., *The Use of Force* (Lanham, Md.: University Press of America, 1983), p. 28. See also Klaus Knorr, "Controlling Nuclear War," *International Security*, 9, no. 4 (Spring 1985): p. 79; John J. Mearsheimer. "Nuclear Weapons and Deterrence in Europe." *International Security*, 9, no. 3 (Winter 1984/85): pp. 25–26; Robert Gilpin, *War and Change in World Politics* (Cambridge: Cambridge University Press, 1981), pp. 213–19.
3. Jonathan Schell, *The Fate of the Earth* (New York: Knopf, 1982), p. 231.
4. Kenneth N. Waltz, *Theory of International Politics* (Reading, Mass.: Addison-Wesley, 1979), p. 190. See also Joseph S. Nye, Jr., "Nuclear Learning and U.S.-Soviet Security Regimes," *International Organization*, 41. no. 3 (Summer 1987): p. 377.
5. Jack Snyder, *The Ideology of the Offensive* (Ithaca N.Y.: Cornell University Press, 1984); Stephen Van Evera, "Why Cooperations Failed in 1914," *World Politics*, 38, no. 1 (October 1985): pp. 80–117. See also the essays on "The Great War and the Nuclear Age" in *International Security*, 9, no. 1 (Summer 1984): pp. 7–186.
6. Matthew A. Evangelista, "Stalin's Postwar Army Reappraised," *International Security*, 7, no. 3 (Winter 1982/83), p. 110.
7. This assumption is strongly questioned in *ibid.*, pp. 110–38.
8. Despite shortages, rationing, and tax surcharges, American consumer spending increased by 12 percent between 1939 and 1944. Richard R. Lingeman, *Don't You Know There's a War On?* (New York: Putnam, 1970), pp. 133, 357, and chap. 4; Alan S. Milward, *War, Economy and Society 1939–1945* (Berkeley and Los Angeles: University of California Press, 1977), pp. 63–74, 271–75; Mercedes Rosebery, *This Day's Madness* (New York: Macmillan, 1944), p. xii.
9. John R. Deane, *The Strange Alliance* (New York: Viking, 1947), pp. 92–95; Robert Huhn Jones, *The Roads to Russia* (Norman: University of Oklahoma Press, 1969), Appendix A. Additional information from Harvey DeWeerd.
10. Adam Ulam, *The Rivals: America and Russia Since World War II* (New York: Penguin, 1971), p. 95 and p. 5. In essence, Stalin seems to have understood that in Great Power wars, as Paul Kennedy put it, "victory has always gone to the side with the greatest material resources." Paul Kennedy, *The Rise and Fall of the Great Powers* (New York: Random House, 1987), p. 439.
11. Samuel P. Huntington, *The Common Defense* (New York: Columbia University Press, 1961), p. 46. See also Walter Mills, ed., *The Forrestal Diaries* (New York: Viking, 1951), pp. 350–51.

12. Thomas, *Armed Truce,* p. 548.

13. James Schlesinger, *On Reading Non-technical Elements to Systems Studies,* P–3545 (Santa Monica, Calif.: RAND, February 1967), p. 6.

14. Warner R. Schilling, "The H-Bomb Decision," *Political Science Quarterly,* 76, no. 1 (March 1961): p. 26. See also Waltz: "Nuclear weapons did not cause the condition of bipolarity. . . . Had the atom never been split, [the US and the USSR] would far surpass others in military strength, and each would remain the greatest threat and source of potential damage to the other." Waltz, *Theory of International Politics,* pp. 180–81.

15. John Lewis Gaddis, *The Long Peace* (New York: Oxford University Press. 1987), pp. 229–232; Gilpin, *War and Change in World Politics,* p. 218; Coit D. Blacker, *Reluctant Warriors* (New York: Freeman, 1987), p. 46.

16. The classic statement of this position is, of course, Albert Wohlstetter. "The Delicate Balance of Terror," *Foreign Affairs,* 27, no. 2 (January 1959): pp. 211–34. See also Glenn H. Snyder, *Deterrence and Defense* (Princeton N.J.: Princeton University Press, 1961), pp. 97–109.

17. Benjamin S. Lambeth, "Deterrence in the MIRV Era," *World Politics,* 24, no. 2 (January 1972), p. 234n.

18. Barry M. Blechman and Stephen S. Kaplan, *Force Without War* (Washington, D.C.: Brookings, 1978), p. 132. See also Jacek Kugler, "Terror Without Deterrence: Reassessing the Role of Nuclear Weapons," *Journal of Conflict Resolution,* 28, no. 3 (September 1984); pp. 470–506.

19. Bernard Brodie, *War and Politics* (New York: Macmillan, 1973), p. 426.

20. Waltz, *Theory of International Politics,* p. 72.

21. Lynn Montross, quoted in Jack S. Levy, *War in the Modern Great Power System* (Lexington: University Press of Kentucky), p. 45. On this issue, see also Brodie, *War and Politics,* p. 314.

22. Norman Angell, *After All* (New York: Farrar, Straus, and Young, 1951), p. 147. See also A.C.F. Beales, *The History of Peace* (New York: Dial, 1931); Roger Chickering, *Imperial Germany and a World Without War* (Princeton N.J. Princeton University Press, 1975).

23. Howard, "The Causes of Wars," p. 92.

24. A.A. Milne, *Peace With Honour* (New York: Dutton, 1935), pp. 9–10. See also Paul Fussell, *The Great War and Modern Memory* (New York: Oxford University Press, 1975); I.F. Clarke, *Voices Prophesying War 1763–1984* (London: Oxford University Press, 1966), chap. 5.

25. Gerhard Weinberg, *The Foreign Policy of Hitler's Germany* (Chicago: University of Chicago Press, 1982), p. 664.

26. MacGregor Knox, *Mussolini Unleashed 1939–1941* (Cambridge: Cambridge University Press, 1982), chap. 3.

27. Herman Kahn, *On Thermonuclear War* (Princeton; N.J.: Princeton University Press, 1961), pp. 574, x, 575.

The Utility of Nuclear Deterrence

Robert Jervis

Perhaps the most striking characteristic of the postwar world is just that—it can be called "postwar" because the major powers have not fought each other since 1945. Such a lengthy period of peace among the most powerful states is unprecedented.[1] Almost as unusual is the caution with which each superpower has treated the other. Although we often model superpower relations as a game of chicken, in fact the United States and USSR have not behaved like reckless teenagers. Indeed, superpower crises are becoming at least as rare as wars were in the past. Unless one strains and counts 1973, we have gone over a quarter of a century without a severe crisis. Furthermore, in those that have occurred, each side has been willing to make concessions to avoid venturing too near the brink of war. Thus the more we see of the Cuban missile crisis, the more it appears as a compromise rather than an American victory. Kennedy was not willing to withhold all inducements and push the Russians as hard as he could if this required using force or even continuing the volatile confrontation.[2]

It has been common to attribute these effects to the existence of nuclear weapons. Because neither side could successfully protect itself in an all-out war, no one could win—or, to use John Mueller's phrase, profit from it.[3] Of course this does not mean that wars will not occur. It is rational to start a war one does not expect to win (to be more technical, whose expected utility is negative), if it is believed that the likely consequences of not fighting are even worse.[4] War could also come through inadvertence, loss of control, or irrationality. But if decision makers are "sensible,"[5] peace is the most likely outcome. Furthermore, nuclear weapons can explain superpower caution: When the cost of seeking excessive gains is an increased probability of total destruction, moderation makes sense.

International Security, Fall 1988 (Vol. 13, No. 2) © 1988 by the President and Fellows of Harvard College and of the Massachusetts Institute of Technology. Portions of the text and some footnotes have been omitted.

Some analysts have argued that these effects either have not occurred or are not likely to be sustained in the future. Thus Fred Iklé is not alone in asking whether nuclear deterrence can last out the century.[6] It is often claimed that the threat of all-out retaliation is credible only as a response to the other side's all-out attack: Thus Robert McNamara agrees with more conservative analysts whose views he usually does not share that the "sole purpose" of strategic nuclear force "is to deter the other side's first use of its strategic forces."[7] At best, then, nuclear weapons will keep the nuclear peace; they will not prevent—and, indeed, may even facilitate—the use of lower levels of violence.[8] It is then not surprising that some observers attribute Soviet adventurism, particularly in Africa, to the Russians' ability to use the nuclear stalemate as a shield behind which they can deploy pressure, military aid, surrogate troops, and even their own forces in areas they had not previously controlled. The moderation mentioned earlier seems, to some, to be only one-sided. Indeed, American defense policy in the past decade has been driven by the felt need to create limited nuclear options to deter Soviet incursions that, while deeply menacing to our values, fall short of threatening immediate destruction of the United States.

Furthermore, while nuclear weapons may have helped keep the peace between the United States and USSR, ominous possibilities for the future are hinted at by other states' experiences. Allies of nuclear-armed states have been attacked: Vietnam conquered Cambodia and China attacked Vietnam. Two nuclear powers have fought each other, albeit on a very small scale: Russia and China skirmished on their common border. A nonnuclear power has even threatened the heartland of a nuclear power: Syria nearly pushed Israel off the Golan Heights in 1973 and there was no reason for Israel to be confident that Syria was not trying to move into Israel proper. Some of those who do not expect the United States to face such a menace have predicted that continued reliance on the threat of mutual destruction "would lead eventually to the demoralization of the West. It is not possible indefinitely to tell democratic republics that their security depends on the mass extermination of civilians . . . without sooner or later producing pacifism and unilateral disarmament."[9]

John Mueller has posed a different kind of challenge to claims for a "nuclear revolution." He disputes, not the existence of a pattern of peace and stability, but the attributed cause. Nuclear weapons are "essentially irrelevant" to this effect; modernity and highly destructive nonnuclear weapons would have brought us pretty much to the same situation had it not been possible to split the atom.[10] Such intelligent revisionism makes us think about questions whose answers had seemed self-evident. But I think that, on closer inspection, the conventional wisdom turns out to be correct. Nevertheless, there is much force in Mueller's arguments, particularly in the importance of what he calls "general stability" and the reminder that the fact that nuclear war would be so disastrous does not mean that conventional wars would be cheap.

Mueller is certainly right that the atom does not have magical properties. There is nothing crucial about the fact that people, weapons, industry, and agriculture may be destroyed as a result of a particular kind of explosion, although fission and fusion do produce special byproducts like fallout and electromagnetic pulse.

What is important are the political effects that nuclear weapons produce, not the physics and chemistry of the explosion. We need to determine what these effect are, how they are produced, and whether modern conventional weapons would replicate them.

POLITICAL EFFECTS OF NUCLEAR WEAPONS

The existence of large nuclear stockpiles influences superpower politics from three directions. Two perspectives are familiar: First, the devastation of an all-out war would be unimaginably enormous. Second, neither side—nor, indeed, third parties—would be spared this devastation. As Bernard Brodie, Thomas Schelling, and many others have noted, what is significant about nuclear weapons is not "overkill" but "mutual kill."[11] That is, no country could win an all-out nuclear war, not only in the sense of coming out of the war better than it went in, but in the sense of being better off fighting than making the concessions needed to avoid the conflict. It should be noted that although many past wars, such as World War II for all the Allies except the United States (and, perhaps, the USSR), would not pass the first test, they would pass the second. For example: Although Britain and France did not improve their positions by fighting, they were better off than they would have been had the Nazis succeeded. Thus it made sense for them to fight even though, as they feared at the outset, they would not profit from the conflict. Furthermore, had the Allies lost the war, the Germans—or at least the Nazis—would have won in a very meaningful sense, even if the cost had been extremely high. But "a nuclear war," as Reagan and Gorbachev affirmed in their joint statement after the November 1985 summit, "cannot be won and must never he fought."[12]

A third effect of nuclear weapons on superpower politics springs from the fact that the devastation could occur extremely quickly, within a matter of days or even hours. This is not to argue that a severe crisis or the limited use of force—even nuclear force—would inevitably trigger total destruction, but only that this is a possibility that cannot be dismissed. At any point, even in calm times, one side or the other could decide to launch an unprovoked all-out strike. More likely, a crisis could lead to limited uses of force which in turn, through a variety of mechanisms, could produce an all-out war. Even if neither side initially wanted this result, there is a significant, although impossible to quantify, possibility of quick and deadly escalation.

Mueller overstates the extent to which conventional explosives could substitute for nuclear ones in these characteristics of destructiveness, evenhandedness, and speed. One does not have to underestimate the horrors of previous wars to stress that the level of destruction we are now contemplating is much greater. Here, as in other areas, there comes a point at which a quantitative difference becomes a qualitative one. Charles De Gaulle put it eloquently: After a nuclear war, the "two sides would have neither powers, nor laws, nor cities, nor cultures, nor cradles, nor tombs."[13] While a total "nuclear winter" and the extermination of human life would not follow a nuclear war, the worldwide effects would be an order of magnitude greater than those of any previous war.[14] Mueller understates the differences in the scale of potential destruction: "World War II did not cause total destruction in the world, but it did utterly annihilate the three national regimes that brought it about. It is probably quite a bit more terrifying to think about a jump from the 50th floor than about a jump from the 5th floor, but anyone who finds life even minimally satisfying is extremely unlikely to do either."[15] The war did indeed destroy these national regimes, but it did not utterly destroy the country itself or even all the values the previous regimes supported. Most people in the Axis countries survived World War II; many went on to prosper. Their children, by and large, have done well. There is an enormous gulf between this outcome—even for the states that lost the war—and a nuclear holocaust. It is far from clear whether societies could ever be reconstituted after a nuclear war or whether economies would ever recover.[16] Furthermore, we should not neglect the impact of the prospect of destruction of culture, art, and national heritage: even a decision maker who was willing to risk the lives of half his population might hesitate at the thought of destroying what has been treasured throughout history.

Mueller's argument just quoted is misleading on a second count as well: The countries that started World War II were destroyed, but the Allies were not. It was more than an accident but less than predetermined that the countries that were destroyed were those that sought to overturn the status quo; what is crucial in this context is that with conventional weapons at least one side can hope, if not expect, to profit from the war. Mueller is quite correct to argue that near-absolute levels of punishment are rarely required for deterrence, even when the conflict of interest between the two sides is great—i.e., when states believe that the gross gains (as contrasted with the net gains) from war would be quite high. The United States, after all, could have defeated North Vietnam. Similarly, as Mueller notes, the United States was deterred from trying to liberate East Europe even in the era of American nuclear monopoly.

But, again, one should not lose sight of the change in scale that nuclear explosives produce. In a nuclear war the "winner" might end up distinguishably less worse off than the "loser," but we should not make too much of this difference. Some have. As Harold Brown put it when he was Secretary of the Air Force, "if the Soviets thought they may be able to recover in some period of time while the U.S. would take three or four times as long, or would never recover, then the Soviets might not be deterred."[17] Similarly, one of the criteria that Secretary of Defense Melvin Laird held necessary for the essential equivalence of Soviet and American forces was: "preventing the Soviet Union from gaining the ability to cause considerably greater urban/industrial destruction than the United States would in a nuclear war."[18] A secret White House memorandum in 1972 used a similar formulation when it defined "strategic sufficiency" as the forces necessary "to ensure that the United States would emerge from a nuclear war in discernably better shape than the Soviet Union."[19]

But this view is a remarkably apolitical one. It does not relate the costs of the war to the objectives and ask whether the destruction would be so great that the "winner," as well as the loser, would regret having fought it. Mueller avoids this trap, but does not sufficiently consider the possibility that, absent nuclear explosives, the kinds of analyses quoted above would in fact be appropriate. Even very high levels of destruction can rationally be compatible with a focus on who will come out ahead in an armed conflict. A state strongly motivated to change the status quo could believe that the advantages of domination were sufficiently great to justify enormous blood-letting. For example, the Russians may feel that World War II was worth the cost not only when compared with being conquered by Hitler, but also when compared with the enormous increase in Soviet prestige, influence, and relative power.

Furthermore, without nuclear weapons, states almost surely would devote great energies to seeking ways of reducing the costs of victory. The two world wars were enormously destructive because they lasted so long. Modern technology, especially when combined with nationalism and with alliances that can bring others to the rescue of a defeated state, makes it likely that wars will last long: Defense is generally more efficacious than offense. But this is not automatically true; conventional wars are not necessarily wars of attrition, as the successes of Germany in 1939–40 and Israel in 1967 remind us. Blitzkrieg can work under special circumstances, and when these are believed to apply, conventional deterrence will no longer be strong.[20] Over an extended period of time, one side or the other could on occasion come to believe that a quick victory was possible. Indeed, for many years most American officials have believed not only that the Soviets could win a conventional war in Europe or the Persian Gulf, but that they could do so at low cost. Were the United States to be pushed off the continent, the considerations Mueller gives might well lead it to make peace rather than pay the price of refighting World War II. Thus, extended deterrence could be more difficult without nuclear weapons. Of course, in their absence, NATO might build up a larger army and better defenses, but each side would continually explore new weapons and tactics that might permit a successful attack. At worst, such efforts would succeed. At best, they would heighten arms competition, national anxiety, and international tension. If both sides were certain that any new conventional war would last for years, the chances of war would be slight. But we should not be too quick to assume that conventional war with modern societies and weapons is synonymous with wars of attrition.

The length of the war is important in a related way as well. The fact that a war of attrition is slow makes a difference. It is true, as George Quester notes, that for some purposes all that matters is the amount of costs and pain the state has to bear, not the length of time over which it is spread.[21] But a conventional war would have to last a long time to do an enormous amount of damage; and it would not *necessarily* last a long time. Either side can open negotiations or make concessions during the war if the expected costs of continued fighting seem intolerable. Obviously, a timely termination is not guaranteed—the fitful attempts at negotiation during World War II and the stronger attempts during World War I were not fruitful. But the possibility of ending the war before the costs become excessive is never foreclosed. Of course, states can believe that a nuclear war would be prolonged, with relatively little damage being done each day, thus permitting intra-war bargaining. But no one can overlook the possibility that at any point the war could escalate to all-out destruction. Unlike the past, neither side could be certain that there would be a prolonged period for negotiation and intimidation. This blocks another path which statesmen in nonnuclear eras could see as a route to meaningful victory.

Furthermore, the possibility that escalation could occur even though neither side desires this outcome—what Schelling calls "the threat that leaves something to chance"[22]—induces caution in crises as well. The fact that sharp confrontations can get out of control, leading to the eventual destruction of both sides, means that states will trigger them only when the incentives to do so are extremely high. Of course, crises in the conventional era also could escalate, but the possibility of quick and total destruction means that the risk, while struggling near the brink, of falling into the abyss is greater and harder to control than it was in the past. Fears of this type dominated the bargaining during the Cuban missile crisis: Kennedy's worry was "based on fear, not of Khrushchev's intention, but of human error, of something going terribly wrong down the line." Thus when Kennedy was told that a U–2 had made a navigational error and was flying over Russia, he commented: "There is always some so-and-so who doesn't get the word."[23] The knowledge of these dangers—which does not seem lacking on the Soviet side as well[24]—is a powerful force for caution.

Empirical findings on deterrence failure in the nuclear era confirm this argument. George and Smoke show that: "The initiator's belief that the risks of his action are calculable and that the unacceptable risks of it can be controlled and avoided is, with very few exceptions, a necessary (though not sufficient) condition for a decision to challenge deterrence."[25] The possibility of rapid escalation obviously does not make such beliefs impossible, but it does discourage them. The chance of escalation means that local military advantage cannot be confidently and safely employed to drive the defender out of areas in which its interests are deeply involved. Were status quo states able to threaten only a war of attrition, extended deterrence would be more difficult.

GENERAL STABILITY

But is very much deterrence needed? Is either superpower strongly driven to try to change the status quo? On these points I agree with much of Mueller's argument—the likely gains from war are now relatively low, thus producing what he calls general stability.[26] The set of transformations that go under the heading of "modernization" have not only increased the costs of war, but have created alternative paths to established goals, and, more profoundly, have altered values in ways that make peace more likely. Our focus on deterrence and, even more narrowly, on matters military has led to a distorted view of international behavior. In a parallel manner, it has adversely affected policy prescriptions. We have not paid sufficient attention to the incentives states feel to change the status quo, or to the need to use inducements and reassurance, as well as threats and deterrence.[27]

States that are strongly motivated to challenge the status quo may try to do so even if the military prospects are bleak and the chances of destruction considerable. Not only can rational calculation lead such states to challenge the status quo, but people who believe that a situation is intolerable feel strong psychological pressures to conclude that it can be changed.[28] Thus nuclear weapons by themselves—and even mutual second-strike capability—might not be sufficient to produce peace. Contrary to Waltz's argument, proliferation among strongly dissatisfied countries would not necessarily recapitulate the Soviet-American pattern of stability.[29]

The crucial questions in this context are the strength of the Soviet motivation to change the status quo and the effect of American policy on Soviet drives and calculations. Indeed, differences of opinion on these matters explain much of the debate over the application of deterrence strategies toward the USSR.[30] Most of this dispute is beyond our scope here. Two points, however, are not. I think Mueller is correct to stress that not only Nazi Germany, but Hitler himself, was exceptional in the willingness to chance an enormously destructive war in order to try to dominate the world. While of course such a leader could recur, we should not let either our theories or our policies be dominated by this possibility.

A second point is one of disagreement: Even if Mueller is correct to believe that the Soviet Union is basically a satisfied power—and I share his conclusion—war is still possible. Wars have broken out in the past between countries whose primary goal was to preserve the status quo. States' conceptions of what is necessary for their security often clash with one another. Because one state may be able to increase its security only by making others less secure, the premise that both sides are basically satisfied with the status quo does not lead to the conclusion that the relations between them will be peaceful and stable. But here too nuclear weapons may help. As long as all-out war means mutual devastation, it cannot be seen as a path to security. The general question of how nuclear weapons make mutual security more feasible than it often was in the past is too large a topic to engage here. But I can at least suggest that they permit the superpowers to adopt military doctrines and bargaining tactics that make it possible for them to take advantage of their shared interest in preserving the status quo. Winston Churchill was right: "Safety [may] be the sturdy child of terror."

NOTES

1. Paul Schroeder, "Does Murphy's Law Apply to History?" *Wilson Quarterly,* 9. no. 1 (New Year's 1985): p. 88; Joseph S. Nye, Jr., "The Long-Term Future of Nuclear Deterrence," in Roman Kolkowicz, *The Logic of Nuclear Terror* (Boston: Allen & Unwin, 1987), p. 234.
2. See the recent information in McGeorge Bundy, transcriber, and James G. Blight, ed., "October 27, 1962: Transcripts of the Meetings of the ExComm," *International Security,* 12, no. 3 (Winter 1987/88): pp. 30–92; and James G. Blight, Joseph S, Nye, Jr., and David A. Welch, "The Cuban Missile Crisis Revisited," *Foreign, Affairs,* 66 (Fall 1987): pp. 178–79. Long before this evidence became available, Alexander George stressed Kennedy's moderation; see Alexander L. George, David K. Hall, and William E. Simons, *The Limits of Coercive Diplomacy: Laos, Cuba, Vietnam* (Boston: Little Brown, 1971), pp. 86–143.

3. "The Essential Irrelevance of Nuclear Weapons: Stability in the Postwar World." But as we will discuss below, it can be rational for states to fight even when profit is not expected.

4. Alternatively, to be even more technical, a decision maker could expect to lose a war and at the same time could see its expected utility as positive if the slight chance of victory was justified by the size of the gains that victory would bring. But the analysis here requires only the simpler formulation.

5. See the discussion in Patrick M. Moran, *Deterrence: A Conceptual Analysis* (Beverly Hills: Sage, 1977), pp. 101–24.

6. Fred Iklé, "Can Nuclear Deterrence Last Out the Century?" *Foreign Affairs,* 51, no. 2 (January 1973): pp. 267–85.

7. Robert McNamara, "The Military Role of Nuclear Weapons," *Foreign Affairs,* 62, no. 4 (Fall 1983): p. 68. For his comments on how he came to this view, see his interview in Michael Charlton, *From Deterrence to Defense* (Cambridge, Mass.: Harvard University Press, 1987), p. 18.

8. See Glenn Snyder's discussion of the "stability-instability paradox," in "The Balance of Power and the Balance of Terror," in Paul Seabury, ed., *The Balance of Power* (San Francisco: Chandler, 1965), pp. 184–201.

9. Henry Kissinger, "After Reykjavik: Current East-West Negotiations," *The San Francisco Meeting of the Tri-Lateral Commission, March 1987* (New York: The Trilateral Commission, 1987), p. 4; see also *ibid.*, p. 7, and his interview in Charlton, *From Deterrence to Defense,* p. 34.

10. Mueller, "The Essential Irrelevance." Waltz offers yet a third explanation for peace and stability—the bipolar nature of the international system, which, he argues, is not merely a product of nuclear weapons. See Kenneth Waltz, *Theory of International Politics* (Reading, Mass.: Addison-Wesley, 1979). But in a later publication he places more weight on the stabilizing effect of nuclear weapons: *The Spread of Nuclear Weapons: More May be Better,* Adelphi, Paper No. 171 (London: International Institute for Strategic Studies, 1981).

11. Bernard Brodie, ed., *The Absolute Weapon: Atomic Power and World Order* (New York: Harcourt Brace, 1946); Thomas Schelling, *Arms and Influence* (New Haven, Conn.: Yale University Press, 1966).

12. *New York Times,* November 22, 1985, p. A12.

13. Speech of May 31, 1960, in Charles De Gaulle, *Discours Et Messages,* 3 (Paris: Plon, 1970): p. 218. I am grateful to McGeorge Bundy for the reference and translation.

14. Starley Thompson and Stephen Schneider, "Nuclear Winter Reappraised," *Foreign Affairs,* 64, no. 5 (Summer 1986): pp. 981–1005.

15. "The Essential Irrelevance," pp. 66–67.

16. For a discussion of economic recovery models, see Michael Kennedy and Kevin Lewis, "On Keeping Them Down: Or, Why Do Recovery Models Recover So Fast?" in Desmond Ball and Jeffrey Richelson, *Strategic Nuclear Targeting* (Ithaca, N.Y.: Cornell University Press, 1986), pp. 194–208.

17. U.S. Senate, Preparedness Investigating Subcommittee of the Committee on Armed Services, *Hearings on Status of U.S. Strategic Power,* 90th Cong., 2d sess., April 30, 1968 (Washington, D.C.: U.S. Government Printing Office, 1968), p. 186.

18. U.S. House of Representatives, Subcommittee on Department of Defense, *Appropriations for the FY 1973 Defense Budget and FY 1973–1977 Program,* 92nd Cong., 2d sess., February 22, 1972, p. 65.

19. Quoted in Gregg Herken, *Counsels of War* (New York: Knopf, 1985), p. 266.

20. John J. Mearsheimer, *Conventional Deterrence* (Ithaca, N.Y.: Cornell University Press, 1983). It should be noted, however, that even a quick and militarily decisive war might

not bring the fruits of victory. Modern societies may be even harder to conquer than are modern governments. A high degree of civilian cooperation is required if the victor is to reach many goals. We should not assume it will be forthcoming. See Gene Sharp, *Making Europe Unconquerable* (Cambridge, Mass.: Ballinger, 1985).

21. George Quester, "Crisis and the Unexpected," *Journal of Interdisciplinary History,* 18, no. 3 (Spring 1988): pp. 701–3.

22. Thomas Schelling, *The Strategy of Conflict* (Cambridge, Mass.: Harvard University Press, 1960), pp. 187–203; Schelling, *Arms and Influence,* pp. 92–125. Also see Jervis, *The Illogic of American Nuclear Strategy* (Ithaca, N.Y.; Cornell University Press, 1984), ch. 5; Jervis, "'MAD is a Fact, not a Policy': Getting the Arguments Straight," in Jervis, *Meaning of the Nuclear Revolution* (Ithaca, N.Y.: Cornell University Press, 1989); and Robert Powell, "The Theoretical Foundations of Strategic Nuclear Deterrence," *Political Science Quarterly,* 100, no. 1 (Spring 1985): pp. 75–96.

23. Arthur M. Schlesinger, Jr., *Robert Kennedy and His Times* (Boston: Houghton Mifflin, 1978), p. 529; quoted in Roger Hilsman, *To Move A Nation* (Garden City, N.Y.: Doubleday, 1964), p. 221.

24. See Benjamin Lambeth, "Uncertainties for the Soviet War Planner," *International Security,* 7, no. 3 (Winter 1982/83): pp. 139–66.

25. Alexander L. George and Richard Smoke, *Deterrence in American Foreign Policy* (New York: Columbia University Press, 1974), p. 529.

26. Mueller, "Essential Irrelevance," pp. 69–70; also see Waltz, *Theory of International Politics,* p. 190.

27. For discussions of this topic, see George, Hall, and Simons, *Limits of Coercive Diplomacy;* George and Smoke, *Deterrence in American Foreign Policy;* Richard Ned Lebow, *Between Peace and War* (Baltimore: Johns Hopkins University Press, 1981); Robert Jervis, "Deterrence Theory Revisited," *World Politics,* 31, no. 2 (January 1979): pp. 289–324; Jervis, Lebow, and Janice Gross Stein, *Psychology and Deterrence* (Baltimore: Johns Hopkins University Press. 1985); David Baldwin, "The Power of Positive Sanctions," *World Politics,* 24, no. 1 (October 1971): pp. 19–38; and Janice Gross Stein, "Deterrence and Reassurance," in Philip E. Tetlock, et al., eds., *Behavior, Society and Nuclear War,* vol. 2 (New York: Oxford University Press. 1991).

28. George and Smoke, *Deterrence in American Foreign Policy;* Lebow, *Between Peace and War;* Jervis, Lebow, and Stein, *Psychology and Deterrence.*

29. Waltz, *Spread of Nuclear Weapons.*

30. See Robert Jervis, *Perception and Misperception in International Politics* (Princeton N.J.: Princeton University Press, 1976), chap. 3.

The Unimpressive Record of Atomic Diplomacy

McGeorge Bundy

In addressing the question of the role of nuclear weapons in diplomacy, it is well to begin with an expression of one's own general position on the nuclear problem. My view of these weapons is that for my own country they are a necessary evil. I do not think it acceptable for the United States to renounce the possession of nuclear capabilities while they are maintained in the Soviet Union. In that most basic sense I accept the need for nuclear deterrence and am unimpressed by arguments that neglect this requirement. . . .

I also believe that not all the consequences of the nuclear arsenals are bad. The very existence of nuclear stockpiles has created and enforced a considerable caution in the relations among nuclear-weapon states, so that where the interests of those states are clear and their political and military engagement manifest, as with the Soviet Union and the United States in Eastern and Western Europe respectively, there is an intrinsic inhibition on adventure which is none the less real for being essentially independent of doctrines—and even of nuclear deployments—on either side. I have elsewhere called this phenomenon "existential deterrence,"[1] and I think it has more to do with the persisting peace—and division—of Europe than all the particular nuclear doctrines and deployments that have so often bedeviled the European scene. . . .

Indeed the acceptance of nuclear deterrence, for me as for the American Catholic bishops, is "strictly conditioned," not only on a constant readiness to move to agreed arms reductions as drastic as the most skillful and dedicated negotiations permit, but also on a reluctance to depend on nuclear weapons for purposes

"The Unimpressive Record of Atomic Diplomacy" by McGeorge Bundy from *The Choice: Nuclear Weapons vs. Security*, edited by Gwyn Prins. Reprinted by permission of Chatto & Windus, one of the publishers in The Random Century Group Ltd. Portions of the text and some footnotes have been omitted.

beyond that of preventing nuclear war. On the historical record since Nagasaki, I think that these weapons have not been of great use to any government for such wider purposes, and I also think a misreading of that record has led to grossly mistaken judgments and to unnecessary, costly, and sometimes dangerous nuclear deployments by both superpowers, and perhaps by others. Let us begin by considering what good these weapons have done the United States, which was their first and for a short four years their only possessor. I am willing to concede, though it cannot be proven, that in the years of American monopoly, and perhaps for a short time thereafter (in my view, not beyond 1955, at the latest) American nuclear superiority had some military and political value in Europe. We must recognize that fear of what the Russians would otherwise do with what was then an enormous advantage in conventional strength was not limited to Winston Churchill. Niels Bohr too believed that the American atomic bomb was a necessary balancing force, and so did many other highly peaceable men. But the time has long since passed when either side could hope to enjoy either monopoly or overwhelming superiority, so from the standpoint of the present and the future it is not necessary to challenge this particular bit of conventional wisdom. We do not really know that the American monopoly saved Europe in the early postwar years, but we do not know it did not, and we need not decide.

What is more interesting is to examine these years of evident American nuclear advantage from another angle, to try, to see what usefulness that advantage may have had in supporting American diplomacy or in restraining specific adventures of others outside Western Europe. Aside from this debatable European case, there is very little evidence that American atomic supremacy was helpful in American diplomacy. Broadly speaking, the years from 1945 to 1949 were a time in which Soviet power and the power of such major Soviet allies as the Chinese communists was expanding and consolidating itself at a rate not remotely equaled since then, and there is no evidence whatever that fear of the American bomb had any restraining effect on this enormous process. It is true that for a short time in the autumn of 1945 Secretary of States James Byrnes believed that the silent presence of the bomb might constructively affect Soviet behavior at the negotiating table, but in fact it had no such impact, and before the end of the year Byrnes himself had changed his tactics. The importance of this brief and foolish flirtation with atomic diplomacy has been grossly exaggerated by students misreading a marginal and passing state of mind into a calculated effort in which Hiroshima itself is read largely as an effort to impress the Russians.[2] But this misreading is less important than the deeper point that to whatever degree atomic diplomacy may have tempted this or that American leader at this or that moment in those years, it did not work.

The point becomes still more evident when we look at moments which American presidents themselves, in later years, came to see as evidence of the power of the atomic possibility. The two most notable cases are the Soviet withdrawal from Iran in 1946 and the armistice agreement that ended the Korean War in 1953.

In April 1952 President Harry Truman told an astonished press conference that not long after the end of World War II he had given Joseph Stalin "an ultimatum"—to get his troops out of Iran—and "they got out." Truman was referring to events in March 1946, when the Soviet union kept troops in northern Iran after the expiration of an agreed date for British and Russian withdrawal that had been honored by the British. The Soviet stance stirred a vigorous international reaction, and after three weeks of increasing tension there came a Soviet announcement of a decision to withdraw that was executed over the following weeks. Truman never doubted that his messages had been decisive. Out of office, in 1957, he described his action still more vividly: "The Soviet Union persisted in its occupation until I personally saw to it that Stalin was informed that I had given orders to our military chiefs to prepare for the movement of our ground, sea and air forces. Stalin then did what I knew he would do. He moved his troops out." If this statement were accurate, it would be an extraordinary confirmation of the effectiveness of American threats in the age of atomic monopoly, because a troop movement of this sort, in 1946, into an area so near the Soviet Union and so far from the United States could only have been ventured, or feared, because of the nuclear monopoly.[3]

The only trouble with this picture is that no such message ever went to Stalin and no such orders to American officers. What actually happened is wholly different. Stalin did indeed attempt to gain a special position in Iran by keeping his troops beyond the deadline, but what made his effort a failure was not an ultimatum from Truman but primarily the resourceful resistance of the Iranian government, supported indeed by American diplomacy (especially at the United Nations) and still more by a wide and general international reaction. Stalin's was a low-stake venture in an area of persistent Soviet hope. He pulled back when he found the Iranian government firm but not belligerent, his Iranian supporters weak, and the rest of the watching world critical. One of the critics was Harry Truman, and we need not doubt the strength of his feelings. But the messages he actually sent (all now published) were careful and genuinely diplomatic. The United States Government "cannot remain indifferent," and "expresses the earnest hope" of immediate Soviet withdrawal, all "in the spirit of friendly association." There is no deadline and no threat. What we have here is no more than an understandable bit of retrospective braggadocio. As George Kennan later remarked—he had been *chargé d'affaires* in Moscow at the time and was the man who would have had to deliver any ultimatum—Truman "had an unfortunate tendency to exaggerate, in later years, certain aspects of the role that he played" in relations with Stalin.[4]

Regrettably, Truman's retrospective version of events was not harmless. Among stouthearted and uncomplicated anticommunists it became a part of the folklore showing that Harry Truman knew how to stop aggression by toughness, when in fact what he and his colleagues knew, in this case, was something much more important: that their task was to help keep up Iranian courage, but precisely *not* to confront Stalin directly. American diplomacy was adroit but not menacing, and Kennan is right again in describing the result: "It was enough for Stalin to learn that a further effort by the Soviet Union to retain its forces in Persia would create serious international complications. He had enough problems at the moment without that." Truman's messages had certainly helped in this learning process, and not least because they had expressly avoided the kind of threat he later came to believe he made. So his faulty memory led others to learn the wrong lesson.

Dwight Eisenhower contributed even more than Harry Truman to the folklore of atomic diplomacy. He believed that it was the threat of atomic war that brought an armistice in Korea in 1953. In his memoirs he cited a number of warnings and signals to make his case, and his Secretary of State, John Foster Dulles, told allied statesmen in private a lurid tale of nuclear deployments made known to the Chinese. But here again the historical record raises questions. The decisive shift in the position of the communists, a shift away from insistence on the forced repatriation of prisoners, occurred before any of these signals was given, shortly after the death of Stalin in March. While Eisenhower certainly intended the whiff of nuclear danger to reach Peking, the records now available make it clear that he in fact held back from any audible threat because of his recognition that it would be as divisive in 1953 as it had been in 1950, when Harry Truman, by a casual press conference response to a question on the possibility of using nuclear weapons, had brought Prime Minister Attlee across the Atlantic to receive assurance that no such step was in prospect. Quite aside from any nuclear threat, there were other and excellent reasons in 1953 for the communist side to want to end the war: their own heavy losses, the absence of any prospect for further gains, and the continuing high cost of unsuccessful probes of United Nations forces on the ground. At the most the springtime signals of a nuclear possibility were a reinforcement to Chinese preferences already established before those signals were conveyed.

Yet Eisenhower clearly did believe that the Korean case showed the value of nuclear threats, and indeed he and Dulles made the threat permanent in the language of a public declaration after the armistice that those who had supported South Korea would respond to any renewed aggression in ways that might not be limited. In two later crises, over the offshore islands of Quemoy and Matsu in 1955 and 1958, Eisenhower used both open references to nuclear weapons and visible deployments of nuclear-armed forces to underline the risks Mao was running. What actually held off the attacking Chinese forces, in both crises, was not these threats but the effective use of local air and naval superiority, but it cannot be denied that the nuclear possibility may have contributed to Chinese unwillingness to raise the stakes. It is also possible that the readiness of the United States to help defend these small and unimportant islands was increased by the fact that against China the United States then held a nuclear monopoly.

In this case too the threat was almost as alarming to friends as to opponents. Fully aware of the fiercely divisive consequences of any actual use of a nuclear weapon, Eisenhower devoted himself in these crises to the energetic and skillful support of the conventional forces and tactics which fended off the Chinese attacks. He was very careful indeed not to lose his control over the nuclear choice, either by any unconditional public threat or by a delegation of authority. The nuclear reply remained a possibility, not a policy. As he told Nixon in 1958, "You should never let the enemy know what you will not do." In the offshore islands affair as in Korea, Eisenhower kept the use of nuclear weapons as something the enemy could not know he would not do, and believed he gained from this stance.[5]

But the President was teaching his Vice President a lesson that was going out of date even as he explained it. The offshore islands crisis of 1958, so far from being a model for the future, turns out to be the last case we have of a crisis between the

United States and a nation not the Soviet Union in which nuclear weapons or threats of their use play any role whatever. Consider the war in Vietnam. Here the president whose inaction proves the point conclusively is the same Richard Nixon who had been Eisenhower's eager student. Nixon came to the White House in 1969 determined to apply to Hanoi the same techniques of credible threat that he thought he had seen used successfully in Korea. If he had continued to believe a nuclear threat would be credible, he would surely have conveyed it. But once he considered the matter carefully he was forced to recognize that there was in reality no way of making a credible nuclear threat because the men in Hanoi knew as well as he did that no American president, by 1969, could in fact have used nuclear weapons in Indochina. To do so would plainly outrage allies and split his own country in half. What you cannot conceivably execute, you cannot plausibly threaten.[6]

The evolution from what Eisenhower believed in 1958 to what Nixon was forced to recognize in 1969 is extraordinarily important, and not all the reasons for it are clear. One of them certainly is the spreading awareness of the danger inherent in the thermonuclear age. The end of the 1950s saw the first large-scale popular reactions to nuclear danger, and the searing experience of the Cuban Missile Crisis gave the threat of nuclear warfare new meaning. More broadly, if less consciously, men had come to believe more and more strongly in the value and importance of respecting the "firebreak" between conventional and nuclear weapons. In September 1964, President Lyndon Johnson had stated the case with characteristic passion and force during his campaign against Barry Goldwater:

> Make no mistake. There is no such thing as a conventional nuclear weapon. For nineteen peril-filled years no nation has loosed the atom against another. To do so now is a political decision of the highest order. And it would lead us down an uncertain path of blows and counterblows whose outcome none may know.[7]

To all these general considerations one must add that by 1969 the morality of the Vietnam War was a profoundly divisive question in the United States. To resort to nuclear weapons in such a war would be to outrage still further the angry opponents of the war and probably to multiply their numbers.

So what Richard Nixon thought he had learned turned out only ten years later not to be so, and by his own wise refusal to present a nuclear threat to Hanoi he reinforced the very tradition whose strength he had not at first understood. If the United States could not threaten the use of nuclear weapons even in such a long and painful contest as Vietnam, in what case was such a threat possible? The answer, today, on all the evidence, is that the only places where a nuclear threat remains remotely plausible are those where it has been present for decades—in Western Europe and in Korea, because of the special historical connections noted above, and much more diffusely and existentially in the general reality that any prospect of direct confrontation between the United States and the Soviet Union presents nuclear risks which enforce caution.

A stronger proposition may be asserted. International support for the maintenance of the nuclear firebreak now operates not only to make nuclear threats largely ineffective, but also to penalize any government that resorts to them. This rule applies as much to the Soviet Union as to the United States. The Soviet government, in the heyday of Nikita Khrushchev, set international records for nuclear bluster. The favorite target was the United Kingdom, not only in the Suez crisis but more generally. Khrushchev clearly believed that his rockets gave him a politically usable superiority and talked accordingly. Yet in fact Soviet threats were not decisive at Suez; they were not even issued until what really was decisive—American opposition to the adventure—had been clear for several days. By 1957 Soviet reminders of British vulnerability, so logical from the point of view of believers in the political value of atomic superiority, were serving only to strengthen the Macmillan government in its determination to maintain and improve its own deterrent. The Soviet triumph in launching Sputnik did indeed help Soviet prestige, but attempts to capitalize on it by crude threats were unproductive.

Still more striking is the failure of Soviet atomic diplomacy in relation to China. Having first made the enormous mistake of helping the Chinese toward nuclear weapons, the Soviets reversed their field at the end of the 1950s and addressed themselves assiduously, but with no success whatever, to an effort to persuade the Chinese that they would be happier without any nuclear weapons of their own. Neither cajolery nor the withdrawal of assistance was effective. Probably nothing could have changed the Chinese purpose, but Soviet unreliability only intensified it, and at no time before the first Chinese explosion in 1964 was the Kremlin prepared to make the matter one of war or peace. By the time that possibility was actively considered, in 1969, the Chinese bomb was a reality requiring caution: In a limited but crucial way the Chinese themselves now had an existential deterrent.

But of course Khrushchev's greatest adventure in atomic diplomacy was also his worst fiasco: the deployment of missiles to Cuba in 1962. It is not clear yet how he hoped to gain from the adventure, but he must have believed that placing these weapons in Cuba would produce advantages of some sort. Whether they were there to be bargained against concessions in Europe, or to demonstrate Soviet will and American impotence, or to establish a less uneven strategic balance, we cannot know. That they were there merely to be traded for a pledge against a U.S. invasion of Cuba we must doubt. Nor need we linger on the fact of the failure.

What deserves attention is rather that in this most important crisis of all we can see clearly three persistent realities: First, it was not what the weapons could actually do but the political impact of the deployment that counted most to both sides; second, both leaders understood that any nuclear exchange would be a personal, political, and national catastrophe; third, as a consequence the determinant of the crisis must be in the level of will and ability to act by less than nuclear means. While this set of propositions does not of itself justify President Kennedy's course, it does make clear the folly of Khrushchev's: He left himself open to the use of conventional superiority by an opponent for whom the choice of inaction was politically impossible. I recognize that many students have asserted the commanding importance of U.S. nuclear superiority in the Cuban Missile Crisis, but I am deeply convinced that they are wrong. Along with five other senior members of the Kennedy Administration, including Dean Rusk and Robert McNamara, I am convinced that the missile crisis illustrates "not the significance but the insignificance of nuclear superiority in the face of survivable thermonuclear retaliatory forces."[8]

The missile crisis had powerful and lasting consequences for the notion of atomic diplomacy. It showed the world that both great governments had a profound lack of enthusiasm for nuclear war, and in so doing it reduced the plausibility of nuclear threats of any kind. It also increased the political costs of such posturing. Even before 1962 Khrushchev had learned to try to couch his threats in relatively civil terms—of course I don't want to crush you, but it's only sensible to note that I can.[9] In October 1962, it was precisely nuclear war that both sides plainly chose to stay clear of, and the world took note. Since that time there has been no open nuclear threat by any government. I think it is not too much to say that this particular type of atomic diplomacy has been permanently discredited.

Even the very occasional use of nuclear signals in a crisis has had low importance in recent decades. The most notable case available is the short alert called in President Nixon's name on October 24, 1973, at the height of Yom Kippur war for the purpose of deterring unilateral Soviet action. This alert, by Henry Kissinger's authoritative account, was intended as a general show of resolution and in no way as a specifically thermonuclear threat. More significantly still, Kissinger's account makes it clear that the alert was unnecessary. The possibility of a unilateral Soviet troop movement to Egypt was effectively blocked by Sadat's overnight decision, before he ever heard of the U.S. alert, to back away from the Soviet proposals.

In recent years there has been one remarkable revival of the notion of atomic diplomacy, together with an equally remarkable demonstration of its lack of content. The revival occurred among frightened American hawks eager to demonstrate that the Soviet nuclear build-up of the 1970s was conferring on Moscow a level of superiority that would inescapably translate into usable political leverage. In its most dramatic form the argument was that the Russians were getting a superiority in large, accurate ICBMs that would soon allow them to knock out our own ICBMs and defy us to reply for fear of annihilation. This was the famous "window of vulnerability," and the argument was that this kind of strategic superiority, because both sides would be aware of it, would make the Soviet Union's political pressures irresistible around the world. It was all supposed to happen before now—in the early 1980s. The argument was riddled with analytical errors, ranging from the over-simplification of the problems of such an attack through the much too facile assumption that no credible reply could be offered, and on to the quite untested notion that a threat of this kind would have useful results for the threat-maker. It is not at all surprising that history has shown the notion empty. There has been no Soviet action anywhere that can be plausibly attributed to the so-called window of vulnerability, and indeed after riding this wave of fear—and others—into the White House, the Reagan Administration eventually managed to discover that the window did not exist. First, in the spring of 1983, the Scowcroft Commission concluded that the existing capabilities of American forces, taken as a whole, made such a scenario implausible, and in early 1984 Ronald Reagan himself concluded that we are all safer now because "America is back—standing tall," though out there in the real world the strategic balance remains almost exactly the one which led to the foolish fears in the first place. The notion of a new vulnerability to nuclear diplomacy was unreal; perhaps we were dealing instead with a little atomic politics. . . .

My general moral is a simple one. The more we learn about living with nuclear arsenals, the less we are able to find any good use for them but one—the deterrence of nuclear aggression by others—and the more we are led to the conclusion that this one valid and necessary role is not nearly as demanding as the theorists of countervailing strategy assert. No sane government wants nuclear war, and the men in the Kremlin, brutal and cynical tyrants to be sure, are eminently sane. There are two places still—Western Europe and South Korea—where we Americans do have outstanding undertakings to go first with nuclear weapons if necessary. I believe those commitments are increasingly implausible and ripe for revision. They may also create pressure for, though they do not in fact require, special and politically neuralgic deployments.

Such deployments are a subset of the competition in weapons systems that is now itself becoming the largest single threat to peace. The systems now coming in sight, especially those that might seem to offer effective prospects for defense, do indeed raise the specter of a world in which at some moment of great tension in the future one side or the other might feel that its only hope was to "preempt"—to go first—to aim at a simultaneous offensive and defensive knockout. That would be another and much nastier world than the one we now have, and it is worth great efforts to see to it that it does not come into being.

Meanwhile what remains remarkable about the enormous arsenals of the superpowers is how little political advantage they have conferred. It is a question for another essay whether other nuclear powers have gained more.

NOTES

1. McGeorge Bundy, "The Bishops and the Bomb." *New York Review of Books,* June 16, 1983.
2. The case for the prosecution was presented by Gar Alperowitz in *Atomic Diplomacy: Hiroshima and Potsdam* (New York. 1956). His thesis has not fared well under analysis by more careful historians, many themselves revisionists—see, e.g., Barton J. Bernstein, ed., *The Atomic Bomb: The Critical Issues* (Boston, 1976), pp. 69–71.
3. Truman's press conference is in the *Public Papers of the Presidents* (1952), at pages 290–96. His 1957 remarks appeared in the *New York Times,* August 25, 1957, and are quoted in Stephen S. Kaplan, *Diplomacy of Power* (Washington, D.C., 1981), pp. 70–71.
4. Truman's message of March 6 is printed in part in his own *Memoirs, II, Years of Trial and Hope* (Garden City, N.Y., 1956), pp. 94–95, and is available also now in *Foreign Relations of the United States* (1946), 7: pp. 340–43. The whole episode is covered with great clarity in Bruce R. Kuniholm, *The Origins of the Cold War in the Near East: Great Power Conflict and Diplomacy in Iran, Turkey and Greece* (Princeton, N.J., 1980), pp.

304–37. Kennan's later remark and the one quoted below are in a letter to Kuniholm printed at 321.

5. Eisenhower to Nixon is in Richard Nixon, *The Real War* (New York, 1980), p. 255.
6. Nixon's recognition that he could not use nuclear weapons in Vietnam is described in his *Memoirs* at p. 347.
7. *Public Papers of the Presidents,* 1963–4, 2: p. 1051.
8. See "The lessons of the Cuban Missile Crisis," *Time,* September 27, 1982, p. 85.
9. For a good example of this sort of thing, see Adam Ulam, *Expansion and Coexistence,* 2nd ed. (New York, 1974), p. 612.

The Political Utility of Force in the Current Era

Complex Interdependence and the Role of Force

Robert O. Keohane and Joseph S. Nye

We live in an era of interdependence. This vague phrase expressed a poorly understood but widespread feeling that the very nature of world politics is changing. The power of nations—that age-old touchstone of analysts and statesmen—has become more elusive: "calculations of power are even more delicate and deceptive than in previous ages."[1] Henry Kissinger, though deeply rooted in the classical tradition, has stated that "the traditional agenda of international affairs—the balance among major powers, the security of nations—no longer defines our perils or our possibilities. . . . Now we are entering a new era. Old international patterns are crumbling; old slogans are uninstructive; old solutions are unavailing. The world has become interdependent in economics, in communications, in human aspirations."[2]

How profound are the changes? A modernist school sees telecommunications and jet travel as creating a "global village" and believes that burgeoning social and economic transactions are creating a "world without borders."[3] To greater or lesser extent, a number of scholars see our era as one in which the territorial state, which has been dominant in world politics for the four centuries since feudal times ended, is being eclipsed by nonterritorial actors such as multinational corporations, transnational social movements, and international organizations. As one economist put it, "the state is about through as an economic unit."[4]

Traditionalists call these assertions unfounded "globaloney." They point to the continuity in world politics. Military interdependence has always existed, and military power is still important in world politics—witness nuclear deterrence; the

---

Vietnam, Middle East, and Indian-Pakistan wars; and Soviet influence in Eastern Europe or American influence in the Caribbean. Moreover, as the Soviet Union has shown, authoritarian states can, to a considerable extent, control telecommunications and social transactions that they consider disruptive. Even poor and weak countries have been able to nationalize multinational corporations, and the prevalence of nationalism casts doubt on the proposition that the nation-state is fading away.

Neither the modernists nor the traditionalists have an adequate framework for understanding the politics of global interdependence.[5] Modernists point correctly to the fundamental changes now taking place, but they often assume without sufficient analysis that advances in technology and increases in social and economic transactions will lead to a new world in which states, and their control of force, will no longer be important.[6] Traditionalists are adept at showing flaws in the modernist vision by pointing out how military interdependence continues, but find it very difficult accurately to interpret today's multidimensional economic, social, and ecological interdependence.

Our task . . . is not to argue either the modernist or traditionalist position. Because our era is marked by both continuity and change, this would be fruitless. Rather, our task is to provide a means of distilling and blending the wisdom in both positions by developing a coherent theoretical framework for the political analysis of interdependence. We shall develop several different but potentially complementary models, or intellectual tools, for grasping the reality of interdependence in contemporary world politics. Equally important, we shall attempt to explore the *conditions* under which each model will be most likely to produce accurate predictions and satisfactory explanations. Contemporary world politics is not a seamless web; it is a tapestry of diverse relationships. In such a world, one model cannot explain all situations. The secret of understanding lies in knowing which approach or combination of approaches to use in analyzing a situation. There will never be a substitute for careful analysis of actual situations. . . .

THE NEW RHETORIC OF INTERDEPENDENCE

During the Cold War, "national security" was a slogan American political leaders used to generate support for their policies. The rhetoric of national security justified strategies designed, at considerable cost, to bolster the economic, military, and political structure of the "free world." It also provided a rationale for international cooperation and support for the United Nations, as well as justification for alliances, foreign aid, and extensive military involvements.

National security became the favorite symbol of the internationalists who favored increased American involvement in world affairs. The key foreign policy coordinating unit in the White House was named the National Security Council. The Truman administration used the alleged Soviet threat to American security to push the loan to Britain and then the Marshall Plan through Congress. The Kennedy administration employed the security argument to promote the 1962

Trade Expansion Act. Presidents invoked national security to control certain sectoral economic interests in Congress, particularly those favoring protectionist trade policies. Congressmen who protested adverse economic effects on their districts or increased taxes were assured—and in turn explained to constituents—that the "national security interests" required their sacrifice. At the same time, special interests frequently manipulated the symbolism of national security for their own purposes, as in the case of petroleum import quotas, promoted particularly by domestic oil producers and their political allies.[7]

National security symbolism was largely a product of the Cold War and the severe threat Americans then felt. Its persuasiveness was increased by realist analysis, which insisted that national security is the primary national goal and that in international politics security threats are permanent. National security symbolism, and the realist mode of analysis that supported it, not only epitomized a certain way of reacting to events, but helped to codify a perspective in which some changes, particularly those toward radical regimes in Third World countries, seemed inimical to national security, while fundamental changes in the economic relations among advanced industrialized countries seemed insignificant.

As the Cold War sense of security threat slackened, foreign economic competition and domestic distributional conflict increased. The intellectual ambiguity of "national security" became more pronounced as varied and often contradictory forms of involvement took shelter under a single rhetorical umbrella.[8] In his imagery of a world balance of power among five major centers (the United States, the Soviet Union, China, Europe, Japan), President Nixon tried unsuccessfully to extend traditional realist concepts to apply to the economic challenge posed by America's postwar allies, as well as the political and military actions of the Soviet Union and China.

As the descriptive accuracy of a view of national security dominated by military concerns declined, so did the term's symbolic power. This decline reflected not only the increased ambiguity of the concept, but also American reaction to the Vietnam imbroglio, to the less hostile relationship with Russia and China summed up by the word *detente,* and to misuse of national security rhetoric by President Nixon in the Watergate affair. National security had to share its position as the prime symbol in the internationalists' lexicon with *interdependence.*

Political leaders often use interdependence rhetoric to portray interdependence as a natural necessity, as a fact to which policy (and domestic interest groups) must adjust, rather than as a situation partially created by policy itself. They usually argue that conflicts of interest are reduced by interdependence, and that cooperation alone holds the answer to world problems.

"We are all engaged in a common enterprise. No nation or group of nations can gain by pushing beyond the limits that sustain world economic growth. No one benefits from basing progress on tests of strength."[9] These words clearly belong to a statesman intending to limit demands from the Third World and influence public attitudes at home, rather than to analyze contemporary reality. For those who wish the United States to retain world leadership, interdependence has become part of the new rhetoric, to be used against both economic nationalism at home and assertive challenges abroad. Although the connotations of interdependence rhetoric may seem quite different from those of national security symbolism, each has often been used to legitimize American presidential leadership in world affairs. . . .

Yet interdependence rhetoric and national security symbolism coexist only uneasily. In its extreme formulation, the former suggests that conflicts of interest are passé, whereas the latter argues that they are, and will remain, fundamental, and potentially violent. The confusion in knowing what analytical models to apply to world politics (as we noted earlier) is thus paralleled by confusion about the policies that should be employed by the United States. Neither interdependence rhetoric nor national security symbolism provides reliable guidelines for problems of extensive interdependence.

Rhetoriticians of interdependence often claim that since the survival of the human race is threatened by environmental as well as military dangers, conflicts of interest among states and people no longer exist. This conclusion would only follow if three conditions were met: an international economic system on which everyone depended or our basic life-supporting ecological system were in danger; all countries were significantly vulnerable to such a catastrophe; *and* there were only one solution to the problem (leaving no room for conflict about how to solve it and who should bear the costs). Obviously these conditions are rarely all present.

Yet balance of power theories and national security imagery are also poorly adapted to analyzing problems of economic or ecological interdependence. Security, in traditional terms, is not likely to be the principal issue facing governments. Insofar as military force is ineffective on certain issues, the conventional notion of power lacks precision. In particular, different power resources may be needed to deal with different issues. Finally, in the politics of interdependence, domestic and transnational as well as governmental interests are involved. Domestic and foreign policy become closely linked. The notion of national interest—the traditionalists' lodestar—becomes increasingly difficult to use effectively. Traditional maxims of international politics—that states will act in their national interests or that they will attempt to maximize their power—become ambiguous.

We are not suggesting that international conflict disappears when interdependence prevails. On the contrary, conflict will take new forms, and may even increase. But the traditional approaches to understanding conflict in world politics will not explain interdependence conflict particularly well. Applying the wrong image and the wrong rhetoric to problems will lead to erroneous analysis and bad policy. . . .

Manipulating economic or sociopolitical vulnerabilities, however, also bears risks. Strategies of manipulating interdependence are likely to lead to counterstrategies. It must always be kept in mind, furthermore, that military power dominates economic power in the sense that economic means alone are likely to be ineffective against the serious use of military force. Thus, even effective manipulation of asymmetrical interdependence within a nonmilitary area can create risks of military counteraction. When the United States exploited Japanese vulnerability to economic embargo in 1940–41, Japan countered by attacking Pearl Harbor and the Philippines. Yet military actions are usually very costly; and for many types of actions, these costs have risen steeply during the last thirty years.

Table 1 shows the three types of asymmetrical interdependence that we have been discussing. The dominance ranking column indicates that the power resources provided by military interdependence dominate those provided by non-military vulnerability, which in turn dominate those provided by asymmetries in sensitivity. Yet exercising more dominant forms of power brings higher costs. Thus, *relative to cost*, there is no guarantee that military means will be more effective than economic ones to achieve a given purpose. We can expect, however, that as the interests at stake become more important, actors will tend to use power resources that rank higher in both dominance and cost. . . .

One's assumptions about world politics profoundly affect what one sees and how one constructs theories to explain events. We believe that the assumptions of political realists, whose theories dominated the postwar period, are often an inadequate basis for analyzing the politics of interdependence. The realist assumptions about world politics can be seen as defining an extreme set of conditions or *ideal type*. One could also imagine very different conditions. In this chapter, we shall construct another ideal type, the opposite of realism. We call it *complex interdependence*. After establishing the differences between realism and complex interdependence, we shall argue that complex interdependence sometimes comes clos-

TABLE 1   ASYMMETRICAL INTERDEPENDENCE AND ITS USES

Source of interdependence	Dominance ranking	Cost ranking	Contemporary use
Military (costs of using military force)	1	1	Used in extreme situations or against weak foes when costs may be slight.
Nonmilitary vulnerability (costs of pursuing alternative policies)	2	2	Used when normative constraints are low, and international rules are not considered binding (including nonmilitary relations between adversaries, and situations of extremely high conflict between close partners and allies).
Nonmilitary sensitivity (costs of change under existing policies)	3	3	A power resource in the short run or when normative constraints are high and international rules are binding. Limited, since if high costs are imposed, disadvantaged actors may formulate new policies.

er to reality than does realism. When it does, traditional explanations of change in international regimes become questionable and the search for new explanatory models becomes more urgent.

For political realists, international politics, like all other politics, is a struggle for power but, unlike domestic politics, a struggle dominated by organized violence. In the words of the most influential postwar textbook, "All history shows that nations active in international politics are continuously preparing for, actively involved in, or recovering from organized violence in the form of war."[10] Three assumptions are integral to the realist vision. First, states as coherent units are the dominant actors in world politics. This is a double assumption: States are predominant; and they act as coherent units. Second, realists assume that force is a usable and effective instrument of policy. Other instruments may also be employed, but using or threatening force is the most effective means of wielding power. Third, partly because of their second assumption, realists assume a hierarchy of issues in world politics, headed by questions of military security: the "high politics" of military security dominates the "low politics" of economic and social affairs.

These realist assumptions define an ideal type of world politics. They allow us to imagine a world in which politics is continually characterized by active or potential conflict among states, with the use of force possible at any time. Each state attempts to defend its territory and interests from real or perceived threats. Political integration among states is slight and lasts only as long as it serves the national interests of the most powerful states. Transitional actors either do not exist or are politically unimportant. Only the adept exercise of force or the threat of force permits states to survive, and only while statesmen succeed in adjusting their interests, as in a well-functioning balance of power, is the system stable.

Each of the realist assumptions can be challenged. If we challenge them all simultaneously, we can imagine a world in which actors other than states participate directly in world politics, in which a clear hierarchy of issues does not exist, and in which force is an ineffective instrument of policy. Under these conditions—which we call the characteristics of complex interdependence—one would expect world politics to be very different than under realist conditions. . . .

We do not argue, however, that complex interdependence faithfully reflects world political reality. Quite the contrary: Both it and the realist portrait are ideal types. Most situations will fall somewhere between these two extremes. Sometimes, realist assumptions will be accurate, or largely accurate, but frequently complex interdependence will provide a better portrayal of reality. Before one decides what explanatory model to apply to a situation or problem, one will need to understand the degree to which realist or complex interdependence assumptions correspond to the situation.

THE CHARACTERISTICS OF COMPLEX INTERDEPENDENCE

Complex interdependence has three main characteristics:

1. *Multiple channels* connect societies, including: informal ties between governmental elites as well as formal foreign office arrangements; informal ties

among nongovernmental elites (face-to-face and through telecommunications); and transnational organizations (such as multinational banks or corporations). These channels can be summarized as interstate, transgovernmental, and transnational relations. *Interstate* relations are the normal channels assumed by realists. *Transgovernmental* applies when we relax the realist assumption that states act coherently as units; *transnational* applies when we relax the assumption that states are the only units.

2. The agenda of interstate relationships consists of multiple issues that are not arranged in a clear or consistent hierarchy. This *absence of hierarchy among issues* means, among other things, that military security does not consistently dominate the agenda. Many issues arise from what used to be considered domestic policy, and the distinction between domestic and foreign issues becomes blurred. These issues are considered in several government departments (not just foreign offices), and at several levels. Inadequate policy coordination on these issues involves significant costs. Different issues generate different coalitions, both within governments and across them, and involve different degrees of conflict. Politics does not stop at the waters' edge.

3. Military force is not used by governments toward other governments within the region, or on the issues, when complex interdependence prevails. It may, however, be important in these governments' relations with governments outside that region, or on other issues. Military force could, for instance, be irrelevant to resolving disagreements on economic issues among members of an alliance, yet at the same time be very important for the alliance's political and military relations with a rival bloc. For the former relationships this condition of complex interdependence would be met; for the latter, it would not.

Traditional theories of international politics implicitly or explicitly deny the accuracy of these three assumptions. Traditionalists are therefore tempted also to deny the relevance of criticisms based on the complex interdependence ideal type. We believe, however, that our three conditions are fairly well approximated on some global issues of economic and ecological interdependence and that they come close to characterizing the entire relationship between some countries. One of our purposes here is to prove that contention. . . .

Multiple Channels

A visit to any major airport is a dramatic way to confirm the existence of multiple channels of contact among advanced industrial countries; there is a voluminous literature to prove it.[11] Bureaucrats from different countries deal directly with one another at meetings and on the telephone as well as in writing. Similarly, nongovernmental elites frequently get together in the normal course of business, in organizations such as the Trilateral Commission, and in conferences sponsored by private foundations.

In addition, multinational firms and banks affect both domestic and interstate relations. The limits on private firms, or the closeness of ties between government and business, vary considerably from one society to another; but the participation of large and dynamic organizations, not controlled entirely by governments, has become a normal part of foreign as well as domestic relations.

These actors are important not only because of their activities in pursuit of their own interests, but also because they act as transmission belts, making government policies in various countries more sensitive to one another. As the scope of governments' domestic activities has broadened, and as corporations, banks, and (to a lesser extent) trade unions have made decisions that transcend national boundaries, the domestic policies of different countries impinge on one another more and more. Transnational communications reinforce these effects. Thus, foreign economic policies touch more domestic economic activity than in the past, blurring the lines between domestic and foreign policy and increasing the number of issues relevant to foreign policy. Parallel developments in issues of environmental regulation and control over technology reinforce this trend.

Absence of Hierarchy Among Issues

Foreign affairs agendas—that is, sets of issues relevant to foreign policy with which governments are concerned—have become larger and more diverse. No longer can all issues be subordinated to military security. As Secretary of State Kissinger described the situation in 1975:

> Progress in dealing with the traditional agenda is no longer enough. A new and unprecedented kind of issue has emerged. The problems of energy, resources, environment, population, the uses of space and the seas now rank with questions of military security, ideology and territorial rivalry which have traditionally made up the diplomatic agenda.[12]

Kissinger's list, which could be expanded, illustrates how governments' policies, even those previously considered merely domestic, impinge on one another. The extensive consultative arrangements developed by the OECD, as well as the GATT, IMF, and the European Community, indicate how characteristic the overlap of domestic and foreign policy is among developed pluralist countries. The organization within nine major departments of the United States government (Agriculture, Commerce, Defense, Health, Education and Welfare, Interior, Justice, Labor, State, and Treasury) and many other agencies reflects their extensive international commitments. The multiple, overlapping issues that result make a nightmare of governmental organization.[13]

When there are multiple issues on the agenda, many of which threaten the interests of domestic groups but do not clearly threaten the nation as a whole, the problems of formulating a coherent and consistent foreign policy increase. In 1975 energy was a foreign policy problem, but specific remedies, such as a tax on gasoline and automobiles, involved domestic legislation opposed by auto workers and companies alike. As one commentator observed, "virtually every time Congress has set a national policy that changed the way people live . . . the action came after a consensus had developed, bit by bit, over the years, that a problem existed and that there was one best way to solve it."[14] Opportunities for delay, for special protection, for inconsistency and incoherence abound when international politics requires aligning the domestic policies of pluralist democratic countries.

Minor Role of Military Force

Political scientists have traditionally emphasized the role of military force in international politics. . . . [F]orce dominates other means of power: *if* there are no constraints on one's choice of instruments (a hypothetical situation that has only been approximated in the two world wars), the state with superior military force will prevail. If the security dilemma for all states were extremely acute, military force, supported by economic and other resources, would clearly be the dominant source of power. Survival is the primary goal of all states, and in the worst situations, force is ultimately necessary to guarantee survival. Thus military force is always a central component of national power.

Yet particularly among industrialized, pluralist countries, the perceived margin of safety has widened: Fears of attack in general have declined, and fears of attacks *by one another* are virtually nonexistent. France has abandoned the *tous azimuts* (defense in all directons) strategy that President de Gaulle advocated (it was not taken entirely seriously even at the time). Canada's last war plans for fighting the United States were abandoned half a century ago. Britain and Germany no longer feel threatened by each other. Intense relationships of mutual influence exist between these countries, but in most of them force is irrelevant or unimportant as an instrument of policy.

Moreover, force is often not an appropriate way of achieving other goals (such as economic and ecological welfare) that are becoming more important. It is not impossible to imagine dramatic conflict or revolutionary change in which the use or threat of military force over an economic issue or among advanced industrial countries might become plausible. Then realist assumptions would again be a reliable guide to events. But in most situations, the effects of military force are both costly and uncertain.[15]

Even when the direct use of force is barred among a group of countries, however, military power can still be used politically. Each superpower continues to use the threat of force to deter attacks by other superpowers on itself or its allies; its deterrence ability thus serves an indirect, protective role, which it can use in bargaining on other issues with its allies. This bargaining tool is particularly important for the United States, whose allies are concerned about potential Soviet threats and which has fewer other means of influence over its allies than does the Soviet Union over its Eastern European partners. The United States has, accordingly, taken advantage of the Europeans' (particularly the Germans') desire for its protection and linked the issue of troop levels in Europe to trade and monetary negotiations. Thus, although the first-order effect of deterrent force is essentially negative—to deny effective offensive power to a superpower opponent—a state can use the force positively—to gain political influence.

Thus, even for countries whose relations approximate complex interdependence, two serious qualifications remain: (1) drastic social and political change could cause force again to become an important direct instrument of policy; and (2) even when elites' interests are complementary, a country that uses military force to protect another may have significant political influence over the other country.

In North-South relations, or relations among Third World countries, as well as in East-West relations, force is often important. Military power helps the Soviet Union to dominate Eastern Europe economically as well as politically. The threat of open or covert American military intervention has helped to limit revolutionary changes in the Caribbean, especially in Guatemala in 1954 and in the Dominican Republic in 1965. Secretary of State Kissinger, in January 1975, issued a veiled warning to members of the Organization of Petroleum Exporting Countries (OPEC) that the United States might use force against them "where there is some actual strangulation of the industrialized world."[16]

Even in these rather conflictual situations, however, the recourse to force seems less likely now than at most times during the century before 1945. The destructiveness of nuclear weapons makes any attack against a nuclear power dangerous. Nuclear weapons are mostly used as a deterrent. Threats of nuclear action against much weaker countries may occasionally be efficacious, but they are equally or more likely to solidify relations between one's adversaries. The limited usefulness of conventional force to control socially mobilized populations has been shown by the United States failure in Vietnam as well as by the rapid decline of colonialism in Africa. Furthermore, employing force on one issue against an independent state with which one has a variety of relationships is likely to rupture mutually profitable relations on other issues. In other words, the use of force often has costly effects on nonsecurity goals. And finally, in Western democracies, popular opposition to prolonged military conflicts is very high.[17]

It is clear that these constraints bear unequally on various countries, or on the same countries in different situations. Risks of nuclear escalation affect everyone, but domestic opinion is far less constraining for communist states, or for authoritarian regional powers, than for the United States, Europe, or Japan. Even authoritarian countries may be reluctant to use force to obtain economic objectives when such use might be ineffective and disrupt other relationships. Both the difficulty of controlling socially mobilized populations with foreign troops and the changing technology of weaponry may actually enhance the ability of certain countries, or nonstate groups, to use terrorism as a political weapon without effective fear of reprisal.

The fact that the changing role of force has uneven effects does not make the change less important, but it does make matters more complex. This complexity is compounded by differences in the usability of force among issue areas. When an issue arouses little interest or passion, force may be unthinkable. In such instances, complex interdependence may be a valuable concept for analyzing the political process. But if that issue becomes a matter of life and death—as some people thought oil might become—the use or threat of force could become decisive again. Realist assumptions would then be more relevant.

It is thus important to determine the applicability of realism or of complex interdependence to each situation. Without this determination, further analysis is likely to be confused. Our purpose in developing an alternative to the realist description of world politics is to encourage a differentiated approach that distinguishes among dimensions and areas of world politics—not (as some modernist observers do) to replace one oversimplification with another.

THE POLITICAL PROCESS OF COMPLEX INTERDEPENDENCE

The three main characteristics of complex interdependence give rise to distinctive political processes, which translate power resources into power as control of outcomes. As we argued earlier, something is usually lost or added in the translation. Under conditions of complex interdependence the translation will be different than under realist conditions, and our predictions about outcomes will need to be adjusted accordingly.

In the realist world, military security will be the dominant goal of states. It will even affect issues that are not directly involved with military power or territorial defense. Nonmilitary problems will not only be subordinated to military ones; they will be studied for their politico-military implications. Balance of payments issues, for instance, will be considered at least as much in the light of their implications for world power generally as for their purely financial ramifications. McGeorge Bundy conformed to realist expectations when he argued in 1964 that devaluation of the dollar should be seriously considered if necessary to fight the war in Vietnam.[18] To some extent, so did former Treasury Secretary Henry Fowler when he contended in 1971 that the United States needed a trade surplus of $4 billion to $6 billion in order to lead in Western defense.[19]

In a world of complex interdependence, however, one expects some officials, particularly at lower levels, to emphasize the *variety* of state goals that must be pursued. In the absence of a clear hierarchy of issues, goals will vary by issue, and may not be closely related. Each bureaucracy will pursue its own concerns; and although several agencies may reach compromises on issues that affect them all, they will find that a consistent pattern of policy is difficult to maintain. Moreover, transnational actors will introduce different goals into various groups of issues.

Linkage Strategies

Goals will therefore vary by issue area under complex interdependence, but so will the distribution of power and the typical political processes. Traditional analysis focuses on *the* international system, and leads us to anticipate similar political processes on a variety of issues. Militarily and economically strong states will dominate a variety of organizations and a variety of issues, by linking their own policies on some issues to other states' policies on other issues. By using their overall dominance to prevail on their weak issues, the strongest states will, in the traditional model, ensure a congruence between the overall structure of military and economic power and the pattern of outcomes on any one issue area. Thus world politics can be treated as a seamless web.

Under complex interdependence, such congruence is less likely to occur. As military force is devalued, militarily strong states will find it more difficult to use their overall dominance to control outcomes on issues in which they are weak. And since the distribution of power resources in trade, shipping, or oil, for example, may be quite different, patterns of outcomes and distinctive political processes are likely to vary from one set of issues to another. If force were readily applicable, and military security were the highest foreign policy goal, these variations in the issue structures of power would not matter very much. The linkages drawn from them to military issues would ensure consistent dominance by the overall strongest states. But when military force is largely immobilized, strong states will find that linkage is less effective. They may still attempt such links, but in the absence of hierarchy of issues, their success will be problematic.

Dominant states may try to secure much the same result by using overall economic power to affect results on other issues. If only economic objectives are at stake, they may succeed: Money, after all, is fungible. But economic objectives have political implications, and economic linkage by the strong is limited by domestic, transnational, and transgovernmental actors who resist having their interests traded off. Furthermore, the international actors may be different on different issues, and the international organizations in which negotiations take place are often quite separate. Thus it is difficult, for example, to imagine a military or economically strong state linking concessions on monetary policy to reciprocal concessions in oceans policy. On the other hand, poor weak states are not similarly inhibited from linking unrelated issues, partly because their domestic interests are less complex. Linkage of unrelated issues is often a means of extracting concessions or side payments from rich and powerful states. And unlike powerful states whose instrument for linkage (military force) is often too costly to use, the linkage instrument used by poor, weak states—international organization—is available and inexpensive.

Thus as the utility of force declines, and as issues become more equal in importance, the distribution of power within each issue will become more important. If linkages become less effective on the whole, outcomes of political bargaining will increasingly vary by issue area.

The differentiation among issue areas in complex interdependence means that linkages among issues will become more problematic and will tend to reduce rather than reinforce international hierarchy. Linkage strategies, and defense against them, will pose critical strategic choices for states. Should issues be considered separately or as a package? If linkages are to be drawn, which issues should be linked, and on which of the linked issues should concessions be made? How far can one push a linkage before it becomes counterproductive? For instance, should one seek formal agreements or informal, but less politically sensitive, understandings? The fact that world politics under complex interdependence is not a seamless web leads us to expect that efforts to stitch seams together advantageously, as reflected in linkage strategies, will, very often, determine the shape of the fabric.

The negligible role of force leads us to expect states to rely more on other instruments in order to wield power. For the reasons we have already discussed, less vulnerable states will try to use asymmetrical interdependence in particular groups of issues as a source of power; they will also try to use international organizations and transnational actors and flows. States will approach economic interdependence in terms of power as well as its effects on citizens' welfare, although welfare considerations will limit their attempts to maximize power. Most economic and ecological interdependence involves the possibility of joint gains or joint losses. Mutual awareness of potential gains and losses and the danger of worsening each actor's position through overly rigorous struggles over the distribution of the gains can limit the use of asymmetrical interdependence.

Agenda Setting

Our second assumption of complex interdependence, the lack of clear hierarchy among multiple issues, leads us to expect that the politics of agenda formation and control will become more important. Traditional analyses lead statesmen to focus on politico-military issues and to pay little attention to the broader politics of agenda formation. Statesmen assume that the agenda will be set by shifts in the balance of power, actual or anticipated, and by perceived threats to the security of states. Other issues will only be very important when they seem to affect security and military power. In these cases, agendas will be influenced strongly by considerations of the overall balance of power.

Yet, today, some nonmilitary issues are emphasized in interstate relations at one time, whereas others of seemingly equal importance are neglected or quietly handled at a technical level. International monetary politics, problems of commodity terms of trade, oil, food, and multinational corporations have all been important during the last decade; but not all have been high on interstate agendas throughout that period.

Traditional analysts of international politics have paid little attention to agenda formation: to how issues come to receive sustained attention by high officials. The traditional orientation toward military and security affairs implies that the crucial problems of foreign policy are imposed on states by the actions or threats of other states. These are high politics as opposed to the low politics of economic affairs. Yet, as the complexity of actors and issues in world politics increases, the utility of force declines and the line between domestic policy and foreign policy becomes blurred: As the conditions of complex interdependence are more closely approximated, the politics of agenda formation becomes more subtle and differentiated.

Under complex interdependence we can expect the agenda to be affected by the international and domestic problems created by economic growth and increasing sensitivity interdependence. . . . Discontented domestic groups will politicize issues and force more issues once considered domestic onto the interstate agenda. Shifts in the distribution of power resources within sets of issues will also affect agendas. During the early 1970s the increased power of oil-producing governments over the transnational corporation and the consumer countries dramatically altered the policy agenda. Moreover, agendas for one group of issues may change as a result of linkages from other groups in which power resources are changing; for example, the broader agenda of North-South trade issues changed after the OPEC price rises and the oil embargo of 1973–74. Even if capabilities among states do not change, agendas may be affected by shifts in the importance of transnational actors. The publicity surrounding multinational corporations in the early 1970s, coupled with their rapid growth over the past twenty years, put the regulation of such corporations higher on both the Union Nations agenda and national agendas.

Politicization—agitation and controversy over an issue that tend to raise it to the top of the agenda—can have many sources, as we have seen. Governments whose strength is increasing may politicize issues by linking them to other issues. An international regime that is becoming ineffective or is not serving important issues may cause increasing politicization, as dissatisfied governments press for change. Politicization, however, can also come from below. Domestic groups may become upset enough to raise a dormant issue, or to interfere with interstate bargaining at high levels. In 1974 the American secretary of state's tacit linkage of a Soviet-American trade pact with progress in detente was upset by the success of domestic American groups working through Congress to link a trade agreement with Soviet policies on emigration.

The technical characteristics and institutional setting in which issues are raised will strongly affect politicization patterns. In the United States, congressional attention is an effective instrument of politicization. Generally, we expect transnational economic organizations and transgovernmental networks of bureaucrats to seek to avoid politicization. Domestically based groups (such as trade unions) and domestically oriented bureaucracies will tend to use politicization (particularly congressional attention) against their transnationally mobile competitors. At the international level, we expect states and actors to "shop among forums" and struggle to get issues raised in international organizations that will maximize their advantage by broadening or narrowing the agenda.

Transnational and Transgovernmental Relations

Our third condition of complex interdependence, multiple channels of contact among societies, further blurs the distinction between domestic and international politics. The availability of partners in political coalitions is not necessarily limited by national boundaries as traditional analysis assumes. The nearer a situation is to complex interdependence, the more we expect the outcomes of political bargaining to be affected by transnational relations. Multinational corporations may be significant both as independent actors and as instruments manipulated by governments. The attitudes and policy stands of domestic groups are likely to be affected by communications, organized or not, between them and their counterparts abroad.

Thus the existence of multiple channels of contact leads us to expect limits, beyond those normally found in domestic politics, on the ability of statesmen to calculate the manipulation of interdependence or follow a consistent strategy of linkage. Statesmen must consider differential as well as aggregate effects of interdependence strategies and their likely implications for politicization and agenda control. Transactions among societies—economic and social transactions more than security ones—affect groups differently. Opportunities and costs from increased transnational ties may be greater for certain groups—for instance,

American workers in the textile or shoe industries—than for others. Some organizations or groups may interact directly with actors in other societies or with other governments to increase their benefits from a network of interaction. Some actors may therefore be less vulnerable as well as less sensitive to changes elsewhere in the network than are others, and this will affect patterns of political action.

The multiple channels of contact found in complex interdependence are not limited to nongovernmental actors. Contacts between governmental bureaucracies charged with similar tasks may not only alter their perspectives but lead to transgovernmental coalitions on particular policy questions. To improve their chances of success, government agencies attempt to bring actors from other governments into their own decision-making processes as allies. Agencies of powerful states such as the United States have used such coalitions to penetrate weaker governments in such countries as Turkey and Chile. They have also been used to help agencies of other governments penetrate the United States bureaucracy.[20] ... [T]ransgovernmental politics frequently characterizes Canadian-American relations, often to the advantage of Canadian interests.

The existence of transgovernmental policy networks leads to a different interpretation of one of the standard propositions about international politics—that states act in their own interest. Under complex interdependence, this conventional wisdom begs two important questions: Which self and which interest? A government agency may pursue its own interests under the guise of the national interest; and recurrent interactions can change official perceptions of their interests. As a careful study of the politics of United States trade policy has documented, concentrating only on pressures of various interests for decisions leads to an overly mechanistic view of a continuous process and neglects the important role of communications in slowly changing perceptions of self-interest.[21]

The ambiguity of the national interest raises serious problems for the top political leaders of governments. As bureaucracies contact each other directly across national borders (without going through foreign offices), centralized control becomes more difficult. There is less assurance that the state will be united when dealing with foreign governments or that its components will interpret national interests similarly when negotiating with foreigners. The state may prove to be multifaceted, even schizophrenic. National interest will be defined differently on different issues, at different times, and by different governmental units. States that are better placed to maintain their coherence (because of a centralized political tradition such as France's) will be better also be manipulate uneven interdependence than fragmented states that at first glance seem to have more resources in an issue area.

NOTES

1. Stanley Hoffman, "Notes on the Elusiveness of Modern Power," *International Journal* 30 (Spring 1975): p. 184.
2. "A New National Partnership," speech by Secretary of State Henry A. Kissinger at Los Angeles, January 24, 1975. News release, Department of State, Bureau of Public Affairs, Office of Media Services, p. 1.

3. See, for example, Lester R. Brown, *World Without Borders: The Interdependence of Nations* (New York: Foreign Policy Association, Headline Series, 1972).

4. Charles Kindleberger, *American Business Abroad* (New Haven, Conn.: Yale University Press, 1969), p. 207.

5. The terms are derived from Stanley Hoffmann, "Choices," *Foreign Policy* 12 (Fall 1973): p. 6.

6. For instance, see Robert Angell, *Peace on the March: Transnational Participation* (New York: Van Nostrand, 1969).

7. See Robert Engler, *The Politics of Oil: Private Power and Democratic Directions* (Chicago: University of Chicago Press, 1962).

8. Arnold Wolfers' "National Security as an Ambiguous Symbol" remains the classic analysis. See his collection of essays, *Discord and Collaboration* (Baltimore: Johns Hopkins University Press, 1962). Daniel Yergin's study of the emergence of the doctrine of national security (in place of the traditional concept of defense) portrays it as a "commanding idea" of the Cold War era. See Daniel Yergin, *The Shattered Peace: The Rise of the National Security State* (Boston: Houghton Mifflin, 1976).

9. Secretary of State Henry A. Kissinger, Address before the Sixth Special Session of the United Nations General Assembly, April 15, 1974. News release, Department of State, Office of Media Services, 2. Reprinted in *International Organization* 28, no. 3 (Summer 1974): pp. 573–83.

10. Hans J. Morgenthau, *Politics Among Nations: The Struggle for Power and Peace,* 4th ed. (New York: Knopf, 1967), p. 36.

11. See Edward L. Morse, "Transnational Economic Processes," in Robert O. Keohane and Joseph S. Nye, Jr., eds., *Transnational Relations and World Politics* (Cambridge, Mass.: Harvard University Press, 1972).

12. Henry A. Kissinger, "A New National Partnership," *Department of State Bulletin,* February 17, 1975, p. 199.

13. See the report of the Commission on the Organization of the Government for the Conduct of Foreign Policy (Murphy Commission) (Washington, D.C.: U.S. Government Printing Office, 1975), and the studies prepared for that report. See also Raymond Hopkins, "The International Role of 'Domestic' Bureaucracy," *International Organization* 30, no. 3 (Summer 1976).

14. *The New York Times,* May 22, 1975.

15. For a valuable discussion, see Klaus Knorr, *The Power of Nations: The Political Economy of International Relations* (New York: Basic Books, 1975).

16. *Business Week,* January 13, 1975.

17. Stanley Hoffmann, "The Acceptability of Military Force," and Laurence Martin, "The Utility of Military Force," in *Force in Modern Societies: Its Place in International Politics* (Adelphi Paper, International Institute for Strategic Studies, 1973). See also Knorr, *The Power of Nations.*

18. Henry Brandon, *The Retreat of American Power* (New York: Doubleday, 1974), p. 218.

19. *International Implications of the New Economic Policy,* U.S. Congress, House of Representatives, Committee on Foreign Affairs, Subcommittee on Foreign Economic Policy, Hearings, September 16, 1971.

20. For a more detailed discussion, see Robert O. Keohane and Joseph S. Nye, Jr., "Transgovernmental Relations and International Organizations," *World Politics* 27, no. 1 (October 1974): pp. 39–62.

21. Raymond Bauer, Ithiel de Sola Pool, and Lewis Dexter, *American Business and Foreign Policy* (New York: Atherton, 1963), chap. 35, esp. pp. 472–75.

Third World Security

Caroline Thomas

The task of addressing the issue of security in the Third World in a single chapter is formidable. We are dealing with over one hundred diverse states within the confines of a few pages. Justice cannot be done to all these states and their millions of inhabitants within such constraints. Therefore the aim of the chapter is to offer guidelines for thought and further study, and to signpost possible pitfalls.

The first task will be to investigate the meaning of the term 'Third World'. The second will be to outline what is meant by security. Here emphasis will be placed both on traditional realist interpretations which are predominantly military in nature, and also on newer, non-military dimensions to security. The third task will be to consider three levels of explanation of Third World states' security problems: the domestic or intra-state level which revolves around the crisis of legitimacy of the state; the regional level which interprets problems and solutions from a local perspective; and finally the global level which stresses that systemic factors, such as bipolarity and the resulting ideologically-motivated superpower competition, inform Third World security problems. Fourthly, we shall turn to the non-traditional aspects of security now confronting not only the Third World but the whole world, particularly the debt crisis and the environmental crisis. The conclusion will argue that the world is even more interdependent in security terms than ever before, and that traditional notions of Third World security must be set aside in favour of a holistic approach to global security.

WHAT IS THE 'THIRD WORLD'?

. . . There is a fundamental problem which we must be aware of before we can proceed with our discussion of the security of the Third World. The 'Third World' grouping consists of well over one hundred states characterised by their *diversity*, politically, economically, geographically, culturally and in terms of religion. We cannot speak of a Third World grouping in the way that we can of a West European group. The latter share secular statehood, developed capitalist economies and pluralist democratic politics. The Third World is a much larger, far less homogeneous grouping. Moreover, with the momentous changes taking place in the Soviet Union and Eastern Europe, it is quite possible that more states will be added to the Third World grouping. This may result both from the disintegration of the Soviet state and the resultant creation of several new states based on national self-determination, and also possibly from the categorisation of some of the East European states, such as Romania, as Third World states at least in terms of their economic indicators. Indeed, the whole category 'Third World' may well come up for reassessment; it may even disappear.

The term has been used until now for less than admirable reasons by scholars and politicians in the developed world, particularly in the West, to refer to all states that are not part of the developed, industrialised West or East. In that sense it is a residual category or a 'catch-all' phrase for referring to all those states which are perceived by the major power blocs not to matter too much in the daily conduct of international politics. It has also been used by some statesmen who locate their own state within that group, feeling that there is a benefit in collective identity. 'Third World' has also come to be used interchangeably with terms such as 'South', 'developing countries' and 'underdeveloped countries'. However, many feel that the term 'Third World' has a derogatory connotation and prefer to use another term.

The most important objective criterion for membership of the Third World is ex-colonial status. This provides a very important psychological backdrop to the grouping; there is a common idea of having been oppressed politically and having won independent sovereign statehood. While this is largely true, it is not universally the case. Ethiopia remained independent for all but a very brief period in the 1930s. China was not a European colony, but suffered at the hands of the Japanese. The USA is a former colony, but is certainly not a Third World state. The states of Latin America are Third World states; they were colonised, but differ from the colonies of Africa and Asia in that independence was won not by indigenous peoples but largely by the European settler population. Hence it is important to keep in mind the rich variety of historical experiences of Third World states.

For many of them, political independence has not resulted in an easy transition to independent nation-statehood. Third World states tend to be artificial constructs, and governments have to try to hold them together after the first wave of anti-colonial nationalism has passed. They undertake nation-building in an effort to forge a common identity within the boundaries of the state which may well cut through ethnic or religious groups. In many cases, the efforts to make state and nation coincide and to forge a high level of domestic consensus have fallen far short of the target. The result is that the main problem facing most Third World states today is that the state itself lacks domestic legitimacy; the methods for resolving domestic differences tend to be based on force and repression rather than any form of participatory process.

Economic criteria are often used to define 'Third World' states. Per capita GNP is a yardstick commonly used by bilateral and multilateral aid and finance organisations. Yet this too is problematic, for it ignores distribution patterns within the society and social indicators such as literacy rates, infant mortality rates and access to healthcare. . . .

WHAT IS SECURITY?

Security is a contested concept; there is no universally accepted definition. P. Saravanamuttu has argued that definitions are influenced by ideology, the time framework being addressed, and the unit of analysis identified.[1] Within the conventional, realist approach to international relations, standard definitions of security usually refer to defence of a state's territorial boundaries and protection of its core values. States are seen as homogeneous units bent on pursuing their national interest above all else and which do not engage in extensive cooperation unless this is motivated by self-interest. The political environment is perceived as being Hobbesian; international anarchy is the order of the day.

In the Third World such definitions of security are problematic for a number of reasons. Firstly, Third World states do not conform to the idea of homogeneous political units. Even the states of Western Europe, which are often regarded as an ideal type of such a model, fall somewhat short of the mark as certain elements within them challenge the authority of the state. In Eastern Europe and the Soviet Union, the idea of homogeneous units does not apply. In January 1990 we witnessed the Soviet army intervene to try to halt a virtual civil war between neighbouring Armenians and Azerbajanis. We have witnessed the Baltic states' call for independence. Similarly in the Eastern European states the fate of ethnic minorities is far from secure. In many Third World states the lack of domestic political consensus means that core values of the populace can be hard to identify, and even the territorial boundaries of the state may come under challenge from groups within the state as well as outside it. In contrast, however, it may well be possible to identify the core values of the ruling elite, and all too often elite security has been mistaken for national security. Indeed we cannot speak of national security in the Third World while nations and states do not coincide.

Secondly, Third World states are extremely vulnerable due to their economic weakness, or in the case of the oil producers, their dependence on a single commodity. This affects their military capability, though it need not determine it. (Client relationships with superpowers can result in a very poor state such as Somalia having a huge arsenal of expensive weaponry.) It also affects how they define insecurity. They are dependent units rather than insulated, separate units. They depend on developed states for technology, money and markets. Due to threats to their sovereignty, they have a great stake in making the international system a less anarchic place in which to function. Hence international cooperation and the rule of law become of great importance for them, for their weakness can invite interventionary activity from stronger states and interference from external organisations such as the International Monetary Fund. Well aware of their vulnerability to economic pressure, the Latin American states began the campaign for recognition of the economic dimension of sovereignty and hence the economic dimension of the non-intervention principle in international law long before the majority of Afro-Asian states won political independence.[2] After the achievement of political independence, the Afro-Asian group joined with the Latin American in the push for economic sovereignty. . . .

In tackling the problem of insecurity, governments in the Third World have to consider issues which have already been taken care of in the more developed states—especially those of the West. Third World states have to try to forge single nations within the boundaries of their state; they need to address basic welfare issues like how to feed, clothe, house and educate their populations; they need to be able to defend themselves in case of internal or external challenge. All this has to be done in circumstances of grave economic and financial insecurity and technological dependence: these states are at the mercy of a fickle oil cartel, fluctuating commodity prices, floating interest rates and unpredictable weather, as well as dictates from the IMF and other multilateral and bilateral lenders. They feel the effects of such influences to varying degrees, but in general we can say that they are more vulnerable to such forces than the developed northern states, and that they have no domestic welfare system to cushion their populations against these things. Thus internal and external security are intimately interlinked. This is demonstrated clearly today in new challenges facing these states, such as the debt crisis and the environmental crisis. The punitive effect of debt repayment, plus increasing protectionism in the North, has encouraged some states to step up their production of arms for export to other Third World states.[3] For example, Brazil has bartered arms for oil with Iraq, but in other cases has sold them for hard currency to go toward debt repayment.

Third World states act individually and collectively to decrease their insecurity. At one level, individual governments do what they can to maintain themselves in power, and they may foster differences or promote cooperation for nation-state building to this end. They will develop traditional security relations with neighbours, regional powers or superpowers, also to this end. At another level, Third World states act together to change the regimes governing international relations in an effort to bring those regimes closer to their common goal of an increased role in managing the system and a more equitable distribution of the benefits. The values of management and equity are extremely important in these concerted security policies emanating from the South. We see them informing both military and non-military security policies. We have witnessed dissatisfaction with the nuclear non-proliferation regime by many Third World statesmen who feel that the nuclear slates have not kept their side of the bargain, and also latterly with the Missile Technology Control Regime. . . .

THIRD WORLD SECURITY: THREE LEVELS OF EXPLANATION

(a) The Internal Dimension

The majority of armed conflicts in the Third World are intra-state rather than interstate. While the Third World states are marked by diversity, they are also commonly characterised by a lack of internal legitimacy. This has resulted in a crisis for many Third World states which has had and continues to have profound implications for security domestically, regionally and globally. Internal challenges to political authority are a more frequent cause of military conflict than border disputes. Moreover, even where border conflicts have occurred, they have almost never resulted in changes in territorial boundaries. The creation of Bangladesh stands out as an exception. This situation exists both because of the manner in which statehood has been achieved since the Second World War (sovereignty has been won by, or endowed on, former colonial units), and because of the international norms governing behaviour, particularly respect for sovereignty and non-intervention. . . .

An examination of the reasons for this preponderance of internal wars leads us to focus on the legitimacy crisis of the state. Here a comparison with the states of Western Europe is important, for the latter are taken as the model for the development of nation-states with high levels of domestic legitimacy. These European states are characterised today by bounded territories, social homogeneity and the monopolisation of violence by a single centre. They have not always been like this. Indeed these states have developed over several centuries, and in the process hundreds of them have been lost, swallowed up by stronger neighbours. They developed in a very hostile international environment and war was frequent. Borders moved with the changing ability of a ruler to defend and extend his hold on territory by force of arms. In order to finance such ventures, taxation had to be extended and increased, and for this to happen leaders had to promote the infrastructural development of the land they held in order to reach people. Rulers realised that the promotion of development was vital to their survival. States in Europe therefore became powerful infrastructurally as well as despotically; in other words, rulers had power over life and death, and thus were strong, but they also derived strength from the bureaucratic powers of the state which they were instrumental in developing. By this gradual process of integration, which was often bloody, nation-states were forged. Thus today a situation exists where multi-party politics is played out without the threat of arms being taken up against the government. This is not to suggest that there are not important differences within states, but rather that the mechanisms for resolving conflicting claims no longer take on a military dimension. Where they do, as is the case in a few European states, those who defy legal channels of opposition are a tiny minority. They do not threaten the integrity of the state.

In complete contrast to this, the majority of Third World states have come into being virtually overnight. International law established that colonial boundaries would be the legitimate boundaries of the new states. Thus it froze into place artificial constructs whose boundaries had been dictated often by colonial whim and bartering among European states in the late nineteenth century. Nation and state did not coincide in the way they had done in Europe. In the case of the older states of Latin and Central America, while territorial boundaries are not under fire the states are often in extreme crisis because the authority of governments is challenged. The benign international environment today, which gives the protection of sovereignty to all states, means that survival as a motor for development is lacking. . . .

The result is that many Third World states exist juridically, but not as 'social facts'. Their governments can take comfort in the fact that the norms of the international community—especially sovereignty and nonintervention—militate against the territorial disintegration of states. Thus even where intervention and occupation have occurred, we have seen occupying armies retreat in the face of international obloquy, as in Vietnam, Afghanistan, Uganda and Kampuchea. For the same reasons we have seen attempts at secession squashed with international approval, as in Nigeria and the Congo. Thus it appears that the survival of these states in their present form is guaranteed by the international community, yet in that very guarantee the same community loses any possibility of legitimate influence over promoting peaceful mechanisms for change within those states and for recognising the legitimacy of social change. . . .

(b) The Regional Dimension

The concept of regional security has become fashionable among politicians and academics in the developed and the developing states.[4] It assumes that many problems faced by Third World states are of a regional nature and potentially could be solved by regional solutions. While on the surface this seems perfectly viable, both the theory and the practice of regional security are fraught with difficulties. Ayoob states that the idea of regional security makes three assumptions: that external actors with interests in the region will refrain from interference; that regional states will have successfully dealt with their own domestic frictions; and that interstate tensions in the region are at a low level and/or can be dealt with easily by institutional mechanisms regionally accepted.[5] Yet he argues quite rightly that these criteria better fit Western Europe, which has had centuries of state-building and political legitimation, than Third World states. A fourth criterion can be added to Ayoob's list: that a region can be defined. Yet even this can pose enormous problems: where does one region end and another begin; are regional problems always the main security concern of all states in the 'region'; is the membership of the region perceived in common by states and peoples within and outside the region?

It is extremely difficult to think of any area in the Third World where all the above criteria are fulfilled simultaneously; indeed it is not an easy task to think of one area where any one of them is fulfilled. If we consider the Middle East, Southern Africa, South East Asia, South Asia and Central America, then examples abound of stateless peoples, the lack of domestic legitimacy of states and regimes, the absence of regionally-accepted mechanisms for conflict resolution, indirect or direct involvement by one or more of the superpowers, ill-defined regional boundaries and pariah states.

The idea of regional security stands in contrast to the notion of global or systemic security which sees the international system as indivisible, i.e. all developments in all parts of the system are interconnected. Whereas in the postwar period global security has been interpreted in the context of the East/West relationship, regional security analysts stress the importance of autonomous indigenous developments and do not look to the ideological superpower competition to explain local developments. While that global rivalry may be exploited by regional powers to enhance their own status and weapons capability, the cause of the regional hostility can be found within the region itself. Moreover, regional solutions are often seen as the most appropriate form of conflict resolution. . . .

Regional problems [can be] caused by the domestic lack of legitimacy of certain governments. However, another type of regional security problem arises from interstate hostilities. South Asia provides a pertinent example of this. The region has been characterised by conflict between India and Pakistan which has already led to two border wars and which will possibly lead to a third over the disputed territory of Kashmir. India is by far the strongest power in the region, and some commentators have suggested that that state has an imperial relationship with the smaller states in the region: Nepal, Bhutan, Sri Lanka and the Maldives. India is also far stronger than Pakistan in terms of economic and military power. However, regional balances have been upset by arms transfers and indigenous arms developments. Since the invasion of Afghanistan, the USA has transferred huge quantities of sophisticated weapons to Pakistan, and India has complained that these represent a threat to her territory as they could never be used to defend Pakistan against the USSR. The USA has not been concerned about this for a number of reasons: firstly, her priority was the global competition with the USSR, and Pakistan, given its proximity to Afghanistan, assumed importance in her global conception of the world; and secondly, despite the fact that India is the largest democracy in the world, the USA has always mistrusted her non-aligned stance and suspected her of tilting toward the USSR.[6] Even if the consequences were unintended, the US transfer of weapons to Pakistan fuelled a regional arms race in the subcontinent which was already simmering.

Efforts have been made to develop regional links through SAARC—the South Asian Association for Regional Cooperation.[7] Yet for India, the South Asian regional aspect of security is but one aspect of her security policies and concerns: China is her most formidable enemy and she has fought border wars with that state. This brings into question the validity of the notion of regional security. Often threats are perceived to come from outside the region, or several regions may overlap with detrimental effects on security. This has happened in the case of Pakistan which has formed part of the USA's picture of West Asia, but which at the same time is a major actor in the South Asian region.

The history of regional organisations for conflict resolution does not inspire hope for the future. The early examples of SEATO and CENTO (the Baghdad Pact) were more the product of the US desire for a global containment policy than of indigenous regional developments. The Organisation of African Unity has been more successful, but has been unable to effect resolutions of the conflicts in Southern Africa, the Horn, Chad and the Western Sahara. The Arab League cannot deal with many key Middle Eastern issues as neither Iran nor Israel belong.[8] . . .

NEW DIMENSIONS IN THE DEBATE ON THIRD WORLD SECURITY

(a) Development and Security

The majority of Third World states and peoples now face non-military threats to their security which no weapons, military alliances or individual governments can counter. Moreover, some such threats are of equal concern to the developed states, and it is becoming increasingly apparent that a holistic strategy to global security must be adopted if the international system as a whole is not to be ravaged by economic chaos, environmental degradation and an unfettered scramble for unaffected resources. The problems of debt, poverty, population growth, the environment and drugs are all interconnected; it is impossible to solve one without tackling the others. Thus development and international cooperation are vital components of any strategy aimed at increasing security in the Third World or globally.

Military strategy and hardware are necessary but not sufficient conditions for security. Weapons are no deterrent against the physical devastation of a state by floods (as in Bangladesh); drought (as in Ethiopia) or hurricanes (as in Jamaica). Nor do they lessen the vulnerability of states to the adverse workings of the international capitalist economy, such as unstable commodity prices, floating interest rates, poor terms of trade, IMF conditionality and high oil prices through OPEC action. Yet such factors can affect security critically, by undermining the social and political fabric of societies, by making states dependent and by forcing governments to act repressively domestically or to engage in foolhardly external policies directed at diverting domestic public opinion away from domestic problems (as with the Argentinian invasion of the Malvinas under the Galtieri government). Food can be a highly effective weapon: dependence on imported food makes the recipient state very insecure indeed. India experienced this in the 1960s when reliance on the US for grain was perceived as a grave threat to her sovereignty. The grain was bought at a price which included agricultural reform, more extensive family planning programmes, a 36.5 per cent devaluation of the rupee, and changes in Indian foreign policy including her attitude to the Vietnam conflict and relations with Pakistan.[9] Health is vital to security. Disease is a transnational phenomenon which can have a devasting effect and whose transmission pays no heed to territorial boundaries. We have yet to see the full impact of the AIDS virus, but it is already thought to have overtaken several armies, for example that of Zaire. The wasted decade of the 1980s, in terms of Third World development, will have repercussions which we can only guess at in the next generation as a whole sector of people in the Third World have suffered from long-term malnutrition, as adjustment has taken place without a human face.

Development and redistribution are preconditions for both domestic and international security. With states the desire to take up arms is often, though not always, motivated by the huge gap between the poverty of the majority and the wealth of a tiny minority. Between states, while the perception of the international order as unjust persists, its rules are bound to come under challenge. The experience of the 1930s shows that economic protectionism can be taken to extremes which ultimately threaten the international political system. Many Third World states feel that the protectionist measures adopted by leading developed states are undermining their development prospects.

While the general problem of underdevelopment has been with Third World states since their independence, the current debt and environmental crises represent a new phase in the predicament and one that makes the problem of security truly global. Moreover, these new challenges are intimately interconnected.

(b) Debt and Security

In 1988, an estimated $30 billion was transferred from the Third World to the West through debt servicing and repayment.[10] This movement of resources threatens the internal stability of debtor states, and in turn this threatens international security, as instability in the South often invites northern military intervention. Given the location of several of the world's major debtors in the US 'backyard', the dangers of political instability are accentuated. Yet the very IMF structural adjustment packages which accompany the borrowing of new money and the rescheduling of old debts intensify social and political unrest by increasing hardship while decreasing welfare provisions such as food subsidies. The riots in democratic Venezuela in 1989 startled the Western World and indicated that austerity measures can destabilise states. The outlook for the states which have only recently undergone transitions from authoritarian to democratic rule is bleak. Third World states remain at the mercy of fluctuating interest rates which are totally beyond their control. In the year ending March 1989, Mexico had over $3 billion added to her repayment bill due to interest rate rises alone. They are also at the mercy of the trading policies of the developed states. All too often, Third World states have found that when they become internationally competitive in a certain product, the Western states put up new restrictions to the entry of such goods. Brazilian steel is an example. Textiles often face such treatment, referred to as the 'new protectionism'. . . .

The debt crisis is no longer a financial crisis for the majority of the banks; however, it remains a financial crisis for the South, and its political, social and economic implications suggest potential security crises for debtor states where governmental legitimacy will be eroded further. This will have repercussions for the international system.

(c) Ecology and Security

Several Third World states will disappear in the next century if the sea level continues to rise at current rates.[11] Thus the security of the Maldives really is about physical survival. Many coastal capital cities will be flooded throughout the world. Rising sea levels are not the only climatic problem: droughts and floods will result in famine, soil erosion and further deforestation, and the latter itself will further affect the climate. The ecological debate is thus intermeshed with the development debate, and both are affected by the debt crisis. Competition for scarce resources will proceed apace between states and individuals. Clearly, international solutions are vital, as particularist answers cannot be of value in the long run. However, agreeing on strategies to alleviate these problems and to distribute resources will be politically difficult. Essentially, a bargain has to be struck between developed and developing states. Unfortunately the lowest common denominator—survival—will not be very helpful when it comes to negotiating agreements on gains and losses as the perceived needs of all states will vary radically.

In 1985 the Vienna Convention for the Protection of the Ozone Layer was signed, followed in 1987 by the addition of the Montreal Protocol. This represented the first global, as opposed to regional, agreement to regulate an environmental problem. The protocol provided for the halving of consumption of chlorofluorocarbons (CFCs) and a freeze on the consumption of halons by the end of the century. These are thought to be the major cause of the depletion of the ozone layer, which results in ultraviolet damage to crops and people. The convention also makes a significant contribution to tackling the greenhouse effect. This refers to the warming of the oceans and atmosphere. CFCs are one of the greenhouse gases, but carbon dioxide produced by burning coal and oil is the major culprit. Global warming will lead to increasingly extreme weather conditions—droughts, floods, hurricanes and rising sea levels. . . . At the London conference on Saving the Ozone Layer in 1989, it was clear that the issue of equity would have to be addressed for any agreement to be acceptable to the developing states. For they perceive the industrialised North to have created the bulk of the problem in the first place by its early industrialisation and by its huge energy consumption. Dr Liu Ming Pu, representing China, stressed that most of the environmental needs of the Third World arise from poverty, and called for levels of economic development and associated special needs to be taken into account in burden-sharing formulas. He indicated that China produced 20 000 tonnes of CFCs annually, compared with 300 000 tonnes by the USA and 130 000 by the USSR. China has 1.1 billion people, and thus suffers most from ozone depletion, yet it has produced only 2 per cent of the world's CFCs and related gases, compared with the 80 per cent produced by the developed world. Other Third World statesmen expressed similar feelings. President Moi of Kenya argued that the polluters must pay, as did Mr Ziul Rahman Ansari, the Indian Minister of the Environment and Forests. Clearly, an international regime governing the issue of the ozone is going to be politically very difficult to achieve, yet it is vital for the security not only of individual states but of the globe. . . .

CONCLUSION

Traditional concepts of security, based on a realist conception of international relations, fail to identify and address the most pressing security concerns of the majority of Third World states. Most Third World military conflicts take place within states, not between them. Military developments within the Third World are certainly very important, and must not be ignored. But they must be seen as one of a whole range of factors affecting the security of Third World states. Moreover, these factors affect each other, as well as affecting *all* states. No group can pursue meaningful security alone: the problems faced are global, and require global solutions.

Poverty intensifies the problem of population growth rather than alleviates it, as children are seen as a form of wealth and protection for the future in societies where there are no social welfare provisions. Poverty is exacerbated by debt, and makes the production of drug crops an attractive prospect to the Latin American and Asian peasant. Environmental problems are also exacerbated by debt. Repayment of debt by the South to the North intensifies the poverty of millions of people in the Third World, and both this and the need to repay generate a huge impetus to pursue ecologically inappropriate land use. Added to northern protectionism, debt stimulates the production of Third World arms industries to supply Third World markets either through barter or to earn foreign exchange. Adjustment puts further strains on already fragile polities, and increases the likelihood of intervention either directly or indirectly through the transfer of arms or logistical support. All these problems make the issue of Third World security far more complex now than it has been in the past. Indeed, a realistic assessment of Third World security must be undertaken in the context of a holistic conception of global security. It is not enough for Third World leaders to recognise this: it is imperative that the leaders of the developed world act on it.

NOTES

1. P. Saravanamuttu. 'Security: an Essentially Contested Concept', unpublished research paper, Southampton University, Department of Politics.
2. For a full discussion see C. Thomas, *New States, Sovereignty and Intervention* (Aldershot: Gower, 1985).
3. M. Brzoska and T. Ohlson, *Arms Production in the Third World* (London: Taylor and Francis/SIPRI, 1986).
4. See M. Ayoob (ed.), *Regional Security in the Third World* (London and Sydney: Croom Helm, 1986).
5. *Ibid.*, p. 4.
6. Raju Thomas, 'Security Relationships in South Asia: Differences in Indian and American Perspectives', *Asian Survey*, July 1981.
7. See articles by Muni, Ayoob, Bokhari and Khatri and Rahman in *Asian Survey*, April 1985.
8. On the Arab League, see Mohammed El Sayed Said, 'The Arab League: Between Regime Security and National Liberation', in Ayoob (ed.), *op. cit.,* 1986.
9. Paarlberg, *Food Trade and Foreign Policy: India, the Soviet Union and the US* (Ithaca and London: Cornell University Press, 1985).
10. See Fidler, *Financial Times,* 15 March 1989; and H. Lever and W. Huhne, *Debt and Danger,* (Harmondsworth: Penguin, 1986), and Susan George, *A Fate Worse than Debt,* (Harmondsworth: Penguin, 1989).
11. For general linkages between environment and security, see N. Brown, 'Climate, ecology and international security', *Survival,* Nov./Dec. 1989, pp. 519–32, and N. Myers, 'Environment and Security', *Foreign Policy,* 74, 1989, pp. 23–41.

Three

THE INTERNATIONAL POLITICAL ECONOMY

*I*n Part One, we examined the meaning of anarchy and saw the consequences for state behavior that flowed from it. In Part Two, we analyzed in more detail one of the primary instruments that states can and must use, namely, military power. In Part Three, we are concerned with the other primary instrument of state action, economic power.

Disparities in power, as we saw earlier, have important effects on state behavior. Such disparities occur, not simply because of the differences in the military power that states wield, but also because of the differences in economic resources that they generate. In the first instance, the force that a nation can field is dependent in part on the economic wealth that it can muster to support and sustain its military forces. Wealth is therefore a component of state power. But the generation of wealth, unlike the generation of military power, is also an end of state action. Except in the rarest of circumstances, military power is never sought as an end in itself, but rather is acquired as a means to attain security or the other ends that a state pursues. By contrast, wealth is both a component of state power and a good that can be consumed by its citizenry. Force is mustered primarily for the external arena. Wealth is sought for both the external and the domestic arena. Moreover, wealth and power differ in the degree that states can pursue each without detriment to the positions and interests of other nations. No situation in international politics is ever totally cooperative or conflictual, but the potential for cooperative behavior is greater in the realm of wealth than in the realm of power.

It is the duality of enonomic power (as a component and end of state action) and its greater potential for common gains that makes the analysis of the role it plays in state behavior and international interactions complex and elusive. The study of international political economy, as it has been traditionally understood, encompasses both these aspects of economic power.

PERSPECTIVES ON POLITICAL ECONOMY

"The science of economics presupposes a given political order, and cannot be profitably studied in isolation from politics." So wrote E. H. Carr in his seminal work, *The Twenty Year's Crisis,* in 1939. Fifty years earlier, in an essay entitled "Socialism: Utopian or Scientific" Friedrich Engels asserted: "The materialist conception of history starts from the proposition that the production of the means to support human life . . . is the basis of all social structure. . . ." These two views—that economic processes are not autonomous but require political structures to support them and that economic factors determine the social and political structures of states—represent the polar extremes on the relationship of politics and economics.

Which view is correct? To this question there is no simple or single answer. Any reply is as much philosophical as it is empirical. The economic interests of individuals in a state and of states within the international arena do powerfully affect the goals that are sought and the degree of success with which they are attained. But the political structure of international action is also a constraint. Anarchy makes cooperative actions more difficult to attain than would otherwise be the case and requires that statesmen consider both relative and absolute positions when framing actions in the international economic realm. And often in international politics the imperatives of security and survival override the dictates of economic interests. War, after all, almost never pays in a strict balance-sheet sense, particularly when waged between states of roughly equal power. The economic wealth lost in fighting is usually not recouped in the peace that follows.

The best answers to the question, what is the relation between politics and economics in international affairs, have been given by the classical theorists of international politics. Robert Gilpin examines three schools of thought—the liberals, the marxists, and the mercantilists. Unlike the other two, liberal political economists have stressed the cooperative, not the conflictual, nature of international economic relations. They have extended Adam Smith's arguments about the domestic economy to the international economy. Smith argued that the specialization of function by individuals within a state, together with their unfettered pursuit of their own self-interests, would increase the wealth of a nation and thereby benefit all. Collective harmony and national wealth could thus be the product of self-interested behavior, if only the government would provide as little restraint on individual action as was necessary. The eighteenth-century Philosophes and the nineteenth- and twentieth-century free traders argued that what was good for the individuals within a state would also be good for states in the international arena. By trading freely with one another, states could specialize according to their respective comparative advantages and the wealth of all nations would, as a consequence, increase. "Make trade not war" has been the slogan of the liberal free traders.

By contrast, both mercantilists and marxists have seen state relations as inherently conflictual. For marxists, this is so because capitalists within and among states compete fiercely with one another to maximize their profits. Driven by their greed, they are incapable of cooperating with one another. Because a state's policy is determined by the capitalist ruling class, states will wage wars for profit and, under

Lenin's dictum, will wage wars to redivide the world's wealth. Imperialism as the highest stage of capitalism is a classic zero-sum situation. Mercantilists also argue that economic factors make relations among states conflictual. But their analysis rests, not on the externalization of class conflict, but on the nature of political and economic power. For eighteenth-century mercantilists, the world's wealth was fixed and could only be redivided. For nineteenth- and twentieth-century mercantilists, wealth could be increased for all, but because wealth contributes to national power and power is relative, not absolute, conflict would continue.

All three schools of thought are motivated by their views on the relation of politics to economics. Mercantilists stress the primacy of politics and the consequent pursuit of national power and relative position in the international arena. Both liberals and marxists stress the primacy of economics. For the former, the potential for economic harmony can override the forces of nationalism if only free trade is pursued. For the latter, economic interests determine political behavior and, since the first is conflictual, the second must be also. Both liberals and marxists want to banish politics from international relations, the former through free trade, the latter through the universal spread of communism. Mercantilists, like realists, view these prescriptions as naive and believe that the national interests of every state are only partly determined by their economic interests.

Contemporary writers continue to wrestle with the relation between politics and economics in international affairs. Robert O. Keohane analyzes what types of international political structures are conducive to economic cooperation among nations. He finds the theory of hegemonic stability—that a dominant power is necessary to create and sustain a stable international economic order—a suggestive but not definitive way to understand the last one hundred years. A hegemonic power can foster economic cooperation among states, as the United States did after World War II, but cooperation can occur in the absence of such a power. A hegemonic power is neither a necessary nor a sufficient condition for interstate cooperation.

Stephen D. Krasner looks at the political-economic relations between the United States and the Third World. He argues that Third World states want both wealth and power and have used international organizations and international regimes to advance their interests in ways that are not beneficial to the United States and the other nations of the industrialized world. Due to a peculiar set of conditions in the 1970s and 1980s, the Third World nations were able to advance their interests, with varying degrees of success, in international fora under the rubric of the New International Economic Order (NIEO).

THE DEBATE ABOUT INTERDEPENDENCE

At the end of the twentieth century, which way will the international political economy go? Can the nations of the world muster the political will necessary to preserve a relatively open international system that has benefitted them all, even if they have benefitted unequally? Or, have the political costs of severe economic dislocations, which the open system of the last two decades has produced, been too great? Will states lapse into protectionism? Does free trade still make sense when factor endowments (land, labor, capital, and technology) are no longer fixed and when, therefore, comparative advantages are no longer static but can be created behind protectionist barriers, as Japan, to take an example, has so successfully shown?

These are difficult questions to answer. How they are answered depends heavily on how economically interdependent one sees the nations of the world today. "Interdependence" is one of those terms that has developed a myriad of meanings. The most fruitful way to use the term, when considering the relationship between this concept and peaceful cooperation among states, is as follows: Interdependence is the size of the stake that a state believes it has in seeing other states' economies prosper, so as to help its own economy prosper too. Interdependence can be high or low. The higher perceived interdependence is, the larger a state's stake in the economic well-being of the countries with which it heavily interacts; the lower interdependence, the smaller is its stake. High levels of interdependence should facilitate cooperation among states for their mutual gain.

After World War II, the United States used its considerable economic and military power to create an open international economic order by working to lower the barriers among nations to the flow of manufactured goods, raw materials other than agriculture, and capital. The result of this international economic openness was a rise in the level of interdependence, particularly among the industrialized nations of the world, but also, to a considerable degree, among the industrializing nations in the Far East and Latin America as well. But interdependence has its costs as well as its benefits. High levels of participation in the international economy can bring the benefits of efficiency that flow from specialization, but also the destruction of national industries that can no longer compete internationally. States today must reconcile the imperatives of what Robert Gilpin has called "Keynes at home" with "Smith abroad": the maintenance of full employment domestically and the competitive participation in the international economy. Through exports and capital inflows, interdependence can help a state increase its wealth; but it also brings vulnerabilities that derive from the need to rely partially on others for one's own prosperity. Balancing the two imperatives is a difficult political act.

How interdependent the world actually is today, how different this era's interdependence is compared to what obtained before 1914, how important ownership of manufacturing assets is compared to where they are located, whether the world is moving towards economic closure, and how significant trade remains in light of the vast daily flows of capital among nations today—all these issues bear upon the nature and resiliency of today's interdependence. None are settled matters among the experts.

Janice Thomson and Stephen Krasner argue that by whatever indices one uses, today's interdependence is little different from that obtained before 1914. Exports as a percentage of gross domestic product are no higher today among the industrialized nations that they were in the four decades before 1914. Neither is the growth of world trade, nor the international movement of capital. Moreover, as Robert Gilpin argues, in the mid–1980s, the world began moving away from openness towards a more closed order characterized by mercantilistic competition, economic regionalism, and sectoral protectionism. This may not bring a return to the economic warfare of the 1930s, but it presages a return to the mercantilism of old, even if a more benign variety.

Richard Rosecrance disagrees with this picture of the contemporary international economic order. He sees this era's interdependence more deeply rooted than the one before 1914 because the nature of cross-national capital investments among the rich nations has changed. There is a greater level of direct, as opposed to indirect (portfolio), investment amongst these nations. As a consequence of the higher levels of direct cross-national investment, a state's interest in seeing other national economies prosper has grown. The reason is that it is easier to dispose of shares in an industry on the stock exchange than it is to sell complete factories and other pieces of real estate.

Robert Reich and Ethan Kapstein approach the question of interdependence by looking at whether firms owe allegiance to any state, especially their home-based state, if, indeed, one can even speak of such a state today. Reich argues that the central question for a nation competing in today's interdependent economy is not who owns the factories within its borders, but how efficient those factories are. Prospering in today's global economy requires an educated, skilled workforce and sufficient capital investment. If capital and other types of investment enhance the efficiency of a nation's workforce, it makes no difference which investor—foreign or national—provided the capital, only that it was provided. Kapstein disagrees in part. States are still powerful and not at the mercy of international businesses. It is states, not firms, that grant access to businesses that wish to operate within their territories. States care about what goes on within their borders, and firms are not as denationalized as many analysts would have one believe. International firms are loyal to the home state in which their corporate headquarters are based. International corporations are a fact of this interdependent world. But it is states that influence corporations more than the latter influence the state. In Kapstein's view, eulogies for the state are premature.

POWER VERSUS PLENTY TODAY

Interdependence is a two-edged sword. States can benefit from participation in the international market and grow richer through the workings of the international division of labor. But states do not grow rich equally. Some will grow richer than others, even if not at the expense of others. An interdependent world may foster growth in world income, but it does so by putting competition on an international, not a national, scale. A truly globalized interdependent world is a fiercely competitive one, especially if wealth is linked to national influence.

This idea is debated by Samuel Huntington and Paul Krugman. In a competitive arena, power counts, so argues Huntington. It is better to be number one than number two. Primacy matters, he argues, even in a world where the terms of competition have shifted from military to economic means. Economic power is still power. Power is still useful for advancing a state's interest. Economic primacy therefore matters today as much as military primacy mattered during the Cold War. For the United States today, the greatest challenge is no longer military but economic: the challenge of Japan. Just as the United States met and defeated the Soviet military threat, so, too, must it now rise to the occasion and defeat the Japanese economic threat.

Paul Krugman takes the contrary view. He stresses not the relative economic position of nations, but rather their absolute wealth. What matters is how wealthy they grow, not how wealthy they grow relative to others. Moreover, Krugman argues that for an economy like that of the United States, how it does internationally matters a lot less than for one highly dependent on international trade. The United States, he points out, has an economy in which 90 percent of its goods and services are produced for its own use. How it does relative to Japan is less important than how it does relative to its own experience.

These two views—Huntington versus Krugman—represent an old and enduring debate in international relations between those who stress absolute power and wealth (Krugman) and those who stress relative power and position (Huntington). It is a debate hard to resolve because both perspectives count. Clearly, absolute wealth matters. But in international politics, as was pointed out in the readings in Part One, so also does relative position. Krugman and Huntington thus represent the two faces of interdependence—the benign view (all grow wealthier) and the not-so-benign view (those who grow wealthiest can exploit the others). The nature of interdependence lies as much in the eye of the beholder as it does in the quantifiable measures of trade, capital, and technology flows across borders.

Perspectives on Political Economy

The Nature of Political Economy

Robert Gilpin

> The international corporations have evidently declared ideological war on the "antiquated" nation state. . . . The charge that materialism, modernization and internationalism is the new liberal creed of corporate capitalism is a valid one. The implication is clear: The nation state as a political unit of democratic decision-making must, in the interest of "progress," yield control to the new mercantile mini-powers.[1]

> While the structure of the multinational corporation is a modern concept, designed to meet the requirements of a modern age, the nation state is a very old-fashioned idea and badly adapted to serve the needs of our present complex world.[2]

These two statements—the first by Kari Levitt, a Canadian nationalist, the second by George Ball, a former United States undersecretary of state—express a dominant theme of contemporary writings on international relations. International society, we are told, is increasingly rent between its economic and its political organization. On the one hand, powerful economic and technological forces are creating a highly interdependent world economy, thus diminishing the traditional significance of national boundaries. On the other hand, the nation-state continues to command men's loyalties and to be the basic unit of political decision making. As one writer has put the issue, "The conflict of our era is between ethnocentric nationalism and geocentric technology."[3]

Ball and Levitt represent two contending positions with respect to this conflict. Whereas Ball advocates the diminution of the power of the nation-state in order to give full rein to the productive potentialities of the multinational corporation, Levitt argues for a powerful nationalism which could counterbalance American corporate domination. What appears to one as the logical and desirable conse-

---

quence of economic rationality seems to the other to be an effort on the part of American imperialism to eliminate all contending centers of power

Although the advent of the multinational corporation has put the question of the relationship between economics and politics in a new guise, it is an old issue. In the nineteenth century, for example, it was this issue that divided classical liberals like John Stuart Mill from economic nationalists, represented by Georg Friedrich List. Whereas the former gave primacy in the organization of society to economics and the production of wealth, the latter emphasized the political determination of economic relations. As this issue is central both to the contemporary debate on the multinational corporation and to the argument of this study, this chapter analyzes the three major treatments of the relationship between economics and politics—that is, the three major ideologies of political economy.

THE MEANING OF POLITICAL ECONOMY

The argument of this study is that the relationship between economics and politics, at least in the modern world, is a reciprocal one. On the one hand, politics largely determines the framework of economic activity and channels it in directions intended to serve the interests of dominant groups; the exercise of power in all its forms is a major determinant of the nature of an economic system. On the other hand, the economic process itself tends to redistribute power and wealth; it transforms the power relationships among groups. This in turn leads to a transformation of the political system, thereby giving rise to a new structure of economic relationships. Thus, the dynamics of international relations in the modern world is largely a function of the reciprocal interaction between economics and politics.

First of all, what do I mean by "politics" or "economics"? Charles Kindleberger speaks of economics and politics as two different methods of allocating scarce resources: the first through a market mechanism, the latter through a budget.[4] Robert Keohane and Joseph Nye, in an excellent analysis of international political economy, define economics and politics in terms of two levels of analysis: those of structure and of process.[5] Politics is the domain "having to do with the establishment of an order of relations, a structure. . . ."[6] Economics deals with "short-term allocative behavior (i.e., holding institutions, fundamental assumptions, and expectations constant). . . ."[7] Like Kindleberger's definition, however, this definition tends to isolate economic and political phenomena except under certain conditions, which Keohane and Nye define as the "politicization" of the economic system. Neither formulation comes to terms adequately with the dynamic and intimate nature of the relationship between the two.

In this study, the issue of the relationship between economics and politics translates into that between wealth and power. According to this statement of the problem, economics takes as its province the creation and distribution of wealth; politics is the realm of power. I shall examine their relationship from several ideological perspectives, including my own. But what is wealth? What is power?

In response to the question, What is wealth?, an economist-colleague responded, "What do you want, my thirty-second or thirty-volume answer?" Basic concepts are elusive in economics, as in any field of inquiry. No unchallengeable definitions are possible. Ask a physicist for his definition of the nature of space, time, and matter, and you will not get a very satisfying response. What you will get is an *operational* definition, one which is usable: It permits the physicist to build an intellectual edifice whose foundations would crumble under the scrutiny of the philosopher.

Similarly, the concept of wealth, upon which the science of economics ultimately rests, cannot be clarified in a definitive way. Paul Samuelson, in his textbook, doesn't even try, though he provides a clue in his definition of economics as "the study of how men and society *choose* ... to employ *scarce* productive resources ... to produce various commodities ... and distribute them for consumption."[8] Following this lead, we can say that wealth is anything (capital, land, or labor) that can generate future income; it is composed of physical assets and human capital (including embodied knowledge).

The basic concept of political science is power. Most political scientists would not stop here; they would include in the definition of political science the purpose for which power is used, whether this be the advancement of the public welfare or the domination of one group over another. In any case, few would dissent from the following statement of Harold Lasswell and Abraham Kaplan:

> The concept of power is perhaps the most fundamental in the whole of political science: The political process is the shaping, distribution, and exercise of power (in a wider sense, of all the deference values, or of influence in general.)[9]

Power as such is not the sole or even the principal goal of state behavior. Other goals or values constitute the objectives pursued by nation-states: welfare, security, prestige. But power in its several forms (military, economic, psychological) is ultimately the necessary means to achieve these goals. For this reason, nation-states are intensely jealous of and sensitive to their relative power position. The distribution of power is important because it profoundly affects the ability of states to achieve what they perceive to be their interests.

The nature of power, however, is even more elusive than that of wealth. The number and variety of definitions should be an embarrassment to political scientists. Unfortunately, this study cannot bring the intradisciplinary squabble to an end. Rather, it adopts the definition used by Hans Morgenthau in his influential *Politics Among Nations:* "man's control over the minds and actions of other men."[10] Thus, power, like wealth, is the capacity to produce certain results.

Unlike wealth, however, power cannot be quantified; indeed, it cannot be over-emphasized that power has an important psychological dimension. Perceptions of power relations are of critical importance; as a consequence, a fundamental task of statesmen is to manipulate the perceptions of other statesmen regarding the distribution of power. Moreover, power is relative to a specific situation or set of circumstances; there is no single hierarchy of power in international relations. Power may take many forms—military, economic, or psychological—though, in the final analysis, force is the ultimate form of power. Finally, the inability to predict the behavior of others or the outcome of events is of great significance. Uncertainty regarding the distribution of power and the ability of the statesmen to control events plays an important role in international relations. Ultimately, the determination of the distribution of power can be made only in retrospect as a consequence of war. It is precisely for this reason that war has had, unfortunately, such a central place in the history of international relations. In short, power is an elusive concept indeed upon which to erect a science of politics.

Such mutually exclusive definitions of economics and politics as these run counter to much contemporary scholarship by both economists and political scientists, for both disciplines are invading the formerly exclusive jurisdictions of the other. Economists, in particular, have become intellectual imperialists; they are applying their analytical techniques to traditional issues of political science with great success. These developments, however, really reinforce the basic premise of this study, namely, the inseparability of economics and politics.

The distinction drawn above between economics as the science of wealth and politics as the science of power is essentially an analytical one. In the real world, wealth and power are ultimately joined. This, in fact, is the basic rationale for a political economy of international relations. But in order to develop the argument of this study, wealth and power will be treated, at least for the moment, as analytically distinct.

To provide a perspective on the nature of political economy, the next section will discuss the three prevailing conceptions of political economy: liberalism, Marxism, and mercantilism, Liberalism regards politics and economics as relatively separable and autonomous spheres of activities; I associate most professional economists as well as many other academics, businessmen, and American officials with this outlook. Marxism refers to the radical critique of capitalism identified with Karl Marx and his contemporary disciples; according to this conception, economics determines politics and political structure. Mercantilism is a more questionable term because of its historical association with the desire of nation-states for a trade surplus and for treasure (money). One must distinguish, however, between the specific form mercantilism took in the seventeenth and eighteenth centuries and the general outlook of mercantilistic thought. The essence of the mercantilistic perspective, whether it is labeled economic nationalism, protectionism, or the doctrine of the German Historical School, is the subservience of economy to the state and its interests—interests that range from matters of domestic welfare to those of international security. It is this more general meaning of mercantilism that is implied by the use of the term in this study.

Following the discussion of these three schools of thought. I shall elaborate my own, more eclectic, view of political economy and demonstrate its relevance for understanding the phenomenon of the multinational corporation.

THREE CONCEPTIONS OF POLITICAL ECONOMY

The three prevailing conceptions of political economy differ on many points. Several critical differences will be examined in this brief comparison. (See Table 1.)

The Nature of Economic Relations

The basic assumption of liberalism is that the nature of international economic relations is essentially harmonious. Herein lay the great intellectual innovation of Adam Smith. Disputing his mercantilist predecessors, Smith argued that international economic relations could be made a positive-sum game; that is to say, everyone could gain, and no one need lose, from a proper ordering of economic relations, albeit the distribution of these gains may not be equal. Following Smith, liberalism assumes that there is a basic harmony between true national interest and cosmopolitan economic interest. Thus, a prominent member of this school of thought has written, in response to a radical critique, that the economic effeciency of the sterling standard in the nineteenth century and that of the dollar standard in the twentieth century serve "the cosmopolitan interest in a national form."[11] Although Great Britain and the United States gained the most from the international role of their respective currencies, everyone else gained as well.

Liberals argue that, given this underlying identity of national and cosmopolitan interests in a free market, the state should not interfere with economic transactions across national boundaries. Through free exchange of commodities, removal of restrictions on the flow of investment, and an international division of labor, everyone will benefit in the long run as a result of a more efficient utilization of the world's scarce resources. The national interest is therefore best served, liberals maintain, by a generous and cooperative attitude regarding economic relations with other countries. In essence, the pursuit of self-interest in a free, competitive economy achieves the greatest good for the greatest number in international no less than in the national society.

Both mercantilists and Marxists, on the other hand, begin with the premise that the essence of economic relations is conflictual. There is no underlying harmony; indeed, one group's gain is another's loss. Thus, in the language of game theory, whereas liberals regard economic relations as a non-zero-sum game, Marxists and mercantilists view economic relations as essentially a zero-sum game.

TABLE 1   COMPARISON OF THE THREE CONCEPTIONS OF POLITICAL ECONOMY

	Liberalism	Marxism	Mercantilism
Nature of economic relations	Harmonious	Conflictual	Conflictual
Nature of the actors	Households and firms	Economic classes	Nation-states
Goal of economic activity	Maximization of global welfare	Maximization of class interests	Maximization of national interest
Relationship between economics and politics	Economics *should* determine politics	Economics *does* determine politics	Politics determines economics
Theory of change	Dynamic equilibrium	Tendency toward disequilibrium	Shifts in the distribution of power

The Goal of Economic Activity

For the liberal, the goal of economic activity is the optimum or efficient use of the world's scarce resources and the maximization of world welfare. While most liberals refuse to make value judgments regarding income distribution, Marxists and mercantilists stress the distributive effects of economic relations. For the Marxist the distribution of wealth among social classes is central; for the mercantilist it is the distribution of employment, industry, and military power among nation-states that is most significant. Thus, the goal of economic (and political) activity for both Marxists and mercantilists is the redistribution of wealth and power.

The State and Public Policy

These three perspectives differ decisively in their view regarding the nature of the economic actors. In Marxist analysis, the basic actors in both domestic and international relations are economic classes; the interests of the dominant class determine the foreign policy of the state. For mercantilists, the real actors in international economic relations are nation-states; national interest determines foreign policy. National interest may at times be influenced by the peculiar economic interests of classes, elites, or other subgroups of the society; but factors of geography, external configurations of power, and the exigencies of national survival are primary in determining foreign policy. Thus, whereas liberals speak of world welfare and Marxists of class interests, mercantilists recognize only the interests of particular nation-states.

Although liberal economists such as David Ricardo and Joseph Schumpeter recognized the importance of class conflict and neoclassical liberals analyze economic growth and policy in terms of national economies, the liberal emphasis is on the individual consumer, firm, or entrepreneur. The liberal ideal is summarized in the view of Harry Johnson that the nation-state has no meaning as an economic entity.[12]

Underlying these contrasting views are differing conceptions of the nature of the state and public policy. For liberals, the state represents an aggregation of private interests: public policy is but the outcome of a pluralistic struggle among interest groups. Marxists, on the other hand, regard the state as simply the "executive committee of the ruling class," and public policy reflects its interests. Mercantilists, however, regard the state as an organic unit in its own right: the whole is greater than the sum of its parts. Public policy, therefore, embodies the national interest or Rousseau's "general will" as conceived by the political elite.

The Relationship Between Economics and Politics: Theories of Change

Liberalism, Marxism, and mercantilism also have differing views on the relationship between economics and politics. And their differences on this issue are directly relevant to their contrasting theories of international political change.

Although the liberal ideal is the separation of economics from politics in the interest of maximizing world welfare, the fulfillment of this ideal would have important political implications. The classical statement of these implications was that of Adam Smith in *The Wealth of Nations*.[13] Economic growth, Smith argued, is primarily a function of the extent of the division of labor, which in turn is dependent upon the scale of the market. Thus he attacked the barriers erected by feudal principalities and mercantilistic states against the exchange of goods and the enlargement of markets. If men were to multiply their wealth, Smith argued, the contradiction between political organization and economic rationality had to be resolved in favor of the latter. That is, the pursuit of wealth should determine the nature of the political order.

Subsequently, from nineteenth-century economic liberals to twentieth-century writers on economic integration, there has existed "the dream . . . of a great republic of world commerce, in which national boundaries would cease to have any great economic importance and the web of trade would bind all the people of the world in the prosperity of peace."[14] For liberals the long-term trend is toward world integration, wherein functions, authority, and loyalties will be transferred from "smaller units to larger ones; from states to federalism; from federalism to supranational unions and from these to superstates."[15] The logic of economic and technological development, it is argued, has set mankind on an inexorable course toward global political unification and world peace.

In Marxism, the concept of the contradiction between economic and political relations was enacted into historical law. Whereas classical liberals—although Smith less than others—held that the requirements of economic rationality *ought* to determine political relations, the Marxist position was that the mode of production does in fact determine the superstructure of political relations. Therefore, it is argued, history can be understood as the product of the dialectical process—the contradiction between the evolving techniques of production and the resistant sociopolitical system.

Although Marx and Engels wrote remarkably little on international economics, Engels, in his famous polemic, *Anti-Duhring*, explicitly considers whether economics or politics is primary in determining the structure of international relations.[16] E. K. Duhring, a minor figure in the German Historical School, had argued, in contradiction to Marxism, that property and market relations resulted less from the economic logic of capitalism than from extraeconomic political factors: "The basis of the exploitation of many by man was an historical act of force which created an exploitative economic system for the benefit of the stronger man or class."[17] Since Engels, in his attack on Duhring, used the example of the unification of Germany through the Zollverein or customs union of 1833, his analysis is directly relevant to this discussion of the relationship between economics and political organization.

Engels argued that when contradictions arise between economic and political structures, political power adapts itself to the changes in the balance of economic forces; politics yields to the dictates of economic development. Thus, in the case of nineteenth-century Germany, the requirements of industrial production had become incompatible with its feudal, politically fragmented structure. "Though political reaction was victorious in 1815 and again in 1848," he argued, "it was unable to prevent the growth of large-scale industry in Germany and the growing participation of German commerce in the world market."[18] In summary, Engels wrote, "German unity had become an economic necessity."[19]

In the view of both Smith and Engels, the nation-state represented a progressive stage in human development, because it enlarged the political realm of economic activity. In each successive economic epoch, advances in technology and an increasing scale of production necessitate an enlargement of political organization. Because the city-state and feudalism restricted the scale of production and the division of labor made possible by the Industrial Revolution, they prevented the efficient utilization of resources and were, therefore, superseded by larger political units. Smith considered this to be a desirable objective; for Engels it was an historical necessity. Thus, in the opinion of liberals, the establishment of the Zollverein was a movement toward maximizing world economic welfare;[20] for Marxists it was the unavoidable triumph of the German industrialists over the feudal aristocracy.

Mercantilist writers from Alexander Hamilton to Frederich List to Charles de Gaulle, on the other hand, have emphasized the primacy of politics; politics, in this view, determines economic organization. Whereas Marxists and liberals have pointed to the production of wealth as the basic determinant of social and political organization, the mercantilists of the German Historical School, for example, stressed the primacy of national security, industrial development, and national sentiment in international political and economic dynamics.

In response to Engels's interpretation of the unification of Germany, mercantilists would no doubt agree with Jacob Viner that "Prussia engineered the customs union primarily for political reasons, in order to gain hegemony or at least influence over the lesser German states. It was largely in order to make certain that the hegemony should be Prussian and not Austrian that Prussia continually opposed Austrian entry into the Union, either openly or by pressing for a customs union tariff lower than highly protectionist Austria could stomach."[21] In pursuit of this strategic interest, it was "Prussian might, rather than a common zeal for political unification arising out of economic partnership, [that] . . . played the major role."[22]

In contrast to Marxism, neither liberalism nor mercantilism has a developed theory of dynamics. The basic assumption of orthodox economic analysis (liberalism) is the tendency toward equilibrium; liberalism takes for granted the existing social order and given institutions. Change is assumed to be gradual and adaptive—a continuous process of dynamic equilibrium. There is no necessary connection between such political phenomena as war and revolution and the evolution of the economic system, although they would not deny that misguided statesmen can blunder into war over economic issues or that revolutions are conflicts over the distribution of wealth; but neither is inevitably linked to the evolution of the productive system. As for mercantilism, it sees change as taking place owing to shifts in the balance of power; yet, mercantilist writers such as members of the German Historical School and contemporary political realists have not developed a systematic theory of how this shift occurs.

On the other hand, dynamics is central to Marxism; indeed Marxism is essentially a theory of social *change*. It emphasizes the tendency toward *dis*equilibrium owing to changes in the means of production and the consequent effects on the everpresent class conflict. When these tendencies can no longer be contained, the sociopolitical system breaks down through violent upheaval. Thus war and revolution are seen as an integral part of the economic process. Politics and economics are intimately joined.

Why an International Economy?

From these differences among the three ideologies, one can get a sense of their respective explanations for the existence and functioning of the international economy.

An interdependent world economy constitutes the normal state of affairs for most liberal economists. Responding to technological advances in transportation and communications, the scope of the market mechanism, according to this analysis, continuously expands. Thus, despite temporary setbacks, the long-term trend is toward global economic integration. The functioning of the international economy is determined primarily by considerations of efficiency. The role of the dollar as the basis of the international monetary system, for example, is explained by the preference for it among traders and nations as the vehicle of international commerce.[23] The system is maintained by the mutuality of the benefits provided by trade, monetary arrangements, and investment.

A second view—one shared by Marxists and mercantilists alike—is that every interdependent international economy is essentially an imperial or hierarchical system. The imperial or hegemonic power organizes trade, monetary, and investment relations in order to advance its own economic and political interests. In the absence of the economic and especially the political influence of the hegemonic power, the system would fragment into autarkic economies or regional blocs. Whereas for liberalism maintenance of harmonious international market relations is the norm, for Marxism and mercantilism conflicts of class or national interests are the norm.

PERSPECTIVE OF THE AUTHOR

My own perspective on political economy rests on what I regard as a fundamental difference in emphasis between economics and politics; namely, the distinction between absolute and relative gains. The emphasis of economic science—or, at least, of liberal economics—is on *absolute* gains; the ultimate defense of liberalism is that over the long run everyone gains, albeit in varying degrees, from a liberal economic regime. Economics, according to this formulation, need not be a zero-sum game. Everyone can gain in wealth through a more efficient division of labor; moreover, everyone can lose, in absolute terms, from economic inefficiency. Herein lies the strength of liberalism.

This economic emphasis on absolute gains is in fact embodied in what one can characterize as the ultimate ideal of liberal economics: the achievement of a "Pareto optimum" world. Such a properly ordered world would be one wherein "by improving the position of one individual (by adding to his possessions) no one else's position is deteriorated." As Oskar Morgenstern has observed, "[e]conomic literature is replete with the use of the Pareto optimum thus for-mulated or in equivalent language."[24] It is a world freed from "interpersonal comparisons of utility," and thus a world freed from what is central to politics, i.e., ethical judgment and conflict regarding the just and relative distribution of utility. That the notion of a Pareto optimum is rife with conceptual problems and is utopian does not detract from its centrality as the implicit objective of liberal economics. And this emphasis of economics on absolute gains for all differs fun-damentally from the nature of political phenomena as studied by political scien-tists: viz., struggles for power as a goal itself or as a means to the achievement of other goals.

The essential fact of politics is that power is always relative; one state's gain in power is by necessity another's loss. Thus, even though two states may be gaining absolutely in wealth, in political terms it is the effect of these gains on relative power positions which is of primary importance. From this *political* perspective, therefore, the mercantilists are correct in emphasizing that in power terms, international relations is a zero-sum game.

In a brilliant analysis of international politics, the relativity of power and its profound implications were set forth by Jean-Jacques Rousseau:

> the state, being an artifical body is not limited in any way. . . . It can always increase; it always feels itself weak if there is another that is stronger. Its security and preservation demand that it make itself more powerful than its neighbors. It can increase, nourish and exercise its power only at their expense . . . while the inequality of man has natur-al limits that between societies can grow without cease, until one absorbs all the others. . . . Because the grandeur of the state is purely relative it is forced to compare itself with that of the others. . . . It is in vain that it wishes to keep itself to itself; it becomes small or great, weak or strong, according to whether its neighbor expands or contracts, becomes stronger or declines. . . .
>
> The chief thing I notice is a patent contradiction in the condition of the human race. . . . Between man and man we live in the condition of the civil state, subjected to laws; between people and people we enjoy natural liberty, which makes the situation worse. Living at the same time in the social order and in the state of nature, we suffer from the inconveniences of both without finding . . . security in either. . . . We see men united by artifical bonds, but united to destroy each other; and all the horrors of war take birth from the precautions they have taken in order to prevent them. . . . War is born of peace, or at least of the precautions which men have taken for the purpose of achieving durable peace.[25]

Because of the relativity of power, therefore, nation-states are engaged in a never-ending struggle to improve or preserve their relative power positions.

This rather stark formulation obviously draws too sharp a distinction between economics and politics. Certainly, for example, liberal economists may be interest-ed in questions of distribution; the distributive issue was, in fact, of central concern to Ricardo and other classical writers. However, when economists stop taking the system for granted and start asking questions about distribution, they have really ventured into what I regard as the essence of politics, for distribution is really a political issue. In a world in which power rests on wealth, changes in the relative distribution of wealth imply changes in the distribution of power and in the political system itself. This, in fact, is what is meant by saying that politics is about relative gains. Politics concerns the effects of groups to redistribute gains to their own advantage.

Similarly, to argue that politics is about relative gains is not to argue that it is a constant-sum game. On the contrary, man's power over nature and his fellow man has grown immensely in absolute terms over the past several centuries. It is certainly the case that eveyone's absolute capabilities can increase due to the development of new weaponry, the expansion of productive capabilities, or changes in the political system itself. Obviously such absolute increases in power are important politically. Who can deny, for example, that the advent of nuclear weapons has profoundly altered international politics? Obviously, too, states can negotiate disarmament and other levels of military capability.

Yet recognition of these facts does not alter the prime consideration that changes in the relative distribution of power are of fundamental significance politically. Though all may be gaining or declining in absolute capability, what will concern states principally are the effects of these absolute gains or losses on relative positions. How, for example, do changes in productive capacity or military weaponry affect the ability of one state to impose its will on another? It may very well be that in a particular situation absolute gains will not affect relative positions. But the efforts of groups to cause or prevent such shifts in the relative distribution of power constitute the critical issue of politics.

This formulation of the nature of politics obviously does not deny that nations may cooperate in order to advance their mutual interest. But even cooperative actions may have important consequences for the distribution of power in the system. For example, the Strategic Arms Limitation Talks (SALT) between the United States and the Soviet Union are obviously motivated by a common interest in preventing thermonuclear war. Other states will also benefit if the risk of war between the superpowers is reduced. Yet, SALT may also be seen as an attempt to stabilize the international distribution of power to the disadvantage of China and other third powers. In short, in terms of the system as a whole, political cooperation can have a profound effect on the relative distribution of power among nation-states.

The point may perhaps be clarified by distinguishing between two aspects of power. When one speaks of absolute gains in power, such as advances in economic capabilities or weapons development, one is referring principally to increases in physical or material capabilities. But while such capabilities are an important component of power, power, as we have seen, is more than physical capability. Power is also a psychological relationship: Who can influence whom to do what? From this perspective, what may be of most importance is how changes in capability affect this psychological relationship. Insofar as they do, they alter the relative distribution of power in the system.

In a world in which power rests increasingly on economic and industrial capabilities, one cannot really distinguish between wealth (resources, treasure, and industry) and power as national goals. In the short run there may be conflicts between the pursuit of power and the pursuit of wealth; in the long run the two pursuits are identical. Therefore, the position taken in this study is similar to Viner's interpretation of classical mercantilism:

What then is the correct interpretation of mercantilist doctrine and practice with respect to the roles of power and plenty as ends of national policy? I believe that practically all mercantilists, whatever the period, country, or status of the particular individual, would have subscribed to all of the following propositions: (1) wealth is an absolutely essential means to power, whether for security or for aggression; (2) power is essential or valuable as a means to the acquisition or retention of wealth; (3) wealth and power are each proper ultimate ends of national policy; (4) there is long-run harmony between these ends, although in particular circumstances it may be necessary for a time to make economic sacrifices in the interest of military security and therefore also of long-run prosperity.[26]

This interpretation of the role of the economic motive in international relations is substantially different from that of Marxism. In the Marxist framework of analysis, the economic factor is reduced to the profit motive, as it affects the behavior of individuals or firms. Accordingly, the foreign policies of capitalist states are determined by the desire of capitalists for profits. This is, in our view, far too narrow a conception of the economic aspect of international relations. Instead, in this study we label "economic" those sources of wealth upon which national power and domestic welfare are dependent.

Understood in these broader terms, the economic motive and economic activities are fundamental to the struggle for power among nation-states. The objects of contention in the struggles of the balance of power include the centers of economic power. As R. G. Hawtrey has expressed it, "the political motives at work can only be expressed in terms of the economic. Every conflict is one of power and power depends on resources."[27] In pursuit of wealth *and* power, therefore, nations (capitalist, socialist, or fascist) contend over the territorial division and exploitation of the globe.

Even at the level of peaceful economic intercourse, one cannot separate out the political element. Contrary to the attitude of liberalism, international economic relations are in reality political relations. The interdependence of national economies creates economic power, defined as the capacity of one state to damage another through the interruption of commercial and financial relations.[28] The attempts to create and to escape from such dependency relationships constitute an important aspect of international relations in the modern era.

The primary actors in the international system are nation-states in pursuit of what they define as their national interest. This is not to argue, however, that nation-states are the only actors, nor do I believe that the "national interest" is something akin to Rousseau's "general will"—the expression of an organic entity separable from its component parts. Except in the abstract models of political scientists, it has never been the case that the international system was composed solely of nation-states. In an exaggerated acknowledgment of the importance of non-state or transnational actors at an earlier time, John A. Hobson asked rhetorically whether "a great war could be undertaken by any European state, or a great state loan subscribed, if the House of Rothschild and its connexions set their face against it."[29] What has to be explained, however, are the economic and political circumstances that enable such transnational actors to play their semi-independent role in international affairs. The argument of this study is that the primary determinants of the role played by these non-state actors are the larger configurations of power among nation-states. What is determinant is the interplay of national interests.

As for the concept of "national interest," the national interest of a given nation-state is, of course, what its political and economic elite determines it to be. In part, as Marxists argue, this elite will define it in terms of its own group or class interests. But the national interest comprehends more than this. More general influences, such as cultural values and considerations relevant to the security of the state itself—geographical position, the evolution of military technology, and the international distribution of power—are of greater importance. There is a sense, then, in which the factors that determine the national interest are objective. A ruling elite that fails to take these factors into account does so at its peril. In short, then, there is a basis for considering the nation-state itself as an actor pursuing its own set of security, welfare, and status concerns in competition or cooperation with other nation-states.

Lastly, in a world of conflicting nation-states, how does one explain the existence of an interdependent international economy? Why does a liberal international economy—that is, an economy characterized by relatively free trade, currency convertibility, and freedom of capital movement—remain intact rather than fragment into autarkic national economies and regional or imperial groupings? In part, the answer is provided by liberalism: economic cooperation, interdependence, and an international division of labor enhance efficiency and the maximization of aggregate wealth. Nation-states are induced to enter the international system because of the promise of more rapid growth; greater benefits can be had than could be obtained by autarky or a fragmentation of the world economy. The historical record suggests, however, that the existence of mutual economic benefits is not always enough to induce nations to pay the costs of a market system or to forgo opportunities of advancing their own interests at the expense of others. There is always the danger that a nation may pursue certain short-range policies, such as the imposition of an optimum tariff, in order to maximize its own gains at the expense of the system as a whole.

For this reason, a liberal international economy requires a power to manage and stabilize the system. As Charles Kindleberger has convincingly shown, this governance role was performed by Great Britain throughout the nineteenth century and up to 1931, and by the United States after 1945.[30] The inability of Great Britain in 1929 to continue running the system and the unwillingness of the United States to assume this responsibility led to the collapse of the system in the "Great Depression." The result was the fragmentation of the world economy into rival economic blocs. Both dominant economic powers had failed to overcome the divisive forces of nationalism and regionalism.

The argument of this study is that the modern world economy has evolved through the emergence of great national economies that have successively become dominant. In the words of the distinguished French economist François Perroux, "the economic evolution of the world has resulted from a succession of dominant economies, each in turn taking the lead in international activity and influence. . . . Throughout the nineteenth century the British economy was the dominant economy in the world. From the [eighteen] seventies on, Germany was dominant in respect to certain other Continental countries and in certain specified fields. In the twentieth century, the United States economy has clearly been and still is the internationally dominant economy."[31]

An economic system, then, does not arise spontaneously owing to the operation of an invisible hand and in the absence of the exercise of power. Rather, every economic system rests on a particular political order; its nature cannot be understood aside from politics. This basic point was made some years ago by E. H. Carr when he wrote that "the science of economics presupposes a given political order, and cannot be profitably studied in isolation from politics."[32] Carr sought to convince his fellow Englishmen that an international economy based on free trade was not a natural and inevitable state of affairs but rather one that reflected the economic and political interests of Great Britain. The system based on free trade had come into existence through, and was maintained by, the exercise of British economic and military power. With the rise after 1880 of new industrial and military powers with contrasting economic interests—namely, Germany, Japan, and the United States—an international economy based on free trade and British power became less and less viable. Eventually this shift in the locus of industrial and military power led to the collapse of the system in World War I. Following the interwar period, a liberal international economy was revived through the exercise of power by the world's newly emergent dominant economy—the United States.

Accordingly, the regime of free investment and the preeminence of the multinational corporation in the contemporary world have reflected the economic and political interests of the United States. The multinational corporation has prospered because it has been dependent on the power of, and consistent with the political interests of, the United States. This is not to deny the analyses of economists who argue that the multinational corporation is a response to contemporary technological and economic developments. The argument is rather that these economic and technological factors have been able to exercise their profound effects because the United States—sometimes with the cooperation of other states and sometimes over their opposition—has created the necessary political framework. As former Secretary of the Treasury Henry Fowler stated several years ago, "it is . . . impossible to overestimate the extent to which the efforts and opportunities for American firms abroad depend upon the vast presence and influence and prestige that America holds in the world."[33]

By the mid-1970s, however, the international distribution of power and the world economy resting on it were far different from what they had been when Fowler's words were spoken. The rise of foreign economic competitors, America's growing dependence upon foreign sources of energy and other resources, and the expansion of Soviet military capabilities have greatly diminished America's presence and influence in the world. One must ask if, as a consequence, the reign of the American multinationals over international economic affairs will continue into the future.

In summary, although nation-states, as mercantilists suggest, do seek to control economic and technological forces and channel them to their own advantage, this is impossible over the long run. The spread of economic growth and industrialization cannot be prevented. In time the diffusion of industry and technology undermines the position of the dominant power. As both liberals and Marxists have emphasized, the evolution of economic relations profoundly influences the nature of the international political system. The relationship between economics and politics is a reciprocal one.

Although economic and accompanying political change may well be inevitable, it is not inevitable that the process of economic development and technological advance will produce an increasingly integrated world society. In the 1930s, Eugene Staley posed the issue.

> A conflict rages between technology and politics. Economics, so closely linked to both, has become the major battlefield. Stability and peace will reign in the world economy only when, somehow, the forces on the side of technology and the forces on the side of politics have once more become accommodated to each other.[34]

Staley believed, as do many present-day writers, that politics and technology must ultimately adjust to one another. But he differed with contemporary writers with regard to the inevitability with which politics would adjust to technology. Reflecting the intense economic nationalism of the period in which he wrote, Staley pointed out that the adjustment may very well be the other way around. As he reminds us, in his own time and in earlier periods economics has had to adjust to political realities: "In the 'Dark Ages' following the collapse of the Roman Empire, technology adjusted itself to politics. The magnificent Roman roads fell into disrepair, the baths and aqueducts and amphitheatres and villas into ruins. Society lapsed back to localism in production and distribution, forgot much of the learning and the technology and the governmental systems of earlier days."[35]

CONCLUSION

The purpose of this chapter has been to set forth the analytical framework that will be employed in this study. This framework is a statement of what I mean by "political economy." In its eclecticism it has drawn upon, while differing from, the three prevailing perspectives of political economy. It has incorporated their respective strengths and has attempted to overcome their weaknesses. In brief, political economy in this study means the reciprocal and dynamic interaction in international relations of the pursuit of wealth and the pursuit of power. In the short run, the distribution of power and the nature of the political system are major determinants of the framework within which wealth is produced and distributed. In the long run, however, shifts in economic efficiency and in the location of economic activity tend to undermine and transform the existing political system. This political transformation in turn gives rise to changes in economic relations that reflect the interests of the politically ascendant state in the system.

NOTES

1. Kari Levitt, "The Hinterland Economy," *Canadian Forum 50* (July–August 1970): p. 163.
2. George W. Ball, "The Promise of the Multinational Corporation," *Fortune,* June 1, 1967, p. 80.

3. Sidney Rolfe, "Updating Adam Smith," *Interplay* (November 1968): p. 15.
4. Charles Kindleberger, *Power and Money: The Economics of International Politics and the Politics of International Economics* (New York: Basic Books, 1970), p. 5.
5. Robert Keohane and Joseph Nye, "World Politics and the International Economic System," in C. Fred Bergsten, ed., *The Future of the International Economic Order: An Agenda for Research* (Lexington, Mass.: D.C. Heath, 1973), p. 116.
6. *Ibid.*
7. *Ibid.*, p. 117.
8. Paul Samuelson, *Economics: An Introductory Analysis* (New York: McGraw-Hill, 1967), p. 5.
9. Harold Lasswell and Abraham Kaplan, *Power and Society: A Framework for Political Inquiry* (New Haven, Conn.: Yale University Press, l950), p. 75.
10. Hans Morgenthau, *Politics Among Nations* (New York: Alfred A. Knopf), p. 26. For a more complex but essentially identical view, see Robert Dahl, *Modern Political Analysis* (Englewood Cliffs, N.J.: Prentice-Hall, 1963).
11. Kindleberger, *Power and Money*, p. 227.
12. For Johnson's critique of economic nationalism, see Harry Johnson, ed., *Economic Nationalism in Old and New States* (Chicago: University of Chicago Press, 1967).
13. Adam Smith, *The Wealth of Nations* (New York: Modern Library, 1937).
14. J. B. Condliffe, *The Commerce of Nations* (New York: W. W. Norton, 1950), p. 136.
15. Amitai Etzioni, "The Dialectics of Supernational Unification" in *International Political Communities* (New York: Doubleday, 1966), p. 147.
16. The relevant sections appear in Ernst Wangerman, ed., *The Role of Force in History: A Study of Bismarck's Policy of Blood and Iron*, trans. Jack Cohen (New York: International Publishers, 1968).
17. *Ibid.*, p. 12.
18. *Ibid.*, p. 13.
19. *Ibid.*, p. 14.
20. Gustav Stopler, *The German Economy* (New York: Harcourt, Brace and World, 1967), p. 11.
21. Jacob Viner, *The Customs Union Issue*, Studies in the Administration of International Law and Organization, no. 10 (New York: Carnegie Endowment for International Peace, 1950), pp. 98–99.
22. *Ibid.*, p. 101.
23. Richard Cooper, "Eurodollars, Reserve Dollars, and Asymmetrics in the International Monetary System," *Journal of International Economics* 2 (September 1972): pp. 325–44.
24. Oskar Morgenstern, "Thirteen Critical Points in Contemporary Economic Theory: An Interpretation," *Journal of Economic Literature* 10 (December 1972): p. 1169.
25. Quoted in F. H. Hinsley, *Power and the Pursuit of Peace* (Cambridge: Cambridge University Press, 1963), pp. 50–51.
26. Jacob Viner, "Power versus Plenty as Objectives of Foreign Policy in the Seventeenth and Eighteenth Centuries," in *The Long View and the Short: Studies in Economic Theory and Practice* (Glencoe, Ill.; The Free Press, 1958), p. 286.
27. R. G. Hawtrey, *Economic Aspects of Sovereignty* (London: Longmans, Green, 1952), p. 120
28. Albert Hirshman, *National Power and the Structure of Foreign Trade* (Berkeley: University of California Press, 1969), p. 16.
29. John A. Hobson, *Imperialism: A Study* (1902; 3rd ed., rev., London: G. Allen and Unwin, 1938), p. 57.

30. Charles Kindleberger, *The World in Depression 1929–1939* (Berkeley: University of California Press, 1973), p. 293.
31. François Perroux, "The Domination Effect and Modern Economic Theory," in *Power in Economics*, ed. K. W. Rothschild (London: Penguin, 1971), p. 67.
32. E. H. Carr, *The Twenty Years' Crisis, 1919–1939* (New York: Macmillan, 1951), p. 117.
33. Quoted in Kari Levitt, *Silent Surrender: The American Economic Empire in Canada* (New York: Liveright Press, 1970), p. 100.
34. Eugene Staley, *World Economy in Transition: Technology vs. Politics, Laissez Faire vs. Planning, Power vs. Welfare* (New York: Council on Foreign Relations [under the auspices of the American Coordinating Committee for International Studies], 1939), pp. 51–52.
35. *Ibid.*, p. 52.

Hegemony in the World Political Economy

Robert O. Keohane

It is common today for troubled supporters of liberal capitalism to look back with nostalgia on British preponderance in the nineteenth century and American dominance after World War II. Those eras are imagined to be simpler ones in which a single power, possessing superiority of economic and military resources, implemented a plan for international order based on its interests and its vision of the world. As Robert Gilpin has expressed it, "the *Pax Britannica* and *Pax Americana*, like the *Pax Romana,* ensured an international system of relative peace and security. Great Britain and the United States created and enforced the rules of a liberal international economic order."

Underlying this statement is one of the two central propositions of the theory of hegemonic stability:[1] that order in world politics is typically created by a single dominant power. Since regimes constitute elements of an international order, this implies that the formation of international regimes normally depends on hegemony. The other major tenet of the theory of hegemonic stability is that the maintenance of order requires continued hegemony. As Charles P. Kindleberger has said, "for the world economy to be stabilized, there has to be a stabilizer, one stabilizer".[2] This implies that cooperation, . . . [the] mutual adjustment of state policies to one another, also depends on the perpetuation of hegemony.

I discuss hegemony before elaborating my definitions of cooperation and regimes because my emphasis on how international institutions such as regimes facilitate cooperation only makes sense if cooperation and discord are not determined simply by interests and power. In this chapter I argue that a deterministic version of the theory of hegemonic stability, relying only on the realist concepts of interests and power, is indeed incorrect. There is some validity in a modest version of the first proposition of the theory of hegemonic stability—that hegemony can facilitate a certain type of cooperation—but there is little reason to believe that hegemony is either a necessary or a sufficient condition for the emergence of cooperative relationships. Furthermore, and even more important for the argument presented here, the second major proposition of the theory is erroneous: Cooperation does not necessarily require the existence of a hegemonic leader after international regimes have been established. Post-hegemonic cooperation is also possible. . . .

The task of the present chapter is to explore in a preliminary way the value and limitations of the concept of hegemony for the study of cooperation. The first section analyzes the claims of the theory of hegemonic stability; the second section briefly addresses the relationship between military power and hegemony in the world political economy; and the final section seeks to enrich our understanding of the concept by considering Marxian insights. Many Marxian interpretations of hegemony turn out to bear an uncanny resemblance to Realist ideas, using different language to make similar points. Antonio Gramsci's conception of ideological hegemony, however, does provide an insightful supplement to purely materialist arguments, whether Realist or Marxist.

EVALUATING THE THEORY OF HEGEMONIC STABILITY

The theory of hegemonic stability, as applied to the world political economy, defines hegemony as preponderance of material resources. Four sets of resources are especially important. Hegemonic powers must have control over raw materials, control over sources of capital, control over markets, and competitive advantages in the production of highly valued goods.

The importance of controlling sources of raw materials has provided a traditional justification for territorial expansion and imperialism, as well as for the extension of informal influence. . . . [S]hifts in the locus of control over oil affected the power of states and the evolution of international regimes. Guaranteed access to capital, though less obvious as a source of power, may be equally important. Countries with well-functioning capital markets can borrow cheaply and may be able to provide credit to friends or even deny it to adversaries. Holland derived political and economic power from the quality of its capital markets in the seventeenth century; Britain did so in the eighteenth and nineteenth centuries; and the United States has similarly benefited during the last fifty years.

Potential power may also be derived from the size of one's market for imports. The threat to cut off a particular state's access to one's own market, while allowing other countries continued access, is a "potent and historically relevant weapon of economic 'power'."[3] Conversely, the offer to open up one's own huge market to other exporters, in return for concessions or deference, can be an effective means of influence. The bigger one's own market, and the greater the government's discretion in opening it up or closing it off, the greater one's potential economic power.

The final dimension of economic preponderance is competitive superiority in the production of goods. Immanuel Wallerstein has defined hegemony in economic terms as "a situation wherein the products of a given core state are produced so efficiently that they are by and large competitive even in other core states, and therefore the given core state will be the primary beneficiary of a maximally free world market."[4] As a definition of economic preponderance this is interesting but poorly worked out, since under conditions of overall balance of payments equilibrium each unit—even the poorest and least developed—will have some comparative advantage. The fact that in 1960 the United States had a trade deficit in textiles and apparel and in basic manufactured goods (established products not, on the whole, involving the use of complex or new technology) did not indicate that it had lost predominant economic status.[5] Indeed, one should expect the economically preponderant state to import products that are labor-intensive or that are produced with well-known production techniques. Competitive advantage does not mean that the leading economy exports *everything*, but that it produces and exports the most profitable products and those that will provide the basis for producing even more advanced goods and services in the future. In general, this ability will be based on the technological superiority of the leading country, although it may also rest on its political control over valuable resources yielding significant rents.

To be considered hegemonic in the world political economy, therefore, a country must have access to crucial raw materials, control major sources of capital, maintain a large market for imports, and hold comparative advantages in goods with high value added, yielding relatively high wages and profits. It must also be stronger, on these dimensions taken as a whole, than any other country. The theory of hegemonic stability predicts that the more one such power dominates the world political economy, the more cooperative will interstate relations be. This is a parsimonious theory that relies on . . . a "basic force model," in which outcomes reflect the tangible capabilities of actors.

Yet, like many such basic force models, this crude theory of hegemonic stability makes imperfect predictions. In the twentieth century it correctly anticipates the relative cooperativeness of the twenty years after World War II. It is at least partially mistaken, however, about trends of cooperation when hegemony erodes. Between 1900 and 1913 a decline in British power coincided with a decrease rather than an increase in conflict over commercial issues. . . . [R]ecent changes in international regimes can only partially be attributed to a decline in American power. How to interpret the prevalence of discord in the interwar years is difficult, since it is not clear whether any country was hegemonic in material terms during those two decades. The United States, though considerably ahead in productivity, did not replace Britain as the most important financial center and lagged behind in volume of trade. Although American domestic oil production was more than sufficient for domestic needs during these years, Britain still controlled the bulk of major Middle Eastern oil fields. Nevertheless, what prevented American leadership of a cooperative world political economy in these years was less lack of economic resources than an absence of political willingness to make and enforce rules for the system. Britain, despite its efforts, was too weak to do so effectively. The crucial factor in producing discord lay in American politics, not in the material factors to which the theory points.

Unlike the crude basic force model, a refined version of hegemonic stability theory does not assert an automatic link between power and leadership. Hegemony is defined as a situation in which "one state is powerful enough to maintain the essential rules governing interstate relations, and willing to do so."[6] This interpretive framework retains an emphasis on power but looks more seriously than the crude power theory at the internal characteristics of the strong state. It does not assume that strength automatically creates incentives to project one's power abroad. Domestic attitudes, political structures, and decision making processes are also important.

This argument's reliance on state decisions as well as power capabilities puts it into the category of what March calls "force activation models." Decisions to exercise leadership are necessary to "activate" the posited relationship between power capabilities and outcomes. Force activation models are essentially *post hoc* rather than *a priori*, since one can always "save" such a theory after the fact by thinking of reasons why an actor would not have wanted to use all of its available potential power. In effect, this modification of the theory declares that states with preponderant resources will be hegemonic except when they decide not to commit the necessary effort to the tasks of leadership, yet it does not tell us what will determine the latter decision. As a causal theory this is not very helpful, since whether a given configuration of power will lead the potential hegemon to maintain a set of rules remains indeterminate unless we know a great deal about its domestic politics.

Only the cruder theory generates predictions. When I refer without qualification to the theory of hegemonic stability, therefore, I will be referring to this basic force model. We have seen that the most striking contention of this theory—that hegemony is both a necessary and a sufficient condition for cooperation—is not strongly supported by the experience of this century. Taking a longer period of about 150 years, the record remains ambiguous. International economic relations were relatively cooperative both in the era of British hegemony during the mid-to-late nineteenth century and in the two decades of American dominance after World War II. But only in the second of these periods was there a trend toward the predicted disruption of established rules and increased discord. And a closer examination of the British experience casts doubt on the causal role of British hegemony in producing cooperation in the nineteenth century.

Both Britain in the nineteenth century and the United States in the twentieth met the material prerequisites for hegemony better than any other states since the Industrial Revolution. In 1880 Britain was the financial center of the world, and it controlled extensive raw materials, both in its formal empire and through investments in areas not part of the Imperial domain. It had the highest per capita income in the world and approximately double the share of world trade and investment of its nearest competitor, France. Only in the aggregate size of its economy had it already fallen behind the United States.[7] Britain's share of world trade gradually declined during the next sixty years, but in 1938 it was still the world's largest trader, with 14 percent of the world total. In the nineteenth century Britain's relative labor productivity was the highest in the world, although it declined rather precipitously thereafter. As Table 1 shows, Britain in the late nineteenth century and the United States after World War II were roughly comparable in their proportions of world trade, although until 1970 or so the United States had maintained much higher levels of relative productivity than Britain had done three-quarters of a century earlier.

Yet, despite Britain's material strength, it did not always enforce its preferred rules. Britain certainly did maintain freedom of the seas. But it did not induce major continental powers, after the 1870s, to retain liberal trade policies. A recent investigation of the subject has concluded that British efforts to make and enforce rules were less extensive and less successful than hegemonic stability theory would lead us to believe they were.[8]

Attempts by the United States after World War II to make and enforce rules for the world political economy were much more effective than Britain's had ever been. America after 1945 did not merely replicate earlier British experience; on the contrary, the differences between Britain's "hegemony" in the nineteenth century and America's after World War II were profound. As we have seen, Britain had never been as superior in productivity to the rest of the world as the United States was after 1945. Nor was the United States ever as dependent on foreign trade and investment as Britain. Equally important, America's economic partners—over whom its hegemony was exercised, since America's ability to make the rules hardly extended to the socialist camp—were also its military allies; but Britain's chief trading partners had been its major military and political rivals. In addition, one reason for Britain's relative ineffectiveness in maintaining a free trade regime is that it had never made extensive use of the principle of reciprocity in trade.[9] It thus

TABLE 1   MATERIAL RESOURCES OF BRITAIN AND THE UNITED STATES AS HEGEMONS: PROPORTIONS OF WORLD TRADE AND RELATIVE LABOR PRODUCTIVITY

	Proportion of world trade	Relative labor productivity*
Britain, 1870	24.0	1.63
Britain, 1890	18.5	1.45
Britain, 1913	14.1	1.15
Britain, 1938	14.0	.92
United States, 1950	18.4	2.77
United States, 1960	15.3	2.28
United States, 1970	14.4	1.72
United States, 1977	13.4	1.45

*As compared with the average rate of productivity in the other members of the world economy
Source: David A. Lake, "International Economic Structures and American Foreign Economic Policy, 1887–1934," World Politics, vol. 35, no. 4 (July 1983), table 1 (p. 525) and table 3 (p. 541).

had sacrificed potential leverage over other countries that preferred to retain their own restrictions while Britain practiced free trade. The policies of these states might well have been altered had they been confronted with a choice between a closed British market for their exports on the one hand and mutual lowering of barriers on the other. Finally, Britain had an empire to which it could retreat, by selling less advanced goods to its colonies rather than competing in more open markets. American hegemony, rather than being one more instance of a general phenomenon, was essentially unique in the scope and efficacy of the instruments at the disposal of a hegemonic state and in the degree of success attained.

That the theory of hegemonic stability is supported by only one or at most two cases casts doubt on its general validity. Even major proponents of the theory refrain from making such claims. In an article published in 1981, Kindleberger seemed to entertain the possibility that two or more countries might "take on the task of providing leadership together, thus adding to legitimacy, sharing the burdens, and reducing the danger that leadership is regarded cynically as a cloak for domination and exploitation."[10] In *War and Change in World Politics,* Gilpin promulgated what appeared to be a highly deterministic conception of hegemonic cycles: "the conclusion of one hegemonic war is the beginning of another cycle of growth, expansion, and eventual decline."[11] Yet he denied that his view was deterministic, and he asserted that "states can learn to be more enlightened in their definitions of their interests and can learn to be more cooperative in their behavior."[12] Despite the erosion of hegemony, "there are reasons for believing that the present disequilibrium in the international system can be resolved without resort to hegemonic war."[13]

The empirical evidence for the general validity of hegemonic stability theory is weak, and even its chief adherents have doubts about it. In addition, the logical underpinnings of the theory are suspect. Kindleberger's strong claim for the necessity of a single leader rested on the theory of collective goods. He argued that "the danger we face is not too much power in the international economy, but too little, not an excess of domination, but a superfluity of would-be free riders, unwilling to mind the store, and waiting for a storekeeper to appear."[14] . . . some of the "goods" produced by hegemonic leadership are not genuinely collective in character, although the implications of this fact are not necessarily as damaging to the theory as might be imagined at first. More critical is the fact that in international economic systems a few actors typically control a preponderance of resources. This point is especially telling, since the theory of collective goods does not properly imply that cooperation among a few countries should be impossible. Indeed, one of the original purposes of Olson's use of the theory was to show that in systems with only a few participants these actors "can provide themselves with collective goods without relying on any positive inducements apart from the good itself."[15] Logically, hegemony should not be a necessary condition for the emergence of cooperation in an oligopolistic system.

The theory of hegemonic stability is thus suggestive but by no means definitive. Concentrated power alone is not sufficient to create a stable international economic order in which cooperation flourishes, and the argument that hegemony is necessary for cooperation is both theoretically and empirically weak. If hegemony is redefined as the ability and willingness of a single state to make and enforce rules, furthermore, the claim that hegemony is sufficient for cooperation becomes virtually tautological.

The crude theory of hegemonic stability establishes a useful, if somewhat simplistic, starting-point for an analysis of changes in international cooperation and discord. Its refined version raises a looser but suggestive set of interpretive questions for the analysis of some eras in the history of the international political economy. Such an interpretive framework does not constitute an explanatory systemic theory, but it can help us think of hegemony in another way—less as a concept that helps to explain outcomes in terms of power than as a way of describing an international system in which leadership is exercised by a single state. Rather than being a component of a scientific generalization—that power is a necessary or sufficient condition for cooperation—the concept of hegemony, defined in terms of willingness as well as ability to lead, helps us think about the incentives facing the potential hegemon. Under what conditions, domestic and international, will such a country decide to invest in the construction of rules and institutions?

Concern for the incentives facing the hegemon should also alert us to the frequently neglected incentives facing other countries in the system. What calculus do they confront in considering whether to challenge or defer to a would-be leader? Thinking about the calculations of secondary powers raises the question of deference. Theories of hegemony should seek not only to analyze dominant powers' decisions to engage in rule-making and rule-enforcement, but also to explore why secondary states defer to the leadership of the hegemon. That is, they need to account for the legitimacy of hegemonic regimes and for the coexistence of cooperation, as defined in the next chapter, with hegemony. We will see later that Gramsci's notion of "ideological hegemony" provides some valuable clues helping us understand how cooperation and hegemony fit together.

MILITARY POWER AND HEGEMONY IN THE WORLD POLITICAL ECONOMY

Before taking up these themes, we need to clarify the relationship between this analysis of hegemony in the world political economy and the question of military power. A hegemonic state must possess enough military power to be able to protect the international political economy that it dominates from incursions by hostile adversaries. This is essential because economic issues, if they are crucial enough to basic national values, may become military-security issues as well. For instance, Japan attacked the United States in 1941 partly in response to the freezing of Japanese assets in the United States, which denied Japan "access to all the vitally needed supplies outside her own control, in particular her most crucial need, oil."[16] During and after World War II the United States used its military power to assure itself access to the petroleum of the Middle East; and at the end of 1974 Secretary of State Henry A. Kissinger warned that the United States might resort to military action if oil-exporting countries threatened "some actual strangulation of the industrialized world."[17]

Yet the hegemonic power need not be militarily dominant worldwide. Neither British nor American power ever extended so far. Britain was challenged militarily during the nineteenth century by France, Germany, and especially Russia; even at the height of its power after World War II the United States confronted a recalcitrant Soviet adversary and fought a war against China. The military conditions for economic hegemony are met if the economically preponderant country has sufficient military capabilities to prevent incursions by others that would deny it access to major areas of its economic activity.

The sources of hegemony therefore include sufficient military power to deter or rebuff attempts to capture and close off important areas of the world political economy. But in the contemporary world, at any rate, it is difficult for a hegemon to use military power directly to attain its economic policy objectives with its military partners and allies. Allies cannot be threatened with force without beginning to question the alliance; nor are threats to cease defending them unless they conform to the hegemon's economic rules very credible except in extraordinary circumstances. Many of the relationships within the hegemonic international political economy dominated by the United States after World War II approximated more closely the ideal type of "complex interdependence"—with multiple issues, multiple channels of contact among societies, and inefficacy of military force for most policy objectives—than the converse ideal type of realist theory.[18]

This does not mean that military-force has become useless. It has certainly played an indirect role even in U.S. relations with its closest allies, since Germany and Japan could hardly ignore the fact that American military power shielded them from Soviet pressure. It has played a more overt role in the Middle East, where American military power has occasionally been directly employed and has always cast a shadow and where U.S. military aid has been conspicuous. Yet changes in relations of military power have not been the major factors affecting patterns of cooperation and discord among the advanced industrialized countries since the end of World War II. Only in the case of Middle Eastern oil have they been highly significant as forces contributing to changes in international economic regimes, and even in that case . . . shifts in economic interdependence, and therefore in economic power, were more important. Throughout the period between 1945 and 1983 the United States remained a far stronger military power than any of its allies and the only country capable of defending them from the Soviet Union or of intervening effectively against serious opposition in areas such as the Middle East. . . .

Some readers may wish to criticize this account by arguing that military power has been more important than claimed here. By considering military power only as a background condition for postwar American hegemony rather than as a variable, I invite such a debate. Any such critique, however, should keep in mind what I am trying to explain [here] . . . not the sources of hegemony (in domestic institutions, basic resources, and technological advances any more than in military power), but rather the effects of changes in hegemony on cooperation among the advanced industrialized countries. I seek to account for the impact of American dominance on the creation of international economic regimes and the effects of an erosion of that preponderant position on those regimes. Only if *these* problems—not other questions that might be interesting—could be understood better by exploring more deeply the impact of changes in relations of military power would this hypothetical critique be damaging to my argument.

MARXIAN NOTIONS OF HEGEMONY

For Marxists, the fundamental forces affecting the world political economy are those of class struggle and uneven development. International history is dynamic and dialectical rather than cyclical. The maneuvers of states reflect the stages of capitalist development and the contradictions of that development. For a Marxist, it is futile to discuss hegemony, or the operation of international institutions, without understanding that they operate, in the contemporary world system, within a capitalist context shaped by the evolutionary patterns and functional requirements of capitalism. Determinists may call these requirements laws. Historicists may see the patterns as providing some clues into a rather open-ended process that is nevertheless affected profoundly by what has gone before: people making their own history, but not just as they please.

Any genuinely Marxian theory of world politics begins with an analysis of capitalism. According to Marxist doctrine, no smooth and progressive development of productive forces within the confines of capitalist relations of production can persist for long. Contradictions are bound to appear. It is likely that they will take the form of tendencies toward stagnation and decline in the rate of profit, but they may also be reflected in crises of legitimacy for the capitalist state, even in the absence of economic crises.[19] Any "crisis of hegemony" will necessarily be at the same time—and more fundamentally—a crisis of capitalism.

For Marxists, theories of hegemony are necessarily partial, since they do not explain changes in the contradictions facing capitalism. Nevertheless, Marxists have often used the concept of hegemony, implicitly defined simply as dominance, as a way of analyzing the surface manifestations of world politics under capitalism for Marxists as well as mercantilists, wealth and power are complementary; each depends on the other . . . the analyses of the Marxist Fred Block and the Realist Robert Gilpin are quite similar: both emphasize the role of U.S. hegemony in creating order after the Second World War and the disturbing effects of the erosion of American power.

Immanuel Wallerstein's work also illustrates this point. He is at pains to stress that modern world history should be seen as the history of capitalism as a world system. Apart from "relatively minor accidents" resulting from geography, peculiarities of history, or luck, "it is the operations of the world-market forces which accentuate the differences, institutionalize them, and make them impossible to surmount over the long run."[20] Nevertheless, when considering particular epochs, Wallerstein emphasizes hegemony and the role of military force. Dutch economic hegemony in the seventeenth century was destroyed not by the operation of the world-market system or contradictions of capitalism, but by the force of British and French arms.[21]

The Marxian adoption of mercantilist categories raises analytical ambiguities having to do with the relationship between capitalism and the state. Marxists who adopt this approach have difficulty maintaining a class focus, since their unit of analysis shifts to the country, rather than the class, for purposes of explaining international events. This is a problem for both Block and Wallerstein, as it often appears that their embrace of state-centered analysis has relegated the concept of class to the shadowy background of political economy. The puzzle of the relationship between the state and capitalism is also reflected in the old debate between Lenin and Kautsky about "ultra-imperialism."[22] Lenin claimed that contradictions among the capitalist powers were fundamental and could not be resolved, against Kautsky's view that capitalism could go through a phase in which capitalist states could maintain unity for a considerable period of time.

The successful operation of American hegemony for over a quarter-century after the end of World War II supports Kautsky's forecast that ultra-imperialism could be stable and contradicts Lenin's thesis that capitalism made inter-imperialist war inevitable. It does not, however, resolve the issue of whether ultra-imperialism could be maintained in the absence of hegemony. An analysis of the contemporary situation in marxian terminology would hold that one form of ultra-imperialism—American hegemony—is now breaking down, leading to increased disorder, and that the issue at present is "whether all this will ultimately result in a new capitalist world order, in a revolutionary reconstitution of world society, or in the common ruin of the contending classes and nations."[23] The issue from a Marxian standpoint is whether ultra-imperialism could be revived by new efforts at inter-capitalist collaboration or, on the contrary, whether fundamental contradictions in capitalism or in the coexistence of capitalism with the state system prevent any such recovery.

The key question of this book—how international cooperation can be maintained among the advanced capitalist states in the absence of American hegemony—poses essentially the same problem. The view taken here is similar to that of Kautsky and his followers, although the terminology is different. My contention is that the common interests of the leading capitalist states, bolstered by the effects of existing international regimes (mostly created during a period of American hegemony), are strong enough to make sustained cooperation possible, though not inevitable. One need not go so far as . . . the "internationalization of capital" to understand the strong interests that capitalists have in maintaining some cooperation in the midst of rivalry. Uneven development in the context of a state system maintains rivalry and ensures that cooperation will be incomplete and fragile . . . but it does not imply that the struggle must become violent or that compromises that benefit all sides are impossible.

Despite the similarities between my concerns and those of many Marxists, I do not adopt their categories in this study. Marxian explications of the "laws of capitalism" are not sufficiently well established that they can be relied upon for inferences about relations among states in the world political economy or for the analysis of future international cooperation. Insofar as there are fundamental contradictions in capitalism, they will surely have great impact on future international cooperation; but the existence and nature of these contradictions seem too murky to justify incorporating them into my analytical framework.

As this discussion indicates, Marxian insights into international hegemony derive in part from combining Realist conceptions of hegemony as dominance with arguments about the contradictions of capitalism. But this is not the only Marxian contribution to the debate. In the thought of Antonio Gramsci and his followers, hegemony is distinguished from sheer dominance. As Robert W. Cox has expressed it:

> Antonio Gramsci used the concept of hegemony to express a unity between objective material forces and ethico-political ideas—in Marxian terms, a unity of structure and superstructure—in which power based on dominance over production is rationalized through an ideology incorporating compromise or consensus between dominant and subordinate groups. A hegemonial structure of world order is one in which power takes a primarily consensual form, as distinguished from a non-hegemonic order in which there are manifestly rival powers and no power has been able to establish the legitimacy of its dominance.[24]

The value of this conception of hegemony is that it helps us understand the willingness of the partners of a hegemon to defer to hegemonial leadership. Hegemons require deference to enable them to construct a structure of world capitalist order. It is too expensive, and perhaps self-defeating, to achieve this by force; after all, the key distinction between hegemony and imperialism is that a hegemon, unlike an empire, does not dominate societies through a cumbersome political superstructure, but rather supervises the relationships between politically independent societies through a combination of hierarchies of control and the operation of markets.[25] Hegemony rests on the subjective awareness by elites in secondary states that they are benefiting, as well as on the willingness of the hegemon itself to sacrifice tangible short-term benefits for intangible long-term gains.

Valuable as the conception of ideological hegemony is in helping us understand deference, it should be used with some caution. First, we should not assume that leaders of secondary states are necessarily the victims of "false consciousness" when they accept the hegemonic ideology, or that they constitute a small, parasitical elite that betrays the interests of the nation to its own selfish ends. It is useful to remind ourselves, as Robert Gilpin has, that during both the *Pax Britannica* and the *Pax Americana* countries other than the hegemon prospered, and that indeed many of them grew faster than the hegemon itself.[26] Under some conditions—not necessarily all—it may be not only in the self-interest of peripheral elites, but conducive to the economic growth of their countries, for them to defer to the hegemon.[27]

We may also be permitted to doubt that ideological hegemony is as enduring internationally as it is domestically. The powerful ideology of nationalism is not available for the hegemon, outside of its own country, but rather for its enemies. Opponents of hegemony can often make nationalism the weapon of the weak and may also seek to invent cosmopolitan ideologies that delegitimize hegemony, such as the current ideology of a New International Economic Order, instead of going along with legitimating ones. Thus the potential for challenges to hegemonic ideology always exists.

CONCLUSIONS

Claims for the general validity of the theory of hegemonic stability are often exaggerated. The dominance of a single great power may contribute to order in world politics, in particular circumstances, but it is not a sufficient condition and there is little reason to believe that it is necessary. But Realist and Marxian arguments about hegemony both generate some important insights.

Hegemony is related in complex ways to cooperation and to institutions such as international regimes. Successful hegemonic leadership itself depends on a certain form of asymmetrical cooperation. The hegemon plays a distinctive role, providing its partners with leadership in return for deference; but, unlike an imperial power, it cannot make and enforce rules without a certain degree of consent from other sovereign states. As the interwar experience illustrates, material predominance alone does not guarantee either stability or effective leadership. Indeed, the hegemon may have to invest resources in institutions in order to ensure that its preferred rules will guide the behavior of other countries.

Cooperation may be fostered by hegemony, and hegemons require cooperation to make and enforce rules. Hegemony and cooperation are not alternatives; on the contrary, they are often found in symbiotic relationships with one another. To analyze the relationships between hegemony and cooperation, we need a conception of cooperation that is somewhat tart rather than syrupy-sweet. It must take into account the facts that coercion is always possible in world politics and that conflicts of interest never vanish even when there are important shared interests. . . . [C]ooperation should be defined not as the absence of conflict—which is always at least a potentially important element of international relations—but as a process that involves the use of discord to stimulate mutual adjustment.

NOTES

1. Robert O. Keohane, "The Theory of Hegemonic Stability and Changes in International Economic Regimes, 1967–1977," in Ole Holsti et al., *Change in the International System* (Boulder, Colo.: Westview Press, 1980), pp. 131–162.
2. Charles P. Kindleberger, *The World in Depression, 1929–1939* (Berkeley: University of California Press, 1973), p. 305.
3. Timothy J McKeown, "Hegemonic Stability Theory and Nineteenth Century Tariff Levels in Europe," *International Organization*, vol. 37, no. 1 (Winter 1980), p. 78.
4. Immanuel Wallerstein, *The Modern World-System II: Mercantilism and the Consolidation of the European World-Economy. 1600–1750* (New York: Academic Press, 1980), p. 38.
5. Stephen D. Krasner, "United States Commercial and Monetary Policy: Unravelling the Paradox of External Strength and Internal Weakness," in Peter J. Katzenstein, ed., *Between Power and Plenty: Foreign Economic Policies of Advanced Industrial States* (Madison: University of Wisconsin Press, 1978), pp. 68–69.
6. Robert O. Keohane and Joseph S. Nye, *Power and Interdependence: World Politics in Transition* (Boston: Little, Brown), p. 44.

7. Stephen D. Krasner, "State Power and the Structure of International Trade," *World Politics,* vol. 28, no. 3 (April 1976), p. 333.

8. McKeown, p. 88.

9. *Ibid.*

10. Charles P. Kindleberger, "Dominance and Leadership in the International Economy," *International Studies Quarterly,* vol. 25, no. 3 (June 1981), p. 252.

11. Robert Gilpin, *War and Change in World Politics* (Cambridge: Cambridge University Press, 1981), p. 210.

12. *Ibid.,* p. 227.

13. *Ibid.,* p. 234.

14. *Ibid.,* p. 253.

15. Mancur Olson, quoted in McKeown, p. 79.

16. Paul Schroeder, *The Axis Alliance and Japanese-American Relations* (Ithaca, N.Y.: Cornell University Press, 1958), p. 53;

17. Seyom Brown, *The Faces of Power: Constancy and Change in United States Foreign Policy from Truman to Reagan* (New York: Columbia University Press, 1983), p. 428.

18. Keohane and Nye, chap. 2.

19. Jurgen Haberman, *Legitimation Crisis* (London: Heinemann, 1976).

20. Immanuel Wallerstein, *The Capitalist World Economy* (Cambridge: Cambridge University Press, 1979), p. 21.

21. Wallerstein, *The Modern World-System II,* pp. 38–39.

22. V. I. Lenin, *Imperialism: The Highest Stage of Capitalism* (New York: International Publishers, 1939), pp. 93–94.

23. Giovanni Arrighi, "A Crisis of Hegemony," in Samir Amin, Giovanni Arrighi, Andre Gunder Frank, and Immanuel Wallerstein, *Dynamics of Global Crisis* (New York: Monthly Review Press, 1982), p. 108.

24. Robert W. Cox, "Social Forces, States, and World Orders: Beyond International Relations Theory," *Journal of International Studies, Millennium,* vol. 10, no. 2 (Summer 1981), p. 153., note 27.

25. Immanuel Wallerstein, *The Modern World System: Capitalist Agriculture and the Origins of the European World-Economy in the Sixteenth Century* (New York: Academic Press, 1974), pp. 15–17.

26. Robert Gilpin, pp. 175–185.

27. This is not to say that hegemony in general benefits small or weak countries. There certainly is no assurance that this will be the case. Hegemons may prevent middle-sized states from exploiting small ones and may construct a structure of order conducive to world economic growth; but they may also exploit smaller states economically or distort their patterns of autonomous development through economic, political, or military intervention. The issue of whether hegemony helps poor countries cannot be answered unconditionally, because too many other factors intervene. Until a more complex and sophisticated theory of the relationships among hegemony, other factors, and welfare is developed, it remains an empirically open question.

Power vs. Wealth in North-South Economic Relations

Stephen D. Krasner

What do Third World countries want? More wealth. How can they get it? By adopting more economically rational policies. What should the North do? Facilitate these policies. How should the North approach global negotiations? With cautious optimism. What is the long-term prognosis for North-South relations? Hopeful, at least if economic development occurs. This is the common wisdom about relations between industrialized and developing areas in the United States and in much of the rest of the North. Within this fold there are intense debates among adherents of conventional liberal, basic human needs, and interdependence viewpoints. But the emphasis on economics at the expense of politics, on material well-being as opposed to power and control, pervades all of these orientations.

[Here], I set forth an alternative perspective. I assume that Third World states, like all states in the international system, are concerned about vulnerability and threat; and I note that national political regimes in almost all Third World countries are profoundly weak both internationally and domestically. This . . . offers a very different set of answers to the questions posed in the preceding paragraph. Third World states want power and control as much as wealth. One strategy for achieving this objective is to change the rules of the game in various international issue areas. In general, these efforts will be incompatible with long-term Northern interests. Relations between industrialized and developing areas are bound to be conflictual because most Southern countries cannot hope to cope with their international vulnerability except by challenging principles, norms, and rules preferred by industrialized countries.

Political weakness and vulnerability are fundamental sources of Third World behavior. This weakness is a product of both external and internal factors. Externally, the national power capabilities of most Third World states are extremely limited. The national economic and military resources at the disposal of their leaders are unlikely to alter the behavior of Northern actors or the nature of international regimes. Southern states are subject to external pressures that they cannot influence through unilateral action. The international weakness of almost all less developed countries (LDCs) is compounded by the internal underdevelopment of their political and social systems. The social structures of most LDCs are rigid, and their central political institutions lack the power to make societal adjustments that could cushion external shocks. They are exposed to vacillations of an international system from which they cannot extricate themselves but over which they have only limited control.[1] The gap between Northern and Southern capabilities is already so great that even if the countries of the South grew very quickly and those of the North stagnated (an unlikely pair of assumptions in any event), only a handful of developing countries would significantly close the power gap within the next one hundred years. The physical conditions of individuals in developing areas may improve dramatically without altering the political vulnerabilities that confront their political leaders.

Third World states have adopted a range of strategies to cope with their poverty and vulnerability. Strategies directed primarily toward alleviating vulnerability are most frequently played out in international forums concerned with the establishment on maintenance of international regimes. Regimes are principles, norms, rules, and decision-making procedures around which actor expectations converge. Principles are a coherent set of theoretical statements about how the world works. Norms specify general standards of behavior. Rules and decision-making procedures refer to specific prescriptions for behavior in clearly defined areas. For instance, a liberal international regime for trade is based on a set of neoclassical economic principles that demonstrate that global utility is maximized by the free flow of goods. The basic norm of a liberal trading regime is that tariff and nontariff barriers should be reduced and ultimately eliminated. Specific rules and decision-making procedures are spelled out in the General Agreement on Tariffs and Trade. Principles and norms define the basic character of any regime. Although rules and decision-making procedures can be changed without altering the fundamental nature of a regime, principles and norms cannot. Regimes define basic property rights. They establish acceptable patterns of behavior. They coordinate decision making. They can enhance global well-being by allowing actors to escape from situations in which individual decision making leads to Pareto-suboptimal outcomes. Changes in regimes can alter the control and allocation of resources among actors in the international system. Every state wants more control over international regimes in order to make its own basic values and interests more secure.[2]

The Third World has supported international regimes that would ameliorate its weakness, As a group, the developing countries have consistently endorsed principles and norms that would legitimate more authoritative as opposed to more market-oriented modes of allocation. Authoritative allocation involves either the direct allocation of resources by political authorities, or indirect allocation by limiting the property rights of nonstate actors, including private corporations. A market-oriented regime is one in which the allocation of resources is determined by the endowments and preferences of individual actors who have the right to alienate their property according to their own estimations of their own best interests.

For developing countries, authoritative international regimes are attractive because they can provide more stable and predictable transaction flows. External shocks and pressures are threatening to developing countries because their slack resources and adjustment capabilities are so limited. Shocks are particularly troubling for political leaders because they are the likely targets of unrest generated by sudden declines in material well-being. Authoritative regimes may also provide a level of resource transfer that developing countries could not secure through market-oriented exchange. Given equal levels of resource transfer, developing states prefer authoritative to market-oriented regimes. Even when market-oriented regimes are accompanied by substantial increases in wealth, as has been the case in the post-World War II period, developing states have still sought authoritative regimes that would provide more security. I do not claim in this study that developing countries prefer control to wealth; rather I argue that authoritative regimes can provide them with both, whereas market-oriented ones cannot. I do not claim the LDCs are uninterested in wealth for its own sake. Purely wealth-oriented activities can he pursued within existing international regimes at the same time that developing states seek basic changes in principles and norms. But I do claim that the South has fundamentally challenged the extant liberal order, most visibly in the call for a New International Economic Order.

The general goal of moving toward more authoritative international regimes has been pursued using two, more specific, strategies. First, the Third World has sought to alter existing international institutions, or create new ones that would be more congruent with its preferred principles and norms. Second, developing countries have pressed for regimes that would legitimate the unilateral assertion of sovereign authority by individual states. With regard to international institutions, Third World states have demanded greater participation in global forums. They have supported universal organizations with one-nation, one-vote decision-making procedures. They have pressed for the creation of new bureaucracies that would be more sympathetic to regimes based on authoritative allocation. For instance, in the area of trade, UNCTAD (the United Nations Conference on Trade and Development) was created to offer a counterweight to the General Agreement on Tariffs and Trade (GATT), which was perceived by developing countries as an institution dedicated to a market-oriented approach. International organizations based on authoritative rather than market-oriented principles can limit the discretionary behavior of Northern actors by redefining property rights including, in the most extreme case, compelling additional resource transfers from the North to the South. For instance, the Law of the Sea Convention provides for the compulsory transfer of technology from multinational corporations to an international entity called the Enterprise, the operating instrument of the International Sea-Bed Authority. The UNCTAD Liner Code states that liners from developing countries (ocean freighters plying regular routes on regular schedules) ought to have 40 percent of the cargo originating in their own home ports.

The second strategy pursued by the Third World has been to support international regimes that legitimate the right of individual states to exercise sovereign control over a wider range of activities than previously. The Third World has sought to enhance the scope of activities that are universally accepted as subject to the unilateral control of the state. For instance, Latin American countries led the fight for extended economic zones in the ocean. By securing international acceptance of this right at the United Nations Conference on the Law of the Sea, developing coastal countries were able to secure both greater economic returns and more control than would have been the case if narrower limits had been recognized. By accepting property-fight claims that were being unilaterally asserted by developing countries, the international community greatly reduced the costs of enforcement. Similarly, in dealing with multinational corporations, the Third World has sought international legitimation of national controls. Such legitimation limits competition among developing countries and makes it more difficult for multinational corporations and their home governments to challenge host-country policies either legally or diplomatically. The South has also resisted Northern efforts to create new international regimes that would delimit existing sovereign powers. For instance, the Third World has rejected Northern efforts to legitimate new international norms regarding population control and individual human rights. The regime objectives pursued by the Third World are designed to limit the market power of the North by enhancing the sovereign prerogatives of the South, either through universal international organizations in which each nation has a single vote, or by widening the scope of activities exclusively subject to the unilateral sovereign will of individual developing states.

The demands associated with proposals for the New International Economic Order (NIEO), which assumed their greatest saliency in the mid–1970s, are the clearest manifestation of Third World efforts to restructure market-oriented international regimes. The NIEO and related proposals covered a wide range of issue areas, including trade, primary commodities, aid, debt, space, multinational corporations, journalism, and shipping. The NIEO was the culmination of Third World efforts that had begun in the 1940s.

The degree to which developing countries have succeeded in altering international regimes has been a function of three variables: the nature of existing institutional structures; the ability to formulate a coherent system of ideas, which set the agenda for international negotiations and cemented Third World unity; and the attitude and power of the North, especially the United States, toward both the demands of the South and the forums in which they have been made.

The nature of existing regime structures, including existing international organizations, has influenced the ability of Third World states to secure an environment governed by authoritative, as opposed to market, allocation. The most important general institutional advantage enjoyed by the Third World has been the acceptance of the principle of the sovereign equality of states. There have always been weak states in the international system, although in recent years disparities in per capita income have magnified distinctions in size and population. Before the twentieth century, however, the great powers were accepted as the dominant actors in the system, possessing rights of unilateral action that were denied to smaller states: the principle of great-power primacy dominated that of sovereign equality. At best, small states could maintain a precarious neutrality, relying on the balance of power to provide them with some freedom of action. In the present system the principle of sovereign equality dominates that of great-power primacy, and states with the most exiguous national power capabilities deny that others have special prerogatives.

The most important organizational manifestation of the principle of sovereign equality has been the United Nations. The UN system provided the major forums at which developing countries could present their demands. Developing states have had automatic access to United Nations agencies. With the exception of international financial institutions and the Security Council, states have had equal voting power. New agencies such as UNCTAD and UNIDO (UN Industrial Development Organization) have been created. The standard operating procedures of agencies have been changed. In areas where existing institutions limited access, such as with the Antarcitc, developing states have had little success. If the United Nations had not existed, it would have been impossible for the Third World to articulate a general program for altering international regimes.

Aside from nonspecialized universal institutions, the principles, norms, rules, and decision-making procedures confronting Third World countries in a number of specific issue areas conditioned their ability to secure their objectives. For developing states the most attractive situations have been ones in which existing international regimes, supported by the North, already embodied norms of authoritative, rather than market, allocation. If developing countries could secure access to these regimes, they could make claims on resources that would have been barred to them in a market-oriented world. For instance, the regime governing civil aviation has, since its inception after World War I, been governed by principles emphasizing state security, and norms that call for an equal allocation of traffic between foreign and domestic carriers in any given national market. Furthermore, fares have been influenced by agreements among airline companies, which are subject to state approval. This regime gave any Third World country that wanted to begin its own national airline a presumptive right to passengers, a reciprocal right to landing privileges, and some guarantee against competitive rate-cutting. Many Third World states took advantage of this situation. In contrast, critical aspects of ocean shipping have been governed by norms and rules (some of whose antecedents stretch back to the late Middle Ages) which are predominantly based on commercial principles emphasizing market allocation. Some rate structures have been negotiated by cartels, to which developing country shipping lines have limited access. The legitimation of flags of convenience has offset some of the competitive advantage that developing countries might have had from cheap labor. Developing countries have been less successful in establishing their own shipping lines than in establishing their own commercial airlines, in part because of the nature of existing international regimes.

The second variable affecting the ability of developing countries to secure their preferred international regimes has been the coherence of the ideological arguments used to rationalize and justify their demands. The degree of coherence has increased over time. Developing states were never entranced with the liberal market-oriented regimes established at the conclusion of the Second World War. But their initial forays were limited to sniping at bits and pieces of this order and calling attention to areas where developed states had violated their own liberal principles. However, beginning with the work of Raul Prebisch at the Economic Commission for Latin America in the late 1940s, spokesmen for Third World countries developed a set of arguments that placed the major reponsibility for underdevelopment on the workings of the international system rather than on the specific characteristics of developing countries and the policies adopted by their leaders. This line of argument was developed and propagated over time, drawing on Marxist as well as conventional economic analyses. The ability of the Third World to present a coherent world view—one which depicted the exploitation of the Third World as an inherent feature of the global economy—provided a rationale for making demands on the North, helped the Group of 77 (formed at the first UNCTAD meeting by seventy-seven LDCs) to coordinate its programs across several issue areas, and reduced negotiating costs among developing countries by suggesting specific policy proposals. By the early 1970s the industrialized world was on the defensive in major international forums. The agenda was being set by the Third World. The Gramscian hegemony enjoyed by liberal doctrines in the immediate post-war period had been totally undermined. It was rejected by almost all Third World leaders and questioned by many specific groups, including some policymakers, in the North.

The final variable influencing the degree of success realized by the Third World in securing international regimes based upon authoritative allocation has been the power of the North, especially that of the United States. This too changed over time. The United States emerged from the Second World War in an extrordinarily dominant position. Its physical plant had not been damaged by the fighting. Its gross national product was three times as large as that of its main rival, the Soviet Union. It had a monopoly on nuclear weapons. It enjoyed a technological advantage over its major competitors in most industrial sectors. Over time this domination has eroded. The Europeans and the Japanese recovered. The Soviet Union and several other countries secured nuclear weapons. The Japanese challenged the United States even in the most technologically advanced industries. Dependence on imported energy supplies increased dramatically. Vietnam undermined the domestic consensus that had supported U.S. foreign policy.[3]

The early 1970s proved to be the most propitious moment for the developing world to launch a major attack on the liberal international order that had been so assiduously cultivated by U.S. policymakers. The United States had been the moving force behind the international organizations created at the conclusion of the Second World War. For a hegemonic power, the purpose of such organizations is to legitimate its preferences, and values. Legitimation requires that the organizations be given autonomy. If they are seen merely as handmaidens of the hegemon, they will be ineffective. Despite formal autonomy, the United States had great influence over specific decisions and general policies in all major international organizations through the 1950s.

Decolonization eroded American influence. In the United Nations, and in other international organizations, voting majorities changed. Third World states questioned both the underlying values and specific policy preferences of the United States. This did not immediately lead to an American renunciation of existing institutions, however, or even to a decline in American commitments. In the absence of alternatives, such a radical shift was unattractive because Third World behavior could be interpreted as a temporary aberration, and the reaction of other countries to a dramatic change could not be easily gauged. At least some American policymakers were committed to the strategy, deeply rooted in basic American attitudes toward international affairs, of resolving conflicts through negotiations and international agreements. Thus, despite a growing inability to influence decisions in the United Nations and other international forums, the United States did not simply walk out. Had it done so the developing world would have been reduced to vacuous rhetoric in chambers devoid of influence, if not of individuals.

The early 1970s offered a unique window of opportunity for the Third World because it was a period characterized by Third World control of major international forums but continued Northern commitment. Through the 1960s the South had not wielded itself into a disciplined voting block or presented a coherent program across many issue areas. By the late 1970s, Northern commitments had begun to erode, especially those of the United States. Financial contributions declined. The United States temporarily withdrew from the International Labor Organization in the late 1970s, and in January 1985 formally withdrew from UNESCO. Other industrialized market-economy states, notably Great Britain, also indicated their deep dissatisfaction with UNESCO. In 1982, several Northern states, including the United States, rejected the United Nations Law of the Sea Convention. Without American participation the Convention is of limited utility. In January 1985 the United States, for the first time, refused to take part in a World Court case, an action in defiance of the Court's rules.

In sum, the desire to secure international regimes embodying authoritative rather than market allocation of resources has been an enduring aspect of Third World policy in the postwar period. It reflects the profound national weakness of most developing countries. This weakness stems from the inability to influence unilaterally or to adjust internally to the pressures of global markets. Larger industrialized states are able to influence the international environment and can adjust internally. Smaller industrialized states have little influence over the global pattern of transactions, but their domestic political economies allow them to adjust. Small size and inflexible domestic structures make Third World states vulnerable: severe domestic political and economic dislocation can occur as a result of shocks and fluctuations emanating from the international system. Such dislocation can be especially painful for political leaders who become the targets of a counter-elite or of popular discontent. By changing the nature of international regimes, Third World leaders hope not only to increase the flow of material resources but also to create a more predictable and stable environment. The success of developing countries in pursuing their regime objectives has depended on the nature of extant institutional arrangements, their ability to articulate a coherent viewpoint, and the willingness of the North, particularly the United States, to tolerate international forums that produced undesired results. These last two factors explain why the North-South conflict reached such intensity during the mid–1970s. At that moment, the South had developed an effective ideological position, the international forums were available, and the United States was still committed to global negotiations. Ironically, it was the last years of the American hegemonic apogee that provided weak states with their greatest opportunity to attack the prevailing order.

This interpretation of Southern behavior draws upon a structural, or third-image, approach to international politics which maintains that the behavior of states is determined by their relative power capabilities.[4] The countries of the South are not purveyors of some new and superior morality, nor are their policies any less reasonable than those of the industrialized world. They are behaving the way states have always behaved; they are trying to maximize their power—their ability to control their own destinies. The claims of the Group of 77 have been based on the equality of sovereign states and have been made for the state and the state alone, not for individual citizens.[5] For developing countries, restructuring regimes was an attractive strategy, particularly in the early 1970s, because of their lack of national power capabilities, their ability to break the ideological hegemony of the North, and the access provided by international organizations.

The implications of this analysis for maintaining universal principles and norms are not sanguine. Effective international regime construction, as opposed to regime maintenance, is difficult. Historically, new regimes are most easily created by hegemonic states possessing overwhelming military, economic, and ideological power. Once regimes are created, narrow calculations of interests, uncertainty about alternatives, and habit may provide support even if the power of the hegemonic state fades and its policy preferences change. The countries of the developing world are, however, interested in altering liberal international regimes, not in maintaining them. They want new principles, norms, rules, and decision-making procedures. They can bring to bear powerful ideological arguments to legitimate their preferences, but they lack national economic and military capabilities.

Existing international regimes are likely to continue to weaken, not only because of attacks from the South but also because of disaffection in the North. Especially for the United States, declining power will make policymakers less willing to tolerate free riders or to bear a disproportionate share of the costs of maintaining international regimes. Although the South will not abandon calls for a New International Economic Order, it will give less emphasis to this program because the prospects for success are dim. The behavior of both the North and the South will be increasingly motivated by short-term calculations of interest rather than by long-term goals that require efficacious regimes. When mutual interests are high, such calculations can lead to cooperative relations. Where specific interests are not present, interaction will decline. For both developing and industrialized states this is not such a daunting prospect. Given fundamental conflicts stemming from outlandish disparities in power, there would be more security in a world with lower levels of transnational interactions. Self-reliance and collective self-reliance rather than interdependence may serve the interests of the North as well as those of the South.

THE VARIETY OF THIRD WORLD GOALS

By emphasizing weakness, vulnerability, and the quest for control in this study, I do not mean to imply that LDCs are uninterested in purely economic objectives. Third World states have pursued a wide variety of goals. These include economic growth, international political equality, influence in international decision-making arenas, autonomy and independence, the preservation of territorial integrity from external invasion or internal fragmentation, the dissemination of new world views at the global level, and the maintenance of domestic regime stability. They have used a wide variety of tactics to promote these objectives, including international commodity organizations such as OPEC and CIPEC (*Conseil Intergouvernment des Pays Exportateurs Cuivre*), regional organizations such as the Organization of African Unity (OAU) and the Association of Southeast Asian Nations (ASEAN), universal coalitions such as the Group of 77 (G–77) at UNCTAD and the United Nations, alliances with major powers, local wars to manipulate major powers, irregular violence such as national liberation movements, bilateral economic arrangements, national regulation of multinational corporations, nationalization of foreign holdings, foreign exchange manipulation, and international loans. . . .

The boundaries of this work can be more clearly delineated by distinguishing between two categories of political behavior. Relational power behavior refers to efforts to maximize values within a given set of institutional structures; meta-power behavior refers to efforts to change the institutions themselves. Relational power refers to the ability to change outcomes or affect the behavior of others within a given regime. Metapower refers to the ability to change the rules of the game.[6]

Outcomes can be changed both by altering the resources available to individual actors and by changing the regimes that condition action. Changing the outcome of struggles fought with relational power requires changing actor capability. But such changes do not necessarily imply an alteration in meta-power. An individual may win more money by learning to become a better poker player without being able to change the rules of poker. A political party may win more offices by attracting more voters without altering the laws governing elections. A state may prevail more frequently in disputes with other international actors by enhancing its national power capabilities without altering the principles, norms, and rules that condition such disputes.

Outcomes can also be changed by changing regimes. Meta-power behavior is designed to do this. When successfully implemented, it usually means a change in relational power as well. Individuals who win at poker may lose at bridge; political parties that secure seats under a proportional representation system might be excluded by single-seat districts; states that secure greater revenue from cartelized exports would be poorer if the price of their product were dictated by those with the greatest military capability. An actor capable of changing the game from poker to bridge, from proportional representation to single-seat, from economic to military capability, possesses meta-power. Actors may seek to enhance their relational power by enhancing their own national capabilities, or they may attempt to secure more favorable outcomes by pursuing a meta-power strategy designed to change regimes. . . .

The exercise of relational power involves only questions of formal rationality. Relational power behavior accepts existing goals and institutional structures. The challenge is to achieve these goals most efficiently. Meta-power rejects existing goals and institutional structures. It employs formal, rational calculations to promote new goals and institutions. Behavior that is formally rational given one set of substantive objectives may be formally irrational given another.

Third World states are interested in employing both relational power and meta-power. Proposals for international regime change, voiced by the less developed countries, are an effort to exercise meta-power. The objective of these proposals, of which the program associated with the New International Economic Order is the most salient, is to alter the principles, norms, rules, and decision-making procedures that condition international transactions. Such transformation is attractive because in a market-oriented regime the ability of Third World states to achieve their objectives solely through the exercise of relational power is limited by the exiguousness of their national capabilities. These capabilities alone could not resolve the vulnerability problems of poorer states. For the Third World, altering international regimes is a relatively attractive way to secure some control over the environment.

Third World efforts to change regimes have been most clearly manifest in international organizations. Debates within these organizations have concerned principles, norms, rules, and decision-making procedures, not just the transfer of resources. LDCs have also used national legislation to try to alter international rules of the game. However, the NIEO and other proposals for regime change have been but one of many kinds of interactions between the North and the South. With regard to actual resource movements, the most important settings have been national and bilateral. In such settings, developing states have used relational power to enhance specific economic interests. When, for instance, a developing country borrows on the Eurodollar market, it attempts to get the best possible terms; it does not, however, challenge the right of private financial institutions to base their decisions on maximizing private economic returns. When a developing country accepts foreign assistance, it tries to alter both the amounts and the terms on which it is dispensed; it does not, however, usually challenge the prerogative of donor countries to base aid allocations on self-determined principles or interests. When a state negotiates a standby agreement with the International Monetary Fund (IMF) it attempts to use relational power to adjust the terms and conditions of the arrangement; it does not, however, challenge the authority of the IMF to sign such an agreement. The modal form of interaction between industrialized and developing areas has involved the transfer of resources and the exercise of relational power, and has taken place in bilateral arenas.

Some examples of relational power and meta-power policies in national and bilateral, as opposed to multilateral, settings are shown in Table 1. Multilateral settings are further broken down into North-South and South-South arrangements.

Behavior that falls within one of the cells is not incompatible with behavior that falls in another. It is not inconsistent for developing countries to pursue different goals in various arenas at the same time. During the 1970s the Group of 77 pressed for generalized debt relief for the least developed states at universal international forums such as UNCTAD and the United Nations General Assembly, while downplaying this issue at multilateral financial institutions such as the World Bank and the IMF.[7] In the area of raw materials, the less developed countries sought both compensatory finance, which would enhance their economic well-being without altering basic regime characteristics, as well as the formation of the Integrated Program for Commodities, which would fundamentally change the principles and norms governing the international movement of primary products. Under the *sexenio* Luis Echeverría, Mexico played a prominent role in the Third World movement. At the same time, the Mexican finance and development ministries were engaged in extensive pragmatic discussions with multinational corporations about conditions for their entry into Mexico. Similarly, Algeria pursued purely economic policies with respect to liquefied natural gas exports while Boumedienne acted as the leader of the Non-Aligned Movement. The pursuit of different goals in various forums is not inconsistent or incoherent.[8] It does not reflect disagreement between politically oriented foreign affairs officials, who do not understand economics, and finance ministry officials, who recognize the "realities" of global interdependence. Rather, the variety of Third World strategies is a manifestation of a variety of objectives. . . .

ALTERNATIVE APPROACHES TO NORTH-SOUTH RELATIONS

The interpretation presented in this study both complements and challenges a number of prominent alternatives: basic human needs, conventional liberalism, and global interdependence. Analysts concerned with basic human needs emphasize the material well-being of individuals rather than the political concerns of states. Advocates of free enterprise and liberal economics focus on problems of economic growth. Those who see interdependence as the defining characteristic of the present international system emphasize the ties that bind the North to the fate of the South. Both those of interdependence orientation and those embracing some variants of the liberal approach are sensitive to the political demands made by developing countries. However, basic human needs, conventional liberal, and interdependence arguments all include the implication that accelerated economic growth accompanied by equitable distribution would eliminate the basic source of

TABLE 1

Negotiating forum		Behavior type	
		Relational power behavior (formal rationality)	Meta-power behavior (substantive rationality)
National and bilateral		Eurodollar loans Taxtreaties Bilateral aid	Some regulation of MNCs (1960s) Control of oil production (1970s) Expansive national claims to ocean resources (1945–1970) Unilateral alteration of loan terms (early 1980s)
Multilateral	South-South	Existing trade arrangements among LDCs	OPEC Andean Pact Collective self-reliance
	Universal, including North-South	Civil aviation Nuclear nonproliferation	New International Information Order (NIIO) NIEO Generalized systems of preferences Commodity agreements Aspects of Lome Convention Integrated Program for Commodities UNCLOS

North-South conflict. Demands for the restructuring of international regimes are understood as instrumental tactics whose ultimate purpose is to enhance economic well-being. Economic well-being for either individuals or the collectivity, rather than state concerns with vulnerability and control, is (tacitly or explicitly) seen as the fundamental motivation for Southern behavior.

As president of the World Bank, Robert McNamara was a prominent exponent of the basic human needs orientation. Under his leadership the bank emphasized the alleviation of absolute poverty. The bank's allocation of funds shifted away from infrastructure and industry toward projects that had a direct effect on the poor, especially small-scale agriculture. In his 1979 address to the board of governors of the bank, McNamara . . . maintained that income gaps between rich and poor are "largely irrelevant for determining the long-term objectives of the developing countries themselves."[9] In a 1977 talk he argued that it would quickly become apparent that "it is relatively unimportant whether the assistance is to take the form of commodity agreements, debt relief, trade concessions, bilateral or multilateral financing—or any particular combination of these—provided the overall total is adequate.[10]

The alleviation of absolute poverty has also been a major theme of American foreign aid doctrines. It has been embodied in legislation and instructions to American executive directors at international financial institutions. Secretary of State Vance maintained in a 1979 speech that "Programs such as those I have mentioned today are not a cure-all. But they come to grips with the most pressing problems of the developing countries, and they will make a difference where it counts most—in the daily lives of people. They will insure that more people in the developing countries will have enough food to eat, that fewer children will die in infancy, that there is sufficient energy to power more irrigation pumps and to bring more heat and light to distant villages."[11]

The emphasis on basic needs exemplifies a wider trend explicated by Robert W. Tucker. Tucker argues that some Western elites are advocates of what he terms the "politics of sensibility." These elites have come to assume that the Third World is primarily concerned with improving the well-being of individuals. They maintain that justice cannot tolerate existing inequalities. They argue that men should no longer distinguish between fellow citizens and the rest of mankind in the provision of basic needs. The countries of the South are seen by such elites, Tucker argues, as expositors of a new international morality that extends across national boundaries.[12]

General economic performance in the South has been a second focus of attention for Northern policymakers and analysts. Discussion of Third World growth has been deeply influenced by the precepts of liberal neoclassical economics. Within this general approach orthodox liberals have emphasized domestic factors in the Third World, while reformist liberals have also taken global systemic factors into account.

For orthodox liberals the problems of developing countries must be resolved internally. Low per capita incomes are the result of inadequate factor endowments. The rate of capital formation is low; infrastructures are underdeveloped; soil conditions are poor; education is limited. To some extent these conditions, and the consequent unsatisfactory economic performance of many developing countries, are blamed on inappropriate economic policies. Underdeveloped countries have authored their own failures. Orthodox liberals are especially perturbed by the Third World's rejection of market mechanisms. Trade barriers promote inefficient domestic industries. Investment regulations discourage multinational corporations. Low payments to farmers reduce food production. Artificial exchange rates distort production and consumption. Taxes on primary exports encourage smuggling. Enforced collectivization destroys individual incentives. . . .

The policy implications for the North of orthodox liberal views are readily apparent. The New International Economic Order (NIEO) program should be rejected in its entirety. There is no need to change the international economic system. Third World policies are responsible for Third World poverty. Indeed, such change would be counterproductive because it would substitute state activity for the market. The NIEO is seen as a cockeyed set of proposals inspired by erroneous dependency arguments at best, and economic stupidity at worst.

Orthodox liberals have not paid much attention to Northern policies that impede the functioning of the market. Such policies are unfortunate, even reprehensible. But the fate of the South will not be determined by anything that the North does; while the present system may be flawed in modest ways, it still offers enormous opportunities to those developing countries, such as Taiwan, South Korea, Hong Kong, and Singapore, which are prepared to seize them.

Reformist liberals start with the same basic presuppositions as orthodox liberals, but place more emphasis on the need for more forthcoming Northern policies. Such policies, they say, should recognize the peculiar circumstances of LDCs as well as making markets work more effectively. Reformist liberals strongly condemn import restrictions imposed by developed countries, which not only discourage adjustment in the North but impede experts from the South. They support criticisms of the system which point to imperfections in existing markets. For instance, the transfer of technology is carried out largely by multinational corporations that often have oligopoly if not monopoly power. International agreements concerning technology-transfer and restrictive business practices are needed because, like American antitrust legislation, they facilitate the functioning of the market.

Reformist liberals are also more tolerant than their orthodox colleagues of domestic policies in developing countries which do not strictly accord with market principles. They more readily accept the infant-industry argument. Given market imperfections, developing countries' domestic subsidies may be the second-best solution. When basic human needs are at stake, the state may have to allocate. But reformist liberals are as unhappy about inefficient domestic policies in developing countries as their orthodox brethren.

This analysis leads reformist liberals to a more sympathetic view of the New International Economic Order. The demands of the Third World are seen as reformist, not revolutionary. The Third World is understood to believe that the world economy can provide benefits for all. Rhetoric that condemns the system as a whole is just rhetoric. Compromise is possible at the international level. Moreover, the North needs to reform its own policies. Northern restrictions on imports from the South can seriously impede economic development. Present structures do not necessarily provide the price signals needed to maximize global efficiency. A more efficient system would provide benefits for both industrialized and developing areas. . . .

The special situation confronting developing countries must be appreciated. Industrialized nations should lower trade barriers and accept some temporary LDC export subsidization. Compensatory finance schemes should be encouraged for primary commodity exporters. Financial flows should be increased by providing more resources for international financial institutions and by creating international tax funds for the poorest countries. There should be more disclosure of information regarding technology to lessen the imperfections resulting from oligopolistic control. . . .

Liberal orientations of one cast or another have dominated American attitudes toward the Third World during the postwar period. Democratic administrations have tended to accept reformist liberal arguments. Such arguments were particularly prevalent under Jimmy Carter. Republicans have been more sympathetic to orthodox liberal perspectives, a viewpoint strongly reflected in the positions taken by the Reagan administration. Undergirding both these approaches is a set of beliefs about the relationship between economic well-being and political behavior which incorporates a reductionist, or second-image, understanding of international politics. Louis Hartz has argued that American views of foreign affairs are dominated by the prevailing liberal approach to politics within the United States. Because America's historical experience isolated it from the mainstream of both conservative and socialist developments in Europe, Lockean liberalism with its emphasis on individualism, free enterprise, and political democracy has set the boundaries of political discourse.[13] The leitmotif of American foreign policy has been to reconstruct the American experience in other parts of the world. The external behavior of states has been understood as a manifestation of their domestic sociopolitical characteristics rather than their international power capabilities.

In a study written before the demands for a New International Economic Order came to dominate North-South relations, Robert Packenham used Hartz's insights to analyze American foreign aid doctrines. He argued that the liberal roots of American attitudes led to four basic precepts. First, change and development are easy. Second, all good things go together. Third, radicalism and revolution are bad. Forth, distributing power is more important than accumulating power. American leaders saw the poorer countries of the world moving along the same path that had been followed by the United States. Economic development would promote political development. Political development meant democracy. Democratic regimes would follow international policies that coincided with the interests of the United States. . . .[14]

The world view of American policymakers has not changed much in the postwar period, and the American response to the New International Economic Order was not very different from the response to earlier Third World demands. Economic development within the countries of the Third World has been seen as the key to their domestic evolution, and domestic political evolution as the key to their international behavior.

For reformist liberals the analogies used to clarify Third World behavior are drawn from domestic politics rather than from international relations. John Sewell of the Overseas Development Council writes that the demands of LDCs bear "some similarity to the emergence of organized labor in this country in the late 1920s and l930s."[15]

Few Northern commentators have perceived the NIEO as a challenge to the basic nature of the liberal regime. Rather, the Third World has been understood to be calling for adjustments within an existing set of principles and norms. Radical transformation was not necessary because a reformed version of the extant liberal order could meet many Third World economic needs. And it was these needs, not the desire to compensate for vulnerability by regime control, which were understood to be the gravamen of LDC dissatisfaction.

While the focus of various liberal and basic human needs perspectives is on the well-being of the South, the emphasis in interdependence approaches is on the links between the North and the South. The fate of all countries is intertwined. The basic assumptions of the realist approach, which underlies this study, are rejected. Viewing states as the only constitutive element of the international system obscures the inability of ostensibly sovereign political institutions to control many transnational flows. The formal imprimatur of sovereignty may remain, but revolutionary changes in the technology of communication and transportation have transformed the global system into a web of interdependence from which states can extricate themselves only at extremely high cost, if at all. Various private and subnational actors have developed their own transnational relations. Multinational corporations orchestrate subsidiaries in various parts of the world. Billions of dollars can be transferred electronically from one financial center to another in a matter of seconds. Domestic economic policies can be undermined or reinforced by choices made by other countries for purely domestic reasons. Partisans of an interdependence perspective maintain that this is a world that cannot be adequately understood by focusing on states and power. Economic failure for the South would have dire consequences for the North.[16]

The first report of the Independent Commission for International Economic Cooperation offers elegant testimony for this approach.[17] The commission was chaired by Willy Brandt, and included notables from the industrialized and developing worlds. The report includes the statement that "the world is now a fragile and interlocking system, whether for its people, its ecology or its resources" (p. 33). Brandt avers that "this Report deals with peace. War is often thought of in terms of military conflict, or even annihilation. But there is a growing awareness that an equal danger might be chaos—as a result of mass hunger, economic disaster, environmental catastrophes, and terrorism" (p. 13). The report contains a number of specific arguments about the way in which developments in the South affect the North. For instance, a surging demand for grain in the South, a result of local crop failures, would contribute to inflation in the North. Rapid population growth could have a deleterious impact on the earth's ecosystem. Developing countries are increasingly important trading partners for the North. Economic collapse in the South could spawn international terrorism and even nuclear blackmail.

The commission's analysis led it to policy conclusions that were more sympathetic to the Third World than those arrived at by analysts with liberal or basic human needs perspectives. While recognizing that the developing countries themselves must carry "the major share of the burden" for effectively attacking poverty, substantial changes in the global economic system were called for in the report (p. 29). Economic forces cannot be left entirely to themselves because they "tend to produce growing inequality" (p. 33). Aid levels should be increased, and the international provision of capital should be more automatic. Levies on armaments and luxury goods trade, taxes on the use of the global commons, or the sale of more gold by the IMF could provide the resources for such transfers. Commodity prices, it is argued in the report, should be stabilized through international agreement. Northern barriers to exports from the South should be eliminated.

The approach taken by the Brandt Commission, and by other analysts who see interdependence as the basic characteristic of the current world system, are closer in some ways to the perspective I have taken in this study than to other interpretations of the North-South situation. Like this study, interdependence arguments have a strong systemic orientation. They address not only the domestic poverty of the South but also the consequences of conditions in the South for the North. While those with basic human needs and liberal orientations focus on the relational power behavior of developing countries, those using interdependence arguments do address meta-power concerns as well. However, while economic growth and prosperity as the center of Third World concerns is stressed in interdependence arguments, I seek to demonstrate in this study that questions of vulnerability and control are more important, at least for some aspects of Third World behavior. Enhancing economic utility will not resolve conflicts between the North and the South. Vulnerability, not simply poverty, is the motivating force for the Third World's meta-power program for transforming international regimes. Those following basic human needs, liberal, and interdependence approaches have failed to comprehend the fundamentally political character of many Third World demands. . . .

CONCLUSION

The meta-political goals of Third World states, and many of their relational goals as well, can be understood in reference to the minimalist objective of preserving political integrity. Most developing countries have very weak domestic political institutions. Nonconstitutional regime changes occur frequently. Domestic violence is common. Slack resources are limited. The material resources controlled by Third World states are typically heavily dependent on international economic transactions, which can be taxed relatively easily compared with domestic transactions. Declines in the value of trade can deprive state officials of revenues that are critical for maintaining domestic political control. Hence, the positions of Third World political leaders are very vulnerable to changes in the international economic environment. Making that environment more predictable and stable would contribute to domestic political stability. Regimes legitimating authoritative, rather than market, allocation can provide more stability as well as greater transfers of wealth.

In this study, however, unlike those presenting conventional structural arguments, I have taken seriously not only international power but also international regimes. Those using conventional structural arguments view international politics as a zero-sum conflict among states. Regimes have little autonomy. They are regarded as being only one small step removed from the underlying power configurations that support them. When national power capabilities change, regimes will change as well. For conventional realists, regimes are purely epiphenomenal. The direct clash of interests among states is the basic characteristic of international life.

Because I have adopted the modified structural, or modified realist, orientation in this study I accept the critical importance of political power for regime creation. It is impossible to establish *de novo* durable principles, norms, rules, and decision-making procedures unless they are supported by the more powerful states in the system. Once regimes are actually in place, however, the relationship between power and regimes can become more attenuated. Established regimes generate inertia if only because of sunk costs and the absence of alternatives.[18] Bureaucrats in international organizations actively cultivate supportive clientele. The distribution of influence within organizations may not reflect underlying national power capabilities, one-nation, one-vote procedures being the most obvious example. Regimes with norms and rules giving open access can be altered by new members. Agendas within established regimes can be influenced not only be voting power but also by the persuasiveness and coherence of intellectual arguments. Hence, regimes do not move in lockstep with changes in underlying national power capabilities. Third World states cannot establish new regimes from scratch, but they have been able to change existing regimes, sometimes in very significant ways.

From a modified structuralist perspective, the normative implications of regime autonomy depend on the degree of disparity between underlying national power capabilities and regime characteristics. Some moderate degree of disparity is acceptable, even desirable. It makes it possible for regimes to have enough longevity and stability to produce mutually beneficial outcomes. The greater the disparity, however, the greater the probability of a sudden rupture. Powerful states can destroy regimes that are antithetical to their interests. By disrupting existing patterns of behavior and introducing high levels of uncertainty, such ruptures can be particularly damaging to global well-being and can exacerbate international tensions.

From a modified structural perspective, therefore, the Third World's quest for regimes based more on authoritative allocation is not quixotic, but it is normatively suspect. Developing states do not have the power to create completely new internatioinal regimes that involve the North. A minimum condition for Southern initiatives has been access to existing international organizations. Given access, the Third World has consistently attempted to move regimes away from market-oriented principles, norms, and rules. Ideological coherence and declining Northern capabilities have made possible some genuine success despite the lack of national power resources in the South. However, Third World accomplishments only rarely contribute to a stable international environment. The greater the success of the Third World in changing regimes against Northern preferences, the more likely the North is to rupture existing practices by withdrawing support.

The tensions between the South and the North, between weak and vulnerable states on the one hand and strong and resilient ones on the other, cannot be resolved through either economic growth or regime change. Even if very optimistic projections of economic performance for the South were realized, national vulnerabilities would not be significantly reduced even with substantial improvements in individual well-being. In only a limited number of cases will the South's support for regimes based on authoritative allocation coincide with the desires of the North. For industrialized states, market-oriented regimes in which resource allocation is determined by present endowments and preferences are more economically attractive and, given developed domestic political and economic structures, disruptions and dislocations can be managed so that political integrity is not put in jeopardy. The international system would be more stable and less conflictual if the North and the South had less to do with each other. From a Northern as well as a Southern perspective collective self-reliance is preferable to greater interdependence.

NOTES

1. The two major exceptions to this generalization are the small number of developing countries that are so large that they can limit external interactions, notably China and India, and a few smaller developing states that have flexible and effective sociopolitical and economic structures that allow them to adjust to international conditions, such as the newly industrializing countries (NICs) in Southeast Asia—South Korea, Taiwan, Singapore, and Hong Kong.

2. Robert Gilpin, *War and Change in World Politics* (New York: Cambridge University Press, 1981), p. 50.

3. Ole Holsti and James N. Rosenau, "Vietnam, Consensus, and the Belief Systems of American Leaders," *World Politics,* vol. 32 (October, 1979).

4. Kenneth N. Waltz, *Man, the State, and War,* (New York: Columbia University Press, 1959); and Waltz, *Theory of International Politics* (Reading, Mass.: Addison-Wesley, 1979).

5. Robert W. Tucker, *The Inequality of Nations* (New York: Basic Books, 1977).

6. The terms are from Tom Baumgartner et al., "Unequal Exchange and Uneven Development," *working paper* no. 45, Institute of Sociology, University of Oslo, 1976.

7. *Wall Street Journal,* October 4, 1976, 8:3; Rothstein, *Global Bargaining,* p. 161.

8. For a similar conclusion, see Branislov Gosovic and John G. Ruggie, "On the Creation of a New International Economic Order," *International Organization,* vol. 30 (Spring 1976), p. 32.

9. Robert S. McNamara, *Address to the Board of Governors,* International Bank for Reconstruction and Development, October 2, 1979, Washington, D.C., p. 6.

10. *The New York Times.* January 15, 1977, 33:6

11. U.S. State Department *Bulletin,* May 1979, p. 37.

12. Tucker, *Inequality of Nations,* esp. pp. 138 ff. Tucker thoroughly rejects the "politics of sensibility."

13. Hartz, *The Liberal Tradition in America* (New York: Harcourt, Brace and World, 1955).

14. Packenham, *Liberal America and the Third World* (Princeton: Princeton University Press, 1973), esp. chap. 3.

15. John Sewell, *The United States and World Development: Agenda 1977* (New York: Prager, 1977) p. 8.

16. See Robert O. Keohane and Joseph Nye, *Power and Interdependence* (Boston: Little, Brown, 1977), for a discussion of complex interdependence.

17. Independent Commission on International Development Issues (Brandt Commission), *North South: A Program for Survival* (Cambridge, Mass.: MIT Press, 1980).

18. Robert O. Keohane, "The Demand for International Regimes," *International Organization,* vol. 36 (Spring 1982).

The Debate About Interdependence

Global Transactions and the Consolidation of Sovereignty

Janice E. Thomson and
Stephen D. Krasner

Challenges to state-centric paradigms are nothing new in the study of international affairs. Before World War I some analysts maintained that the level of economic interdependence in Europe was so high that war was basically unthinkable. After World War II functionalists argued that specific functions could be assumed by political entities that would eventually supersede individual states. Advocates of the concept of transnational relations saw a world not only of interaction among national-states but also a transnational world involving interactions among nonstate actors or between nonstate actors and states (Keohane and Nye 1972). Some analysts saw multinational corporations escaping from the jurisdiction of any one state or any set of states. Hence the concern with the relationship between micro-macro interactions expressed in James Rosenau's micro formulation (Rosenau 1988), and especially the impact of greater individual competence on macro-processes, has a lengthy intellectual pedigree.

One thread that runs through most of these arguments is that technological innovation is the most important factor explaining changes in the international system. Technological change is itself an exogenous variable; it is left unexplained, at least in relation to the political system. Technological change has reduced transactions costs. Transportation and communication are much cheaper than they have

Reprinted with permission of Lexington Books, an imprint of Macmillan, Inc. from *Global Changes and Theoretical Challenges* by Ernst-Oho Czempiel and James N. Rosenau. Copyright © 1989 by the publisher. Portions of the text and some footnotes have been omitted.

been in the past. The importance of geographic propinquity, of the territoriality that is at the core of the modern state system, has declined. Japan could become the world's most efficient steel producer even though both its coal and iron are thousands of miles away, a feat that would have been impossible in the nineteenth and early twentieth centuries before the development of bulk shipping. Billions of dollars can be transferred from one end of the world to the other in a matter of seconds—a far cry from the Rothschilds' use of carrier pigeons to secure information on the outcome of the Battle of Waterloo so that they could decide whether to buy or sell British sovereigns. Technological change may increase the competence of specific actors, whether individuals or organizations, by providing them with a vastly improved knowledge base.

The argument that interdependence has undermined the effective sovereignty of the state (the ability of the state to control activities that are nominally or juridicially subject to authoritative decisions) has been most fully elaborated for economic transactions. International flows have made it more difficult for national governments to independently manage their own economies. Policies could be nullified by new international transactions over which national decision makers had no control. For instance, the effort by a small state to dampen domestic economic activity by raising interest rates could be frustrated by international capital inflows attracted by these same higher interest rates, which would increase the state's money supply and lead to lower interest rates (Cooper 1968). Formal sovereignty remains but actual control diminishes or even disappears. The basic causal sequence is as follows: Technological change leads to increased economic flows, which erodes state control.

Realists have been extremely skeptical of all variants of the interdependence position. Realism has attempted to incorporate, to swallow up, the kinds of empirical evidence pointed to by interdependence formulations and to endogenize their theoretical variables. Realists argued first that growing interdependence has been a function of political power and political choice, not of exogenous technological change. The international rules of the game that are necessary for an open international economic system (the precondition for growing interdependence) precede, rather than follow, technological change. These rules had to be created by political choice and political power. In the postwar world only the United States could play an effective leadership role and even then only for those political entities that were not part of the Soviet bloc. The United States' desire for global liberalism has been explained in a variety of ways, including domestic preferences: a desire to internationalize the market-oriented economy that characterized the domestic U.S. economy; lessons drawn from the past; the conclusion accepted by U.S. leaders that the protectionism of the 1930s, especially the Smoot-Hawley Tariff Act, had contributed to economic breakdown, economic breakdown to authoritarian regimes, and authoritarian regimes to war; and finally to the realpolitik and national interest preferences that would be natural for any dominant state (Goldstein 1986; Krasner 1976; Maier 1977; Gilpin 1975). All of these arguments presuppose a hegemonic position for the United States, a level of dominance that would allow it to propagate its domestic preferences, act on the lessons its leaders drew from the past, and attain its realpolitik goals. The fact that technology has not led to an integration of the communist and noncommunist worlds strongly suggests that technology alone is not an adequate explanation for the pattern of international economic transactions.

Some realists, notably Kenneth Waltz, took a somewhat different tack. They argued that interdependence and global power were being confused. Transactions in and of themselves did not have any political significance. What counted was the ability of a state to adjust to change or to use its economic position for political leverage. A state that is heavily involved in the international economy, but could easily shift to relative autarky, is not vulnerable. Such a state may even be in a strong position to exercise political leverage over its economic partners because the relative opportunity costs of change weigh heavily in its favor (Waltz 1970; Hirschman 1945).

This chapter points to three other problems with arguments that see the macro structure of the international system (national-states) being undermined by micro processes driven by changes in individual competencies. First, such arguments lack historical perspective, often tacitly assuming that states have, in some golden age in the past, been able to effortlessly control transborder movements, or taking recent changes as indicative of long-term trends. In comparison with the past, contemporary changes in the level of international transactions do not appear particularly spectacular. The kinds of technological changes that have reduced international transaction costs have also reduced domestic transaction costs. Although some ratios of international to domestic transactions have increased, others have gone down. To the extent that historical data can be obtained they do not suggest any powerful long-term trends.

Second, interdependence arguments have ignored different trajectories of state consolidation that have occurred in different issue areas. They have focused on economic transactions and ignored military and security concerns. Indeed, the analysis of international security issues has, with a few exceptions such as discussions of terrorism, hardly dealt with any of the concerns raised by the interdependence literature. In the past, however, the ability of states to control the international use of force was not at all clear. Mercenaries were an important component of European militaries into the nineteenth, and in some cases even the twentieth, centuries. States would charter private, that is, nonstate actors to conduct military as well as commercial activities. Mercantile companies acted like quasi-states, maintaining their own courts and armed forces. Privateers were authorized to attack foreign shipping. Private citizens did engage in military intervention. (The fact that the activities of private citizens associated with Irangate are considered illegitimate is an indication of how much attitudes and legal stipulations have changed since the early nineteenth century.) One of the achievements of the state over the last two centuries has been to curtail the number, activities, and kinds of nonstate actors in the security issue area. Thus, though some aspects of international economic relations might suggest that micro processes have become more important, others, such as the private use of coercion, indicate that they have declined.

Third, and most important, interdependence arguments ignore the relationship between the growing level of some transactions, both domestic and international, and the consolidation of sovereignty; that is, of the control of a defined territory by a stable government that exercises final authority. High levels of exchange and market-rational outcomes (outcomes that reach the Pareto-optimal frontier given existing preferences and distributions of income) require stable property rights which, in a capitalist economic system, internalize costs and benefits. The only actors currently able to provide such rights are national-states. National-states may not always establish such property rights: socialist states will not routinely vest the right to freely alienate property in private entities; many states have arbitrarily altered the distribution of property rights. Nevertheless, in the modern world consolidated national states are the necessary if not sufficient condition for stable property rights that internalize costs and benefits. Other things being equal, the more stable the pattern of property rights the higher the level of economic transactions. Hence the commonplace notion that there is an inherent conflict between sovereignty and economic transactions is fundamentally misplaced. The consolidation of sovereignty—that is, the establishment of a set of institutions exercising final authority over a defined territory—was a necessary condition for more international economic transactions.

CHALLENGES TO STATE CONTROL

At least some of the literature on economic interdependence regards recent challenges to state control as qualitatively different from challenges that have arisen in the past. There has not, however, been any golden age of state control. States, conceived of as central administrative apparatuses, have never been able to free themselves from concerns about external and internal challenges. The Peace of Westphalia went some way toward domesticating and routinizing the international and civil conflicts generated by religious differences. The eighteenth century saw persistent conflict between the major European powers, culminating in Napoleon's attempt to establish complete dominance over the continent of Europe, an effort that was also a threat to the existing domestic orders of the major European states. High levels of war placed persistent strains on the financial resources of states, compelling them to alter their relationships with their own civil societies.[1]

Compared to earlier periods the nineteenth century was relatively peaceful. The number of international challenges to state boundaries, or even the existence of states, declined. In the center of Europe, however, internal challenges increased. The enervation of the Ottoman and Hapsburg empires precipitated a series of nationalist challenges that led to the creation of new states in the Balkans. In Germany and Italy fragmented political entities were consolidated into nation-states. There has been no past golden age in which Machiavelli's Prince could take a nap secure in the knowledge that external and internal challenges had disappeared.

The kinds of international economic flows that have attracted the attention of analysts who see micro phenomena altering macro structures in the international system are not unprecedented. Technological change has reduced transaction costs domestically as well as internationally. The direction of the long-term trend in the relative importance of international as opposed to domestic flows has not always been clear.

State control over the movement of capital and goods in the international system is the primary focus of interdependence arguments. Huge increases in the absolute volume of world trade, international capital movements, and multinational manufacturing are taken as indicators of declining state control. If these observations are put in the context of domestic activities, it is not clear that international flows are relatively more important today than they were a century or more ago.

Table 1 presents a measure of the volume of international flows of goods, corrected for changes in world GNP. With some exceptions (1900 and 1910), world trade progressively increased, and grew more rapidly than GNP, until World War I. From 1830 to 1913 the volume of world trade increased more than twice as fast as world GNP. In the post-World War II period, trade has also outstripped the growth in world GNP. However, the ratio of trade to GNP did not reach its pre–World War I high of 11 percent until the early 1970s. During the thirty years immediately following World War II, the trade-to-GNP ratio was at a level comparable to that of the 1850–70 period. One interpretation of these data is that between 1950 and 1975, world trade was simply recovering from the disruptions caused by two world wars.

TABLE 1   WORLD TRADE

Year	World exports/world GNP
1830	0.046
1840	0.057
1850	0.068
1860	0.093
1870	0.098
1880	0.114
1890	0.111
1900	0.104
1910	0.104
1913	0.114
1950	0.081
1960	0.092
1965	0.090
1970	0.100
1975	0.139
1980	0.169

Sources: Paul Bairoch, *Commerce Extérieur et Dévelopment Économique de l'Europe au XIXe Siècle* (Paris: École des Hautes Études en Sciences Sociales, 1976); 78; *UN Statistical Yearbook,* various years; UNCTAD, *1983 Handbook of International Trade and Development Statistics;* and B.R. Mitchell. *International Historical Statistics: The Americas and Australasia* (Detroit: Gale Research): pp. 886–89.

Note: Data for 1830–1913 only include the United States and Europe (including European and Asian Russia, but not Turkey). The gap in the data (1913–1950) is due to the paucity of reliable figures in the war and interwar years.

It is true that world trade increased much more rapidly than GNP in the 1970s, but the differential slowed markedly during the recession of the early 1980s. Whether the increased level of trade to GNP will persist remains to be seen.

Disaggregated figures for world output and exports in agricultural products, minerals, and manufactures are presented in Table 2. Between 1950 and 1970, exports increased more rapidly than production in all three categories. Agricultural production grew by 70 percent as exports more than doubled. Although the output of minerals nearly tripled during the twenty-year period, exports in 1970 were four times their 1950 level. In manufacturing, output quadrupled, while exports grew by a factor of six.

After 1970, however, the picture is decidedly mixed. Though the export of manufactures more than doubled between 1970 and 1985, and production increased by nearly 80 percent, increases in the other commodity categories were more modest. No real trend is evident in agricultural commodities, though it appears that exports and output have increased at about the same rate. As of 1985, production was up about 41 percent over the 1970 level; exports were up 50 percent. More striking are the post–1970 trends in the minerals category. Here exports have consistently grown less rapidly than output. In 1985, mineral production was only 15 percent greater than in 1970; the volume of exports was actually less than the 1970 level.

Both output and trade in manufactures have increased dramatically over the past thirty-five years, but this does not necessarily imply an increase in interdependence—if growing interdependence is meant to imply increasing vulnerability to external forces. Rather, the agricultural and mineral commodities production and export statistics suggest that dependence on items that are basic to the reproduction of labor and the production of manufactures has stabilized or even declined. This implies that vulnerability to disruptions in the flow of basic raw materials, and therefore at least one measure of interdependence, has diminished.

TABLE 2   INDICES OF WORLD OUTPUT AND TRADE OF COMMODITIES[a]

	Agricultural products		Minerals[b]		Manufactures	
Year	Output	Exports	Output	Exports	Output	Exports
1950	58	42	38	23	26	16
1955	66	50	49	35	38	25
1960	78	68	59	50	49	37
1965	88	82	79	64	72	58
1970	100	100	100	100	100	100
1975	114	106	109	103	122	143
1980	124	141	131	118	152	199
1985	141	150	115	98	177	252

Source: GATT, *International Trade 1985–86.* Geneva, 1986, p. 139.

[a]*Based on volume.*

[b]Includes fuels and nonferrous metals

Moreover, one of the striking characteristics of trade in manufactures is the growth of intrasectoral trade. This is especially true for the United States and Western Europe. Trade has increased most in commodities where countries are most able to adjust to external changes.

In the area of trade, institutional structures (as opposed to actual patterns of behavior) have deteriorated. There are more departures from the General Agreement on Tariffs and Trade (GATT) principles of nondiscrimination and reductions in trade barriers. Efforts to expand the GATT regime to nontariff barriers (NTBs) have met with mixed results. Only relatively few countries have signed the NTB codes negotiated during the Tokyo Round, and the provisions of these codes are limited to the signatories. The Department of Commerce has estimated that barter trade rose from 2 to 3 percent of world trade in 1976 to 25 to 30 percent in 1983. The percentage of automobile trade among advanced industrialized countries affected by NTBs increased from 1 percent in 1973 to 50 percent in 1983 (Gilpin 1987, 195, 207).

Another indicator of the volume of international economic transactions is capital flows, including direct foreign investment, loans, and bonds. Table 3 presents the ratio of foreign investments to GNP for Western industrialized countries. Here again, the pre–World War I period was one in which foreign investment increased much faster than GNP. Unlike world trade, however, foreign investment has yet to reattain the level it reached in 1913. Foreign investment in the 1950s and 1960s stabilized at 12 percent of GNP, well below the 19 percent it reached in 1840.

The Western industrialized countries have been investing relatively decreasing amounts of capital abroad since 1965. From 0.25 percent of GNP in 1965, to 0.22 percent in 1970, the amount of new foreign investment declined to 0.17 percent in 1981 (United National Conference on Trade and Development, 1983, 446; Organisation for Economic Co-operation and Development 1981, 39, 52).

Bank loans and bonds emanating from Eurocurrency markets are other forms of international capital movements that have attracted a great deal of attention. This involves lending in currencies other than that of the country in which the venture is taking place, such as dollar transactions in London, or yen transactions in Frankfurt. Eurocurrency markets first developed in the 1950s when the Soviet Union and China deposited dollars in European banks because they were afraid that holdings in the United States might be seized. U.S. corporations began making Eurodollar deposits in the 1960s to secure higher interest rates, and they greatly increased their borrowing in Eurodollar markets when capital controls were imposed in the United States in the mid–1960s. The influx of petrodollars during the 1970s further enlarged Euromarkets, although activity decelerated sharply with the onset of the Third World debt crisis in the 1980s. In aggregate Eurocurrency markets in the European reporting area grew from $12 billion in 1964 to $920 billion in 1984. This was a rate of growth far higher than for any other major international economic activity (Frieden 1987, 81–84; Cohen 1986, 21–25).

The increase in size of international capital markets has been accompanied by what appears to be a dramatic change in institutional structures. National capital markets have become integrated. Staggering sums of money can be transferred across international boundaries almost instantaneously by modern communication

TABLE 3   TOTAL FOREIGN INVESTMENT

Year	Foreign investment/GNP
1840	0.19
1870	0.57
1900	1.02
1913	1.08
1929	0.24
1938	0.27
1960	0.12
1970	0.12

Source: Bairoch (1976), p. 99.

Note: Data for 1840–1913 include only Germany, Belgium, France, Sweden, Switzerland, the United Kingdom, and Holland. All Western developed countries are included for 1929 and later.

links. Bankers can respond instantaneously to developments in any part of the globe (Frieden 1987, 80). There is always a major financial market open in some part of the world.

Both the size and institutional character of Eurocurrency markets have led many observers to regard them as a quintessential example of the impact of micro developments on macro structures. Eurocurrency markets have not been subject to much supervision by national regulatory authorities. The size of the international currency pool has made it extremely difficult for central banks to intervene effectively to manage exchange rates. Walter Wriston, president of Citibank during the 1970s, has argued that there is a new world information standard that "is exerting discipline on the countries of the world, which they all hate. For the first time in history, the politicians can't stop it. It's beyond the political control of the world, and that's good news" (quoted in Frieden 1987, 115).

As in the area of trade, however, this viewpoint is woefully lacking in historical perspective. International banking has been important since the Renaissance. Lending rose dramatically during the nineteenth century, with Britain at the core of the system. Almost half of all British savings were lent overseas. The United States replaced Britain as the world's leading creditor after World War I, and lending grew considerably during the 1920s. The amount owed to U.S. banks by foreign borrowers was, as a percentage of GNP, about the same in 1929 as in the mid 1980s—in both cases around 12 percent (Frieden 1987, 89; Cohen 1986, 84–90). The Depression and the aftermath of World War II were the aberrant periods. In the 1970s, as in the case of trade, international lending approximated levels that had been reached in the nineteenth century and the 1920s.

Nor is it obvious that new institutional structures and the ability to rapidly deploy capital around the world indicate that state control is more tenuous than it has been in the past. At least some Renaissance sovereigns were more dependent on international capital markets than contemporary rulers. International capital movements were seen as a threat to domestic financial stability by the end of the nineteenth century. When a major British banking house, Baring Brothers, was threatened with bankruptcy in the early 1890s by Argentine defaults, an international rescue operation was put together by the Bank of England which included not only the Bank but also the British Treasury, the Bank of France, other London banks, and J.P. Morgan (Cohen 1986, 94–95; Frieden 1987, 117–18).

In general national governments, especially Britain, took a more laissez-faire attitude toward international lending in the nineteenth century than is presently the case. Most lending was in the form of bonds rather than bank loans, making it easier for states to argue that responsibility lay with private bondholders, rather than with the national regulatory authorities that were, in any event, much less well developed. Despite the increase in international banking operations in New York during the 1920s, the U.S. government was extremely reluctant to become involved, an attitude that contributed to the onset of the Great Depression (Cohen 1986, 110–11). There were private bondholder committees in the nineteenth century that tried to deal with default, and as gunboat diplomacy (which was often prompted by defaults) indicates, governments did become involved. But the institutional structure for state or at least official involvement in international lending is much more elaborated now, including Paris Clubs and the IMFs as well as private arrangements.

Jeffrey Frieden, who is in many ways quite sympathetic to the autonomy of international capital markets, sums up the present situation in the following terms:

> Nevertheless, the Euromarkets are not stateless; they rest on the implicit, and sometimes explicit support of major western governments. The offshore markets arose, after all, in response to actions by national governments, and they grew because national governments tolerated or encouraged them. At any point in the last thirty years, the U.S. government could have put a stop to much Euromarket activity by prohibiting American banks from participating and by blocking the use of the U.S. dollar offshore [1987, 116].

We do not mean to imply that states cannot be affected by international capital markets that they cannot directly control, but it is critical to recognize that this is not a new development and that these markets have only been able to develop within a broader institutional structure delineated by the power and policies of states.

International travel is another area in which microprocesses have been seen as challenging or altering macrostructures. Technological developments in transportation have facilitated world travel, making it economically feasible for millions of people. Yet the increase in the international flows of people is not so striking if we look at the ratio of foreign to domestic travel. Table 4 presents data on air travel for the world and for the United States. Since 1950, the number of foreign travelers has fluctuated between 20 and 30 percent of the number of domestic travelers. The data for U.S. air travel shows similar fluctuations, but between 7 and 11 percent of the domestic volume. Although the number of international travelers leaving the United States in 1980 was almost six hundred times what it was in 1930, the number of domestic air travelers has increased even more rapidly. In fact, the postwar high for the United States, 11 percent in 1970, was still less—albeit mar-

TABLE 4   AIR TRAVEL

Year	International/domestic (world)	International/domestic (U.S.)
1930		0.114
1940		0.075
1950	0.29	0.097
1955	0.21	
1960	0.27	0.105
1965	0.29	
1970	0.31	0.110
1980		0.088

Sources: ICAO, *Digest of Statistics: Traffic 1961–71;* Air Transport Association of America, *Air Transport Facts and Figures,* various years; and FAA, *Airport Activity Statistics,* various years.

ginally—than it was in 1930. Neither U.S. nor world air traffic demonstrates any trend in the ratio of international to domestic travel.

James Rosenau and others have placed considerable emphasis on the communications revolution as a source of micro changes that may alter macro structures. Telecommunications and computer technology make possible dramatic increases in the flow of information across state borders. They make, so the argument goes, state control of information problematic. Though it is premature to gauge the impact these developments will have on state control of international communications, it is instructive to examine what happened with an earlier communication technology. Table 5 presents data on the ratio of international to domestic mail flows for the world, Europe, and the United States. Europe and the world as a whole reattained their pre-World War II highs only in the late 1960s and 1970s; the United States has yet to reach the level it saw in 1928–29. By the late 1970s, the ratio of foreign to domestic mail had reached new highs both worldwide and in Europe, though not in the United States.

The ratio of international to domestic telephone calls for selected countries is presented in Table 6. Data on telephone traffic are more difficult to obtain and—at best—available for only the last twenty years.[2] However, the figures in Table 6 do suggest a general trend toward the internationalization of this mode of communication. With only four exceptions, the number of international calls has increased more rapidly than that of domestic calls. The four exceptions (Mozambique, Rwanda, Pakistan, and Burma) are all LDCs whose flat or declining ratios are due not so much to a reduction in their international telephone calls as to rapid growth in the amount of domestic traffic. Though these data must be interpreted with a great deal of caution, they do suggest that in the realm of telephone communications, international flows are growing more rapidly than domestic ones.

These data on the flow of goods, money, people, and information do not definitively answer the question of whether state control has eroded. All of the data presented here are in the form of ratios between international and domestic flows. The worldwide flow of goods has reached new highs since the 1970s, but it took ninety years to attain the previous historic high achieved in the 1880s. Capital flows, in the

TABLE 5   MAIL FLOWS

	Foreign mail sent/total domestic mail		
Year	World	United States	Europe
1928–29	0.072	0.018	0.067
1936–38	0.058	0.014	0.051
1948–49	0.058	0.009	0.054
1958–59	0.069	0.009	0.065
1967–68	0.068	0.008	0.071
1975–77	0.093	0.010	0.083

Source: U.N. Statistical Yearbook, various years.

form of foreign investment, increased dramatically until World War I, but consistently declined after 1938. Lending in the 1970s was at a level comparable to that of the nineteenth century. International air travel in comparison with domestic has been relatively stable for the past thirty years. Mail flows in the late 1960s were about the same as they were in the 1920s, though they increased slightly in the 1970s. Among the indicators we have considered here, it is only the pattern of telephone communications that is consistent with growing interdependence.

International flows of all kinds have increased dramatically during the last century. But domestic transactions have increased as well. The relative importance of domestic and international flows has not followed any clear trend. Perhaps states have lost control over all kinds of economic and noneconomic activities in domestic society, and interdependence analyses of the loss of control at the international level could be married with similar arguments about domestic activities. But given the growing scope of state activities, and the steady increase in the ability of states to extract resources from their own societies, arguments about the domestic loss of state control are problematic at best. At the very least the effectiveness of state control domestically, coupled with the absence of any clear increase in the relative importance of international transactions, suggest that there is no prima facie case for the assertion that international flows are more of a challenge to state control now than they have been in the past.

THE CONSOLIDATION OF SOVEREIGNTY

A second problem with interdependence arguments is that they ignore the consolidation of final authority within a defined territory. Historically, the overarching problem for statesmen has been the survival of their state. Although Kant was right to argue that the state of nature of the international system was less malignant than the state of nature for individuals, the existence of states, or at least their geographic boundaries, has often been threatened (Kant 1963). The minimalist goals of preserving territorial and political integrity could not be taken for granted in the past.

TABLE 6   TELEPHONE TRAFFIC

	International/domestic traffic (%)				
Country	1966	1970	1975	1980	1984
Bahamas	0.48	0.91	0.78	1.78	—
Burma	0.008	0.006	0.005	0.008[a]	—
Canada	0.15	0.18	0.25	0.35	0.38[b]
Chile	0.014	0.028	0.024	0.042[a]	—
Costa Rica	—	0.26	0.24	0.30	0.33
Czechoslovakia	0.04	0.05	0.05	0.12	0.13
Gambia	0.29	0.51	0.63	1.36[a]	—
Mexico	—	0.14[d]	0.17	0.23	0.26
Mozambique	0.62	1.05	0.56	0.33[a]	0.36[b]
Pakistan	1.06	1.05	0.36	0.98	0.90[b]
Philippines	—	11.2	12.5	18.8	25.0
Poland	0.18	0.16	0.24	0.07	0.25
Rwanda	0.43	0.58	0.57	0.39	0.27[c]
United Kingdom	0.12	0.16	0.23	0.54	0.81[b]
West Germany	0.43	0.60	0.85	1.18	1.42

Source: International Telecommunication Union. *Yearbook of Common Carrier Telecommunication Statistics.* Geneva: various years.

[a]Data are for 1979.

[b]Data are for 1983.

[c]Data are for 1981.

[d]Data are for 1971.

Annihilation Rates

The contemporary international system is not nirvana, but the situation for individual states has become more secure. The number of official actors in the international system declined until the Napoleonic Wars; it began to increase in the nineteenth century. After World War II the number of states in the international system exploded. At the same time the number of states that have disappeared has continued at a low level. Figures for the last two centuries are shown in Table 7.

The low annihilation rate of states since World War II can be explained in several ways. Nuclear weapons have made force less usable. The weapons themselves are most credible when they are associated with maintaining the central balance between the Soviet Union and the United States, although even here their utility has been challenged.[3] Nuclear weapons may also, however, play some role in deterring conventional conflicts because of the fear of escalation.[4]

The survival rate of states may also be enhanced by the growing significance of juridical sovereignty. Jackson and Rosberg (1982) have pointed out that many of the states created since the conclusion of World War II do not have the attributes that have been traditionally associated with the recognition of sovereignty. Some have not been able to effectively control activities within their own territory. Most lack the material resources that would be needed to resist an external attack by more powerful states in the system. Despite this they have survived. Jackson and Rosberg argue that the most efficacious resource that these states have is juridical sovereignty: the fact that they are recognized as sovereign by other states in the international system. This gives them access to international resources and discourages depredations by other states.

Finally, the high survival rate of states since World War II may reflect the bipolar balance of power. The interests of the two superpowers in Europe are well defined. Any change, particularly a change as dramatic as the elimination of a state, would be very threatening to either the Soviet Union or the United States, a development that neither would welcome. In the Third World the superpowers have cautiously tracked each other's initiatives. There is no playing field where the superpowers are indifferent to outcomes. The most recent disappearance of an arguably sovereign entity, South Vietnam, occurred only after an extended and bloody conflict in which one of the superpowers committed its own forces. Hence, the bipolar distribution of power, which engenders balancing by the poles, may also contribute to the security of states in the postwar world.

Regardless of whether the consolidation of the state system (as indicated by the low annihilation rate for states in the postwar period) is attributable to nuclear weapons, juridical sovereignty, or bipolarity, the pattern of development here does not suggest that basic macro structures are being undermined by micro processes or anything else.

The Control of Military Activity

State control over the use of violence in the international system today is substantially greater than it was as recently as the mid-nineteenth century. In the eighteenth century, most European armies depended on large contingents of foreign mercenaries. Privateers played an important role in sea warfare. The great mercantile companies of Britain, France, and the Netherlands fought wars with each other, governments, and pirates. Piracy was rampant everywhere. Filibustering—"private" military expeditions into neighboring states launched by adventurers, politicians, and renegade military officers, often in collusion with local government officials—flourished in the Americas until the 1860s.

These activities suggest that as recently as the mid-nineteenth century, state control over the exercise of coercion beyond its borders was far from complete. Control was incomplete because state authority claims on coercion were minimal, conflictual, or unsettled. States did not claim the exclusive authority to raise an army within their own borders. They did not claim the exclusive right to employ the military services of individuals residing in their jurisdiction. Individuals were quite free to exercise violence in the international system for their own ends.

The story of how the state gained a monopoly over the coercive forces domestically is well known (Tilly 1975). Less familiar is the process through which the state achieved the exclusive right to deploy violence beyond its borders. This process involved the assertion of new authority claims and the development of

TABLE 7   CREATION AND DISAPPEARANCE OF STATES

Decade	Number created	Number destroyed	Total
			34
1816–25	7	0	41
1826–35	5	0	46
1836–45	6	0	52
1846–55	1	0	53
1856–65	2	6[a]	49
1866–75	3	9[b]	43
1876–85	3	0	46
1886–95	1	0	47
1896–1905	5	1[c]	51
1906–15	3	0	54
1916–25	14	3[d]	65
1926–35	1	0	66
1936–45	1	4[e]	63
1946–55	21	0	84
1956–65	43	1[f]	126
1966–73	17	0	143

Source: Arthur S. Banks, Cross-National Time Series Data Archive User's Manual. Bingham: SUNY. 1975.

[a]These were Modena, the Papal States, Parma, Sardinia, Tuscany, and Two Sicilies in 1862.

[b]The nine were Hanover, Hesse (Electorate), Hesse (Grand Duchy), Mecklenburg, Prussia, and Saxony in 1867, and Württemburg, Baden, and Bavaria in 1870.

[c]In 1905 Russia recognized Japan's "paramount interest" in Korea, though Japan did not formally annex Korea until 1910.

[d]These were Austria-Hungary (1918), Montenegro (1919) and Serbia (1919).

[e]These were Estonia, Latvia, and Lithuania (1940) and Germany (1945).

[f]This was Zanzibar, which joined Tanganyika in 1964 to form Tanzania.

appropriate enforcement capabilities. It began in the fourteenth and fifteenth centuries when the Hundred Years' War (1337–1453) marked the demise of the feudal methods of warfare (Preston and Wise 1970, 85) and culminated in the late eighteenth and early nineteenth centuries.

One way to view the process is in terms of the allocation of military capabilities. Valued goods, including coercive forces, can be allocated by the market or an authoritative body.[5] The feudal levy was an authoritative allocation of military capabilities. Nobles and knights had a duty to provide military force in behalf of the king in exchange for the privilege of landholding. Men served, not for pay, but because they were obligated to serve. By the time of the Hundred Years' War, however, the market had already begun to erode this system, with many knights fighting for pay. In Europe, the fifteenth and sixteenth centuries were the age of the mercenaries (Mockler 1969, 25–27). Market forces were even more evident in sea warfare where "until the end of the fifteenth century maritime warfare was largely in the hands of privateers" (Jessup and Deak 1935, 12). Mercenaries, mercantile companies, privateers, pirates, and filibusters appeared as authoritative allocations gave way to more market-oriented allocations.

Yet by the end of the nineteenth century, all of these nonstate actors had virtually disappeared. Market forces had been supplanted by state authority. State claims to a monopoly on the use of violence in the international system had replaced market allocation of military forces. State control, which for centuries had been problematic, was virtually uncontested in 1990. . . .

PROPERTY RIGHTS AND THE CONSOLIDATION OF SOVEREIGNTY

Let us accept for the moment the proposition that the relative importance of international economic transactions has increased and that effective state control has been eroded. This is a position that supports the contention that major changes may be afoot in the international system. At the same time, however, state control has been consolidated in other areas, especially core areas related to survival and the use of force; this is a development that supports the contention that the existing macro structure (that is, a world of national states) will persist. In fact, these apparently contradictory trends may be causally related.

Optimal market resource allocation, and the high levels of economic exchange with which such allocation is likely to be associated, requires secure property rights. Property rights can be thought of as a set of economic and social relations among individuals that defines "the position of each individual with respect to the utilization of scarce resources" (Furubotn and Pejovich 1972, 1139). Without secure property rights market activities would be constrained because of uncertainty about the possessor's right to sell the commodity and the threat to achieve transfers through force and coercion rather than voluntary exchange.[6] Individuals would place a high discount rate on the future. Capital allocation would be aimed at maximizing short-term gain—getting out before the rules of the game were changed. International trade would concentrate on luxury goods that offered the possibility of very high payoffs if a transaction were successfully completed.

In the present environment the state is the only actor capable of establishing stable property rights. The transaction costs of allocating such rights privately could be prohibitive, especially in cases involving externalities and collective goods (Calabresi and Melamed 1972). The state also has the most developed legal apparatus for enforcing property rights including contractual arrangements.

Stability alone, however, is not a guarantee of an optimal market allocation of economic resources. To achieve this end, property rights must also internalize costs and benefits. States are more than capable of establishing stable property rights that encourage suboptimal economic behavior. Douglass North (1981) has argued that states are torn between securing revenue by seizing a larger slice of the existing pie (which discourages market rational economic behavior), and limiting revenues to encourage a more productive allocation of resources. Robert Bates

(1981) has elegantly delineated how the policies pursued by many African states have discouraged agricultural production. Hence the extent to which a particular pattern of exchange approaches market rationality is a function of both the stability of property rights and their specific substance. These two dimensions are depicted in Figure 1.

The highest level of exchange activity will occur in the upper right quadrant, where property rights are both stable and market rational. (We assume here that all other things being equal, optimal allocation will be associated with higher levels of exchange at least up to the point where transaction costs outweigh further market activity.) Industrialized market economy states fall somewhere in this quadrant. Market activity will be least in the lower left quadrant. Perhaps Afghanistan is now an example. Centrally planned economies fall in the upper left quadrant. Neoclassicla economists have also generally argued that many Third World states also belong in this quadrant by having established stable property rights that encourage misallocation. To some extent economists have tended to view entitlements through property rules as a natural state of affairs and restrictions on such entitlements as a product of misinformed or pernicious government policies.[7] The economist's prescription calls for moving from the upper-left-hand quadrant to the upper-right-hand quadrant of Figure 1.

The history of property rights is, however, much richer than this economist's prescription suggests. Property rights, as Hobbes, Locke, and Smith recognized, were not endowed by nature. Rights are not always stable. Political authority can disappear. New revolutionary regimes may, or may not, honor the international commitments of their predecessors. Private actors caught in the midst of boundary changes may have their property rights radically altered.[8] The movement from feudalism to capitalism was not always functionally optimal; that is, it did not always represent a shift from the upper-left quadrant to the upper-right quadrant of Figure 1. Japan did, in fact, make such a move after the Meiji Restoration. In Europe, however, some areas moved from the upper-left to the lower-right quadrant only later shifting to the upper-right quadrant. Depending on how colonial property rights are assessed some might argue that recently independent states have moved from the upper-right to the upper-left quadrant or even from the upper-right to the lower-left.

The increase in international economic transactions (absolute if not relative) to which the adherents of interdependence arguments so frequently point has occurred primarily in countries that fall in the upper-right-hand quadrant. But almost all areas of the world have, to some extent, participated in the absolute growth of international transactions. At least in part this must be attributed to the consolidation of sovereignty at the global level. Property rights are, in the contemporary world, only rarely threatened by external invasion or boundary changes. Disorder has emanated primarily from internal sources.[9] The consolidation of the state system has facilitated, indeed made possible, increased levels of exchange, both domestic and international.

At the international level, as suggested earlier in this chapter, the hegemonic distribution of power in the noncommunist world did facilitate the creation of a set of international property rights that encouraged international exchange. The trad-

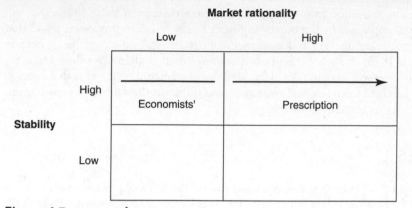

Figure 1 Property rights.

ing regime embodied in GATT gave some assurance that the international flow of goods would not be arbitrarily changed by states.[10] Bilateral treaties helped to secure stable treatment for direct foreign investment. The Bretton Woods agreements, which reflected U.S. initiatives, power, and values, contributed to stability in international capital markets. National laws were, however, the base on which these international arrangements were erected. Without stable property rights enforced by national governments, international regimes would have been meaningless. In a world of national states, transactions take place within national jurisdictions.

CONCLUSION

Arguments that contend that changes in micro processes driven by exogenous technological innovations are fundamentally altering macro structures are vulnerable to several objections. First, they have exaggerated the growth in international transactions relative to domestic ones and have ignored the difficulties that states have always encountered in trying to control at least some transborder movements. Second, such conceptualizations have not taken sufficient account of the importance of hegemonic powers in at least initially creating stable international regimes. Third, they have not confronted the fact that in some issues areas, especially those related to security and the international use of coercion, states have become more consolidated: they have successfully eliminated almost all nonstate actors; and their existence and borders have become more secure. Finally, interdependence arguments have paid little attention to the way in which the consolidation of sovereignty has facilitated the creation of stable property rights that are a necessary if not sufficient condition for a market-rational allocation of resources.

If macro structures crumbled micro processes would almost certainly collapse as well. The transition from the present macro structure to some alternative will not be accomplished by the burrowing from below of micro processes, a fact that students of functionalism and neofunctionalism recognized more than a decade ago (Haas 1975). If such a transition is accomplished at all, more subtle and symbiotic changes will have to take place, and the new institutional forms that emerge will be different from any that exist now, and different than those the more mundane among us could even imagine.

NOTES

1. Skocpol (1979) argues that in one case, France, the financial pressures were so great that the king was compelled to enter into negotiations with civil society (through the Estates General) which ultimately precipitated the French Revolution. For a discussion of the relationship between war and taxation see Tilly (1975) and Ardant (1975). For a discussion of the benefits of an efficient domestic tax system for international military power see Rasler and Thompson (1983).
2. Problems with the ITU series are numerous. Many countries did not provide any statistics before the 1970s; others use different means for measuring international and domestic telephone traffic (for example, pulses versus number of calls), or change the method of measurement in the middle of the series. Of the countries for which twenty years of consistently reported data exist, we have selected countries from as many geographical regions, levels of development, and political systems as possible.
3. Jonathan Schell (1982), for instance, has argued that once a first strike has been launched, the original rationale for retaliation (which was to prevent that strike) has disappeared. But if the rationale is undermined by a preemptive strike then the logic of deterrence unravels. The standard response to this line of argument is the threat that leaves something to chance.
4. For a discussion of the declining utility of force see Keohane and Nye (1977) and Rosecrance (1986). For the ability of nuclear weapons to deter nonnuclear conflict see Robert Jervis (1984).
5. McNeill (1982) argues that the history of modern European warfare reflects the transition from the feudal command (that is, authoritative) allocation of military capabilities to a market-based system, and back to a command system.
6. Calabresi and Melamed (1972, 1092) have argued that an entitlement may be protected by property rules, liability rules, or it may be inalienable. If an entitlement is protected by property rules then its ownership or use can only be changed through the voluntary agreement of the current owner by, for instance, sale in a market. An entitlement protected by liability rules may be destroyed by another party so long as that party is willing to pay an objectively determined value. A right is inalienable if it cannot be transferred, even if there are willing buyers and willing sellers.
7. For example, see Furubotn and Pejovich (1972, 1140).
8. The movie *The Mission* gives a graphic example of such a change when the shift from Spanish to Portuguese rule transformed some South American Indians from recognized Christian individuals into slaves.
9. As U.S. assistance to the Nicaraguan contras illustrates, however, external intervention has hardly come to an end.

10. It is not clear whether the recent U.S. imposition of tariffs on $300 million worth of Japanese goods, given a bilateral trade deficit of tens of billions of dollars, should be taken as an indication of the strength of existing rules or of their malleability.

REFERENCES

Ardant, Gabriel (1975). "Financial Policy and Economic Infrastructure of Modern States and Nations." In C. Tilly, ed., *The Formation of National States in Western Europe.* Princeton, N.J.: Princeton University Press.

Bairoch, Paul (1976). *Commerce extérieur et développement économique de l'Europe au XIXe siécle.* Paris: École des Hautes Études en Sciences Sociales.

Bates, Robert (1981). *Markets and States in Tropical Africa: The Political Basis of Agricultural Policies.* Berkeley: University of California Press.

Baumgart, Winfried (1981). *The Peace of Paris 1856.* Santa Barbara, Calif.: ABC-Clio.

Bayley, C. C. (1977). *Mercenaries for the Crimea.* London: McGill-Queen's University Press.

Brown, Charles H. (1980). *Agents of Manifest Destiny.* Chapel Hill: University of North Carolina Press.

Burchett, Wilfred, and Derek Roebuck (1977). *The Whores of War.* New York: Penguin Books.

Calabresi, Guido, and A. Douglas Melamed (1972). "Property Rules, Liability Rules, and Inalienability: One View of the Cathedral." *Harvard Law Review* 85 (April).

Cohen, Benjamin J. (1986). *In Whose Interest? International Banking and American Foreign Policy.* New Haven, Conn.: Yale University Press.

Cooper, Richard (1968). *The Economics of Interdependence.* New York: McGraw-Hill.

Frieden, Jeffrey (1987). *Banking on the World: The Politics of American International Finance.* New York: Random House.

Furubotn, Eirik G., and Svetozar Pejovich (1972). "Property Rights and Economic Theory: A Survey of Recent Literature." *Journal of Economic Literature* 10 (December).

Gilpin, Robert (1975). *U. S. Power and the Multinational Corporation.* New York: Basic Books.

————(1987). *The Political Economy of International Relations.* Princeton, N.J.: Princeton University Press.

Goldstein, Judith (1986). "The Political Economy of Trade: Institutions of Protection." *American Political Science Review* 80, no. 1 (March).

Gooch, John (1980). *Armies in Europe.* London: Routledge & Kegan Paul.

Haas, Ernst (1975). *The Obsolescence of Regional Integration Theory.* Berkeley: Institute for International Studies.

Hall, William E. (1924). *A Treatise on International Law.* Oxford: Clarendon Press.

Hirschman, Albert (1945). *National Power and the Structure of Foreign Trade.* Berkeley: University of California Press.

Jackson, Robert H., and Carl G. Rosberg (1982). "Why Africa's Weak States Persist: The Empirical and Juridical in Statehood." *World Politics* 35 (October).

Jervis, Robert (1984). *The Illogic of American Nuclear Strategy.* Ithaca, N.Y.: Corner University Press.

Jessup, Philip, and Francis Deak (1935). *Neutrality: Its History, Economics, and Law.* Vol. 1. New York: Columbia University Press.

Kant, Immanuel (1963). *On History.* New York: Bobbs-Merrill.

Keohane, Robert, and Joseph Nye (1972). *Transnational Relations and World Politics.* Cambridge, Mass.: Harvard University Press.

———(1977). *Power and Interdependence.* Boston: Little, Brown.

Krasner, Stephen (1976). "State Power and the Structure of International Trade." *World Politics* 28 (April).

McNeill, William H. (1982). *The Pursuit of Power.* Chicago: University of Chicago Press.

Maier, Charles (1977). "The Politics of Productivity." In Peter J. Katzenstein, ed., *Between Power and Plenty.* Madison: University of Wisconsin Press.

Malloy, William M. (1910). *Treaties, Conventions, International Acts, Protocols, and Agreements between the United States of America and Other Powers, 1776–1909.* Washington, D.C.: G.P.O.

Mitchell, B.R. (1983). *International Historical Statistics: The Americas and Australasia.* Detroit: Gale Research.

Mockler, Anthony (1969). *The Mercenaries.* New York: Macmillan.

Mukherjee, Ramkrishna (1974). *The Rise and Fall of the East India Company.* New York: Monthly Review Press.

Murdoch, Richard K. (1951). *The Georgia-Florida Frontier 1793–96: Spanish Reaction to French Intrigue and American Designs.* University of California Publications in History, J.W. Caughey, D.K. Bjork, and R.H. Fisher, eds., Vol. 40. Berkeley: University of California Press.

North, Douglass (1981). *Structure and Change in Economic History.* New York: Norton.

Organisation for Economic Co-operation and Development (OECD) (1981). *International Investment and Multinational Enterprises.* Paris: OECD.

Phillips, W.A., and Arthur H. Reede (1936). *Neutrality: Its History, Economics, and Law.* New York: Columbia University Press.

Preston, Richard A., and Sydney E. Wise (1970). *Men in Arms.* New York: Praeger.

Rasler, Karen, and William Thompson (1983). "Global Wars, Public Debts, and the Long Cycle," *World Politics* 35.

Ritchie, Robert C. (1986). *Captain Kidd and the War against the Pirates.* Cambridge, Mass.: Harvard University Press.

Roche, James J. (1891). *The Story of the Filibusters.* New York: Macmillan.

Rosecrance, Richard (1986). *The Rise of the Trading State.* New York: Basic Books.

Rosenau, James N. (1988). "Post-International Politics: The Micro Dimension." Paper presented at the fourteenth World Congress of the International Political Science Association. Washington, D.C., 28 August–1 September.

Schell, Jonathan (1982). *The Fate of the Earth.* New York: Knopf.

Sherry, Frank (1986). *Raiders and Rebels.* New York: Hearst Marine Books.

Skocpol, Theda (1979). *States and Social Revolutions.* New York: Cambridge University Press.

Stout, Joseph A. (1973). *The Liberators.* Los Angeles: Westernlore Press.

Tilly, Charles (1975). *The Formation of National States in Western Europe.* Princeton, N.J.: Princeton University Press.

United Nations Conference on Trade and Development (UNCTAD) (1983). *1983 Handbook of International Trade and Development Statistics.* Geneva: UNCTAD.

United Nations (various years). *U.N. Statistical Yearbook.* New York: United Nations.

Wallace, Edward S. (1957). *Destiny and Glory.* New York: Coward-McCann.

Waltz, Kenneth (1970). "The Myth of National Interdependence." In Charles P. Kindleberger, ed., *The International Corporation.* Cambridge, Mass.: MIT Press.

———(1979). *Theory of International Relations.* Reading, Mass.: Addison-Wesley.

The Trading State— Then and Now

Richard Rosecrance

The Second World War initially strengthened both the military-political world and the trading world, but the second impetus was more enduring. After most major conflicts in Western history, peacetime brought a respite, a period of consolidation and agreement. This period did not last long after World War I when the victors concentrated on keeping Germany down, economically and militarily. After World War II, a peace of reconciliation was effected with the defeated powers, Germany and Japan, in part because the Cold War with the Soviet Union broke out at its close. As a new enemy emerged, the Western victors effected a rapprochement with the reformed ex-enemy states. The new trading system might have been undermined at the outset as political hostility and the threat of war overshadowed all other events. It was not, because despite the antagonism between Soviet and Western camps neither side wanted another round of war. Both Western Europe and the Soviet Union needed time to rebuild their economies and restore their devastated homelands. On the Western side there was a much greater understanding of the means by which liberal economies with convertible currencies could contribute to the rebuilding process. Part of the pressure for open economies came from the United States, no doubt desirous of extending her export markets. Part was based on conclusions reached in the 1930s that when financial collapse cuts the commercial links between societies, all nations will suffer, and some will move to seize what they cannot acquire through trade. Economic crisis and depression had been the fare that nourished domestic desperation and brought radical and nationalist leaders to power in more than one state. Prosperity, on the other hand, contributed to stable governments and to a more relaxed foreign policy stance.

The 1930s had also witnessed a transformation in domestic politics in a series of states. The Great Depression of 1929–37 convinced both peoples and governments that employment and social welfare were major national responsibilities: they were too important to be left to the private market and the workings of free enterprise. Henceforth governments in democratic countries—indeed in many others—would act to ensure basic levels of social and economic living. They could do this not only through domestic pump-priming or Keynesian deficit financing: the economic outcomes in one country were likely to be affected by policies in other nations. Depression could easily be communicated from America to Europe as had in fact happened in 1929–31. Depression could partly be avoided by holding export markets open to countries in need. But it was even more important to provide the international funds that would temporarily solve their balance of payments deficits. They would then not have to place restrictions upon their own trade or capital movements, restrictions which would hurt other nations. "Exporting one's unemployment" was a recipe for disaster for the developed world, and it could be avoided by mutual agreement.

The creation of the International Monetary Fund at Bretton Woods in 1944 was a giant step toward a trading system of international relations. The new regime called for an open world economy with low tariffs and strictly limited depreciation of currencies. Tariff hikes and competitive devaluation of currencies were to be restricted by the General Agreement on Tariffs and Trade (GATT) and by the Fund. Unlike the situation after World War I, nations were to be persuaded not to institute controls by offering them liquid funds to float over any period of imbalance in international payments. They would then have a grace period to get their economies in order, after which they could repay the loans.

The plethora of small nations created after the war by the decolonization process in Africa, Asia, the Middle East, and Oceania were generally not large or strong enough to rely on domestic resources, industry, agriculture, and markets for all their needs. Unless they could trade, they could not live. This meant that the markets of the major Western and industrial economies had to take their exports and they in return would need manufacturing exports from the developed countries. The open international economy was critical to their growth and stability. This is not to say that there were no other factors which supported the independence of new nations in the post–World War II period. Military factors and superpower rivalries made the reconquest of colonial areas very costly; ethnic and cultural differences limited the success of attempts to subdue one country or another. But political and military viability were not enough. Small states could not continue to exist as independent entities unless they could earn an economic livelihood. To some degree economic assistance from developed nations or from multilateral agencies met this need. If tariffs and restrictions had inhibited the trade of new nations, however, they would not have been able to function as independent units.

But the open economy of the trading world did not benefit only small nations. The growth of world trade, which increased faster than gross national product until

1980, attracted larger states as well. As the cost of using force increased and its benefits declined, other means of gaining national welfare had to be found. The Federal Republic of Germany, following Hanseatic precedents, became more dependent on international trade than the old united Germany had been. The United Kingdom, France, Italy, Norway, Switzerland, Germany, Belgium, Holland, and Denmark had imports and exports which equalled 30 percent or more of their gross national product, nearly three times the proportion attained in the United States. Japan's huge economy was fueled by foreign trade, which amounted to 20 percent of her GNP total.

The role of Japan and Germany in the trading world is exceedingly interesting because it represents a reversal of past policies in both the nineteenth century and the 1930s. It is correct to say that the two countries experimented with foreign trade because they had been disabused of military expansion by World War II. For a time they were incapable of fighting war on a major scale; their endorsement of the trading system was merely an adoption of the remaining policy alternative. But that endorsement did not change even when the economic strength of the two nations might have sustained a much more nationalistic and militaristic policy. Given the choice between military expansion to achieve self-sufficiency (a choice made more difficult by modern conventional and nuclear weapons in the hands of other powers) and the procurement of necessary markets and raw materials through international commerce, Japan and Germany chose the latter.

It was not until the nineteenth century that this choice became available. During the mecantilist period (1500–1775) commerce was hobbled by restrictions, and any power that relied on it was at the mercy of the tariffs and imperial expansion of other nations. Until the late eighteenth century internal economic development was slow, and there seemed few means of adding to national wealth and power except by conquering territories which contained more peasants and grain. With the Industrial Revolution the link between territory and power was broken; it then became possible to gain economic strength without conquering new lands.[1] New sources of power could be developed within a society, simply by mobilizing them industrially. When combined with peaceful international trade, the Industrial Revolution allowed manufactured goods to find markets in faraway countries. The extra demand would lengthen production runs and increase both industrial efficiency (through economies of scale) and financial return. Such a strategy, if adhered to by all nations, could put an end to war. There was no sense in using military force to acquire power and wealth when they could be obtained more efficiently through peaceful economic development and trade.

The increasing prevalence of the trading option since 1945 raises peaceful possibilities that were neglected during the late nineteenth century and the 1930s. It seems safe to say that an international system composed of more than 160 states cannot continue to exist unless trade remains the primary vocation of most of its members. Were military and territorial orientations to dominate the scene, the trend to greater numbers of smaller states would be reversed, and larger states would conquer small and weak nations.

The possibility of such amalgamations cannot be entirely ruled out. Industrialization had two possible impacts: it allowed a nation to develop its wealth peacefully through internal economic growth, but it also knit new sinews of strength that could coerce other states. Industrialization made territorial expansion easier but also less necessary. In the mid-nineteenth century the Continental states pursued the expansion of their territories while Britain expanded her industry. The industrialization of Prussia and the development of her rail network enabled her armies to defeat Denmark, Austria, and France. Russia also used her new industrial technology to strengthen her military. In the last quarter of the century, even Britain returned to a primarily military and imperialist policy. In his book on imperialism Lenin declared that the drive for colonies was an imminent tendency of the capitalist system. Raw materials would run short and investment capital would pile up at home. The remedy was imperialism with colonies providing new sources for the former and outlets for the latter. But Lenin did not fully understand that an open international economy and intensive economic development at home obviated the need for colonies even under a capitalist, trading system.

The basic effect of World War II was to create much higher world interdependence as the average size of countries declined. The reversal of past trends toward a consolidation of states created instead a multitude of states that could not depend on themselves alone. They needed ties with other nations to prosper and remain viable as small entities. The trading system, as a result, was visible in defense relations as well as international commerce. Nations that could not stand on their own sought alliances or assistance from other powers, and they offered special defense contributions in fighting contingents, regional experience, or particular types of defense hardware. Dutch electronics, French aircraft, German guns and tanks, and British ships all made their independent contribution to an alliance in which no single power might be able to meet its defense needs on a self-sufficient basis. Israel developed a powerful and efficient small arms industry, as well as a great fund of experience combating terrorism. Israeli intelligence added considerably to the information available from Western sources, partly because of its understanding of Soviet weapons systems accumulated in several Arab-Israeli wars.

Defense interdependencies, however, are only one means of sharing the burdens placed upon the modern state. Perhaps more important is economic interdependence among countries. One should not place too much emphasis upon the existence of interdependence per se. European nations in 1913 relied upon the trade and investment that flowed between them; that did not prevent the political crisis which led to a breakdown of the international system and to World War I. Interdependence only constrains national policy if leaders accept and agree to work within its limits. In 1914 Lloyds of London had insured the German merchant marine but that did not stop Germany attacking Belgium, a neutral nation, or England from joining the war against Berlin.[2] The United States was Japan's best customer and source of raw materials in the 1930s, but that did not deter the Japanese attack on Pearl Harbor.

At least among the developed and liberal countries, interdependent ties since 1945 have come to be accepted as a fundamental and unchangeable feature of the situation. This recognition dawned gradually, and the United States may perhaps have been the last to acknowledge it, which was not surprising. The most powerful economy is ready to make fewer adjustments, and America tried initially to pursue its domestic economic policies without taking into account the effect on others, on itself, and on the international financial system as a whole. Presidents Kennedy and Lyndon B. Johnson tried to detach American domestic growth strategies from the deteriorating United States balance of payments, but they left a legacy of needed economic change to their successors. Finally, in the 1980s two American administrations accepted lower United States growth in order to control inflation and began to focus on the international impact of United States policies. The delay in fashioning a strategy of adjustment to international economic realities almost certainly made it more difficult. Smaller countries actively sought to find a niche in the structure of international comparative advantage and in the demand for their goods. Larger countries with large internal markets postponed that reckoning as long as they could. By the 1980s, however, such change could no longer be avoided, and United States leaders embarked upon new industrial and tax policies designed to increase economic growth and enable America to compete more effectively abroad.

The acceptance of new approaches was a reflection of the decline in economic sovereignty. As long as governments could control all the forces impinging upon their economies, welfare states would have no difficulty in implementing domestic planning for social ends. But as trade, investment, corporations, and to some degree labor moved from one national jurisdiction to another, no government could insulate and direct its economy without instituting the extreme protectionist and "beggar thy neighbor" policies of the 1930s. Rather than do this, the flow of goods and capital was allowed to proceed, and in recent years it has become a torrent. In some cases the flow of capital has increased to compensate for barriers or rigidities to the movement of goods.

In both cases the outcome is the result of modern developments in transportation and communications. Railway and high-speed highway networks now allow previously landlocked areas to participate in the international trading network that once depended on rivers and access to the sea. Modern communications and computers allow funds to be instantaneously transferred from one market to another, so that they may earn interest twenty-four hours a day. Transportation costs for a variety of goods have reached a new low, owing to container shipping and handling. For the major industrial countries, (member countries of the Organization for Economic Cooperation and Development, which include the European community, Austria, Finland, Iceland, Portugal, Norway, Spain, Sweden, Switzerland, Turkey, Australia, Canada, Japan, New Zealand, and the United States) exports have risen much faster than either industrial production or gross domestic product since 1965, with the growth of GDP (in constant prices) at 4 percent and that of exports at 7.7 percent.[3] Only Japan's domestic growth has been able to keep pace with the increase in exports (see Table 1).

Foreign trade (the sum of exports and imports) percentages were roughly twice as large as these figures in each case. The explosion of foreign trade since 1945 has, if anything, been exceeded by the enormous movement of capital.

In 1950 the value of the stock of direct foreign investment held by U.S. companies was $11.8 billion, compared with $7.2 billion in 1935, $7.6 billion in 1929 and $3.9 billion

TABLE 1   EXPORTS OF GOODS AND SERVICES (AS A PERCENTAGE OF GDP)

Country	1965	1979
United States	5	9
Japan	11	12
Germany	18	26
United Kingdom	20	29
France	14	22

Source: Michael Stewart, *The Age of Interdependence* (Cambridge, Mass.: MIT Press, 1981), p. 21 (derived from United Nations *Yearbook of National Accounts Statistics*, 1980, vol. 2, table 2A).

in 1914. In the following decade, these investments increased by $22.4 billions, and at the end of 1967 their total value stood at $59 billion.[4]

In 1983, it had reached $226 billion.[5] And direct investment (that portion of investment which buys a significant stake in a foreign firm) was only one part of total United States investment overseas. In 1983 United States private assets abroad totaled $774 billion, or about three times as much.

The amounts, although very large, were not significant in themselves. In 1913, England's foreign investments, equaled one and one-half times her GNP as compared to present American totals of one-quarter of United States GNP. England's foreign trade was more than 40 percent of her national income as compared with contemporary American totals of 15–17 percent. England's pre–World War I involvement in international economic activities was greater than America's today.

Part of what must be explained in the evolution of interdependence is not the high level reached post–1945, but how even higher levels in 1913 could have fallen in the interim. Here the role of industrialization is paramount. As Karl Deutsch, following the work of Werner Sombart, has shown, in the early stages of industrial growth nations must import much of their needed machinery: rail and transportation networks are constructed with equipment and materials from abroad. Once new industries have been created, in a variety of fields, ranging from textiles to heavy industry, the national economy can begin to provide the goods that previously were imported.[6] The United States, the Scandinavian countries, and Japan reached this stage only after the turn of the century, and it was then that the gasoline-powered automobile industry and the manufacturing of electric motors and appliances began to develop rapidly and flourish. The further refinement of agricultural technology also rested on these innovations. Thus, even without restrictions and disruptions of trade, the 1920s would not have seen a rehabilitation of the old interdependent world economy of the 1890s. The further barriers erected in the 1930s confirmed and extended this outcome. If new industrial countries had less need for manufacturing imports, the growth and maintenance of general trade would then come to depend upon an increase in some other category of commerce than the traditional exchange of raw materials for finished goods. In the 1920s, as Albert Hirschman shows, the reciprocal exchange of industrial goods increased briefly, but fell again in the 1930s.[7] That decrease was only made up after 1945 when there was a striking and continuing growth in the trade of manufactured goods among industrial countries.[8] Some will say that this trade is distinctly expendable because countries could produce the goods they import on their own. None of the trade that the United States has today with Western Europe or Japan could really be dubbed "critical" in that the United States could not get along without it. American alternatives exist to almost all industrial products from other developed economies. Thus if interdependence means a trading link which "is costly to break,"[9] there is a sense that the sheer physical dependence of one country upon another, or upon international trade as a whole, has declined since the nineteenth century.

But to measure interdependence in this way misses the essence of the concept. Individuals in a state of nature can be quite independent if they are willing to live at a low standard of living and gather herbs, nuts, and fruits. They are not forced to depend on others but decide to do so to increase their total amount of food and security. Countries in an international state of nature (anarchy) can equally decide to depend only on themselves. They can limit what they consume to what they can produce at home, but they will thereby live less well than they might with specialization and extensive trade and interchange with other nations.

There is no shortage of energy in the world, for example, and all energy needs that previously have been satisfied by imported petroleum might be met by a great increase in coal and natural gas production, fission, and hydropower. But coal-generated electric power produces acid rain, and coal liquification (to produce fuel for automobiles) is expensive. Nuclear power leaves radioactive wastes which have to be contained. Importing oil is a cheaper and cleaner alternative. Thus even though a particular country, like the United States, might become energy self-sufficient if it wanted to, there is reason for dependence on the energy supplies of other nations. Does this mean treating a "tie that is costly to break"? Yes, in the sense that we live less well if we break the tie; but that doesn't mean that the tie could not be broken. Any tie can be broken. In this respect, all ties create "vulnerability interdependence" if they are in the interest of those who form them. One could get along without Japanese cars or European fashions, but eliminating them from the market restricts consumer choice and in fact raises opportunity costs. In this manner, trade between industrial countries may be equally important as trade linking industrial and raw material producing countries.

There are other ways in which interdependence has increased since the nineteenth century. Precisely because industrial countries imported agricultural commodities and sold their manufactured goods to less developed states, their dependence upon each other was much less in the nineteenth century and the 1920s than it is today. Toward the end of the nineteenth century Britain increasingly came to depend upon her empire for markets, food, and raw materials or upon countries in the early stages of industrialization. As Continental tariffs increased, Britain turned to her colonies, the United States, and Latin America to find markets for her exports. These markets provided

> ready receptacles for British goods when other areas became too competitive or unattractive: for example, Australia, India, Brazil and Argentina took the cotton, railways,

steel and machinery that could not be sold in European markets. In the same way, whilst British capital exports to the latter dropped from 52 percent in the 1860s to 25 percent in the few years before 1914, those to the empire rose from 36 percent to 46 percent, and those to Latin America from 10.5 percent to 22 percent.[10]

The British foreign trade which totalled 43.5 percent of GNP in 1913 went increasingly to the empire; thus, if one takes Britain and the colonies as a single economic unit, that unit was much less dependent upon the outside world than, say, Britain is today with a smaller (30.4 percent) ratio of trade to GNP. And Britain alone had much less stake in Germany, France, and the Continental countries' economies than she does today as a member of the European Common Market.

In the nineteenth century trade was primarily vertical in character, taking place between countries at different stages of industrial development, and involving an exchange of manufactured goods on the one hand for food and raw materials on the other. But trade was not the only element in vertical interdependence.

British investment was also vertical in that it proceeded from the developed center, London, to less developed capitals in the Western Hemisphere, Oceania, and the Far East. Such ties might contribute to community feeling in the British Empire, later the Commonwealth of Nations, but it would not restrain conflicts among the countries of Western Europe. Three-quarters of foreign investment of all European countries in 1914 was lodged outside of Europe. In 1913, in the British case 66 percent of her foreign investment went to North and South America and Australia, 28 percent to the Middle and Far East, and only 6 percent to Europe.

In addition, about 90 percent of foreign investment in 1913 was portfolio investment, that is, it represented small holdings of foreign shares that could easily be disposed of on the stock exchange. Direct investment, or investment which represented more than a 10 percent share of the total ownership of a foreign firm was only one-tenth of the total. Today the corresponding figure for the United States is nearly 30 percent. The growth of direct foreign investment since 1945 is a reflection of the greater stake that countries have in each other's well-being in the contemporary period.

In this respect international interdependence has been fostered by a growing interpenetration of economies, in the sense that one economy owns part of another, sends part of its population to live and work in it, and becomes increasingly dependent upon the progress of the latter.[11] The multinational corporation which originates in one national jurisdiction, but operates in others as well, is the primary vehicle for such investment ownership. Stimulated by the demands and incentives of the product life cycle, the multinational corporation invests and produces abroad to make sure of retaining its market share. That market may be in the host country, or it may be in the home country, once the foreign production is imported back into the home economy. Foreign trade has grown enormously since 1945. But its necessary growth has been reduced by the operation of multinational companies in foreign jurisdictions: production abroad reduces the need for exports. In this way an interpenetrative stake has increased between developed economies even when tariffs and other restrictions might appear to have stunted the growth

of exports. The application of a common external tariff to the European Economic Community in the 1960s greatly stimulated American foreign investment in
Europe, which became such a massive tide that Europeans reacted against the
"American challenge," worrying that their prized national economic assets might
be preempted by the United States.

They need not have worried. The reverse flow of European and Japanese
investment in the United States is reaching such enormous proportions that America has become a net debtor nation: A country that has fewer assets overseas than
foreigners have in the United States. The threatened imposition of higher American tariffs and quotas on imports led foreign companies to invest in the United
States in gigantic amounts, thereby obviating the need to send exports from their
home nation. Such direct investment represents a much more permanent stake in
the economic welfare of the host nation than exports to that market could ever be.
Foreign production is a more permanent economic commitment than foreign
sales, because large shares of a foreign company or subsidiary could not be sold on
a stock exchange. The attempt to market such large holdings would only have the
effect of depressing the value of the stock. Direct investment is thus illiquid, as
opposed to the traditional portfolio investment of the nineteenth century.

After 1945 one country slowly developed a stake in another, but the process
was not initially reciprocal. Until the beginning of the 1970s, the trend was largely
for Americans to invest abroad, in Europe, Latin America, and East Asia. As the
American dollar cheapened after 1973, however, a reverse flow began, with Europeans and Japanese placing large blocs of capital in American firms and acquiring
international companies. Third World multinationals, from Hong Kong, the OPEC
countries, and East Asia also began to invest in the United States. By the end of the
1970s world investment was much more balanced, with the European stake in the
American economy nearly offsetting the American investment in Europe. Japan
also moved to diversify her export offensive in the American market by starting to
produce in the United States. But Japan did not benefit from a reciprocal stake in
her own economy. Since foreign investors have either been kept out of the Japanese market or have been forced to accept cumbersome joint ventures with Japanese firms, few multinationals have a major commitment to the Japanese market.
Japan imports the smallest percentage of manufactured goods of any leading
industrial nation. Thus when economic policy makers in America and Europe formulate growth strategies, they are not forced to consider the Japanese economy on
a par with their own because Americans and Europeans have little to lose if Japan
does not prosper. In her own self-interest Japan will almost certainly have to open
her capital market and economy to foreign penetration if she wishes to enjoy corresponding access to economies of other nations. Greater Japanese foreign direct
investment will only partly mitigate the pressures on Tokyo in this respect.

It is nonetheless true that interpenetration of investment in industrial
economies provides a mutual stake in each other's success that did not exist in the
nineteenth century or before World War I. Then Germany cared little if France
progressed and the only important loan or investment stake between major powers
was that between France and Russia, a factor that could hardly restrain conflict in
1914. It is very important at the moment that the Arab oil countries have substan-

tial investments in Europe and North America because their profitability will be influenced by changes in the oil price. Too high oil prices, throwing the industrial West into depression, would have the effect of cutting returns on Arab overseas investments. It would therefore restrain OPEC from precipitate price increases. American business interests with a large stake in Europe would hardly encourage their government to take steps to export American unemployment to other industrial economies for this would only depress their own holdings abroad. A recognition of the degree to which all industrial economies are in the same boat has led to a series of economic summit meetings of seven developed nations in hopes that policies of multilateral growth could be agreed upon to benefit all. These have not solved economic problems, but they have contributed to much greater understanding of the difficulties and policies of other states and perhaps to a greater tolerance for them.

Between the developed countries and the Third World, energy and mineral interdependence fostered a more equal relationship (see Table 2). Australia was the leading producer of bauxite and a huge provider of iron ore in 1982. South Africa was an important source of manganese. Otherwise many of the world's minerals were found in developing nations like Zimbabwe (chromium), Zaire (cobalt), Malaysia (tin), Guinea and Jamaica (bauxite), Zambia (cobalt). Brazil and India (iron ore), and Gabon (manganese). Indian production of iron ore exceeds that of the United States, and Brazilian output is nearly three times as much as America's. In 1982 the twenty-four OECD countries imported eighteen million barrels of oil per day from the OPEC countries and Mexico. Only the United Kingdom and Norway, among Western industrial countries, were virtually self-sufficient in oil supplies. In this way the Third World obtained a considerable leverage in Western industrial economies, and they were bound to obtain more as industrial dependence on imported minerals and oil increased with time.

Yet the great dependence of industrial economies upon each other for markets and the need for Third World minerals and oil would not produce political interdependence between countries in all circumstances. If governments were committed to reducing or eliminating their interdependence with others, the network of economic ties could actually be a factor for conflict. One of the fundamental differences between the Western and democratic industrial countries in 1914 and today—was the lack of commitment to maintain the structure of international economic relations prior to World War I. War between such economies was accepted as a natural outcome of the balance of power system. No pre–1914 statesman or financier was fully aware of the damage that war would do to the European body economic because of the belief that it would be over very quickly. Few bankers or finance ministers interceded with their foreign office brethren to seek to reduce the probability of war.

But the economic interdependence of 1913 had little restraining effect in another respect. Depression and economic disturbances were believed to be natural events like earthquakes and floods; they were not expected to be mediated by governmental intercession or economic policy. It was not until the 1930s that one of the chief functions of the modern democratic state became the achievement of domestic welfare with full employment and an avoidance of inflation. Because it

TABLE 2 DEPENDENCE ON FOREIGN MINERALS (50 Percent or More)

Country/region	Bauxite	Copper	Nickel	Zinc	Tin	Cobalt	Iron ore	Manganese	Chromium
United States	X	—	X	X	X	X	—	X	X
Japan	X	X	X	X	X	X	X	X	X
European Economic Community	X	X	X	X	X	X	X	X	X

Source: Directorate of Intelligence, Handbook of Economic Statistics, 1983 (Washington, D.C., Sept. 1983), p. 13.

was not the business of government in 1914 to prevent economic disruption and dislocation, little effort was made to minimize the effect of a prolonged war upon society, and no effort to prevent war altogether. Between Western industrial countries and Japan today, war is virtually unthinkable. Even if economic interdependence was lower after 1945 than it had been in 1913 (and this is not the case), the political significance of interdependence is still much greater today. Governments in the present era cannot achieve the objectives of high employment without inflation except by working together.

NOTES

1. It is true that the greatest imperial edifices were constructed after the start of the Industrial Revolution. It was precisely that revolution, however, which prepared the groundwork for their demise.
2. Paul Kennedy, *Strategy and Diplomacy 1870–1945* (London: Fontana Paperbacks 1984), pp. 95–96.
3. Michael Stewart, *The Age of Interdependence* (Cambridge, Mass.: MIT Press, 1984), p. 20.
4. John H. Dunning, *Studies in International Investment* (London: George Allen and Unwin, 1970), p. 1.
5. "International Investment Position of the United States at Year End" in *Survey of Current Business* (Washington, D.C.: Department of Commerce, June 1984).
6. Karl W. Deutsch and Alexander Eckstein, "National Industrialization and the Declining Share of the International Economic Sector, 1890–1959" in *World Politics*, 13 (January 1961), pp. 267–99.
7. *National Power and the Structure of Foreign Trade* (Berkeley: University of California Press, 1980), pp. 129–43.
8. Richard Rosecrance and Arthur Stein, "Interdependence: Myth or Reality" in *World Politics* (July 1973), pp. 7–8.
9. Kenneth Waltz, "The Myth of National Interdependence" in Charles Kindleberger, ed., *The International Corporation* (Cambridge, Mass.: MIT Press, 1970), p. 206.
10. Paul Kennedy, *The Rise and Fall of British Naval Mastery* (London: Allen Lace, 1976), pp. 187–88.
11. Nothing could be more misleading than to equate these interrelations with those of nineteenth-century imperialism. The imperial dictates went in one direction—military, economic, and social. The metropole dominated the colony. Today, does North America become a colony when Chicanos and Hispanics move to it in increasing numbers or England a tributary of the West Indies? Does Chinese or Korean investment in the United States render it a peripheral member of the system? The point is that influence goes in both directions just as does investment and trade in manufactured goods.

Who Is Us?

Robert B. Reich

Who is "us"? Is it IBM, Motorola, Whirlpool, and General Motors? Or is it Sony, Thomson, Philips, and Honda?

Consider two successful corporations:

- Corporation A is headquartered north of New York City. Most of its top managers are citizens of the United States. All of its directors are American citizens, and a majority of its shares are held by American investors. But most of Corporation A's employees are non-Americans. Indeed, the company undertakes much of its R&D and product design, and most of its complex manufacturing, outside the borders of the United States in Asia, Latin America, and Europe. Within the American market, an increasing amount of the company's product comes from its laboratories and factories abroad.
- Corporation B is headquartered abroad, in another industrialized nation. Most of its top managers and directors are citizens of that nation, and a majority of its shares are held by citizens of that nation. But most of Corporation B's employees are Americans. Indeed, Corporation B undertakes much of its R&D and new product design in the United States. The company exports an increasing proportion of its American-based production, some of it even back to the nation where Corporation B is headquartered.

Now, who is "us"? Between these two corporations, which is the American corporation, which the foreign corporation? Which is more important to the economic future of the United States?

As the American economy becomes more globalized, examples of both Corporation A and B are increasing. At the same time, American concern for the competitiveness of the United States is increasing. Typically, the assumed vehicle for improving the competitive performance of the United States is the American corporation—by which most people would mean Corporation A. But today, the competitiveness of American-owned corporations is no longer the same as American competitiveness. Indeed, American ownership of the corporation is profoundly less relevant to America's economic future than the skills, training, and knowledge commanded by American workers—workers who are increasingly employed within the United States by foreign-owned corporations.

So who is us? The answer is, the American work force, the American people, but not particularly the American corporation. The implications of this new answer are clear: If we hope to revitalize the competitive performance of the United States economy, we must invest in people, not in nationally defined corporations. We must open our borders to investors from around the world rather than favoring companies that may simply fly the U.S. flag. And government policies should promote human capital in this country rather than assuming that American corporations will invest on "our" behalf. The American corporation is simply no longer "us."

GLOBAL COMPANIES

American corporations have been abroad for years, even decades. So in one sense, the multinational identity of American companies is nothing new. What is new is that American-owned multinationals are beginning to employ large numbers of foreigners relative to their American work forces, are beginning to rely on foreign facilities to do many of their most technologically complex activities, and are beginning to export from their foreign facilities—including bringing products back to the United States.

Around the world, the numbers are already large—and still growing. Take IBM—often considered the thoroughbred of competitive American corporations. Forty percent of IBM's world employees are foreign, and the percentage is increasing. IBM Japan boasts 18,000 Japanese employees and annual sales of more than $6 billion, making it one of Japan's major exporters of computers.

Or consider Whirlpool. After cutting its American work force by 10 percent and buying Philips's appliance business, Whirlpool now employs 43,500 people around the world in 45 countries—most of them non-Americans. Another example is Texas Instruments, which now does most of its research, development, design, and manufacturing in East Asia. TI employs over 5,000 people in Japan alone, making advanced semiconductors—almost half of which are exported, many of them back to the United States.

American corporations now employ 11 percent of the industrial work force of Northern Ireland, making everything from cigarettes to computer software, much of which comes back to the United States. More than 100,000 Singaporians work for more than 200 U.S. corporations, most of them fabricating and assembling electronic components for export to the United States. Singapore's largest private employer is General Electric, which also accounts for a big share of that nation's growing exports. Taiwan counts AT&T, RCA, and Texas Instruments among its largest exporters. In fact, more than one-third of Taiwan's notorious trade surplus with the United States comes from U.S. corporations making or buying things there, then selling or using them back in the United States. The same corporate sourcing practice accounts for a substantial share of the U.S. trade imbalance with Singapore, South Korea, and Mexico—raising a question as to whom complaints about trade imbalances should be directed.

The pattern is not confined to America's largest companies. Molex, a suburban Chicago maker of connectors used to link wires in cars and computer boards, with revenues of about $300 million in 1988, has 38 overseas factories, five in Japan. Loctite, a midsize company with sales in 1988 of $457 million, headquartered in Newington, Connecticut, makes and sells adhesives and sealants all over the world. It has 3,500 employees—only 1,200 of whom are Americans. These companies are just part of a much larger trend: according to a 1987 McKinsey & Company study, America's most profitable midsize companies increased their investments in overseas production at an annual rate of 20 percent between 1981 and 1986.

Overall, the evidence suggests that U.S. companies have not lost their competitive edge over the last 20 years—they've just moved their base of operations. In 1966, American-based multinationals accounted for about 17 percent of world exports; since then their share has remained almost unchanged. But over the same period, the share of exports from the United States in the world's total trade in manufactures fell from 16 percent to 14 percent. In other words, while Americans exported less, the overseas affiliates of U.S.owned corporations exported more than enough to offset the drop.

The old trend of overseas capital investment is accelerating: U.S. companies increased foreign capital spending by 24 percent in 1988, 13 percent in 1989. But even more important, U.S. businesses are now putting substantial sums of money into foreign countries to do R&D work. According to National Science Foundation figures, American corporations increased their overseas R&D spending by 33 percent between 1986 and 1988, compared with a 6 percent increase in R&D spending in the United States. Since 1987, Eastman Kodak, W.R. Grace, Du Pont, Merck, and Upjohn have all opened new R&D facilities in Japan. At Du Pont's Yokohama laboratory, more than 180 Japanese scientists and technicians are working at developing new materials technologies. IBM's Tokyo Research Lab, tucked away behind the far side of the Imperial Palace in downtown Tokyo, houses a small army of Japanese engineers who are perfecting image-processing technology. Another IBM laboratory, the Kanagawa arm of its Yamato Development Laboratory, houses 1,500 researchers who are developing hardware and software. Nor does IBM confine its pioneering work to Japan: Recently, two European researchers at IBM's Zurich laboratory announced major breakthroughs into superconductivity and microscopy—earning them both Nobel Prizes.

An even more dramatic development is the arrival of foreign corporations in the United States at a rapidly increasing price. As recently as 1977, only about 3.5 percent of the value added and the employment of American manufacturing originated in companies controlled by foreign parents. By 1987, the number had grown to almost 8 percent. In just the last two years, with the faster pace of foreign acquisitions and investments, the figure is now almost 11 percent. Foreign-owned companies now employ 3 million Americans, roughly 10 percent of our manufacturing workers. In fact, in 1989, affiliates of foreign manufacturers created more jobs in the United States than American-owned manufacturing companies.

And these non-U.S. companies are vigorously exporting from the United States. Sony now exports audio- and videotapes to Europe from its Dothan, Alabama factory and ships audio recorders from its Fort Lauderdale, Florida plant. Sharp exports 100,000 microwave ovens a year from its factory in Memphis, Tennessee. Last year, Dutch-owned Philips Consumer Electronics Company exported 1,500 color televisions from its Greenville, Tennessee plant to Japan. Its 1990 target is 30,000 televisions; by 1991, it plans to export 50,000 sets. Toshiba America is sending projection televisions from its Wayne, New Jersey plant to Japan. And by the early 1990s, when Honda annually exports 50,000 cars to Japan from its Ohio production base, it will actually be making more cars in the United States than in Japan.

THE NEW AMERICAN CORPORATION

In an economy of increasing global investment, foreign-owned Corporation B, with its R&D and manufacturing presence in the United States and its reliance on American workers, is far more important to America's economic future than American-owned Corporation A, with its platoons of foreign workers. Corporation A may fly the American flag, but Corporation B invests in Americans. Increasingly, the competitiveness of American workers is a more important definition of "American competitiveness" than the competitiveness of American companies. Issues of ownership, control, and national origin are less important factors in thinking through the logic of "who is us" and the implications of the answer for national policy and direction.

Ownership Is Less Important

Those who favor American-owned Corporation A (that produces overseas) over foreign-owned Corporation B (that produces here) might argue that American ownership generates a stream of earnings for the nation's citizens. This argument is correct, as far as it goes. American shareholders do, of course, benefit from the global successes of American corporations to the extent that such successes are reflected in higher share prices. And the entire U.S. economy benefits to the extent that the overseas profits of American companies are remitted to the United States.

But American investors also benefit from the successes of non-American companies in which Americans own a minority interest—just as foreign citizens benefit from the successes of American companies in which they own a minority interest, and such cross-ownership is on the increase as national restrictions on foreign

356 THE INTERNATIONAL POLITICAL ECONOMY

ownership fall by the wayside. In 1989, cross-border equity investments by Americans, British, Japanese, and West Germans increased 20 percent, by value, over 1988.

The point is that in today's global economy, the total return to Americans from their equity investments is not solely a matter of the success of particular companies in which Americans happen to have a controlling interest. The return depends on the total amount of American savings invested in global portfolios comprising both American and foreign-owned companies—and on the care and wisdom with which American investors select such portfolios. Already Americans invest 10 percent of their portfolios in foreign securities; a recent study by Salomon Brothers predicts that it will be 15 percent in a few years. U.S. pension managers surveyed said that they predict 25 percent of their portfolios will be in foreign-owned companies within 10 years.

Control Is Less Important

Another argument marshaled in favor of Corporation A might be that because Corporation A is controlled by Americans, it will act in the best interests of the United States. Corporation B, a foreign national, might not do so—indeed, it might act in the best interests of its nation of origin. The argument might go something like this: Even if Corporation B is now hiring more Americans and giving them better jobs than Corporation A, we can't be assured that it will continue to do so. It might bias its strategy to reduce American competitiveness; it might even suddenly withdraw its investment from the United States and leave us stranded.

But this argument makes a false assumption about American companies—namely, that they are in a position to put national interests ahead of company or shareholder interests. To the contrary: Managers of American-owned companies who sacrificed profits for the sake of national goals would make themselves vulnerable to a takeover or liable for a breach of fiduciary responsibility to their shareholders. American managers are among the loudest in the world to declare that their job is to maximize shareholder returns—not to advance national goals.

Apart from wartime or other national emergencies, American-owned companies are under no special obligation to serve national goals. Nor does our system alert American managers to the existence of such goals, impose on American managers unique requirements to meet them, offer special incentives to achieve them, or create measures to keep American managers accountable for accomplishing them. Were American managers knowingly to sacrifice profits for the sake of presumed national goals, they would be acting without authority, on the basis of their own views of what such goals might be, and without accountability to shareholders or to the public.

Obviously, this does not preclude American-owned companies from displaying their good corporate citizenship or having a sense of social responsibility. Sensible managers recognize that acting "in the public interest" can boost the company's image; charitable or patriotic acts can be good business if they promote long-term profitability. But in this regard, American companies have no particular edge over foreign-owned companies doing business in the United States. In fact, there is every reason to believe that a foreign-owned company would be even more eager to demonstrate to the American public its good citizenship in America than would the average American company. The American subsidiaries of Hitachi, Matsushita, Siemens, Thomson, and many other foreign-owned companies lose no opportunity to contribute funds to American charities, sponsor community events, and support public libraries, universities, schools, and other institutions. (In 1988, for example, Japanese companies operating in the United States donated an estimated $200 million to American charities; by 1994, it is estimated that their contributions will total $1 billion.)[1]

By the same token, American-owned businesses operating abroad feel a similar compulsion to act as good citizens in their host countries. They cannot afford to be seen as promoting American interests; otherwise they would jeopardize their relationships with foreign workers, consumers, and governments. Some of America's top managers have been quite explicit on this point. "IBM cannot be a net exporter from every nation in which it does business," said Jack Kuehler, IBM's new president. "We have to be a good citizen everywhere." Robert W. Galvin, chairman of Motorola, is even more blunt: should it become necessary for Motorola to close some of its factories, it would not close its Southeast Asian plants before it closed its American ones. "We need our Far Eastern customers," says Galvin, "and we cannot alienate the Malaysians. We must treat our employees all over the world equally." In fact, when it becomes necessary to reduce global capacity, we might expect American-owned businesses to slash more jobs in the United States than in Europe (where labor laws often prohibit precipitous layoffs) or in Japan (where national norms discourage it).

Just as empty is the concern that a foreign-owned company might leave the United States stranded by suddenly abandoning its U.S. operation. The typical argument suggests that a foreign-owned company might withdraw for either profit or foreign policy motives. But either way, the bricks and mortar would still be here. So would the equipment. So too would be the accumulated learning among American workers. Under such circumstances, capital from another source would fill the void; an American (or other foreign) company would simply purchase the empty facilities. And most important, the American work force would remain, with the critical skills and capabilities, ready to go back to work.

After all, the American government and the American people maintain jurisdiction—political control—over assets within the United States. Unlike foreign assets held by American-owned companies that are subject to foreign political control and, occasionally, foreign expropriation, foreign-owned assets in the United States are secure against sudden changes in foreign governments' policies. This not only serves as an attraction for foreign capital looking for a secure haven; it also benefits the American work force.

Work Force Skills Are Critical

As every advanced economy becomes global, a nation's most important competitive asset becomes the skills and cumulative learning of its work force. Consequently, the most important issue with regard to global corporations is whether and to what extent they provide Americans with the training and experience that enable them to add greater value to the world economy. Whether the company happens to be headquartered in the United States or the United Kingdom is fundamentally unimportant. The company is a good "American" corporation if it equips its American work force to compete in the global economy.

Globalization, almost by definition, makes this true. Every factor of production other than work force skills can be duplicated anywhere around the world. Capital now sloshes freely across international boundaries, so much so that the cost of capital in different countries is rapidly converging. State-of-the-art factories can be erected anywhere. The latest technologies flow from computers in one nation, up to satellites parked in space, then back down to computers in another nation— all at the speed of electronic impulses. It is all fungible: capital, technology, raw materials, information—all, except for one thing, the most critical part, the one element that is unique about a nation: its work force.

In fact, because all of the other factors can move so easily any place on earth, a work force that is knowledgeable and skilled at doing complex things attracts foreign investment. The relationship forms a virtuous circle: Well-trained workers attract global corporations, which invest and give the workers good jobs; the good jobs, in turn, generate additional training and experience. As skills move upward and experience accumulates, a nation's citizens add greater and greater value to the world—and command greater and greater compensation from the world, improving the country's standard of living.

Foreign-Owned Corporations Help American Workers Add Value

When foreign-owned companies come to the United States, they frequently bring with them approaches to doing business that improve American productivity and allow American workers to add more value to the world economy. In fact, they come here primarily because they can be more productive in the United States than can other American rivals. It is not solely America's mounting external indebtedness and relatively low dollar that account for the rising level of foreign investment in the United States. Actual growth of foreign investment in the United States dates from the mid–1970s rather than from the onset of the large current account deficit in 1982. Moreover, the two leading foreign investors in the United States are the British and the Dutch—not the Japanese and the West Germans, whose enormous surpluses are the counterparts of our current account deficit.

For example, after Japan's Bridgestone tire company took over Firestone, productivity increased dramatically. The joint venture between Toyota and General Motors at Fremont, California, is a similar story: Toyota's managerial system took many of the same workers from what had been a deeply troubled GM plant and turned it into a model facility, with upgraded productivity and skill levels.

In case after case, foreign companies set up or buy up operations in the United States to utilize their corporate assets with the American work force. Foreign-owned businesses with better design capabilities, production techniques, or managerial skills are able to displace American companies on American soil precisely because those businesses are more productive. And in the process of supplanting the American company, the foreign-owned operation can transfer the superior know-how to its American work force—giving American workers the tools they need to be more productive, more skilled, and more competitive. Thus foreign companies create good jobs in the United States. In 1986 (the last date for which such data are available), the average American employee of a foreign-owned manufacturing company earned $32,887, while the average American employee of an American-owned manufacturer earned $28,954.[2]

This process is precisely what happened in Europe in the 1950s and 1960s. Europeans publicly fretted about the invasion of American-owned multinationals and the onset of "the American challenge." But the net result of these operations in Europe has been to make Europeans more productive, upgrade European skills, and thus enhance the standard of living of Europeans.

NOW WHO IS US?

American competitiveness can best be defined as the capacity of Americans to add value to the world economy and thereby gain a higher standard of living in the future without going into ever deeper debt. American competitiveness is not the profitability or market share of American-owned corporations. In fact, because the American-owned corporation is coming to have no special relationship with Americans, it makes no sense for Americans to entrust our national competitiveness to it. The interests of American-owned corporations may or may not coincide with those of the American people.

Does this mean that we should simply entrust our national competitiveness to any corporation that employs Americans, regardless of the nationality of corporate ownership? Not entirely. Some foreign-owned corporations are closely tied to their nation's economic development—either through direct public ownership (for example, Airbus Industrie, a joint product of Britain, France, West Germany, and Spain, created to compete in the commercial airline industry) or through financial intermediaries within the nation that, in turn, are tied to central banks and ministries of finance (in particular the model used by many Korean and Japanese corporations). The primary goals of such corporations are to enhance the wealth of their nations, and the standard of living of their nations' citizens, rather than to enrich their shareholders. Thus, even though they might employ American citizens in their world-wide operations, they may employ fewer Americans—or give Americans lower value-added jobs—than they would if these corporations were intent simply on maximizing their own profits.[3]

On the other hand, it seems doubtful that we could ever shift the goals and orientations of American-owned corporations in this same direction—away from profit maximization and toward the development of the American work force. There is no reason to suppose that American managers and shareholders would accept new regulations and oversight mechanisms that forced them to sacrifice proftis for the sake of building human capital in the United States. Nor is it clear that the American system of government would be capable of such detailed oversight.

The only practical answer lies in developing national policies that reward *any* global corporation that invests in the American work force. In a whole set of public policy areas, involving trade, publicly supported R&D, antitrust, foreign direct investment, and public and private investment, the overriding goal should be to induce global corporations to build human capital in America.

Trade Policy

We should be less interested in opening foreign markets to American-owned companies (which may in fact be doing much of their production overseas) than in opening those markets to companies that employ Americans—even if they happen to be foreign-owned. But so far, American trade policy experts have focused on representing the interests of companies that happen to carry the American flag—without regard to where the actual production is being done. For example, the United States recently accused Japan of excluding Motorola from the lucrative Tokyo market for cellular telephones and hinted at retaliation. But Motorola designs and makes many of its cellular telephones in Kuala Lumpur, while most of the Americans who make cellular telephone equipment in the United States for export to Japan happen to work for Japanese-owned companies. Thus we are wasting our scarce political capital pushing foreign governments to reduce barriers to American-owned companies that are seeking to sell or produce in their market.

Once we acknowledge that foreign-owned Corporation B may offer more to American competitiveness than American-owned Corporation A, it is easy to design a preferable trade policy—one that accords more directly with our true national interests. The highest priority for American trade policy should be to discourage other governments from invoking domestic content rules—which have the effect of forcing global corporations, American and foreign-owned alike, to locate production facilities in those countries rather than in the United States.

The objection here to local content rules is not that they may jeopardize the competitiveness of American companies operating abroad. Rather, it is that these requirements, by their very nature, deprive the American work force of the opportunity to compete for jobs, and with those jobs, for valuable skills, knowledge, and experience. Take, for example, the recently promulgated European Community nonbinding rule on television-program production, which urges European television stations to devote a majority of their air time to programs made in Europe. Or consider the European allegations of Japanese dumping of office machines containing semiconductors, which has forced Japan to put at least 45 percent European content into machines sold in Europe (and thus fewer American-made semiconductor chips).

Obviously, U.S.-owned companies are already inside the EC producing both semiconductors and television programs. So if we were to adopt American-owned Corporation A as the model for America's competitive self-interest, our trade policy might simply ignore these EC initiatives. But through the lens of a trade policy focused on the American work force, it is clear how the EC thwarts the abilities of

Americans to excel in semiconductor fabrication and filmmaking—two areas where our work force already enjoys a substantial competitive advantage.

Lack of access by American-owned corporations to foreign markets is, of course, a problem. But it only becomes a crucial problem for America to the extent that both American and foreign-owned companies must make products within the foreign market—products that they otherwise would have made in the United States. Protection that acts as a domestic content requirement skews investment away from the United States—and away from U.S. workers. Fighting against that should be among the highest priorities of U.S. trade policy.

Publicly Supported R&D

Increased global competition, the high costs of research, the rapid rate of change in science and technology, the model of Japan with its government-supported commercial technology investments—all of these factors have combined to make this area particularly critical for thoughtful public policy. But there is no reason why preference should be given to American-owned companies. Dominated by our preoccupation with American-owned Corporation A, current public policy in this area limits U.S. government-funded research grants, guaranteed loans, or access to the fruits of U.S. government-funded research to American-owned companies. For example, membership in Sematech, the research consortium started two years ago with $100 billion annual support payments by the Department of Defense to help American corporations fabricate complex memory chips, is limited to American-owned companies. More recently, a government effort to create a consortium of companies to catapult the United States into the HDTV competition has drawn a narrow circle of eligibility, ruling out companies such as Sony, Philips, and Thomson that do R&D and production in the United States but are foreign-owned. More generally, long-standing regulations covering the more than 600 government laboratories and research centers that are spread around the United States ban all but American-owned companies from licensing inventions developed at these sites.

Of course, the problem with this policy approach is that it ignores the reality of global American corporations. Most U.S.-owned companies are quite happy to receive special advantages from the U.S. government—and then spread the technological benefits to their affiliates all over the world. As Sematech gets under way, its members are busily going global: Texas Instruments is building a new $250 million semiconductor fabrication plant in Taiwan; by 1992, the facility will produce four-megabit memory chips and custom-made, application-specific integrated circuits—some of the most advanced chips made anywhere. TI has also joined with Hitachi to design and produce a super chip that will store 16 million bits of data. Motorola, meanwhile, has paired with Toshiba to research and produce a similar generation of futurist chips. Not to be outdone, AT&T has a commitment to build a state-of-the-art chip-making plant in Spain. So who will be making advanced chips in the United States? In June 1989, Japanese-owned NEC announced plans to build a $400 million facility in Rosedale, California, for making four-megabit memory chips and other advanced devices not yet in production anywhere.

The same situation applies to HDTV. Zenith Electronics is the only remaining American-owned television manufacturer, and thus the only one eligible for a government subsidy. Zenith employs 2,500 Americans. But there are over 15,000 Americans employed in the television industry who do not work for Zenith—undertaking R&D, engineering, and high-quality manufacturing. They work in the United States for foreign-owned companies: Sony, Philips, Thomson, and others (see Table 1). Of course, none of these companies is presently eligible to participate in the United States's HDTV consortium—nor are their American employees.

Again, if we follow the logic of Corporation B as the more "American" company, it suggests a straightforward principle for publicly supported R&D: We should be less interested in helping *American-owned companies* become technologically sophisticated than in helping *Americans* become technologically sophisticated. Government-financed help for research and development should be available to any corporation, regardless of the nationality of its owners, as long as the company undertakes the R&D in the United States—using American scientists, engineers,

TABLE 1   U.S. TV SET PRODUCTION, 1988

Company name	Plant type	Location	Employees	Annual production
Bang & Olufsen	Assembly	Compton, Calif.	n.a.†	n.a.
Goldstar	Total*	Huntsville, Ala.	400	1,000,000
Harvey Industries	Assembly	Athens, Tex.	900	600,000
Hitachi	Total	Anaheim, Calif.	900	360,000
JVC	Total	Elmwood Park, N.J.	100	480,000
Matsushita	Assembly	Franklin Park, Ill.	800	1,000,000
American Kotobuki (Matsushita)	Assembly	Vancouver, Wash.	200	n.a.
Mitsubishi	Assembly	Santa Ana, Calif.	550	400,000
Mitsubishi	Total	Braselton, Ga.	300	285,000
NEC	Assembly	McDonough, Ga.	400	240,000
Orion	Assembly	Princeton, Ind.	250	n.a.
Philips	Total	Greenville, Tenn.	3,200	2,000,000+
Samsung	Total	Saddle Brook, N.J.	250	1,000,000
Sanyo	Assembly	Forrest City, Ark.	400	1,000,000
Sharp	Assembly	Memphis, Tenn.	770	1,100,000
Sony	Total	San Diego, Calif.	1,500	1,000,000
Tatung	Assembly	Long Beach, Calif.	130	17,500
Thomson	Total	Bloomington, Ind.	1,766	3,000,000+
Thomson	Components	Indianapolis, Ind.	1,604	n.a.
Toshiba	Assembly	Lebanon, Tenn.	600	900,000
Zenith	Total	Springfield, Mo.	2,500	n.a.

Source: Electronic Industries Association, HDTV Information Center, Washington, D.C.

*Total manufacturing involves more than the assembling of knocked-down kits. Plants that manufacture just the television cabinets are not included in this list.

†Not available.

and technicians. To make the link more explicit, there could even be a relationship between the number of Americans involved in the R&D and the amount of government aid forthcoming. It is important to note that this kind of public-private bargain is far different from protectionist domestic content requirements. In this case, the government is participating with direct funding and thus can legitimately exact a quid pro quo from the private sector.

Antitrust Policy

The Justice Department is now in the process of responding to the inevitability of globalization; it recognizes that North American market share alone means less and less in a global economy. Consequently, the Justice Department is about to relax antitrust policy—for American-owned companies only. American-owned companies that previously kept each other at arm's length for fear of prompting an inquiry into whether they were colluding are now cozying up to one another. Current anti-trust policy permits research joint ventures; the attorney general is on the verge of recommending that antitrust policy permit joint production agreements as well, when there may be significant economies of scale and where competition is global—again, among American-owned companies.

But here again, American policy seems myopic. We should be less interested in helping American-owned companies gain economies of scale in research, production, and other key areas, and more interested in helping corporations engaged in research or production within the United States achieve economies of scale— regardless of their nationality. U.S. antitrust policy should allow research or production joint ventures among any companies doing R&D or production within the United States, as long as they can meet three tests: They could not gain such scale efficiencies on their own, simply by enlarging their investment in the United States; such a combination of companies would allow higher levels of productivity within the United States; and the combination would not substantially diminish global competition. National origin should not be a factor.

Foreign Direct Investment

Foreign direct investment has been climbing dramatically in the United States: last year it reached $329 billion, exceeding total American investment abroad for the first time since World War I (but be careful with these figures, since investments are valued at cost and this substantially understates the worth of older investments). How should we respond to this influx of foreign capital?

Clearly, the choice between Corporation A and Corporation B has important implications. If we are most concerned about the viability of American-owned corporations, then we should put obstacles in the way of foreigners seeking to buy controlling shares in American-owned companies, or looking to build American production facilities that would compete with American-owned companies.

Indeed, current policies tilt in this direction. For example, under the so-called Exon-Florio Amendment of the Omnibus Trade and Competitiveness Act of 1988, foreign investors must get formal approval from the high-level Committee on Foreign Investments in the United States, comprising the heads of eight federal agencies and chaired by the secretary of the treasury, before they can purchase an American company. The expressed purpose of the law is to make sure that a careful check is done to keep "national security" industries from passing into the hands of foreigners. But the law does not define what "national security" means: Thus it invites all sorts of potential delays and challenges. The actual effect is to send a message that we do not look with favor on the purchase of American-owned assets by foreigners. Other would-be pieces of legislation send the same signal. In July 1989, for instance, the House Ways and Means Committee voted to apply a withholding capital gains tax to foreigners who own more than 10 percent of a company's shares. Another provision of the committee would scrap tax deductibility for interest on loans made by foreign parents to their American subsidiaries. A third measure would limit R&D tax credits for foreign subsidiaries. More recently, Congress is becoming increasingly concerned about foreign takeovers of American airlines. A subcommittee of the House Commerce Committee has voted to give the Transportation Department authority to block foreign acquisitions.

These policies make little sense—in fact, they are counterproductive. Our primary concern should be the training and development of the American work force, not the protection of the American-owned corporation. Thus we should encourage, not discourage, foreign direct investment. Experience shows that foreign-owned companies usually displace American-owned companies in just those industries where the foreign businesses are simply more productive. No wonder America's governors spend a lot of time and energy promoting their states to foreign investors and offer big subsidies to foreign companies to locate in their states, even if they compete head-on with existing American-owned businesses.

Public and Private Investment

The current obsession with the federal budget deficit obscures a final, crucial aspect of the choice between Corporation A and Corporation B. Conventional wisdom holds that government expenditures "crowd out" private investment, making it more difficult and costly for American-owned companies to get the capital they need. According to this logic, we may have to cut back on public expenditures in order to provide American-owned companies with the necessary capital to make investments in plant and equipment.

But the reverse may actually be the case—particularly if Corporation B is really more in America's competitive interests than Corporation A. There are a number of reasons why this is true.

First, in the global economy, America's public expenditures don't reduce the amount of money left over for private investment in the United States. Today capital flows freely across the national borders—including a disproportionately large inflow to the United States. Not only are foreign savings coming to the United States, but America's private savings are finding their way all over the world. Sometimes the vehicle is the far-flung operations of a global American-owned company, sometimes a company in which foreigners own a majority stake. But the old notion of national boundaries is becoming obsolete. Moreover, as I have stressed, it is a mistake to associate these foreign investments by American-owned companies with any result that improves the competitiveness of the United States. There is simply no necessary connection between the two.

There is, however, a connection between the kinds of investments that the public sector makes and the competitiveness of the American work force. Remember: A work force that is knowledgeable and skilled at doing complex things attracts foreign investment in good jobs, which in turn generates additional training and experience. A good infrastructure of transportation and communication makes a skilled work force even more attractive. The public sector often is in the best position to make these sorts of "pump priming" investments—in education, training and retraining, research and development, and in all of the infrastructure that moves people and goods and facilitates communication. These are the investments that distinguish one nation from another—they are the relatively nonmobile factors in the global competition. Ironically, we do not ordinarily think of these expenditures as investments; the federal budget fails to distinguish between a capital and an operating budget, and the national income accounts treat all government expenditures as consumption. But without doubt, these are precisely the investments that most directly affect our future capacity to compete.

During the 1980s, we allowed the level of these public investments either to remain stable or, in some cases, to decline. As America enters the 1990s, if we hope to launch a new campaign for American competitiveness, we must substantially increase public funding in the following areas:

- *Government spending on commerical R&D.* Current spending in this critical area has declined 95 percent from its level two decades ago. Even as late as 1980, it comprised 0.8 percent of gross national product; today it comprises only 0.4 percent—a much smaller percentage than in any other advanced economy.
- *Government spending to upgrade and expand the nation's infrastructure.* Public investment in critical highways, roads, bridges, ports, airports, and waterways dropped from 2.3 percent of GNP two decades ago to 1.3 percent in the 1980s. Thus many of our bridges are unsafe, and our highways are crumbling.
- *Expenditures on public elementary and secondary education.* These have increased, to be sure. But in inflation-adjusted terms, per pupil spending has shown little gain. Between 1959 and 1971, spending per student grew at a brisk 4.7 percent in real terms—more than a full percentage point above the increase in the GNP—and teachers' salaries increased almost 3 percent a year. But since then, growth has slowed. Worse, this has happened during an era when the demands on public education have significantly increased, due to the growing incidence of broken homes, unwed mothers, and a rising population of the poor. Teachers' salaries, adjusted for inflation, are only a bit higher than they were in 1971. Despite the rhetoric, the federal government has all but retreated from the field of education. In fact, George Bush's 1990 education budget is actually smaller than Ronald Reagan's in 1989. States and municipalities, already staggering under the weight of

These are the priorities of an American strategy for national competitiveness—a strategy based more on the value of human capital and less on the value of financial capital. The simple fact of American ownership has lost its relevance to America's economic future. Corporations that invest in the United States, that build the value of the American work force, are more critical to our future standard of living than are American-owned corporations investing abroad. To attract and keep them, we need public investments that make America a good place for any global corporation seeking talented workers to set up shop.

NOTES

1. Craig Smith, editor of *Corporate Philanthropy Report*, quoted in *Chronicle of Higher Education*, November 8, 1989, p.A–34.
2. Bureau of Economic Analysis, *Foreign Direct Investment in the U.S.: Operations of U.S. Affiliates, Preliminary 1986 Estimates* (Washington, D.C.: U.S. Department of Commerce, 1988) for data on foreign companies; Bureau of the Census, *Annual Survey of Manufacturers: Statistics for Industry Groups and Industries, 1986* (Washington, D.C., 1987) for U.S. companies.
3. Robert B. Reich and Eric D. Mankin, "Joint Ventures with Japan Give Away Our Future," *Harvard Business Review* (March–April 1986) p.78.

We Are US: The Myth of the Multinational

Ethan B. Kapstein

In public debate of policy issues it has become commonplace for the anecdote to replace data, the witty phrase to replace analysis. Intellectual fads overwhelm cumulative research, and normative assertions precede observation. Searching for the television camera and radio microphone instead of the truth, policy analysts are all too willing to generalize from isolated cases.

A striking recent example is Robert Reich's compellingly titled article, "Who Is US?"[1] Reich asserts that large, corporations have lost their national identity, as these profit-maximizing firms go abroad in search of markets, employees, and new technology. As proof of this broad assertion, he cites a number of specific cases, including IBM, where foreigners make up 40 percent of total employment, and Du Pont, where "180 Japanese scientists" are working in Yokohama to develop "new materials and technologies." Reich concludes that ownership and control over multinational corporations have lost importance, and that "American-owned corporations . . . have no special relationship with Americans."

This analysis, of course, has a long pedigree in the "interdependence" literature that goes back at least to the early 1900s. Such theorists of interdependence as Norman Angell posited that the deepening of economic transactions among the advanced industrial states would lead to the erosion of national boundaries; this early view exploded with the First World War.[2] During the late 1960s and early 1970s Robert Keohane and Joseph Nye identified a "modernist school" of interdependence theory, which held that changes in technology were creating a "global village," a "world without borders."[3] Many authors during this period spoke of the "cosmo-corp," and books with tides such as *Global Reach* became best-sellers.

Some critics of this view called it "globaloney," and suggested that state actors continued to exercise considerable authority over the behavior of even the largest corporations.[4] In one of the most influential articles on transnationalism of that era, Samuel Huntington argued that the phenomenon of global business expansion after World War II had actually *increased* the power of states. As firms expanded beyond their national territory, they needed access to foreign countries, a right only national governments could grant. Since governments retained a monopoly over corporate access to the domestic market, this gave them considerable authority in negotiations with transnational corporations. Indeed, according to Huntington, governments could exploit the capabilities of the firms to meet national policy objectives.[5]

The power of the home country over the multinational has not diminished; if anything, it has continued to increase. Corporations have not became anational, multinational, or transnational; they remain wedded to their home governments for both political and economic reasons. The question "Who is US?" is an interesting one, but it is not asked by business executives.

To be sure, the foreign activities of large corporations pose some special problems for governments, and public officials remain concerned with export controls, technology transfer, and foreign investment. In search of profit, private firms will sometimes act in ways that the home government does not like; in any relationship, one side will exhibit behavior that the other party does not appreciate. But these examples do not undermine the inextricable link that exists between firms and their home country.

Indeed, the very firms that are seen as being anational often act in explicit support of state functions and needs. The gathering of economic intelligence, the promotion of national values and symbols, and the building of economic alliances may reflect the explicit desires of advanced industrial states. The benefits provided to home governments by large firms must surely overwhelm the costs associated with their international business; if they did not, social scientists really *would* have a puzzle to explain.

In general, large corporations are not only aware of the identity of their home country, they wish to maintain a close relationship with the government. Only the state can defend corporate interests in international negotiations over trade, investment, and market access. Agreements over such things as airline routes, the opening of banking establishments, and the right to sell insurance are not decided by corporate actors who gather around a table; they are determined by diplomats and bureaucrats. Corporations must turn to governments when they have interests to protect or advance. In the words of Raymond Vernon and Louis Wells, "Accordingly, we find the U.S. Ambassador to Liberia inviting the Liberian government to deal gently with the U.S.-owned firms in that country; and the Japanese government assuring Indonesia of certain aid projects if Japanese firms receive rights to a source of hydropower for an aluminum smelter."[6] When talks on debt restructuring take place, the pre-eminent actors are states, not banks. In its singular ability to tax and to make laws and treaties, the state remains the large corporation's worst adversary and most critical ally.

Americans often tend to view the world in their own image, and the question "Who is US?" is indeed distinctively American. I have never heard colleagues from Japan or France or Germany ask a similar question of *their* corporate identity. They seem to know who they are. Nor have Japanese officials recently been heard to complain that Honda and Sony have lost their national character, despite substantial investments in the United States. Does anyone seriously doubt that Siemens is German, Dassault French? Yet both these firms have significant foreign activities, and they are both lodged within the European Community, the strongest of all multinational organizations. It seems that some Americans, especially those who spend their waking hours in universities, are doomed to struggle with a perpetual identity crisis. As Karel van Wolferen recently wrote in these pages, "Theories of a global, borderless economy and of economic interdependence only console those who seem unaware of the political forces at play."[7]

These comments suggest that the question "Who Is US?" is misguided; most of us know who we are, and the numbers prove it.

SOME SURPRISING NUMBERS

Good social science is often inspired by an analysis of data. And, an analysis of American data on both inward and outward direct investment and on the activities of "transnational" firms generates many interesting questions, but "Who Is US?" is not one of them.

American firms invest overseas, and foreign firms invest in the United States. In both cases the numbers are small from the perspective of GNP. In neither case do they suggest the "transnationalization" of the American economy.

In 1990, about 7 percent of America's GNP was invested overseas. At that time, many foreigners feared the launching of an "American invasion." They need not have worried. Today, somewhat less than 7 percent of GNP is invested abroad; the number has hardly changed in almost a century.

Regarding the alleged takeover of America, Reich reports that "foreign direct investment has been climbing dramatically in the United States; last year it reached $329 billion." How big is this number? In absolute terms, it is somewhat larger than the defense budget—which translates approximately to the 7 percent of GNP that seems to be a ubiquitous number in this context. . . .

Of course, this is not surprising when you consider the size of the American economy relative to that of all its major competitors. . . . The types of investment may have changed over time, as have the investors (we don't find many Englishmen investing in railroads or the whaling industry any more), but at the aggregate level, the numbers hardly suggest a foreign takeover, and from a historical perspective foreign investment has actually *decreased* in importance for the American economy.[8]

With the end of the Cold War, it has become increasingly popular to point to Japan as the source of all American woes. It is frequently asserted that "America is for sale" and that the Japanese have purchased our nation on the cheap, given the value of the yen. Such arguments greatly exaggerate Japanese investment in the United States, from the perspective of each country. Japanese activity has indeed risen in the United States: in 1989 the Japanese executed over 2,000 direct investment transactions with a total value of some $32 billion.[9] For the United States, Japanese direct investment that year constituted somewhat over 2 percent of GNP, which hardly suggests a takeover.

Yet another concern of the "Who Is us?" crowd concerns foreign takeovers of American business. The numbers are surprising here as well. The General Accounting Office reports that foreign mergers and acquisitions have actually *declined* in the United States since 1980, when they peaked at 12 percent of all such activity. Transactions *among* U.S. firms have far-outpaced activity *between* Americans and foreigners.

All these numbers would seem to support the conclusion of a recent United Nations report that "the transnationalization of United States firms peaked somewhere between 1965 and 1975."[10] That is to say, prior to this period a trend can be observed in which the stock of foreign direct investment held by American corporations was continuously increasing relative to domestic investment; after 1965 a plateau was reached and since the early 1970s the trend has reversed; over the past decade the relative importance of domestic over foreign assets has actually increased.

The domestic to foreign employment ratio lends further support to this analysis. In "Who Is us?" Reich devotes a substantial amount of his attention to the alleged globalization of the corporate workforce. But the proportion of foreign to domestic employees in American manufacturing firms peaked in 1977 at about 25 percent, and the number has declined since that time to about 23 percent. Multinationals based in other major home countries have even lower percentages of foreign workers. Less than 8 percent of the workforce employed by German multinationals is foreign, and the number for Japanese firms is about 2 percent.[11]

Regarding the American workforce, only a small percentage is employed by foreign firms. According to the U.S. Department of Commerce, 2.1 million Americans were employed in foreign-owned manufacturing plants, or about 7 percent of all manufacturing employees. (In "Who Is us?" Reich, without providing a source for the number, asserts that 3 million Americans are so employed). Another 2 million are employed in foreign-owned service industries and again the number is significantly below 10 percent of the total.

The importance of the home country is further suggested by corporate earnings. To be sure, several American-based multinational corporations now earn a significant share of their profits, if not the majority share, from their overseas operations. But in almost every case the United States remains the single largest market and profit center. Of the 100 largest corporations in America, foreign sales as a percentage of total sales peaked in 1980 at about 33 percent; the number has since declined to about 25 percent. For the 50 largest firms based in Japan, foreign sales accounted for just 8 percent of total sales.[12]

In sum, only the most xenophobic among us would find cause for concern in the aggregate data on multinational corporations. This is not to minimize the serious economic problems that face the United States; the country *does* have many such problems, including a desperate need for more investment. However, the numbers suggest that the problems must be largely of our own making since the American economy remains, for better or for worse, largely American.

FIRM STRATEGY

There is now a substantial literature on the operations of large corporations. Far from suggesting that these firms have evolved into transnational actors without any national identity, this body of work points to the enduring importance of the home country. As Philip Wellons has pointed out in a study of international banking, "The home's impact is much more pervasive and important than the impact of other governments. . . . Home governments affect the banks' relations with competitors . . . other governments, and other borrowers."[13]

Indeed, there is substantial evidence that large corporations are becoming *localized* rather than *globalized*. That is, instead of establishing transnational structures with global ownership, global employment, and global products, they are becoming increasingly sensitive to state policies. A Harvard Business School study found that "the most important force for localization has been the reactions of national governments." It points out that even the Reagan administration, "one of the strongest advocates of free trade," enacted a number of policy measures aimed at greater regulation of international business. These regulations "defined necessary levels of local content, technology transfer, and a variety of other conditions."[14]

One might argue that this localization trend will only work to obscure further the identity of multinational firms. If firms are responding to the demands of a home government and several hosts at the same time, then it might well be asked "Who Is us?" Home governments, however, will not permit firms to make foreign investments that are perceived to be detrimental to the national interest. States possess both formal and informal means to block such investments. Of course, an investment made today may *over time* have consequences for the home government that were not originally foreseen; such could be the case with contemporary interest in investing in the Soviet Union. But mistaken policy should not be confused with an absence of policy.

The business literature suggests that both inward and outward foreign investment decisions are not made solely in response to market opportunities, but in response to government policies as well. During the 1960s, it was official U.S. policy to discourage foreign investment by American multinationals in order to keep capital at home, and a number of onerous restrictions were placed on private enterprise. During the 1980s, the government moved to block inward foreign direct investment in some sectors of the economy, particularly those related to the "military-industrial complex." Governments prevent the export of many goods and services, and technology transfer is generally regulated. As Vernon and Wells have concluded, "the scrutiny of home governments is becoming increasingly common" in corporate life.[15]

Some analysts have responded that the multinational enterprise can simply circumvent government regulations by going offshore. They should consult a good lawyer. The United States government has put into place an elaborate set of laws controlling both the onshore and offshore activities of American-owned corporations. Further, the United States has demonstrated its ability to punish severely foreign firms whose activities are deemed to be at odds with the national interests; witness Toshiba's sale of sensitive technology to the Soviet Union and the penalties it subsequently faced. Access to the American market is a powerful incentive for good behavior on the part of corporate actors; denial of that market is a heavy penalty.[16]

The literature on business strategy, then, also argues against the proposition that multinational firms have lost their sense of allegiance. If anything, they are becoming increasingly sensitive to national concerns in a myriad of issue-areas, from affirmative action to technology policy to the environment. Again, most firms know who their home government is, and they recognize the importance of maintaining a good relationship with it.

The preceding sections have utilized aggregate data and the general business literature in suggesting that most firms know who they are. But since the main weapon in the arsenal of the "Who Is US?" group has been the anecdote, it may be useful to provide some specific examples here as well. I would argue that these are "easy" cases from the "Who Is US?" perspective, and "hard" cases for those of us who continue to believe in powerful states. The cases are drawn from banking— arguably the most global of all industries—and remote sensing, an area in which no state seems in control of its territory.

BANKING

Of all economic sectors, none would appear so global as finance. As Professor Stephen Kobrin of the Wharton School of Business has argued, "The financial market is global in the sense that transactions are linked in an electronic network and borders and territoriality are virtually irrelevant." Citing such acute observers of the international business scene as Walter Wriston and Keniche Ohmae in support of this view, Professor Kobrin concludes that "government control over flows of funds and thus the value of currencies or monetary policy is very limited."[17]

Once again, there is a long pedigree for the contention that finance is global, and not subject to any government. In his classic 1944 work *The Great Transformation*, Karl Polanyi reminded his readers that the greatest of all banking families, the Rothschilds, was held out during the nineteenth century as the exemplification of the interdependent world economy. "As a family," he wrote, "they embodied the abstract principle of internationalism; their loyalty was to a firm." But in fact, their "independence sprang from the needs of the time."

Such is the case with international banks today, though their ties to home governments and countries are so strong that it would appear to be stating the obvious. First, each international bank has a central bank that acts as its lender of last resort, and a national supervisory authority that acts as the primary regulator of its activities. It is doubtful that the management of Continental Illinois Bank or the Bank of New England asked "Who Is US?" as their institutions tumbled toward bankruptcy.

Second, in most important international financial negotiations states, not banks, determine policy. The Plaza Accord, which is widely held as being influential in bringing down the value of the dollar in the late 1980s, was negotiated by ministers of foreign affairs and the treasury, not by private banks. The problem of Third World debt, in which debt restructuring has become the rule, is managed largely by state actors and international organizations. Finally, in terms of market access, it is states that establish the rules of the game; market opening in Japanese financial markets was due to heavy political pressure by the United States, not by the dictates of modern financial engineering.

Third, in many countries banks are state-owned, or the capital markets are highly controlled by state actors. The major French banks (e.g. Crédit Lyonnais) are owned by the state, as are those of such developing countries as Brazil. Within Western Europe, access to stock markets is rigidly controlled by governments; free-market Britain (the free market itself being a consequence of state action) is the exception, not the rule. Within and between states, the heavy hand of government is found throughout the financial marketplace.

Finally, to follow on the preceding point, in most industrial countries the largest borrower on the capital markets is the state. Over 80 percent of the debt outstanding in Britain, 75 percent in France, 65 percent in Japan, and 55 percent in the United States is held by the government.[18] Indeed, a recent agreement reached by the central bankers of the Group of Ten industrial countries, the so-called "Basle Accord," provides a new set of incentives for international banks to hold government debt.[19] In finance, no actor is more important than the state.

To be sure, the BCCI scandal would indicate that "rogue empires" exist in the financial world, just as pirates, mercenaries, and criminals continue to operate. But if the existence of the state is in doubt, just ask the depositors of BCCI in some fifty countries who woke up one morning in July to find their accounts frozen, the result of a coordinated action on the part of central bankers under the leadership of the Bank of England. These individuals are now dealing with state officials in making their claims.

It is somewhat surprising to find the "cosmo-corp" intellectuals still using international finance as their primary example of globalization and of the state's demise. Indeed, probably no economic sector is more rigidly controlled and regulated than finance. Domestically, every country has a central bank and major supervisory authority. Internationally, a host of formal and informal organizations supervise and—when deemed necessary—direct world financial flows (do you believe the Third World would have received any money at all since 1982 had it not been for the state?). In short, finance is too important for public officials to leave in the hands of bankers.

REMOTE SENSING

In the global world of high technology, you don't get any higher than remote sensing by satellite. As Stephen Kobrin asks, "What do borders mean when the United States or the Soviet Union can scan any territory in the world?" He argues that, owing to new satellite and data technology, "it is virtually impossible for any government" to control the flow of information across borders; indeed, the idea of borders, which cannot be seen from on high, is rendered meaningless.

A recent analysis by Professor Stephen Krasner of Stanford University, however, suggests the conclusion that remote sensing takes place because powerful states wish to engage in this activity, and they permit others to do so as well.[20] If the United States wanted to prevent the gathering or transmission of information by satellite, it could easily do so by shooting the satellite down, or by "blinding" a remote sensor.

Nor need we be so melodramatic. Krasner argues that, from the beginning, the United States has reaped economic and political benefits from remote sensing. In so doing, "it backed the development of local receiving states and made the raw data secured from its LANDSAT available to all comers at affordable prices." The United States thus used the technology to promote alliance relationships; in short, remote sensing supported the traditional objectives of American economic and foreign policy.

The examples of remote sensing and banking suggest that even the easiest cases for the "cosmo-corp" believers break down upon close examination. In each sector, the state looms large, a discovery that should not be surprising. After all, both finance and high technology are of vital interest to governments. While most industrial states have placed renewed emphasis on market mechanisms in recent years, they have certainly not surrendered their authority over the economy. It is a long way from deregulation to "Who Is us?"

The past decade has been a troubled one for the American economy. Strong growth during the Reagan era was coupled with growing budget and trade deficits. A recent cyclical recession has been harsh for many regions and has endured longer than most economists predicted. Clearly, a profound sense of insecurity sweeps the land when it comes to the nation's economic future.

This insecurity was brilliantly captured by Robert Reich with the question "Who Is us?" In an age when every home is filled with Japanese products, when individuals invest their pensions in international stock funds, when universities are crowded with foreign students, it is easy—and perhaps beneficial to some degree—to question our national identity.

But it is unlikely that, even with the end of the Cold War, we will soon witness a "great transformation" to a single, integrated world economy where borders are no longer meaningful. Indeed, one could also imagine that economic conflict among the leading industrial powers will increase, as economic security replaces military security as the primary goal of state actors. Further, as the war with Iraq recently demonstrated, there is still plenty of firepower in the international system. The state may be anachronistic, but we have yet to develop an alternative form of societal organization that is able to provide its members with both wealth and power.

Corporations certainly recognize the importance of their home state as much as any other societal actor. In most cases, the home country provides the single largest source of employee talent, of earnings, and of investment opportunities. In negotiations over market access, the corporation must rely on the state to advance its interests. Firms retain a national identity because they must, even if that identity is kept hidden at times from their critics.[21]

NOTES

1. *Harvard Business Review* (January–February 1990).
2. *The Great Illusion* (New York: Putnam, 1911). For a pre–World War II argument along similar lines, see Eugene Staley, *World Economy in Transition* (New York: Council on Foreign Relations, 1939).
3. *Power and Interdependence* (Boston: Little, Brown, 1977).
4. For one of the classic critiques, see Kenneth Waltz, "The Myth of National Interdependence," in Charles P. Kindleberger, ed., *The International Corporation* (Cambridge, Mass.: MIT Press, 1970).
5. "Transnational Organizations in World Politics," *World Politics* (April 1973).
6. *Manager in the International Economy* (Englewood Cliffs, N.J.: Prentice Hall, 1981).
7. "No Brakes, No Compass," *The National Interest* (Fall 1991). Van Wolferen articulates the strongest case I know concerning the links between the Japanese state and Japanese corporations.
8. See Mira Wilkins, *A History of Foreign Investment in the United States to 1914* (Cambridge, Mass.: Harvard University Press, 1989).
9. Japanese Ministry of International Trade and Investment, September 1991.
10. *Transnational Corporations in World Development* (New York: United Nations, 1989).
11. *Ibid.*
12. *Ibid.*
13. "International Debt: The Behavior of Banks in a Politicized Environment," *International Organization* (Summer 1985).
14. Christopher A. Bartlett and Sumantra Ghoshal, *Managing Across Borders* (Boston: Harvard Business School Press, 1989).
15. *Manager in the International Economy.*
16. See, for example, Jeffrey Bialos, "The Detection and Disclosure of U.S. Export Control Violations: Management Choices and their National Security Ramifications," (Washington, D.C.: Weil, Gotshal & Manges, 1989).
17. "Transnational Integration, National Markets and Nation-States," (Working Paper, Reginald Jones Center, The Wharton School, August 1991).
18. Michael Sesit, "Industrial Nations' Appetite for Debt Surged 15% in '90," *Wall Street Journal,* September 30, 1991.
19. See Ethan B. Kapstein, *The Basle Accord: Origins and Implications* (Princeton N.J.: Princeton Essays in International Finance, 1991).
20. "Global Communications and National Power," *World Politics* (April 1991).

Power Versus Plenty Today

Why International Primacy Matters

Samuel P. Huntington

Does international primacy matter? The answer seems . . . obvious. . . . On further thought, however, one sees that while the answer may be obvious for most people, the reasons why it is obvious may not be all that clear and may have been forgotten or lost in the other concerns of political scientists and economists studying international relations. . . .

PRIMACY IN WHAT?

First, what do we mean by primacy? Primacy in what? Politics is concerned with primacy in power. In international politics power is the ability of one actor, usually but not always a government, to influence the behavior of others, who may or may not be governments. International primacy means that a government is able to exercise more influence on the behavior of more actors with respect to more issues than any other government can. Or, as Lasswell and Kaplan put it in their classic formulation, the amount of power an actor possesses is a function of weight (degree of participation in decision-making), scope (the values that are influenced), and domain (the people who are influenced).[1]

To ask whether primacy matters is to ask whether power matters. And the answer can only be: of course, it matters in most human relationships, even in families, and it obviously matters in national and international affairs. It does make a difference whether one party, politician, branch of government, interest group, public official, or national government has more or less power than another. It mat-

Excerpt from Samuel Huntington, "Why International Primacy Matters" in *International Security*, Spring 1993, Vol. 17:4. Reprinted by permission of MIT Press. Portions of the text and some footnotes have been omitted.

tered to a hundred million American voters whether George Bush or Bill Clinton or Ross Perot has primacy in shaping decisions affecting the United States. It matters to hundreds of millions of people throughout the world whether the United States, Japan, Germany, Europe, Russia, China, or some other entity has primacy in shaping decisions affecting the world. Political science is, indeed, the study of why, how, and with what consequences people get and exercise power in major collective entities. If power and primacy did not matter, political scientists would have to look for other work.

Those who are skeptical concerning the value of primacy often approach the issue in terms of relative and absolute gains. The argument is that, given a choice, Actor A should prefer to achieve a gain of x even though Actor B is scoring a gain of $x + y$, rather than achieving a gain of $x - y$ while Actor B is scoring a gain of $x - 2y$. The crucial issue, however, in the debate of absolute versus relative gains is: gain in what? Whether absolute or relative gains are to be preferred depends on the values at stake. If it is gains in health, Actor A probably will prefer a gain of x as against a gain of $x - y$, no matter what health gains Actor B may be achieving. With respect to wealth, in some circumstances actors may prefer absolute gains and in others relative gains. In Olympic competitions, probably most athletes would prefer to run the 1,000 meters in time t and win a gold medal than to run it in time $t - y$ if another athlete was making off with the gold by running it in time $t - 2y$. With respect to power, however, absolute gains are meaningless. An actor gains or loses power compared to other people. Since it concerns the ability of people to influence each other, power is only relative. Lord Acton and others may have talked about "absolute power," but they do not mean absolute in the meaning it has in the term absolute gains. Absolute power itself is relative: it means that relative to other actors, Actor A monopolizes decision-making on all issues concerning all people in a given universe. International primacy means a state has more power than other actors and hence primacy is inherently relative.

Even if power is relative, the question remains: Why do people want power? A variety of motives are possible. The contest for power itself may be satisfying and enjoyable. So also may be the exercise of power once it is acquired. To be powerful and to be viewed by others as such surely enhances the self-esteem of individuals and nations. Power enables an actor to shape his environment so as to reflect his interests. In particular it enables a state to protect its security and prevent, deflect, or defeat threats to that security. It also enables a state to promote its values among other peoples and to shape the international environment so as to reflect its values. States and other actors who are powerful can, and do, do evil. But power is also the prerequisite to doing good and promoting collective goods. Almost nothing beneficial in the world happens except by the exercise of power.

IS HISTORY ENDING?

It is a fact well-known since Thucydides that it matters which state exercises the most power in the international system. At no time in history has this been more true than in the twentieth century: one has only to consider what the world would have looked like if Nazi Germany had won World War II or the Soviet Union won the Cold War.[2] No reason exists to assume that what has been true for millennia will cease to be true in the next hundred years.

Does it matter to the United States or the world that American primacy be maintained? Obviously that depends on what the alternative distributions of power might be. Logically there are two other possibilities. Some other state could displace the United States as the only superpower in the world, or there could be a condition in which no state was in a position of international primacy and there was a rough equilibrium of power among the major states. Would either of these situations be more desirable for the United States or for the world than the maintenance of U.S. primacy?

It is quite erroneous to think that the principal reason states pursue international primacy is to be able to win wars, and that hence if war is unlikely primacy is unimportant. States pursue primacy in order to be able to insure their security, promote their interests, and shape the international environment in ways that will reflect their interests and values. Primacy is desirable not primarily to achieve victory in war but to achieve the state's goals without recourse to war. Primacy is thus an alternative to war. A state such as the United States that has achieved international primacy has every reason to attempt to maintain that primacy through peaceful means so as to preclude the need of having to fight a war to maintain it.

Some argue that the end of the Cold War means the end of history as we have known it. Unfortunately every day's newspaper contains dramatic and tragic evidence that the end of the Cold War means the return to history as we used to know it. Conflicts among nations and ethnic groups are escalating. Controversies are intensifying between the United States and other major powers. This is to be expected. The end of a significant war or conflict, whether among individuals, groups, or states, creates the basis for the generation of new conflicts. The end of war leads to the breakup of the coalition of powers fighting the war. There is no reason why the end of the Cold War should have any different consequences. The alliances of the United States with Japan and with the Western European countries in NATO rested on three fundamentals: shared political and economic values; common economic interests; and the Soviet security threat. Without the last of these three, the alliances would never have come into existence. Now, however, the Soviet threat is gone, and common economic interests are giving way to competing economic interests. Shared political and economic values remain the principal glue holding together the grand alliances of the Cold War. Those common values are real, and they mean that wars are most unlikely between these countries.[3] They do not mean that these countries will have shared or even congruent interests. Instead the disappearance of the common enemy means that conflicting interests that were subordinated to the common need to unite against the Soviet security threat during the Cold War will now emerge with a vengeance. This is not likely to lead to the physical mayhem that occurred in Bosnia, but it will lead to intense conflicts over political and economic interests. Competition—the struggle for primacy—we all recognize as natural among individuals, corporations, political parties, athletes, and universities; it is no less natural among countries.

DOES ECONOMIC PRIMACY MATTER?

In the coming years, the principal conflicts of interests involving the United States and the major powers are likely to be over economic issues. U.S. economic primacy is now being challenged by Japan and is likely to be challenged in the future by Europe. Obviously the United States, Japan, and Europe have common interests in promoting economic development and international trade. They also, however, have deeply conflicting interests over the distribution of the benefits and costs of economic growth and the distribution of the costs of economic stagnation or decline. The idea that economics is primarily a non-zero-sum game is a favorite conceit of tenured academics. It has little connection to reality. In the course of the economic competition that may produce economic growth, companies go bankrupt; bankers forfeit their investments; factories are closed; managers and workers lose their jobs; money, wealth, well-being, and power are shifted from one industry, region, or country to another.

Economists argue that in economic competition what counts are absolute not relative gains; to economists this is a self-evident truth. It is, however, self-evident to almost no one but economists. The American public as a whole, various groups in American society, and the leaders and publics in other societies do not buy it for a moment.[4] Why are the economists out in left field? They are there because they are blind to the fact that economic activity is a source of power as well as well-being. It is, indeed, probably the most important source of power, and in a world in which military conflict between major states is unlikely, economic power will be increasingly important in determining the primacy or subordination of states. Precisely for this reason Americans have every reason to be concerned by the current challenge to American economic primacy posed by Japan and the possible future challenge that could come from Europe.

The threat to American economic primacy from Japan is serious because Japanese policy makes it serious. Since the 1950s Japan has pursued a strategy designed not to promote Japanese economic welfare but to maximize Japanese economic power. For decades Japan has acted in a way totally consistent with the "realist" theory of international relations, which holds that international politics is basically anarchic and that to insure their security states act to maximize their power.[5] Realist theorists have focused overwhelmingly on military power. Japan has accepted all the assumptions of realism but applied them purely in the economic realm. Abjuring military power, it has acted precisely as realist theory would predict in the pursuit of economic power. In the realm of military competition, the instruments of power are missiles, planes, warships, bombs, tanks, divisions. In the realm of economic competition, the instruments of power are productive efficiency, market control, trade surplus, strong currency, foreign exchange reserves, ownership of foreign companies, factories, and technology. These are the objectives that Japan has unremittingly pursued. . . .

The Japanese challenge to American economic primacy affects the United States in a variety of ways. First, American national security, in a narrow sense, could be affected if the Japanese expand their lead in a variety of militarily important technologies. In 1988, for instance, the Defense Science Board identified 22 areas of critical technology and judged the Soviet Union to be "significantly" ahead of the United States in "some niches of technology" in two areas, but Japan to be ahead in six.[6] A 1990 Commerce Department study found Japan to be ahead of the United States in five of twelve emerging technologies and rapidly gaining in another five.[7] American national security obviously is weakened to the extent to which the United States becomes dependent upon Japanese technology for its sophisticated weapons. In the Gulf War, U.S. defense contractors had to obtain from Japan semiconductors, video display equipment, circuits for missile guidance systems, and other key electronic products. As a senior Japanese Foreign Ministry official noted, Japan supplied these products, but the Japanese public has "a strong abhorrence" to exporting arms, and the sale of weapons parts to the United States "meets some psychological resistance."[8] In a future war where the United States was not so dearly fighting in Japan's interests, the willingness to supply those parts could easily evaporate.

Second, the growth of Japanese economic power threatens American economic well-being. The loss of markets means that American factories close and jobs migrate offshore. Profits go down, businesses go bankrupt, investors suffer. American per capita income increases at a slower rate or even decreases. The economic decline and even collapse manifest in so many industries targeted by the Japanese will appear in still others. The Japanese government, for instance, has targeted aerospace for rapid development with government "subsidies, loans, and political support."[9] If Japan is successful, the future of Seattle can be seen in Detroit.

The Japanese also use their financial resources to acquire and to transfer to their country technologies critical for military or essential civilian purposes and generally to move home the high-value-added operations of the companies they acquire. In contrast to European and Canadian firms, Japanese firms investing in the United States "have been prone to keep top management, high value-added productions, and research and development operations at home, often preferring to build 'screwdriver' assembly plants [abroad] that pay lower wages."[10]

Third, American influence in third countries declines relative to that of Japan. In 1989 Japan supplanted the United States as the largest provider of economic assistance. Japanese influence over Third World developing countries has increased compared to that of the United States.[11] By the early 1990s the tremendous expansion of Japanese investment and trade with Southeast Asia, combined with economic and technological assistance, had made Japan the most influential outside power in that region. Japanese influence in southern Asia has also risen, fueled by Japan's concerns for its oil supplies. The Japanese similarly moved to expand their involvements in Mexico, Brazil and other Latin American countries, constructing factories there whose products they plan to export to the United States.

Fourth, the influence that Japan exercises over the United States increases. To the extent that the United States becomes dependent on imports of goods and money from Japan, it also becomes vulnerable to Japanese threats to restrict those outflows. The United States, as Kiichi Miyazawa pointed out just before becoming prime minister, requires Japanese electronic components for its weapons, and cutting the flow of Japanese exports would produce "problems in the U.S. economy." "The real trigger" of the October 19, 1987, stock market crash, according to Treasury Secretary Nicholas Brady, "was that the Japanese came in for their own reasons and sold an enormous amount of government bonds, and drove the 30-year government bond rate up through 10 percent. And when it got through 10 percent, that got a lot of people thinking, Gee, that's four times the return you get on equity. Here we go, inflation again. That, to me, is what really started the 19th—a worry by the Japanese about U.S. currency."[12]

Japan has regularly used its financial power as a threat against the United States. "During the tensest period of the Super–301 [trade] negotiations with the U.S.," one leading Japanese journalist reports, "voices in the leadership argued, for the first time, for retaliation over concessions. They hinted that in financial markets, Japanese institutional investors would begin dumping dollar-denominated securities." In January 1991, the vice minister of finance "indicated Tokyo's awareness of its leverage. He bluntly commented, in public, that Japan would reduce capital investments in America if the United States applied sanctions for not giving U.S. financial institutions opportunities in Japan similar to those Japanese firms have in America." In the fall of 1991, as controversies intensified over Japanese exports of automobiles and other goods, reports repeatedly surfaced of Japan threatening a "'second strike': if Washington cuts off Japanese imports, Tokyo can strangle the American economy by cutting off investments or purchases of Treasury bonds." Japan, two distinguished economists concluded, "has the financial capacity—and begins, in public, to threaten to use that capacity—to influence American exchange rate and monetary conditions."[13]

Economic power increases Japan's ability to shape American public attitudes and decision-making so as to favor Japanese interests. In the 1940s the Soviet Union used its ideology to enlist influential Americans to serve its interests; in the 1990s Japan uses its money to enlist influential Americans to serve its interests. The Japanese government and Japanese corporations have worked closely together to achieve this goal and they have achieved significant success. In 1989 more than 250 Japanese government agencies and Japanese corporations were funding Washington lobbyists; second-place Canada had only 90 groups so engaged. Japanese spending on Washington lobbying was variously estimated from $60 to $100 million, the latter figure being more than that spent by the next six largest spenders combined. With this money Japanese organizations hire well-placed and well-connected former executive branch officials, members of Congress, and congressional staffers.[14]

Japanese investments in the United States expand Japanese political influence and in part appear to be designed to have that effect. In the 1980s, for instance, the Japanese government targeted the U.S. movie industry and began to provide substantial tax incentives for Japanese investments in that industry. By 1990 about 40 percent of the investment in new Hollywood movies came from Japan. The result was the ability to influence public opinion: the chairman of Matsushita made it clear that MCA would not be allowed to produce movies critical of or offensive to Japan.[15]

The Japanese effort to influence policy outcomes in Washington necessarily leads Japan to attempt to influence who becomes a policymaker in Washington. "Japan should use its economic power," said Keniche Ohmae, a leading Tokyo economic analyst, "to put a stop to one-sided Japan-bashing in the U.S." Akio Morita agreed: "If a congressman or a politician bashes his friend [Japan], than that politician will lose the election." He is right. In 1988 candidates supported by the Auto Dealers and Drivers for Free Trade PAC (AUTOPAC), the political action committee representing Japanese auto dealers and the importers of Japanese cars in the United States, won six of their seven congressional races. AUTOPAC financial support was crucial to the victory of Republican Connie Mack in a very close Florida Senate race over the Democratic candidate Buddy MacKay, who said afterwards, "I was beaten in Tokyo." Two years later AUTOPAC targeted Sen. John Durkin (D-N.H.) for defeat, and late in the campaign bought $357,000 worth of television time in New Hampshire to attack Durkin, effectively securing the election of his Republican opponent, Bob Smith. "We depend heavily on the element of surprise," AUTOPAC's director remarked.[16]

The Japanese also make substantial efforts to cultivate intellectuals and scholars and to influence the output of universities and research centers. Japanese corporations have endowed thirteen professorships at MIT and nine at Harvard. Between 1970 and 1991, Harvard received $30 million from Japanese corporations. "According to Harvard insiders," the Harvard alumni magazine reported, "these donors wanted the funds to provide an antidote to 'Japan-bashing' through the creation at Harvard of a public forum for explaining Japan's position on such sensitive issues as investment and trade with the United States." The head of at least one think tank that received Japanese support resigned "after protesting efforts by Japanese sponsors to influence the organization's research."[17] "The U.S. has been *penetrated*," a 1989 study prepared at the U.S. Foreign Service Institute concluded, "not only by Japanese autos and VCRs, but by Japanese influence peddling at every level. Thousands of American lawyers, lobbyists, former officials, bankers, and scholars are funded by Japanese corporations or the Government of Japan."[18]

"Economics," as Daniel Bell has said, "is the continuation of war by other means."[19] Economic primacy matters because economic power is both the most fundamental and the most fungible form of power. For the United States, the loss of economic primacy to Japan could be highly damaging, as would have been the loss of political-military primacy to the Soviet Union. This loss to Japan would, first, make U.S. influence in world affairs subordinate to that of Japan and, second, reduce long-term U.S. economic welfare, as Japan used its power, as its leaders and policies have said that it would, to accumulate high-technology, high-value-added industries in Japan, and to reduce the United States to the status of a "giant Denmark." The American public, in the phrase that provoked Robert Jervis, very justifiably "is obsessed with Japan for the same reasons that it was once obsessed with the Soviet Union. It sees that country as a major threat to its primacy in a crucial arena of power." Does Professor Jervis really believe that Americans are wrong for not wanting to live in a world where the major decisions affecting them economically are made in Tokyo? Does he really think that those decisions would be the same as decisions made in Washington, New York, Chicago, Atlanta, Houston, and Los Angeles?

To restore its economic primacy *vis-à-vis* Japan requires the United States to take two bread types of measures. First, the United States needs to recognize the Japanese economic power maximization strategy for what it is and to pursue a much more concerted and consistent course to prevent Japan from exploiting the openness of the American economy and to induce Japan to open its own economy further to foreign goods, investment, and participation. Second, the United States needs to take the measures which it should take in any event to renew its economic health: reducing the federal deficit, increasing savings and investment, increasing productivity, promoting research and development, improving its educational system. Good reason exists to do all of these things even if there were no Japanese challenge. The existence of such a challenge provides additional incentive for these actions in order to insure America's primacy in the world.

WHAT'S THE WORLD'S INTEREST?

The maintenance of U.S. primacy matters for the world as well as for the United States.

First, no other country can make comparable contributions to international order and stability. The security consequences of a multipolar world have been dramatically evident in the dismal failure of the major European powers to deal with the Yugoslav catastrophe on their doorstep. Leaders and publics throughout the world recognize the need for an American presence and American leadership in maintaining stability in their region. These are, as the prime ministers of Japan and Korea said, "indispensable" to Asian security.[20] Crowds chanting "Americans go home!" are not much in evidence these days. The fear is, instead, that Americans may well turn isolationist again and do exactly that. The ability of the United States to provide international order is obviously limited and, despite the constant demands, the United States cannot settle every dispute in every part of the world. Yet the fact remains that, as General Colin Powell, chairman of the Joint Chiefs of Staff, put it, "One of the fondest expressions around here is that we can't be the world's policeman. But guess who gets called when suddenly someone needs a cop?"[21] As Bosnia, Somalia, and many other places evidence, the answer to that question is obvious. And, given the nature of the world as it is, is there any remotely plausible alternative answer or better answer? If the United States is unable to maintain security in the world's trouble spots, no other single country or combination of countries is likely to provide a substitute.

Second, the collapse of the Soviet Union leaves the United States as the only major power whose national identity is defined by a set of universal political and economic values. For the United States these are liberty, democracy, equality, private property, and markets. In varying degrees other major countries may from time to time support these values. Their identity, however, is not defined by these values, and hence they have far less commitment to them and less interest in promoting them than does the United States. This is not, obviously, to argue that these values are always at the forefront of American foreign policy; other concerns and needs have to be taken into consideration. It is, rather, to argue that the promotion of democracy, human rights, and markets are far more central to American policy than to the policy of any other country. Following in the footsteps of both Jimmy Carter and Ronald Reagan, Bill Clinton has committed himself to a foreign policy of "democratic realism" in which the central goal of the United States will be the promotion of democracy in the world. The maintenance of American primacy and the strengthening of American influence in the world are indispensable to achieving that goal. To argue that primacy does not matter is to argue that political and economic values do not matter and that democracy does not or should not matter.

A world without U.S. primacy will be a world with more violence and disorder and less democracy and economic growth than a world where the United States continues to have more influence than any other country in shaping global affairs. The sustained international primacy of the United States is central to the welfare and security of Americans and to the future of freedom, democracy, open economies, and international order in the world.

NOTES

1. Harold D. Lasswell and Abraham Kaplan, *Power and Society: A Framework for Political Inquiry* (New Haven, Conn.: Yale University Press, 1950), p. 77.
2. For an imaginative and quite persuasive picture (which could not be published in Germany) of what a Nazi victory would have meant, and also for a good read, see Richard Harris, *Fatherland* (New York: Random House, 1992). For a brilliant discussion of this book, see Josef Joffe, "The Mother of All Fatherlands," *The National Interest*, No. 29 (Fall 1992), pp. 85–88.
3. Michael N. Doyle, "Liberalism and World Politics," *American Political Science Review*, Vol. 80, No. 4 (December 1986), pp. 1151–69; and Doyle, "Kant, Liberal Legacies, and Foreign Affairs," *Philosophy and Public Affairs*, Vol. 12 (Summer/Fall 1983), pp. 205–35, 323, 353.
4. See, e.g., Michael Mastanduno, "Do Relative Gains Matter? America's Response to Japanese Industrial Policy," *International Security*, Vol. 16, No. 1 (Summer 1991), pp. 73–74.
5. Here and a few other places in this essay, I draw on my "America's Changing Strategic Interests," *Survival*, Vol. 33 (January/February 1991), pp. 3–7; and "The Economic Renewal of America," *The National Interest*, No. 28 (Spring 1992), pp. 14–18.
6. U.S. Department of Defense, *Critical Technologies Plan* (Washington, D.C.: Department of Defense, March 15, 1990), pp. 10–12.
7. U.S. Department of Commerce, Technology Administration, *Emerging Technologies: A Survey of Technical and Economic Opportunities* (Washington, D.C.: Department of Commerce, Spring 1990), pp. 12–14.
8. *Washington Post National Weekly Edition*, April 1–7, 1991, p. 11.
9. Richard W. Stevenson, "Will Aerospace Be the Next Casualty?" *New York Times*, March 15, 1992, Sec. 3, pp. 1, 6.
10. Thomas Omestad, "Selling Off America," *Foreign Policy*, No. 76 (Fall 1989), pp. 134–35.
11. See, e.g., Victor H. Palmieri, "U.S. Takes Back Seat in Third World," *New York Times*, August 26, 1990, p. F13.
12. Kiichi Miyazawa, *International Herald Tribune*, October 19–20, 1991, p. 5; Nicholas Brady, quoted in Catherine Collins, "Could Japan Realty Holdings Hurt U.S.?" *Los Angeles Times*, May 7, 1989, Sect. VIII, p. 3.
13. Yoichi Funabashi, "Japan as Superpower: Will It Say 'Yes' or 'No'?" *Economic Insights*, Vol. 1 (July–August 1990), p. 20: William J. Barnds, "The United States and Japan: A Time of Troubles," CAPA Report No. 2, June 1991, The Asia Foundation, Center for

Asian Pacific Affairs, p. 2; Steven R. Weisman, "Pearl Harbor in the Mind of Japan," *New York Times Magazine,* November 3, 1991, p. 68; Nickerson, "U.S., Japan Drift Dangerously Apart"; Steven R. Weisman, "Japanese-U.S. Relations Undergoing a Redesign," *New York Times,* June 4, 1990, p. A2; *Washington Post National Weekly Edition,* February 19–25, 1990, p. 23; C. Michael Aho and Bruce Stokes, "The Year the World Economy Turned," *Foreign Affairs,* Vol. 70, No. 1 (America and the World 1990–91), p. 166; Michael Borrus and John Zysman, "The Highest Stakes: Industrial Competitiveness and National Strategy," BRIE Working Paper No. 39, April 1991, Berkeley Roundtable on the International Economy, p. 41.

14. Clyde Farnsworth, "Japan's Loud Voice in Washington," *New York Times,* December 10, 1989, p. F1; James Fallows, "Agents of Influence: How Japan's Lobbyists in the United States Manipulate America's Political and Economic System," *New York Review of Books,* November 8, 1990, p. 35; James Fallows, "The Japan-Handlers," *Atlantic Monthly,* Vol. 264 (August 1989), p. 18; Pat Choate, *Agents of Influence* (New York: Alfred A. Knopf, 1990), pp. 109–20.

15. David E. Sanger, "Politics and Multinational Movies," *New York Times,* November 27, 1990, p. D7; Eamon Fingleton, "YMCA," *New Republic,* December 31, 1990, pp. 13–14.

16. Akio Morita, quoted in William J. Holstein, *The Japanese Power Game* (New York: Charles Scribner's Sons, 1990) pp. 234–35; Choate, *Agents of Influence,* pp. 110–12; David Nyhan, "The GOP-Japanese Connection in N.H.," *Boston Globe,* February 9, 1992, p. 77.

17. Sol Hurwitz, "The Japanese Connection," *Harvard Magazine,* Vol. 94 (January–February 1992), p. 94; Choate, *Agents of Influence,* pp. 39–11: Holstein, *Japanese Power Game,* pp. 230–32. Steven Kelman, "The 'Japanization' of America." *The Public Interest,* No. 98 (Winter 1990), p. 81.

18. Kenneth J. Dillon, *Worlds in Collision: The U.S. and Japan Beyond the Year 2000* (U.S. Department of State, Foreign Service Institute, Center for the Study of Foreign Affairs, Center Paper No. 2, April 1989), p. 27 (emphasis added).

19. Daniel Bell, "Germany: The Enduring Fear," *Dissent,* Vol. 37 (Fall 1990), p. 466.

20. "Asian Allies Say U.S. Military Presence Is Indispensable," *Christian Science Monitor,* November 10, 1992, p. 3.

21. "The Global Constable," *The Economist,* September 1, 1990, p. 26.

Competitiveness: A Dangerous Obsession

Paul Krugman

. . . The idea that a country's economic fortunes are largely determined by its success on world markets is a hypothesis, not a necessary truth; and as a practical, empirical matter, that hypothesis is flatly wrong. That is, it is simply not the case that the world's leading nations are to any important degree in economic competition with each other, or that any of their major economic problems can be attributed to failures to compete on world markets. The growing obsession in most advanced nations with international competitiveness should be seen, not as a well-founded concern, but as a view held in the face of overwhelming contrary evidence. And yet it is clearly a view that people very much want to hold—a desire to believe that is reflected in a remarkable tendency of those who preach the doctrine of competitiveness to support their case with careless, flawed arithmetic.

This article makes three points. First, it argues that concerns about competitiveness are, as an empirical matter, almost completely unfounded. Second, it tries to explain why defining the economic problem as one of international competition is nonetheless so attractive to so many people. Finally, it argues that the obsession with competitiveness is not only wrong but dangerous, skewing domestic policies and threatening the international economic system. This last issue is, of course, the most consequential from the standpoint of public policy. Thinking in terms of competitiveness leads, directly and indirectly, to bad economic policies on a wide range of issues, domestic and foreign, whether it be in health care or trade.

MINDLESS COMPETITION

Most people who use the term "competitiveness" do so without a second thought. It seems obvious to them that the analogy between a country and a corporation is reasonable and that to ask whether the United States is competitive in the world market is no different in principle from asking whether General Motors is competitive in the North American minivan market.

In fact, however, trying to define the competitiveness of a nation is much more problematic than defining that of a corporation. The bottom line for a corporation is literally its bottom line: if a corporation cannot afford to pay its workers, suppliers, and bondholders, it will go out of business. So when we say that a corporation is uncompetitive, we mean that its market position is unsustainable—that unless it improves its performance, it will cease to exist. Countries, on the other hand, do not go out of business. They may be happy or unhappy with their economic performance, but they have no well-defined bottom line. As a result, the concept of national competitiveness is elusive.

One might suppose, naively, that the bottom line of a national economy is simply its trade balance, that competitiveness can be measured by the ability of a country to sell more abroad than it buys. But in both theory and practice a trade surplus may be a sign of national weakness, a deficit a sign of strength. For example, Mexico was forced to run huge trade surpluses in the 1980s in order to pay the interest on its foreign debt since international investors refused to lend it any more money; it began to run large trade deficits after 1990 as foreign investors recovered confidence and began to pour in new funds. Would anyone want to describe Mexico as a highly competitive nation during the debt crisis era or describe what has happened since 1990 as a loss in competitiveness?

Most writers who worry about the issue at all have therefore tried to define competitiveness as the combination of favorable trade performance and something else. In particular, the most popular definition of competitiveness nowadays runs along the lines of the one given in Council of Economic Advisors Chairman Laura D'Andrea Tyson's *Who's Bashing Whom?*: competitiveness is "our ability to produce goods and services that meet the test of international competition while our citizens enjoy a standard of living that is both rising and sustainable." This sounds reasonable. If you think about it, however, and test your thoughts against the facts, you will find out that there is much less to this definition than meets the eye.

Consider, for a moment, what the definition would mean for an economy that conducted very little international trade, like the United States in the 1950s. For such an economy, the ability to balance its trade is mostly a matter of getting the exchange rate right. But because trade is such a small factor in the economy, the level of the exchange rate is a minor influence on the standard of living. So in an economy with very little international trade, the growth in living standards—and thus "competitiveness" according to Tyson's definition—would be determined almost entirely by domestic factors, primarily the rate of productivity growth. That's domestic productivity growth, period—not productivity growth relative to other countries. In other words, for an economy with very little international trade, "competitiveness" would turn out to be a funny way of saying "productivity" and would have nothing to do with international competition.

But surely this changes when trade becomes more important, as indeed it has for all major economies? It certainly could change. Suppose that a country finds that although its productivity is steadily rising, it can succeed in exporting only if it repeatedly devalues its currency, selling its exports ever more cheaply on world markets. Then its standard of living, which depends on its purchasing power over imports as well as domestically produced goods, might actually decline. In the jargon of economists, domestic growth might be outweighed by deteriorating terms of trade.[1] So "competitiveness" could turn out really to be about international competition after all.

There is no reason, however, to leave this as a pure speculation; it can easily be checked against the data. Have deteriorating terms of trade in fact been a major drag on the U.S. standard of living? Or has the rate of growth of U.S. real income continued essentially to equal the rate of domestic productivity growth, even though trade is a larger share of income than it used to be?

To answer this question, one need only look at the national income accounts data the Commerce Department publishes regularly in the *Survey of Current Business.* The standard measure of economic growth in the United States is, of course, real GNP—a measure that divides the value of goods and services produced in the United States by appropriate price indexes to come up with an estimate of real national output. The Commerce Department also, however, publishes something called "command GNP." This is similar to real GNP except that it divides U.S. exports not by the export price index, but by the price index for U.S. imports. That is, exports are valued by what Americans can buy with the money exports bring. Command GNP therefore measures the volume of goods and services the U.S. economy can "command"—the nation's purchasing power—rather than the volume it produces.[2] And as we have just seen, "competitiveness" means something different from "productivity" if and only if purchasing power grows significantly more slowly than output.

Well, here are the numbers. Over the period 1959–73, a period of vigorous growth in U.S. living standards and few concerns about international competition, real GNP per worker-hour grew 1.85 percent annually, while command GNP per hour grew a bit faster, 1.87 percent. From 1973 to 1990, a period of stagnating living standards, command GNP growth per hour slowed to 0.65 percent. Almost all (91 percent) of that slowdown, however, was explained by a decline in domestic productivity growth: real GNP per hour grew only 0.73 percent.

Similar calculations for the European Community and Japan yield similar results. In each case, the growth rate of living standards essentially equals the growth rate of domestic productivity—not productivity relative to competitors, but simply domestic productivity. Even though world trade is larger than ever before, national living standards are overwhelmingly determined by domestic factors rather than by some competition for world markets.

How can this be in our interdependent world? Part of the answer is that the world is not as interdependent as you might think: countries are nothing at all like corporations. Even today, U.S. exports are only 10 percent of the value-added in the economy (which is equal to GNP). That is, the United States is still almost 90 percent an economy that produces goods and services for its own use. By contrast, even the largest corporation sells hardly any of its output to its own workers; the "exports" of General Motors—its sales to people who do not work there—are virtually all of its sales, which are more than 2.5 times the corporation's value-added.

Moreover, countries do not compete with each other the way corporations do. Coke and Pepsi are almost purely rivals: only a negligible fraction of Coca-Cola's sales go to Pepsi workers, only a negligible fraction of the goods Coca-Cola workers buy are Pepsi products. So if Pepsi is successful, it tends to be at Coke's expense. But the major industrial countries, while they sell products that compete with each other, are also each other's main export markets and each other's main suppliers of useful imports. If the European economy does well, it need not be at U.S. expense; indeed, if anything a successful European economy is likely to help the U.S. economy by providing it with larger markets and selling it goods of superior quality at lower prices.

International trade, then, is not a zero-sum game. When productivity rises in Japan, the main result is a rise in Japanese real wages; American or European wages are in principle at least as likely to rise as to fall, and in practice seem to be virtually unaffected.

It would be possible to belabor the point, but the moral is clear: while competitive problems could arise in principle, as a practical, empirical matter the major nations of the world are not to any significant degree in economic competition with each other. Of course, there is always a rivalry for status and power—countries that grow faster will see their political rank rise. So it is always interesting to *compare* countries. But asserting that Japanese growth diminishes U.S. status is very different from saying that it reduces the U.S. standard of living—and it is the latter that the rhetoric of competitiveness asserts.

One can, of course, take the position that words mean what we want them to mean, that all are free, if they wish, to use the term "competitiveness" as a poetic way of saying productivity, without actually implying that international competition has anything to do with it. But few writers on competitiveness would accept this view. They believe that the facts tell a very different story, that we live, as Lester Thurow put it in his best-selling book, *Head to Head,* in a world of "win-lose" competition between the leading economies. How is this belief possible?

CARELESS ARITHMETIC

One of the remarkable, startling features of the vast literature on competitiveness is the repeated tendency of highly intelligent authors to engage in what may perhaps most tactfully be described as "careless arithmetic." Assertions are made that sound like quantifiable pronouncements about measurable magnitudes, but the writers do not actually present any data on these magnitudes and thus fail to notice that the actual numbers contradict their assertions. Or data are presented that are supposed to support an assertion, but the writer fails to notice that his own numbers imply that what he is saying cannot be true. Over and over again one finds books and articles on competitiveness that seem to the unwary reader to be full of convincing evidence but that strike anyone familiar with the data as strangely, almost eerily inept in their handling of the numbers. Some examples can best illustrate this point. Here are three cases of careless arithmetic, each of some interest in its own right.

Trade Deficits and the Loss of Good Jobs. In a recent article published in Japan, Lester Thurow explained to his audience the importance of reducing the Japanese trade surplus with the United States. U.S. real wages, he pointed out, had fallen six percent during the Reagan and Bush years, and the reason was that trade deficits in manufactured goods had forced workers out of high-paying manufacturing jobs into much lower-paying service jobs.

This is not an original view; it is very widely held. But Thurow was more concrete than most people, giving actual numbers for the job and wage loss. A million manufacturing jobs have been lost because of the deficit, he asserted, and manufacturing jobs pay 30 percent more than service jobs.

Both numbers are dubious. The million-job number is too high, and the 30 percent wage differential between manufacturing and services is primarily due to a difference in the length of the workweek, not a difference in the hourly wage rate. But let's grant Thurow his numbers. Do they tell the story he suggests?

The key point is that total U.S. employment is well over 100 million workers. Suppose that a million workers were forced from manufacturing into services and as a result lost the 30 percent manufacturing wage premium. Since these workers are less than 1 percent of the U.S. labor force, this would reduce the average U.S. wage rate by less than 1/100 of 30 percent—that is, by less than 0.3 percent.

This is too small to explain the 6 percent real wage decline *by a factor of 20.* Or to look at it another way, the annual wage loss from deficit-induced deindustrialization, which Thurow clearly implies is at the heart of U.S. economic difficulties, is on the basis of his own numbers roughly equal to what the U.S. spends on health care every week.

Something puzzling is going on here. How could someone as intelligent as Thurow, in writing an article that purports to offer hard quantitative evidence of the importance of international competition to the U.S. economy, fail to realize that the evidence he offers clearly shows that the channel of harm that he identifies was *not* the culprit?

High Value-Added Sectors. Ira Magaziner and Robert Reich, both now influential figures in the Clinton Administration, first reached a broad audience with their 1982 book, *Minding America's Business.* The book advocated a U.S. industrial policy, and in the introduction the authors offered a seemingly concrete quantitative basis for such a policy: "Our standard of living can only rise if (i) capital and labor increasingly flow to industries with high value-added per worker and (ii) we maintain a position in those industries that is superior to that of our competitors."

Economists were skeptical of this idea on principle. If targeting the right industries was simply a matter of moving into sectors with high value-added, why weren't private markets already doing the job?[3] But one might dismiss this as simply the usual boundless faith of economists in the market; didn't Magaziner and Reich back their case with a great deal of real-world evidence?

Well, *Minding America's Business* contains a lot of facts. One thing it never does, however, is actually justify the criteria set out in the introduction. The choice of industries to cover clearly implied a belief among the authors that high value-added is more or less synonymous with high technology, but nowhere in the book do any numbers compare actual value-added per worker in different industries.

Such numbers are not hard to find. Indeed, every public library in America has a copy of the *Statistical Abstract of the United States,* which each year contains a table presenting value-added and employment by industry in U.S. manufacturing. All one needs to do, then, is spend a few minutes in the library with a calculator to come up with a table that ranks U.S. industries by value-added per worker.

The table on this page shows selected entries from pages 740–744 of the 1991 *Statistical Abstract.* It turns out that the U.S. industries with really high value-added per worker are in sectors with very high ratios of capital to labor, like cigarettes and petroleum refining. (This was predictable: because capital-intensive industries must earn a normal return on large investments, they must charge prices that are a larger markup over labor costs than labor-intensive industries, which means that they have high value-added per worker). Among large industries, value-added per worker tends to be high in traditional heavy manufacturing sectors like steel and autos. High-technology sectors like aerospace and electronics turn out to be only roughly average.

This result does not surprise conventional economists. High value-added per worker occurs in sectors that are highly capital-intensive, that is, sectors in which an additional dollar of capital buys little extra value-added. In other words, there is no free lunch.

But let's leave on one side what the table says about the way the economy works, and simply note the strangeness of the lapse by Magaziner and Reich. Surely they were not calling for an industrial policy that would funnel capital and labor into the steel and auto industries in preference to high-tech. How, then, could they write a whole book dedicated to the proposition that we should target high value-added industries without ever checking to see which industries they meant?

Labor Costs. In his own presentation at the Copenhagen summit, British Prime Minister John Major showed a chart indicating that European unit labor

TABLE 1   VALUE ADDED PER WORKER, 1988

	(IN THOUSANDS OF DOLLARS)
Cigarettes	488
Petroleum Refining	283
Autos	99
Steel	97
Aircraft	68
Electronics	64
All manufacturing	66

costs have risen more rapidly than those in the United States and Japan. Thus he argued that European workers have been pricing themselves out of world markets.°

But a few weeks later Sam Brittan of the *Financial Times* pointed out a strange thing about Major's calculations: the labor costs were not adjusted for exchange rates. In international competition, of course, what matters for a U.S. firm are the costs of its overseas rivals measured in dollars, not marks or yen. So international comparisons of labor costs, like the tables the Bank of England routinely publishes, always convert them into a common currency. The numbers presented by Major, however, did not make this standard adjustment. And it was a good thing for his presentation that they didn't. As Brittan pointed out, European labor costs have not risen in relative terms when the exchange rate adjustment is made.

If anything, this lapse is even odder than those of Thurow or Magaziner and Reich. How could John Major, with the sophisticated statistical resources of the U.K. Treasury behind him, present an analysis that failed to make the most standard of adjustments?

These examples of strangely careless arithmetic, chosen from among dozens of similar cases, by people who surely had both the cleverness and the resources to get it right, cry out for an explanation. The best working hypothesis is that in each case the author or speaker wanted to believe in the competitive hypothesis so much that he felt no urge to question it; if data were used at all, it was only to lend credibility to a predetermined belief, not to test it. But why are people apparently so anxious to define economic problems as issues of international competition?

THE THRILL OF COMPETITION

The competitive metaphor—the image of countries competing with each other in world markets in the same way that corporations do—derives much of its attractiveness from its seeming comprehensibility. Tell a group of businessmen that a country is like a corporation writ large, and you give them the comfort of feeling that they already understand the basics. Try to tell them about economic concepts like comparative advantage, and you are asking them to learn something new. It should not be surprising if many prefer a doctrine that offers the gain of apparent sophistication without the pain of hard thinking. The rhetoric of competitiveness has become so widespread, however, for three deeper reasons.

First, competitive images are exciting, and thrills sell tickets. . . .

Second, the idea that U.S. economic difficulties hinge crucially on our failures in international competition somewhat paradoxically makes those difficulties seem easier to solve. The productivity of the average American worker is determined by a complex array of factors, most of them unreachable by any likely government policy. So if you accept the reality that our "competitive" problem is really a domestic productivity problem pure and simple, you are unlikely to be optimistic about any dramatic turnaround. But if you can convince yourself that the problem is really

---

°Editors' Note: The Copenhagen Summit of the European Community was held in June 1993. One of the prime topics was the problem of Europe's high level of unemployment.

one of failures in international competition—that imports are pushing workers out of high-wage jobs, or subsidized foreign competition is driving the United States out of the high value-added sectors—then the answers to economic malaise may seem to you to involve simple things like subsidizing high technology and being tough on Japan.

Finally, many of the world's leaders have found the competitive metaphor extremely useful as a political device. The rhetoric of competitiveness turns out to provide a good way either to justify hard choices or to avoid them. . . .

[T]he well-received presentation of Bill Clinton's initial economic program in February 1993 showed the usefulness of competitive rhetoric as a motivation for tough policies. Clinton proposed a set of painful spending cuts and tax increases to reduce the Federal deficit. Why? The real reasons for cutting the deficit are disappointingly undramatic: the deficit siphons off funds that might otherwise have been productively invested, and thereby exerts a steady if small drag on U.S. economic growth. But Clinton was able instead to offer a stirring patriotic appeal, calling on the nation to act now in order to make the economy competitive in the global market—with the implication that dire economic consequences would follow if the United States does not.

Many people who know that "competitiveness" is a largely meaningless concept have been willing to indulge competitive rhetoric precisely because they believe they can harness it in the service of good policies. An overblown fear of the Soviet Union was used in the 1950s to justify the building of the interstate highway system and the expansion of math and science education. Cannot the unjustified fears about foreign competition similarly be turned to good, used to justify serious efforts to reduce the budget deficit, rebuild infrastructure, and so on?

A few years ago this was a reasonable hope. At this point, however, the obsession with competitiveness has reached the point where it has already begun dangerously to distort economic policies.

THE DANGERS OF OBSESSION

Thinking and speaking in terms of competitiveness poses three real dangers. First, it could result in the wasteful spending of government money supposedly to enhance U.S. competitiveness. Second, it could lead to protectionism and trade wars. Finally, and most important, it could result in bad public policy on a spectrum of important issues.

During the 1950s, fear of the Soviet Union induced the U.S. goverment to spend money on useful things like highways and science education. It also, however, led to considerable spending on more doubtful items like bomb shelters. The most obvious if least worrisome danger of the growing obsession with competitiveness is that it might lead to a similar misallocation of resources. To take an example, recent guidelines for government research funding have stressed the importance of supporting research that can improve U.S. international competitiveness. This exerts at least some bias toward inventions that can help manufacturing firms, which generally compete on international markets, rather than service producers, which generally do not. Yet most of our employment and value-added is now in services, and lagging productivity in services rather than manufactures has been the single most important factor in the stagnation of U.S. living standards.

A much more serious risk is that the obsession with competitiveness will lead to trade conflict, perhaps even to a world trade war. Most of those who have preached the doctrine of competitiveness have not been old-fashioned protectionists. They want their countries to win the global trade game, not drop out. But what if, despite its best efforts, a country does not seem to be winning, or lacks confidence that it can? Then the competitive diagnosis inevitably suggests that to close the borders is better than to risk having foreigners take away high-wage jobs and high-value sectors. At the very least, the focus on the supposedly competitive nature of international economic relations greases the rails for those who want confrontational if not frankly protectionist policies.

We can already see this process at work, in both the United States and Europe. In the United States, it was remarkable how quickly the sophisticated interventionist arguments advanced by Laura Tyson in her published work gave way to the simple-minded claim by U.S. Trade Representative Mickey Kantor that Japans bilateral trade surplus was costing the United States millions of jobs. And the trade rhetoric of President Clinton, who stresses the supposed creation of high-wage jobs rather than the gains from specialization, left his administration in a weak position when it tried to argue with the claims of NAFTA foes that competition from cheap Mexican labor will destroy the U.S. manufacturing base.

Perhaps the most serious risk from the obsession with competitiveness, however, is its subtle indirect effect on the quality of economic discussion and policy-making. If top government officials are strongly committed to a particular economic doctrine, their commitment inevitably sets the tone for policy-making on all issues, even those which may seem to have nothing to do with that doctrine. And if an economic doctrine is flatly, completely and demonstrably wrong, the insistence that discussion adhere to that doctrine inevitably blurs the focus and diminishes the quality of policy discussion across a broad range of issues, including some that are very far from trade policy per se. . . .

To make a harsh but not entirely unjustified analogy, a government wedded to the ideology of competitiveness is as unlikely to make good economic policy as a government committed to creationism is to make good science policy, even in areas that have no direct relationship to the theory of evolution. . . .

So let's start telling the truth: competitiveness is a meaningless word when applied to national economies. And the obsession with competitiveness is both wrong and dangerous.

NOTES

1. An example may be helpful here. Suppose that a country spends 20 percent of its income on imports, and that the prices of its imports are set not in domestic but in foreign currency. Then if the country is forced to devalue its currency—reduce its value in foreign currency—by 10 percent, this will raise the price of 20 percent of the country's

spending basket by 10 percent, thus raising the overall price index by 2 percent. Even if domestic *output* has not changed, the country's real *income* will therefore have fallen by 2 percent. If the country must repeatedly devalue in the face of competitive pressure, growth in real income will persistently lag behind growth in real output.

It's important to notice, however, that the size of this lag depends not only on the amount of devaluation but on the share of imports in spending. A 10 percent devaluation of the dollar against the yen does not reduce U.S. real income by 10 percent—in fact, it reduces U.S. real income by only about 0.2 percent because only about 2 percent of U.S. income is spent on goods produced in Japan.

2. In the example in the previous footnote, the devaluation would have no effect on real GNP, but command GNP would have fallen by two percent. The finding that in practice command GNP has grown almost as fast as real GNP therefore amounts to saying that events like the hypothetical case in footnote one are unimportant in practice.

3. "Value-added" has a precise, standard meaning in national income accounting: the value added of a firm is the dollar value of its sales, minus the dollar value of the inputs it purchases from other firms, and as such it is easily measured. Some people who use the term, however, may be unaware of this definition and simply use "high value-added" as a synonym for "desirable."

PART
Four

CENTRAL ISSUES IN CONTEMPORARY WORLD POLITICS

With the end of the Cold War, a new era in international politics is upon us. A few of the selections in the previous parts of this book discussed some of the changes that we are already experiencing and speculated on those that we will likely soon see. The selections in Part Four deal more systematically with these matters. In particular, they ponder the question of how much is new and how much is familiar in the era we are now entering. We have picked four issues that we consider central to this debate even though they do not exhaust all of them: the future of war, the future of the global economy, the protection of the global environment, and the prospects for international intervention.

THE FUTURE OF WAR

War is as old as the time when human beings first organized themselves into groups. Will the world be as ravaged by war in the decades to come as it has been since the dawn of civilization? Or are we now entering a new era in which war will be banished from the face of the earth?

Robert Jervis and Stephen Van Evera provide insights into this question. Jervis argues that war among the rich democracies of North America, Western Europe, and Japan is a thing of the past. For the rest of the world, however, war will be endemic, even if not total. We have already seen some of the reasons why the first and third worlds will experience conflict differently in Parts One and Two. Nuclear weapons, democratic states, and high levels of economic interdependence in the first world make war among these states unlikely. These conditions are not duplicated within the third world, where ethnic conflicts within and between nations rage, where leaders seek foreign adventures to solidify their rule at home, and where disputes over borders and access to resources provide proximate reasons for conflict. But as Stephen Van Evera points out, even the first world experiences conflicts where nationalism waxes. Van Evera analyzes the relation between nationalism and war and shows under what conditions the former is likely to produce the latter. Nationalism is not a thing of the past but is alive and well in many parts of the globe. To tame it, or at least to prevent its causing destructive wars, requires active intervention by states in the affairs of others.

THE FUTURE OF THE GLOBAL ECONOMY

Will the global economy continue toward greater openness, and will interdependence increase? Recent progress in the creation of a new World Trade Organization to replace GATT (the General Agreement on Trade and Tariffs) suggests that this may be the case. But as noted by some of the readings in Part Three, it is not a future without its costs.

Both Peter Drucker and Lester Thurow portray a world that will become economically more competitive as it becomes more interdependent, but for different reasons. Drucker argues that the daily movement of capital among nations now overwhelms the exchange of goods among them. This is what is new in the global economy, and this is what now binds states ever closer together economically. The globalization of finance reduces the ability of states to insulate themselves from one another's capital markets. Drucker's vision is one of lessened state autonomy. But as Lester Thurow points out, another development has occurred in the international economy: Competition is becoming more intense because the nature of the products in which states compete has changed. It has become head-to-head, not niche competition. The world's powerful industrial economies now compete directly in the production and export of the same goods, rather than exchanging largely complementary goods as in the past. It is also a world where comparative advantages are more easily created by national policies that foster technology and that give industries tax breaks and protection against imports. Drucker's vision is one of national economies more tightly bound by the globalization of finance. Thurow's is one of national economies competing more fiercely than ever before.

THE PROTECTION OF THE GLOBAL ENVIRONMENT

Protection of the global environment is not a new issue, but its importance has increased within the last decade. This is partly a natural result of the demise of the Cold War. As the American–Soviet rivalry faded and then ended, other issues could more easily rise on the international agenda. But the increasing salience of global environmental problems has also resulted from the demonstrated increase in damage to the world environment. The depletion of the ozone layer and the threat of global warming, two issues that received prominence just within the last decade, together with the 1992 United Nations Conference on the Environment in Rio, have brought global environmental issues to the very top of the international agenda.

A particular class of environmental problems—called "commons" or "collective action" or "public goods" problems—makes it especially difficult to concert action among states. For truly global commons resources, like ozone and the overall global temperature, the situation looks like this: No single state owns the resource, but all use it (and can abuse it); and none can be prevented from using and abusing it. A commons (or a public) good is one that no single individual or entity owns, but that all can utilize. For such commons resources, no individual or state has an incentive to minimize its degradating effects unless it is persuaded that all others will act in similar fashion. There is little incentive for India to reduce its carbon-dioxide emissions into the atmosphere unless it is convinced that the United States and the other industrialized nations will do so. The three central tasks for solving international collective action problems are: first, to obtain agreement that there are serious problems; second, to reach consensus on how to solve the problems; and third, to devise institutional agreements for monitoring compliance and for punishing offenders.

The four selections by Wijkman, Mathews, Simon, and Homer-Dixon deal with these issues. Per Magnus Wijkman lays out the problem of dealing with abuses of the global commons, sets forth the nature of the institutional arrangements that must be devised to deal with them, and surveys how states have dealt with selected commons issues. Jessica Tuchman Mathews calls for a new definition of state security. The next decade will require that states focus their intellectual and financial resources less on armaments and more on the environment. Environmental degradation is at war with the traditional assumptions and practices of international relations. Environmental problems know no borders; solutions based on customary views of national sovereignty are no longer appropriate to deal with them. Cross-national environmental challenges will require transnational institutions.

Julian Simon challenges the view that mankind must husband its natural resources because he argues that the supply of natural resources is infinite, or at least not finite in an economic sense. He challenges us to think like an economist: to consider not just the absolute supply of a good, but rather how much of it is available at a given price. In this sense, no resource is finite because substitutes are always available if the price of a good rises too high compared to other goods that can be substituted for it. In short, the market will solve the problem of the availability of resources. And, by extension, the market can deal with the degradation of the environment if the costs of cleaning it up are included in the price of those goods that contribute to its degradation. Thomas Homer-Dixon takes exception to Simon's view. He gives seven reasons why Simon-type arguments no longer apply in today's world. What drives all these factors, in his view, is the size of the world's population and its continued rapid growth. At a certain point, quantity can overwhelm the demonstrated ingenuity of humans to invent their way out of problems. In Homer-Dixon's view, we are at that point now.

THE PROSPECTS FOR INTERNATIONAL INTERVENTION

The fourth issue concerns the obligations states have to one another and the rights they possess as sovereign states. The United Nations was founded on the principle of the sovereignty of the state—on its presumed right to be the final arbiter within its geographic borders. Yet, also incorporated within the United Nations system is the Universal Declaration on Human Rights, which was discussed in Part One. This declaration attests to the universality of human rights that transcends state borders. The opposition between these two principles—state sovereignty and universal rights—was never resolved during the Cold War. In our era, their contradictory prescriptions remain unresolved.

The four selections by Trachtenberg, Mandelbaum, Fisher, and Gamba deal with various aspects of this tension. Marc Trachtenberg looks at intervention in historical perspective and shows that states, or at least the great powers, regularly intervened in the affairs of other states when it suited their interests. Intervention per se is not new, even if the reasons for it have changed. Michael Mandelbaum demonstrates that intervention, especially for humanitarian reasons, is an illusion. If one state intervenes in another to avert an imminent humanitarian disaster, such as mass starvation or ethnic genocide, it must realize that such intervention cannot be truly effective unless it solves the political dispute that caused the disaster in the first place. Apart from purely natural disasters, most such humanitarian disasters have deep roots in politics. As a consequence, an apolitical humanitarian intervention is likely to fail unless it deals with the underlying political conditions that first caused it. This, to state the obvious, is never an easy task.

David Fisher provides a more abstract discussion of the ethics of intervention. He applies what is called "just war" theory to the matter and shows the conditions under which forcible intervention in the affairs of another state can be justified. Finally, Virginia Gamba looks at the matter of intervention from the perspective of the South. Having been subjected to colonialism from the western industrialized world, these states are understandably suspicious of the whole concept. To prevent intervention from being simply the strong lording it over the weak, she suggests a truly global cooperative effort to "internationalize" the rules under which third-party intervention can take place.

The Future of War

The Future of World Politics

Robert Jervis

History usually makes a mockery of our hopes or our expectations. The events of 1989, perhaps more welcomed than those of any year since 1945, were unforeseen. Much of what analysts anticipate for the 1990s is unpleasant. Nevertheless, it is clear that we are entering a new world. . . . It appears that while international politics in much of the world will follow patterns that are familiar in outline although unpredictable in detail, among the developed states we are likely to see new forms of relations. . . .

WHAT IS CONSTANT; WHAT HAS CHANGED

Cyclical thinking suggests that, freed from the constraints of the Cold War, world politics will return to earlier patterns.[1] Many of the basic generalizations of international politics remain unaltered: it is still anarchic in the sense that there is no international sovereign that can make and enforce laws and agreements.[2] The security dilemma remains as well, with the problems it creates for states who would like to cooperate but whose security requirements do not mesh. Many specific causes of conflict also remain, including desires for greater prestige, economic rivalries, hostile nationalisms, divergent perspectives on and incompatible standards of legitimacy, religious animosities, and territorial ambitions. To put it more generally, both aggression and spirals of insecurity and tension can still disturb the peace. But are the conditions that call these forces into being as prevalent as they were in the past? Are the forces that restrain violence now as strong, or stronger, than they were?

International Security, Winter 1991/92 (Vol. 16, No. 3) © 1991 by the President and Fellows of Harvard College and of the Massachusetts Institute of Technology. Portions of the text and some footnotes have been omitted.

The answers may be different for different regions of the world. Even where fundamental changes have not occurred, the first seven impediments to prediction remain in place; but there we can at least say that the variables and relationships that acted in the past should continue. Where time's arrow predominates, on the other hand, our first task may be negative: to argue that some familiar patterns are not likely to re-appear. On some questions we may be able to discern at least the outlines of the new arrangements; on others, what will emerge may not yet be determined.

The Developed World

Time's arrow is most strikingly at work in the developed world: it is hard to see how a war could occur among the United States, Western Europe, and Japan, at least in the absence of revolutionary domestic changes, presumably linked to severe economic depression. Indeed, peace among these countries is over-determined: there are many reasons, each of which is probably sufficient, why they should remain at peace.[3] One indication of the profound change is that although Britain's primary aim always was to prevent any power from dominating the continent of Europe, even those Britons who opposed joining the European Community or who remain opposed to seeing it develop political sovereignty would laugh at the idea of going to war to prevent its formation. The United States, too, fought to prevent Germany from dominating Europe, but sponsored European integration during the Cold War and still looks on it with favor, even though Germany is its leader.[4] Similarly, if international politics in the West had not changed, in the absence of bipolarity it would be hard to understand how the United States would not now fear the French and British nuclear forces which, after all, could obliterate it. A test of whether the standard logic of international politics will continue to apply among the developed states will be whether this fear will emerge. A parallel—and more disturbing—test will be whether Germany and Japan, freed from the security and constraints of the Cold War, will seek nuclear weapons, following the previous rule that great powers seek the most prestigious and powerful military weapons available even in the absense of a clear threat. (A decision to "go nuclear" would not prove the point, however, if it was motivated by fear of the Soviet Union or China.)

These dramatic breaks from the past and the general peacefulness of the West are to be explained by increases in the costs of war, decreases in its benefits and, linked to this, changes in domestic regimes and values. Earlier I argued that specific events sometimes send history into a different path. But these changes in the developed world are so deep, powerful, and interlocked that they cannot readily be reversed by any foreseeable event.

The Increased Costs of War The costs of war among developed states probably would be enormous even it there were no nuclear weapons.[5] But such weapons do exist, and by increasing still more the costs of war, they also increase the chances of peace. This much is generally agreed upon. Many analysts believe that mutual deterrence means not only that each nuclear power can deter a direct attack, but also that nothing else can be deterred—i.e., that allies cannot be sheltered under the nuclear umbrella and that "extended deterrence" is a fiction. As I have argued elsewhere, however, both logic and the historical record indicates that this position is not true.[6] Because inadvertent escalation is always a possibility, a conventional war that involves a nuclear power—or that could draw in a nuclear power—could lead to nuclear devastation.

During the Cold War the risks of escalation meant that the United States could protect Western Europe even if the West had neither a first-strike capability nor an adequate conventional defense; in the current era it means that the European states gain some of the deterrent advantages of nuclear weapons even if they do not own them. Because statesmen realize that any European war could lead to a nuclear conflagration, aggression and even crises will be discouraged. This sharply decreases the incentives for proliferation: nuclear weapons are not necessary to ensure the security of European states like Germany that lack them, and would not greatly help such countries realize expansionist aims if they should develop them. Because the French and British nuclear forces increase the chance that any fighting in Europe could escalate, they decrease the likelihood of war and so, far from threatening the United States, should continue to be welcomed by it.

The Declining Benefits of War Because the expected costs of armed conflict among the developed countries are so high, only the strongest pressures for war could produce such an outcome. Yet it is hard to conjure up any significant impulses toward war. The high level of economic interdependence among the developed states increases not only the costs of war, but the benefits of peace as well. Even in the case that shows the greatest strain—U.S.-Japan relations—no one has explained how a war could serve either country's interests.[7] The claim that a high degree of integration prevents war by making it prohibitively costly for states to fight each other has often been incorrectly attributed to Norman Angell's *The Great Illusion,* and the outbreak of World War I a few years after this book was published is cited as proof of the error of the position. But the title of Angell's book gives its actual argument: it is an illusion to believe that war will provide economic gain.[8] The argument was as much prescription as description, and the former would not have been necessary had the latter been self-evident. The implications for today are obvious: while the objective facts of interdependence are important, one must also ask how they are viewed by the general public, elites, and statesmen.

Not only the degree but also the kinds of interdependence matter. If statesmen examine the situation with any sophistication, they will be concerned not about the size of the flows of trade and capital, but rather with what will happen to their states' welfare if these flows are halted.[9] Thus the fact that levels of trade are higher among the developed countries today than they were in 1914 may be less significant than the fact that direct foreign investment is greater and that many firms, even if they are not formally multinational, have important international ties.[10] It would be harder for states and firms to arrange for substitutes if conflict or war severed these financial ties than would be the case if it were only goods that were being exchanged.

The other side of this coin is that continued high levels of economic intercourse may significantly increase each state's wealth. This, of course, is the foundation of the argument for the advantage of open international economic systems, and the postwar history of the developed world is strongly consistent with it. Even those who call for some protection do not doubt that trade is necessary for prosperity. Most importantly for a consideration of the political relations among the developed countries, no one in any of these states believes that his or her country can grow richer by conquering any of the others than it can by trading with it, in part because the techniques of controlling an occupied country are not compatible with making a post-industrial economy function well.[11] People in each country can believe, sometime with good reason, that their own fortunes would improve more if others do less well or may attribute their difficulties to extreme—and unfair— economic competition, but this does not mean that they believe that they are likely to thrive if their partners suffer significant economic misfortune.

The belief that one's economic well-being is linked to that of others is not sufficient to bring peace, however. Many values are more important to people than wealth. High levels of economic interdependence have not prevented civil wars, although it may have inhibited them; perhaps more internal conflicts would have occurred had countries not been fairly well integrated. This could help explain why modern countries rarely experience these bloody disturbances. Alternative explanations are possible, however, and the Spanish Civil War and current unrest in Yugoslavia, Czechoslovakia, and the Soviet Union at minimum show that a higher level of economic integration than that which characterizes the current international system does not prevent armed conflict.

In international politics it is particularly true that wealth is not the primary national goal. Not only will states pay a high price to maintain their security, autonomy, and the spread of their values, but the calculus of economic benefit is affected by the international context. While economic theory argues that the actor should care only about how the outcome of an economic choice affects him, those who fear that they may have to fight need to worry about relative advantage as well as absolute gains.[12] Furthermore, states that become more dependent on others than others are on them will be vulnerable to pressure, as the Balkan states discovered before World War II.[13]

Both the fear of dependence and concern about relative gains are less when states expect to remain at peace with each other. Indeed, expectations of peaceful relations were a necessary condition for the formation of the European Common Market; the growth of interdependence in the developed world is as much a symptom as a cause of the basic change in international politics. Had the Europeans thought there was a significant chance that they would come to blows, they would not have permitted their economies to grow so interdependent. The price of greater wealth would have been excessive if they felt their security would be endangered, and so it is not surprising that other regions have not imitated the successful European experience.

When states fear each other, interdependence can increase conflict.[14] Thus there is at least an element of reinforcing feedback in the current situation: interdependence has developed in part because of the expectations of peace, and the economic benefits of close economic relations in turn make peace more likely. The political implications of the economic situation were very different in the early twentieth century when Britain and Germany, although trading heavily with each other, each feared that economic endeavors that strengthened the other would eventually weaken its own security. As one British observer put it after an extended tour of Germany: "Every one of these new factory chimneys is a gun pointed at England."[15] The growth of another state's political and economic power now is worrisome only if it causes harm to the first in some direct way; it is no longer automatically seen as decreasing the first state's ability to protect its interests in the next war. Samuel Huntington argues that the answer to the question of why Americans are so concerned about the Japanese challenge is straightforward: "The United States is obsessed with Japan for the same reason that it was once obsessed with the Soviet Union. It sees that country as a major threat to its primacy in a crucial arena of power."[16] But it is far from clear that one state's economic progress constitutes a threat to another unless the two are likely to fight, the former's relative advantage will diminish the other's absolute wealth, or the former will gain leverage it can use in important political disputes. The first condition does not hold in the U.S.-Japan case, and it is certainly debatable whether either of the other two do. Rivalry is different in its meaning and implications when it is conducted with an eye to future fighting than when the interactions are expected to be peaceful.

Changes in Domestic Regimes and Values   The change in relations among the developed states is partly a result of a shift in basic outlook and values. As John Mueller has noted, war is no longer seen as good, or even as honorable, in anything less than desperate circumstances.[17] No Western leader would speak—or even think—in terms like those expressed by Chief of the German General Staff Helmuth von Moltke in a letter to his wife during the 1911 Moroccan Crisis:

> If we again slip away from the affair with our tail between our legs and if we cannot bring ourselves to put forward a determined claim which we are prepared to force through with the sword, I shall despair of the future of the German Empire. I shall then resign. But before handing in my resignation, I shall move to abolish the Army and to place ourselves under Japanese protectorate; we shall then be in a position to make money without interference and to develop into ninnies.[18]

These sentiments seem archaic: we may now be seeing, among developed states, the triumph of interests over passions, as Angell and Joseph Schumpeter foresaw.[19]

As the Gulf War reminds us, it is not as though developed states do not feel a sense of pride, or even self-identity, in asserting themselves abroad. But the impulse is more episodic than it once was, is not directed against other democracies, and is more often exercised in the service of economic values than counterposed to them. Part of the explanation for this change is the waning of nationalism, perhaps in the sense of pride in the achievements of one's nation, and certainly in the sense of a belief that one's country is superior to others and should dominate them. The progress toward West European unification both facilitated and is made possible by a weakening of the attachment to one's nation as a source of identity and personal satisfaction. The residual feelings may be sufficient to prevent Europe from completely unifying, but the process never could have moved this far had nationalism remained even at the level of the fairly benign late 1920s, let alone of any other era. I doubt if we will see a return to these periods: reduced national-ism is now closely associated with economic and political gains and has been embodied in institutions that have become the focus of power and perhaps loyalty. Nationalism was discredited in some European states (although not Germany) after 1918, but this was because it had brought failure, not because being less nationalistic had produced success.

Change in values is also evident from the absence of territorial disputes. Ger-mans no longer seem to care that Alsace and Lorraine are French: The French, who permitted the Saar to return to Germany in a plebiscite, are not bothered by this loss, and indeed do not see it as a loss at all. The Germans did feel sufficient Germanness to seek the unification of their country, but the desire to regain the "lost territories" to the east seems extremely low. Furthermore, unification was not accomplished against the will of any other country and, unlike manifestations of more disturbing nationalism, did not involve the assertion of the rightful domina-tion of one country over another.

Equally important, the developed states are now democratic and it appears that liberal democracies rarely, if ever, fight each other.[20] Here too values play a large role. What would one democracy gain by conquering another? The United States could conquer Canada, for example, but why would it want to do so when much of what it would want to see there is already in place? Neither security considerations nor the desire to improve the world would impel one liberal democ-racy to attack another.

Implications of Changed Relations Among the Developed States   In summary, war among the developed states is extremely unlikely because its costs have greatly increased, the gains it could bring have decreased, especially com-pared to the alternative routes to those goals, and the values states seek have altered. Four qualities of these changes are particularly important. First, they are powerful determinants of behavior: compared to these factors, the influence of the polarity of the international system is slight. Even if multipolar systems are less sta-ble than bipolar ones and even if the future world will be multipolar, it is hard to see how the overall result could be dangerous. The forces for peace among the developed countries are so overwhelming that impulses which under other cir-cumstances would be destabilizing will not lead to violence.

Second, the three kinds of changes interact and reinforce each other. The high costs of war permit economic interdependence by reducing each state's fear of armed conflict with others. The joining of economic fates reciprocally gives each state a positive stake in the others' well-being, thus limiting political conflict. But these developments would not have had the same impact were it not for the spread of democracy and the shift of values. These changes in turn support the perceived advantages of peace. If hyper-nationalism and the belief that one's country was destined to rule over others were rampant, then violence would be the only way to reach state goals. If statesmen thought expansion brought national honor, they might risk the high costs of war as an instrument of coercion. So focusing on any one of these elements in isolation from the others misunderstands how and why the world has changed.

Third, many of the changes in West European politics and values were caused in part by the Cold War. The conflict with the Soviet Union generated an unprecedented sense of unity and gave each state an important stake in the welfare of the others. To the extent that each was contributing to the anti-Soviet coalition, each reaped political benefit from the others' economic growth and strength.[21] Since the coalition could be undermined by social unrest or political instability, each country also sought to see that the others were well-off, that social problems were adequately managed, and that sources of discontent were minimized. It would then have been costly for any country to have tried to solve its own domestic problems by exporting them to its neighbors. Indeed, since the coalition would have been disrupted if any country had developed strong grievances against others in the coalition, each had incentives to moderate its own potentially disturbing demands and to mediate if conflicts developed between others.

But the end of the Cold War will not bring a return to the older patterns. Rather, the changes are irreversible, especially if the developed countries remain democratic, which is likely. The ties of mutual interest and identification, the altered psychology, whereby individuals identify less deeply with their nations and more with broader entities, values, and causes, the new supra-national institutions, and the general sense that there is no reason for the developed countries to fight each other will remain.

Finally, these changes represent time's arrow: international politics among the developed nations will be qualitatively different from what history has made familiar. War and the fear of war have been the dominant motor of politics among nations. The end of war does not mean the end of conflict, of course. Developed states will continue to be rivals in some respects, to jockey for position, and to bargain with each other. Disputes and frictions are likely to be considerable; indeed the shared expectation that they will not lead to fighting will remove some restraints on vituperation. But with no disputes meriting the use of force and with such instruments being inappropriate to the issues at hand, we are in unmapped territory: statesmen and publics will require new perspectives if not new concepts; scholars will have to develop new variables and new theories. Although Karl Deutsch and his colleagues explored some of the paths that could lead to the formation of what they called a pluralistic security community—a group of states among whom war was unthinkable[22]—there are few systematic treatments of how countries in such a configuration might conduct themselves.[23]

Eastern Europe

In other areas of the world, however, we are likely to see time's cycle. The resurgent ethnic disputes in Eastern Europe and the Soviet Union appear much as they were when they were suppressed by Soviet power 45 and 70 years ago. It is almost as though we had simply turned back the clock or, to change the analogy, as though they were the patients described by Oliver Sacks who came back to life after medication had released them from the strange disease that had frozen them.[24] The prospects for international politics in this region are worrisome at best.

Most of the arguments made in the preceding section about the prospects for peace in Western Europe do not apply to the Eastern part of the continent. The

latter is not filled with stable, democratic governments that have learned to cooperate and have developed a stake in each other's well-being. Nationalism and militarism are dangerous and grievances abound, especially those rooted in ethnic and
border disputes. Even if Stephen Van Evera is correct to argue that the decrease in
social stratification will remove one of the causes of hyper-nationalism,[25] the traditional sources of international strife are sufficient to lead the relations among these
states to be permeated by the fear of war.

War is not inevitable, however. Statesmen realize that the costs of fighting are
likely to be high, even if the likelihood of Soviet intervention has diminished. Also
powerful will be the new factor of the East Europeans' knowledge that economic
prosperity depends on access to the markets of the European Community and that
such access is not likely to be granted to unstable, authoritarian, or aggressive
regimes. Thus the very existence of the EC should encourage peace and stability
in the East.[26] The West can also support democracy and moderation in Eastern
Europe and the Soviet Union by seeking to build appropriate institutions, habits,
and processes, although the extent of this influence is difficult to determine.[27]

Much is likely to depend on internal developments within each East European country (and the way one country develops may influence what happens in
others as well). If the forces of nationalism and militarism are kept under control,
the chances for peace will be increased.[28] This, in turn, depends in part on the success of the countries' economic programs. But whether the results are peaceful or
violent, the general determinants of international politics in this region are likely to
be fairly traditional ones, such as the presence or absence of aggressive regimes,
the offense/defense balance in military strategy and technology, and the level of
political and diplomatic skill of the national leaders. Our inability to predict the
results stems from the fact that we cannot be certain about the values of a number
of the key variables. But, with the exception of the pacifying influence of the hope
for acceptance by West Europe, the variables at work and the ways they relate to
each other should be quite familiar.

Because Eastern Europe is not alone on its continent, the optimism I stated
earlier about the developed countries needs to be qualified. Probably the greatest
danger—but still slight—to the peace and stability of Western Europe, and by
extension to the United States, is large-scale violence—either international or
civil—in Eastern Europe and the Soviet Union. The power, location, and history of
Germany mean that the most disturbing scenarios involve that country, which
could easily be drawn into the East by strife, generating fears that the result if not
the intention would be German dominance of the continent.

This chain of events seems unlikely, however. Offensive motivations are not
strong: neither the West in general nor Germany in particular is likely to see a great
deal to be gained by using force in the East. More troublesome would be the threat
that unrest in the East could pose to established Western interests. This problem
would be greater if and when the West has extensive economic ties to the East, but
even under these conditions the costs of using force probably would outweigh the
expected benefits. Security could be a more potent motivator in the face of extensive violence. But quarantine probably would be a more effective response than
intervention. Violence in the East could also set in motion large flows of refugees

that would create an economic and political menace,[29] but here too military force would not be the most appropriate remedy. Ideology might pull the West in: the urge to protect a newly-democratic regime could be a strong one. But while active diplomacy would certainly be expected in this situation, force would only be a last resort. In all of these possible cases what would be crucial for the West would be the extent of its solidarity. The danger would be least if any intervention were joint, greater if any one country—especially Germany—proceeded on its own, and greatest if different Western states were linked to opposing factions or countries in the East. To a large extent, then, the West can contain the consequences of violence in Eastern Europe even if it fails to prevent it. Indeed, maintaining Western unity is perhaps the most important function of NATO, and 1991 discussions of a joint NATO force for potential use in Eastern Europe seem to have been motivated largely by the shared desire to avoid unilateral interventions.

The Third World

To include all of Africa, Asia, and Latin America under one rubric is to wield an even broader brush than I have employed so far. The crudeness of this residual category is indicated by the name "Third World," which is surely a confession of intellectual failure. That being neither economically developed nor communist gives countries much in common is to be doubted; the patterns of politics are likely to be different in different regions.[30] Also, perhaps, for better and for worse, international politics in Central and South America will continue to be strongly influenced by the United States. International politics among the states of sub-Saharan Africa are likely to continue to show at least some restraint because the lack of legitimacy of borders makes them all vulnerable and thus gives them powerful incentives to avoid fighting each other.[31] Furthermore, most African countries have quite weak states, a characteristic that will continue to influence both their domestic and foreign policies by limiting both the resources that leaders can extract and the extent to which national as opposed to personal and societal interests can be expected to prevail.[32]

The question I want to ask here may not require much detail: is the end of the Cold War likely to increase or decrease international conflict in the Third World? To put this another way, did the Cold War dampen or exacerbate conflict? It probably did both: dampened it in some respects, exacerbated it in others; dampened it in some areas of the globe, exacerbated it in others; dampened it under some circumstances, exacerbated it under others. In the net, however, it generally dampened conflict and we can therefore expect more rather than less conflict in the future.[33]

Many analysts argued that superpower competition spread conflict to the Third World. On some occasions, strife might not have developed at all had not a superpower sought out or been receptive to the pleas of a local actor to undermine or at least to preoccupy the other superpower's client. In other cases, conflict would have been less bloody and prolonged had the states or factions not expected that they could compensate for local weakness by garnering increased aid from abroad. Furthermore, the aid itself, especially financial and military, made these conflicts more intense and destructive. The civil war in Angola epitomizes these processes, although traces can be found in many other countries as well.

This is only the most visible part of the story, however. The extent to which superpower involvement dampened Third World conflicts is more difficult to discern because it resulted in non-events. But it is at least as important. Each superpower had an interest in seeing that the other did not make significant gains in the Third World, and also realized that the other had a parallel interest. Each knew that under most circumstances to succeed too well, or to permit its clients to do so, would invite a forceful response. Of course the Soviet Union in its desire to change the status quo welcomed and assisted disruptive movements and sought clients who, in part because of the nature of their domestic regimes, challenged their neighbors. But often it was indigenous forces that created violence and were restrained from abroad. The civil strife in Sri Lanka and the Punjab shows that even without superpower involvement, internal conflict can be prolonged and bloody. Furthermore, it is no accident that the only protracted armed conflicts in the Middle East were those that did not engage the Soviet-American rivalry (the Iran-Iraq War and Egypt's intervention in Yemen). The Arab-Israeli wars were short because they were dangerous not only to the local actors, but also to the superpowers who therefore had an interest in seeing that they did not get out of hand. In some cases, such as Angola and Afghanistan, extensive superpower involvement was compatible with a lengthy conflict, and indeed may have prolonged it. But when the superpower stakes were great, the area volatile, and the Third World actors not completely under control, the superpowers could not be content to fuel the conflict by indiscriminate assistance but also had to see that it did not lead them to a dangerous confrontation.

The 1991 Gulf War, the first case of major post–Cold War violence, might not have taken place in the earlier era. The United States could not have afforded to act as it did had the Soviet Union been Iraq's ally and a threat in Europe. The latter factor would have made the United States unable to deploy such a large military force; the former would have made it fear that a military response could call in the Soviet Union. On the other hand, aggression by a client of the Soviet Union would have been more of a threat than was Iraq's action in the actual event. So the United States would have been more strongly motivated to respond. Indeed, the Soviet Union would have realized this and might have restrained its client. Iraq's behavior also would have been different. With Soviet assistance, its need for Kuwait's wealth would have been slightly diminished. Furthermore, to the extent that it acted out of fear of isolation or the hope that the new international constellation provided it with a "window of opportunity," a continuation of the Cold War would have made the aggression less likely.[34]

The superpowers offered security to their Third World clients as well as restraining them. Unless other forces and mechanisms that would serve these functions develop, aggression will be less difficult and, partly for this reason, status quo states in the Third World will worry more about self-protection. Even absent aggressive motives, conflict will often result through the security dilemma: states' efforts to make themselves more secure will threaten others. These traditional sources of international conflict will work themselves out in a context that for at least several years will be changing rapidly as the states seek to adjust to the decreased superpower presence. Indeed, in some cases weak clients will collapse or be overthrown (e.g., Ethiopia), heightening the possibilities for regional disturbances.

The Third World may not necessarily recapitulate the international history of developed states. What Alexander Gerschenkron showed about domestic politics is true for international relations as well—the countries that go first change the environment so that the paths of late-comers are different. Even without their Cold War hyper-involvement, the superpowers and European states will continue to exert some influence. Third World leaders may also seek to emulate the First, in part in the hope of thereby earning greater aid, investment, and access to markets. Nevertheless, as in Eastern Europe, a decrease in superpower influence will permit more of the display of aggression and mutual insecurity that constitute the standard patterns of international conflict. Nationalism, ethnic disputes, and regional rivalries are likely to be prominent. Undoubtedly there will be surprises in the details, and specific predictions are beyond reach, but there is no reason to think that the basic contours of international politics will be unfamiliar. . . .

CONCLUSION

The end of the Cold War bears witness both to time's cycle and to time's arrow. Politics among the developed countries will not return to what it was before 1939. The costs of war have drastically increased while the benefits, especially compared with those available from alternative means, have decreased. Part of the reason for the latter change, in turn, is that the values of states and the individuals that compose them have changed. Although such constant factors as rivalry, the security dilemma, and the desire for advantage over others will continue, they are not likely to produce violence. And without the recurring threat of war, the patterns of international politics in the developed world cannot be the same. This is not true elsewhere on the globe. While Eastern Europe and the Third World are not likely to simply recapitulate the West's history from which so many of our theories of international politics are derived, neither should we expect a basic change from the familiar ways in which nations relate to each other.

The combination of the end of traditional threats to American security and the continuation of violence in many parts of the world confronts the United States with a wide range of choice. Without the clear framework that constituted the Cold War, there will be conflicts between security interests and other interests. New possibilities arise but not all of them can be pursued simultaneously. While the new era will be a less constrained one for the developed states in general and the United States in particular, by the same token the intellectual and political tasks are considerably increased. How involved America should be in world politics and what values it should seek to foster—and at what cost and risk—are questions that remain open, unanswered, and largely unaddressed.

NOTES

1. A good example is Mearsheimer, "Back to the Future: Instability in Europe, After the Cold War," *International Security,* Vol. 15, No. 1 (Summer 1990), pp. 5–56.
2. The best critique of the utility of theorizing based on the assumption of anarchy is Helen Milner, "The Assumption of Anarchy in International Relations Theory: A Critique," *Review of International Studies,* Vol. 17, No. 1 (January 1991), pp. 67–85.
3. See Stephen Van Evera, "Primed for Peace: Europe After the Cold War," *International Security,* Vol. 15, No. 3 (Winter 1990/91), pp. 7–57; and Richard H. Ullman, *Securing Europe* (Princeton, N.J.: Princeton University Press, 1991).
4. George Bush states that the "United States has deemed it a vital interest to prevent any hostile power or group of powers from dominating the Eurasian land mass," but in fact neither the United States nor Britain was willing to trust the benign intentions of any state that seemed likely to control the continent. George Bush, *The National Security Strategy of the United States, 1990–1991* (Washington, D.C.: Brassey's, 1990), p. 5.
5. This point is stressed in John Mueller, *Retreat from Doomsday: The Obsolescence of Major War* (New York: Basic Books, 1989).
6. Robert Jervis, *The Illogic of American Nuclear Strategy* (Ithaca, N.Y.: Cornell University Press, 1984), chaps. 5 and 6; Jervis, *The Meaning of the Nuclear Revolution* (Ithaca, N.Y.: Cornell University Press, 1989), chap. 3.
7. For an unconvincing attempt, see George Friedman and Meredith LeBard. *The Coming War with Japan* (New York: St. Martin's, 1990).
8. See the discussion in J.D.B. Miller. *Norman Angell and the Futility of War* (New York: St. Martin's, 1986).
9. See the discussion of vulnerability and sensitivity interdependence in Richard Cooper. *The Economics of Interdependence* (New York: McGraw-Hill, 1968); and Robert Keohane and Joseph S. Nye, Jr., *Power and Interdependence* (Boston: Little Brown, 1977); as well as the pathbreaking study by Albert Hirschman, *National Power and the Structure of International Trade* (Berkeley: University of California Press, 1980 [originally published in 1945]).
10. Richard Rosecrance, *The Rise of the Trading State* (New York: Basic Books, 1986), chap. 7: Helen Milner, *Resisting Protectionism* (Princeton, N.J.: Princeton University Press, 1988).
11. Stephen Van Evera, "Why Europe Matters, Why the Third World Doesn't: America's Grand Strategy After the Cold War," *Journal of Strategic Studies,* Vol. 13, No. 2 (June 1990), p. 5; Van Evera, "Primed for Peace," pp. 14–16; Carl Kaysen, "Is War Obsolete? A Review Essay," *International Security,* Vol. 14, No. 4 (Spring 1990), pp. 53–57.
12. Waltz, *Theory of International Politics,* (Reading, Mass.: Addison-Wesley, 1979); Arthur Stein, "The Hegemon's Dilemma: Great Britain, the United States, and the International Economic Order," *International Organization,* Vol. 38, No. 2 (Spring 1984), pp. 355–386; Robert Jervis, "Realism, Game Theory, and Cooperation," *World Politics,* Vol. 40, No. 3 (April 1988), pp. 334–336; Joseph Grieco, "Anarchy and the Limits of Cooperation: A Realist Critique of the Newest Liberal Institutionalism," *International Organization,* Vol. 42, No. 3 (Summer 1988), pp. 485–507; Michael Mastanduno, "Do Rela-

tive Gains Matter? America's Response to Japanese Industrial Policy," *International Security*, Vol. 16, No. 1 (Summer 1991), pp. 73–113. Of course even in purely economic exchanges, actors must be concerned about relative gain if getting a smaller share now means that their absolute as well as relative gains will be less in the future. This is one of the concerns of strategic trade theory. For an exposition and application see Helen Milner and David Yoffie, "Between Free Trade and Protectionism: Strategic Trade Policy and a Theory of Corporate Trade Demands," *International Organization*, Vol. 43, No. 2 (Spring 1989), pp. 237–72; and J. David Richardson, "The Political Economy of Strategic Trade Theory," *International Organization*, Vol. 44, No. 1 (Winter 1990). pp. 107–35. The broader dynamic in which a small relative advantage leads to much greater absolute (and relative) gains later is the heart of the argument in E. J. Hobsbawm, *Industry and Empire* (New York: Pantheon, 1968); and Immanuel Wallerstein, *The Modern World-System*, 3 vols. (New York: Academic Press, 1974–88).

13. Hirschman, *National Power.*

14. Waltz, *Theory of International Politics.* pp. 151–160.

15. Quoted in Paul Kennedy, *The Rise of the Anglo-German Antagonism, 1860–1914* (Boston: George Allen and Unwin, 1980), p. 315.

16. Samuel Huntington, "America's Changing Strategic Interests," *Survival*, Vol. 23, No. 1 (January/February 1991), p. 8.

17. Mueller, *Retreat From Doomsday.* For a discussion of changes in values among Europeans on matters of domestic society and ways of life, see Ronald Inglehart, *The Silent Revolution* (Princeton, N.J.: Princeton University Press, 1977); and Inglehart, *Culture Shift in Advanced Industrial Society* (Princeton, N.J.: Princeton University Press, 1990). For a rebuttal, see Harold Clarke and Nitish Dutt, "Measuring Value Change in Western Industrialized Societies," *American Political Science Review*, Vol. 85, No. 3 (September 1991), pp. 905–20.

18. Quoted in V.R. Berghahn, *Germany and the Approach of War in 1914* (New York; St. Martin's, 1973), p. 97.

19. Norman Angell, *The Great Illusion*, 4th ed. (New York: Putnam's, 1913); Joseph Schumpeter, "The Sociology of Imperialisms," in *Imperialism and Social Classes* (New York: Kelley, 1951). The phrase is borrowed from Albert Hirschman (although the story Hirschman tells is much more complex), in *The Passions and the Interests* (Princeton, N.J.: Princeton University Press, 1977).

20. Michael Doyle, "Kant, Liberal Legacies and Foreign Affairs," Part 1. *Philosophy and Public Affairs*, Vol. 12. No. 3 (Summer 1983), pp. 205–35; and Part 2, ibid., No. 4 (Fall 1983), pp. 323–53.

21. Joanne Gowa, "Bipolarity, Multipolarity, and Free Trade," *American Political Science Review*, Vol. 83, No. 4 (December 1989), pp. 1245–56.

22. Karl Deutsch, et al., *Political Community and the North Atlantic Area: International Organization in the Light of Historical Experience* (Princeton, N.J.: Princeton University Press, 1957).

23. Keohane and Nye, *Power and Interdependence,* developed a model of complex interdependence that applies when force is not central, but much of the subsequent debate concerned whether the conditions for it were met, rather than elaborating and testing theories of how relations within a pluralistic security community would be conducted. Furthermore, the previous behavior was strongly influenced by the Cold War setting and so may be different, although still peaceful, in the future.

24. Oliver Sacks, *Awakenings* (New York: Dutton, 1983). The analogy should not be carried too far, however. The history of the intervening years has left strong, damaging marks: see George Kennan, "Communism in Russian History," *Foreign Affairs*, Vol. 69, No. 5

(Winter 1990/91), pp. 168–86. Alexander Motyl argues that *perestroika* has not merely permitted the rise of ethnic nationalism in the USSR, but has made it a necessity for economic survival: Motyl, "Empire or Stability? The Case for Soviet Dissolution," *World Policy Journal*, Vol. 8, No. 3 (Summer 1991), pp. 499–524.

25. Van Evera, "Primed for Peace," pp. 9–10, 43–44.
26. The incentives of ties to the rest of Europe, in conjunction with the active assistance of European politicians, facilitated Spain's transition to democracy: see Edward Malefakis, "Spain and its Francoist Heritage." in John Herz, ed., *From Dictatorship to Democracy* (Westport, Conn.: Greenwood, 1982), pp. 217–19; and Mary Barker, "International Influences in the Transition to Democracy in Spain" (unpublished ms., Columbia University, Spring 1988).
27. Jack Snyder, "Avoiding Anarchy in the New Europe," *International Security*, Vol. 14, No. 4 (Spring 1990), pp. 5–41.
28. This is central to Snyder's policy prescriptions in "Avoiding Anarchy," Mearsheimer also sees hyper-nationalism as "the most important domestic cause of war," but exaggerates the extent to which "its causes lie . . . in the international system"; Mearsheimer, "Back to the Future," p. 21.
29. For an excellent discussion of the links between migration and security, see Myron Weiner, "Security, Stability, and International Migration," *International Security*, Vol. 17, No. 3 (Winter 1992/93), pp. 91-126.
30. For general overviews of Third World security, see Yezid Sayigh, *Confronting the 1990s: Security in the Developing Countries*, Adelphi Paper No. 251 (London: International Institute of Strategic Studies, Summer 1990); and Mohammed Ayoob, "The Security Problematic of the Third World," *World Politics*, Vol. 43, No. 2 (January 1991), pp. 257–83.
31. See, for example, Jeffrey Herbst, "The Creation and Maintenance of National Boundaries in Africa," *International Organization*, Vol. 43, No. 4 (Fall 1989), pp. 673–92.
32. Robert Jackson and Carl Rosberg, "Why Africa's Weak States Persist: The Empirical and the Juridical in Statehood," *World Politics*, Vol. 35, No. 1 (October 1982), pp. 1–24; Jeffrey Herbst, "War and the State in Africa," *International Security*, Vol. 14, No. 4 (Spring 1990), pp. 117–39. As these articles note, more wars might lead to stronger states. See also Robert H. Jackson, *Quasi States: Sovereignty, International Relations, and the Third World* (Cambridge and New York: Cambridge University Press, 1990).
33. It should be noted, however, that the conclusion about the future follows from the judgment of the past only if all other things remain equal. This ignores the possibility that the end of the Cold War will trigger processes that could compensate for the removal of the superpower restraint or, on the other hand, that would alter politics in the Third World in ways that are difficult to foresee. For reasoning of this type, see Jervis, "Systems Effects."
34. See Milton Viorst, "Report from Baghdad," *New Yorker*, June 24, 1991, pp. 67–68; Saddam Hussein's speech to the Arab Summit Meeting on February 24, 1990, *Foreign Broadcast Information Service: Near East and South Asia*, February 27, 1990, pp. 1–5.

Hypotheses on Nationalism and War

Stephen Van Evera

Scholars have written widely on the causes of nationalism but said little about its effects, especially its effects on international politics. Most strikingly, the impact of nationalism on the risk of war has barely been explored. Most authors take the war-causing character of nationalism for granted, assuming it without proof or explanation. Factors that govern the size of the dangers posed by nationalism are neglected. What types of nationalism are most likely to cause war? What background conditions catalyze or dampen this causal process? These questions are largely undiscussed, hence the causal nexus between nationalism and war presents an important unsolved riddle.

This article explores that nexus. I define nationalism as a political movement having two characteristics: (1) individual members give their primary loyalty to their own ethnic or national community;[1] this loyalty supersedes their loyalty to other groups, e.g., those based on common kinship or political ideology; and (2) these ethnic or national communities desire their own independent state. I leave the origins of nationalism unexplored, instead focusing on its effects on the risk of war. Seven questions are addressed: Does nationalism cause war? If so, what types

Thanks to Robert Art, Don Blackmer, David Laitin, John Mearsheimer, Barry Posen, Jack Snyder, and Stephen Walt for sharing their thoughts on nationalism and their comments on this paper. A version of this article appears in 1994 in a Council on Foreign Relations volume edited by Charles Kupchan. Bibliographic footnotes have been omitted.

Excerpt from Stephen Van Evera, "Hypothesis on Nationalism and War" in *International Security*, Spring 1994. Reprinted by permission of MIT Press. Portions of the text and some footnotes have been omitted.

of nationalism are most likely to cause war? How and why do they cause war? What causes these war-causing nationalisms? Under what conditions are they most dangerous? How, if at all, can the war-causing attributes of nationalism be suppressed or neutralized? How large are the risks to peace posed by nationalism in today's Europe, and how can these risks be minimized? In answer I offer unproven hypotheses that I leave untested for now. Our stock of hypotheses on the consequences of nationalism is meager, hence our first order of business should be to expand it. This can set the stage for empirical inquiry by others.

Causes of war or peace can be classified as proximate (causes that directly affect the odds of war) or remote (causes of these proximate causes, or background conditions required for their activation.) I explore proximate causes first, then turn to remote causes. Specifically, the next section of this article identifies varieties of nationalism that are most likely to cause war (including both civil and inter-state war). The section that follows it identifies the causes of these dangerous varieties of nationalism and the conditions that govern the size of the dangers they produce. Twenty-one hypotheses are proposed in all—nine main hypotheses and twelve sub-hypotheses. Some focus on the impact of the environment that surrounds

TABLE 1 HYPOTHESES ON NATIONALISM AND WAR: SUMMARY

I. IMMEDIATE CAUSES
1. The greater the proportion of state-seeking nationalities that are stateless, the greater the risk of war.
2. The more that nationalities pursue the recovery of national diasporas, and the more they pursue annexationist strategies of recovery, the greater the risk of war.
3. The more hegemonistic the goals that nationalities pursue toward one another, the greater the risk of war.
4. The more severely nationalities oppress minorities living in their states, the greater the risk of war.

II. CAUSES OF THE IMMEDIATE CAUSES AND CONDITIONS REQUIRED FOR THEIR OPERATION

Structural Factors:
1. Stateless nationalisms pose a greater risk of war if they have the strength to plausibly reach for freedom, and the central state has the will to resist their attempt.
2. The more densely nationalities are intermingled, the greater the risk of war.
   a. The risks posed by intermingling are larger the more local (house-by-house) rather than regional (province-by-province) the pattern of intermingling.
   b. The risks posed by intermingling are larger if the rescue of diasporas by homelands is difficult but possible; smaller if rescue is either impossible or easy.
3. The greater the defensibility and legitimacy of borders, and the greater the correspondence between these political borders and communal boundaries, the smaller the risk of war.
   a. The less secure and defensible the borders of emerging nation-states, the greater the risk of war.
   b. The greater the international legitimacy of the borders of emerging nation-states, the smaller the risk of war.
   c. The more closely the boundaries of emerging nation-states follow ethnic boundaries, the smaller the risk of war.

TABLE 1 (Continued)

Political/Environmental Factors:

4. The greater the past crimes committed by nationalities toward one another, the greater the risk of war.
   a. The better these crimes are remembered by the victims, the greater the risk of war.
   b. The more that responsibility for past crimes can be attached to groups still on the scene, the greater the risk of war.
   c. The less contrition and repentance shown by the guilty groups, the greater the risk of war.
   d. The greater the coincidence of power and victimhood, the greater the risk of war.
5. The more severely nationalities oppress minorities now living in their states, the greater the risk of war. (This restates Hypothesis No. 1.4; I list it twice because it operates as both a direct and a remote cause of war.)

Perceptual Factors:

6. The more divergent are the beliefs of nationalities about their mutual history and their current conduct and character, the greater the risk of war.
   a. The less legitimate the governments or leaders of nationalist movements, the greater their propensity to purvey mythical nationalist beliefs, hence the greater the risk of war.
   b. The more the state must demand of its citizens, the greater its propensity to purvey mythical nationalist beliefs, hence the greater the risk of war.
   c. If economic conditions deteriorate, publics become more receptive to scapegoat myths, hence such myths are more widely believed, hence war is more likely.
   d. If independent evaluative institutions are weak or incompetent, myths will more often prevail, hence war is more likely.

---

nationalist movements; this environment can incline the movement toward peaceful or toward warlike behavior. Others focus on the impact of the movement's internal character, especially its ideology and vision of history; this, too, can incline the movement toward peace or war. These hypotheses are highlighted because they are deductively sound, survive plausibility probes, and in some cases generate policy prescriptions. They are summarized in Table 1.[2] Viewed together, they suggest that the effects of nationalism are highly varied: some types of nationalism are far more dangerous than other types, all types of nationalism are more dangerous under some conditions than under others, and nationalism can even dampen the risk of war under some conditions.

If accepted, these hypotheses provide a checklist for assessing the dangers posed by a given nationalist movement or by the spread of nationalism in a given region. To illustrate, I use them in the concluding section to assess the risks that nationalism now poses in Europe, because Europe is a region in flux whose future is much debated. This exercise suggests that nationalism poses very little danger of war in Western Europe, but poses large dangers in the East, especially in the former Soviet Union. Current Western European nationalisms are benign, and the conditions required for a return to the malignant nationalisms of 1870–1945 are almost wholly absent. In contrast, many Eastern nationalisms have many (though not all) of the attributes that I argue make nationalism dangerous; hence the risk of large-scale violence stemming from the now-rising tide of Eastern nationalism is substantial.

What prescriptions follow? The character and consequences of nationalism are not written in stone. The Western powers have some capacity to influence the character and consequences of Eastern nationalist movements, and should try to channel it in benign directions. Most importantly, the Western powers should promote full respect for minority rights, democracy, and official respect for historical truth; if Eastern nationalisms adopt these programs, the risks they pose will sharply diminish.

VARIETIES OF NATIONALISM: WHICH CAUSE WAR?

Four primary attributes of a nationalist movement determine whether it has a large or small potential to produce violence. These are: (1) The movement's political status: is statehood attained or unattained? (2) The movement's stance toward its national diaspora (if it has one): if the movement has a national state, but some members of the nation are dispersed or entrapped beyond the state's borders, does the nation accept continued separation from this diaspora, or does it seek to incorporate the diaspora in the national state? And if it seeks the diaspora's incorporation, will it accomplish this by immigration or by territorial expansion? (3) The movement's stance toward other nations: does it respect or deny other nationalities' right to national independence? (4) The movement's treatment of its own minorities: are these minorities respected or abused?

Is National Statehood Attained or Unattained?

Nationalist movements without states raise greater risks of war because their accommodation requires greater and more disruptive change. Their struggle for national freedom can produce wars of secession, which in turn can widen to become international wars. Their freedom struggle can also injure the interests of other groups, displacing populations whose new grievances sow the seeds of future conflict, as Zionism's displacement of the Palestinian Arabs in 1948 sowed the seeds of later Arab-Israeli wars. Finally, the appearance of new states creates a new, less mature regional international system that lacks "rules of the game" defining the rights and obligations of its members toward one another, and norms of international conduct; these rights, obligations, and norms can take years to define, raising the risk of crises and collisions in the meantime.

The international system tolerates change poorly, but the accommodation of new nationalist movements requires it.[3] Thus the first measure of the risks to the peace of a region posed by nationalism is found in the proportion of its nationalist movements that remain unfulfilled in statehood, a factor expressed in the nation-to-state ratio. Are the supply of and demand for states in equilibrium or disequilibrium? Peace in a region is more likely the more closely a supply/demand equilibrium is approached.[4] Modern nationalism disrupted peace over the past two centuries partly because so many of the world's current nationalist movements were stateless at the outset, requiring vast change to accommodate their emergence. Nationalism still threatens peace because its full accommodation would require vast additional change: the number of states in the world has more than tripled since World War II (up from the 50 signers of the UN Charter in 1945, to 180-odd states today), but many nationalities remain stateless; the world has some 6000 language groups, many of which have dormant or manifest aspirations for statehood.

In Western Europe the transition of nations to statehood is largely behind us: that region's remaining stateless nationalities are relatively few and weak. In Eastern Europe and the former Soviet Union, the problem is more serious because the transition to statehood, while largely fulfilled, is still incomplete. The bulk of these stateless nationalities are found in the former Soviet Union; 15 of the 104 nationalities in the former USSR have attained states, but the other 89 have not; these stateless nationalities total 25.6 million people, comprising 10 percent of the former USSR's total population. Most of these nationalities are not potential candidates for statehood (e.g., the Jews) but some might be (e.g., the Tatars, Chechen, Ingush, and Ossetians), and their reach for statehood could sow future friction.

Attitude Toward the National Diaspora: Is Partial or Total National Unity Pursued? Are Immigrationist or Expansionist Tactics Used?

Does the nationalist ideology posit that all or only a part of the national ethnic community must be incorporated in the national state? And if the whole nationality must be incorporated, will this be accomplished by immigration (bringing the diaspora to the state) or by territorial expansion (bringing the state to the diaspora)?

These questions suggest a distinction among three types of nationalism: "diaspora-accepting," "immigrationist," and "diaspora-annexing." Some nationalisms (the diaspora-accepting variety) are content with partial union (e.g., Chinese nationalism); such nationalisms are less troublesome because they make fewer territorial demands on their neighbors. Some nationalisms (the immigrationist type) seek to incorporate their diasporas in the national state, but are content to pursue union by seeking immigration of the diaspora (current German nationalism and Zionist Jewish nationalism.) Such immigrationist nationalisms are also easy to accommodate. Finally, some nationalisms seek to incorporate their diasporas by means of territorial expansion (pre–1914 Pan-Germanism and current Pan-Serbianism are examples.) Such diaspora-annexing nationalisms are the most dangerous of the three, since their goals and tactics produce the greatest territorial conflict with others. Thus one scenario for war in the former Soviet Union lies in the possible appearance of a Pan-Russian nationalism that would seek to reincorporate by force the vast Russian diaspora now living in the non-Russian republics. This diaspora includes some 24 million Russians, or 17 percent of all Russians. The future hinges heavily on whether Russian nationalism accepts separation from this diaspora (or seeks to ingather it by immigration), or instead forcibly seeks to annex it.

Attitude Toward Other Independent Nationalities: Tolerant or Hegemonistic?

Does the ideology of the nationalism incorporate respect for the freedom of other nationalities, or does it assume a right or duty to rule them? In other words, is the national ideology symmetrical (all nationalities deserve states) or asymmetrical (only our nationality deserves statehood; others should be denied it)?

Hegemonistic, or asymmetrical, nationalism is both the rarest and the most dangerous variety of nationalism. Interwar Nazi nationalism in Germany, fascist nationalism in Mussolini's Italy, and militarist nationalism in imperial Japan illustrate such hegemonistic nationalism; the wars they caused illustrate its results. No European nationalism today displays such hegemonism, but the vast trouble that it caused in the past advises alertness to its possible reappearance in Europe or elsewhere.

The Degree of National Respect for Minority Rights: High or Low?

Is the nationalism minority-respecting, or minority-oppressing? A minority-respecting nationalism grants equal rights to other nationalities lying within the boundaries of its claimed state; it may even grant their right to secede and establish their own state. A minority-oppressing nationalism denies such rights to these other nationalities, subjugating them instead. Many of the nationalisms of immigrant nations (American, Anglo-Canadian) have been relatively minority-respecting (in the Canadian case this includes a tacit right to secession, which the Quebecois may soon exercise.) Non-immigrant nationalisms often display far less tolerance for their minorities: prominent current examples include Iraq's and Turkey's oppression of their Kurdish minorities, Bulgaria's oppression of its Turks, China's cruelties in Tibet, Croatia's intolerance toward its Serb minority, and Serbian oppression of its Slavic Moslem and Albanian minorities. Nazi German nationalism was an extreme case of a minority-oppressing nationalism.

The first three attributes—is statehood attained? attitude toward diaspora? attitude toward other independent nationalities?—define the scope of a nationalist movement's claims against others; conversely, the fourth attribute—policy toward minorities?—helps determine the scope of others' claims against the movement. The larger these others' goals become, the more they will collide with the movement's goals, raising the risk of war. Minority-oppressing nationalism can cause war in two ways: (1) by provoking violent secessions by its captive nations; or (2) by spurring the homelands of these captive nations to move forcefully to free their oppressed co-nationals[5] (as Croatian threats against the Serb minority in Croatia helped spawn the Serb attack on Croatia in 1991). Minority-oppressing nationalism is most dangerous if the oppressed minorities have nearby friends who have the capacity to protect the oppressed nation by force. (The Serbo-Croat war exploded partly because Croatia's Serbs had such a friend in Serbia). The attitude of many nationalisms in Eastern Europe and the former Soviet Union toward their minorities remains undefined, and the future hinges on whether they evolve toward minority respect or oppression.

These four attributes can be used to create a nationalism "danger-scale," expressing the level of danger posed by a given nationalism, or by the spread of nationalism in a given region. If all four attributes are benign, the nationalism poses little danger of war, and may even bolster peace. Specifically, a nationalism is benign if it has achieved statehood; has limited unity goals (i.e., accepts the existence of any unincorporated diaspora) or adopts an immigrationist strategy for ingathering its diaspora; posits no claim to rule other nationalities living beyond its national territory; and respects the rights of minorities found in this territory. Multiplied, such nationalisms may even dampen the risk of war, by making conquest more difficult: where these nationalisms are prevalent, conquest is harder because nation-states are among the most difficult type of state to conquer (since nationalism provides an inspirational liberation doctrine that can be used to mobilize strong popular resistance to conquest). As a result strong states will be deterred from reaching for regional or global hegemony, and will also be less fearful that others might achieve it; hence all states will compete less fiercely with one another. In contrast, a nationalism is bound to collide with others if all four attributes are malign: If the nationalism has no state, the risk of civil war arising from its struggle for national independence is increased; this also raises the risk of inter-state war, since civil war can widen to engulf nearby states. If, after achieving statehood, the nationalism seeks to incorporate a diaspora by force, oppresses minorities found in its claimed national territory, and seeks hegemony over nationalities lying beyond that territory, violence between the nationalism and its neighbors is inevitable.

CAUSES AND CONDITIONS FOR WAR-CAUSING NATIONALISM

What factors determine whether these four variables will have benign or malignant values? What conditions are required for malignant values to have malignant effects? The deciding factors and conditions are grouped below into three broad families: structural (those arising from the geographic and demographic arrangement of a nation's people); political-environmental (those arising from the past or present conduct of a peoples neighbors); and perceptual (those arising from the nationalist movement's self-image and its images of others, including its images of both sides' past and present conduct and character).

Structural Factors: The Geographic, Demographic, and Military Setting

The size of the risks posed by nationalism is influenced by the balance of power and of will between stateless nationalisms and the central states that hold them captive; by the degree and pattern of regional ethnic intermingling; by the defensibility and legitimacy of the borders of new national states; and by the correspondence of these borders with ethnic boundaries.

The Domestic Balance of Power and of Will   Unattained nationalisms are more troublesome under two conditions: (1) the movement has the strength to reach plausibly for statehood: and (2) the central state has the will to resist this attempt.

Stateless nationalisms whose statehood is unattainable will lie dormant, their emergence deterred by the power of the central state.[6] Nationalism becomes manifest and can produce war when the power-balance between the central state and the captive nationalism shifts to allow the possibility of successful secession. Thus two safe conditions exist: where national statehood is already attained; and where it is not attained, but clearly cannot be. The danger zone lies between, in cases where statehood has not been attained yet is attainable or appears to be.[7] In this zone we find wars of nationalist secession.[8] Such conflicts can, in turn, grow into international wars: examples include the 1912–14 Balkan secessionist struggles that triggered World War I, and the 1991–92 Serbo-Croatian conflict.

The Third World nationalisms of the twentieth century erupted partly because the spread of small arms and literacy shifted the balance of power in favor of these nationalisms, and against their imperial captors. Nationalism emerged because it could. Likewise, nationalism exploded in the former Soviet Union in the late 1980s partly because Soviet central power had waned.

War is inevitable if central states have the will to resist emerging nationalist/secessionist movements, but these movements can win freedom without violence if that will is missing. Many sub-Saharan African states gained freedom in the 1960s without violence because the European colonial powers lost their imperial will. Likewise, the emergence of non-Russian nationalisms in the former Soviet Union was accompanied by (and encouraged by) the loss of imperial will in Moscow; this loss of will at the center allowed the non-Russians to escape the Soviet empire without waging wars of secession. French decolonization was far more violent, spawning large wars in Vietnam and Algeria, because the French metropole retained its will even after nationalism gained momentum in the French empire.

The will of the central state is largely governed by its domestic politics, but is also determined partly by demographic facts. Specifically, central governments can allow secession more easily if secession would leave a homogeneous rump central state, since permitting secession then sets a less damaging precedent. Thus the Czechs could accept Slovak independence without fear of setting a precedent that would trigger another secession, since there is no potential secessionist group in the rump Czech Republic. Likewise, the United States could grant independence to the Philippines fairly easily in 1946 because the United States had few other colonies, and none of these were large or valuable, hence Philippine independence set no dangerous precedents. Conversely, the Austro-Hungarian empire strongly resisted secessions before 1914 because the empire contained many potential secessionists who might be encouraged if any secession were allowed.

The Demographic Arrangement of National Populations: Are They Intermingled or Homogeneous?   Are nationality populations densely intermingled? If they are, does this create large or small national diasporas? Intermingling raises the risk of communal conflict during the struggle for national freedom, as groups that would be trapped as minorities in a new national state oppose its reach for freedom. Dispersion and intermingling will also trap some co-ethnics outside the boundaries of their nation-states; this raises the danger that new nation-states will pursue diaspora-recovering expansionism after they gain statehood, and the possibility that their abuse of minorities will trigger attack from outside.[9]

These dangers are reduced if national populations are compact and homogenous—diasporas and minorities then occur only if political boundaries fail to follow ethnic boundaries. They are intensified if the nationality is dispersed abroad, and intermingled with others at home. The Czechs, for example, can pursue nationalism with little risk to the peace of their neighborhood, because they have no diaspora abroad, and few minorities at home. They need not limit their goals or learn to accommodate minorities. The 1947 partition of India was a far bloodier process than the 1992 Czech-Slovak divorce partly because Hindus and Moslems were far more intermingled than Czechs and Slovaks. The partition of Yugoslavia has been especially violent partly because nationalities in former Yugoslavia are more densely intermingled than any others in Eastern or Western Europe outside the former Soviet Union.

Overall, nationalism poses greater dangers in Eastern than Western Europe because the peoples of Eastern Europe are more densely intermingled. A survey of Eastern Europe reveals roughly a dozen minority group pockets that may seek independence or be claimed by other countries.[10] The ethnographic structure of the former Soviet Union is even more ominous; an ethnographic map of the former USSR reveals massively intermingled nationalities, scattered in scores of isolated pockets, a mosaic far more tangled and complex than any found elsewhere in Europe except the former Yugoslavia.

Two aspects of intermingling determine the size of the dangers it poses: the scope of intermingling, and the pattern of intermingling. All intermingling causes trouble, but some patterns of intermingling cause more trouble than others.

Groups can be intermingled on a regional scale (regions are heterogeneous, small communities are homogeneous) or local scale (even small communities are heterogeneous, as in Sarajevo.) Regional intermingling is more easily managed, because inter-group relations can be negotiated by elites. In contrast, elites can lose control of events when intermingling extends to the local level: conflict can flare against the wishes of elites when unofficial killers seize the agenda by sparking a spiral of private violence. Local intermingling can also produce conflict-dampening personal friendships and inter-ethnic marriages, but the Bosnian conflict shows the limits of this tempering effect. Overall, local intermingling is more dangerous.

The most dangerous pattern of regional intermingling is one that leaves elements of one or both groups insecurely at the mercy of the other, but also allows for the possibility of forcible rescue—either by self-rescue (secession) or external rescue (intervention by an already-free homeland).

If rescue is impossible, then the goal of secession or reunion with a homeland will be abandoned. Israel cannot rescue Soviet Jewry, except by immigration, and

Ukraine cannot rescue the Ukrainian diaspora in Russia; hence neither considers forceful rescue. This lowers the risk of war.

If rescue is easy, it may not be attempted, since the threat of rescue is enough to deter abuse of the diaspora. Russia could fairly easily rescue the Russian minority in the Baltics and perhaps elsewhere on the Russian periphery, because much of the Russian diaspora lies clustered near the Russian border, and Russia holds military superiority over its neighbors. These power realities may deter Russia's neighbors from abusing their Russian minorities, leaving Russia more room to take a relaxed attitude.

It is in-between situations—those where rescue is possible, but only under optimal conditions—that are most dangerous. This situation will tempt potential rescuers to jump through any windows of opportunity that arise. Forceful rescue is then driven by both fear and opportunity—fear that later the abuse of diasporas cannot be deterred by threatening to rescue them (since the difficulty of rescue will rob that threat of credibility), and by the opportunity to rescue the diaspora now by force. Thus Serbia would have probably been unable to rescue the Serb diaspora in normal times: Serbia is too weak, and the Serbian diasporas in Croatia and Bosnia are too distant from Serbia. But rescue was feasible if Serbia made the attempt at a moment of peak Serbian military advantage. Such a moment emerged in 1990, after Serbia consolidated the weaponry of the Yugoslav army under its control, but before the Croatian and Bosnian states could organize strong militaries. In contrast, such a moment may never emerge for Russia, because it can always rescue large parts of its diaspora should the need ever arise, leaving less need to seize an early opportunity.

These in-between situations are most troublesome when the diaspora is separated from the homeland by lands inhabited by others: wars of rescue then cause larger injury. In such cases rescue requires cutting a secure corridor through these lands; this, in turn, requires the forcible expulsion of the resident population, with its attendant horrors and cruelties. In 1991 the Serbian diaspora in Croatia and Bosnia was cut off from the Serb homeland by walls of Moslem-inhabited territory, and the vast Serbian cruelties against the Bosnian Moslems during 1992–93 grew mainly from Serbia's effort to punch corridors through these walls in order to attach these diasporas to Serbia proper. In contrast, more of Russia's diaspora is contiguous to Russia, hence a Russian war of rescue would do relatively less harm to others innocently in the way (though it would still do plenty of harm.)

Borders: Defensibility, Legitimacy, and Border/Ethnic Correspondence

The risks to peace posed by a nationalism's emergence are governed partly by the defensibility and international legitimacy of the nation's borders, and by the degree of correspondence between these political borders and ethnic boundaries.

The satisfaction of national demands for statehood extends international anarchy by creating more states: hence nationalism's effects are governed partly by the character of the extended anarchy that it creates. Some anarchies are relatively peaceful, others more violent. The acuteness of the security dilemma is a key factor governing the answer. Anarchy is a precondition for international war, hence extending anarchy may expand the risk of war, but this is not always the case: the fragmentation of states can deepen peace if it leaves the world with states that are more difficult to conquer, hence are more secure, than the older states from which they were carved. The character of boundaries helps decide the issue: if the new borders are indefensible, the net impact of the creation of new national states will be warlike; if borders are highly defensible, the net impact may be peaceful.

Defensible boundaries reduce the risk of war because they leave new states less anxious to expand for security reasons, while also deterring others from attacking them. The nations of Western Europe can be more peaceful than those of the East because they are endowed with more defensible borders: the French, Spanish, British, Italian, and Scandinavian nations have natural defenses formed by the Alps and the Pyrenees, and by the waters of the English Channel, the Baltic, and the North Sea. Icelandic nationalism is especially unproblematic because geography makes Iceland unusually secure, and almost incapable of attack. In contrast, the nationalities living on the exposed plains of Eastern Europe and western Asia contend with a harsher geography: with few natural barriers to invasion, they are more vulnerable to attack, hence are more tempted to attack others in preemptive defense. They are therefore more likely to disturb the status quo, or to be victims of other disturbers.

The international legitimacy of a new nation's borders helps determine the level of danger raised when it gains independence: if borders lack international legitimacy or are unsettled altogether, demands for border changes will arise, providing new occasions for conflict. The successor states of the former Soviet Union find themselves with borders drawn by Stalin or other Bolshevik rulers; these have correspondingly small legitimacy. Israel's post–1948 boundaries at first lacked international legitimacy because they had no historical basis, having arisen simply from truce lines expressing the military outcome of the 1948 war. In contrast, the borders of the recently-freed states of Eastern Europe have greater legitimacy because they have firmer grounding in history, and some were the product of earlier international negotiation and agreement.

Borders may bisect nationalities, or may follow national demographic divides. Nation-bisecting borders are more troublesome, because they have the same effect as demographic intermingling: they entrap parts of nationalities within the boundaries of states dominated by other ethnic groups, giving rise to expansionism by the truncated nation. Thus Hungary's borders bisect (and truncate) the Hungarian nation, giving rise to a (now dormant but still surviving) Hungarian revanchism against Slovakia, Serbia, and Rumania. The Russian/Ukrainian border bisects both nationalities, creating the potential for movements to adjust borders in both countries.

The borders of new states can arise in two main ways: from violent military struggle (e.g., Israel) or as a result of cession of sovereignty to existing administrative units whose boundaries were previously defined by the parent multiethnic state (e.g., former Soviet Union). War-born borders often have the advantage of following ethnic lines, because the cruelties of war often cause ethnic cleansing, and offensives lose strength at ethnic boundaries; inherited administrative borders (e.g., the boundaries of Azerbaijan, which entrap the Armenians of Nagorno-Karabakh) more often plant the charge of future conflict by dividing nations and creating diasporas. The peaceful dissolution of the former Soviet Union was thus a mixed blessing: its successor states emerged without violence, but with borders that captured unhappy diasporas behind them.

Political/Environmental Factors: How Have Neighbors Behaved? How Do They Now Behave?

The conduct of nationalities and nation-states mirrors their neighbors' past and present conduct.

Past Conduct: Were Great Crimes Committed?   The degree of harmony or conflict between intermingled nationalities depends partly on the size of the crimes committed by each against the other in the past; the greater these past crimes, the greater the current conflict. Memories of its neighbors' cruelties will magnify an emerging nation's impulse to ingather its diaspora, converting the nation from a diaspora-accepting to a diaspora-annexing attitude. Thus the vast Croatian mass-murders of Serbs during the 1940s were the taproot that fed violent pan-Serbianism after 1990: Serbs vowed "never again," and argued that they must incorporate the Serbian diaspora in Croatia to save it from new pogroms. Past suffering can also spur nations to oppress old tormentors who now live among them as minorities, sparking conflict with these minorities' home countries. Thus the past horrors inflicted on the Baltic peoples by Stalinism fuels their discrimination against their Russian minorities today; this discrimination, in turn, feeds anti-Baltic feeling in Russia. In contrast, non-victim nations are less aggressive toward both neighbors and minorities. Czech nationalism is benign partly because the Czechs have escaped real victimhood; Quebec nationalism is mild for the same reason.

Mass murder, land theft, and population expulsions are the crimes that matter most. Past exterminations foster diaspora-recovering ideologies that are justified by self-protection logic. Past land theft fosters territorial definitions of nationhood (e.g., the Israeli Likud's concept of "the Land of Israel," a place including once-Jewish lands that Likud argues were wrongfully taken by others) and claims to land that excludes the rights of peoples now on that land (the Likud rejects equal rights for the Palestinian inhabitants of these once-Jewish lands; Serbs likewise reject equal rights for Albanian Kosovars who Serbs claim wrongfully took Serb land.) Past expulsions and dispersions feed diaspora-intolerance: if others created the diaspora, it is argued, then others should pay the price for restoring the diaspora to the nation by making territorial concessions.

The scope of the dangers posed by past crimes is a function, in part, of whether these crimes are remembered, and whether victims can attach responsibility for crimes to groups that are still present. Crimes that have faded in the victims' memories have a less corrosive effect on intergroup relations; thus mayhem that occurred before written records poses fewer problems than more recent crimes that are better-recorded.

Crimes committed by groups still on the scene pose more problems than crimes committed by vanished groups. This, in turn, is a matter of interpretation: who committed the crime in question? Can inherited blame be attached to any present group? Thus the Ukrainians can assess responsibility for Stalin's vast murders of Ukrainians in several ways. Were they committed by a crazed Georgian? This interpretation is benign: it points the finger at a single man who is long gone from the scene. Were they committed by that now-vanished tribe, the Bolsheviks? This interpretation is also benign: those responsible have miraculously disappeared, leaving no target for violence. Or, more ominously, were these the crimes of the Russian empire and the Russian people? This interpretation would guarantee bitter Russian-Ukrainian conflict, because the crimes in question were so enormous, and many of the "criminals" live in Ukraine, making ready targets for hatred, and setting the stage for a Russian-Ukrainian conflict-spiral. Such a spiral is more likely because Russians would not accept the blame assigned them: they count themselves among the victims, not the perpetrators, of Bolshevism's crimes, and they would view others' demands that they accept blame as a malicious outrage.

The danger posed by past crimes also depends on the criminal group's later behavior: has it apologized or otherwise shown contrition? Or has it shown contempt for its victims' suffering? Nazi Germany's crimes were among the greatest in human history, but Germany has re-established civil relations with its former victims by acknowledging its crimes and showing contrition, e.g., by postwar German leaders' public apologies and symbolic acts of repentance. Conversely, Turkey has denied the great crimes it committed against the Armenian people during World War I; this display of contempt has sustained an Armenian hatred that is still expressed in occasional acts of violent anti-Turkish retribution.

A final significant factor lies in the degree of coincidence of power and victimhood. Are the groups with the greatest historic grievances also the groups with the greatest power today? Or is past victimhood confined to today's weaker groups? Things are more dangerous when power and aggrievement coincide, since this combination brings together both the motive and the capacity to make trouble; when power and aggrievement are separated, grievances have less effects. On this count the past crimes of the Russian and Bolshevik states leave a less dangerous legacy than the crimes committed in the former Yugoslavia during World War II, because the strongest group in the former Soviet Union (the Russians) is the least aggrieved; in contrast, in former Yugoslavia the strongest group (the Serbs) is the most aggrieved.

Current Conduct: Are Minority Rights Respected?   As noted earlier, nations are less diaspora-accepting if others abuse the rights of that diaspora; such abuse magnifies the impulse to incorporate the territory of the diaspora by force. Thus Serbia's 1991 attack on Croatia was spurred partly by Croatian threats against the Serbian minority. Likewise, Russia's attitude toward the Russian diaspora will be governed partly by the treatment of the Russian diaspora in their new homelands. Oppressive policies will provoke wider Russian aims.

Perceptual Factors: Nationalist Self-Images and Images of Others

The effects of nationalism depend heavily on the beliefs of nationalist movements, especially their self-images and their images of their neighbors. Nations can coexist most easily when these beliefs converge—when they share a common image of their mutual history, and of one another's current conduct and character. This can be achieved either by common convergence of images on something close to the "truth," or by convergence on the same distortion of the truth. Relations are worst if images diverge in self-justifying directions. This occurs if nations embrace self-justifying historical myths, or adopt distorted pictures of their own and others' current conduct and character that exaggerate the legitimacy of their own cause. Such myths and distortions can expand a nation's sense of its right and its need to oppress its minorities or conquer its diaspora. If carried to extreme such myths can also transform nationalism from symmetrical to asymmetrical—from a purely self-liberating enterprise into a hegemonistic enterprise.

Chauvinist mythmaking is a hallmark of nationalism, practiced by nearly all nationalist movements to some degree. These myths are purveyed through the schools, especially in history teaching, through literature; or by political elites. They come in three principal varieties: self-glorifying, self-whitewashing, and other-maligning. Self-glorifying myths incorporate claims of special virtue and competence, and false claims of past beneficence toward others. Self-whitewashing myths incorporate false denial of past wrongdoing against others. Both types of myths can lead a nation to claim a right to rule others ("we are especially virtuous, so our expansion benefits those we conquer"). They also lead a nation to view others' complaints against them as expressions of ungrateful malice: ("we have never harmed them; they slander us by claiming otherwise"). This can produce conflict-spirals, as the nation responds to others' legitimate complaints with hostility, in expectation that the claimant knows its claims are illegitimate and will back down if challenged. The targets of this hostility, in turn, will take it as further evidence of the nation's inherent cruelty and injustice. Self-glorifying myth, if it contains claims of cultural superiority, can also feed false faith in one's capacity to defeat and subdue others, causing expansionist wars of optimistic miscalculation.

Other-maligning myths can incorporate claims of others' cultural inferiority, false blame of others for past crimes and tragedies, and false claims that others now harbor malign intentions against the nation. Such myths support arguments for the rightness and necessity of denying equal rights to minorities living in the national territory, and for subjugating peoples further afield. These minorities and distant peoples will appear to pose a danger if they are left unsuppressed; moreover, their suppression is morally justified by their (imagined) misconduct, past and planned.

Self-whitewashing myths are probably the most common of these three varieties. The dangers they pose are proportional to the gravity of the crimes they whitewash. If small crimes are denied, their denial is disrespect that victims can choose to overlook. The denial may even spring from simple ignorance; if so, it conveys little insult. If great crimes are denied, however, their denial conveys contempt for the victims' very humanity. The denial cannot be ascribed to unintended ignorance; if truly great crimes are forgotten, the forgetting is willful, hence it conveys greater insult. And being willful, the denial implies a dismissal of the crime's wrongness, which in turn suggests an ominous willingness to repeat it. As a result, the denial of great crimes provokes greater hostility from the victims than the denial of minor crimes. Thus Croatian historians and politicians who whitewashed the Croatian Ustashi's vast murders of Serbs during World War II were playing with especially powerful dynamite: the crimes they denied were enormous, hence their denial had serious ramifications, feeding Serb hostility that led to the Serbo-Croatian war of 1991–92. Likewise, the question of historical responsibility for Stalin's crimes in the former Soviet Union is especially explosive because the crimes in question are so vast.

Why are myths purveyed? They emanate largely from nationalist political elites, for whom they serve important political functions. Some of these functions also serve the nation as a whole, while others serve only the narrow interests of the elite. Self-glorifying myths encourage citizens to contribute to the national community—to pay taxes, join the army, and fight for the nation's defense. These purposes are hard to fault, although the myths purveyed to achieve them may nevertheless have pernicious side-effects. Myths also bolster the authority and political power of incumbent elites: self-glorifying and self-whitewashing myths allow elites to shine in the reflected luster of their predecessors' imagined achievements and the imagined glory of the national institutions they control; other-maligning myths bolster the authority of elites by supporting claims that the nation faces external threats, thus deflecting popular hostility away from national elites and toward outsiders. Myths that serve only these purposes injure intercommunal relations without providing countervailing benefits to the general community.

Although mythmaking is ubiquitous among nationalisms, the scope and character of mythmaking varies widely across nations. Myths flourish most when elites need them most, when opposition to myths is weakest, and when publics are most myth-receptive. Four principal factors govern the level of infection by nationalist myth.

The Legitimacy of the Regime (or, if the national movement remains stateless, the legitimacy of the movement's leaders).   As just noted, nationalist myths can help politically frail elites to bolster their grip on power. The temptation for elites to engage in mythmaking is therefore inversely proportional to their political legitimacy: the less legitimate their rule, the greater their incentive to make myths.

A regime's legitimacy is in turn a function of its representativeness, its competence and efficiency, and the scope of the tasks that face it. Unrepresentative regimes will face challenge from under-represented groups, and will sow myths to build the support needed to defeat this challenge. This motive helped fuel the extreme nationalism that swept Europe in the late nineteenth century: oligarchic regimes used chauvinist myths, often spread through the schools, to deflect demands from below for a wider sharing of political and economic power.[11] Corrupt regimes or regimes that lack competence due to underinstitutionalization will likewise deploy chauvinist myths to divert challenges from publics and elites. This is a common motive for mythmaking in the Third World. Finally, regimes that face overwhelming tasks—e.g., economic or social collapse, perhaps caused by exogenous factors—will be tempted to use myths to divert popular impatience with their inability to improve conditions. Thus the Great Depression fueled nationalist mythmaking in some industrial states during the 1930s.

These factors correlate closely with the ebb and flow of nationalist mythmaking through history. Nationalist mythmaking reached high tide in Europe when Europe's regimes had little legitimacy, during 1848–1914. It then fell dramatically as these regimes democratized and their societies became less stratified, which greatly lessened popular challenge to elites.

The Scope of the Demands Posed by the State on its Citizenry   The more the regime asks of its citizens, the harder it must work to persuade its citizens to fulfill these demands; this increases its temptation to deploy nationalist myths for purposes of social mobilization. Regimes at war often use myths to motivate sacrifice by their citizens and to justify their cruelties against others. These myths can live on after the war to poison external relations in later years. Mass revolutionary movements often infuse their movements with mythical propaganda for the same reason; these myths survive after the revolution is won. Regimes that are forced by external threats to sustain large peacetime military efforts are likewise driven to use myths to sustain popular support. This is especially true if they rely on mass armies for their defense. Finally, totalitarian regimes place large demands on their citizens, and use correspondingly large doses of myth to induce their acquiescence.

Domestic Economic Crisis   In societies suffering economic collapse, myth-making can take scapegoating form—the collapse is falsely blamed on domestic or international malefactors. Here the mythmaking grows from increased receptivity of the audience: publics are more willing to believe that others are responsible when they are actually suffering pain; when that pain is new and surprising, they search for the hand of malevolent human agents. Germany in the 1930s is the standard example.

The Strength and Competence of Independent Evaluative Institutions
Societies that lack free-speech traditions, a strong free press, and free universities are more vulnerable to mythmaking because they lack "truth squads" to counter the nationalist mythmakers. Independent historians can provide an antidote to official historical mythmaking; an independent press is an antidote to official myth-making about current events. Their absence is a permissive condition for nationalist mythmaking. Wilhelmine Germany illustrates: the German academic community failed to counter the official myths of the era, and often helped purvey them.

Several conclusions follow from this discussion. Democratic regimes are less prone to mythmaking, because such regimes are usually more legitimate and are free-speech tolerant; hence they can develop evaluative institutions to weed out nationalist myth. Absolutist dictatorships that possess a massive military superiority over their citizens are also less prone to mythmaking, because they can survive without it. The most dangerous regimes are those that depend on some measure of popular consent, but are narrowly governed by unrepresentative elites. Things are still worse if these governments are poorly institutionalized, are incompetent or corrupt for other reasons, or face overwhelming problems that exceed their governing capacities. Regimes that emerged from a violent struggle, or enjoy only precarious security, are also more likely to retain a struggle-born chauvinist belief-system.

CONCLUSION: PREDICTIONS AND PRESCRIPTIONS

What predictions follow? These hypotheses can be used to generate forecasts; applied to Europe, they predict that nationalism will pose little risk to peace in Western Europe, but large risks in Eastern Europe.

Most of the nationalisms of the West are satisfied, having already gained states. Western diasporas are few and small, reflecting the relative homogeneity of Western national demography, and Western minorities are relatively well-treated. The historic grievances of Western nationalities against one another are also small—many of the West's inter-ethnic horrors have faded from memory, and the perpetrators of the greatest recent horror—the Germans—have accepted responsibility for it and reconciled with their victims. The regimes of the West are highly legitimate, militarily secure, and economically stable; hence chauvinist mythmaking by their elites is correspondingly rare. The West European nationalism that caused the greatest recent troubles, those of Germany and Italy, are now clearly benign, and the conditions for a return to aggressive nationalism are absent in both countries. Outsiders sometimes fear that outbreaks of anti-immigrant extremism in Germany signal the return of German fascism, but the forces of tolerance and decency are overwhelmingly dominant in Germany, and the robust health of German democracy and of German academic and press institutions ensures they will remain dominant. As a result nationalism should cause very little trouble in Western Europe.

In the East the number of stateless nationalisms is larger, raising greater risk that future conflicts will arise from wars of liberation. The collapse of Soviet power shifted the balance of power toward these nationalisms, by replacing the Soviet state with weaker successor states. This shift has produced secessionist wars in Georgia and Moldova, and such wars could multiply. The tangled pattern of ethnic intermingling across the East creates large diasporas. Eastern societies have little tradition of respect for minority rights, raising the likelihood that these diasporas will face abuse; this in turn may spur their homelands to try to incorporate them by force. The borders of many emerging Eastern nations lack natural defensive barriers, leaving the state exposed to attack; some borders also lack legitimacy, and correspond poorly with ethnic boundaries. Some new Eastern regimes, especially those in the former Soviet Union, lack legitimacy and are under-institutionalized, raising the risk that they will resort to chauvinist mythmaking to maintain their political viability. This risk is heightened by the regional economic crisis caused by the transition from command to market economies. Evaluative institutions (free universities and a free press) remain weak in the East, raising the risk that myths will go unchallenged. The Soviet regime committed vast crimes against its subject peoples; this legacy will embitter relations among these peoples if they cannot agree on who deserves the blame.[12]

The Eastern picture is not all bleak. The main preconditions for democracy—high levels of literacy, some degree of industrial development, and the absence of a landed oligarchy—exist across most of the East. As a result the long-term prospects for democracy are bright. Moreover, the East's economic crisis is temporary: the conditions for prosperous industrial economies (a trained workforce and adequate natural resources) do exist, so the crisis should ease once the market transition is completed. These relatively favorable long-term prospects for democracy and prosperity dampen the risk that chauvinist mythmaking will get out of hand. The fact that the new Eastern states managed to gain freedom without violent struggles also left them with fewer malignant beliefs, by allowing them to forgo infusing their societies with chauvinist war propaganda. The power and ethnographic structures of the East, while dangerous, are less explosive than those of Yugoslavia: historic grievances and military power coincide less tightly—there is no other Eastern equivalent of Serbia, having both military superiority and large historical grievances; and ethnographic patterns create less imperative for a diaspora-rescue operation by the state most likely to attempt such a rescue, Russia.

All in all, however, conditions in Eastern Europe are more bad than good; hence nationalism will probably produce a substantial amount of violence in the East over the next several decades.

What policy prescriptions follow? The Western powers should move to dampen the risks that nationalism poses in the East, by moving to channel manipulable aspects of Eastern nationalism in benign directions. Some aspects of Eastern nationalist movements are immutable (e.g., their degree of intermingling, or the history of crimes between them). Others, however, can be decided by the movements themselves (e.g., their attitude toward minorities, their vision of history, and their willingness to reach final border settlements with others); these can be influenced by the West if the movements are susceptible to Western pressure or persuasion. The Western powers should use their substantial economic leverage to bring such pressure to bear.

Specifically, the Western powers should condition their economic relations with the new Eastern states on these states' conformity with a code of peaceful conduct that proscribes policies that make nationalism dangerous. The code should have six elements: (1) renunciation of the threat or use of force; (2) robust guarantees for the rights of national minorities, to include, under some stringent conditions, a legal right to secession;[13] (3) commitment to the honest teaching of history in the schools,[14] and to refrain from the propagation of chauvinist or other hate propaganda; (4) willingness to adopt a democratic form of government and to accept related institutions—specifically, free speech and a free press (5) adoption of market economic policies, and disavowal of protectionist or other beggar-thy-neighbor economic policies toward other Eastern states; and (6) acceptance of current national borders, or agreement to settle contested borders promptly though peaceful means. This list rests on the premise that "peaceful conduct" requires that nationalist movements renounce the use of force against others (element 1), and also agree to refrain from policies that the hypotheses presented here warn against (elements 2–6).

Hypothesis I.4 (see Table 1) warns that the risk of war rises when nationalist movements oppress their minorities; hence the code requires respect for minority rights (element 2). Hypothesis II.6 warns that divergent beliefs about mutual history and current conduct and character raise the risk of war; hence the code asks for historical honesty and curbs on official hate propaganda (element 3). Hypothesis II.6.a warns that illegitimate governments have a greater propensity to myth-make, and hypothesis II.6.d warns that chauvinist myths prevail more often if independent evaluative institutions are weak; hence the code asks that movements adopt democracy (to bolster legitimacy) and respect free speech and free press rights (to bolster evaluation) (element 4). Hypothesis II.6.c warns that economic collapse promotes chauvinist mythmaking; hence the code asks movements to adopt market reforms, on grounds that prosperity requires marketization (element 5). Hypothesis II.3.b warns that the risk of war rises if the borders of emerging nation states lack legitimacy; hence the code asks movements to legitimize their borders through formal non-violent settlement (element 6).

The Western powers should enforce this code by pursuing a common economic policy toward the states of the East: observance of the code should be the price for full membership in the Western economy, while non-observance should bring exclusion and economic sanctions. This policy should be married to an economic aid package to assist marketization, also conditioned on code observance.

The Bush and Clinton administrations have adopted elements of this policy, but omitted key aspects. In September 1991, then-Secretary of State James Baker outlined five principles that incorporate most of the six elements in the code of conduct outlined above (only element 3—honest treatment of history—was unmentioned), and he indicated that American policy toward the new Eastern states would be conditioned on their acceptance of these principles. During the spring and summer of 1992 the administration also proposed a substantial economic aid package (the Freedom Support Act) and guided it through Congress.

However, Baker's principles later faded from view. Strangely, the Bush administration failed to clearly condition release of its aid package on Eastern compliance with these principles. It also failed to forge a common agreement among the Western powers to condition their economic relations with the Eastern states on these principles. The principles themselves were not elaborated; most importantly, the minority rights that the Eastern states must protect were not detailed, leaving these states free to adopt a watered-down definition. The Bush administration also recognized several new Eastern governments (e.g., Azerbaijan's) that gave Baker's principles only lip service while violating them in practice. The Clinton administration has largely followed in Bush's footsteps: it continued Bush's aid program, but omitted clear political conditions.

There is still time for such a policy, but the clock is running out. A policy resting on economic sticks and carrots will be too weak to end major violence once it begins; hence the West should therefore move to avert trouble while it still lies on the horizon.

NOTES

1. My usage of "ethnic community" follows Anthony Smith, who suggests that an ethnic community has six characteristics: a common name, a myth of common ancestry, shared memories, a common culture, a link with a historic territory or homeland (which it may or may not currently occupy), and a measure of common solidarity. See Smith, *Ethnic Origins of Nations*, pp. 22–30.

2. The text of this article identifies factors that govern the size of the risk posed by nationalism, and explains the proposed causal relationship. Table 1 restates these factors and explanations as hypotheses.

3. The dichotomy between stateless and state-possessing nationalist movements is analogous to the dichotomy in international relations between "satisfied" and "dissatisfied" powers; the latter disturb the peace in their effort to gain satisfaction, while the former cause less trouble.

4. Wars can result from having too many states, as well as too few. If states are too many, wars of national unification will result, as they did in Germany and Italy in the nineteenth century, and as they might someday in the Arab world. In Europe, however, the problem everywhere is an excess of demand for states over the supply.

5. Thus the second and fourth attributes are related: if some states oppress their minorities (the fourth attribute) this affects other states' propensity to pursue diaspora recovery (the second attribute).

6. If nationalism is unattainable it may not even appear: the captive nation will submerge the nationalist thought. This is similar to the realist argument that imperialism is a function of capability: states imperialize simply when and where they can. Likewise, and conversely, nationalism is in part simply a function of capability: it emerges where it can.

7. We can scale up this logic from single states to regions by asking: do nations have states in proportion to their power? That is, does the state-to-nation ratio correspond with the state-to-nation power ratio? Or do nations have fewer states than their power justifies? If the former is the case, peace is more likely. But if nations have fewer states than their power would allow, trouble results in the form of wars of secession.

8. Overall, then, three variables matter: (1) the supply of states; (2) the demand for states; (3) the capacity of submerged nations to acquire states. Peace is stronger if supply and demand are in equilibrium; or if supply and capacity are in equilibrium. In one case, nationalism is satisfied; in the other, it is dissatisfied but impotent. Dangers arise if both supply and demand, and supply and capacity, are not in equilibrium. We then have submerged nationalisms that both desire and can assert the demand for statehood.

9. The scope and structure of intermingling governs the acuteness of what might be called the "inter-ethnic security dilemma": this dilemma is posed where one group cannot achieve physical security without diminishing the physical security of other groups. It is analogous to the interstate security dilemma of international relations, except that the clashing units are ethnic or culture groups, not states.

10. These include Hungarians in Romania, Slovakia, and Serbia; Poles in Lithuania, Belarus, Ukraine, and the Czech Republic; Germans in Poland and the Czech Republic; Turks in Bulgaria; Greeks in Albania; Albanians in Serbia and Macedonia; Croats in Bosnia-Herzegovina; and Serbs in Croatia and Bosnia-Herzegovina.

11. Regime illegitimacy provides the largest motive for elite mythmaking when the state cannot rule by pure force: mythmaking is then the elite's only means to preserve its rule. The proximate cause of mythmaking can therefore sometimes be found in the decline of the state monopoly of force, not the decline of elite legitimacy. This was the case in Europe in the nineteenth century: nationalist mythmaking rose with the rise of mass armies and popular literacy, which diminished the capacity of the state to govern by pure coercion. Elites were therefore forced to resort to persuasion, hence to mythmaking. (Mass literacy in this context proved a double-edged sword for newly-literate publics. Literacy enabled mass political mobilization by spreading social knowledge and ideas; this led to popular empowerment, but literacy also made publics easier to control

from above, by enabling elites to purvey elite-justifying myths through the written word; this limited or reduced popular power.)

12. The emerging nations of the former USSR now stand knee-deep in the blood of Stalin's victims, and in the economic ruin that Bolshevism left behind. If every nation blames only others for these disasters, civil relations among them will be impossible; each will hope to someday settle accounts. Civil relations depend, then, on a convergence toward a common history of the Bolshevik disaster. Things would be best if all converged on a version that blamed the Bolshevisks—who, having vanished, can be blamed painlessly. (Bolshevism would then usefully serve as a hate-soaker—its final, and among its few positive, functions in Soviet history.) Absent that, things would be better if the successor nations agree on how to allocate blame among themselves.

13. Minority rights should be defined broadly, to include fair minority representation in the legislative, executive, and judicial branches of the central government. The definition of minority rights used in most international human rights agreements is more restrictive: it omits the right to share power in the national government, and includes only the right to political autonomy and the preservation of minority language, culture, and religion.

    When should minority rights be defined to include the right to secession and national independence? Universal recognition of this right would require massive redrawing of boundaries in the East, and would raise the question of Western recognition of scores of now-unrecognized independence movements worldwide. One solution is to recognize the right to secede in instances where the central government is unwilling to fully grant other minority rights, but to decline to recognize the right to secede if all other minority rights are fully recognized and robustly protected. In essence, the West would hold its possible recognition of a right to secede in reserve, to encourage governments to recognize other minority rights.

14. States should not be asked to accept externally-imposed versions of history in their texts, since no society can arbitrarily claim to know the "truth" better than others. But states could be asked to commit to international dialogue on history, on the theory that free debate will cause views to converge. Specifically, they could be asked to accept the obligation to subject their school curricula to foreign criticism, perhaps in the context of textbook exchanges, and to allow domestic publication of foreign criticisms of their curricula. Schemes of this sort have a long history in Western Europe, where they had a substantial impact after 1945. See Dance, *History the Betrayer,* pp. 127–28, 132, 135–50. This West European experience could serve as a template for an Eastern program.

The Future of the Global Economy

The Changed World Economy

Peter F. Drucker

The talk today is of the "changing world economy." I wish to argue that the world economy is not "changing"; it has *already changed*—in its foundations and in its structure—and in all probability the change is irreversible.

Within the last decade or so, three fundamental changes have occurred in the very fabric of the world economy:

- The primary-products economy has come "uncoupled" from the industrial economy.
- In the industrial economy itself, production has come "uncoupled" from employment.
- Capital movements rather than trade (in both goods and services) have become the driving force of the world economy. The two have not quite come uncoupled, but the link has become loose, and worse, unpredictable.

These changes are permanent rather than cyclical. We may never understand what caused them—the causes of economic change are rarely simple. It may be a long time before economic theorists accept that there have been fundamental changes, and longer still before they adapt their theories to account for them. Above all, they will surely be most reluctant to accept that it is the world economy in control, rather than the macroeconomics of the nation-state on which most economic theory still exclusively focuses. Yet this is the clear lesson

---

of the success stories of the last 20 years—of Japan and South Korea; of West Germany (actually a more impressive though far less flamboyant example than Japan); and of the one great success within the United States, the turnaround and rapid rise of an industrial New England, which only 20 years ago was widely considered moribund.

Practitioners, whether in government or in business, cannot wait until there is a new theory. They have to act. And their actions will be more likely to succeed the more they are based on the new realities of a changed world economy.

First, consider the primary-products economy. The collapse of non-oil commodity prices began in 1977 and has continued, interrupted only once (right after the 1979 petroleum panic), by a speculative burst that lasted less than six months; it was followed by the fastest drop in commodity prices ever registered. By early 1986 raw material prices were at their lowest levels in recorded history in relation to the prices of manufactured goods and services—in general as low as at the depths of the Great Depression, and in some cases (e.g., lead and copper) lower than their 1932 levels.[1]

This collapse of prices and the slowdown of demand stand in startling contrast to what had been confidently predicted. Ten years ago the Club of Rome declared that desperate shortages for *all* raw materials were an absolute certainty by the year 1985. In 1980 the Carter Administration's *Global 2000 Report to the President: Entering the Twenty-First Century* concluded that world demand for food would increase steadily for at least 20 years; that worldwide food production would fall except in developed countries; and that real food prices would double. This forecast helps to explain why American farmers bought up all available farmland, thus loading on themselves the debt burden that now so threatens them.

Contrary to all these expectations, global agricultural output actually rose almost one-third between 1972 and 1985 to reach an all-time high. It rose the fastest in less-developed countries. Similarly, production of practically all forest products, metals and minerals has gone up between 20 and 35 percent in the last ten years—again with the greatest increases in less-developed countries. There is not the slightest reason to believe that the growth rates will slacken, despite the collapse of commodity prices. Indeed, as far as farm products are concerned, the biggest increase—at an almost exponential rate of growth—may still be ahead.[2]

Perhaps even more amazing than the contrast between such predictions and what has happened is that the collapse in the raw materials economy seems to have had almost no impact on the world industrial economy. If there was one thing considered "proven" beyond doubt in business cycle theory, it is that a sharp and prolonged drop in raw material prices inevitably, and within 18 to 30 months, brings on a worldwide depression in the industrial economy.[3] While the industrial economy of the world today is not "normal" by any definition of the term, it is surely not in a depression. Indeed, industrial production in the developed non-communist countries has continued to grow steadily, albeit at a somewhat slower rate in Western Europe.

Of course, a depression in the industrial economy may only have been postponed and may still be triggered by a banking crisis caused by massive defaults on the part of commodity-producing debtors, whether in the Third World or in Iowa. But for almost ten years the industrial world has run along as though there were no raw material crisis at all. The only explanation is that for the developed countries—excepting only the Soviet Union—the primary-products sector has become marginal where before it had always been central.

In the late 1920s, before the Great Depression, farmers still constituted nearly one-third of the U.S. population and farm income accounted for almost a quarter of the gross national product. Today they account for less than 5 percent of population and even less of GNP. Even adding the contribution that foreign raw material and farm producers make to the American economy through their purchases of American industrial goods, the total contribution of the raw material and food producing economies of the world to the American GNP is, at most, one-eighth. In most other developed countries, the share of the raw materials sector is even lower. Only in the Soviet Union is the farm still a major employer, with almost a quarter of the labor force working on the land.

The raw material economy has thus come uncoupled from the industrial economy. This is a major structural change in the world economy, with tremendous implications for economic and social policy as well as economic theory, in developed and developing countries alike.

For example, if the ratio between the prices of manufactured goods and the prices of non-oil primary products (that is, foods, forest products, metals and minerals) had been the same in 1985 as it had been in 1973, the 1985 U.S. trade deficit might have been a full one-third less—$100 billion as against an actual $150 billion. Even the U.S. trade deficit with Japan might have been almost one-third lower, some $35 billion as against $50 billion. American farm exports would have bought almost twice as much. And industrial exports to a major U.S. customer, Latin America, would have held; their near-collapse alone accounts for a full one-sixth of the deterioration in the U.S. foreign trade over the past five years. If primary-product prices had not collapsed, America's balance of payments might even have shown a substantial surplus.

Conversely, Japan's trade surplus with the world might have been a full 20 percent lower. And Brazil in the last few years would have had an export surplus almost 50 percent higher than its current level. Brazil would then have had little difficulty meeting the interest on its foreign debt and would not have had to endanger its economic growth by drastically curtailing imports as it did. Altogether, if raw material prices in relationship to manufactured goods prices had remained at the 1973 or even the 1979 level, there would be no crisis for most debtor countries, especially in Latin America.[4]

What accounts for this change?

Demand for food has actually grown almost as fast as the Club of Rome and the *Global 2000 Report* anticipated. But the supply has grown much faster; it not only has kept pace with population growth, it has steadily outrun it. One cause of this, paradoxically, is surely the fear of worldwide food shortages, if not world famine, which resulted in tremendous efforts to increase food output. The United States led the parade with a farm policy of subsidizing increased food production.

The European Economic Community followed suit, and even more successfully. The greatest increases, both in absolute and in relative terms, however, have been in developing countries: in India, in post-Mao China and in the rice-growing countries of Southeast Asia.

And there is also the tremendous cut in waste. In the 1950s, up to 80 percent of the grain harvest of India fed rats and insects rather than human beings. Today in most parts of India the wastage is down to 20 percent. This is largely the result of unspectacular but effective "infrastructure innovations" such as small concrete storage bins, insecticides and three-wheeled motorized carts that take the harvest straight to a processing plant instead of letting it sit in the open for weeks.

It is not fanciful to expect that the true "revolution" on the farm is still ahead. Vast tracts of land that hitherto were practically barren are being made fertile, either through new methods of cultivation or through adding trace minerals to the soil. The sour clays of the Brazilian highlands or the aluminum-contaminated soils of neighboring Peru, for example, which never produced anything before, now produce substantial quantities of high-quality rice. Even greater advances have been registered in biotechnology, both in preventing diseases of plants and animals and in increasing yields.

In other words, just as the population growth of the world is slowing down quite dramatically in many regions, food production is likely to increase sharply.

Import markets for food have all but disappeared. As a result of its agricultural drive, Western Europe has become a substantial food exporter plagued increasingly by unsalable surpluses of all kinds of foods, from dairy products to wine, from wheat to beef. China, some observers predict, will have become a food exporter by the year 2000. India is about at that stage, especially with wheat and coarse grains. Of all major non-communist countries only Japan is still a substantial food importer, buying abroad about one-third of its food needs. Today most of this comes from the United States. Within five or ten years, however, South Korea, Thailand and Indonesia—low-cost producers that are fast increasing food output—are likely to try to become Japan's major suppliers.

The only remaining major food buyer on the world market may then be the Soviet Union—and its food needs are likely to grow.[5] However, the food surpluses in the world are so large—maybe five to eight times what the Soviet Union would ever need to buy—that its food needs are not by themselves enough to put upward pressure on world prices. On the contrary, the competition for access to the Soviet market among the surplus producers—the United States, Europe, Argentina, Australia, New Zealand (and probably India within a few years)—is already so intense as to depress world food prices.

For practically all non-farm commodities, whether forest products, minerals or metals, world demand is shrinking—in sharp contrast to what the Club of Rome so confidently predicted. Indeed, the amount of raw material needed for a given unit of economic output has been dropping for the entire century, except in wartime. A recent study by the International Monetary Fund calculates the decline as one and one-quarter percent a year (compounded) since 1900.[6] This would mean that the amount of industrial raw materials needed for one unit of industrial production is now no more than two-fifths of what it was in 1900. And the decline is accelerating. The Japanese experience is particularly striking. In 1984, for every unit of industrial production, Japan consumed only 60 percent of the raw materials consumed for the same volume of industrial production in 1973, 11 years earlier.

Why this decline in demand? It is not that industrial production is fading in importance as the service sector grows—a common myth for which there is not the slightest evidence. What is happening is much more significant. Industrial production is steadily switching away from heavily material-intensive products and processes. One of the reasons for this is the new high-technology industries. The raw materials in a semiconductor microchip account for 1 to 3 percent of total production cost; in an automobile their share is 40 percent, and in pots and pans 60 percent. But also in older industries the same scaling down of raw material needs goes on, and with respect to old products as well as new ones. Fifty to 100 pounds of fiberglass cable transmit as many telephone messages as does one ton of copper wire.

This steady drop in the raw material intensity of manufacturing processes and manufacturing products extends to energy as well, and especially to petroleum. To produce 100 pounds of fiberglass cable requires no more than 5 percent of the energy needed to produce one ton of copper wire. Similarly, plastics, which are increasingly replacing steel in automobile bodies, represent a raw material cost, including energy, of less than half that of steel.

Thus it is quite unlikely that raw material prices will ever rise substantially as compared to the prices of manufactured goods (or high-knowledge services such as information, education or health care) except in the event of a major prolonged war.

One implication of this sharp shift in the terms of trade of primary products concerns the developed countries, both major raw material exporters like the United States and major raw material importing countries such as Japan. For two centuries the United States has made maintenance of open markets for its farm products and raw materials central to its international trade policy. This is what it has always meant by an "open world economy" and by "free trade."

Does this still make sense, or does the United States instead have to accept that foreign markets for its foodstuffs and raw materials are in a long-term and irreversible decline? Conversely, does it still make sense for Japan to base its international economic policy on the need to earn enough foreign exchange to pay for imports of raw materials and foodstuffs? Since Japan opened to the outside world 120 years ago, preoccupation—amounting almost to a national obsession—with its dependence on raw material and food imports has been the driving force of Japan's policy, and not in economics alone. Now Japan might well start out with the assumption—a far more realistic one in today's world—that foodstuffs and raw materials are in permanent oversupply.

Taken to their logical conclusion, these developments might mean that some variant of the traditional Japanese policy—highly mercantilist with a strong de-emphasis of domestic consumption in favor of an equally strong emphasis on capital formation, and protection of infant industries—might suit the United States better than its own tradition. The Japanese might be better served by some variant of America's traditional policies, especially a shifting from favoring savings and capital formation to favoring consumption. Is such a radical break with more than a century of political convictions and commitments likely? From now on the fundamentals of economic policy are certain to come under increasing criticism in these two countries—and in all other developed countries as well.

These fundamentals will, moreover, come under the increasingly intense scrutiny of major Third World nations. For if primary products are becoming of marginal importance to the economies of the developed world, traditional development theories and policies are losing their foundations.[7] They are based on the assumption—historically a perfectly valid one—that developing countries pay for imports of capital goods by exporting primary materials—farm and forest products, minerals, metals. All development theories, however much they differ otherwise, further assume that raw material purchases by the industrially developed countries must rise at least as fast as industrial production in these countries. This in turn implies that, over any extended period of time, any raw material producer becomes a better credit risk and shows a more favorable balance of trade. These premises have become highly doubtful. On what foundation, then, can economic development be based, especially in countries that do not have a large enough population to develop an industrial economy based on the home market? As we shall presently see, these countries can no longer base their economic development on low labor costs.

The second major change in the world economy is the uncoupling of manufacturing production from manufacturing employment. Increased manufacturing production in developed countries has actually come to mean *decreasing* blue-collar employment. As a consequence, labor costs are becoming less and less important as a "comparative cost" and as a factor in competition.

There is a great deal of talk these days about the "de-industrialization" of America. In fact, manufacturing production has risen steadily in absolute volume and has remained unchanged as a percentage of the total economy. Since the end of the Korean War, that is, for more than 30 years, it has held steady at 23–24 percent of America's total GNP. It has similarly remained at its traditional level in all of the other major industrial countries.

It is not even true that American industry is doing poorly as an exporter. To be sure, the United States is importing from both Japan and Germany many more manufactured goods than even before. But it is also exporting more, despite the heavy disadvantages of an expensive dollar, increasing labor costs and the near-collapse of a major industrial market, Latin America. In 1984—the year the dollar soared—exports of American manufactured goods rose by 8.3 percent; and they went up again in 1985. The share of U.S.-manufactured exports in world exports was 17 percent in 1978. By 1985 it had risen to 20 percent—while West Germany accounted for 18 percent and Japan 16. The three countries together thus account for more than half of the total.

Thus it is not the American economy that is being "de-industrialized." It is the American labor force.

Between 1973 and 1985, manufacturing production (measured in constant dollars) in the United States rose by almost 40 percent. Yet manufacturing employment during that period went down steadily. There are now five million fewer people employed in blue-collar work in American manufacturing industry than there were in 1975.

Yet in the last 12 years total employment in the United States grew faster than at any time in the peacetime history of any country—from 82 to 110 million between 1973 and 1985—that is, by a full one-third. The entire growth, however, was in non-manufacturing, and especially in non-blue-collar jobs.

The trend itself is not new. In the 1920s one out of every three Americans in the labor force was a blue-collar worker in manufacturing. In the 1950s the figure was one in four. It now is down to one in every six—and dropping. While the trend has been running for a long time, it has lately accelerated to the point where—in peacetime at least—no increase in manufacturing production, no matter how large, is likely to reverse the long-term decline in the number of blue-collar jobs in manufacturing or in their proportion of the labor force.

This trend is the same in all developed countries, and is, indeed, even more pronounced in Japan. It is therefore highly probable that in 25 years developed countries such as the United States and Japan will employ no larger a proportion of the labor force in manufacturing than developed countries now employ in farming—at most, 10 percent. Today the United States employs around 18 million people in blue-collar jobs in manufacturing industries. By 2010, the number is likely to be no more than 12 million. In some major industries the drop will be even sharper. It is quite unrealistic, for instance, to expect that the American automobile industry will employ more than one-third of its present blue-collar force 25 years hence, even though production might be 50 percent higher.

If a company, an industry or a country does not in the next quarter century sharply increase manufacturing production and at the same time sharply reduce the blue-collar work force, it cannot hope to remain competitive—or even to remain "developed." It would decline fairly fast. Britain has been in industrial decline for the last 25 years, largely because the number of blue-collar workers per unit manufacturing production went down far more slowly than in all other non-communist developed countries. Even so, Britain has the highest unemployment rate among non-communist developed countries—more than 13 percent.

The British example indicates a new and critical economic equation: a country, an industry or a company that puts the preservation of blue-collar manufacturing jobs ahead of international competitiveness (which implies a steady shrinkage of such jobs) will soon have neither production nor jobs. The attempt to preserve such blue-collar jobs is actually a prescription for unemployment.

So far, this concept has achieved broad national acceptance only in Japan.[8] Indeed, Japanese planners, whether in government or private business, start out with the assumption of a doubling of production within 15 to 20 years based on a cut in blue-collar employment of 25 to 40 percent. A good many large American companies such as IBM, General Electric and the big automobile companies have similar forecasts. Implicit in this is the conclusion that a country will have less over-all unemployment the faster it shrinks blue-collar employment in manufacturing.

This is not a conclusion that American politicians, labor leaders or indeed the general public can easily understand or accept. What confuses the issue even more is that the United States is experiencing several separate and different shifts in the manufacturing economy. One is the acceleration of the substitution of knowledge and capital for manual labor. Where we spoke of mechanization a few decades ago, we now speak of "robotization" or "automation." This is actually more a change in terminology than a change in reality. When Henry Ford introduced the assembly line in 1909, he cut the number of man-hours required to produce a motor car by some 80 percent in two or three years—far more than anyone expects to result from even the most complete robotization. But there is no doubt that we are facing a new, sharp acceleration in the replacement of manual workers by machines—that is, by the products of knowledge.

A second development—and in the long run this may be even more important—is the shift from industries that were primarily labor-intensive to industries that, from the beginning, are knowledge-intensive. The manufacturing costs of the semiconductor microchip are about 70 percent knowledge—that is, research, development and testing—and no more than 12 percent labor. Similarly with pre-scription drugs, labor represents no more than 15 percent, with knowledge representing almost 50 percent. By contrast, in the most fully robotized automobile plant labor would still account for 20 to 25 percent of the costs.

Another perplexing development in manufacturing is the reversal of the dynamics of size. Since the early years of this century, the trend in all developed countries has been toward ever larger manufacturing plants. The economies of scale greatly favored them. Perhaps equally important, what one might call the "economies of management" favored them. Until recently, modern management techniques seemed applicable only to fairly large units.

This has been reversed with a vengeance over the last 15 to 20 years. The entire shrinkage in manufacturing jobs in the United States has occured in large companies, beginning with the giants in steel and automobiles. Small and especially medium-sized manufacturers have either held their own or actually added employees. In respect to market standing, exports and profitability too, smaller and middle-sized businesses have done remarkably better than big ones. The reversal of the dynamics of size is occurring in the other developed countries as well, even in Japan where bigger was always better and biggest meant best. The trend has reversed itself even in old industries. The most profitable automobile company these last years has not been one of the giants, but a medium-sized manufacturer in Germany—BMW. The only profitable steel companies, whether in the United States, Sweden or Japan, have been medium-sized makers of specialty products such as oil drilling pipe.

In part, especially in the United States, this is a result of a resurgence of entre-preneurship.[9] But perhaps equally important, we have learned in the last 30 years how to manage the small and medium-sized enterprise to the point where the advantages of smaller size, e.g., ease of communications and nearness to market and customer, increasingly outweigh what had been forbidding management limitations. Thus in the United States, but increasingly in the other leading manufacturing nations such as Japan and West Germany as well, the dynamism in the economy has shifted from the very big companies that dominated the world's industrial economy for 30 years after World War II to companies that, while much smaller, are professionally managed and largely publicly financed.

Two distinct kinds of "manufacturing industry" are emerging. One is material-based, represented by the industries that provided economic growth in the first three-quarters of this century. The other is information- and knowledge-based: pharmaceuticals, telecommunications, analytical instruments and information processing such as computers. It is largely the information-based manufacturing industries that are growing.

These two groups differ not only in their economic characteristics but especially in their position in the international economy. The products of material-based industries have to be exported or imported as "products." They appear in the balance of trade. The products of information-based industries can be exported or imported both as "products" and as "services," which may not appear accurately in the overall trade balance.

An old example is the printed book. For one major scientific publishing company, "foreign earnings" account for two-thirds of total revenues. Yet the company exports few, if any, actual books—books are heavy. It sells "rights," and the "product" is produced abroad. Similarly, the most profitable computer "export sales" may actually show up in trade statistics as an "import." This is the fee some of the world's leading banks, multinationals and Japanese trading companies get for processing in their home office data arriving electronically from their branches and customers around the world.

In all developed countries, "knowledge" workers have already become the center of gravity of the labor force. Even in manufacturing they will outnumber blue-collar workers within ten years. Exporting knowledge so that it produces license income, service fees and royalties may actually create substantially more jobs than exporting goods.

This in turn requires—as official Washington seems to have realized—far greater emphasis in trade policy on "invisible trade" and on abolishing the barriers to the trade in services. Traditionally, economists have treated invisible trade as a stepchild, if they noted it at all. Increasingly, it will become central. Within 20 years major developed countries may find that their income from invisible trade is larger than their income from exports.

Another implication of the "uncoupling" of manufacturing production from manufacturing employment is, however, that the choice between an industrial policy that favors industrial *production* and one that favors industrial *employment* is going to be a singularly contentious political issue for the rest of this century. Historically these have always been considered two sides of the same coin. From now on the two will increasingly pull in different directions; they are indeed already becoming alternatives, it not incompatible.

Benign neglect—the policy of the Reagan Administration these last few years—may be the best policy one can hope for, and the only one with a chance of success. It is probably not an accident that the United States has, after Japan, by far the lowest unemployment rate of any industrially developed country. Still, there is surely need also for systematic efforts to retrain and to place redundant blue-collar workers—something no one as yet knows how to do successfully.

Finally, low labor costs are likely to become less of an advantage in international trade simply because in the developed countries they are going to account for less of total costs. Moreover, the total costs of automated processes are lower than even those of traditional plants with low labor costs; this is mainly because automation eliminates the hidden but high costs of "not working," such as the expense of poor quality and rejects, and the costs of shutting down the machinery to change from one model of a product to another. Consider two automated American producers of televisions, Motorola and RCA. Both were almost driven out of the market by imports from countries with much lower labor costs. Both subsequently automated, with the result that these American-made products now successfully compete with foreign imports. Similarly, some highly automated textile mills in the Carolinas can underbid imports from countries with very low labor costs such as Thailand. On the other hand, although some American semiconductor companies have lower labor costs because they do the labor-intensive work offshore, e.g., in West Africa, they are still the high-cost producers and easily underbid by the heavily automated Japanese.

The cost of capital will thus become increasingly important in international competition. And this is where, in the last ten years, the United States has become the highest-cost country—and Japan the lowest. A reversal of the U.S. policy of high interest rates and costly equity capital should thus be a priority for American decision-makers. This demands that reduction of the government deficit, rather than high interest rates, becomes the first defense against inflation.

For developed countries, especially the United States, the steady downgrading of labor costs as a major competitive factor could be a positive development. For the Third World, especially rapidly industrializing countries such as Brazil, South Korea or Mexico, it is, however, bad news.

In the rapid industrialization of the nineteenth century, one country, Japan, developed by exporting raw materials, mainly silk and tea, at steadily rising prices. Another, Germany, developed by leap-frogging into the "high-tech" industries of its time, mainly electricity, chemicals and optics. A third, the United States, did both. Both routes are blocked for today's rapidly industrializing countries—the first because of the deterioration of the terms of trade for primary products, the second because it requires an infrastructure of knowledge and education far beyond the reach of a poor country (although South Korea is reaching for it). Competition based on lower labor costs seemed to be the only alternative: is this also going to be blocked?

The third major change that has occurred in the world economy is the emergence of the "symbol" economy—capital movements, exchange rates and credit flows—as the flywheel of the world economy, in place of the "real" economy—the flow of goods and services. The two economies seem to be operating increasingly independently. This is both the most visible and the least understood of the changes.

World trade in goods is larger, much larger, than it has ever been before. And so is the "invisible trade," the trade in services. Together, the two amount to around $2.5 trillion to $3 trillion a year. But the London Eurodollar market, in which the world's financial institutions borrow from and lend to each other, turns over $300 billion each working day, or $75 trillion a year, a volume at least 25 times that of world trade.[10]

In addition, there are the foreign exchange transactions in the world's main money centers, in which one currency is traded against another. These run around $150 billion a day, or about $35 trillion a year—12 times the worldwide trade in goods and services.

Of course, many of these Eurodollars, yen and Swiss francs are just being moved from one pocket to another and may be counted more than once. A massive discrepancy still exists, and there is only one conclusion: capital movements unconnected to trade—and indeed largely independent of it—greatly exceed trade finance.

There is no one explanation for this explosion of international—or more accurately, transnational—money flows. The shift from fixed to floating exchange rates in 1971 may have given an initial impetus (though, ironically, it was meant to do the exact opposite) by inviting currency speculation. The surge in liquid funds flowing to petroleum producers after the two oil shocks of 1973 and 1979 was surely a major factor.

But there can be little doubt that the U.S. government deficit also plays a big role. The American budget has become a financial "black hole," sucking in liquid funds from all over the world, making the United States the world's major debtor country.[11] Indeed, it can be argued that it is the budget deficit that underlies the American trade and payments deficit. A trade and payments deficit is, in effect, a loan from the seller of goods and services to the buyer, that is, to the United States. Without it Washington could not finance its budget deficit, at least not without the risk of explosive inflation.

The way major countries have learned to use the internationl economy to avoid tackling disagreeable domestic problems is unprecedented: The United States has used high interest rates to attract foreign capital and avoid confronting its domestic deficit; the Japanese have pushed exports to maintain employment despite a sluggish domestic economy. This politicization of the international economy is surely also a factor in the extreme volatility and instability of capital flows and exchange rates.

Whichever of these causes is judged the most important, together they have produced a basic change: In the world economy of today, the "real" economy of goods and services and the "symbol" economy of money, credit and capital are no longer bound tightly to each other: they are, indeed, moving further and further apart. . . .

Traditional international economic theory is still neoclassical, holding that trade in goods and services determines international capital flows and foreign exchange rates. Capital flows and foreign exchange rates since the first half of the 1970s have, however, moved quite independently of foreign trade, and indeed (e.g., in the rise of the dollar in 1984–85) have run counter to it. . . .

From now on exchange rates between major currencies will have to be treated in economic theory and business policy alike as a "comparative-advantage" factor, and a major one.

Economic theory teaches that the comparative-advantage factors of the "real" economy—comparative labor costs and labor productivity, raw material costs, energy costs, transportation costs and the like—determine exchange rates. Practically all businesses base their policies on this notion. Increasingly, however, it is exchange rates that decide how labor costs in country A compare to labor costs in country B. Exchange rates are thus a major "comparative cost" and one totally beyond business control. Any firm exposed to the international economy has to realize that it is in two businesses at the same time. It is both a maker of goods (or a supplier of services) and a "financial" business. It cannot disregard either.

Specifically, the business that sells abroad—whether as an exporter or through a subsidiary—will have to protect itself against three foreign exchange exposures: proceeds from sales, working capital devoted to manufacturing for overseas markets, and investments abroad. This will have to be done whether the business expects the value of its own currency to go up or down. Businesses that buy abroad will have to do likewise. Indeed, even purely domestic businesses that face foreign competition in their home market will have to learn to hedge against the currency in which their main competitors produce. If American businesses had been run this way during the years of the overvalued dollar, from 1982 through 1985, most of the losses in market standing abroad and in foreign earnings might have been prevented. They were management failures, not acts of God. Surely stockholders, but also the public in general, have every right to expect management to do better the next time around. . . .

We are left with one conclusion: economic dynamics have decisively shifted from the national economy to the world economy.

Prevailing economic theory—whether Keynesian, monetarist or supply-side—considers the national economy, especially that of the large developed countries, to be autonomous and the unit of both economic analysis and economic policy. The international economy may be a restraint and a limitation, but it is not central, let alone determining. This "macroeconomic axiom" of the modern economist has become increasingly shaky. The two major subscribers to this axiom, Britain and the United States, have done least well economically in the last 30 years, and have also had the most economic instability.

West Germany and Japan never accepted the "macroeconomic axiom." Their universities teach it, of course, but their policymakers, both in government and in business, reject it. Instead, both countries all along have based their economic policies on the world economy, have systematically tried to anticipate its trends and exploit its changes as opportunities. Above all, both make the country's competitive position in the world economy the first priority in their policies—economic, fiscal, monetary, even social—to which domestic considerations are normally subordinat-ed. And these two countries have done far better—economically and socially—than Britain and the United States these last 30 years. In fact, their focus on the world economy and the priority they give it may be the real "secret" of their success.

Similarly the "secret" of successful businesses in the developed world—the Japanese, the German carmakers like Mercedes and BMW, Asea and Erickson in Sweden, IBM and Citibank in the United States, but equally of a host of medium-sized specialists in manufacturing and in all kinds of services—has been that they base their plans and their policies on exploiting the world economy's changes as opportunities.

From now on any country—but also any business, especially a large one—that wants to prosper will have to accept that it is the world economy that leads and that domestic economic policies will succeed only if they strengthen, or at least do not impair, the country's international competitive position. This may be the most important—it surely is the most striking—feature of the changed world economy.

NOTES

1. When the price of petroleum dropped to $15 a barrel in February 1986, it was actually below its 1933 price (adjusted for the change in the purchasing power of the dollar). It was still, however, substantially higher than its all-time low in 1972–73, which in 1986 dollars amounted to $7–$8 a barrel.
2. On this see two quite different discussions by Dennis Avery, "U.S. Farm Dilemma: The Global Bad News Is Wrong," *Science,* Oct. 25, 1985; and Barbara Insel, "A World Awash in Grain," *Foreign Affairs,* Spring 1985.
3. The business cycle theory was developed just before World War I by the Russian math-ematical economist, Nikolai Kondratieff, who made comprehensive studies of raw material price cycles and their impacts all the way back to 1797.
4. These conclusions are based on static analysis, which presumes that which products are bought and sold is not affected by changes in price. This is of course unrealistic, but the flaw should not materially affect the conclusions.
5. Although the African famine looms large in our consciousness, the total population of the affected areas is far too small to make any dent in world food surpluses.
6. David Sapsford, *Real Primary Commodity Prices: An Analysis of Long-Run Movements,* International Monetary Fund Internal Memorandum, May 17, 1985, (unpublished).
7. This was asserted as early as 1950 by the South American economist Raúl Prebisch in *The Economic Development of Latin America and its Principal Problems* (E/CN.12/89/REV.1), United Nations Economic Commission for Latin America. But then no one, including myself, believed him.
8. The Japanese government, for example, sponsors a finance company that makes long-term, low interest loans to small manufacturers to enable them to automate rapidly.
9. On this see my book, *Innovation and Entrepreneurship: Practice and Principles,* New York: Harper & Row, 1985.
10. A Eurodollar is a U.S. dollar held outside the United States.
11. This is cogently argued by Stephen Marris, for almost 30 years economic adviser to the Organization for Economic Cooperation and Development (OECD), in his *Deficits and the Dollar: The World Economy at Risk,* Washington: Institute of International Eco-nomics, December 1985.

Head to Head: A New Economic Game

Lester B. Thurow

NEW COMPETITORS

Looking backward, future historians will see the twentieth century as a century of niche competition and the twenty-first century as a century of head-to-head competition. In 1950 the United States had a per capita GNP four times that of West Germany and fifteen times that of Japan. What were high-wage products from the Japanese perspective were low-wage products in West Germany. What were high-wage products in West Germany were low-wage products in America. As a result, imports from West Germany or Japan were not seen as threatening the good jobs that Americans wanted. Conversely, America's exports did not threaten good jobs in West Germany or Japan. The United States exported agricultural products that they could not grow, raw materials that they did not have, and high-tech products, such as civilian jet airliners, that they could not build.

The 1990s start from a very different place. In broad terms there are now three relatively equal contenders—Japan; the European Community, centered around its most powerful country, Germany; and the United States. Measured in terms of external purchasing power (how much can be bought if one's income is spent abroad), the per capita GNPs of Japan and Germany are slightly larger than that of the United States. The exact amount depends upon the precise value of the dollar, mark, and yen when the measurements are made. Measured in terms of internal purchasing power (how much can be bought if one's income is spent at home), America's per capita GNP is higher than that of West Germany or Japan. . . .[1]

Portions of the text and some footnotes have been omitted.

Consumer standards of living are one aspect of success, but production abilities are another. Depending upon the industry under consideration, leadership can now be found in Germany, Japan, and the United States. The United States no longer leads in everything. In some areas, such as automobiles, it is a follower, and in others, such as consumer electronics, it is not even a player.

Where American firms used to dwarf their competitors, they now find themselves increasingly on the small side. In 1970, 64 of the world's 100 largest industrial corporations were found in the United States, 26 were found in Europe, and only 8 in Japan. By 1988 only 42 of the 100 largest were located in the United States, 33 were located in Europe, and 15 were located in Japan. . . .

But starting from approximately the same level of economic development, each country or region now wants exactly the same industries to insure that its citizens have the highest standards of living in the twenty-first century. Ask Japan, Germany, and the United States to name those industries that they think are necessary to give their citizens a world-class standard of living in the first half of the twenty-first century, and they will return remarkably similar lists—microelectronics, biotechnology, the new materials-science industries, telecommunications, civilian aviation, robotics plus machine tools, and computers plus software.[2]

What was an era of niche competition in the last half of the twentieth century will become an era of head-to-head competition in the first half of the twenty-first century. Niche competition is win-win. Everyone has a place where they can excel; no one is going to be driven out of business. Head-to-head competition is win-lose. Not everyone will get those seven key industries. Some will win; some will lose. . . . Conflicts in economic self-interest will also be sharper than they otherwise would have been because of the disappearance of the Soviet military bear. In the next haft century no one has to moderate economic positions to preserve the military alliances that were necessary to contain the USSR. In the past half century military needs prevented economic conflicts from getting out of hand. From now on, economic cooperation will have to stand on its own, and economic arrangements will not be held together with military glue.

On one level a prediction that economic warfare will replace military warfare is good news. Vigorous competition may spur economic growth. There is nothing morally wrong with an aggressive invasion of well-made, superbly marketed German or Japanese products. Being bought is not the same thing as being militarily occupied. At the same time the military metaphor is fundamentally incorrect. The economic game that will be played in the twenty-first century will have cooperative as well as competitive elements. As we shall later see, a cooperative macroeconomic locomotive will have to be built to prevent the cycles that are inherent in capitalism. The world's common environment will require global cooperation if it is to be livable for anyone.

Economics abhors a vacuum no less than Mother Nature. The economic competition between communism and capitalism is over, but another competition between two different forms of capitalism is already under way. Using a distinction first made by George C. Lodge, a Harvard Business School professor, the individualistic Anglo-Saxon British-American form of capitalism is going to face off against the communitarian German and Japanese variants of capitalism. The

Japanese variant of capitalism will be examined in detail in Chapter 4, but the essential difference between the two forms of capitalism is their stress on communitarian versus individualistic values as the route to economic success[3]—the "I" of America or of the United Kingdom versus "Das Volk" and "Japan Inc."

America and Britain trumpet individualistic values: the brilliant entrepreneur, Nobel Prize winners, large wage differentials, individual responsibility for skills, easy to fire and easy to quit, profit maximization, and hostile mergers and take-overs—their hero is the Lone Ranger. In contrast, Germany and Japan trumpet communitarian values: business groups, social responsibility for skills, teamwork, firm loyalty, industry strategies, and active industrial policies that promote growth. Anglo-Saxon firms are profit maximizers; Japanese business firms play a game that might better be known as "strategic conquest." Americans believe in "consumer economics"; Japanese believe in "producer economics."

In the Anglo-Saxon variant of capitalism, the individual is supposed to have a personal economic strategy for success, and the business firm is supposed to have an economic strategy that is a reflection of the wishes of its individual shareholders. Since shareholders want income to maximize their lifetime consumption, their firms must be profit maximizers. For the profit-maximizing firm, customer and employee relations are merely a means to the end of higher profits for the shareholders. Wages are to be beaten down where possible, and when not needed, employees are to be laid off. Lower wages equal higher profits. Workers in the Anglo-Saxon system are expected to change employers whenever opportunities arise to earn higher wages elsewhere. They owe their employer nothing. In contrast, many Japanese firms still refer to voluntary quits as "treason."[4]

In communitarian capitalism individual and firm strategies also exist but are built on quite different foundations. The individual does not play as an individual. One joins a team and is then successful as part of that company team. The key decision in an individual's personal strategy is to join the *right* team. From then on their own personal success or failure will be closely bound up with the success or failure of the firm for which they work. In the Anglo-Saxon world, company loyalty is somewhat suspect. The individual succeeds as an individual—not as a member of a team.

In both Germany and Japan, job switching is a far less prevalent phenomenon than it is in the United States or Great Britain. Labor-force turnover is bad in communitarian capitalism, since no one will plant apple trees (make sacrifices for the good of the company) if they do not expect to be around when the apples are harvested. In contrast, turnover rates are viewed positively in America and Great Britain. Firms are getting rid of unneeded labor when they fire workers, and individuals are moving to higher wage (higher productivity) opportunities when they quit. Job switching, voluntary or involuntary, is almost a synonym for efficiency.

The communitarian business firm has a very different set of stakeholders who must be consulted when its strategies are being set. In Japanese business firms employees are seen as the number one stakeholder, customers number two, and the shareholders a distant number three. Since the employee is the prime stakeholder, higher employee wages are a central goal of the firm in Japan. Profits will be sacrificed to maintain either wages or employment. Dividend payouts to the shareholders are low.

Communitarian societies expect companies to invest in the skills of their work forces. In the United States and Great Britain, skills are an individual responsibility. Firms exist to promote efficiency by hiring skills at the lowest possible wage rates. Labor is not a member of the team. It is just another factor of production to be rented when it is needed, and laid off when it is not.

Beyond personal and firm strategies, communitarian capitalism believes in having strategies at two additional levels. Business groups such as the Mitsui group or the Deutsche Bank group are expected to have collective strategies. Companies should be financially interlocked and work together to strengthen each other's activities. The Japanese break up into vertical *keiretsu* made up of suppliers, producers, and retailers, and horizontal *keiretsu* made up of firms in different industries. At the top of the pyramid of Japanese business groups are the major former *zaibatsu* groups: Mitsui group (23 member firms), Mitsubishi group (28 member firms), Sumitomo group (21 member firms), Fuji group (29 member firms), Sanwa group (39 member firms), Dai-Ichi Kangyo group (45 member firms).[5] The members of each of these groups will own a controlling block of shares in other firms in the group. In addition each member firm would have a secondary group of smaller customers and suppliers, its *keiretsu*, organized around it. Hitachi counts 688 firms in its family; Toyota, 175 primary members and 4,000 secondary members.[6]

Similar patterns exist in Germany. The Deutsche Bank directly owns 10 percent or more of the shares in 70 companies: 28 percent of Germany's largest company, Daimler-Benz; 10 percent of Europe's largest reinsurance company, Munich Rai; 25 percent of Europe's largest department-store chain, Karstady; 30 percent of Germany's largest construction company, Philipp Holzmann; and 21 percent of Europe's largest sugar producer, Sudzucker. Indirectly, it controls many more shares that don't have to be publicly disclosed through its trust department. Deutsche Bank executives sit on four hundred corporate boards.[7] Outside of Germany, it owns 4 percent of the shares in Italy's Fiat. Similar if smaller empires exist at the other universal banks. Among the one hundred largest industrial corporations in Germany, the large universal banks own 10 to 25 percent of the shares in 48 of the largest 100 firms, 25 to 50 percent of the shares in 43 others, and over 50 percent of the shares in 9 of the 100 biggest firms. . . .[8]

Both Europe and Japan believe that government has a role to play in economic growth. Airbus Industries, a civilian aircraft manufacturer owned by the British, French, German, and Spanish governments, is an expression of a pan-European strategy. It was designed to break the American monopoly and get Europe back into civilian aircraft manufacturing. Today it is a success, as it has captured 20 percent of the aircraft market and announced plans to double production and capture one third of the worldwide market by the mid–1990s.

Germany, the dominant European economic power, sees itself as having a *"social-market"* economy and not just a "market" economy. Codetermination is required to broaden the ranks of corporate stakeholders beyond that of the traditional capitalistic owners to include workers. German governments (state and federal) own more shares in more industries (airlines, autos, steel, chemicals, electric power, transportation—some outright, some partially) than any noncommunist country on the face of the globe. Public investments such as Airbus Industries are not controversial political issues. Privatization is not sweeping across Germany as it did across Great Britain.

Government is believed to have an important role in insuring that everyone has the skills necessary to participate in the market. Germany's socially financed apprenticeship system is the envy of the world. Social-welfare policies are seen as a necessary part of a market economy. Unfettered capitalism is believed to generate levels of income inequality that are unacceptable.

In contrast, in the United States social-welfare programs are seen as regrettable necessities, since people will not provide for their own futures (old age, unemployment, ill health), but there are continual reminders that the higher taxes necessary to pay for social-welfare benefits will reduce work incentives for those paying taxes and that the benefits will undercut work incentives for those receiving them. In the ideal Anglo-Saxon market economy, social-welfare policies would not be necessary.

In Japan industry representatives working with the Ministry of International Trade and Industry present "visions" of where the economy should be going. In the past these visions served as guides to the allocation of scarce foreign exchange or capital flows. Today they are used to guide R&D funding. Key industries are targeted. What the Japanese know as "administrative guidance" is a way of life.

Like the European policy in aircraft, the Japanese strategy in semiconductor chips was also lengthy and expensive. The government-financed very-large-integrated-circuit-chip-research project was just part of a much larger effort. In the end a combination of patience, large investments, and American mistakes (a reluctance to expand capacity during cyclical downturns) succeeded in breaking the dominance of American semiconductor firms.

In America's economic theology, government has no role in investment funding and a *legitimate* one only in basic R&D. These rules are sometimes violated in practice, but the theology is clear. In the Anglo-Saxon view governments should protect private-property rights, then step back, get out of the way, and let individuals do their thing. Profit maximization will lead capitalism in the right directions.

These different conceptions of capitalism flow from very different histories. The Industrial Revolution began in Great Britain. In the formative years of British capitalism during the nineteenth century, it did not have to play catch-up with anyone. It was the leader. It was the most powerful country in the world. The United States similarly had a quick start in the Industrial Revolution. Situated between two great oceans, the United States did not feel militarily threatened by Britain's early economic lead. In the last quarter of the nineteenth century, when it was moving faster than Great Britain, Americans could see that they were going to catch up without deliberate government efforts to throw more coal into America's economic steam engines.

By way of contrast, nineteenth-century Germany had to catch up with Great Britain if it was not to be run over in the wars of Europe. . . . To have its rightful place at the European table, Prussia had to have a modern industrial economy. German capitalism needed help to catch up. Similarly, the Japanese system did not occur by accident. Admiral Perry arrived in the mid–1800s and, with a few cannon balls, forced Japan to begin trading with the rest of the world. But the mid-nineteenth century was the height of colonialism. If Japan did not quickly develop, it would become a colony of someone—the British, the French, the Dutch, the Germans, or the Americans. Economic development was part of national defense—perhaps a more important part than the army itself. A modern army could not be built without a modern economy.

In both Germany and Japan economic strategies were important elements in military strategies for remaining politically independent. Governments pushed actively to insure that the economic combustion did indeed take place. They had to up the intensity of that combustion so that the economic gaps and, hence, military gaps, between themselves and their potential enemies could be cut in the shortest possible time. In these circumstances it was not surprising that business firms were organized along military lines or that the line between public and private disappeared. Government and industry had to work together to design the national economic strategies necessary for national independence. In a very real sense business firms become the front line of national defense. Military strategies and economic strategies were woven so closely together that they could not be separated.

American history is very different. Government's first significant economic act (the establishment of the Interstate Commerce Commission) prevented the railroads from using their monopoly power to set freight rates so high as to rip off everyone else. A few decades later, its second significant act (the passage of antitrust laws) prevented Mr. Rockefeller from using his control over the supply of lighting oil to extract monopoly rents. The third major source of government economic activity flowed from the collapse of capitalism in the 1930s. Government had to pick up capitalism's mess. As a result adversarial relations between government and the private sector and deep suspicions of each other's motives are deeply embedded in American history.

While very different histories have led to very different systems, today those very different systems face off in the same world economy. Let me suggest that the military metaphors now so widely used should be replaced by the language of football. Despite its competitive element—the desire to win—football also has a cooperative element. Everyone has to agree on the rules of the game, the referees, and how to split the proceeds. One can want to win yet still remain friends both during and after the game. But what the rest of the world knows as football is known in America as soccer. What Americans like about American football—frequent time-outs, lots of huddles, and unlimited substitutions—is not found in world football. It has no time-outs, no huddles, and very limited substitutions. It is a faster game. So too is the economic game ahead. All sides will call themselves capitalists, but participants will be playing two very different games.

NEW SOURCES OF STRATEGIC ADVANTAGE

Historically, individuals, firms, and countries became rich if they possessed more natural resources, were born rich and enjoyed the advantages of having more capital (plant and equipment) per person, employed superior technologies, or had more skills than their competitors. Putting some combination of these four factors together with reasonable management was the route to success.

In the nineteenth century natural resources (coal) and technology (the invention of the steam engine, the spinning jenny, and the Bessemer steel furnace) gave the United Kingdom the edge. Having gotten rich first, higher incomes allowed the British to save more than those in poorer lands. With more savings, more could be invested in plant and equipment. More capital led to higher productivity and, hence, to higher wages. With more income, more could be saved. Being rich, it was easy to stay rich—a virtuous circle.

Historians trace much of America's economic success to cheap, plentiful, well-located raw materials and farm land. America did not become rich because it worked harder or saved more than its neighbors. A small population lived in a very large, resource-rich environment. Natural resources were combined with the first compulsory public K–12 education system and the first system of mass higher education in the world. Together they gave America an economic edge. While Americans may not have worked harder, they were better skilled and worked smarter. Once rich, America also found it easy to stay rich.

New technologies and new institutions are combining to substantially alter these four traditional sources of competitive advantage. Natural resources essentially drop out of the competitive equation. Being born rich becomes much less of an advantage than it used to be. Technology gets turned upside down. New product technologies become secondary; new process technologies become primary. And in the twenty-first century, the education and skills of the work force will end up being the dominant competitive weapon.

Natural Resources

With the exception of a few very lightly populated countries that possess massive amounts of oil, natural resources have essentially ceased to be a major source of competitive advantage. . . .

The green revolution worked in both the developed and the developing world. A very small number of farmers grow more food than those who have money to pay for it want to eat. The growth in farm productivity easily outpaces the demand for more food. The biotech revolution on the horizon can only speed up the process. Simply reducing today's huge farm surpluses will require many fewer farmers tomorrow—something on the order of five million fewer in the developed world. In the nineteenth century, Russia was the world's biggest agricultural exporter. If Middle and Eastern Europe return to being efficient producers, a huge importing area will become a huge exporting area. The numbers that must leave farming could easily double. . . .

The green revolution is being matched by a materials-science revolution, where less and less natural resources are being used per unit of GNP. America uses less steel in 1990 than it did in 1960, while its GNP is two and one half times as large.[9] Reductions in usage have brought about sharp reductions in raw-material prices. After correcting for inflation, raw-material prices in 1990 were 30 percent below where they were in 1980—almost 40 percent below where they were in

1970.[10] The materials-science revolution now under way is going to accelerate in the years ahead, and further reductions in the use of almost all scarce natural resources per unit of GNP are to be expected. Traditional raw-material suppliers in the Third World will find ever-smaller markets for their ever-cheaper resources.

In the twenty-first century a lack of natural resources may in fact be an advantage. The Japanese have the world's best steel industry, though they have neither iron ore nor coal. To some extent they are the best precisely because they do not have iron ore or coal. They are not locked into poor-quality, high-cost local sources of supply. There is no need to buy low-quality British coal or American iron ore. They can buy wherever quality and price are best.

For all practical purposes natural resources have dropped out of the competitive equation. Having them is not the way to become rich. Not having them is not a barrier to becoming rich. Japan doesn't have them and is rich; Argentina has them and is not rich.

Capital

Since it is much easier for the rich to save, living in a rich country has traditionally meant that workers would automatically work with more plant and equipment per capita than those born in poor countries. Working with more capital led to higher productivity, which resulted in wages automatically being higher. Being born in a rich country almost insured that one would die in a rich country.

In the twenty-first century being born rich becomes less of a competitive advantage. Advances in telecommunications, computers, and air transportation have led to a logistics revolution where global sourcing is possible. Multinational companies bring First World capital availability with them when they build production facilities in Third World countries. Those same factors have created a world capital market where a Thai entrepreneur can borrow money to build facilities that are just as capital intensive as those built in a rich country such as Japan—especially if he has sales contracts with retailers in the First World. Today's Korean consumer-electronics factories don't look much different from those found in Japan, despite the fact that Japan has a per capita GNP six times that of Korea.

For those in the highly indebted Third World or Second World, "country risk" can intervene to lock them out of the world capital market. A good business firm with a good project in Brazil won't get a loan. With existing Brazilian debt, no lender can be confident that a Brazilian borrower will be allowed to acquire the dollars needed to pay interest and repay principal from the Brazilian Central Bank. Small companies and those that live in unstable economies with high country risk still don't have the same access as large companies and those that live in stable economies, but the differences in access to capital have sharply narrowed.

A world capital market has arisen partly because of institutional changes (deregulation of financial markets) and partly because of technological developments. In the 1950s an Italian who wanted to move money into Switzerland had to fill her backpack with lira and walk across the Alps. Today she can move her money on a personal computer. When money can be moved on a PC, there is no such thing as governments stopping money from flowing around the world. The last of the post–World War II capital controls are now being abolished (Italy did so in early 1990; France and Japan still have some controls left), but even those that are not abolished will have little impact. Transactions will simply move electronically to someplace on the globe where the offending regulations are not in force.

In principle, once adjustments are made for expected swings in foreign-exchange rates, inflation rates, and local default risks, a world capital market should insure roughly equal access—similar real interest rates and capital avail-abilities wherever one is geographically located. Wealthy countries will still save more, but their savings will flow into a world capital market where they will be allo-cated to the regions generating the highest returns. . . . At the firm level capital availability clearly has become less important in the competitive equation. There will be factories in poor countries that can match the capital intensity of those in rich countries. To some extent these plants will be owned by local firms who have access to world capital markets, and to some extent they will be the offshore pro-duction facilities of multinational firms that bring their access (local or interna-tional) to capital markets with them. Either way, many fewer workers will be guar-anteed high wages in the twenty-first century simply by virtue of the fact that they were born in a rich country.

Technology

In the past comparative advantage was a function of natural-resources endow-ments and factor proportions (capital-labor ratios). Cotton was grown in the Amer-ican South because the climate and soil were right. Slavery provided abundant labor. Cotton was spun in New England because it had the capital to harness avail-able waterpower. Each industry had its natural location.

Consider what are commonly believed to be the seven key industries of the next few decades—microelectronics, biotechnology, the new materials industries, civilian aviation, telecommunications, robots plus machine tools, and computers plus software. All are brainpower industries. Each could be located anywhere on the face of the globe. Where they will be located depends upon who can organize the brainpower to capture them. In the century ahead comparative advantage will be man-made.

Since technology lies behind man-made comparative advantage, research and development becomes critical. In the past the economic winners were those who invented new products. The British in the nineteenth century and the Americans in the twentieth century got rich doing so. But in the twenty-first century sustain-able competitive advantage will come much more out of newprocess technologies and much less out of newproduct technologies. Reverse engineering has become an art form. New products can easily be reproduced. What used to be primary (inventing new products) becomes secondary, and what used to be secondary (inventing and perfecting new processes) becomes primary.

If R&D spending by private firms is examined, American firms spend two thirds of their money on new products and one third on new processes. The Japan-ese do exactly the opposite—one third on new products, two thirds on new processes. Not surprisingly, both sets of firms do well where they concentrate their talent. While the Americans earn higher rates of return on new product technologies, Japanese firms earn higher rates of return on new processes.[11]

Someone, however, is making a mistake.[12] Both strategies cannot be correct. In this case the someone is the United States. Its spending patterns are wrong, but they are wrong because they used to be right. In the early 1960s it was conventional wisdom, and also true, that the rate of return on investment in new product R&D was almost always higher than that on new process R&D. A new product gave the inventor a monopoly power to set higher prices and earn higher profits. With a new product, there were no competitors.

In contrast, a new process left the inventor in a competitive business. Competitors knew how to make the product, and they would always lower their prices to match the inventor's prices as long as they were covering marginal costs in their old facilities. To make monopoly rents on process technologies, it was necessary to drive one's competitors out of business. To do this, new process technologies had to have average costs below the marginal costs of old process technologies. Since marginal costs are typically far below average costs, an enormous (and very unlikely) process breakthrough was necessary if one were to establish a monopoly position with better process technologies. Driving one's competitor out of business was also likely to get one into trouble with the antitrust laws. It was simply rational to spend most of a firm's R&D money on new product development.

While Americans focused on product technologies, Japan and West Germany focused on process technologies. They did so not because they were smarter than Americans but because the United States had such a technical lead in the 1950s and 1960s that it was virtually impossible for either Japan or West Germany to become leaders in the development of new products. They could only hope to compete in existing markets that Americans were exiting. As a result, Japan and West Germany invested less of their GNP in R&D, and what they did invest was invested more heavily in process R&D. They had no choice.

But what was a good American strategy thirty years ago, a focus on new product technologies, is today a poor strategy. Levels of technical sophistication in Germany, Japan, and the United States are now very different, and reverse engineering has become a highly developed art form. The nature of the change can be seen in the economic history of three leading new products introduced into the mass consumer market in the past two decades—the video camera and recorder, the fax, and the CD player. Americans invented the video camera and recorder and the fax; Europeans (the Dutch) invented the CD player. But measured in terms of sales, employment, and profits, all three have become Japanese products.

The moral of the story is clear. Those who can make a product cheaper can take it away from the inventor. In today's world it does very little good to invent a new product if the inventor is not the cheapest producer of that product. What necessity forced upon West Germany and Japan thirty years ago happens to be the right long-run R&D strategy today. . . .

In the twenty-first century man-made comparative advantage, with an emphasis on process technologies, will be the starting point for economic competition. Many parts of the world are going to develop strategies to capture what they see as the key industries of the future. As in chess, the economic player who is planning his game five moves ahead loses to the player that is thinking six moves ahead. . . .

Skills

While technology creates man-made comparative advantage, seizing that man-made comparative advantage requires a work force skilled from top to bottom. The skills of the labor force are going to be the key competitive weapon in the twenty-first century. Brainpower will create new technologies, but skilled labor will be the arms and legs that allow one to employ—to be the low-cost masters of—the new product and process technologies that are being generated. In the century ahead natural resources, capital, and new-product technologies are going to rapidly move around the world. People will move—but more slowly than anything else. Skilled people become the only sustainable competitive advantage.

If the route to success is inventing new products, the education of the smartest 25 percent of the labor force is critical. Someone in that top group will invent the new products of tomorrow. If the route to success is being the cheapest and best producer of products, new or old, the education of the bottom 50 percent of the population moves to center stage. This part of the population must staff those new processes. If the bottom 50 percent cannot learn what must be learned, new high-tech processes cannot be employed.

Firms have to be able to use new computer-based CAD-CAM technologies, employ statistical quality control, manage just-in-time inventories, and operate flexible manufacturing systems. Information technologies have to be integrated into the entire production process, from initial designs through marketing to final sales and supporting services such as maintenance. To do this requires the office, the factory, the retail store, and the repair service to have average workers with levels of education and skill that they have never had to have in the past. To employ statistical quality control, every production worker must be taught some simple operations research. To learn what must be learned, every worker must have a level of basic mathematics that is far beyond that achieved by most American high school graduates. Without statistical quality control, today's high-density semiconductor chips cannot be built. They can be invented, but they cannot be built.

In a global economy where goods can be sourced in low-wage Third World countries, the effective supply of unskilled workers has expanded enormously. As a consequence, wages must fall for the unskilled who live in rich countries. Quite simply, supply and demand require it. In a global economy a worker has two things to offer—skills or the willingness to work for low wages. Since products can be built anywhere, the unskilled who live in rich societies must work for the wages of the equally unskilled who live in poor societies. If they won't work for such wages, unskilled jobs simply move to poor countries[13]. . . .

If sustainable competitive advantage swirls around work-force skills, Anglo-Saxon firms have a problem. Human-resource management is not traditionally seen as central to the competitive survival of the firm in America or Great Britain. Skill acquisition is an individual responsibility, and business firms exist to beat wages down. Labor is simply another factor of production to be hired—rented at the lowest possible cost—much as one buys raw materials or equipment. Workers are not members of the team. Adversarial labor-management relations are part of the system.

The lack of importance attached to human-resource management can be seen in the corporate pecking order. In an American firm the chief financial officer (CFO), is almost always second in the pecking order. The post of head of human resource management is usually a specialized, off-at-the-edge-of-the-corporation job, and the executive who holds it is never consulted on major strategic decisions and has no chance to move up to chief executive officer (CEO). By way of contrast, in Japan the head of human resource management is usually the second most important person after the CEO. To become CEO, it is a job that one must have held.

While American firms often talk about the vast amounts spent on training their work forces, in fact, they invest less in the skills of their workers than do either Japanese or German firms. What they do invest is also more highly concentrated on professional and managerial employees. The more limited investments that are made in average workers are also much more narrowly focused on the specific skills necessary to do the next job rather than on the basic background skills that make it possible to absorb new technologies.

As a result, problems emerge when new breakthrough technologies arrive. If American workers, for example, take much longer to learn to operate new flexible manufacturing stations than those in Germany (as they do), the effective costs of buying those flexible manufacturing stations is lower in Germany than it is in the United States. More time is required before equipment is up and running at capacity, and the need for extensive retraining generates costs and creates bottlenecks that limit the speed with which new equipment can be employed. The result is less American investment and a slower pace of technical change.

In Germany there is an extensive training system for the non-college bound. The non-college bound enter a dual school-industry apprenticeship system at age fifteen to sixteen. At the end of three years, after passing written and practical examinations, they become journeymen with known skill levels. After another three years of work and additional courses in business management, law, and technology, a journeyman can become a master—a credential necessary to open one's own business.[14] Outside observers often cite this training system as the key ingredients in German economic success. The Germans are not the best educated at the top (America, with its superb graduate schools, is far better at this level), nor are they the best educated at the very bottom (the Japanese win there), but they are the world's very best over a broad range of midlevel, noncollege skills.

In the end the skills of the bottom half of the population affect the wages of the top half. If the bottom half can't effectively staff the processes that have to be operated, the management and professional jobs that go with these processes disappear. This effect can be seen in something near and dear to my heart. American economics professors make two to three times as much money as British economics professors but 20 to 30 percent less than German economics professors. We do so not because we know more economics than the British and less economics than the Germans but because we play on a more productive team than the British and a less productive team than the Germans. The quality of my team makes a difference to my income.

NEW RULES FOR PLAYING THE GAME

The late 1920s and early 1930s began with a series of worldwide financial crashes that ultimately spiraled downward into the Great Depression. As GNPs fell, the dominant countries each created trading blocks (the Japanese Co-Prosperity Sphere, the British Empire, the French Union, Germany plus eastern Europe, America with its Monroe Doctrine) to minimize imports and preserve jobs. If only one country had kept imports out, limiting imports would have helped it avoid the Great Depression, but with everyone restricting trade, the downward pressures were simply magnified. In the aggregate, fewer imports must equal fewer exports. Eventually, those economic blocks evolved into military blocks, and World War II began.

In the aftermath of World War II, the GATT-Bretton Woods trading system was built to prevent a repetition of these events. Trade restrictions and tariff barriers were gradually reduced in a series of trading rounds such as the Kennedy round or the Tokyo round. Under the rules, each country had to treat all other countries in exactly the same way—the most-favored-nation principle. The best deal (the lowest tariffs, the easiest access, the fewest restrictions) given to anyone must be given to everyone–effectively prohibiting trading blocks.

This system . . . was unilateral in that the United States was "single-handedly prepared to direct and maintain the system." The dollar was the medium of exchange and the standard of value. America was the manager of the system. It practiced "global Keynesianism" (tightening monetary and fiscal policies when inflation threatened; loosening monetary and fiscal politics when recession threatened) so that it could be an economic locomotive for the rest of the world. It provided a "market of first resort" where countries could export relatively easily and the United States did not insist on strict reciprocity in its commercial dealings with other countries. The system was also very Anglo-Saxon—a universal rule-driven system as opposed to a deal-driven system.

America performed these functions not because it was altruistic, although it might have been, but because, as the world's biggest economy, it had more to gain from an open global economy than anyone else. America believed that it could not be prosperous unless the world was prosperous and everyone had equal access to raw materials and markets.

History will record that the GATT-Bretton Woods trading system was one of the world's all-time great successes. In the forty years after it was adopted, the world economy grew faster than it had grown in all of human history. That growth was also much more widely shared. With the exception of a handful of countries, mostly in Africa, everyone had much higher real per capita incomes in 1990 than they had had in 1945. Where the United States was once much richer than the rest of the world, by the late 1980s it had become just one of a number of approximately equally wealthy countries. As America's position shifted from one of effortless economic superiority to one of equality. . . .

In the first three decades after World War II, everyone played a win-win economic game. Imports that looked small to the United States (3 to 5 percent of GNP) provided large markets to the rest of the world because of America's great wealth and giant size. Export opportunities were abundant for anyone who wanted to sell in the U.S. market, and the jobs that were associated with these exports were high-wage jobs by the standards of the exporting countries. Viewed from the American perspective, these imports were not threatening. Foreign market shares were small, and import penetration came in what were in America labor-intensive, low-wage industries that were being phased out anyway.

These imports were just an expression of what came to be known as the "product cycle." America would invent a new high-tech product and learn to mass produce it. Gradually, the product would shift to being a mid-tech product best produced in mid-wage countries such as Japan or Europe, from whence it would eventually move as a low-tech product to low-wage countries in the Third World.

Balancing America's trading accounts was not a problem. America could grow farm products that the rest of the world could not grow, supply raw materials such as oil that the rest of the world did not have, and manufacture unique high-tech products such as the Boeing 707 that the rest of the world could not build. America's exports did not compete with products from the rest of the world. They filled gaps that the rest of the world could not fill. In the jargon of today's strategic planners, each country had a noncompetitive niche where it could be a winner. America grew rapidly; the rest of the world grew even more rapidly.

Because of its size, America served as a locomotive for the world economy. When the system was established, memories of the Great Depression were still sharp. Whenever the world sank into a recession, to prevent it from becoming a depression the United States would use its fiscal and monetary policies to stimulate demand—benefiting both American and foreign producers. Foreign exports to America would rise, pulling the exporting countries out of their economic slump. With higher export earnings, these countries would buy more unique American products.

But with success, the American locomotive gradually grew too small to pull the rest of the world. The last gasp of the old macroeconomic locomotive was seen in the aftermath of the 1981–1982 recession. American macroeconomic stimulus, starting in the fall of 1982, pulled the industrial world out of its sharpest post-World War II recession. In 1983 and 1984 most of the growth in both Europe and Japan could be traced to exports to the American market. But for the first time the United States found itself burdened with a large trade deficit as a consequence. It's exports did not automatically rise to balance its imports.

America's effortless exports were a thing of the past. The green revolution in the developed and underdeveloped world had sharply curtailed foreign markets for American farm products. America had gradually shifted from being a large exporter of raw materials, such as oil, to being a large importer. The unique high-tech products that the rest of the world could not build had disappeared in a world of technical parity. They could be gotten many other places. What in the past had been a temporary cyclical trade deficit became a permanent structural trade deficit. . . .

In response, slowly but surely, trade is increasingly being managed by governments. Nontariff import barriers are rising everywhere. . . .

To work, a multipolar, integrated, open world economy requires fiscal and monetary coordination among the major countries—Germany, Japan, and the United States. A common locomotive is needed, and it can only exist if the major countries stimulate or restrict their economies in unison. . . .

Coordination is one of those words that is easy to say but hard to do. It means that each country must occasionally take actions that it does not want to take. The reasons for the resistance to coordination are easy to understand. In February 1991 Germany and America would have had to agree on whether the world's major problem was recession or inflation. Coordination would have required the United States to balance its budget to allow the world to move to lower real interest rates. The world needs more savings to handle the investment demands of the Second World and Third World and to repair the damage in Kuwait. America should not be the world's biggest borrower. But Americans neither want to raise taxes nor cut government services. . . .

The need to construct a new macroeconomic locomotive has gotten a lot of attention, if not much action, but a market of first resort is no less important. All of the successful developing countries in the past half century have gone through a phase where they sent most of their exports to the United States. The United States has effectively been the open market of first resort on which any country that wished to join the industrial world focused its attention during the takeoff phase of economic growth. . . . While America represents only 23 percent of world GNP, in 1987 it took 48 percent of the manufactured exports from all of the Third World countries combined.[15] In contrast, the European Economic Community (EEC) took 29 percent and Japan, 12 percent. Yet the aggregate EEC GNP is larger than that of the United States, and Japan's GNP is only 40 percent smaller. Earlier, during the dollar-shortage era of the 1950s, Europe was equally dependent upon access to the U.S. market for its success. The United States has been the market where successful developing countries earned the foreign exchange they needed to grow.

The American market cannot forever absorb most of the exports from the Third World. At some point in the future, the United States will have to generate a trade surplus to pay interest on its accumulated international debts. When it does so, it will cut back on its foreign purchases and go through a period where its market is effectively closed to developing countries.

Everyone is now unilaterally judging their own trade disputes—no one more so than the United States. . . . The need to do what it was designed to do—judge trade disputes and enforce decisions resolving those disputes—has only become more obvious in recent years. Increasingly, countries are making themselves judges of their own trade disputes. When this happens, multi-lateralism ceases to have any real meaning. . . .

The GATT-Bretton Woods trading system is dead. It died not in failure but at the normal end of a very successful life. Logically, a new Bretton Woods conference should now be under way. But politically, it cannot be called. Such a conference can only occur if there is a dominant political power that can force everyone to agree. In 1944 the United States was such a power (Germany and Japan were not even represented). Today there is no such power. If the Uruguay round cannot succeed, much more fundamental negotiations certainly could not succeed.

The required economic changes cannot, however, wait for the right political moment to call such a conference. Success is forcing the rules of the game to change, even if no one formally writes a new set of rules. In this case the rules of the new game will be informally written in Europe. Those who control the world's largest market get to write the rules. That is as it always has been. When the United States had the world's largest market, it got to write the rules. As the Europeans negotiate the rules for their internal common market and decide how outsiders relate to that market, they will effectively be writing the rules for world trade in the next century. Everyone else will gradually adopt Europe's rules as the world's de facto operating system.

The Europeans are going to write the rules for a system of "managed trade" and "quasi trading blocks.". . . I will call the blocks quasi trading blocks to distinguish them from the trading blocks of the 1930s. The quasi trading blocks of the 1990s will attempt to manage trade, but they will not attempt to reduce or eliminate it as the trading blocks of the 1930s did.

NEW OPPORTUNITIES

At temperatures near absolute zero, and now at much higher temperatures in some ceramic materials, superconductivity occurs. The rules that govern the propagation of electricity suddenly change. Old constants are no longer constant. New rules suddenly apply. Resistance disappears, and electrical devices that could not previously be built can now be built, but the currents that are unleashed are difficult to control.

Much the same is happening in the world economy. New players, technologies, and rules are coming together to generate an economic form of superconductivity. Old constants will have to be discarded. Suddenly, new rules will emerge in a very different game. Potentially, much more productive economies can be built, but controlling the currents that will be unleashed will be equally difficult.

NOTES

1. *The Economist,* July 28, 1990, p. 83.
2. Nomura Research Institute of America, *New Directions in Corporate Management and the Capital Market* (New York: The Institute, 1990), p. 1.
3. H. Brest, *The New Competition* (Cambridge, Mass.: Harvard University Press, 1990). Robert Kuttner, "Atlas Unburdened: America's Economic Interests in a New World Era," *The American Prospect,* Summer 1990: 90.

4. "Graduates Take Rites of Passage into Japanese Corporate Life," *Financial Times,* April 8, 1991, p. 4.
5. Masaru Yoshitomi, "Keiretsu: An Insider's Guide to Japan's Conglomerates," *International Economic Insights,* Sept/Oct 1990: 10.
6. "Inside the Charmed Circle," *The Economist,* January 5, 1991, p. 54.
Carla Rapoport, "Why Japan Keeps Winning," *Fortune,* July 15, 1991, p. 77.
7. John Dornberg, "The Spreading Might of Deutsche Bank," *New York Times Business World,* September 23, 1990, p. 28.
8. "The Old Bank Network," *The Economist,* March 14, 1987, p. 64.
9. Council of Economic Advisers, *Economic Report of the President, 1990* (Washington, D.C.: GPO, 1990) p. 296. U.S. Department of Commerce, *Survey of Current Business,* June 1990: S–25. U.S. Department of Commerce, *Business Statistics,* 1982 (Washington, D.C.: GPO, 1982) p. 104.
10. International Monetary Fund, *Primary Commodities: Market Development and Outlook,* July 1990: 26.
11. Joint Economic Committee of Congress, Testimony of Edwin Mansfield, 99th Cong., 1st sess., December 2, 1986, p. 4.
12. Michael L. Dertouzos, Richard Lester, and Robert Solow, *Made in America: Regaining the Productive Edge* (Cambridge, Mass.: MIT Press, 1989), p. 72. Edwin Mansfield, p. 6.
13. Walter Russell Mead, *The Low Wage Challenge to Global Growth.* (Washington, D.C.: Economic Policy Institute, 1990), p. 1.
14. William E. Nothdurft, "Reinventing Public Schools to Create the Workforce of the Future," German Marshall Fund, as summarized in *Transatlantic Perspectives,* Autumn 1989: 11.
15. World Bank, *Handbook of International Trade and Development* (Washington, D.C.: The Bank, 1989), p. A36–A37.

The Protection of the Global Environment

Managing the Global Commons

Per Magnus Wijkman

Our planet contains some natural resources over which no single nation has a generally recognized exclusive jurisdiction. Familiar examples are the resources of the continental margin and the deep seabed, the water column beyond territorial seas, celestial bodies and orbits in outer space, the electromagnetic frequency spectrum, and the Antarctic. Less familiar but ultimately more important resources are the planet's ozone layer and carbon dioxide balance.

These resources have long been a global commons, free of national or international regulations. With growing world population and improving technology, however, the absence of exclusive property rights and well-defined management rights is leading inevitably to economic inefficiency and to international contention. Garrett Hardin's "tragedy of the commons" is enacted through depletion of fishing stocks and the ozone layer, congestion of orbital slots by satellites, and overheating of the atmosphere.[1] Once theoretical possibilities, these are now acute problems.

Increasing awareness of the need to manage the global commons has led to attempts to redefine property rights. The effect of these ongoing negotiations within and without the United Nations Organization has been to award some resources to the international community and others to nation states.[2]

This development evokes several major questions. Will national jurisdiction over resources that traditionally have been open to all increase or decrease the efficiency of exploitation? How will extension of national jurisdiction over previously shared resources redistribute income between countries? Should national or international organizations manage these resources?[3]

This article considers these fundamental policy issues. Section I considers why firms or individuals may prefer communal ownership to private ownership, while Section II considers why governments may favor internationally shared jurisdiction over national jurisdiction. In both cases, joint ownership or management confers economic benefits at the price of some elements of sovereignty; and the more extensive are the joint management powers involved, the greater the costs in terms of abrogated sovereignty. Section III outlines an international organization for efficiently managing a common resource (assuming that the parties can agree on the distribution of its benefits). Section IV considers some current proposals for managing internationally shared resources and illustrates the practical problems involved in achieving agreement. It assesses whether the proposed regimes are efficient and pays particular attention to how the new entitlements will redistribute income between countries.

I. WHY COMMONS EXIST

A commons is a resource to which no single decision-making unit holds exclusive title. This can mean that it is owned by no one (*res nullius*) or by everyone (*res communis*). This seems an anomaly in a world of private property and national jurisdiction. Why does it persist?

Traditionally, access to a commons has been free for all, and any individual could exploit the resource independently of others. As long as the resource is plentiful, users are unlikely to interfere with each other. However, when it becomes scarce, uncontrolled access results in congestion and overuse. Access must be limited in some way to prevent use by one from inflicting costs on another. One possibility is to subdivide the resource and award each commoner private property rights to some part of it, leaving to each new owner the decision on how to use his own share. I shall call this procedure "enclosing the commons," in reference to the most famous historical example—enclosure of the village commons.[4]

While private ownership and national appropriation have been usual historically, dissolution of the commons is not the inevitable outcome. Another possibility is for the users or other interested parties to form an organization to manage the resource jointly. Which form of management and ownership is more efficient depends on the relative costs and benefits of extending property rights in each particular case.[5]

If exclusive ownership reduces interference, enclosure should both result in more efficient use and conserve the resource. If these benefits exceed the costs of negotiating, transacting, and policing enclosure, subdivision should be socially profitable. However, these costs are not always included though they are often considerable. In the past, some users excluded others without compensation and some existing users forcibly prevented new entry.[6] Uncompensated appropriation has been frequent historically, and even the Third United Nations Conference on the Law of the Sea (UNCLOS III) does not require coastal states to pay when they extend their resource jurisdiction seaward. Excessive claims result when possibly valuable resources can be obtained for free.

Enclosure will come about through market forces if actual or potential users can buy out others and still be better off. Assume, for instance, that the commons is appropriated by giving all commoners transferable rights to use the resource. Voluntary market transactions may, as a first step, consolidate user rights in the hands of a limited number of users. As a second step, these owners may agree to divide the commons into private lots of sizes proportional to their user rights if the economic benefits of enclosure exceed its costs. Voluntary, informed market transactions will provide the optimal amount of enclosure. Such transactions have the additional advantage that those who give up user rights are adequately compensated by those who gain property rights. Enclosure through markets is a Pareto-sanctioned change; that is, society as a whole benefits from the introduction of private property rights and no single member is worse off as a result.

Unfortunately, the legal nature of communally owned resources usually precludes the existence of marketable user rights. Enclosure must be accomplished by means other than market forces. Unless legislative measures determine whether enclosure occurs, might becomes right and possession becomes nine-tenths of the law. The English enclosure movement provides notable examples during the last half of the nineteenth century of legislative measures designed to ensure that those who lost rights through enclosure were compensated by those who gained.

While a failure to pay adequate compensation stimulates private or state appropriation of the commons, three other factors work to maintain communal ownership: high risks associated with subdividing resources of uncertain value, high costs of defining and policing private property rights or enforcing national jurisdiction, and significant external economies in production. By contrast, prime candidates for enclosure are those resources that are easily subdivided, have a definite value, and lack external economies.

When the value of the resource being divided is uncertain, an individual nation risks obtaining a worthless share. This risk is especially great when the resource consists of heterogeneous parts about which a government lacks information. It must invest resources in finding out which fishing grounds are richer than others, which orbital slots are more useful than others, or which nodule fields are cheaper to mine than others. Already complex political negotiations to divide a resource become even more difficult to resolve when the value of the resource is also at issue. The key element in these negotiations is determining appropriate compensation upon enclosure. Two basic issues are involved—how to divide the resource and distribute its parts between the new owners, and how to compensate those who lose historical rights. These issues require assessing the value of respective user rights in order to determine how much a user either should pay to acquire property rights or should receive to part with user rights. Of course, a decision *not* to compensate is a possible outcome of negotiations: Only some commoners may receive property rights, those who do may receive their deeds gratis, and losers of historical rights may not be compensated.

Subdividing and distributing in parts of a largely unexplored resource more closely resembles a lottery than a deliberate distribution of wealth. A government averse to risk may prefer to own a share in the whole asset rather than to subdivide an asset the value of whose parts is uncertain, especially if the administrative costs of communal ownership are small. This preference saves both the prospecting cost necessary to reduce risk and the cost of negotiating a subdivision of the commons.

In addition, private ownership of the parts of a commons may be impractical or undesirable when property rights to parts of the resource cannot be economically enforced (the resource is not divisible); when the size of the resource is unknown; and when exploitation of the resource involves external economies. Resources possessing these characteristics are sometimes called common property resources.[7] Considerations of economic efficiency caution against enclosing such common property resources and argue for communal ownership and joint management. Consider some examples of this important group of resources.

Many oil or water pools and fishing stocks are shared by several owners or are under the jurisdiction of several nations. Enclosing part of an oil or water pool . . . or a fishing ground . . . common to several parties may be prohibitively expensive. Fluid flows among sections of the pool indiscriminately; fishing stocks migrate among different areas of the shared habitat in the course of their life cycles.

When a habitat cannot be enclosed at reasonable cost, it is necessary to enforce property rights to the individual animals. Sometimes this is feasible; large animals with a tendency to move in herds (such as reindeer, cattle, and goats) can be rounded up, caught, and marked at little cost relative to their value. If property rights can be enforced in the face of poaching and rustling, the animals can graze on the common habitat. In other cases, as with most fish and fowl, the costs of acquiring and enforcing property rights to individual animals are too high.[8] Even such large animals as whales are prohibitively expensive to mark. In these cases, the animals themselves are a common property resource.

An important consequence for public resource policy follows from failure to define and enforce property rights. When several owners have overlapping rights to a resource, it is rational for each to attempt to exploit the resource before the others. Such competition depletes stocks, and fisheries provide many familiar examples of this process. To maintain the resource, whether grazing ground or herd, at an optimal level, the user rights of commoners must be restricted. Restriction can take the form of a voluntary agreement by the joint owners to exclude new entrants and to limit their own use of the resource. This requires a unanimous decision by all the parties that claim user rights to the resource.

When the precise size of the resource is unknown, harvesting quotas may be difficult to establish.[9] Often the parties sharing a resource cannot agree upon its size due, perhaps, to insufficient prospecting or to imperfect prospecting techniques. For instance, the sampling necessary to estimate the size of fishing stocks is so extensive that an estimate with a normal margin of error is prohibitively expensive to obtain. Thus, policy makers are usually uncertain about the size of individual fish stocks.

Resource size may be uncertain also because it is determined by available production technology and by relative factor and commodity prices; as these change, so does the size of the resource. For instance, the amount of "recoverable oil" in a well depends among other considerations on the price of oil. Similarly, the number of telecommunications that the electromagnetic spectrum can accommodate depends on production technology and on the amount of capital invested in sending and receiving equipment. The size of many important natural resources is thus inherently uncertain because it depends on changing economic and technological factors. Finally, even if the size of the resource can be known accurately, owners may have different views on what size is optimal to maintain because they employ different interest rates to discount future benefits. In theory, the parties can achieve a mutually beneficial solution in these cases if capital movements are free or if side-payments are allowed.[10] But in practice this is not always possible.

Even if the owners could agree both on the actual and on the desired size of the resource, and on each other's share of the harvest, the occurrence of external economies creates problems when each exploits his own share of the resource independently of the others.[11] While the parts of a resource might be legally separated, they are then joined through production effects and can be exploited separately only at extra cost. Assume that a firm from country A is the first to drill an oil or artesian well . . . or to fish the grounds. . . . This exploitation lowers the pressure in the common pool or thins the common fishing stock and raises costs for a firm from country B that arrives later to pump from the pool or to catch fish. The prospect of lower exploitation costs prompts each co-owner of a shared resource to extract his share of the resource first. In this way, external economies lead to an overly rapid rate of harvesting. To prevent this, production quotas must be expressed as a flow (units per time period) rather than as a share of the resource stock.

In summary, the crucial characteristic of common property resources is that property rights to parts of the resource cannot be economically defined and enforced. Additional complications in sharing the resource arise when the size of the resource is unknown and its exploitation involves significant external economies. In such a situation the many small firms of the perfectly competitive model fail to exploit the resource efficiently. Each firm lacks incentives to limit its harvest and strives instead to exploit the resource before its competitors do, thereby harvesting more and faster than is socially efficient. Not only is the resource depleted, but too much capital and labor are employed in the industry. Rational pursuit of private profit by firms is therefore wasteful of capital, labor, and natural resources alike.

II. COOPERATIVE OR COERCIVE MANAGEMENT

Some form of regulation is necessary to realize fully the economic benefits from exploiting common property resources. I shall discuss first the problems of regulation when the participating parties agree to maximize pecuniary benefits and agree on their distribution. The main issue in this case is whether management can be based on voluntary cooperation or requires some coercive power. Thereafter, I shall discuss some of the problems that arise when countries include nonpecuniary

or political benefits among their objectives, which makes agreement more difficult.

Regulation can be organized either by the private interests involved in exploiting the resource or by a public authority endowed with coercive powers. Sometimes private interests find it profitable to regulate use of the resource themselves
on a voluntary basis. This is likely to occur if only a few owners have overlapping
rights to the resource. For instance, if two firms of roughly equal size share the
resource . . . and neither can be certain of being the first to exploit it, an awareness
of the external economies could influence them to coordinate their exploitation.
They could set up a joint venture (i.e., drilling one oil well) if each believes that its
share of the larger joint profits available through coordinated effort will exceed
what it would get through individual, uncoordinated exploitation (i.e., drilling two
independent oil wells). Joint ventures are a way to internalize externalities and to
approximate the efficiency of sole ownership.

When firms are few and of equal size, and have similar perceptions of the
future, each may find it advantageous to coordinate use of the commons. Thus, voluntary regulation may achieve efficient use.[12]

When many firms exploit the resource . . . and interfere with one another's
activities, public regulation is necessary. The task of the manager is to restrict the
commoners' rights of access and to coordinate exploitation in order to minimize
externalities. The selection of appropriate regulatory tools is a complex issue, not
treated here. The basic choices are regulating by means of quotas, by taxes and
subsidies, or by a system of liability rules enforced through the courts.

The difficult problems of public regulation are compounded when the common property resource is internationally shared and several governments are
involved. A key question is whether these governments will voluntarily cooperate
in managing the resource. Failing cooperation, efficient regulation requires use of
coercive powers, that is, creation of a management authority with the power to
impose its decisions on any uncooperative co-owner of the resource. Few examples
of this exist in fact, and in this section I suggest why this is so.

The prospects for voluntary joint management depend critically on how many
governments share the resource. If two governments share it equally . . . both may
perceive the interdependence of their national harvests. Each government therefore has an incentive to agree to control the rate and the amount of exploitation of
the shared resource by its own nationals. It will do this only if it can rely on the
other government's willingness and ability to enforce its part of the agreement.[13]

The greater the number of nations sharing resource jurisdiction, the less likely
it is that voluntary agreements between governments to manage the resource will
work. Each government is a potential free rider on any management regime; each
is tempted clandestinely to ignore the system of production controls that it espous-
es publicly. This occurs when the individual government retains all the benefits of
cheating but bears only a small fraction of the costs.[14] Voluntary agreements among
many governments quickly break down—they contain strong incentives to cheat
and they lack effective enforcement mechanisms. The history of international
fisheries commissions is replete with examples of ineffectual voluntary agreements
to limit harvest of the stocks, the best known, perhaps, being the Northeast

Atlantic Fisheries Commission. When many governments share a resource, the management authority must be given power to determine harvesting limitations unilaterally and to enforce the observance of national quotas allocated within this general limit. Management of the commons requires, in Garrett Hardin's words, a "system of mutual coercion mutually agreed upon."

Most governments are reluctant on principle to surrender sovereignty even in minor issues. Substantive factors contribute to this reluctance. Sovereignty allows a government greater freedom in formulating its policy goals and a greater choice of instruments with which to pursue these goals. The more a government's goals differ from those of others, the greater the perceived cost of surrendering sovereignty. For instance, a government may want its nationals to participate in production not solely to generate profits but also to ensure security of supply of strategic commodities, to maintain employment in a particular occupation or region, or to increase national prestige. Several governments view deep seabed mining as important for each of these different reasons. No standard exists by which to measure the value of one unit of nonpecuniary benefit: the value of a given level of self-sufficiency or of employment maintenance can only be determined by the government concerned, and it will differ from government to government. Consequently, the distribution of nonpecuniary benefits by an international bureaucracy is inherently arbitrary. If these values are important to a country, it will preserve its freedom to pursue them and will be reluctant to depend on other nations' decisions. This complicates the management of common property resources, since countries have non-comparable objectives.

In summary, economically efficient exploitation of global common property resources requires restrictions on national sovereignty. Governments must abide by decisions made by a supranational authority and accept supranational enforcement of these decisions. The "tragedy of the commons" occurs on the international level because governments are either unable to design appropriate international authorities or unwilling to accept the consequent "stinting" of their national sovereign rights. The basic reason for this reluctance is the absence of a sufficient community of interest among the participating governments. A government that holds minority opinions is unlikely to surrender power to an authority where it may be outvoted consistently, even if this refusal entails an economic loss.

III. A MANAGEMENT PARADIGM

Section I gave some reasons why internationally shared resources may remain under communal ownership and shared jurisdiction in spite of the historical trend to private ownership and national jurisdiction. Defining and enforcing property rights may make subdivision unreasonably expensive; if subdivision is possible, it may reduce efficiency because individual owners cannot exploit their parts independently of each other, or it may increase their risk because of the uncertain value of the parts they receive. Finally, like heirs to an estate, the commoners simply may fail to agree on how to divide the inheritance and none may be inclined to appropriate it unilaterally. When a scarce resource is maintained as a commons for any of the above reasons, open access will result in inefficient use. Section II considered the conditions under which voluntary cooperation between governments was unlikely to occur. When many governments are involved, efficient management requires the creation of a supranational authority. A government will surrender jurisdiction only if it feels it has sufficient common interests with other governments. Inevitably, some governments will not feel that this is the case.

This section presents a paradigm of an international management institution in order to illustrate clearly the different interests involved. Any management regime for common property resources discharges three primary functions. First, it assesses the harvesting or carrying capacity of the commons and determines an annual quota to be harvested. Second, it allocates rights to participate in harvesting this quota. Third, it distributes the benefits derived from exploiting the resource among its co-owners. A condominium designed to exercise separately each of these functions of allocation, distribution, and scientific assessment provides a useful comparison norm when analyzing management problems.[15] I shall use it to distinguish reconcilable from irreconcilable conflicts of interest between parties.

Allocation of User Rights

Deciding who gets to use a scarce common resource is a controversial issue when valuable rights are given away for free. Nonmarket methods of allocating rights of access to a resource are inherently discretionary and inevitably arbitrary. An alternative is the market method, whereby the right of access is sold on an open market. For instance, leases to drill on the continental shelf to log public forest lands in the United States are commonly sold at public auctions. The first task of the condominium is to auction user rights to the resource.

Competitive bidding ensures that the most efficient firms obtain harvesting rights, since normally they outbid less efficient firms. In the absence of monopoly power this minimizes production costs, which benefits consumers, and maximizes rents from the commons, which benefits its owners. A user fee that reflects the scarcity value of the natural resource provides users with the information they need to produce commodities with the least possible expenditure of real resources. Resources are thereby put to the best possible use.[16]

Nonmarket methods mean that an institution other than the market assigns access rights according to some criterion other than the users' willingness to pay. Bureaucratic allocation normally results in less efficient production, since it allows less efficient firms to produce. Discrimination on the grounds of equity rather than of efficiency has been claimed to be justified when granting access to common property resource. Each co-owner, it is claimed, should have "equal" use of the resource. However, this is the case only if economic institutions are imperfect. An efficient allocation results in greater pecuniary benefits and is therefore preferable if social institutions (tax and transfer systems) exist to redistribute those benefits in a generally acceptable manner.

As noted previously, access to a common property resource may provide a government with nonpecuniary benefits. However, this is not an argument for non-market methods of allocating user rights—on the contrary. By their nature, nonpecuniary benefits are distributed imperfectly by bureaucracies. Market methods of allocation allow a government that values nonpecuniary benefits highly to reflect its evaluation in a premium on its bid for user rights. Ironically, market methods achieve the most efficient allocation of nonpecuniary benefits. Also, it is just as illogical from a distributional viewpoint for the international community to provide nonpecuniary benefits to a government free of charge as it is for it to provide pecuniary benefits gratis.

The distribution of pecuniary benefits, not the allocation of user rights, is therefore the key to achieving equity.

Distribution of Pecuniary Benefits

A commons generates three forms of pecuniary benefits. Rents from the natural resource normally accrue to its owner; producers' surplus accrues to the firms that use the resource as an input to produce commodities; and, finally, consumers' surplus is enjoyed by those who consume these commodities or their close substitutes. Residents of a country benefit from increased exploitation of a communally owned resource to the extent that they can claim some of the resource rents, and consume or produce commodities (or close substitutes) that use the resource as an input. For instance, low-cost seabed production of nickel lowers its price, benefits consumers, and harms landbased producers, in addition to providing benefits in the form of seabed rents.

The second task of the condominium is to accommodate the conflicting interests of nations as consumers, producers, and *rentiers* by providing a mechanism to distribute rents and to transfer income from consumers to existing producers. I shall treat these functions separately for clarity.

Rents can be distributed by awarding nations shares in the condominium, shares that entitle them to a portion of the revenues generated by auctioning user rights to the highest bidder. The initial distribution of shares between nations must reflect a consensus about the appropriate distribution of rents from the commons. On this political question opinions will inevitably differ; the following factors are bound to enter into the decision. First, it is necessary to identify those who are entitled to claim an ownership interest in the commons. Is a resource the property of a few states, or is it the common heritage of mankind? If the latter, what representative of mankind is the appropriate recipient of shares in the condominium? Shares could be distributed to individuals themselves, to national governments as representatives of individuals, or to the United Nations and its agencies as representatives of national governments.[17] There is clearly a trade-off between the degree of representativeness of a given distribution and the transaction costs it entails. The most representative alternative—distributing rents directly to each individual—involves high transaction costs. Letting the United Nations Organization receive the rents involves the lowest transaction costs but is less representative. An intermediate solution is to distribute the shares in the condominium to national governments. They could be distributed in proportion to the population subject to each national government, on the assumption that each person has an equal claim on rents from the commons. But there is no *objective* basis for determining the best distribution. The explicit determination of national interests in a commons is probably the most emotionally loaded aspect of management.

Since countries consume and produce in different proportions those commodities that use the communally owned resource as an input, exploitation of the commons will change consumer and producer surplus for most countries. This redistribution of benefits can be so large that the losers demand compensation before they will permit exploitation of the commons (if this is in their power). For instance, the government of a land-based producer of copper and nickel can expect to lose significant amounts of producer surplus and tax revenues when seabed mining starts; a net consuming country will gain a substantial consumer surplus. The condominium may therefore have to set up a compensation fund to effect lump-sum transfers from consumer to producer nations. Ideally, governments of net consumer countries would annually pay into this fund an amount reflecting their gain of consumer surplus, while governments of traditional net producer countries would receive corresponding payments from the fund. These payments and disbursements should be assessed separately from the determination of the international distribution of rents for two reasons. First, national consumption and production patterns change more rapidly than population, requiring more frequent reassessments of compensation payments than of rents. Second, the distribution of rents is a permanent phenomenon while it can be argued that compensation payments should be transitory.

The distribution of shares in the condominium and the establishment of a compensation fund would inevitably be subject to intense controversy. This is desirable, because it would force an explicit discussion of the distribution of benefits and would separate decisions about who gets the rents from decisions about who gets to exploit the resource. This is a major advantage of the proposed condominium: In sum, rents are distributed at the conference table and user rights are allocated in the marketplace. The resource can therefore be managed efficiently while demands for equity can be satisfied through political compromise. The cost of failing to strike a compromise can be measured as the reduced efficiency in exploiting the commons. This cost is likely to materialize when government views on equity consist of mutually inconsistent claims for absolute levels of income or shares in decision-making powers.

Determination of Harvesting Capacity

Decentralized decision making by private firms or individuals who possess perfect information and well-defined property rights, and act on competitive markets, results in efficient allocation of resources among competing present and future uses. This well-known and attractive property of competitive markets is lost in the case of common property resources. Market imperfections caused by external economies and by the absence of effective property rights must be corrected by a central decision maker.

The third task of the condominium, therefore, is to determine the optimal rate at which the resource should be harvested and to ensure that this rate is not exceeded. This is normally a very complex task since the optimal harvesting rate must be determined in spite of imperfect knowledge of the state of the resource, changing costs of production, and difficult time preferences of consumer nations. In addition, the condominium must have the authority and the resources to enforce observance of its rulings. Ideally the scientific council would be independent of national producer and consumer interests. This might be achieved if council members were to be nominated by national academies of science and voted for by governments with votes proportionate to their share in resource rents. This might encourage a decision-making structure that maximizes rents. However, achieving such an institution encounters problems familiar from the theory of regulation and public choice.[18] I shall not deal with this complex issue here.

International resource commissions have seldom been empowered to exercise all three of the above functions. A classic exception is the Interim Convention on the Conservation of North Pacific Fur Seals of 1957, which the U.S. Senate is currently considering extending. The fur seal breeds on North Pacific islands under the sovereignty of the Soviet Union and of the United States, in particular the Pribilof Islands. In the nineteenth century, hunters from these two countries and Japan and Canada caught seals as common property on the high seas and depleted the herd. The 1957 Convention, like its predecessor of 1912, bans open-sea hunting. A North Pacific Fur Seal Commission coordinates research to determine the maximum sustainable yield. Hunting is limited to the breeding islands, where the agreed-upon quota is caught by local hunters employed by Soviet and U.S. government agencies. Profits from the commercial sale of pelts are shared with Japan and Canada, whose citizens must abstain from their traditional high-seas hunting. The Pribilof Treaty contains on a small scale the elements of an efficient management regime for a common property resource: an efficient allocation and enforcement of harvesting rights, an acceptable distribution of the resource rents among the interested parties, and a scientifically determined harvesting quota. The question is whether such a management regime can be duplicated when more countries are involved. . . .

IV. CURRENT MANAGEMENT PROPOSALS

Technical progress has opened previously inaccessible resources for exploitation. As the exploitation of marginal resources becomes worthwhile, prime resources generate more rents. Distrustful of international organizations, nations strive to enclose the resources and to appropriate the rents. The common heritage is thus transformed into national inheritances.

Whether national enclosure is more efficient than managing these resources through a supranational resource regime, and whether it is as fair, must be judged from case to case. It depends on the answers to three questions. First, does the resource possess such common property characteristics that coordination of use provides benefits sufficiently large to offset the management costs? Second, can the voluntary cooperation of co-owners achieve coordinated use more cheaply than a centralized decision-making authority? Third, how do awards of new property rights and the loss of historical rights affect the distribution of wealth?. . .

Fisheries and Antarctic living resources fall in the category of resources that are costly to subdivide. The amount harvested must be limited and harvesting rights allocated. The difficulties of the distributional issue are compounded by efficiency considerations. The resources of the deep seabed and the continental margin constitute a commons that can be partitioned, and its parts individually exploited, without much extra cost. Subdivision poses mainly a question of equity, and the primary function of an international authority should be to negotiate an acceptable initial distribution of private property rights. . . .

Fishing Stocks

Fishing stocks are a classic example of a common property resource. Early in the Third United Nations Conference on the Law of the Sea delegates agreed on the principle of an exclusive economic zone (EEZ), whereby each coastal state would be granted exclusive management and fishing rights within two hundred nautical miles of its coastline. In most cases, this broader includes the continental shelf, in whose shallow waters are located the richest fishing grounds. The world's annual fish catch was worth close to $20 billion in the late seventies, and virtually all of this is caught in the proposed EEZs. Thus, UNCLOS III proposes in effect that eighty coastal states enclose the world's major fishing grounds.[19]

For the purpose of conserving fishing stocks, two hundred-mile EEZs are superior to the current regime of nonexistent or voluntary management, but they probably are inferior to a supranational management regime. National management will result in efficient management of stocks only if the extension of fishing limits brings the fishing stock, and sometimes also the fish it preys upon and those that prey upon it, entirely within the coastal state's jurisdiction. The key question therefore is how often this occurs. Many stocks that migrate along coasts remain transboundary resources even after the outward extension of fishing limits. In Africa, where coastlines tend to be short, fishing stocks pass through the waters of several countries in their seasonal or life-cycle migrations. The waters of both Chile and Peru contain the Pacific anchovy stock; the North Sea remains a common fishing ground for five European countries. Georges Bank is shared by Canada and the United States, even with limits of two hundred nautical miles. With some exceptions—Icelandic cod is notable—major fishing stocks will remain common property resources, though common now to fewer states than before.

The fewer the states, the more willing each government will be to limit the catch in its EEZ and to rely on other governments' promises to do likewise. Will this extension of fishing limits reduce the number of co-owners of fishing stocks sufficiently to induce effective voluntary cooperation? The answer to this requires a detailed study stock by stock, but no such studies were made prior to UNCLOS

III. Thus, its Draft Convention proposes dispensing management rights to coastal states without any assurances that management will be effective.*

In addition to imperfectly managing stocks, government will be tempted to follow protectionist policies. The political difficulties encountered by a government that attempts to introduce effective management programs should not be underestimated. Programs to control harvesting are unpopular with fishermen, who are extended fishing limits as a means to protect domestic fishermen rather than fishing stocks. The Draft Convention produced by UNCLOS III condones protectionist use of extended fishing limits. It does not require that entry to fishing grounds be controlled in a nondiscriminatory way, for example by requiring domestic and foreign fishermen to pay the same price for fishing licenses. In many of the eighty countries that now claim two hundred nautical mile fishing limits, domestic fishermen have replaced foreign fishermen and domestic political opposition has postponed the introduction of effective controls on total catch. The effect of protectionist policies is to reduce the efficiency of the world's fishing fleet by forcing parts of it to move to new waters and to convert to new types of fishing.

The Draft Convention proposals would also have significant income redistribution effects. The creation of EEZs permits the coastal state to appropriate all the rents from fishing grounds should it wish to.[20] These rents have been estimated to be at least $2 billion annually. Compared with the existing situation, this would redistribute income from nations with long-distance fishing fleets to states with long coasts bordering on rich fishing grounds. Since the richest fishing grounds, like the richest countries, are located in the temperate zones, the benefit go mainly to developed coastal states. One may debate the fairness of this redistribution, but one cannot deny either that it fails to compensate those who lose historical fishing rights or that it favors rich countries more than poor countries.

Hydrocarbon Resources and Manganese Nodules

The continental margin and the deep seabed traditionally have been international commons under the doctrine of the freedom of the high seas. However, since the Truman proclamation in 1945 an increasing number of coastal states have extended their resource jurisdiction over the adjoining continental shelf. UNCLOS III proposes to place the resources of the continental margin and those of the deep seabed under separate regimes. It would confirm the coastal states' jurisdiction over most of the continental margin while placing the remaining area of the seabed under an International Seabed Authority. Do the resource characteristics of these areas justify these different assignments?

The main resources of the deep seabed are currently believed to be manganese nodules, containing most notably manganese, nickel, cobalt, and copper. Deep-seabed mining holds out the prospect of commercial success, especially for prime mine sites in the Pacific. In the absence of limits on production the seabed might provide the major part of world consumption of these minerals in twenty or thirty years.

---

*Editor's Note: Such management by coastal states has not been effective. Overfishing has taken place and fishing stocks have been depleted.

Hydrocarbons are the main resource of the continental margin. Currently, off-shore oil and gas come entirely from the continental shelf (e.g., from the North Sea and the Gulf of Mexico); large areas remain to be exploited—Georges Bank, the Arctic Sea, and the China Sea. The average water depth of the shelf is two hundred meters. Recently, however, deposits have been discovered on the continental slope, which descends down to about two thousand meters. Recovering hydrocarbons from these water depths is already technically possible, and will become commercially feasible as the relative price of oil increases. Today offshore reserves account for about 20 percent of the world's total oil and gas production, a share that may double by the year 2000.[21]

Efficiency considerations do not justify regulating the exploitation of manganese nodules or of hydrocarbons, except in rare cases.

Manganese nodules present none of the characteristics of common property resources that make private ownership or national jurisdiction inefficient. On the contrary, efficient mining requires exclusive rights to mine a well-defined site.[22] The seabed regime proposed by UNCLOS III provides exclusive mining rights, but it also proposes to limit the volume of seabed mineral production. Pollution aside, seabed mining does not exhibit the external economies that require coordination of mining activities. Production limitation, therefore, reduces the economic efficiency of mining.

Hydrocarbon exploitation on the continental margin may provide examples of common pools, which would benefit from coordinated management. Common pools occur in the North Sea and elsewhere (e.g., fields off Newfoundland and the Aleutian Islands). However, it is unlikely that more than two governments, or one government and the International Seabed Authority, will share a pool. This increases the likelihood that the involved parties will be able to negotiate a solution to the common-pool problem on their own. Even if they cannot, this problem is likely to remain no matter where the boundary between national and international jurisdiction over resources is drawn.

In the case of the continental margin and the deep seabed, in contrast to international fisheries, efficiency considerations argue for allowing private property rights but not for imposing central production control. The primary function of an international authority should be to distribute resource rents and consumer surplus, not to regulate production. National enclosure of the deep seabed would award its rents to the new owners unless they paid a market price for seabed real estate. However, auctioning off large tracts of the seabed would favor large countries and those rich in capital, while allowing coastal states alone to enclose the deep seabed would preclude the possibility of extracting a market price. Consequently, distributional considerations argue against national enclosure of the seabed and in favor of allowing an International Seabed Authority to sell or lease mine sites at market prices and to distribute the resulting revenues among governments.

The Antarctic

The Antarctic is a disputed commons. Seven countries claim sovereignty over parts of the continent. The claims of Argentina, Chile, and the United Kingdom partially overlap; Australia, France, New Zealand, Norway, and the United Kingdom recognize one another's claims. These seven, together with six non-claimant states, are parties to the Antarctic Treaty of 1959.

The treaty is designed to ensure the exclusively peaceful use of the continent—one tenth of the globe's land surface—and to facilitate scientific research by allowing scientists access to the whole area. It sidesteps the issue of territorial claims by freezing existing claims and prohibiting new ones. It does not deal with the issue of the exploitation of Antarctic resources.

The natural resources of the Antarctic consist of onshore and offshore oil and gas reserves estimated to be about one-half of Alaskan offshore reserves.[23] There are also large but currently inaccessible coal and iron ore deposits. The living resources include fur seals, crabs, lobsters, fish, and krill; the last may be the most important. The annual sustainable catch of krill has been estimated at between 50 and 150 million tons, and thus perhaps equivalent to the current annual world catch of all other seafoods.[24]

The Treaty's tenth consultative meeting (1979) initiated negotiation of a convention to regulate the exploitation of living marine animals other than whales and fur seals (which are covered by separate conventions). The treaty, signed by the parties in December 1980, adopts a comprehensive ecosystem management approach. Krill is the base of a complex food web in the Antarctic ecosystem. The amount of krill harvested annually affects the stocks of animals that prey upon it and, in particular, affects the already severely decimated population of Antarctic baleen whales. During the Antarctic winter, these whales migrate toward the equator and are caught by countries other than Antarctic claimant states. The amount of krill harvested thus affects a group of countries and interests wider than just the krill fishing nations (USSR, Japan, West Germany) or even the thirteen nations party to the Antarctic Treaty.

Furthermore, the circular flow of ocean currents around the Antarctic continent makes the planktonic krill a common property resource. No single claimant state can by itself control the size of the stocks of krill under its jurisdiction. The governments must agree upon and enforce a common management policy and extend their jurisdiction beyond two hundred nautical miles if they are to manage all krill stocks.

Comprehensive management of the Antarctic's living resources is thus essential, and must cover the major animal groups of the food web and their habitats. It is therefore unfortunate that the harvesting of whales and seals is regulated by separate conventions. Another weakness is that the convention, while establishing a scientific committee, provides no financial support to make it independent of the treaty members; nor does it empower the committee to determine the annual harvesting capacity of the resource. There is no political mechanism to allocate national quotas, since this might prejudge the issue of territorial claims, and consequently there is no enforcement mechanism to ensure that the actual harvest does not exceed the allowable catch. Given the large number of countries involved either as claimant states or as exploiters of the resources, management based on voluntary observance may well prove ineffective. Interests not represented in the decision-making process may be especially reluctant to comply with the committee's recommendations. . . .

V. CONCLUSION

The appropriate organization for managing a commons depends on a variety of factors, the most important being why communal ownership is maintained to begin with and how many co-owners are involved.

When the resource is held as a commons simply because the parties cannot agree on how to subdivide it, the organization serves primarily to pool risks, distributing to co-owners the revenues that result from auctioning user rights.

If communal ownership is maintained because external diseconomies in resource use are significant, the organization in addition must limit production to a level that is socially optimal. When several governments share jurisdiction over the resource, interdependence between the firms exploiting it results in policy interdependence of the governments. In some countries politicians may resent this interdependence, but refusal to recognize it will result in less efficient use of the resource.

When few governments share jurisdiction over the resource, strong economic incentives exist for them to cooperate voluntarily in managing the commons in order to avoid inefficiency. They are more likely to do this if their respective national interests in the resource are roughly equal and if they share common values. On the other hand, when many governments share jurisdiction over the resource, experience shows that effective management requires that the organization have coercive powers, that is, the power to make decisions binding on members and to monitor and enforce compliance.

Sovereign governments are normally reluctant to surrender jurisdiction, although their reluctance may be less in regional organizations than in international organizations with more heterogenous membership. It is easy to despair, therefore, about the ability of international organizations to deal effectively with the problems posed by transborder fisheries, ozone layer depletion, and atmospheric carbon dioxide accumulation.

Nevertheless, let us hope that governments will be persuaded to pool modest jurisdictional powers before the global commons suffer large and irreversible damage. They may do this if they recognize that the unique physical characteristics of common property resources require governments to coordinate their management powers regardless of any distributional considerations; that distributional goals can be achieved independently of resource use given political willingness to effectuate income transfers; and that the price mechanism can be an effective facilitator of compromise for conflicts over resource use.

NOTES

1. Garrett Hardin, "The Tragedy of the Commons," *Science*, 13 December 1968.
2. In 1970 the General Assembly declared the deep seabed the "common heritage of mankind" and convened UNCLOS III to draft a comprehensive new law of the sea. The Conference holds its eleventh session in March and April 1982. In 1979 the General Assembly declared outer space the "common province of all mankind" and declared its intention to negotiate an international regime for the exploration of outer space

resources. The second World Administrative Radio Conference met in 1979 under the auspices of the International Telecommunications Union to allocate radio frequencies and orbital slots for the next 20 years; it reconvenes in 1982. In 1980; the consultative parties of the Antarctic treaty concluded a treaty for the conservation of Antarctic living marine resources and are currently negotiating a treaty for mineral resources.

3. For analysis of these problems leading to different policy conclusions see S. Brown, N. Cornell, L. Fabian, and E. Weiss, *Regimes for the Ocean, Outer Space and Weather* (Washington, D.C.: Brookings, 1977); and R. Eckert, *The Enclosure of Ocean Resources: Economics and the Law of the Sea* (Stanford, Cal.: Hoover Institution Press, 1979). See also the thematic issue entitled "Managing International Commons" of *Journal of International Affairs*, 31, no. 1 (Spring Summer 1977); Ann Hollick's contribution to R. W. Arad et al., *Sharing Global Resources* (New York: McGraw-Hill, 1979); O. Schachter. *Sharing the World's Resources* (New York: Columbia University Press, 1977).

4. Villages in medieval Europe contained tracts of land, especially pasture and woodland, to which commoners as well as the lord of the manor had access. Their rights were usually clearly specified, allowing them to graze cattle, to gather wood, etc. These user rights were personal, and customarily the produce collected was not sold to others, so there were no markets affiliated with these rights. The rising price of agricultural produce created incentives to "enclose" the commons by hedge or by fence. When the price of wool rose in 13th century England, for instance, the lord of the manor characteristically attempted to reduce the commons by converting some land to pasture for his exclusive personal use. In response to rising food prices in 19th century Europe, common pasture was enclosed and converted to private farmland. By now enclosure was closely regulated in most countries and included consolidation of private holdings of land and compensation for loss of rights in the commons. For one view see J. S. Cohen and M. L. Weitzman, "A Marxian Model of Enclosures," *Journal of Development Economics* (1975).

5. Ricardo noted the possibility that property rights might be extended to certain "gifts of nature which exist in boundless quantity," such as air and water, once they became sufficiently scarce to generate rents to their owners. "If air, water, the elasticity of steam, and the pressure of the atmosphere were of various qualities; if they could be appropriated, and each quality existed only in moderate abundance, they, as well as the land, would afford a rent, as the successive qualities were brought into use." *The Principles of Political Economy and Taxation*, 3rd ed. (1821), chap. 2, "On Rent." Compare this to the reaction of the Indian chief Tecumseh, a contemporary of Ricardo, when the white man offered to buy Indian land: "What! Sell land! As well sell air and water. The Great Spirit gave them in common to all, the air we breathe, the water we drink, and the land we live upon."

6. H. Demsetz, "Toward a Theory of Property Rights," *American Economic Review* 57 (May 1967.) Demsetz argues that property rights develop to internalize externalities when the gains exceed the costs of internalization. He illustrates his argument by pointing out that the emergence of property rights among the Indians of the Labrador Peninsula in the 18th century was due to the low cost of enclosing the relatively stationary beaver combined with a high return as foreign trade increased the demand for furs. The absence of property rights to land among the Plains Indians was due to higher costs relative to benefits of enclosing grazing cattle.

7. While a commons is characterized by the legal form of ownership, the term "common property resource" refers to certain physical rather than legal characteristics. High costs of enforcing individual property rights and high returns from coordinated use make it socially inefficient to subdivide the resource. Thus, common property resources are exploited more efficiently if production is coordinated. For other resources, private

property rights are socially more efficient than communal ownership when the resource is scarce; a classical proof of this statement is provided by M. L. Weitzman, "Free Access vs. Private Ownership as Alternative Systems for Managing Common Property." *Journal of Economic Theory* 8 (1974).

8. See Cyrille de Klemm, "The Conservation of Migratory Animals through International Law," *Natural Resources Journal* 12, 2 (April 1972). An international convention on the conservation of migratory species of wild animals was signed in June 1978. The text, with comments, is published in *Environmental Policy and Law Journal* no. 5 (1979).

9. Indeed, when the size of the resource is unknown, it may in practice be difficult to convince those who exploit the resource of the need to limit the harvest.

10. See G. R. Munro, "The Optimal Management of Transboundary Renewable Resources," *Canadian Journal of Economics* 12 (August 1979).

11. An external economy occurs if the rate at which A exploits the resource affects the exploitation costs for B, or vice versa, or both. Its occurrence serves to define common property resources, according to Robert Dorfman: "Any economic unit's behavior can affect the welfare or productivity of others in a vast number of different ways, through altruism, envy, congestion, pollution, and a myriad of other kinds of connection. Sometimes the connection is physical. That is to say, sometimes there is an identifiable physical medium through which the effects of one agent's activities are transmitted to other agents. Such a medium is what I shall mean by a common property resource. . . . [This] means that all problems attributable to the misuse or abuse of common property resources are instances of externalities, and the entire theory of externalities applies to them." See "The Technical Basis for Decision Making," in E. T. Haefele, ed., *The Governance of Common Resources* (Washington, D.C.: Resources for the Future, 1974). I have argued in the text that the infeasibility of defining exclusive property rights and the resulting overlapping of rights is a distinctive feature of common property resources leading to the characteristic depletion of the resource. This is often related to the externality.

12. Some historical examples of voluntary management of a commons are provided by T. L. Anderson and T. J. Hill, "Property Rights as a Common Pool Resource," in J. Baden and R. Stroup, eds., *Bureaucrats vs. Environment* (Ann Arbor: University of Michigan Press, 1981).

13. For instance, an international convention to abate pollution of the Rhine River in Europe has been difficult to achieve because of the many countries involved (five), and because of the asymmetry in the interdependence of "downstream" and "upstream" countries.

14. This is the familiar thesis of M. Olson, *The Logic of Collective Action: Public Goods and the Theory of Groups* (Cambridge: Harvard University Press, 1965). See also his "Increasing the Incentives for International Cooperation," *International Organization* 25, 4 (Autumn 1971). The point is illustrated by H. V. Muhsam in "An Algebraic Theory of the Commons," in G. Hardin and J. Baden, eds., *Managing the Commons* (San Francisco: W. H. Freeman, 1977), pp. 34–37. For a practical illustration of the management problems posed by an internationally shared resource, see P. Bohm, "CFC Emissions Control in an International Perspective," in J. Cumberland, J. Hibbs, and I. Hoch, eds., *The Economics of Managing Chlorofluorocarbons: Stratospheric Ozone and Climate Issues* (Washington, D.C.: Resources for the Future, 1982).

15. Discussions of international resource management would benefit from more explicit application of this distinction, which corresponds to the classical distinction in economics between the allocation, distribution, and stabilization branches of government. It is spelled out clearly by some economists dealing with this subject. See R. D. Tollison and T. D. Willett, "Institutional Mechanisms for Dealing with International Externalities: A

Public Choice Perspective," in R. C. Amacher and R. J. Sweeney, *The Law of the Sea: U.S. Interests and Alternatives* (Washington, D. C.: American Enterprise Institute, 1976); F. T. Christy Jr., "Economic Criteria for Rules Governing Exploitation of Deep Sea Minerals," *International Lawyer* 2, 2 (April 1968); *Alternative Arrangements for Marine Fisheries: An Overview* (Washington, D.C.: Resources for the Future, May 1973); and R. Cooper, "An Economist's View of the Oceans," *Journal of World Trade Law* 9, 4 (1975).

16. Demsetz speaks in this connection of the valuation function of the price system: "The Exchange and Enforcement of Property Rights," *Journal of Law and Economics* 7, 1 (October 1964). By guiding resources to their most valuable use, the price mechanism contributes to efficiency. Consequently, free use of the scarce orbit-spectrum frequency means that too much of the spectrum is devoted to satellite communications instead of to other purposes, and that more labor and capital are devoted to constructing and launching satellites than would be required to lay an equivalent amount of transatlantic cable. Similarly, if the charges levied on seabed mining are in excess of the rent due to the mine site, more capital and labor will be devoted to landbased mining than would be required to mine the same amount of ore from the seabed.

17. For instance, Richard Cooper interprets the concept "common heritage of mankind" to mean that any rents "from use of the oceans or seabed should be used for internationally agreed purposes. That is, the international community as a whole should hold title to the property" and any net revenues be "used for a variety of common purposes: budgetary support for the United Nations, which is frequently strapped for funds; U.N. peace-keeping activities; and most obviously, development assistance to the poor countries of the world." Cooper, "Economist's View of Oceans," p. 370. A similar approach has been presented by Tollison and Willett, "Institutional Mechanisms," pp. 91–97.

18. See S. Zamora, "Voting in International Economic Organizations," *American Journal of International Law* 74, 3 (July 1980). For an interesting example see A. Klevorick and G. H. Kramer, "Social Choice on Pollution Management: The Genossenschaften," *Journal of Public Economics* 2 (1973), pp. 101–146; and K. A. Mingst, "The Functionalist and Regime Perspectives: The Case of Rhine River Cooperation," *Journal of Common Market Studies* 20, 2 (December 1981).

19. S. Holt estimates the world marine catch, excluding whales, to have been $15 billion (U.S.) in 1974, or about 0.44% of world GNP. FAO statistics of the value of fish landings have been discontinued since then, but allowance for inflation places the yearly value of the world marine catch at the end of the 1970s at roughly $20 billion. See Holt's "Marine Fisheries," in E. M. Borgese and N. Ginsburg, eds., *Ocean Yearbook 1* (Chicago: University of Chicago Press, 1978), p. 53. J. Gulland notes that only 1% of the total world catch of marine fish is caught beyond 200 nautical miles from shore. This 1% consists mainly of tuna. See his "Developing Countries and the New Law of the Sea," *Oceanus* 22, 1 (Spring 1979), p. 36.

20. The Draft Convention of UNCLOS III allows the coastal state to give domestic fishermen prior claim to the resources of the EEZ, to determine unilaterally if these resources are sufficiently large to permit foreign fishermen to share in harvesting them, and to charge foreigners an entry fee upon admitting them. Such a fee may be larger than that charged domestic fishermen. Noncoastal states and others with an interest or a tradition of fishing in a foreign EEZ are dependent on the host country's permission.

21. See G. J. Mangone, ed., *The Future of Gas and Oil from the Sea* (New York: Van Nostrand, 1982), for an informed survey of current and future technologies for exploring and exploiting offshore hydrocarbon resources. See Wijkman, "UNCLOS," pp. 34–37, for estimates of offshore hydrocarbon wealth and its distribution.

22. Nodule fields are divisible and property rights to sites can be enforced cheaply in the courts once nations have agreed on a legal regime. While one firm's mining costs are not affected by mining conducted on other sites, they are affected if other firms mine the *same* site. This is because of the characteristics of the resource and of the exploitation technology. Nodules will be recovered from about 4000 meters of water depth by complex dredging systems. Unlike wild berries on a commons, they are evenly distributed on certain parts of the seafloor so that harvesting costs are lower when firms systematically comb a given area than where they sweep it randomly. When several firms work the same field, harvesting becomes random and, because of the large sunk costs of the dredging equipment, recovery costs rise significantly. Thus, exclusive mining rights to a site are important for minimizing costs.

    The minimum economic size of a single site may be large. Since processing plans evidence economies of scale and each one is adapted specifically to process nodules possessing the chemical composition characteristic of that site, each site must be large enough to supply three million metric tons annually for 20 to 25 years. It has been estimated that this requires that mine sites be about 40,000 square kilometers in size assuming that profitability requires at least 10 kg of nodules per square meter and nickel and copper content of 2.25% in the nodules. See J.P. Levy, "Evolution of a Resource Policy," pp. 23–24. Such prime sites may be few and expensive to find and consequently need to be husbanded.

23. This estimate is based on a recent U.S. Geological Survey report quoted in Barbara Mitchell and Lee Kimball, "Conflict over the Cold Continent," *Foreign Policy* no. 35 (Summer 1979). See also Ursula Wassermann, "The Antarctic Treaty and Natural Resources," *Journal of World Trade Law* 12, 2 (March–April 1978).

24. See S. Z. El-Sayed and Mary A. McWhinnie, "Antarctic Krill: Protein of the Last Frontier," *Oceanus* 22, 1 (Spring 1979), p. 13. A resource survey is provided by Inigo Everson, *The Living Resources of the Southern Ocean*, FAO/UNDP, Southern Ocean Fisheries Survey Programme, GLO/SO/77/1 (Rome, September 1977).

Redefining Security

Jessica Tuchman Mathews

The 1990s will demand a redefinition of what constitutes national security. In the 1970s the concept was expanded to include international economics as it became clear that the U.S. economy was no longer the independent force it had once been, but was powerfully affected by economic policies in dozens of other countries. Global developments now suggest the need for another analogous, broadening definition of national security to include resource, environmental and demographic issues.

The assumptions and institutions that have governed international relations in the postwar era are a poor fit with these new realities. Environmental strains that transend national borders are already beginning to break down the sacred boundaries of national sovereignty, previously rendered porous by the information and communication revolutions and the instantaneous global movement of financial capital. The once sharp dividing line between foreign and domestic policy is blurred, forcing governments to grapple in international forums with issues that were contentious enough in the domestic arena.

Despite the headlines of 1988—the polluted coastlines, the climatic extremes, the accelerating deforestation and flooding that plagued the planet—human society has not arrived at the brink of some absolute limit to its growth. The planet may ultimately be able to accommodate the additional five or six billion people projected to be living here by the year 2100. But it seems unlikely that the world will be

From "Redefining Security" by Jessica Tuchman Mathews, from *Foreign Affairs* (Spring, 1989). Copyright © 1989 by the Council on Foreign Relations, Inc. Reprinted by permission of *Foreign Affairs*, (Spring, 1989). Portions of the text and some footnotes have been omitted.

able to do so unless the means of production change dramatically. Global economic output has quadrupled since 1950 and it must continue to grow rapidly simply to meet basic human needs, to say nothing of the challenge of lifting billions from poverty. But economic growth as we currently know it requires more energy use, more emissions and wastes, more land converted from its natural state, and more need for the products of natural systems. Whether the planet can accommodate all of these demands remains an open question.

Individuals and governments alike are beginning to feel the cost of substituting for (or doing without) the goods and services once freely provided by healthy ecosystems. Nature's bill is presented in many different forms: the cost of commercial fertilizer needed to replenish once naturally fertile soils; the expense of dredging rivers that flood their banks because of soil erosion hundreds of miles upstream; the loss in crop failures due to the indiscriminate use of pesticides that inadvertently kill insect pollinators; or the price of worsening pollution, once filtered from the air by vegetation. Whatever the immediate cause for concern, the value and absolute necessity for human life of functioning ecosystems is finally becoming apparent.

Moreover, for the first time in its history, mankind is rapidly—if inadvertently—altering the basic physiology of the planet. Global changes currently taking place in the chemical composition of the atmosphere, in the genetic diversity of species inhabiting the planet, and in the cycling of vital chemicals through the oceans, atmosphere, biosphere, and geosphere are unprecedented in both their pace and scale. If left unchecked, the consequences will be profound and, unlike familiar types of local damage, irreversible.

Population growth lies at the core of most environmental trends. It took 130 years for world population to grow from one billion to two billion: It will take just a decade to climb from today's five billion to six billion. More than 90 percent of the added billion will live in the developing world, with the result that by the end of the 1990s the developed countries will be home to only 20 percent of the world's people, compared to almost 40 percent at the end of World War II. Sheer numbers do not translate into political power, especially when most of the added billion will be living in poverty. But the demographic shift will thrust the welfare of developing nations further toward the center of international affairs.

The relationship linking population levels and the resource base is complex. Policies, technologies and institutions determine the impact of population growth. These factors can spell the difference between a highly stressed, degraded environment and one that can provide for many more people. At any given level of investment and knowledge, absolute population numbers can be crucial. For example, traditional systems of shifting agriculture—in which land is left fallow for a few years to recover from human use—can sustain people for centuries, only to crumble in a short time when population densities exceed a certain threshold. More important, though, is the *rate* of growth. A government that is fully capable of providing food, housing, jobs and health care for a population growing at one percent per year (therefore doubling its population in 72 years), might be completely overwhelmed by an annual growth rate of 3 percent, which would double the population in 24 years.

Today the United States and the Soviet Union are growing at just under one percent annually (Europe is growing only half that fast). But Africa's population is expanding by almost 3 percent per year. Latin America's by nearly 2 percent and Asia's somewhat less. By 2025 the working-age population in developing countries alone will be larger than the world's current total population. This growth comes at a time when technological advance requires higher levels of education and displaces more labor than ever before. For many developing countries, continued growth at current rates means that available capital is swallowed up in meeting the daily needs of people, rather than invested in resource conservation and job creation. Such policies inescapably lay the foundations of a bleak future.

An important paradox to bear in mind when examining natural resource trends is that so-called nonrenewable resources—such as coal, oil and minerals—are in fact inexhaustible, while so-called renewable resources can be finite. As a nonrenewable resource becomes scarce and more expensive, demand falls, and substitutes and alternative technologies appear. For that reason we will never pump the last barrel of oil or anything close to it. On the other hand, a fishery fished beyond a certain point will not recover, a species driven to extinction will not reappear, and eroded topsoil cannot be replaced (except over geological time). There are, thus, threshold effects for renewable resources that belie the name given them, with unfortunate consequences for policy.

The most serious form of renewable resource decline is the deforestation taking place throughout the tropics. An area the size of Austria is deforested each year. Tropical forests are fragile ecosystems, extremely vulnerable to human disruption. Once disturbed, the entire ecosystem can unravel. The loss of the trees causes the interruption of nutrient cycling above and below the soil, the soil loses fertility, plant and animal species lose their habitats and become extinct, and acute fuelwood shortages appear (especially in the dry tropical forests). The soil erodes without the ground cover provided by trees and plants, and downstream rivers suffer siltation, causing floods and droughts, and damaging expensive irrigation and hydroelectric systems. Traced through its effects on agriculture, energy supply and water resources, tropical deforestation impoverishes about 2 billion people. This pattern is endemic throughout Central America, much of Asia, sub-Saharan Africa and South America.

The planet's evolutionary heritage—its genetic diversity—is heavily concentrated in these same forests. It is therefore disappearing today on a scale not seen since the age of the dinosaurs, and at an unprecedented pace. Biologists estimate that species are being lost in the tropical forests 1,000–10,000 times faster than the natural rate of extinction.[1] As many as 20 percent of all the species now living may be gone by the year 2000. The loss will be felt aesthetically, scientifically and, above all, economically. These genetic resources are an important source of food, materials for energy and construction, chemicals for pharmaceuticals and industry, vehicles for health and safety testing, natural pest controls and dozens of other uses.

The only reason that species loss is not a front-page issue is that the majority of species have not yet been discovered, much less studied, so that none but a few conservation biologists can even guess at the number and kinds of species that are vanishing. The bitter irony is that genetic diversity is disappearing on a grand scale at the very moment when biotechnology makes it possible to exploit fully this resource for the first time.

Soil degradation is another major concern. Both a cause and a consequence of poverty, desertification, as it is generally called, is causing declining agricultural productivity on nearly two billion hectares, 15 percent of the earth's land area. The causes are overcultivation, overgrazing, erosion, and salinization and waterlogging due to poorly managed irrigation. In countries as diverse as Haiti, Guatemala, Turkey and India, soil erosion has sharply curtailed agricultural production and potential, sometimes destroying it completely. Though the data are uncertain, it is estimated that the amount of land permanently removed from cultivation due to salinization and waterlogging is equal to the amount of land newly irrigated at great expense each year.

Finally, patterns of land tenure, though not strictly an environmental condition, have an immense environmental impact. In 1975, 7 percent of landowners of Latin America possessed 93 percent of all the arable land in this vast region. In Guatemala, a typical case, 2 percent of the population in 1980 owned 80 percent of the land, while 83 percent of farmers lived on plots too small to support a household. At the same time, even in Costa Rica, with its national concern for social equity, 3 percent of landowners held 54 percent of the land. These large holdings generally include the most desirable land. The great mass of the rural population is pushed onto the most damage-prone land, usually dry or highly erodible slopes, and into the forests. Land reform is among the most difficult of all political undertakings, but without it many countries will be unable to create a healthy agricultural sector to fuel economic growth.

Environmental decline occasionally leads directly to conflict, especially when scarce water resources must be shared. Generally, however, its impact on nations' security is felt in the downward pull on economic performance and, therefore, on political stability. The underlying cause of turmoil is often ignored; instead governments address the poverty and instability that are its results.

In the Philippines, for example, the government regularly granted logging concessions of less than ten years. Since it takes 30–35 years for a second-growth forest to mature, loggers had no incentive to replant. Compounding the error, flat royalties encouraged the loggers to remove only the most valuable species. A horrendous 40 percent of the harvestable lumber never left the forests but, having been damaged in the logging, rotted or was burned in place. The unsurprising result of these and related policies is that out of 17 million hectares of closed forests that flourished early in the century only 1.2 million remain today. Moreover, the Philippine government received a fraction of the revenues it could have collected if it had followed sound resource management policies that would have also preserved the forest capital. This is biological deficit financing writ large.

Similarly, investments in high-technology fishing equipment led to larger harvests but simultaneously depleted the stock. Today, 10 of 50 major Philippine fishing grounds are believed to be overfished; the net result of heavy investment is that the availability of fish per capita has actually dropped. These and other self-destructive environmental policies, combined with rapid population growth, played a significant role in the economic decline that led to the downfall of the Marcos regime.

Conditions in sub-Saharan Africa, to take another case, have reached catastrophic dimensions. In the first half of this decade export earnings fell by almost one-third, foreign debt soared to 58 percent of GNP, food imports grew rapidly while consumption dropped, and per capita GNP fell by more than 3 percent. A large share of those woes can be traced to Africa's dependence on a fragile, mismanaged and overstressed natural resource base.

Exports of mineral and agricultural commodities alone account for a quarter of the region's GNP, and nearly three-quarters of the population makes its living off the land, which also supplies, as fuelwood, 80 percent of the energy consumed. The land's capacity to produce is ebbing away under the pressure of rapidly growing numbers of people who do not have the wherewithal to put back into the land what they take from it. A vicious cycle of human and resource impoverishment sets in. As the vegetative cover—trees, shrubs and grass—shrinks from deforestation and overgrazing, soil loses its capacity to retain moisture and nourish crops. The decline accelerates as farmers burn dung and crop residues in place of fuelwood, rather than using them to sustain the soil. Agricultural yields then fall further, and the land becomes steadily more vulnerable to the naturally variable rainfall that is the hallmark of arid and semiarid regions, turning dry spells into droughts and periods of food shortage into famines. Ethiopia is only the most familiar case. The sequence is repeated throughout the region with similarly tragic results.

If such resource and population trends are not addressed, as they are not in so much of the world today, the resulting economic decline leads to frustration, resentment, domestic unrest or even civil war. Human suffering and turmoil make countries ripe for authoritarian government or external subversion. Environmental refugees spread the disruption across national borders. Haiti, a classic example, was once so forested and fertile that it was known as the "Pearl of the Antilles." Now deforested, soil erosion in Haiti is so rapid that some farmers believe stones grow in their fields, while bulldozers are needed to clear the streets of Port-au-Prince of topsoil that flows down from the mountains in the rainy season. While many of the boat people who fled to the United States left because of the brutality of the Duvalier regimes, there is no question that—and this is not widely recognized—many Haitians were forced into the boats by the impossible task of farming bare rock. Until Haiti is reforested, it will never be politically stable.

Haitians are by no means the world's only environmental refugees. In Indonesia, Central American and sub-Saharan Africa, millions have been forced to leave their homes in part because the loss of tree cover, the disappearance of soil, and other environmental ills have made it impossible to grow food. Sudan, despite its civil war, has taken in more than a million refugees from Ethiopia, Uganda and Chad. Immigrants from the spreading Sahel make up one-fifth of the total population in the Ivory Coast. Wherever refugees settle, they flood the labor market, add to the local demand for food and put new burdens on the land, thus spreading the environmental stress that originally forced them from their homes. Resource mismanagement is not the only cause of these mass movements, of course. Religious and ethnic conflicts, political repression and other forces are at work. But the environmental causes are an essential factor.

A different kind of environmental concern has arisen from mankind's new ability to alter the environment on a planetary scale. The earth's physiology is shaped by the characteristics of four elements (carbon, nitrogen, phosphorous and sulfur); by its living inhabitants (the biosphere); and by the interactions of the atmosphere and the oceans, which produce our climate.

Mankind is altering both the carbon and nitrogen cycles, having increased the natural carbon dioxide concentration in the atmosphere by 25 percent. This has occurred largely in the last three decades through fossil-fuel use and deforestation. The production of commercial fertilizer has doubled the amount of nitrogen nature makes available to living things. The use of a single, minor class of chemicals, chlorofluorocarbons, has punched a continent-sized "hole" in the ozone layer at the top of the stratosphere over Antarctica, and caused a smaller, but growing loss of ozone all around the planet. Species loss is destroying the work of three billion years of evolution. Together these changes could drastically alter the conditions in which life on earth has evolved.

The greenhouse effect results from the fact that the planet's atmosphere is largely transparent to incoming radiation from the sun but absorbs much of the lower energy radiation reemitted by the earth. This natural phenomenon makes the earth warm enough to support life. But as emissions of greenhouse gases increase, the planet is warmed *un*naturally. Carbon dioxide produced from the combustion of fossil fuels and by deforestation is responsible for about half of the greenhouse effect. A number of other gases, notably methane (natural gas), nitrous oxide, ozone (in the lower atmosphere, as distinguished from the protective ozone layer in the stratosphere) and the man-made chlorofluorocarbons are responsible for the other half.

Despite important uncertainties about aspects of the greenhouse warming, a virtually unanimous scientific consensus exists on its central features. If present emission trends continue, and unless some as yet undocumented phenomenon (possibly increased cloudiness) causes an offsetting cooling, the planet will, on average, get hotter because of the accumulation of these gases. Exactly how large the warming will be, and how fast it will occur, are uncertain. Existing models place the date of commitment to an average global warming of 1.5–4.5°C (3–8°F) in the early 2030s. The earth has not been this hot for two million years, long before human society, and indeed, even Homo sapiens, existed.

Hotter temperatures will be only one result of the continuing greenhouse warming. At some point, perhaps quite soon, precipitation patterns are likely to shift, possibly causing dustbowl-like conditions in the U.S. grain belt. Ocean currents are expected to do the same, dramatically altering the climates of many regions. A diversion of the Gulf Stream, for example, would transform Western Europe's climate, making it far colder than it is today. Sea level will rise due to the expansion of water when it is warmed and to the melting of land-based ice. The oceans are presently rising by one-half inch per decade, enough to cause serious erosion along much of the U.S. coast. The projected rise is one to four feet by the year 2050. Such a large rise in the sea level would inundate vast coastal regions, erode shorelines, destroy coastal marshes and swamps (areas of very high biological productivity), pollute water supplies through the intrusion of salt water, and put at high risk the vastly disproportionate share of the world's economic wealth that is packed along coastlines. The great river deltas, from the Mississippi to the Ganges, would be flooded. Estimates are that a half-meter rise in Egypt would displace 16 percent of the population, while a two-meter rise in Bangladesh would claim 28 percent of the land where 30 million people live today and where more than 59 million are projected to live by 2030.

Positive consequences would be likely as well. Some plants would grow more quickly fertilized by the additional carbon dioxide. (Many of them, however, will be weeds.) Rainfall might rise in what are now arid but potentially fertile regions, such as parts of sub-Saharan Africa. Conditions for agriculture would also improve in those northern areas that have both adequate soils and water supplies. Nonetheless, as the 1988 drought in the United States vividly demonstrated, human societies, industrial no less than rural, depend on the normal, predictable functioning of the climate system. Climate undergoing rapid change will not only be less predictable because it is different, but may be inherently more variable. Many climatologists believe that as accumulating greenhouse gases force the climate out of equilibrium, climate extremes—such as hurricanes, droughts, cold snaps and typhoons—will become more frequent and perhaps more intense.

Since climate change will be felt in every economic sector, adapting to its impact will be extremely expensive. Developing countries with their small reserves of capital, shortages of scientists and engineers, and weak central governments will be the least able to adapt, and the gap between the developed and developing worlds will almost certainly widen. Many of the adaptations needed will be prohibitively costly, and many impacts, notably the effects on wildlife and ecosystems, will be beyond the reach of human correction. A global strategy that relies on future adaption almost certainly means greater economic and human costs, and vastly larger biological losses, than would a strategy that attempts to control the extent and speed of the warming.

Greenhouse change is closely linked to stratospheric ozone depletion, which is also caused by chlorofluorocarbons. The increased ultraviolet radiation resulting from losses in that protective layer will cause an increase in skin cancers and eye damage. It will have many still uncertain impacts on plant and animal life, and may suppress the immune systems of many species.

Serious enough in itself, ozone depletion illustrates a worrisome feature of man's newfound ability to cause global change. It is almost impossible to predict accurately the long-term impact of new chemicals or processes on the environment. Chlorofluorocarbons were thoroughly tested when first introduced, and found to be benign. Their effect on the remote stratosphere was never considered.

Not only is it difficult to anticipate all the possible consequences in a highly interdependent, complex system, the system itself is poorly understood. When British scientists announced the appearance of a continent-sized "hole" in the ozone layer over Antarctica in 1985, the discovery sent shock waves through the scientific community. Although stratospheric ozone depletion had been the subject of intense study and debate for more than a decade, no one had predicted the Antarctic hole and no theory could account for it.

The lesson is this: Current knowledge of planetary mechanisms is so scanty that the possibility of surprise, perhaps quite nasty surprise, must be rated rather high. The greatest risk may well come from a completely unanticipated direction. We lack both crucial knowledge and early warning systems.

Absent profound change in man's relationship to his environment, the future does not look bright. Consider the planet without such change in the year 2050. Economic growth is projected to have quintupled by then. Energy use could also quintuple; or if post–1973 trends continue, it may grow more slowly, perhaps only doubling or tripling. The human species already consumes or destroys 40 percent of all the energy produced by terrestrial photosynthesis, that is, 40 percent of the food energy potentially available to living things on land. While that fraction may be sustainable, it is doubtful that it could keep pace with the expected doubling of the world's population. Human use of 80 percent of the planet's potential productivity does not seem compatible with the continued functioning of the biosphere as we know it. The expected rate of species loss would have risen from perhaps a few each day to several hundred a day. The pollution and toxic waste burden would likely prove unmanageable. Tropical forests would have largely disappeared, and arable land, a vital resource in a world of ten billion people, would be rapidly decreasing due to soil degradation. In short, sweeping change in economic production systems is not a choice but a necessity.

Happily, this grim sketch of conditions in 2050 is not a prediction, but a projection, based on current trends. Like all projections, it says more about the present and the recent past than it does about the future. The planet is not destined to a slow and painful decline into environmental chaos. There are technical, scientific and economical solutions that are feasible to many current trends, and enough is known about promising new approaches to be confident that the right kinds of research will produce huge payoffs. Embedded in current practices are vast costs in lost opportunities and waste, which, if corrected, would bring massive benefits. Some such steps will require only a reallocation of money, while others will require sizable capital investments. None of the needed steps, however, requires globally unaffordable sums of money. What they do demand is a sizable shift in priorities.

For example, family-planning services cost about $10 per user, a tiny fraction of the cost of the basic human needs that would otherwise have to be met. Already identified opportunities for raising the efficiency of energy use in the United States cost one-half to one-seventh the cost of new energy supply. Comparable savings are available in most other countries. Agroforestry techniques, in which carefully selected combinations of trees and shrubs are planted together with crops, can not only replace the need for purchased fertilizer but also improve soil quality, make more water available to crops, hold down weeds, and provide fuelwood and higher agricultural yields all at the same time.

But if the technological opportunities are boundless, the social, political and institutional barriers are huge. Subsidies, pricing policies and economic discount rates encourage resource depletion in the name of economic growth, while delivering only the illusion of sustainable growth. Population growth remains a controversial subject in much of the world. The traditional prerogatives of nation states are poorly matched with the needs for regional cooperation and global decision-making. And ignorance of the biological underpinning of human society blocks a clear view of where the long-term threats to global security lie.

Overcoming these economic and political barriers will require social and institutional inventions comparable in scale and vision to the new arrangements conceived in the decade following World War II. Without the sharp political turning point of a major war, and with threats that are diffuse and long term, the task will be more difficult. But if we are to avoid irreversible damage to the planet and a heavy toll in human suffering, nothing less is likely to suffice. A partial list of the specific changes suggests how demanding a task it will be.

Achieving sustainable economic growth will require the remodeling of agriculture, energy use and industrial production after nature's example—their reinvention, in fact. These economic systems must become circular rather than linear. Industry and manufacturing will need processes that use materials and energy with high efficiency, recycle by-products and produce little waste. Energy demand will have to be met with the highest efficiency consistent with full economic growth. Agriculture will rely heavily upon free ecosystem services instead of nearly exclusive reliance on man-made substitutes. And all systems will have to price goods and services to reflect the environmental costs of their provision.

A vital first step, one that can and should be taken in the very near term, would be to reinvent the national income accounts by which gross national product is measured. GNP is the foundation on which national economic policies are built, yet its calculation does not take into account resource depletion. A country can consume its forests, wildlife and fisheries, its minerals, its clean water and its topsoil, without seeing a reflection of the loss in its GNP. Nor are ecosystem services—sustaining soil fertility, moderating and storing rainfall, filtering air and regulating the climate—valued, though their loss may entail great expense. The result is that economic policymakers are profoundly misled by their chief guide.

A second step would be to invent a set of indicators by which global environmental health could be measured. Economic planning would be adrift without GNP unemployment rates, and the like, and social planning without demographic indicators—fertility rates, infant mortality, literacy, life expectancy—would be impossible. Yet this is precisely where environmental policymaking stands today.

Development assistance also requires new tools. Bilateral and multilateral donors have found that project success rates climb when nongovernmental organizations distribute funds and direct programs. This is especially true in agriculture, forestry and conservation projects. The reasons are not mysterious. Such projects are more decentralized, more attuned to local needs and desires, and have a much higher degree of local participation in project planning. They are usually quite small in scale, however, and not capable of handling very large amounts of development funding. Often, too, their independent status threatens the national government. Finding ways to make far greater use of the strengths of such groups without weakening national governments is another priority for institutional innovation.

Better ways must also be found to turn the scientific and engineering strengths of the industrialized world to the solution of the developing world's problems. The challenges include learning enough about local constraints and conditions to ask the right questions, making such research professionally rewarding to the individual scientist, and transferring technology more effectively. The international centers for agricultural research, a jointly managed network of thirteen institutions launched in the 1960s, might be improved upon and applied in other areas.

On the political front, the need for a new diplomacy and for new institutions and regulatory regimes to cope with the world's growing environmental interdependence is even more compelling. Put bluntly, our accepted definition of the limits of national sovereignty as coinciding with national borders is obsolete. The government of Bangladesh, no matter how hard it tries, cannot prevent tragic floods, such as it suffered last year. Preventing them requires active cooperation from Nepal and India. The government of Canada cannot protect its water resources from acid rain without collaboration with the United States. Eighteen diverse nations share the heavily polluted Mediterranean Sea. Even the Caribbean Islands, as physically isolated as they are, find themselves affected by others' resource management policies as locusts, inadvertently bred through generations of exposure to pesticides and now strong enough to fly all the way from Africa, infest their shores.

The majority of environmental problems demand regional solutions which encroach upon what we now think of as the prerogatives of national governments. This is because the phenomena themselves are defined by the limits of watershed, ecosystem, or atmospheric transport, not by national borders. Indeed, the costs and benefits of alternative policies cannot often be accurately judged without considering the region rather than the nation.

The developing countries especially will need to pool their efforts in the search for solutions. Three-quarters of the countries in sub-Saharan Africa, for example, have fewer people than live in New York City. National scientific and research capabilities cannot be built on such a small population base. Regional cooperation is required.

Dealing with global change will be more difficult. No one nation or even group of nations can meet these challenges, and no nation can protect itself from the actions—or inaction—of others. No existing institution matches these criteria. It will be necessary to reduce the dominance of the superpower relationship which so often encourages other countries to adopt a wait-and-see attitude (you solve your problems first, then talk to us about change).

The United States, in particular, will have to assign a far greater prominence than it has heretofore to the practice of multilateral diplomacy. This would mean changes that range from the organization of the State Department and the language proficiency of the Foreign Service, to the definition of an international role that allows leadership without primacy, both in the slogging work of negotiation and in adherence to final outcomes. Above all, ways must soon be found to step around the deeply entrenched North-South cleavage and to replace it with a planetary sense of shared destiny. Perhaps the successes of the UN specialized agencies can be built upon for this purpose. But certainly the task of forging a global energy policy in order to control the greenhouse effect, for example, is a very long way from eradicating smallpox or sharing weather information. . . .

Today's negotiating models—the Law of the Sea Treaty, the Nuclear Nonproliferation Treaty, even the promising Convention to Protect the Ozone Layer—are inadequate. Typically, such agreements take about 15 years to negotiate and enter into force, and perhaps another ten years before substantial changes in behavior are actually achieved. (The NPT, which required only seven years to complete these steps, is a notable exception.) Far better approaches will be needed.

Among these new approaches, perhaps the most difficult to achieve will be ways to negotiate successfully in the presence of substantial scientific uncertainty. The present model is static: years of negotiation leading to a final product. The new model will have to be fluid, allowing a rolling process of intermediate or self-adjusting agreements that respond quickly to growing scientific understanding. The recent Montreal agreement on the ozone layer supplies a useful precedent by providing that one-third of the parties can reconvene a scientific experts group to consider new evidence as it becomes available. The new model will require new economic methods for assessing risk, especially where the possible outcomes are irreversible. It will depend on a more active political role for biologists and chemists than they have been accustomed to, and far greater technical competence in the natural and planetary sciences among policymakers. Finally, the new model may need to forge a more involved and constructive role for the private sector. Relegating the affected industries to a heel-dragging, adversarial, outsiders role almost guarantees a slow process. The ozone agreement, to cite again this recent example, would not have been reached as quickly, and perhaps not at all, had it not been for the cooperation of the chlorofluorocarbon producers.

International law, broadly speaking, has declined in influence in recent years. With leadership and commitment from the major powers it might regain its lost status. But that will not be sufficient. To be effective, future arrangements will require provisions for monitoring, enforcement and compensation, even when damage cannot be assigned a precise monetary value. These are all areas where international law has traditionally been weak.

This is only a partial agenda for the needed decade of invention. Meanwhile, much can and must be done with existing means. Four steps are most important: prompt revision of the Montreal Treaty, to eliminate completely the production of chlorofluorocarbons no later than the year 2000; full support for and implementation of the global Tropical Forestry Action Plan developed by the World Bank, the UN's Development Programme, the Food and Agricultural Organization, and the World Resources Institute; sufficient support for family planning programs to ensure that all who want contraceptives have affordable access to them at least by the end of the decade; and, for the United States, a ten-year energy policy with the goal of increasing the energy productivity of our economy (i.e., reducing the amount of energy required to produce a dollar of GNP) by about 3 percent each year. While choosing four priorities from dozens of needed initiatives is highly arbitrary, these four stand out as ambitious yet achievable goals on which a broad consensus could be developed, and whose success would bring multiple, long-term global benefits touching every major international environmental concern.

Reflecting on the discovery of atomic energy, Albert Einstein noted "everything changed." And indeed, nuclear fission became the dominant force—military, geopolitical, and even psychological and social—of the ensuing decades. In the same sense, the driving force of the coming decades may well be environmental change. Man is still utterly dependent on the natural world but now has for the first time the ability to alter it, rapidly and on a global scale. Because of that difference, Einstein's verdict that "we shall require a substantially new manner of thinking if mankind is to survive" still seems apt.

NOTES

1. E.O. Wilson, ed., *Biodiversity*, Washington, D.C.: National Academy Press, 1988. pp. 3–18.

The Infinite Supply of Natural Resources

Julian Simon

Natural resources are not finite. Yes, you read correctly. This chapter shows that the supply of natural resources is not finite in any economic sense, which is why their cost can continue to fall in the future.

On the face of it, even to inquire whether natural resources are finite seems like nonsense. Everyone "knows" that resources are finite, from C.P. Snow to Isaac Asimov to as many other persons as you have time to read about in the newspaper. And this belief has led many persons to draw far-reaching conclusions about the future of our world economy and civilization. A prominent example is the *Limits to Growth* group, who open the preface to their 1974 book, a sequel to the *Limits,* as follows:

> Most people acknowledge that the earth is finite. . . . Policy makers generally assume that growth will provide them tomorrow with the resources required to deal with today's problems. . . . Recently, however, concern about the consequences of population growth, increased environmental pollution, and the depletion of fossil fuels has cast doubt upon the belief that continuous growth is either possible or a panacea.[1]

(Note the rhetorical device embedded in the term "acknowledge" in the first sentence of the quotation. That word suggests that the statement is a fact, and that anyone who does not "acknowledge" it is simply refusing to accept or admit it.)

The idea that resources are finite in supply is so pervasive and influential that the President's 1972 Commission on Population Growth and the American Future based its policy recommendations squarely upon this assumption. Right at the beginning of its report the commission asked, "What does this nation stand for and where is it going? At some point in the future, the finite earth will not satisfactorily accommodate more human beings—nor will the United States. . . . It is both proper and in our best interest to participate fully in the worldwide search for the good life, which must include the eventual stabilization of our numbers."[2]

The assumption of finiteness is responsible for misleading many scientific forecasters because their conclusions follow inexorably from that assumption. From the *Limits to Growth* team again, this time on food: "The world model is based on the fundamental assumption that there is an upper limit to the total amount of food that can be produced annually by the world's agricultural system."[3]

THE THEORY OF DECREASING NATURAL-RESOURCE SCARCITY

We shall begin with a far-out example to see what contrasting possibilities there are. (Such an analysis of far-out examples is a useful and favorite trick of economists and mathematicians.) If there is just one person, Alpha Crusoe, on an island, with a single copper mine on his island, it will be harder to get raw copper next year if Alpha makes a lot of copper pots and bronze tools this year. And if he continues to use his mine, his son Beta Crusoe will have a tougher time getting copper than did his daddy.

Recycling could change the outcome. If Alpha decides in the second year to make new tools to replace the old tools he made in the first year, it will be easier for him to get the necessary copper than it was the first year because he can reuse the copper from the old tools without much new mining. And if Alpha adds fewer new pots and tools from year to year, the proportion of copper that can come from recycling can rise year by year. This could mean a progressive decrease in the cost of obtaining copper with each successive year for this reason alone, even while the total amount of copper in pots and tools increases.

But let us be "conservative" for the moment and ignore the possibility of recycling. Another scenario: If there are two people on the island, Alpha Crusoe and Gamma Defoe, copper will be more scarce for each of them this year than if Alpha lived there alone, unless by cooperative efforts they can devise a more complex but more efficient mining operation—say, one man on the surface and one in the shaft. Or, if there are two fellows this year instead of one, and if copper is therefore harder to get and more scarce, both Alpha and Gamma may spend considerable time looking for new lodes of copper. And they are likely to be successful in their search. This discovery may lower the cost of copper to them somewhat, but on the average the cost will still be higher than if Alpha lived alone on the island.

Alpha and Gamma may follow still other courses of action. Perhaps they will invent better ways of obtaining copper from a given lode, say a better digging tool, or they may develop new materials to substitute for copper, perhaps iron.

The cause of these new discoveries, or the cause of applying ideas that were discovered earlier, is the "shortage" of copper—that is, the increased cost of getting copper. So a "shortage" of copper causes the creation of its own remedy. This has been the key process in the supply and use of natural resources throughout history.

Discovery of an improved mining method or of a substitute product differs, in a manner that affects future generations, from the discovery of a new lode. Even after the discovery of a new lode, on the average it will still be more costly to obtain copper, that is, more costly than if copper had never been used enough to lead to a "shortage." But discoveries of improved mining methods and of substitute products, caused by the shortage of copper, can lead to lower costs of the services people see from copper. Let's see how.

The key point is that a discovery of a substitute process or product by Alpha or Gamma can benefit innumerable future generations. Alpha and Gamma cannot themselves extract nearly the full benefit from their discovery of iron. (You and I still benefit from the discoveries of the uses of iron and methods of processing it that our ancestors made thousands of years ago.) This benefit to later generations is an example of what economists call an "externality" due to Alpha and Gamma's activities, that is, a result of their discovery that does not affect them directly.

So, if the cost of copper to Alpha and Gamma does not increase, they may not be impelled to develop improved methods and substitutes. If the cost of getting copper does rise for them, however, they may then bestir themselves to make a new discovery. The discovery may not immediately lower the cost of copper dramatically, and Alpha and Gamma may still not be as well off as if the cost had never risen. But subsequent generations may be better off because their ancestor suffered from increasing cost and "scarcity."

This sequence of events explains how it can be that people have been using cooking pots for thousands of years, as well as using copper for many other purposes, and yet the cost of a pot today is vastly cheaper by any measure than it was 100 or 1,000 or 10,000 years ago.

It is all-important to recognize that discoveries of improved methods and of substitute products are not just luck. They happen in response to "scarcity"—an increase in cost. Even after a discovery is made, there is a good chance that it will not be put into operation until there is need for it due to rising cost. This point is important: Scarcity and technological advance are not two unrelated competitors in a race; rather, each influences the other.

The last major U.S. governmental inquiry into raw materials was the 1952 President's Materials Policy Commission (Paley Commission), organized in response to fears of raw-material shortages during and just after World War II. The Paley Commission's report is distinguished by having some of the right logic, but exactly the wrong predictions, for its twenty-five year forecast.

There is no completely satisfactory way to measure the real costs of materials over the long sweep of our history. But clearly the manhours required per unit of output declined heavily from 1900 to 1940, thanks especially to improvements in production technology and the heavier use of energy and capital equipment per worker. This long-term decline in real costs is reflected in the downward drift of prices of various groups of materials in relation to the general level of prices in the economy.

> [But since 1940 the trend has been] soaring demands, shrinking resources, the
> consequences pressure toward rising real costs, the risk of wartime shortages, the
> strong possibility of an arrest or decline in the standard of living we cherish and hope
> to share.[4]

For the quarter century for which the commission predicted, however, costs
declined rather than rose.

The two reasons why the Paley Commission's cost predictions were topsy-
turvy should help keep us from making the same mistakes. First, the commission
reasoned from the notion of finiteness and from a static technological analysis.

> A hundred years ago resources seemed limitless and the struggle upward from meager
> conditions of life was the struggle to create the means and methods of getting these
> materials into use. In this struggle we have by now succeeded all too well. . . . The na-
> ture of the problem can perhaps be successfully over-simplified by saying that the con-
> sumption of almost all materials is expanding at compound rates and is thus pressing
> harder and harder against resources which whatever else they may be doing are not
> similarly expanding.[5]

The second reason the Paley Commission went wrong is that it looked at the wrong
facts. Its report gave too much emphasis to the trends of costs over the short period from 1940 to 1950, which included World War II and therefore was almost
inevitably a period of rising costs, instead of examining the longer period from
1900 to 1940, during which the commission knew that "the man-hours required
per unit of output declined heavily."[6]

We must not repeat the same mistakes. We should look at cost trends for the
longest period, rather than focus on a historical blip; the OPEC-led price rise in all
resources after 1973 is for us as the temporary 1940–50 wartime reversal for the
Paley Commission. And the long-run trends make it very clear that the costs of
materials, and their scarcity, continuously decline with the growth of income and
technology.

RESOURCES AS SERVICES

As economists or as consumers, we are interested in the particular services that
resources yield, not in the resources themselves. Examples of such services are an
ability to conduct electricity, an ability to support weight, energy to fuel autos,
energy to fuel electrical generators, and food calories.

The supply of a service will depend upon (a) which raw materials can supply
that service with the present technology; (b) the availabilities of these materials at
various qualities; (c) the costs of extracting and processing them; (d) the amounts
needed at the present level of technology to supply the services that we want; (e)
the extent to which the previously extracted materials can be recycled; (f) the cost
of recycling; (g) the cost of transporting the raw materials and services; and (h) the
social and institutional arrangements in force. What is relevant to us is not whether
we can find any lead in existing lead mines but whether we can have the services of
lead batteries at a reasonable price; it does not matter to us whether this is accom-

plished by recycling lead, by making batteries last forever, or by replacing lead batteries with another contraption. Similarly, we want intercontinental telephone and television communication, and, as long as we got it, we do not care whether this requires 100,000 tons of copper for cables or just a single quarter-ton communications satellite in space that uses no copper at all.[7]

Let us see how this concept of services is crucial to our understanding of natural resources and the economy. To return to Crusoe's cooking pot, we are interested in a utensil that we can put over the fire and cook with. After iron and aluminum were discovered, quite satisfactory cooking pots, perhaps even better than pots of copper, could be made of these materials. The cost that interests us is the cost of providing the cooking service rather than the cost of copper. If we suppose that copper is used only for pots and that iron is quite satisfactory for the same purpose, as long as we have cheap iron it does not matter if the cost of copper rises sky high. (But in fact that has not happened. As we have seen, the prices of the minerals themselves, as well as the prices of the services they perform, have fallen over the years.)

ARE NATURAL RESOURCES FINITE?

Incredible as it may seem at first, the term "finite" is not only inappropriate but is downright misleading when applied to natural resources, from both the practical and philosophical points of view. As with many of the important arguments in this world, the one about "finiteness" is "just semantic." Yet the semantics of resource scarcity muddle public discussion and bring about wrong-headed policy decisions.

The word "finite" originates in mathematics, in which context we all learn it as schoolchildren. But even in mathematics the word's meaning is far from unambiguous. It can have two principal meanings, sometimes with an apparent contradiction between them.[8] For example, the length of a one-inch line is finite in the sense that it is bounded at both ends. But the line within the endpoints contains an infinite number of points; these points cannot be counted, because they have no defined size. Therefore the number of points in that one-inch segment is not finite. Similarly, the quantity of copper that will even be available to us is not finite, because there is no method (even in principle) of making an appropriate count of it, given the problem of the economic definition of "copper," the possibility of creating copper or its economic equivalent from other materials, and thus the lack of boundaries to the sources from which copper might be drawn.

Consider this quote about potential oil and gas from Sheldon Lambert, an energy forecaster. He begins, "It's like trying to guess the number of beans in a jar without knowing how big the jar is." So far so good. But then he adds, "God is the only one who knows—and even He may not be sure."[9] Of course Lambert is speaking lightly. But the notion that some mind might know the "actual" size of the jar is misleading, because it implies that there is a fixed quantity of standard-sized beans. The quantity of a natural resource that might be available to us—and even more important the quantity of the services that can eventually be rendered to us by that natural resource—can never be known even in principle, just as the number of points in a one-inch line can never be counted even in principle. Even if the "jar" were fixed in size, it might yield ever more "beans." Hence resources are not "finite" in any meaningful sense.

To restate: A satisfactory *operational* definition of the quantity of a natural resource, or of the services we now get from it, is the only sort of definition that is of any use in policy decisions. The definition must tell us about the quantities of a resource (or of a particular service) that we can expect to receive in any particular year to come, at each particular price, conditional on other events that we might reasonably expect to know (such as use of the resource in prior years). And there is no reason to believe that at any given moment in the future the available quantity of any natural resource or service at present prices will be much smaller than it is now, or non-existent. Only such one-of-a-kind resources as an Arthur Rubenstein concert or a Julius Erving basketball game, for which there are no close replacements, will disappear in the future and hence are finite in quantity.

Why do we become hypnotized by the word "finite"? That is an interesting question in psychology, education, and philosophy. A first likely reason is that the word "finite" seems to have a precise and unambiguous meaning in any context, even though it does not. Second, we learn the word in the context of mathematics, where all propositions are tautologous definitions and hence can be shown logically to be true or false (at least in principle). But scientific subjects are empirical rather than definitional, as twentieth-century philosophers have been at great pains to emphasize. Mathematics is not a science in the ordinary sense because it does not deal with facts other than the stuff of mathematics itself, and hence such terms as "finite" do not have the same meaning elsewhere that they do in mathematics.

Third, much of our daily life about which we need to make decisions is countable and finite—our weekly or monthly salaries, the number of gallons of gas in a full tank, the width of the backyard, the number of greeting cards you sent out last year, or those you will send out next year. Since these quantities are finite, why shouldn't the world's total possible salary in the future, or the gasoline in the possible tanks in the future, or the number of cards you ought to send out, also be finite? Though the analogy is appealing, it is not sound. And it is in making this incorrect analogy that we go astray in using the term "finite."

A fourth reason that the term "finite" is not meaningful is that we cannot say with any practical surety where the bounds of a relevant resource system lie, or even if there are any bounds. The bounds for the Crusoes are the shores of their island, and so it was for early man. But then the Crusoes found other islands. Mankind traveled farther and farther in search of resources—finally to the bounds of continents, and then to other continents. When America was opened up, the world, which for Europeans had been bounded by Europe and perhaps by Asia too, was suddenly expanded. Each epoch has seen a shift in the bounds of the relevant resource system. Each time, the old ideas about "limits," and the calculations of "finite resources" within those bounds, were thereby falsified. Now we have begun to explore the sea, which contains amounts of metallic and other resources that dwarf any deposits we know about on land. And we have begun to explore the moon. Why shouldn't the boundaries of the system from which we derive resources continue to expand in such directions, just as they have expanded in the past? This is one more reason not to regard resources as "finite" in principle.

You may wonder, however, whether "non-renewable" energy resources such as oil, coal, and natural gas differ from the recyclable minerals in such a fashion that the foregoing arguments do not apply. Energy is particularly important because it is the "master resource"; energy is the key constraint on the availability of all other resources. Even so, our energy supply is non-finite, and oil is an important example. (1) The oil potential of a particular well may be measured, and hence is limited (though it is interesting and relevant that as we develop new ways of extracting hard-to-get oil, the economic capacity of a well increases). But the number of wells that will eventually produce oil, and in what quantities, is not known or measurable at present and probably never will be, and hence is not meaningfully finite. (2) Even if we make the unrealistic assumption that the number of potential wells in the earth might be surveyed completely and that we could arrive at a reasonable estimate of the oil that might be obtained with present technology (or even with technology that will be developed in the next 100 years), we still would have to reckon the future possibilities of shale oil and tar sands—a difficult task. (3) But let us assume that we could reckon the oil potential of shale and tar sands. We would then have to reckon the conversion of coal to oil. That, too, might be done; yet we still could not consider the resulting quantity to be "finite" and "limited." (4) Then there is the oil that we might produce not from fossils but from new crops—palm oil, soybean oil, and so on. Clearly, there is no meaningful limit to this source except the sun's energy. The notion of finiteness does not make sense here, either. (5) If we allow for the substitution of nuclear and solar power for oil, since what we really want are the services of oil, not necessarily oil itself, the notion of a limit makes even less sense. (6) Of course the sun may eventually run down. But even if our sun were not as vast as it is, there may well be other suns elsewhere.

About energy from the sun: The assertion that our resources are ultimately finite seems most relevant to energy but yet is actually more misleading with respect to energy than with respect to other resources. When people say that mineral resources are "finite" they are invariably referring to the earth as a boundary, the "spaceship earth," to which we are apparently confined just as astronauts are confined to their spaceship. But the main source of our energy even now is the sun, no matter how you think of the matter. This goes far beyond the fact that the sun was the prior source of the energy locked into the oil and coal we use. The sun is also the source of the energy in the food we eat, and in the trees that we use for many purposes. In coming years, solar energy may be used to heat homes and water in many parts of the world. (Much of Israel's hot water has been heated by solar devices for years, even when the price of oil was much lower than it is now.) And if the prices of conventional energy supplies were to rise considerably higher than they now are, solar energy could be called on for much more of our needs, though this price rise seems unlikely given present technology. And even if the earth were sometime to run out of sources of energy for nuclear processes—a prospect so distant that it is a waste of time to talk about it—there are energy sources on other planets. Hence the notion that the supply of energy is finite because the earth's fossil fuels even its nuclear fuels are limited is sheer nonsense.

Whether there is an "ultimate" end to all this—that is, whether the energy supply really is "finite" after the sun and all the other planets have been exhausted—is a question so hypothetical that it should be compared with other metaphysical entertainments such as calculating the number of angels that can dance on the head of a pin. As long as we continue to draw energy from the sun, any conclusion about whether energy is "ultimately finite" or not has no bearing upon present policy decisions. . . .

SUMMARY

A conceptual quantity is not finite or infinite in itself. Rather, it is finite or infinite if you make it so—by your own definitions. If you define the subject of discussion suitably, and sufficiently closely so that it can be counted, then it is finite—for example, the money in your wallet or the socks in your top drawer. But without sufficient definition the subject is not finite—for example, the thoughts in your head, the strength of your wish to go to Turkey, your dog's love for you, the number of points in a one-inch line. You can, of course, develop definitions that will make these quantities finite; but that makes it clear that the finiteness inheres in you and in your definitions rather than in the money, love, or one-inch line themselves. There is no necessity either in logic or in historical trends to suggest that the supply of any given resource is "finite."

NOTES

1. Meadows, Dennis L.; William W. Behrens, III; Donella H. Meadows; Roger F. Naill; Jorgen Randers; and Erich K. O. Zahn, *Dynamics of Growth in a Finite World* (Cambridge, Mass.: Wright-Allen, 1974) p. vii.
2. U.S. The White House, Population and the American Future, *The Report of the Commission on Population Growth and the American Future* (New York: Signet, 1972) pp. 2–3.
3. Meadows, Dennis L. et al., *op. cit.*, p. 265.
4. U.S. The White House, The President's Materials Policy Commission (The Paley Commission), *Resources for Freedom*, 4 vols. (Washington, D.C.: GPO, 1952) summary of vol. 1, pp. 12–13; *idem*, p. 1.
5. *Ibid.*, p. 2.
6. *Ibid.*, p. 1.
7. Fuller, Buckminster, *Utopia or Oblivion: The Prospect for Humanity* (New York: Bantam, 1969) p. 4, quoted by Weber, James A., *Grow or Die!* (New Rochelle, N.Y.: Arlington House, 1977) p. 45.
8. I appreciate a discussion of this point with Alvin Roth.
9. Sheldon Lambert, quoted in *Newsweek*, June 27, 1977, p. 71.

Cornucopians and Neo-Malthusians

Thomas Homer-Dixon

Experts in environmental studies now commonly use the labels "cornucopian" for optimists like [Julian] Simon and "neo-Malthusian" for pessimists like Paul and Anne Ehrlich. Cornucopians do not worry much about protecting the stock of any single resource, because of their faith that market-driven human ingenuity can always be tapped to allow the substitution of more abundant resources to produce the same end-use service. . . .

Historically, cornucopians have been right to criticize the idea that resource scarcity places fixed limits on human activity. Time and time again, human beings have circumvented scarcities, and neo-Malthusians have often been justly accused of "crying wolf." But in assuming that this experience pertains to the future, cornucopians overlook seven factors.

First, whereas serious scarcities of critical resources in the past usually appeared singly, now we face multiple scarcities that exhibit powerful interactive, feedback, and threshold effects. An agricultural region may, for example, be simultaneously affected by degraded water and soil, greenhouse-induced precipitation changes, and increased ultraviolet radiation. This makes the future highly uncertain for policymakers and economic actors; tomorrow will be full of extreme events and surprises. Furthermore, as numerous resources become scarce simultaneously, it will be harder to identify substitution possibilities that produce the same end-use services at costs that prevailed when scarcity was less severe. Second, in the past the scarcity of a given resource usually increased slowly, allowing time for social, economic, and technological adjustment. But human populations are much

Excerpt from Thomas Homer-Dixon, "Environmental Change & Acute Conflict" in *International Security*, Fall 1991. Copyright 1991 by MIT Press. Reprinted by permission. Portions of the text and some footnotes have been omitted.

larger and activities of individuals are, on a global average, much more resource-intensive than before. This means that debilitating scarcities often develop much more quickly: whole countries may be deforested in a few decades; most of a region's topsoil can disappear in a generation; and critical ozone depletion may occur in as little as twenty years. Third, today's consumption has far greater momentum than in the past, because of the size of the consuming population, the sheer quantity of material consumed by this population, and the density of its interwoven fabric of consumption activities. The countless individual and corporate economic actors making up human society are heavily committed to certain patterns of resource use; and the ability of our markets to adapt may be sharply constrained by these entrenched interests.

These first three factors may soon combine to produce a daunting syndrome of environmentally induced scarcity: humankind will face multiple resource shortages that are interacting and unpredictable, that grow to crisis proportions rapidly, and that will be hard to address because of powerful commitments to certain consumption patterns.

The fourth reason that cornucopian arguments may not apply in the future is that the free-market price mechanism is a bad gauge of scarcity, especially for resources held in common, such as a benign climate and productive seas. In the past, many such resources seemed endlessly abundant; now they are being degraded and depleted, and we are learning that their increased scarcity often has tremendous bearing on a society's well-being. Yet this scarcity is at best reflected only indirectly in market prices. In addition, people often cannot participate in market transactions in which they have an interest, either because they lack the resources or because they are distant from the transaction process in time or space; in these cases the true scarcity of the resource is not reflected by its price.

The fifth reason is an extension of a point made earlier: market-driven adaptation to resource scarcity is most likely to succeed in wealthy societies, where abundant reserves of capital, knowledge, and talent help economic actors invent new technologies, identify conservation possibilities, and make the transition to new production and consumption patterns. Yet many of the societies facing the most serious environmental problems in the coming decades will be poor; even if they have efficient markets, lack of capital and know-how will hinder their response to these problems.

Sixth, cornucopians have an anachronistic faith in humankind's ability to unravel and manage the myriad processes of nature. There is no *a priori* reason to expect that human scientific and technical ingenuity can always surmount all types of scarcity. Human beings may not have the mental capacity to understand adequately the complexities of environmental-social systems. Or it may simply be impossible, given the physical, biological, and social laws governing these systems, to reduce all scarcity or repair all environmental damage. Moreover, the chaotic nature of these systems may keep us from fully anticipating the consequences of various adaptation and intervention strategies. Perhaps most important, scientific and technical knowledge must be built incrementally—layer upon layer–and its diffusion to the broader society often takes decades. Any technical solutions to environmental scarcity may arrive too late to prevent catastrophe.

Seventh and finally, future environmental problems, rather than inspiring the wave of ingenuity predicted by cornucopians, may instead reduce the supply of ingenuity available in a society. The success of market mechanisms depends on an intricate and stable system of institutions, social relations, and shared understandings. Cornucopians often overlook the role of *social* ingenuity in producing the complex legal and economic climate in which *technical* ingenuity can flourish. Policymakers must be clever "social engineers" to design and implement effective market mechanisms. Unfortunately, however, the syndrome of multiple, interacting, unpredictable, and rapidly changing environmental problems will increase the complexity and pressure of the policymaking setting. It will also generate increased "social friction" as elites and interest groups struggle to protect their prerogatives. The ability of policymakers to be good social engineers is likely to go *down*, not up, as these stresses increase.

Population size and growth are key variables producing the syndrome of environmental scarcity I have described. While sometimes population growth does not damage the environment, often this growth—in combination with prevailing social structures, technologies, and consumption patterns—makes environmental degradation worse. During the 1970s and early 1980s, family size dropped dramatically in many countries from six or seven children to three or four. But family planners have discovered that it is much more difficult to convince parents to forgo a further one or two children to bring family size down to replacement rate. . . . These developments have recently led the United Nations to increase its mid-range estimate of the globe's population when it stabilizes (predicted to occur towards the end of the twenty-first century) from 10.2 to 11 billion, which is over twice the size of the planet's current population.

Consequently, many countries will have to keep boosting their agricultural production by 2 to 4 percent per year well into the next century to avoid huge food imports. But, for the seven reasons discussed above, the social and technical engineers in these countries might not be able to supply the ever-increasing ingenuity required over this extended period. In particular, in many developing countries the effects of land scarcity and degradation are likely to become much more evident as the potential gains from green revolution technologies are fully realized. Unfortunately, there is no new generation of agricultural technologies waiting in the wings to keep productivity rising. Genetic engineering may eventually help scientists develop nitrogen-fixing, salinity-resistant, and drought-resistant grains, but their widespread use in the developing world is undoubtedly decades in the future.

Although we must be careful not to slip into environmental determinism, when it comes to the poorest countries on this planet we should not invest too much faith in the potential of human ingenuity to respond to multiple, interacting, and rapidly changing environmental problems once they have become severe. The most important of the seven factors above is the last: growing population, consumption, and environmental stresses will increase social friction. This will reduce the capacity of policymakers in developing countries to intervene as good social engineers in order to chart a sustainable development path and prevent further social disruption. Neo-Malthusians may underestimate human adaptability in *today's* environmental-social system, but as time passes their analysis may become ever more compelling.

The Prospects for International Intervention

Intervention in Historical Perspective

Marc Trachtenberg

. . . With the end of the Cold War, the issue of intervention has suddenly emerged as a major focus of political discussion. In the recent past, intervention was treated as a political problem—that is, as something that the major powers simply *did*, for political reasons. The current focus is on the question of whether a new "right to intervene"[1] is taking shape—of whether, in this new world of cooperation among great and small powers, the line between permissible and unacceptable uses of force is being redrawn. The idea that the international community has a right to intervene, albeit in exceptional cases, in the internal affairs of independent states—that sovereignty is in important ways limited by the existence of an international community—has suddenly become widely accepted. In particular, it is now often argued that the world community has a right to prevent countries like Iraq, Libya, and North Korea from developing nuclear capabilities—by force if necessary, many would add. It is also increasingly taken for granted that the world community has a right, and maybe even an obligation, to intervene when certain limits are transgressed—when ethnic or religious minorities are being massacred, for example, or when a state allows its territory to be used as a base for terrorist activity, or even perhaps if countries are ruled by dictators.

Clearly, something important is going on. New norms seem to be emerging. The international system may be changing in fundamental ways. But how should such a process be managed? What sort of system should we be trying to create? Such issues can scarcely be approached simply on an abstract and theoretical level, where notions of legitimacy are drawn deductively from first principles. The sort of attitude one should take toward this set of issues also needs to be based to a certain

From Marc Trachtenberg, "Intervention in Historical Perspective" in *Emerging Norms of Justified Intervention*, 1993. Reprinted by permission of American Academy of Arts & Sciences. Portions of the text and some footnotes have been omitted.

extent on a study of the past. For it certainly matters whether one views oneself as writing on a completely blank slate and developing something essentially new, or whether one thinks of oneself as building on historical tradition and historical experience. It makes a difference whether one thinks that the world is in the process of dismantling a set of norms, based on national sovereignty and nonintervention, that is deeply embedded in the international system, the product of a very basic, long-term historical process, or whether one views that set of norms as a relatively superficial feature of the international system, reflecting the political circumstances of a particular historical period.

For this reason, it makes sense to take a look at the whole phenomenon of intervention from a historical point of view. When we talk about intervention in the modern world, are we dealing with something fundamentally new or with something that has long been a familiar feature of international political life—indeed, a feature whose legitimacy has been sanctioned by a body of thought that is still politically relevant?

To answer that question, it is important to define what is meant by the term "intervention." Intervention in the sense of interference, by force or the threat of force, in the internal affairs of another country, is a very broad concept. Many examples leap to mind: the expansion of Islam, the wars of religion in Europe, the military actions set off by the French and Russian revolutions, the whole phenomenon of imperialism. Or consider the relatively brief history of the United States, a nation which, because of its great size and favorable geographical position, had less reason than many others to get involved in foreign affairs. But even in this case, one finds a whole series of interventions, "from the halls of Montezuma to the shores of Tripoli"—military action in the Mediterranean, in Latin America, in the Philippines, in Europe during and after both world wars, in Korea and Vietnam and the Middle East. To talk about intervention in this broad sense is therefore, as many writers have noted, virtually tantamount to talking about international politics as a whole.[2]

But the problem of the legitimacy of intervention has traditionally not been concerned with intervention in this very broad sense. It has a distinct historical meaning, and in fact derives historically from the rise of nationalism and the nation-state in the nineteenth century. The idea that a nation should be free to determine its own destiny implied a *general* norm of nonintervention. But the emergence of this general norm led inevitably to the question of when it did *not* apply. "Intervention" therefore meant the use of force in those exceptional cases in which a line had been crossed and national sovereignty, the legitimacy of which was recognized in principle, no longer had to be respected. The problem of intervention, in other words, was, in the Western political tradition, the problem of defining which *exceptions* to the general norm were permissible.[3]

Thus, the nature of the problem, as it has taken shape historically, defines what we are interested in when we review the evidence. What sort of pattern emerges when one looks at intervention, in this sense, as an historical phenomenon? What was the line of thinking that rationalized constraints on sovereignty and sanctioned forcible interference in the internal affairs of a foreign state?

Looking back, one can identify not one but two distinct lines of thought limiting sovereignty and rationalizing intervention. The first relates to constraints on national rights, supported by the threat or the reality of armed intervention, in order to maintain a given balance of power. In this case the interests of the international system, and in particular the need to deal preemptively with possible threats to the peace, set limits to the sovereign powers of great and small states alike. The second has to do with relations between "civilized" nations at the core of the system and other states, viewed as less civilized, whose sovereignty was viewed as more problematic. One set of rules applied when the European states were dealing with each other, and quite a different set applied when the European powers were dealing with countries like China, Persia, Morocco, or Turkey, and the second interventionist tradition reflected this double standard.

THE FIRST TRADITION: GUARANTEEING INTERNATIONAL STABILITY

In July 1900 the historian William Lingelbach published an article on "The Doctrine and Practice of Intervention in Europe."[4] Lingelbach objected to the way almost all writers interested in the question of intervention had dealt with the issue. It was as though they were engaged in an exercise in moral philosophy: "Almost without exception they treat the subject in an 'a priori' manner. From the premises that nations are independent, politically equal and possessed of the same rights, they deduce what the doctrine of intervention must be and what the conditions are which justify its use." But this method, he said, was totally unsatisfactory: "In every other branch of international law, writers arrive at the doctrine and principles from the practice and precedents established by nations in their dealings with each other. There is no adequate reason why this should not be done with regard to intervention."[5] It was therefore necessary to base a "theory of intervention" on a study of historical reality, and for Lingelbach the basic reality was that "states are not independent of each other; that they are not politically equal; and that their so-called independence is constantly called in question."

Limitations on sovereignty, he stressed, were traditionally sanctioned by the principle of the balance of power. In the Treaty of Utrecht of 1713, for example, Spain and France were forbidden to unite, even if they both wanted to; the aim, the treaty explicitly said, was "to perpetuate the equilibrium of Europe." The balance of power principle—the idea that national rights could be overridden in the name of European equilibrium—applied to great and small powers alike. Belgium, regardless of her own wishes, was not allowed to merge herself into France without the consent of the European powers. The powers "had the right," they declared, to provide that Belgium, "having become independent, shall not endanger the general security and the European equilibrium. Every nation has its rights, but Europe also has her rights."[6] This final sentence is of particular interest because it reflects a sense of principles in conflict, of a clash between the idea of national sovereignty and the principle of the balance of power.

For Lingelbach, limitations on sovereignty such as those embodied in the 1831 treaty on Belgium were paradigmatic. Intervention was "based on the principle that there are certain obligations which states owe to each other, and which no state is at liberty to violate; that there is a power residing outside the individual state superior to it, which assumes to dictate what the individual state may or may not do in its dealings with others; that there is a right superior to national right, and which in a measure controls national will, and that the practice of intervention is a means admissible for enforcing these higher claims against the individual state." *"Intervention, therefore,"* he concluded (and the sentence was italicized in the original text), *"instead of being outside the pale of the law of nations and antagonistic to it, is an integral and essential part of it; an act of police for enforcing recognized rights, and the only means, apart from war, for enforcing the rules of International Law."*[7]

Lingelbach had without question identified a powerful tradition supporting limitations on the sovereign rights of independent states. But he had mistakenly assumed that the right of intervention was "becoming more and more recognized as the legal means by which the society of nations enforces its rights." Writing at the time of the international intervention against the Boxers in China, he thought that "modern practice" was showing "a strong tendency towards action in concert."[8] But things in fact were moving in exactly the opposite direction.

Intervention in Lingelbach's sense, as "an act of police" for enforcing international norms, was already in decline when he did his study. The principle of national sovereignty was still on the rise, propelled first by the great wave of European nationalism in the nineteenth century and then by the gradual awakening of national feeling in the Third World, which was encouraged in particular by Japan's victory in the war with Russia just after the turn of the century. The First World War accelerated the process, as each side sought to use national sentiment as a political weapon against its adversary, and after 1945 the Cold War led to a further increase in the power and autonomy of the "nonaligned" states, as America and Russia competed for their favor. After World War I, furthermore, the very idea of the balance of power came to be viewed as rather disreputable—as tied into an old order of arms and alliances that had itself supposedly been a cause of the war.

Moreover, a balance of power system, in the sense of the great powers acting as a group to maintain international stability, no longer corresponded to political reality. The fact was that the great powers could lay down the rules only when they were united, or at least when the powers that constituted the dominant coalition were as a bloc strong enough to keep any recalcitrant power in line. This had been the case at various times in the nineteenth century, but it was not to be the case in the twentieth, at least not until now. In the decade before World War I, Germany and Austria-Hungary moved increasingly toward the idea of a military intervention against Serbia—not to conquer territory, which the Austrians, and especially the Hungarians, did not want, but to intimidate the Serbs and prevent Serbia from being used as a base for undermining the Habsburg monarchy. The Central Powers defended the policy in terms of the need to maintain the European equilibrium by preserving Austria as a great power; the Entente in the final analysis did not accept the argument. So with Europe divided into two increasingly hostile blocs of approximately equal power, and with one of those blocs ultimately siding with the Serbs, an interventionist policy became very risky, with the result that in the end what one had was not "intervention," but general war.

Similarly, after World War I the victorious Allies imposed their peace terms on Germany in the Treaty of Versailles. Germany's population and industrial resources were such that without restraints on her sovereign rights, she would again become the strongest power in Europe. The restraints were thus justified by the need to provide for European security—to prevent Germany from again becoming a threat to the peace. The German military establishment was limited and subjected to Allied control; the Rhineland was demilitarized and temporarily occupied; Austria was forbidden to merge herself into Germany. These constraints on Germany's sovereign rights were policed by the threat, and at two points—in 1920, with the occupation of Frankfurt, and in 1923, with the occupation of the Ruhr—by the reality, of foreign intervention. But the bloc of status quo powers was not strong enough to enforce these constraints. Of the powers that had fought the war against Germany, America had defected, Britain had half-defected, Russia was hostile, and France by herself was not strong or resolute enough to bear the enormous burden of policing the system. The policy of keeping Germany down was therefore increasingly viewed as futile, and even France's former allies in the war frowned on the very idea of military intervention to support such a policy.

Nevertheless, the tradition of intervention for power-political reasons never really died out. This tradition naturally carries most weight in time of war. In World War II especially, even those governments that took seriously the principle of non-intervention in the affairs of independent states were quite willing to infringe on the sovereign rights of neutral powers. Thus, nonbelligerents like Iran were occupied; French North Africa was invaded and occupied, even though it belonged to a neutral power; the British even destroyed the French fleet at Mers-el-Kebir after France had dropped out of the war and opted for neutrality. In World War I also, the rights of neutrals—even their right to trade with each other—had not been respected; and the war began, of course, with the German invasion of neutral Belgium.

This familiar pattern of wartime conduct, in which respect for national sovereignty takes a back seat to security concerns, for obvious reasons carries over to postwar periods as well. Thus, the deep involvement of the Allies in the remaking of German and Japanese society after World War II was a natural consequence of the war. The same general point explains the many interventions of the Cold War period—the active and latent use of power by both sides to prevent defections from their respective blocs and to influence civil conflicts in Third World countries. The most important of these interventions, the limited use of American force in 1962 to bring about the withdrawal of the Soviet missiles from Cuba, was in fact explicitly defended in balance of power terms.

Both the persistence and the relative decline of the balance of power tradition can perhaps best be illustrated by turning to the case of Germany. During the Cold War period, a regime gradually took shape to govern Germany's political status. . . .

But unlike the system that was created to control post-Napoleonic France—or, much less successfully, post–World War I Germany—the existence of the Cold War system for the control of Germany was never openly proclaimed. The regime of constrained German sovereignty was not policed by the threat of armed intervention sanctioned by the four powers that had created it; it operated in a much more subtle way, and in fact depended on a degree of tension between the Soviets and the West for its viability.

More generally, one senses a definite ebbing of the force of the balance of power tradition. Territorial insecurity among the major powers is no longer the problem it was in the past, and the sensitivity of states to shifts in the balance of power has declined accordingly. So intervention to maintain a given balance is no longer as important as it once was.

But this is not to say that the balance of power interventionist tradition is totally moribund. As long as political problems have not completely vanished, the threat of force will remain a possible way of dealing with them. To reduce the risk that force will ultimately be used, security regimes may therefore be constructed. But a regime is basically a set of rules, some of which way limit the traditional rights of sovereign powers—the right, for example, to decide for oneself the size and nature of one's own military establishment, and the right to conclude alliances and to allow one's allies to base forces on one's own territory. And the rules may constrain sovereignty in various other ways—by providing, for example, for the rights of ethnic minorities.

If a security regime is a set of rules, that regime has real meaning only if those rules, if tested, can be enforced. The act of enforcement, then, would be an intervention in Lingelbach's sense. The existence of the system is what legitimates the use of force. The "right of intervention" and the existence of the regime are two sides to a coin; the two notions are inseparable, and one cannot analyze either without thinking about the other. . . .

This whole analysis has a number of implications. The first point is that the way we think about intervention is often too narrow and apolitical. There is a common tendency to think that "legitimate" intervention is divorced from normal political life—that a line has been crossed, that the normal rules no longer apply, that humanitarian principles, for example, should now govern policy, and that to go further and think in terms of political involvement and a political settlement somehow taints the legitimacy of the whole interventionist enterprise. The argument here, to the contrary, is that as a rule the problem of intervention is not to be treated in a political vacuum, and that broad political considerations are not to be ignored. An intervention in Bosnia, for example, would have implications with regard to what is permissible throughout the ethnically mixed region of East Central Europe. What sort of precedent one would want to create would depend on the sort of system one wanted for the region as a whole, and policy on the Bosnian problem should certainly be elaborated with those broader considerations in mind.

The second point has to do with the way interventionist policy relates to a regime of constrained sovereignty. The two go together hand in hand, but not in the sense of a correlation—that the more you have of one, the more you have of the other. In fact, one can say almost the opposite: that the more effective the regime, the less need there is for actual intervention as the means of enforcement. What this implies is that the problem of intervention is most salient when the system has not yet established itself but rather is still taking shape—most commonly in the aftermath of some great political upheaval, such as a war, or the collapse of communism in the East—and that the decisions on intervention made at that time will thus play a key role in determining the sort of system that eventually does emerge.

The final point is that the balance of power tradition is most alive today in one specific area: the international regime for the control of nuclear weapons. This is in particular one of the key issues facing the major powers as they deal with the Third World. Indeed, it is in this area that the second interventionist tradition also comes into play.

THE SECOND TRADITION: IMPOSING EUROPEAN VALUES

It was in Britain at the beginning of the nineteenth century that an explicit norm of nonintervention began to emerge. In 1818, at the Congress of Aix-la-Chapelle, the Russian Tsar Alexander I proposed the creation of an international army to guarantee the existing political status quo—that is, to protect conservative regimes against revolution. After a revolt overthrew the absolutist regime in Spain in 1820, Alexander pressed forcefully for an interventionist policy. At the Congress of Troppau in December 1820, and largely at his instigation, the rulers of Russia, Prussia, and Austria issued a circular that was taken as the "manifesto of their political faith." They claimed for themselves an unrestricted right to intervene to suppress revolution, to check "according to their means the evils resulting from the violation of all the principles of order and morality.". . . The British government was asked to support intervention in Spain, but the foreign secretary, Lord Castlereagh, refused, and laid down his reasoning in an important document, his State Paper of May 5, 1820.

Castlereagh, it is important to note, was not opposed to intervention on principle: there was no talk in his State Paper of any pretended right of national sovereignty that took precedence over all other considerations of policy. To him, "the principle of one state interfering by force in the internal affairs of another, in order to enforce obedience to the governing authority, is always a question of the greatest possible moral as well as political delicacy." He was very much against any generalized system of intervention. The alliance that had brought down Napoleon had remained together after his defeat, and, in conformity with a treaty provision that Castlereagh had personally drafted, allied representatives met together in periodic congresses in the post-Napoleonic period. But the alliance, Castlereagh stressed, never was "intended as an Union for the Government of the World, or for the superintendence of the internal affairs of other states."[9]

Although the alliance did not have the general function of running European affairs, it did have specific responsibilities related to the internal affairs of particular states, and in outlining what these were, Castlereagh was defining the limits of legitimate intervention. These corresponded to what could be justified in terms of the balance of power interventionist tradition discussed above.

The alliance, Castlereagh wrote, had "designated the revolutionary power which had convulsed France and desolated Europe as an object of its constant solicitude; but it was the revolutionary power more particularly in its military character actual and existent within France against which it intended to take precautions, rather than against the democratic principles, then as now, but too generally spread throughout Europe." It was when the balance of power, and thus the peace of the world, was at stake, and only then, that outside powers had the right to intervene in the internal affairs of other countries. As far as Britain was concerned, the Low Countries provided the best example of this general point: "the importance of preventing the Low Countries, the military barrier of Europe, from being lost, by being melted down into the general mass of French power, whether by insurrection or by conquest, might enable the British government to act more promptly upon this than perhaps upon any other case of an internal character that can be stated." Unless the peace of the world was at stake, all kinds of arguments pointed to a policy of nonintervention: the danger, for example, of the interventionist armies being "contaminated," the disturbing effect of an interventionist policy at home, the cost of the intervention, and (since the armies would not stay on indefinitely) the possibly limited political reach of the intervention. A "rational statesman," he argued, would therefore have to conclude "that the only necessity which could in wisdom justify such an attempt is that which, temperately considered, appears to leave to Europe no other option than that of either going to meet that danger which they cannot avoid, or having it poured in the full tide of military invasion upon their own states. The actual existence of such a danger may indeed be inferred from many circumstances short of the visible preparations for attack, but it is submitted that on this basis the conclusion should always be examined."[10]. . .

But even the most cursory glance at British policy in the course of the century shows that Britain was highly interventionist—indeed, especially during the periods when Palmerston and Gladstone headed the government—and that Britain's interventions went well beyond what Castlereagh's doctrine would warrant.

For there was in fact a second interventionist tradition at play at the time, and this had little to do with balance of power principles. It focused not on Europe, where Castlereagh's ideas really did form the basis of British policy, but rather on the rest of the world, where a totally different set of rules applied.

The phrase "gunboat diplomacy" is by no means a mere cliche. The nineteenth century was an era of naval demonstrations, blockades, and bombardments directed at weak and relatively backward countries. One incident, a little extreme, nevertheless gives some indication of the prevailing practice. A Chinese-built and -owned vessel called the *Arrow*, illegally "flying the British flag as a screen for piratical acts," was seized by the Chinese authorities in 1856. The British governor of Hong Kong then demanded an apology, "and when this was declined he requested Admiral Seymour to bombard first the forts and then the city" of Canton. This led to war with China. The issue evoked indignation in the British Parliament, and the government was actually defeated on the issue in the Commons, but then called a general election and, after a jingoistic campaign, "returned triumphantly to power.". . .

The important point to note about such interventions—and they were rather common in this period—is that they were directed at only certain areas of the world: at Latin America and especially at what Lord Salisbury called the "dying nations," the broad band of oriental despotisms stretching from Morocco in the west to China in the east, and including also Egypt, Turkey, and Persia. Intervention as such was not an issue when it came to the expansion of Europe into sub-Saharan Africa, or of Russia into Central Asia. It was only in relations with states that possessed a modicum of sovereignty, a recognized international status, that "intervention" was the appropriate concept. And it is also important to remember in this context that the Christian powers had for centuries been intervening on behalf of non-Muslim minorities in the Muslim East. This was a tradition that one writer traced back to the year 1250, when St. Louis promised the Maronites in the Levant "protection as though they had been French subjects."[11]

So by the end of the nineteenth century, a double standard had taken shape. The "civilized" nations of Europe, it was assumed, had the right to control their own destiny, free of foreign intrusion, but the backward and less civilized oriental and Latin American states could be the targets of intervention. . . .

The Americans also took it for granted that a different set of rules applied outside the circle of the "civilized" countries. Woodrow Wilson, for example, the great champion of self-determination for the European nationalities, sent American forces into Santo Domingo and Haiti, and into Mexico twice.[12]

The whole phenomenon of intervention up to the period of the First World War thus underscored and dramatized the fact that the society of nations was not a society of equals—that there were in fact two castes of states. To be a target of intervention—indeed, even of humanitarian intervention—was to be stigmatized as of inferior status. Intervention was in this sense a two-edged sword. On the one hand, the purpose of intervention was often in large part to intimidate and humiliate. It was this purpose that lay behind the extraordinary sensitivity of the Europeans to real and imagined slights. The Kaiser's notorious speech to the German troops about to be sent off to help put down the Boxer uprising in 1900 is perhaps an extreme example: "Let all who fall into your hands be at your mercy. Just as the Huns a thousand years ago, under the leadership of Attila, gained a reputation by virtue of which they still live in historical tradition, so may the name of Germany become known in such a manner in China, that no Chinese will ever again dare to look askance at a German."[13] But as the many references at the time to the "salutary" effect of such interventions make clear, the sentiment itself was by no means uncommon before World War I.[14]

On the other hand, the goal of intervention was not always to push down the target countries; often the aim was to pull them up to European standards. The actions to suppress piracy and end the slave trade are to be understood in this sense, and indeed, the interventions on behalf of private economic interests—on behalf of the principle of the sanctity of contracts, for example—can also be viewed in this light.

In either case, much of the political meaning of intervention derives from the fact that it stigmatizes its target as less than civilized and thus as not worthy of the respect that civilized states have for each other. Indeed, it is because it carries this connotation even today that the threat of intervention—that is, the threat of stigmatization, of being placed outside the circle of the civilized nations—can carry real weight as a means of enforcing international norms.

One problem, however, is that the great powers do not always agree on which countries are appropriate targets of intervention, and this disagreement can sometimes be an important source of international conflict. It is for this reason, in fact, that intervention can escalate into a major war. One can look, for example, at the Serbian question in 1914 as an argument over whether Serbia was a European state and thus entitled to have its sovereign rights respected, or "oriental" and uncivilized and thus an appropriate target for Austrian intervention. The Central Powers, of course, argued that the latter was the case. "The Serbs," said the Kaiser, "are Orientals, therefore liars, tricksters, and masters of evasion," and a *"douce violence"* in the form of a military occupation of Belgrade was necessary to ensure their compliance with Austria's demands for the suppression of Serb-based terrorism.[15] But a large section of British opinion, which knew how quick Britain had been to take punitive action against small countries that infringed on British interests, was inclined to sympathize with Austria.[16] And certainly, the whole Balkan area, in British eyes, did not quite have European status (as Palmerston's extraordinary bullying of Greece at the time of the Don Pacifico affair in 1850 had made abundantly clear). Other factors of course came into play, and in the end the Triple Entente supported the Serbs. But the failure of the powers to agree on Serbia's status—that is, whether she was "oriental" or "European"—was in a sense one of the major factors that led to the war.

The rationales for intervention in the pre–1914 world were certainly very different from what they are today. One is struck repeatedly by how overt the appeal then was to national interest (even in the narrow sense of purely commercial interest) and national prestige in the period before 1914, although this appeal was frequently mixed together with more idealistic arguments. President McKinley's rationale for intervention in Cuba in April 1898 (and at this point the plan was only for intervention, not for war) is a good example. He referred first to the need "to put an end to the barbarities, bloodshed, starvation, and horrible miseries now existing there, and which the parties to the conflict are either unable or unwilling to stop or mitigate," but then stressed that "the right to intervene may be justified by the very serious injury to the commerce, trade and business of our people."[17]

Intervention for humanitarian reasons was not unknown in the nineteenth century, although the protection of European (and American) lives was a more compelling motive than more general humanitarian concerns.[18] It was really only in 1876, however, that outrage at political massacre—and in particular at the "Bulgarian Horrors," the massacres visited upon the Bulgarians by the Turks—was able to have an important impact on the policy of a great European power. England (or, really, half of England—the mainly Nonconformist, Liberal half) was deeply moved by the stories of the atrocities in the Bulgarian parts of Turkey; the agitation was able to prevent the Conservative government from pursuing its traditional pro-

Turkish (because anti-Russian) policy. There was nothing equivalent in any of the continental countries; even in Russia, the policy of supporting the subject nationalities in the Balkans was rooted in part in a sense of racial and religious kinship, and in part in a desire to use the issue as an instrument for advancing Russian interests, and in particular for moving Russian power closer to control of the Turkish Straits. From the mid–1870s on, in fact, the European powers had made many efforts to get the Turks to make life more bearable for their subject nationalities, and the reform effort had involved a series of threats of force. But all this had been motivated by the goal of avoiding the more radical alternative of carving up European Turkey and allowing new nations of unclear political orientation to come into being there. The Turks, however, were recalcitrant, and force was eventually used against them; the Russo-Turkish War of 1877 led to important territorial changes in the interest of the Balkan peoples, especially the creation of a Bulgarian state. But only on the British side was disinterested sympathy for oppressed people— that is, a relatively pure humanitarian concern—in any way a major factor in policy.[19]

The basis for intervention has certainly changed a good deal since the end of the nineteenth century. Intervention for the defense of economic interests gradually lost legitimacy.[20] Indeed, many of the old interventionist rationales were in decline, especially after 1945. The need to "restore order," for example, was no longer considered an entirely respectable basis for intervention. Even intervention to protect one's own nationals gradually became suspect; the tendency today is to urge one's nationals to pull out if real risks develop (with the implication that if they choose to stay on, they do so at their own risk).

The First World War marked a real watershed. . . .

And the process of change accelerated after 1945. The Cold War almost totally delegitimated armed intervention for economic purposes. For example, during the conflict between Iran and Great Britain in the early 1950s over the control of Iranian oil, the American government came down hard against the British for threatening intervention that might lead to the fall of Iran to the Communists. Secretary of State Dean Acheson in 1951 was appalled that the "cardinal purpose of British policy" was not "to prevent Iran from going Commie," but that Britain's fundamental purpose was instead "to preserve what they believe to be the last remaining bulwark of British solvency; that is, their overseas investment and property position."[21] . . .

On the other hand, certain rationales for intervention became more widely accepted in the twentieth century, most notably the idea of intervention for humanitarian purposes. But even so, it is important to note that at no point has the actual use of force for humanitarian purposes been a familiar feature of the international political scene.

The story of the "minorities treaties" that the Allies imposed on a series of states after World War I provides a good case in point. These treaties sought to prevent political discrimination against ethnic and religious minorities in those states, and also to assure them of certain cultural rights—for example, the right to set up their own schools and religious institutions. This system was "placed under the guarantee of the League of Nations."[22] The postwar system for the protection of minorities was rooted not just in humanitarian concerns, but even more in a desire to prevent threats to the peace from emerging, most notably through the possible mistreatment of their large German minority by the new Polish state. So the treaties are important for having laid down the principle that the civilized world had a double interest in assuring that minorities were treated fairly.

But the minority treaty system is also significant for two other reasons. First, it provides a rather striking example of the persistence of the double standard governing intervention into the post–World War I period. The treaty regime applied mainly to a belt of states in East-Central Europe, running from Estonia in the north to Greece and Turkey in the south.[23] It included both new states and old; it covered both Allied states and ex-enemies. But the traditional great powers were not included in the system: the German-speaking minority that lived in the territory Italy had acquired from the old Austrian empire was given no protection, and even Germany herself, although the defeated power, was not obliged to respect the rights of any Poles still living on German territory, although Poland was required to protect the rights of its German-speaking minority. And in western Europe, neither France nor Belgium nor Denmark had to sign treaties to safeguard the rights of the German populations in the lands they acquired after the war. A basic distinction was made between civilized and backward countries. The treaty states thus felt singled out for discriminatory treatment, and this was perhaps the main reason they so deeply resented the system.

The second point relates to the reasons for the failure of the system. At its best, in the immediate postwar period, the League system provided a framework for the mediation of disputes between the minorities and the governments of the treaty states. Agreements were sometimes worked out, but even the League Council tended to focus its attention on such trivial cases as the "denial of a liquor license to an innkeeper," and the Council "failed completely in dealing with flagrant atrocities, massacres and pogroms. In such instances, a word of censure, sometimes years after the event, was all the satisfaction the minority could expect."[24] In fact, the great powers represented on the Council had leverage over the treaty states only because of the political benefits they could confer—above all, security against Russia and Germany. As the years went by, the ability of those powers to provide security in eastern Europe was called increasingly into question. By the early 1930s countries like Poland had turned away from the League system and sought instead to deal with their powerful neighbors on a bilateral basis, and it is certainly no mere coincidence that by this point the treaty regime had essentially collapsed. The moral here is that a system like the post–World War I minorities treaty regime can be run only by a very powerful bloc of states; an interventionist system makes sense only if the great powers are already more or less united politically.

INTERNATIONAL ORGANIZATION

It was something of a paradox that although the nineteenth century was an era of relatively unbridled self-assertion on the part of the European powers in their dealings with the non-European world, the interventionist tradition at that time placed a considerable premium on international sanction. From the outset it was understood that interference was most effective when the powers were most united. The British, for example, were supported by the French in their intervention in China in the late 1850s; the French were careful to obtain international sanction for their intervention in Syria in 1860; the French-dominated intervention in Mexico in 1862 had been authorized by a convention signed in October 1861 by Britain, Spain, and France. The 1882 British intervention in Egypt was originally supposed to be a joint Anglo-French operation on behalf of the European powers. And as the intervention turned into a semipermanent occupation, the British authorities did not feel free to do what they wanted in Egypt; their hands were to a certain extent tied by the need to obtain international sanction. The United States, for its part, was interested in obtaining European support for its intervention in Cuba—more interested, in fact, than in acting jointly with the Latin American republics. And the Americans did actually cooperate with the Europeans in 1900, when they took part in the international expedition to put down the Boxers—the most striking example of the concert of the great powers in action against a Third World nationalist movement.

The tradition that intervention was to be governed by the great powers acting, if possible, as a semiformal bloc, was quite strong in the nineteenth century. The "Concert of Europe" is by no means a mere label that historians have applied after the fact to the system of great power collaboration that existed at various times in the nineteenth century. Indeed, the term was commonly used by statesmen at the time, and the system was rooted in a sense that the interest of Europe had a claim on the policies of the individual states—that national interest had to be subordinated to the interest of Europe as a whole.

The assumption throughout the period, therefore, was that the great powers, acting as a semiformal entity and often meeting in great congresses and conferences, should govern the system of foreign intervention. In 1823 Britain, as a member of the European concert, had the recognized right to place limits on the French intervention in Spain—that is, to keep it from becoming anything more than an intervention in the strict sense of the term.[25] Similarly, British pressure on Russia—and indeed, an overt threat of war—forced a rollback of the extensive changes Russia had dictated in the Treaty of San Stefano, following her victory over the Turks in 1877, to the modest levels that conformed basically to what the powers had agreed on before the conflict. It is important to note, moreover, that although the basic terms of the settlement had been agreed on in bilateral negotiations between Salisbury and Shuvalov, the terms were worked out in greater detail and given formal international sanction at the Congress of Berlin in 1878.

Indeed, in the generation or two before World War I, the assumption was that the powers, acting in concert, had the right to oversee intervention in such politically sensitive areas as Morocco and especially the Balkans. In the First Moroccan Crisis, the Germans tried to use the system to their political advantage. The French "penetration" of Morocco was contrary to the Act of Madrid, which recognized the sovereignty of the Sultan of Morocco and had been adopted by the powers in 1880. The Germans, mistakenly calculating that they would have the upper hand at a new international meeting, demanded a new conference of the powers.

But at that meeting, held at Algeciras in 1906, the French were able to turn the tables on the hapless Germans and received international sanction for their increasingly intrusive Moroccan policy.

With regard to the Balkans, the assumption was that the powers had the right to control what went on there, especially since changes in Balkan arrangements were constantly being threatened, and these changes generally conflicted with previous arrangements the powers had more or less formally adopted.[26] The system worked with increasing difficulty in the years before World War I: during the Bosnian crisis of 1908–1909 and again during the Balkan Wars of 1912–13, conferences met and arrangements were hammered out. There was still some sense that a vestige of a system existed. Even during the July crisis in 1914, the original Russian advice to Serbia was not to resist an Austrian invasion and to "entrust her fate to the judgment of the Great Powers."[27] If the Russian government had kept to this position, the result would have been an intervention in the traditional sense, and not European war.

But this example serves mainly to draw out the obvious problem with the Concert system (and with its successors, the League of Nations and the United Nations). The system works only when the major powers are relatively united.[28] It thus cannot serve as a means of regulating basic political differences *among* the great powers; it essentially provides a legal framework for joint action in dealing with weaker countries when the political basis for such joint action exists. For most of the twentieth century the great powers were more sharply divided than they had been in the nineteenth, and the area in which common action was possible had shrunk significantly. The instruments for great power collaboration were more highly formalized, but fundamental political division meant that for most of the twentieth century these institutions provided little basis for the control of intervention. . . .

THE FUTURE OF INTERVENTION

Using this brief historical survey as a springboard, what can be said about the future of intervention? It is clear that there are longstanding traditions that support the idea that there are limits to what a state should be free to do within its own borders; and that these traditions, for a variety of reasons but which mainly have to do with the Cold War, led for many years a kind of subterranean existence. The long-term historical trend was toward increasing recognition of the right of the civilized world to uphold certain standards of behavior—that states, for example, should not be free to massacre their own citizens or allow their territory to serve as a base for piracy or terrorism. As a political force, this factor was held in suspension by the Cold War, but the ending of that conflict can be expected to free it up. Similarly, international political institutions, whose main function has always been to provide a framework through which the major powers govern a system of intervention, can once again be expected to come into their own.

One of the key points to emerge from this survey is that intervention should generally be thought of as part of a *system*—a system of constrained sovereignty, whose rules are not applied capriciously and whose legitimacy is broadly accepted. The common tendency is to think of intervention, or at least of *legitimate* intervention, as a relatively isolated action taking place at the margin of international political life. The standard view is that intervention is permissible only in extreme cases, when a line has been crossed and the norms of civilized behavior have been so egregiously violated that the rest of the world can no longer remain passive. And the conclusion is drawn that the act of intervention must be limited to what is necessary to ensure respect for those norms: it must be brief, relatively narrow in scope, and more or less untainted by a concern with political considerations that go beyond the immediate issue at hand.

But many interventions need to be viewed, to one extent or another, in systemic terms, as "acts of police" sustaining a regime of constrained sovereignty. In those cases one should take the opposite view: one should in such circumstances analyze an intervention in terms of its system-wide, and often essentially political, implications.

Consider, for example, the whole question of nuclear proliferation in the Third World. This issue is bound to lie at the center of the debate on intervention in coming years. Indeed, it is bound to be of special interest from the standpoint of the present analysis, because it marks one of the key areas in which the two interventionist traditions identified above happen to converge. . . .

More generally, what the systemic approach implies is that the sole test of the legitimacy of intervention should not be narrow, apolitical, and legalistic. If the problem in what used to be Yugoslavia is that the different ethnic groups there can no longer live together peacefully, and if for reasons having to do with precedent, proximity, and spillover effects in general, the Western world decides that the continuation of such violence is intolerable, then there is no compelling reason that intervention should be limited to preventing starvation or controlling atrocities— that is, to action aimed only at the most extreme violations of international norms. There is no reason why the outside powers should rule out as illegitimate the very idea of trying to get at the root of the problem—for example, by arranging for an orderly, equitable, and humane exchange of populations. As many nineteenth-century statesmen understood, interventions in any case have a natural tendency to expand their reach. If one is going to intervene at all, one should understand that extrication may be difficult, that the pressure to deepen involvement in a political direction will be great—that, in short, intervention is a very serious business, not a limited, "easy-in, easy-out" affair.

What this implies is that one often has to think of intervention in political terms—as governed far more by political considerations than, say, by legal principles. This is scarcely a problem at present, since the norms governing intervention are still relatively unconstrained by firmly established legal structures. . . .

Many people, of course, are trying to grapple with the problem of developing clear principles for intervention, and a number of ideas have been put forward. In the literature on intervention, for example, there is a great emphasis on process, and the argument is frequently made that one of the major tests of legitimacy is international sanction. Unilateral intervention is said to be impermissible; intervention is legitimate only when the UN or one of the major regional organizations, such as the OAS, authorizes the action. Such principles are not to be dismissed out of hand, but there is a risk in pushing them too far and taking them as absolutely binding. It is not simply that the governments of the world are not always right about these matters. A more basic argument is that a policy of consensualism is often a policy of the lowest common denominator. It may be better in certain cases to pursue a more radical policy aimed at a decisive settlement. But (as in the case of the confrontation with Iraq) consensualism ties one's hands, truncates one's goals, and thus may stand in the way of a real resolution of the problem that gave rise to the intervention in the first place.

That being said, a real preference for international sanction, and, if possible, multilateral action, certainly makes sense, and even if one does not think formal international authorization is absolutely essential, one should still be willing to pay a certain price to obtain it.

For the effectiveness of intervention rests on something more than the firepower of the armed forces of the more developed states. The power of intervention is, as argued above, in large measure the power to stigmatize. This is a power that can easily backfire on those who would wield it. Political meaning is in large measure rooted in historical memory, and even a cursory survey of the past should make it clear that for much of the world, intervention is suspect; it is bound to evoke memories of imperialism, colonialism, racism, and national humiliation. The problem for the intervening powers, especially when a Third World country is the target of an intervention, is how to counteract this effect, how to make sure that it is outweighed by other considerations—that is, how to make stigmatization support the values of the whole civilized world, so that it will be supported honestly by most of the Third World countries themselves.

Or, to put the issue in somewhat different terms: the problem is to figure out how the second interventionist tradition, which sanctioned the right of powerful European states to impose their standards on countries they viewed as less civilized, can be transmuted into a set of more broadly based principles sanctioning intervention when certain norms of civilized behavior are violated—when populations are being slaughtered, when terrorist groups are sheltered, perhaps when civil strife seems to be out of control. The problem is difficult because the powerful states at the center of the system will never themselves be the target of interventions of this sort. This group of states, not just powerful but also rich, democratic, and mainly white, will be the force behind interventionist policy, while the interventions themselves will still be directed mainly at weaker states on the periphery, mostly in the Third World. For this reason alone, the legitimacy of intervention is bound to be suspect in the eyes of most of the world's population.

What all this adds up to is the conclusion that much of the enthusiasm lying behind the new interventionism is misplaced. Intervention does have a role to play in international political life, but an interventionist policy has to be elaborated with considerable care. For an interventionist system to be viable, it needs in particular to have a general aura of legitimacy. In the case of intervention in the Third World, the system needs to be supported especially by the major Third World countries that can be expected to be very suspicious of it.

This means more than just solving the tactical problems of getting Third World governments to vote for interventionist actions in the UN and various regional bodies, or even to send in their own military contingents. It means figuring out how whole populations, or at least their politically active components, react to intervention—what excites hostility, which aspects of an interventionist policy can generate support—and then framing one's own policy with this understanding in mind. It means listening to people we are not used to listening to, and understanding the limits on our own power and, especially, on our own wisdom. In short, it means that we have to approach these issues not timidly but with great care— that we need to think through much better than we have the implications and purposes of interventionist policy.

NOTES

1. This was the title of William Safire's column in the *New York Times*, November 30, 1992.
2. Stanley Hoffman, "The Problem of Intevention," in Hedley Bull, ed., *Intervention in World Politics* (Oxford: Clarendon Press, 1984), p. 8; Kenneth Younger, "Intervention: The Historical Development I," in Louis Jaquet, ed., *Intervention in International Politics* (The Hague: Nijhoff, 1971), p. 12.
3. Note Kenneth Younger's very effective argument on this point in Younger, "Intervention," pp. 12–18. See also Paul A. Neuland, "Traditional Doctrine on Intervention in the Law of Nations," unpub. diss., Georgetown University, 1971; note especially chap. 11, "Basic Norm of Nonintervention," and chap. 12, "Exceptional Right of Intervention."
4. William Lingelbach, "The Doctrine and Practice of Intervention in Europe," *Annals of the American Academy of Political and Social Science* (July 1900), pp. 1–32.
5. *Ibid.*, pp. 1–2.
6. *Ibid.*, pp. 2, 4, 5, 7.
7. *Ibid.*, pp. 28–32.
8. *Ibid.*, p. 32. There is a totally uncritical reference to the Boxer intervention on p. 20.
9. State Paper of May 5, 1820, in Harold Temperley and Lillian Penson, eds., *Foundations of British Foreign Policy, 1792–1902* (New York: Barnes and Noble, 1966), pp. 54, 61.
10. *Ibid.*, pp. 54, 60, 62.
11. C.A. Macartney, *National States and National Minorities* (London: Oxford University Press, 1934), p. 161.
12. See Frederick S. Calhoun, *Power and Principle: Armed Intervention in Wilsonian Foreign Policy* (Kent, Ohio: Kent State University Press, 1986); David Healy, *Gunboat Diplomacy in the Wilson Era: The US Navy in Haiti, 1915–1916* (Madison: University of Wisconsin Press, 1976); Whitney Perkins, *Constraint of Empire: The United States and Caribbean Interventions* (Westport, Conn.: Greenwood, 1981).
13. Quoted in William Langer, *The Diplomacy of Imperialism* (New York: Knopf, 1935), p. 699.
14. Note even the comments of the American minister in China, quoted in Langer, *The Diplomacy of Imperialism*, p. 704.
15. William II to Jagow, July 28, 1914, in I. Geiss, ed., *July 1914* (New York: Scribner's, 1967), p. 256. Note also Gladstone's comment in 1880: "The mind of the Sultan, who *is*

the Turkish Government, is a bottomless pit of fraud and falsehood, and he will fulfil *nothing* except under force or the proximate fear of *force.*" Quoted in Temperley and Penson, *Foundations,* p. 408.

16. See D.C. Watt, "The British Reactions to the Assassination at Sarajevo," *European Studies Review,* vol. 1, no. 3 (July 1971).

17. Quoted in Charles E. Martin, *The Policy of the United States as Regards Intervention* (New York: AMS Press, 1967; originally written in 1920), pp. 155–156.

18. Perhaps the best example of a humanitarian intervention, and one frequently cited in the literature, is the French intervention in Lebanon after massacres of Christians in the Levant in 1860. The French expedition was sanctioned (in advance) by a convention with Britain. See Seton-Watson, *Britain in Europe,* pp. 419–420. See also the list of historical examples of humanitarian intervention in the nineteenth century cited in Michael Reisman, "Humanitarian Intervention to Protect the Ibos," in Richard B. Lillich, *Humanitarian Intervention and the United Nations* (Charlottesville: University Press of Virginia, 1973), pp. 178–183.

19. See especially R.W. Seton-Watson, *Disraeli, Gladstone and the Eastern Question* (London: Macmillan, 1935), and B.H. Sumner, *Russia and the Balkans, 1870–1880* (Oxford: Clarendon, 1937).

20. For an economic interpretation of the decline of American interventionist policy, see Jeffry Frieden, "The Economics of Intervention: American Overseas Investments and Relations with Underdeveloped Areas, 1890–1950," *Comparative Studies in Society and History,* vol. 31, no. 1, January 1989. This important article is full of original arguments and striking data, and its footnotes provide an excellent introduction to the important literature on this subject.

21. Acheson to State Department, November 10, 1951, Foreign Relations of the United States, 1951–54, vol. 10.

22. From Article 12 of the Polish Minorities Treaty, in Appendix I of C.A. Macartney, *National States and National Minorities.* (London: Oxford University Press, 1934). The other minorities treaties contained similar provisions for League of Nations supervision of the regime.

23. The following states were included in the system: Poland, Yugoslavia, Czechoslovakia, Romania, Greece, Austria, Bulgaria, Hungary, Turkey, Albania, Estonia, Finland (with regard to the Aland Islands), Latvia, Lithuania, and (somewhat later) Iraq.

24. Jacob Robinson et al., *Were the Minorities Treaties a Failure?* (New York: Antin Press, 1943), pp. 122–123.

25. The British were also able to place limits on France's ability to draw political dividends from the invasion in the form of an extension of French influence over the Spanish colonies in the New World. See ibid., pp. 114–121.

26. Thus, the annexation of Bosnia by Austria in 1908 was contrary to the Treaty of Berlin of 1878, which provided only for Austrian occupation of Bosnia. This provided a legal basis for Russian objection and was one of the factors that led to the Bosnian crisis of 1908–1909.

27. Special Journal of the Russian Council of Ministers, July 24, 1914, and Sazonov to Strandmann, July 24, 1914, in I. Geiss, ed., *July 1914* (New York: Scribner 1967) pp. 186–188.

28. The support of the smaller powers, even as a bloc, is less important in practice, but it does play a certain legitimating role, both within regional systems (like NATO and the OAS) and in the UN system.

The Reluctance to Intervene

Michael Mandelbaum

At first, the post–Cold war era appeared to be a golden age for American military power abroad. In the Persian Gulf crisis the Bush administration responded to an act of international aggression by assembling a great multinational coalition, gaining approval for a military campaign from both the United Nations and the Congress, winning a swift, decisive, inexpensive victory, and bringing the troops home quickly.

The Gulf war was, however, a false dawn—less the harbinger of the future than the last gasp of a morally and politically clearer age. It was a replay of World War II, on a far smaller and less costly scale. The first glimpse of the real future of military intervention appeared in northern Iraq only after the war was won. There the United States mounted an operation to protect the Kurds, who had risen in rebellion against Iraqi president Saddam Hussein and suffered his vengeful retaliation.

Two similar American interventions followed shortly: one in Somalia, on the Horn of Africa; the other in Southern Europe, in the former Yugoslav republic of Bosnia-Herzegovina. Geographically disparate as the three episodes were, together they defined the issues surrounding intervention in the post–Cold War era.

The three conflicts shared several features. Intervention had been approved by the U.N. None bore any trace of the single great issue of the Cold War era—the contest of political ideas and military power between the United States and the Soviet Union. Instead, each conflict was among the fundamental groups of organized social life: clans, tribes, and nations.

Each episode proved to be messy, confusing, and frustrating for the United States. The reason was that there was no longer a clear rationale for American intervention, as during the Cold War. In northern Iraq, Somalia, and Bosnia in 1993 the United States found what at first seemed to be a compelling substitute. The United States was drawn into each place to alleviate the suffering of civilians, suffering that television brought into America's living rooms. In all three countries, the heart of the mission was to feed starving people. In each case the operation relied on the American military's transport and logistical capabilities rather than on its firepower.

In the wake of the Cold War, a new American policy was born: humanitarian intervention. Unfortunately, strictly speaking, there is no such thing. Intervention for humanitarian purposes leads inevitably to . . . two quintessentially political tasks: guaranteeing the borders of countries under challenge, and constructing an apparatus of government in places where it is absent. Those are familiar tasks. The first was a principal aim of American intervention during the Cold War. The second was a common practice of the European great powers for much of the modern era, particularly during the nineteenth century.

Despite their historical precedents, the two types of post–Cold War intervention present the United States with vexing choices. The main difficulty with the first type is conceptual. While defending a country is usually a straightforward (though not necessarily easy) task, it is difficult to decide which groups ought to have their own countries. The obstacle to the second is practical. The desired end of effective government is clear enough, but mustering the means to achieve it in the post–Cold War world is difficult, and for the United States perhaps impossible.

CLAN CONFLICT

Since the end of the Cold War there has been an explosion of claims for sovereignty. Politics in many rates during the Cold War consisted of one group suppressing others. The end of the Cold War made guns and money, once-plentiful resources for suppression, suddenly scarce. As a result, restraints on powerful centrifugal political tendencies were removed.

The Cold War imposed what can be seen retrospectively as artificial loyalty— or at least obedience—to abstractions: to the principles of democracy and the market or to the precepts of Marxism-Leninism, and to sovereign states, a number of them created by the victorious powers after World War I. With the end of the Cold War, primary group loyalties came to the fore. The governments of Iraq, Somalia, and Bosnia might have been considered legitimate by the international community, but not by the people who lived under them. Most of those people identified themselves as clan members, not as Somalis; as Serbs, Croats, and Muslims, not as Bosnians or Yugoslavs; and as Sunnis, Shiites, or Kurds, not as Iraqis. Such groups have tended to seek their own states, or at least dominant power in the states in which they reside. The result has been the ethnic conflicts that drew the United States into Iraq and Bosnia, as well as secessionist movements in Moldova, Georgia, and Azerbaijan and the potential for similar conflicts throughout Eurasia and much of Central Asia and Africa.

To stop the epidemic of conflict, the international community would need to decide upon a single principle or set of principles to govern the various outbreaks of secession. A coherent international effort requires a rule that could be consistently applied to apportion sovereignty. Thus far, it has not been possible to settle on such a rule. One reason is that the drive for independence brings into conflict two strongly held and widely supported international principles: the sanctity of existing borders and the right to national self-determination.

The case for respecting existing borders is, at its heart, an argument in favor of order. International boundaries must be based on *some* principle. Support for the status quo is the simplest one available. If it is discarded, all borders are suspect, and the potential for chaos is considerable.

The sanctity of existing borders was a widely held principle during the Cold War, with the international community generally shunning secessionist movements. Members of that community obviously had a strong self-interest in the principle, for that community is composed of sovereign states, none of whose governments want groups they govern to break away to form their own states. Each state is therefore comfortable endorsing a principle that effectively prohibits secession.

However, that norm has proven untenable in the post–Cold War era. In the second half of the nineteenth and the first half of the twentieth centuries, boundaries all over the planet were drawn arbitrarily and—in the view of many living within them—unjustly. Almost nowhere were the boundaries established with the consent of the governed. In Yugoslavia and the Soviet Union they were often drawn with the intent of dividing ethnic and national groups in order to weaken them and set them against one another rather than against the imperial power.

Those boundaries had been grudgingly accepted because there was no prospect of overturning them. The end of the Cold War, however, made them vulnerable. Once some groups achieved independence—in the former Yugoslavia and Soviet Union for instance—others aspired to follow their examples. So the Cold War principle for determining sovereignty—accepting the legacy of history—can no longer be, and is not being, sustained. Moreover, national or other groups that seek to overturn existing boundaries and to acquire their own states can invoke a second, widely accepted international principle: the right to national self-determination.

It, too, has a persuasive rationale. Sovereign states must, of course, have some principle of composition. And basing the state on the nation, tribe, or other primary group seems to offer the best prospect for internal cohesion and stability. It is that social grouping that commands the most intense political loyalty. Enormous suffering, ingenuity, and persistence have fueled the campaigns for self-determination of self-identified nations. The Germans and the Italians are the most prominent instances of national self-determination in the nineteenth century; the Poles, Jews, and Eritreans are perhaps the most dramatic of the many twentieth-century examples.

Yet that principle cannot be applied consistently. For if every district group were given its own state, the international community would divide and subdivide until there were two or three or four times as many members of the United Nations as currently belong. It would be a recipe for chaos.

There is no widely accepted criterion for deciding which groups deserve their own state and which do not—nor is it likely that there could be. Historically, the prize of independence has gone to those powerful or clever or fortunate or merely numerous enough to achieve it.

Even if there were such a criterion, a problem would remain. Some groups are not concentrated geographically but rather dispersed among other peoples; they cannot be given their own homogeneous state simply by redrawing lines on a map. That is the tragedy of Bosnia. Since Muslims, Serbs, and Croats are scattered throughout that former republic, partition would leave hundreds of thousands of people outside their national territories. The only way to concentrate them would be through the mass transfer of populations, a familiar and terrible feature of the twentieth century known as "ethnic cleansing."

Thus, a consistent policy on secession is not feasible. Not surprisingly, when the United States has been drawn into the midst of political conflicts over secession through its humanitarian intervention, American policy has not been consistent. Washington supported the territorial integrity of Somalia, although a secessionist movement was active in the northern part of the country, the former British colony of Somaliland. The United States initially insisted upon, and indeed seemed prepared to use force to safeguard, the territorial integrity of Bosnia within its former borders as a constituent republic of Yugoslavia. Yet the American government had come to accept the disintegration of Yugoslavia itself, which had enjoyed international recognition for almost 75 years. Then, in the summer of 1993, the United States accepted the Owen-Stoltenberg peace plan for Bosnia, which effectively partitioned what the Clinton administration had publicly insisted was a single sovereign state.

In northern Iraq, the United States never recognized any Kurdish claim to independence, in part because of the objections of neighboring countries the United States does not wish to offend, particularly Turkey. But the Kurds of northern Iraq are now independent in all but name thanks to American military protection.

The international community and the United States have not found, and are unlikely to find, a consistent approach to the question, "who is to be sovereign?" Nevertheless, they can and do decide that question—albeit inconsistently—on a case-by-case basis. And where they decide, the issue of enforcing their decisions arises. Unfortunately, the international community has had as much difficulty mustering the means required as it has had deciding on desirable ends.

In the post–Cold War era the world has a favored response to conflicts over sovereignty: the dispatch of U.N. "peacekeepers" to the site of the conflict. The list of peacekeeping operations, the number of troops involved, and the size of the U.N. peacekeeping budget all have increased substantially since the end of the Cold War. Peacekeeping has enjoyed some success where the parties to a conflict want peace but distrust each other too much to achieve it unassisted. On the Golan Heights and in Cyprus, for instance, peacekeepers have played the role of impartial witness, certifying that the two sides are doing what they have promised to do.

However, when the parties in dispute are *not* prepared to carry out the terms of agreement, a far more formidable military force is needed to assure compliance than the U.N. is ordinarily able to field. In that case, peacekeepers must act as police. In Bosnia, for example, a peacekeeping effort would almost certainly require policing contested borders, ensuring the free flow of traffic, controlling heavy weapons, and supervising the return of millions of refugees to their homes. The United Nations is plainly unprepared for those tasks.

Various reforms have been proposed to correct the U.N.'s shortcomings: establishing standing forces that could be sent rapidly to trouble spots around the world; strengthening the operations of its secretariat; and equipping it with the capacity to gather information worldwide. None of those changes, however, would solve the organization's fundamental problem because the roots of that problem are not in the design of the United Nations but in its basic character: It cannot conduct military operations on its own. That is the business of sovereign states. States, not multinational organizations, have the authority to raise and deploy troops. Their authority springs from their political legitimacy; that legitimacy—stemming from a common history and sense of common destiny—cannot be transferred by fiat to an international organization.

The U.N. is a trade association of sovereign states. Just as a trade association of hospitals can issue resolutions on health care policy, the U.N. is an appropriate forum for passing resolutions expressing the will of the international community. However, where the execution of U.N. decrees is difficult or costly, responsibility must be assumed by sovereign states, acting under the authorization of the Security Council or the General Assembly. The U.N. itself can no more conduct military operations on a large scale on its own than a trade association of hospitals can perform heart surgery.

In Somalia, borders were not the central issue. The suffering that attracted American humanitarian attention to the Horn of Africa was caused by a civil war. The different factions—with the exception of the Somali National Movement in the north—were fighting not for their own states but for control of the one state that included them all. Somalia—as well as Cambodia and Haiti, where the U.N. has also been involved—is an example of what is being called a "failed state." Humanitarian intervention in such states leads to the task of putting them back together. That in turn requires restoring order, which is a military, or quasi-military, undertaking. It also requires reestablishing functioning institutions of government, which have disintegrated under the pressure of war. Reconstructing a state is a political matter.

The U.N. has chosen to call the process "peacebuilding." According to Secretary-General Boutros Boutros-Ghali, it entails "support for the transformation of deficient national structures and capabilities, and for the strengthening of democratic institutions." The U.N. is trying to accomplish all of that in Cambodia. There the United Nations Transitional Authority in Cambodia (UNTAC) is responsible not only for policing the country but also for helping to establish a civilian administration, including a judicial system.

The U.N. has limited experience and very modest competence at "peacebuilding." Historically, however, the task is not unfamiliar. When it was most widely and successfully practiced it went by another name: imperialism.

Many of the functioning states outside Europe were built under Western imperial tutelage. In the greatest of all imperial possessions, India, the British laid the foundations of a modern state. They created a single administrative structure embracing the disparate linguistic groups of the subcontinent and bequeathed to its people a superior system of railways, a civil service of high quality, and a democratic tradition on the basis of which India has been governed for almost five decades.

International organizations have limited experience in building states, but the major powers have an impressive track record. After the two world wars, efforts were made to use the state-building skills of the major powers under the auspices of an international organization, first with the League of Nations mandate system, then as U.N. trusteeships.

The lesson of the mandate and trusteeship systems for contemporary peacebuilding is familiar: While peacekeeping and peacebuilding may be approved by the international community as a whole, they are likely to be tasks for individual states. Cambodia is an exception to that rule. If successful, UNTAC could set a precedent for reconstructing failed states through genuine international cooperation with minimal outside military force. But it is not certain that the effort there will succeed; even if it does, it will not easily be replicated elsewhere.

What is required for peacebuilding can be costly, and it is inconsistent with the preferred American pattern of intervention. In the wake of Vietnam, the American public has come to expect military engagement in other countries to correspond to surgery: The United States diagnoses the problem, performs the appropriate operation—the shorter, cheaper, and cleaner the better—and then moves on. However, state building is more likely to resemble psychiatry: long and frustrating treatment bringing only incremental change, with no obvious or speedy date for termination.

THE "I" WORD

Humanitarian intervention thus leads, ineluctably, to political intervention, and political intervention by the strong in the affairs of the weak is as old as international politics itself. Whether, when, and how the strong intervene all depend both on international norms concerning intervention and on national incentives to intervene. That is, intervention depends both on what the international community says and on what its member states want. The U.N. Security Council may authorize armed mediation, the establishment of a protectorate, or an effort at nation building, but it is individual states—and, in practice, the most powerful state of all, the United States—that must assume the burden of carrying out such policies. Here a development both curious and dramatic is taking place. Both determinants of intervention, international norms and national incentives, are shifting in the wake of the Cold War—but they are moving in opposite directions.

Throughout modern history, countries have expected their neighbors to stay out of their internal affairs. The international norm has long been *against* intervention in another's domestic domain. In international politics the word intervention itself has come to have an unsavory connotation, as something illicit and illegal, an international version of assault or burglary. National sovereignty has been understood to include the right of governments to do what they wish within their own borders, without interference from others.

In the second half of the twentieth century, as the world came to be dominated by two nuclear superpowers sharply polarized along ideological lines, the norm of nonintervention became increasingly popular. It was all the stronger because of nuclear weapons, which gave great-power intervention the potential for global annihilation.

In the 1960s and 1970s the U.N. began to reverse that norm by censuring the white governments of South Africa and Rhodesia. With the end of the Cold War, that trend has accelerated. A milestone came in the wake of the Gulf war when the U.N. General Assembly adopted a resolution demanding that Saddam Hussein's government end its repression of people whom the U.N. recognized as Iraq's own citizens. Javier Pérez de Cuellar, BoutrosGhali's predecessor as secretary-general, remarked that the world was "clearly witnessing what is probably an irresistible shift in public attitudes toward the belief that the defense of the oppressed in the name of morality should prevail over frontiers and legal documents."

There are two reasons for that shift. One is the end of the Cold War, which eliminated one of the main purposes of the norm of nonintervention: the prevention of conflict among great powers trying to impose their own models of legitimacy on other countries. With the collapse of communism, there is greater consensus than ever before on proper domestic order.

The second reason for the shift in the international attitude toward intervention is the increasing acceptance of the protection of individual rights as an international norm. That emerging tenet is in conflict with the principle of the inviolability of national sovereignty. Indeed, it *encourages* intervention because the rights of individuals are often violated by their own governments—as were the rights of the Kurds in Iraq.

The norm of nonintervention, however widely accepted in theory, was often violated in practice during the Cold War. The United States and the Soviet Union intervened militarily, both directly and indirectly, all over the world. Indeed, the history of politics among sovereign nations is in no small part the history of intervention, which is a consequence of the perpetually unequal distribution of power in the international community. The strong have always intervened in the affairs of the weak, and for the same reasons. What is remarkable, perhaps even revolutionary, about the post–Cold War world is that the age-old motives for intervention are suddenly all but extinct.

The search for economic gain was one such motive. Wars of plunder have been recurrent features of international affairs. Empires have repeatedly been established to enrich their administrators and home countries. The sixteenth-through eighteenth-century Spanish domain in the Americas is the example closest to home but hardly the only one. An important tenet of Leninist theory argues that capitalist economies require continual imperial expansion and that imperialism is therefore the highest stage of capitalism. Here Lenin was wrong. Empire *ceased* to be a paying proposition with the rise of capitalism. As Adam Smith observed in *The Wealth of Nations* in opposing the British war to retain the American colonies, a country with a market economy will profit much more from international trade and investment in other independent countries than from trying to enrich itself through direct political control over them.

Another venerable motive for intervention is glory. For brave, energetic, and bloodthirsty Europeans from Columbus to Cecil Rhodes, the greatest of all adventures was the conquest of alien lands in the name of their sovereign. Larger and less self-interested versions of glory were also at work in the construction of Europe's overseas empires. . . .

Some nineteenth-century Europeans were genuinely devoted to spreading what they saw as the inestimable benefits of Christianity and Western civilization to the peoples of Africa and Asia under the auspices of imperial rule. Imperialism was for them an act of altruism. However, rising skepticism and cultural relativism since World War I have sharply reduced the level of religious commitment and cultural self-confidence that had once led Europeans to export their religious faith and their political institutions. As a result, that motive has lost much of its power.

The most powerful and enduring motive for intervention has been security. Strong states fear each other; in the great board game of international politics they treat the weak as lesser pieces, or as spaces to be occupied.

American intervention beyond North America during the Cold War was driven almost exclusively by the great rivalry with the Soviet Union. Korea and Vietnam, where the United States fought the most protracted wars of the Cold War era, were spaces on the board of global geopolitics; the United States was attempting to defend those spaces for feat that, if the Soviet Union and its clients occupied them, the Soviets would be emboldened to challenge Western positions elsewhere. America's Cold War efforts at state building—the Marshall Plan, the Agency for International Development, the Alliance for Progress—modest though they were compared to the great European empires, were undertaken for strategic reasons: to contain Soviet power and resist Soviet influence.

Now the contest is over. America's opponent first retired, then disintegrated. Regions that seemed vital during the Cold War have lost their importance. For the moment, the forces that have historically driven the governments of the powerful to intervene beyond their borders have all but vanished. A notable exception to the trend is Russia, which has adopted a proprietary interest in neighbors that only recently were its imperial provinces. Moscow has designated the other former Soviet republics—known as Russia's "near abroad"—as its own preserve. Russian troops remain in the Caucasus and Central Asia. The motive, as in the past, is fear—not so much of a rival great power, but of disorder. The Russians are concerned that turbulence in those regions, if not checked, could creep north.

For the United States, however, what lies behind intervention in the post–Cold War era is neither gold, nor glory, nor strategic calculation. It is, rather, sympathy. The televised pictures of starving people in northern Iraq, Somalia, and Bosnia created a political clamor to feed them, which propelled the U.S. military into those three distant parts of the world.

Sympathy is a powerful human emotion and a precious one. Whether it can—or should—be a decisive motive in the conduct of foreign policy, however, remains doubtful. Americans approved of the dispatch of troops abroad to relieve suffering under the misunderstanding that the forces would be able to steer clear of local politics. The public believed that the interventions would be costless, especially in our most valuable currency: American lives. The stark lesson of Iraq, Bosnia, and especially Somalia is that this belief is a delusion.

When the siege of Sarajevo was at least partially lifted in February 1994 by the threat to bomb Serb artillery positions circling the city, the United States showed no inclination to enforce a political settlement in Bosnia with tens of thousands of American troops. More representative of the American public's attitude toward intervention in the post–Cold War era was its response to the death of 18 soldiers in October 1993 in Somalia: an urgent, widespread demand to withdraw all American forces from the Horn of Africa.

A distinctive pattern regarding intervention has thus emerged in the international community: agreement in principle, paralysis in practice. Since the end of the Cold War, the U.N. Security Council has become a font of resolutions authorizing international action. But the United Nations lacks the means to carry out its resolution, and its member states lack the will to do so.

That combination represents a notable transformation. During the Cold War the international community was divided on what to do, which, in its many forms, is the central issue of politics. Today, however, it cannot reach a consensus on how to apportion the costs of doing what all agree ought to be done; that is essentially the problem of government.

The world is ready for a government; or rather, it is ready for more international governance than ever before. But the U.N. is not a world government and it will not become one. The instruments of order are sovereign states. But there is no effective method of extracting resources from states to pay for governance. Further, the most powerful state, the United States, has shown little interest in making the large-scale contributions necessary to fulfill the international mandate arising from the end of the Cold War.

Thus, for large parts of the world beyond the secure, prosperous triad of Western Europe, North America, and Japan, one of the great developments of the modern era is being reversed. The revolution in the technology of transportation and warfare over the past several centuries led to the expansion of European power throughout the world. Although in historical perspective that expansion was not in all ways a benign development, it did bring order to much of the world. Tribes, nations, and sects that had fought one another with primitive weapons were forced to submit to the superior firepower of alien conquerors and to accept their institutions.

Now, however, the Europeans and their North American offspring have gone home and are disinclined to return. The response of the West to the ensuing disorder has not been to intervene; instead, it has tried to wall itself off from the misery that disorder brings. For many parts of the world where Europeans once governed it will be as if they had never come, with two exceptions: The traditional indigenous sources of order have long since been weakened if not destroyed, and the arms available are more numerous and deadlier than ever before. Saddam Hussein, Mohammad Farah Aidid, and Slobodan Milošević, the political descendants of premodern chieftains, have equipment such as rocket-propelled grenades, long-range artillery, and jet aircraft, which can do far more damage than anything in the possession of their equally brutal predecessors. Thus, in much of the world beyond the prosperous industrial triad, continued suffering and carnage of the kind northern Iraq, Somalia, and Bosnia have experienced is a very real prospect.

Even if some of the consequences of the revolution in transportation are reversed, however, the results of the more recent but equally profound revolution in communications will remain. Technology will continue to make images from obscure countries instantly available virtually everywhere. Thus, life in the world's nether regions may not only become nastier, more brutish, and shorter than before the Europeans arrived, but it will also be televised.

The Ethics of Intervention

David Fisher

Two conflicting nightmares haunt the moral philosopher. One is the fear that morality might ultimately prove to be without rational foundation: that there might be no good reason to act morally. The other is that morality is only too well founded from a rational standpoint: that there are such good reasons to act morally that the demands of morality may become too insistent. We may then become plagued with the universal guilt experienced by Father Zossima's younger brother in *The Brothers Karamazov*, who was convinced that 'every one of us is responsible for everyone else in every way, and I most of all'.[1]

Universal guilt has begun to haunt foreign policy-makers and military strategists in recent years, as media demands have become ever more incessant for interventions in disputes and disasters throughout the world, and television images of maimed bodies lead to cries for action. This article explores the extent to which moral philosophy can provide guidance to policy-makers in determining whether and when interventions might be ethically permissible or, even, ethically required.

CHANGING INTERNATIONAL CIRCUMSTANCES

One of the reasons why this problem has only become acute within the last few years is the rediscovery of the diverse utility of military force as a result of the ending of the Cold War. As long as the Eastern and Western power blocs confronted each other in a nuclear stalemate, direct military intervention by one side in the other's sphere of influence was deemed too dangerous. The West accordingly turned deaf ears to the cries for help from Hungary in 1956 and Czechoslovakia in

From David Fisher, "The Ethics of Intervention" in *Survival*, Spring 1994. Reprinted by permission of Oxford University Press. Portions of the text and some footnotes have been omitted.

1968, 'preferring them to be red than us dead'. Moreover, the interventions by the superpowers outside each other's sphere of influence (the United States in Vietnam and the Soviet Union in Afghanistan) proved, in general, far more hazardous and difficult than their proponents had initially supposed. The West subsequently failed to intervene when the Pol Pot regime committed genocide against the people of Cambodia.

During the Cold War, the habit of non-intervention was induced not just by nuclear prudence, but was also supported by ethical, political and legal considerations. Following the European experience in the first half of the twentieth century of wars resulting from the interventions of great powers, the international order established after the end of the Second World War was founded on the principle or non-intervention, as enshrined in Article 2 (4) of the United Nations (UN) Charter:

> All members shall refrain in their international relations from the threat or use of force against the territorial integrity or political independence of any State.[2]

The only recognised exception to this—'the inherent right of individual or collective self-defence if an armed attack occurs' (as provided for under Article 51)— was designed to strengthen rather than weaken the principle of non-intervention by providing a mechanism for its enforcement. Moreover, there was no recognised right within international law to intervene for humanitarian reasons, even to prevent atrocities being committed by another state. A 1984 UK Foreign Office Planning Staff paper concluded that 'the best case that can be made in support of humanitarian intervention is that it cannot be said to be unambiguously illegal'.[3]

The sanctity of the state and the need to ensure its security from external interference was also proclaimed by political philosophers, most eloquently by Michael Walzer:

> The boundaries that exist at any moment in time are likely to be arbitrary, poorly drawn, the products of ancient wars. The mapmakers are likely to have been ignorant, drunken, or corrupt. Nevertheless, these lines establish a habitable world. Within that world, men and women (let us assume) are safe from attack; once the lines are crossed, safety is gone . . . It is only common sense, then, to attach great importance to boundaries. Rights in the world have value only if they also have dimension.[4]

With a bipolar nuclear stalemate, the demands of prudence, morality and law appeared conveniently to coincide: it was far too dangerous to intervene and intervention would, in any case, breach the sanctity of the state. With the ending of the Cold War, the risk of nuclear holocaust has receded and international relations have reacquired their multi-dimensional complexity. The cries of those clamouring for intervention can, therefore, perhaps no longer be dismissed quite so readily.

AN ETHICAL FRAMEWORK

To appraise such demands an ethical framework is required, which is most appropriately provided by the just war tradition. The relevance of this tradition may not at first be apparent because of the sheer variety of possible interventions, many of which do not involve warfare, such as diplomacy and economic sanctions. While the just war tradition is certainly of most relevance to military intervention, economic intervention can involve the threat or use of physical harm against civilians and is hence an activity that requires careful ethical appraisal. Military interventions can take several forms: support for one state against external aggression by another; support for one or another side in a civil war; peacemaking or peacekeeping operations; and humanitarian interventions to prevent genocide or assist in bringing aid to war-torn people. While the just war tradition may be most relevant when a state is deliberating over whether to enter a war, military interventions on a smaller scale also involve the threat or use of potentially lethal military force. The just war tradition does, therefore, provide a helpful framework for the ethical appraisal of all economic and military interventions—when they involve the threat or use of harm.

The just war tradition defines circumstances in which a state may legitimately resort to war—the *jus ad bellum*—and the way in which the war should be conducted—the *jus in bello*. The *jus ad bellum* prescribes that war is permissible if and only if: war is declared by a competent authority; all available peaceful means of settling the dispute have been tried and failed; a just cause exists; and the harm likely to result from the war is not disproportionate to the likely good to be achieved, taking into account the probability of success. The *jus in bello* adds two further conditions governing the conduct of war: the harm likely to result from a particular military action should not be disproportionate to the good it might achieve; and non-combatant casualties should be minimised.[5]

This article discusses how military and, where appropriate, other interventions might be judged against each of these conditions. The first requirement—that war should be declared by a competent authority—is usually interpreted within the tradition to mean by a government of a state. This reflects the fact that the wielding of military force is regarded as the monopoly of governments, not individuals, although governments may forfeit that monopoly if they behave so tyrannously as to provoke a just rebellion. This condition would appear readily applicable to military interventions since we are concerned with the interventions of one state in the affairs of another.

The second requirement—that military interventions should only be undertaken as a last resort—is sensible given that the application of military force, even in a limited mode, can have harmful and, indeed, lethal consequences. It is, therefore, necessary that other ways of achieving one's objective should also have been considered. It does not follow, however, that the use of military force in a limited mode (for example, to assist a humanitarian, food-distribution operation) should never be undertaken in preference to other measures, because economic sanctions, for example, can sometimes be a greater threat to human life than limited military force.

Indeed, it is arguable that economic sanctions have been imposed by the international community too readily because they are perceived as an easy, low-cost option. This may be true of selective, carefully targeted sanctions, such as arms embargoes. The imposition of more general economic sanctions, however, are far from low-cost to the people upon whom they are imposed, who may be faced with widespread hardship, starvation and death. The imposition of such indiscriminate harm would at least require an assurance that some overriding good could only be achieved through such action. Given the poor, not to say non-existent, success rate of general economic sanctions in achieving their objectives, the readiness with which they have been applied is difficult to justify. Indeed, it may be morally preferable to use limited military force against carefully targeted military objectives *before* applying such an indiscriminate weapon as general economic sanctions.

The third condition of the just war theory is that there should be a just cause for the use of force. As the sixteenth-century writer Vitoria put it: 'there is one and only one just cause for waging war—an injury received'.[6] Until recently, most modern interpreters of the just war tradition have tended to restrict this to individual or collective self-defence against aggression, as provided for by Article 51 of the UN Charter.

On the basis of such a restrictive interpretation, the coalition operations to eject Iraq from Kuwait would have been justified, but subsequent allied operations to protect the Kurds in northern Iraq, the Shi'ite Muslims in southern Iraq and current allied operations in the former Yugoslavia would not. As international opinion now considers such actions to be justified there has clearly been a shift in thinking, with a readiness to interpret what constitutes a just cause less restrictively than previously. The question—which this article seeks to answer—is whether such a relaxation is justified.

Assisting a country to defend itself against aggression constitutes the paradigm just cause for intervention. The article will now discuss whether deviations from this paradigm still constitute legitimate interventions.

A frequent pretext for intervention has been to support one side in a civil war. This does not on its own, however, constitute a just cause. The writer Montague Bernard argued against such interventions in the nineteenth century:

> The interference in the case supposed either turns the balance, or it does not. In the latter event, it misses its aim; in the former it gives superiority to the side which would not have been uppermost without it and establishes a sovereign or a form of government, which the nation, if left to itself, would not have chosen.[7]

Suppose, however, that one of the parties to the dispute has successfully established its *bona fides* in representing a distinctive political community and has gained control of a sizeable area of territory. It is being prevented from achieving full statehood only by a repressive colonial or imperial power. It could, perhaps, be argued that this case fits the self-defence paradigm, with the repressive colonial power representing the role of the external aggressor. In such a case, intervention on behalf of the oppressed community could be considered legitimate. Suppose further that an outside power has moved to prop up the crumbling imperial regime and crush the movement for national liberation. Support for the struggling people could then be regarded as a special case of the self-defence paradigm and so be justified.

This was certainly the view of John Stuart Mill, who generally regarded interventions as futile. In his view, only a political community by its own struggles could determine its own freedom. He, nonetheless, argued in favour of intervention in the case of Hungary's revolt against the Hapsburg Empire in 1848–49:

It might not have been right for England (even apart from the question of prudence) to have taken part with Hungary in its noble struggle against Austria; although the Austrian government in Hungary was in some sense a foreign yoke. But when the Hungarians having shown themselves likely to prevail in this struggle, the Russian despot interposed, and joining his force to that of Austria, delivered back the Hungarians, bound hand and foot, to their exasperated oppressors, it would have been an honourable and virtuous act on the part of England to have declared that this should not be, and that if Russia gave assistance to the wrong side, England would aid the right.[8]

In the event, Britain did not intervene since Palmerston feared that such a move could upset the balance of power and so risk general war, which were similar reasons to those offered by the West in 1956 when it did not support Hungary for a second time against Russian aggression.

There are occasions when intervention in a civil war is an option not to assure victory to one side or the other but to try to prevent further bloodshed by keeping the warring factions apart and so impose a peace—currently known as 'peacemaking'. The aim of bringing peace to a war-torn region by using superior force, perhaps under the authority of the UN, to separate belligerent parties could constitute a just cause for intervention. Whether it is justified depends on whether the next requirement of the just war theory is also satisfied—is there a reasonable prospect of achieving this laudable objective at a proportionate cost? It is on these grounds that peacemaking operations have often been resisted: the fear being that the intervening party may be drawn into the civil war without achieving peace.

Both of these conditions are far more readily satisfied when what is at issue is peacekeeping—the use of military force to enforce a peace settlement or truce which has already been agreed. Peacekeeping would certainly constitute a just cause.

Finally, there are humanitarian interventions, undertaken not to achieve any particular political objective but to prevent suffering. These range from interventions to prevent genocide or large-scale massacres to more humble, but still worthy, interventions such as those currently being undertaken by British, French and other troops in the former Yugoslavia, where the primary aim is to provide military protection for humanitarian aid convoys. Such humanitarian motives constitute *prima facie* just causes for intervention, although even here a degree of caution is required. The burden of proof for any intervention must rest with its advocate because it is a regrettable breach of the integrity of a sovereign state with potentially harmful consequences. When human rights are at risk on a limited scale or where redress is available within the legal system of the state concerned, external interference would not be warranted. When people are threatened with large-scale torture, massacre or even genocide, however, the prevention of such suffering would constitute a just cause for humanitarian intervention.

The more interesting question is whether intervention can also be ethically required—that is, whether we have a duty to intervene to prevent suffering when it is readily within our power to do so. Such an extension of moral responsibility would hardly be welcome. It may, therefore, be tempting to suppose that foreign atrocities can be kept at a safe moral distance by the use of the act/omission distinction. This distinction argues that whereas we have a clear moral duly not to take the life of another person (an act), we have no such duty to prevent a life being taken by someone else (an omission), particularly when the lives are at risk as a result of 'a quarrel in a far away country between people of whom we know nothing'.[9] The problem is that it is extremely difficult to clarify the act/omission distinction sufficiently for it to bear the moral weight thus placed upon it.

The hospital ward orderly, who has inveigled a terminally ill patient to bequeath him all her money, hardly seems less culpable if he deliberately fails to switch her life-support machine on (an omission) than if he deliberately turns it off (an act). In either case he intended the patient to die. It might then appear that a moral distinction can be drawn between what we intend and what we merely foresee. We may foresee that our failure to act will lead to many deaths, but those deaths are hardly intended and hence not our moral responsibility.

Once again, however, the distinction is not sufficiently clear-cut to bear the moral weight placed upon it. In the celebrated case of *Regina v Desmond, Barrett and others*, the accused had attempted to free two Fenians by blowing up the wall of Clerkenwell prison, causing the death of a number of people living nearby. Their defence was that they had not intended to kill them even though they may have foreseen their deaths as a consequence of their actions. Their plea was rejected, with Lord Coleridge concluding that it was murder 'if a man did an act not with the purpose of taking life but with the knowledge or belief that life was likely to be sacrificed by it'.[10] A similar conclusion can be drawn by considering the excuses proffered for the US bombing of the air raid shelter at Amiriyah during the Gulf War, an attack which killed 300 civilians. Rather than seeking to justify this on the grounds that the deaths, while foreseen, were not intended, the US spokesman pleaded that the US leaders did not foresee, and could not reasonably have been expected to have foreseen, that there would be civilians in the facility as they believed it was solely a military communications centre.

These considerations suggest that the moral dividing line is perhaps better drawn not between those consequences we intend and those we foresee, but between those consequences that are within our control, and consented to by us, and those which are not. If we do not know about something (the US plea in the case of the Amiriyah bombing) we cannot be held to have consented to its occurrence (unless the ignorance was in some way culpable). Nor can we be held responsible when we have knowledge but no control over what is happening. But when the consequences are within our control (as was the case with the Fenian rescuers because those living near the wall would not have died if the Fenians had not blown it up) and when by persisting with an action the consequences, even if not intended, are to that extent consented to by us (as was true in the Clerkenwell case) then we can be regarded as morally responsible.

If this is how the moral dividing line is drawn then the arguments against humanitarian intervention, when there are large-scale abuses of human rights, are less convincing. For if it is readily within our power to stop genocide and we fail to act are we not in a sense consenting to what is happening? Do we not, in such circumstances, have a duty to intervene and prevent the appalling suffering? Of course, in many cases we may not be aware of what is happening or, if we are, may not be able to do anything about it. But what if both conditions are fulfilled? What if the atrocities are happening within our own continent, under the glare of our own television cameras, and we have sufficient military force to do something about it? In such circumstances there would appear to be at least a *prima facie* case to intervene.

Even if there is a just cause to intervene, however, the next condition of the just war theory must also be met: that the harm likely to result from war must not be disproportionate to the likely good to be achieved, taking into account the probability of success. This is a very important condition. Many of those who have recently demanded military action have had no clear idea of what the objective is that they wish to achieve, by what means, at what cost and with what likelihood of success. This attitude was well caricatured in a cartoon published in the *Guardian* newspaper entitled 'The Bosnian Drill'. In the cartoon a squad of soldiers are being drilled by a sergeant who is bellowing out the command: 'On the order "something", do something!' It is important to make a careful assessment of the likely consequences of one's actions before military force is applied and to ensure that the good to be achieved will indeed outweigh the harm (often unintended) that may result. Hastily prepared and ill-conceived interventions—however worthy their motive may be—would not, therefore, be sanctioned by the just war tradition.

These are the *jus ad bellum* requirements that have to be met before any military intervention is undertaken. There are two further conditions that have to be satisfied in the conduct of any military operation—the *jus in bello* conditions. These are that the harm likely to result from a particular military action should not be disproportionate to the good aimed at, and that noncombatant casualties should be minimised.[11]

These requirements would not appear to need special interpretation to be applied to all kinds of military interventions and not simply to the conduct of military operations in war. The requirement to minimise non-combatant casualties is, however, one that may, as we have seen, make the imposition of general economic sanctions difficult to justify.

CONCLUSION

The just was tradition, with suitable modifications, provides a helpful guide through the tangled maze of issues raised by the question of whether to intervene, militarily or otherwise. Intervention has to be justified because of the potential harmful consequences flowing from it. Indeed, the moral presumption should be against intervention. Nonetheless, intervention can, on occasion, be ethically permissible and may, even, be ethically required.

Judged against the just war criteria, the coalition operations to liberate Kuwait would appear—in both their conception and conduct (in so far as the latter adhered to the principles of proportion and discrimination)—to be justified. The allies' operations to prevent the massacre of the Kurds in northern Iraq and of the Shi'ite Muslims in southern Iraq, and current UN humanitarian operations in the former Yugoslavia, would also appear to be justified against just war criteria as interpreted here. Indeed, it is arguable, on the basis of the ethical theory outlined above, that morality would require more rather than less action in the former Yugoslavia: to prevent, in so far as it is in our power so to do, the medieval barbarities being perpetrated by Serbs against Croats, Croats against Serbs, and both against the Bosnian Muslims. The injured stranger we were called upon to help in the Gospel story lay on the road to Jericho. He or she could equally be lying now on the road from Split.

NOTES

1. Fyodor Dostoyevsky, *The Brothers Karamazov*, translated by David Magarshack (London: Penguin Books, 1958 (reissued 1982)), p. 339.
2. Department of Public Information, *Charter of the United Nations and Statute of the International Court of Justice* (New York: United Nations, 1945), p. 4.
3. The Foreign and Commonwealth Planning Staff, 'Is Intervention ever Justified?' Policy Document No. 148, 1984, quoted in Christopher Greenwood, 'New World Order or Old? The Invasion of Kuwait and the Rule of Law', *The Modern Law Review*, vol. 55, no. 2, March 1992, p. 176.
4. Michael Walzer, *Just and Unjust Wars* (London: Allen Lane, 1977), pp. 57–58. Walzer does, however, concede that intervention may sometimes be permissible: see chap. 6.
5. The just war criteria are so described in David Fisher, *Morality and the Bomb* (London: Croom Helm, 1985; New York: St. Martin's Press, 1985), chaps. 2–3.
6. Francisco de Vitoria, *De Indis Recenter Inventis et de Jure Belli Hispanorum in Barbaros*, 13, Walter Schätzel (ed.) (Tübingen: J. C. B. Mohr (Paul Siebeck), 1952).
7. Montague Bernard, 'On the Principle of Non-Intervention' (Oxford, 1860), p. 21; quoted in Walzer, *Just and Unjust Wars*, p. 96.
8. 'A Few Words on Non-Intervention', in J. S. Mill, *Dissertations and Discussions* (New York, 1873), III, pp. 261–62.
9. This is Neville Chamberlain's infamous description of Czechoslovakia on the occasion of the Munich agreement.
10. Quoted in H. L. A. Hart, *Punishment and Responsibility* (Oxford: Oxford University Press, 1968), p. 120.
11. The arguments for interpreting the principle of non-combatant immunity as a non-absolute requirement to minimise civilian casualties are set out in Fisher, *Morality and the Bomb*, chap. 3. This chapter also develops more fully the arguments for drawing a moral distinction between those consequences that are within our control and consented to and those that are not.

Justified Intervention? A View from the South

Virginia Gamba

Depending on their needs, their relative power, and the times, nations have alternatively looked for their right to intervene and their right to prevent intervention. Thus, the term *intervention* has both positive and negative connotations, depending not only on whether the point of view is that of the intervenor or the intervened-upon, but also on the nature of the political environment at the time. Therefore, the allure of justified intervention in the affairs of another state changes with time and circumstances. Usually, the weaker the state, the more interested it will be in consolidating principles of nonintervention.

The post–Cold War world has brought about discussion of international governance issues. Central to this discussion is the question of enforcement, which has led to a rekindling of the issue of justified third-party intervention in the internal affairs of other states. . . .

Nations of the developing world have had unfortunate experiences as the objects of both direct and indirect interventions. These actions, ranging from economic sanctions to direct military interventions, have shaped the nature of the sociopolitical evolution of the societies against which they were directed. At different times in the past several decades, less-developed nations have attempted to generate a front against superpower manipulation. These efforts, varied and often ideologically charged in themselves, have ranged from the Movement of the Nonaligned Nations in the 1960s to ad hoc subregional groupings such as the Contadora Group, which initiated effective conflict-resolution efforts in Central America during the 1980s.

The author wishes to thank Dr. Pedro Villagra Delgado, Dr. Sergey Plekhanov, and Dr. Sally Falk Moore for their reviews of the first draft of this paper. Their comments have been taken into account and, when applicable, have been incorporated into the text. This paper was written while the author was at King's College, London. Portions of the text and some footnotes have been omitted.

Nevertheless, the perceptual result of clustering issues and nations together has been the perpetuation of an adversarial relationship in the international community. The idea of East versus West has given way to the idea of North versus South. The end of the Cold War has not brought about a change in this perception; indeed, this is nothing more than the continuation of a Cold War mindset applied to other circumstances. . . .

UNDERSTANDING THE NEGATIVE CONNOTATIONS OF INTERVENTION

A sense of impotence and distrust concerning intervention, prevalent among nations today, is based on a mix of historical issues and Cold War practices—mainly the Cold War doctrine of deterrence, the use of intervention as an alternative to open confrontation between superpowers, the psychological linkage between Cold War interventions and colonialism, suspicions aroused within the United Nations by the permanent membership of the Security Council, and the role of existing regional defense organizations in superpower intervention.

1. *The doctrine, policy, and strategy of bipolar deterrence,* in both its material and nonmaterial dimensions, generated the belief that there was a distinction between acceptable uses of force and unacceptable forms of violence. The judgment that certain forms of violence were unacceptable was based on the value system of the more powerful nations (i.e., the deterrers), which avoided nuclear war and protracted conventional warfare. This value system embodied the belief that protracted warfare was evil/unacceptable—which, paradoxically, made it possible to find many other forms of violence and coercion good/acceptable. Both military and nonmilitary intervention mechanisms were thus considered acceptable forms of pressure, policy, influence, coercion, and violence. Recipient states, however, found these actions totally unacceptable.

Tied in to this doctrine of deterrence were a host of other issues that corroded international trust, fueled suspicion among nations, and now obstruct common action. Some had to do with conflicting ideas as to the causes of war. Since the First World War, developed nations have frequently believed that aggressive and preemptive uses of force (whether military, economic, diplomatic, or political) were justified to secure peace. The emphasis was on deterrence, and on prevention and preemption as part of the credible base of deterrence. The doctrine of deterrence also incorporated the need to construct "enemy" images, since deterrence is useless without an enemy. This is a heavy legacy today, and it underscores the importance of constructing confidence-building measures among nations.

2. *In a constrained bipolar world fearful of ultimate nuclear war, top priority was given to policy opportunities to increase influence or coercion without ultimate censure.* Intervention became one of these policies: a "sophisticated" way in which to conduct international relations, often with acceptable results for the competing powers but disastrous results for the recipients of such conduct. . . .

Intervention was seen as playing a role in bipolar balance-of-power considerations. Today there is a variation in this belief, based on the relative power between industrialized and developing nations. Therefore, in the South, the belief that international policies were primarily influenced by the East-West conflict interaction has been replaced by the belief that it will now be influenced chiefly by interactions between the haves and have-nots.

Moreover, there is a psychological link between intervention and colonialism. . . . This must be taken seriously: the nuclear politics of the Cold War coincided with the age of decolonization. Thus, in many cases, the struggle for independence became associated with foreign direct and indirect intervention to influence the course of that struggle in favor of one or the other superpower.

This has posed two problems: the fear of the powerless that coercive measures—as opposed to mutually accepted norms and regulations—would be applied against them by the powerful; and the fear of the powerful nations that the delicate stability of their world order would be upset by the crude manipulations of this equation by the powerless. . . .

Powerless states have come to view intervention with deep misgivings, either because they have been direct recipients of it or because they have had to condition their options so as to avoid it. Again, examples abound, from the military interventions in Hungary, Czechoslovakia, Angola, Afghanistan, and Grenada to the maintenance of authoritarian regimes in Haiti, the Philippines, and Latin America; from the physical divisions of nations in Southeast Asia and the Middle East to the military and economic support of armed groups to support progressive or democratic forces. Intervention has become associated with the loss of freedom.[1]

3. *The psychological linkage that developing nations make between intervention and colonialism.*. . . Intervention was often seen as a manifestation of the need of powerful nations to meddle in the affairs of new, weaker nations. . . . And the loss of freedom associated with indirect intervention during the Cold War reinforced this perception.

The ways in which nations regard intervention and nonintervention are tied up with their notions and value systems related to revolution, independence, sovereignty, democracy, and human rights, as well as their definitions of security threats and national interests. The new types of global security threats, such as population flows, environmental degradation, the drug trade, and international crime and terrorism, have boosted a fear among weaker states that intervention might be used to crush the South's own definitions of security threats. Overall, these global security threats have been identified by the developed nations' analysts and scientists, using a powerful technological and communications base that is unavailable to the South. Statistics, to give but one example, are generated in the North and developing nations lack the capability to interpret the data or to produce their own. This has fueled suspicion as to which are the real global security threats that all nations can agree and act upon.

Thus, for powerless states, the issue of intervention is still tinted by the larger issues of independence and sovereignty, the impact of relative power between intervening and intervened-upon states, and the nature of international and regional organizations today. . . .

Conspiracy theorists in developing nations usually use very crude elements to judge third-party intentions and to interpret the underlying designs behind intervention. They usually concentrate on the issue of relative power between intervenor and intervened-upon, because unlike wars almost all interventions have to do with relative power and muscle flexing. Relative military power means that most nations that decide to intervene militarily have greater military power than the target state. Thus, it is often possible for intervened-upon states to accuse intervening nations of using their military might to force their policies on the weaker.

Because intervention has come to be seen as having to do with relative power, it is very difficult to justify it in universal terms. But precisely because of the power element of the ability to intervene, developing countries perceive that the more powerful they get, the less tempted other nations will be to carry out third-party interventions against them. This need to overinsure—to become powerful rather than powerless—is what threatens the stability of a system. It is the struggle to change power ratios that brings about international political change. . . .

Nationalism, a need to overinsure so as to defend, and an almost pathological need for self-reliance are often the consequences of insecurities that lie at the heart of young nations. The need for development can also be explained in this way rather than in terms of humanitarian reasons for improving standards of living. In the worst case the push for development is primarily fostered by the need to develop indigenous power, and in the best case it is undertaken in order to diminish negative dependencies.

4. *Suspicion related to the unequal power distribution within the UN, as reflected in the differences between the Security Council and the General Assembly.*

The UN was not a product of the Cold War, but it became its victim very early on. . . .

And yet, . . . the incipient Cold War soon paralyzed the UN Security Council, and the prospect of making the blueprint a reality evaporated. Then began a series of improvisations to sidestep East-West tension. Bitterly divided, the Security Council was unable to carry out preventive actions or to provide convincing security. The divisions within the Security Council not only hampered the original mission of the UN; it also fueled distrust among countries in the South. The impact of the Cold War within the Security Council generated a perception that the powerful nuclear nations of the world were attempting to control and retain the status quo, either through limited alliances among themselves or through the veto power of the Security Council.

This in turn generated a perception that the powers-that-be always attempt to control and retain the status quo, either through limited alliances among themselves (as since the beginning of the century) or through control of relevant international organizations. It is therefore possible to make a perceptual link among old powers, colonialism, military alliances of developed nations, the permanent members of the Security Council of the UN as it emerged at the end of World War II, and the present status of the Security Council in the new world order.

Thus, intervention as mandated by Security Council decisions could be used as a tool by the five permanent member states, who represent the status quo. Because intervention has historically been seen as protecting the powerful against change by maintaining the status quo, developing countries are naturally suspicious of it.

5. *Suspicion regarding the potential role in the new world order of existing regional organizations that were generated during the Cold War and that mostly served the interests of one or the other superpower.* Just as the Security Council of the UN was seen as a club apart in the international arena, the role of existing regional organizations has also fueled suspicion in the present context.

Intervention, particularly military intervention as conducted in the past forty years, was often perceived as needing a regional justification to soften the responsibility that the intervening nation had to face when using force. Most interventions were excused internationally by demonstrating that a regional organization or a group of countries "requested" one or more powers to intervene to solve a problem. The consultation (and often coercion) of other nations to request forceful action was the normal procedure that more powerful countries applied when deciding an intervention of any kind, as seen in the role of the Warsaw Pact in the Soviet interventions in Hungary end Czechoslovakia or the role of Caribbean states in the US intervention in Grenada. For powerful nations, mostly in the developed world, it was not politically acceptable to use force directly or go it alone; thus, lobbying for other nations to share the responsibility of the action became prevalent. The Warsaw Pact justified some Soviet interventions in Eastern Europe, and the Organization of American States (OAS), as well as coalitions of Caribbean countries, justified some US interventions in Central America and the Caribbean. Powerful nations had difficulty in applying force directly, so lobbying other, smaller nations to share in that responsibility became prevalent, and regional organizations often became the mechanism for this type of action. . . .

The past role of organizations in aiding and abetting military intervention by the powerful against the powerless constrains the potential for truly collaborative actions today. The deep-rooted suspicion that things are not what they seem when an intervention is planned or executed hampers cooperation in today's political climate. Any group of nations, even if it does not mirror the structure of formal regional organizations, faces today the difficult task of deciding on joint action and convincing observers that its member states are not the tools of a larger, secret and often more powerful agent.

JUSTIFIED INTERVENTION IN A NEW WORLD ORDER

With the end of the Cold War, the international community was liberated from the constraints of a rigid system. Nevertheless, this did not mean that the international climate would improve automatically. Much as the end of communism in Eastern Europe and the Soviet Union brought about the collapse of systems that had artificially sustained entire regions, the collapse of the bipolar world order has brought about a need to find workable systems of communication among nations. . . .

At the end of the Cold War, much lip service was given to the emergence of a "new world order," but no such thing is yet in evidence. The beginning of the 1990s is marked by a double standard: the remnants of the old power balance and doctrines are mingling with emerging elements of a new international order. Deterrence interacts with cooperation; bipolarity interacts with multipolarity; unilateral action interacts with international mechanisms for action; old definitions of security threats interact with new ones, much as old definitions of the role of military forces interact with new ones as nations address nonmilitary threats to security.

Thus, it is not surprising that third-party intervention also maintains a double standard. Is intervention viewed as the continuation of terror tactics of the powerful versus the weak in a new format? Or is it seen as the first brick of the wall of future cooperation and international interaction?

Just as the collapse of the Cold War prompted a return to the search for the first UN Charter blueprint, the discussions on cooperative modes of preserving peace are returning to the original ideas of collective security. Intervention in the internal affairs of other states is an issue charged with negative connotations. Before any norm for justified intervention is agreed upon, nations must address the fears and distrust that this mode of action has brought about. This must be done quickly.

Now, at the end of the twentieth century, there is enough knowledge and information to permit nations to engage in discussions about their common threats. There is also a growing realization that many problems cannot be successfully dealt with by any nation acting alone. Nations are turning to serious consideration of collective action to solve collective problems. But distrust and the persistence of Cold War images among nations do not permit a fresh look at this discourse. As Argentine diplomat Pedro Villagra Delgado has observed:

> I believe that the establishment of some kind of international mechanism to defend, for example, human rights and democracy could be helpful to all emerging democracies. Nevertheless, the principal obstacle is to surmount the distrust that past interventions have created. For these reasons it will not be easy to convince our people that this time, this type of action (i.e., intervention) is for a good cause and that it will benefit our right to freely choose those who will govern us. I do believe that to start this campaign to restore trust is worthwhile. The big countries, on the other hand, must demonstrate that things are now different and the causes for this type of action are—this time—really just. I believe that what is interesting about this topic is that on the one hand it opens an ethical dilemma (to be in favor or not of interventions to help people to exert their rights), and, on the other hand, not to fall in the ingenuousness of believing that justice or morals are the "normal" reasons for intervention.[2]

The past three years have seen increased action by a number of nations to work collectively on security issues. Nations have joined forces to obtain results that were outside the reach of existing structures and of their own limited resources.

This trend toward more imaginative use of collective action to either prevent or resolve military and nonmilitary conflicts has not yet been institutionalized as a new mode of international behavior. Yet we desperately need new ways in which nations can communicate their common problems and find common solutions. For example, there is too much talk of coercive multilateral action and too little of preventive diplomacy. Common problems are generating a need for cooperative processes, which are difficult for many nations to accept. In such processes, every nation involved must want to have its individual options curtailed so as to benefit the whole and manage the transition in peace; every nation involved must wish to cede power to international organizations so as to assist in the administration of the new world order. Unfortunately, this has not yet come to pass.

If these perceptual problems could be overcome, a collective security system could be set up. More important, if such a system were deemed trustworthy, it would also be possible to envisage the multilateral use of force in specific situations, especially within the practices of the UN. Achieving this will require a truly international effort, implemented by the UN:

> It will require a transition from the sheriff's posse to the beginnings of a regularly established, and respected, international police force, monitoring the implementation of international decisions and agreements. If the Security Council does begin to develop a real system of peace and security instead of the largely reactive measures and safety nets to which it has been limited so far, the technique of peace-keeping will have to be developed and strengthened as an essential practical part of it.[3]

RECOMMENDATIONS

Perhaps new norms of justified intervention can be found in theory, but in practice, any type of intervention is doomed to fail if it is perceived to perpetuate the status quo and value systems of only a handful of nations.

There are some actions that could be undertaken so that third-party intervention acquires a workable and positive dimension in the future world system. These all depend on the successful reversal of negative perceptions relating to the usefulness of intervention. Toward this end it would be necessary to:

1. Boost the feeling that international norms help regulate world affairs in peace, in a just and equitable manner. Strengthening international law and the rule of law is of the first importance in restoring global political confidence that will permit action. . . .

2. Boost the positive values in the international community, such as the possibility of self-reliance; the dignity of independence; the common sense of interdependence; the recognition of developmental needs; the true nature of democracy; the rule and guarantee of international law based on equality of principle, not of force. If these positive values are then linked to the notion of intervention, the notion itself might revert to a positive value.

3. Recognize that the things that make nations different from the way they were in the past are education, information, democracy, and law. Therefore, the roles of all four elements, which are relatively new in universal society, should be boosted. Intervention will lose its negative trait if linked to these types of "guarantees" of civilized behavior.

Education, information, democracy, and law could become the basis for a new kind of international dialogue, which might lead to a revival of notions of international cooperation and human solidarity.

The improvement of communication among nations is the first modest step toward this goal. Javier Pérez de Cuéllar, the former Secretary-General of the UN, faced just such a task in 1986 as he witnessed the beginning of the end of the Cold War era. He understood the power of building on communications:

A better understanding of the global nature of their problems—of their complexity and correlation—would make governments aware that the only solution is through co-operation. Is the accumulation of armaments inevitable? Are oppression and underdevelopment inevitable? What we do have is the lack of capabilities or lack of will to stop this isolationism. All tragic situations are reversible as long as nations are willing to reject resignation and willing to act in unison.[4]

4. Show real advancement toward the building of a just, equitable new world order. Toward this end, new participatory mechanisms must be designed and regulated—mechanisms that promote the value of international ethics and of clear, nondiscriminatory international law. The best way to achieve this objective is to construct confidence-building measures that will improve international participation and break the mold of old discriminatory world orders.

> For a plural future, benign indifference to multiculturalism is no better than intolerance. Genuine multiculturalism is a profound new world we have to discover. It is a new moral universe we have to navigate, a new ethic we all have to acquire. . . . In a world torn by domination, conflicts, and conflicting loyalties, our best hopes lie in the liberating power of truth and moral ideals. We must re-learn to cherish the idea, that power of truth, the power of a truthful word, the strength of a free spirit, conscience and responsibility, can actually transform the world. This is not a naive idea but rooted, though often forgotten, in the deepest core of human nature.[5]

5. Talk over each nation's fears in order to redefine the nature of a security threat and to design participatory solutions. We have to renegotiate the terms upon which all nations communicate with each other and the perceptions of what they stand for. We must understand what all of us are really talking about.

To restore confidence it is first necessary to strive to understand the value systems of all parties, so as not to judge causes and effects by alien standards. Perhaps the best way to explain this is to say that nations must strive to rediscover one another.

As to the actual mechanisms for intervention, most of the opposition to this type of action will be removed if the previous five points are developed. Even so, some specific issues must be addressed, such as defining the different types of intervention (e.g., voluntarily supported by all parties, imposed, requested by one party); agreeing on the voting mechanisms for deciding upon intervention or non-intervention (e.g., veto, consensus, majority); deciding on the mechanisms for implementation of intervention; differentiating between multilateral enforcement operations and peace-enforcement and peacekeeping operations in the internal affairs of other states; and perhaps even deciding to use a totally different word when referring to this new positive type of intervention.

CONCLUSION

Justified third-party intervention is a difficult concept for many nations in the South to accept. Nevertheless, the transition to a new world order has made many nations hopeful that new forms for collective action, particularly if related to humanitarian issues, can be found. The UN seems to be the repository of most of these hopes.

Intervention is only one way in which nations might conceivably act together for the common good. How the international community views intervention will depend on the rationale, objective, and mode of intervention. Fundamentally, it will also depend on the dialogue established among nations, the level of decision sharing and humanitarian awareness, and the creation of participatory mechanisms to make this new dialogue meaningful.

Solidarity is a powerful tool in development, peace, and progress, but it cannot exist among individuals or nations unless they believe they have something in common with each other. The prospect of a new world order has brought about a new willingness to explore our commonalities.

In using this newfound will to create a new reality, our greatest challenge will be not the creation of new mechanisms for action but the removal of distrust from existing ones.

NOTES

1. Editorial comment, *Third World Quarterly*, Vol. 10, no. 4 (October 1988), p. 9.
2. Comments of Pedro Villagra Delgado on the first draft of this paper.
3. Brian Urquhart, "Beyond the Sheriff's Posse," *Survival*, Vol. 31, no. 3 (May/June 1990), p. 198.
4. Javier Pérez de Cuéllar, "Anarquia o armonia: un mundo interdependiente en busca del multilateralismo," keynote speech at the Consejo Argentino para las Relaciones Internacionales, Buenos Aires, Argentina, 1986, p. 25. [Please note that the translation from Spanish was done by the author of this paper.]
5. Datuk Seri Anwar Ibrahim, Minister of Finance of Malaysia, in an interview in *New Straits Times* (November 18, 1992), p. 12.